ADAPTING EARLY CHILDHOOD CURRICULA
suggestions for meeting special needs

With deep gratitude to
Curtis, Christopher, Kimberly
Ray, Bob, and **Bill**

ADAPTING EARLY CHILDHOOD CURRICULA
suggestions for meeting special needs

RUTH E. COOK, Ph.D.

Graduate Division of Counseling and Education,
The University of Santa Clara, Santa Clara, California;
formerly Special/Early Childhood Education,
Southern Illinois University at Edwardsville, Edwardsville, Illinois

VIRGINIA B. ARMBRUSTER, M.A., CCC-Sp

Early Childhood Special Educator, Alton Public Schools,
Alton, Illinois; Visiting Lecturer, Southern Illinois University
at Edwardsville, Edwardsville, Illinois

with 67 illustrations

The C. V. Mosby Company

ST. LOUIS • LONDON • TORONTO   1983

MOSBY

A TRADITION OF PUBLISHING EXCELLENCE

Editor: Julia Allen Jacobs
Manuscript editors: Ivie Lewellen Davis, Dale Woolery
Book design: Susan Trail
Cover design: Suzanne Oberholtzer
Production: Susan Trail

Cover photo: J. Myers, H. Armstrong Roberts

Printed in the United States of America

The C.V. Mosby Company
11830 Westline Industrial Drive, St. Louis, Missouri 63141

Library of Congress Cataloging in Publication Data

Cook, Ruth E.
  Adapting early childhood curricula.

  Includes bibliographies and index.
  1. Handicapped children—Education (Preschool).
2. Handicapped children—Education (Preschool)—
Curricula. 3. Mainstreaming in education.
I. Armbruster, Virginia B. II. Title.
LC4019.2.C66   371.9   81-18904
ISBN 0-8016-1149-0   AACR2

AC/VH/VH 9 8 7 6 5 4 3 2 1   01/B/041

Preface

As the necessity to accommodate special needs within early childhood education expands, so does the new field of Early Childhood Special Education. This book provides teachers, parents, and paraprofessionals with the information and techniques needed to develop curricula and instruction to meet unique needs of individual children within any preschool classroom. Teachers working with groups of handicapped children in special education classrooms will also find the curricula adaptations suggested throughout this book to be useful.

As more is learned about the effectiveness of early education, perspectives change. Currently the goal is to identify high risk children as soon as possible and to provide their parents with guidance in nurturing them mentally and physically. Although it is generally acknowledged that all children are more alike than different, the unique differences must be identified and conscientiously considered when programs are planned. To meet the special needs of children, instruction oriented toward individualization is advocated. Environments are tailored to help all children achieve their full potential by building on individual task capabilities.

Although terms such as *retarded, physically handicapped, blind,* and *deaf* continue to be used, most professionals recognize that these terms are often not helpful. Children do not come in packages. Two children will respond very differently even though their handicaps may appear to be very similar. For example, although two children have the same hearing loss, each child presents a unique combination of educational strengths and weaknesses.

We provide high risk signals for specific handicapping conditions and suggest teaching strategies for working with children "diagnosed" as having certain problems. However, the plan and focus of this book are different from many others. The content is not organized around traditional handicapping categories. In fact, we suggest that "labels" be avoided whenever possible. Individual needs can be identified best by close observation and analysis of what the child actually can and cannot do. Sensitive awareness of individual strategies is encouraged.

Emphasis is on individualizing educational programs while including children within a group activity or lesson. Learning to analyze a child's learning style and then matching this with an effective teaching strategy is described in detail. Ways to determine the steps children need to take to learn a new skill are explained. Adaptations to daily routines are described and specific suggestions are provided through vignettes, dialogues, and illustrations as well as guidelines. In this way, effective individualization is demonstrated.

Our aim is to reflect a workable integration of the theories, research, and practical applications from both the fields of early childhood education and special education. Because this blend is in an initial stage of development, we may have left some questions unanswered or issues unresolved and placed heavy emphasis on others. Our rationale for the inclusion of material is highlighted in this overview of the chapters.

The purpose of Chapter 1 is to explore some of the current knowledge and issues related to the education of young handicapped children. The historical, theoretical, and legal overviews presented in Chapter 2 are designed to foster an understanding of why and how the new field of early childhood special education has come to be. Chapter 3 is intended to help teachers realize the importance of their role as daily observers of children. To teachers fall the awesome responsibilities of noticing high risk signals, assessing children to develop programs based on individual developmental levels, and working closely with numerous professionals to provide the most appropriate education for each child. The purpose of this chapter is to help teachers effectively use information gained from informal classroom observation in recognizing each child's educational needs.

Chapter 4 presents the framework necessary for the construction and use of a developmental curriculum checklist designed to create the type of individualization advocated earlier. Although teachers cannot be expected to accomplish this level of individualization immediately, by understanding the process they can avoid wasting time getting started. This process has been implemented, over time, by numerous teachers with impressive success. In each case, they have remarked about the time saved once the process is in place. The result has been and continues to be worth the effort.

Chapters 5 to 8 are characteristic of most books on early childhood education. However, we have given new and different examples along with many of the "tried and true." In all cases, every activity or strategy suggested has been used successfully in classrooms of young chil-

dren with and without handicaps. In Chapter 7 an adaptation of introductory activities from The McGinnis Association Method is described. This adaptation has been found especially helpful in working with overly active children as well as those who have speech and language problems. In addition, these activities are a useful introduction to the auditory discrimination skills required for beginning reading readiness in kindergarten. Extra attention is given to suggestions for working with overly active children and reluctant children because these special needs are found in nearly every classroom.

The length of Chapter 9 reflects the importance of the topic—working in partnership with parents. Research supports the influence of parents in the lives of young children, and we believe that the parents' role cannot be underestimated. They are indeed the primary teachers of their children. This realization motivated us to cover so much in this one chapter. Finally, Chapter 10 focuses on a critical area often neglected. Making effective use of paraprofessionals is becoming of greater importance as the numbers of volunteer and paid aides increase. The format of this chapter is somewhat different because we believe that teachers must learn to be "managers" of the human resources available to them. If not, precious time and skills are wasted.

We present this book with gratitude to the hundreds of children and parents who have been our teachers. From them we have learned to value and nurture the uniqueness of each individual child no matter what his or her background, skills, or abilities. We believe we have found a way to meet unique needs in whatever setting they appear. It has been our purpose to convey the essence of this process to anyone interested in working with young children.

We wish to thank colleagues Dr. William Whiteside, Dr. Thomas Shea, and Dr. Norma Jean Havlin for their encouragement and expert opinions. We are indebted to Marion Boris for excellence in typing and for saving the manuscript from a tornado that destroyed her home. Sincere appreciation goes to Peggy Ellis for many hours given to proofreading, to Ray Ellis for careful indexing, to Julia Allen Jacobs, Fawn Chapel, and Elaine Steinborn for continued assistance as our editors, and to Robbie Crane and Nyla Snyder for their overall helpfulness.

Ruth E. Cook
Virginia B. Armbruster

Contents

1

Introduction

The butterfly

Her mother thought the butterfly was dead,
But didn't tell her crippled child, whose head
Was bent inspecting him . . . in wonderment.
"I know you can, if only you will try . . .
Just spread your wings and show how you can fly."
She murmured low—about an hour or so.
Once while she watched, she thought she saw him
   stir,
Was it the wind? she couldn't quite be sure. . . .
And then to her delight, he rose in flight!
He circled round her head a time or two,
Then fluttered to a wider, higher view.
the child's enraptured eyes looked to the skies
At black and orange wings against a cloud.
The joy she felt caused her to cry aloud,
"You're free, you're free! Why don't you wait for
   me?"
Forgetting that her chair had wheels, she stood—
(The butterfly in her had known she could)
And as her mother wept . . . she took a step.

*Nancy H. Wiley**

Helping children discover the butterfly within, that they may recognize their own capabilities—what a challenge that is! Parents and teachers together can provide each child with the opportunity to develop his or her own unique potential, beginning with that first step. For those children who appear to have developmental disabilities or characteristics that interfere with normal growth and learning, the stage must be more thoughtfully prepared. Parents and teachers need to work together to create a nurturing environment sensitive to, but not solicitous of, children's handicapping conditions.

Many aspects of mental and physical development seem to "just happen" to most children. They are, however, the result of interaction be-

*Written especially for this introduction by Nancy H. Wiley.

tween innate capacities and appropriate environmental experiences. With most children comparatively little deliberate effort has to be made to synchronize capacities and experiences. Most have a repertoire of skills and interests that motivate them to explore, experiment, and therefore learn (Allen, 1981). However, children with special needs may not be able to learn spontaneously from the play experiences they naturally encounter. Teachers must carefully adapt materials, equipment, space, instructions, and expectations to provide environmental experiences conducive to learning.

Bijou (1977) concisely captures the basic aim of all early childhood education: "Such a general goal would be the maximization of development of each child in the context of his or her circumstance of living" (p. 13). It is toward this goal that the theory, lessons, and adaptations suggested in this book are focused. Guidelines for analyzing the tasks typical of any early childhood curriculum are offered rather than the proposal of a special curriculum designed for each disability. Suggestions are given for adapting strategies to accommodate individual styles of learning. The intent is to identify ways and means to make it possible for children with special needs to be educated appropriately in regular early childhood programs with nonhandicapped peers. However, these same adaptations are useful to special education teachers in any environment.

WHY INCLUDE HANDICAPPED CHILDREN IN "REGULAR" PRESCHOOL PROGRAMS?

Currently educational literature is replete with convincing arguments in favor of educating handicapped and nonhandicapped children in the same classroom. Among the most cited reasons for the integration of preschool handicapped and nonhandicapped children are three arguments advanced by Bricker (1978): social-ethical, legal-legislative, and psychological-educational.

1. Social-ethical arguments seek to discourage a negative view of handicapped children. This view is perpetuated by isolating such children. Inclusion of handicapped children in programs with nonhandicapped children contributes to altering societal perceptions; at the same time educational resources are used more efficiently.

2. Legal-legislative arguments evolve from the recent court decisions and legislative acts that mandate that handicapped children are to be educated in the most "normal" appropriate setting.

3. Psychological-educational arguments consider the need for children to interact with a progressively more demanding environment. An integrated program is thought to be more characteristic of such an environment. Studies suggest that learning through imitation occurs when suitable models are available, and activities are arranged to elicit imitative behavior. Integrated intervention programs have been successful when carefully planned and evaluated.

Is "mainstreaming" appropriate for all handicapped children?

Terms such as *mainstreaming, integration,* and *least restrictive environment* are often used interchangeably and seldom are well defined. They usually describe the practice of educating handicapped and nonhandicapped children in the same environment. (This meaning of integration is similar in process to but differs from the popular usage that combines children of various races and cultures within the same environment.) The term *mainstreaming* developed as a result of legislation demanding that children be educated in the least restrictive environment (legal-legislative argument). As a result, confusion has occurred. Some believe that the least restrictive environment is automatically a mainstreamed environment. Believing this, some

children in special education were quickly returned to the regular classroom. Negative feelings arose from an apparent lack of regard for the unique needs of the children or for preparation of the environment into which they were being placed.

However, Public Law 94-142, which is discussed at length in Chapters 2 and 3 emphasizes the desirable principle of *appropriate* education within the least restrictive environment. When describing mainstreaming, Safford and Rosen (1981, p. 3) state: "Mainstreaming means providing experiences most likely to ensure that handicapped children can realize maximum potential for full participation in society and independence of functioning." They go on to emphasize that the amount or kind of contact with nonhandicapped age peers appropriate for any given child must be individually determined. Only through careful study and analysis of each child and the available educational alternatives can the most appropriate placement be determined.

THE PRESCHOOL YEARS: THE BEST TIME TO INTEGRATE CHILDREN WITH SPECIAL NEEDS?

It is not unusual to find handicapped children enrolled in regular preschool classrooms. Many teachers welcome handicapped children and try to provide worthwhile experiences even with limited resources. However, it is also not unusual to find that handicapped children are included only through the untiring efforts of parents and other child advocates. Sometimes mothers have had to accompany their child to the preschool and serve as an aide in order for the child to be accepted. Only recently have educators begun to consider the regular preschool classroom as an appropriate placement alternative. The 1972 mandate requiring Head Start to enroll handicapped children certainly gave the proponents of mainstreaming a chance to demonstrate the wisdom of their beliefs.

Systematic research into the effectiveness of integrating or mainstreaming young handicapped children is still in its infancy. Researchers tend to agree "that simply placing handicapped children in the same educational settings with nonhandicapped children does not accomplish all the goals of mainstreaming" (Cooke, Ruskus, Apolloni, and Peck, 1981, p. 73). However, studies suggest that it is possible to structure interactions so that handicapped children acquire more competent behaviors (Dunlop, Stoneman, and Cantrell, 1980). At the very least, mainstreamed programs can be supported on moral and ethical grounds. Detrimental effects have not been revealed in literature (Vincent, Brown, and Getz-Sheftel, 1981).

The optimal preschool years

One can easily speculate on the factors that may interact to make the preschool years optimal ones for mainstreaming children with handicaps. First, most preschool programs expect children to mature at varying rates during these years of enhanced growth and development. Differences in skills are expected and accommodated within the curriculum. The range of preschool "normalcy" is much broader than that usually found in elementary school classrooms. Teachers also tend to focus on the process more than the product of learning. They are busy setting up centers to allow for sensory exploration rather than grading spelling papers or preparing the next day's language test. In addition, the methods and materials usually found in preschool centers are conducive to the development of all young children. Exploration, manipulation, expression, sharing, and active involvement provide easy opportunities for teachers to structure and reinforce meaningful interaction between handicapped and nonhandicapped children.

Anyone who has worked with young children is readily aware of children's natural ability to accept and even appreciate individual differences. Children respond to one another without making judgments and comparisons. Spontaneous friendships abound with little in the way of ongoing expectations. When differences are observed, questions reflect a natural curiosity. If answered in genuine, thoughtful ways, children accommodate and accept the child who is different.

Labels can be hazardous. The diagnosis of children with presumed learning handicaps traditionally results in the application of categorizing labels such as mentally retarded, emotionally disturbed, and learning handicapped. Advocates argue that labels lead to efficiency of "treatment" and are often required for financial reimbursement. But most who make recommendations for children in the preschool years try to avoid attaching labels because they realize how tenuous the testing results are for children of this age. Fortunate are the children who are accepted into early childhood programs through open enrollment policies, because they experience a lower probability of being labeled. However, children who are referred because of special problems may arrive with labels. Research suggests that such labels bias the behavior of others toward those who are labeled (Kronick, 1977).

The following two points merit consideration in regard to the practice of labeling young children:

1. Does the label help the teacher plan a better program for the child? Labels can be helpful if teachers use them as guides in their search for teaching strategies relevant to each individual's needs. If, on the other hand, the labels are so broad and vague that they are not useful, they should be ignored. Siegel and Spradlin (1978) believe "the instructional tasks seem to be the same, regardless of whether the child is labeled autistic, brain damaged, retarded or congenitally aphasic" (p. 378). In every case it is the child's characteristics that must be observed closely.

What is observed may or may not fit the characteristics implied by a label. Furthermore, labels are static; children are dynamic.

2. Is there a chance that a label will be detrimental to the individual being labeled? If indeed labels do create a type of "self-fulfilling prophecy," then caution must be taken. Consider this situation in a preschool. Perhaps a teacher does act or feel differently because of his or her image of a characteristic suggested by a label. Young children are such keen observers that they will readily absorb the teacher's attitudes and behavior. Those who are not handicapped will model the teacher's behavior and reflect his or her feelings. The labeled child may begin to act as expected and may even become isolated.

Because of the obvious dangers involved in labeling, the format of this book has avoided the traditional categorical approach. (Although several terms are used throughout the book (for example, *handicapped, special needs, developmentally delayed, slow,* and *visually, physically, or hearing impaired*), their use does not suggest that labeling should occur.) These terms are used for clarity of communication, not as diagnostic labels.

Public school programs are not enough. Consideration must be given to the fact that public school preschools have been provided only for handicapped children. It is impossible to develop a mainstreamed program unless classes are provided for nonhandicapped children as well. Of course, one solution would be to include special children in nonpublic preschools. Certified early childhood special education teachers could assist with the implementation of the individual education programs. Currently, plans for a reduced federal budget may jeopardize existing public school services. If present programs are rescinded, parents and teachers will seek educational adaptations for young children in day-care centers and private preschools.

TEACHERS: THEIR ROLE IN THE INTEGRATION OF HANDICAPPED CHILDREN

"The ability and attitude of the teacher appear to be *the* most important factors in the success of an integrated program" (Wynne, Ulfelder, and Dakof, 1975, p. 75). There is no doubt that the role of the teacher is central to the successful integration of special needs children. It is the teacher who must structure the environment, adapt the materials, determine the child's most profitable mode of learning, initiate the desired responses, and reinforce those that should be encouraged.

To fulfill such a multifaceted role teachers are expected to develop competencies characteristic of both the early childhood educator and the special educator. Fortunately, the skills needed are basically the same as those necessary to work with any child between the ages of 2 and 6. However, there are certain areas in which added emphasis or expertise is desirable. Safford (1978, p. 31) and Allen (1981, p. 51) list several skill areas. These areas and others often found in the literature are listed below:

1. Knowledge of normal and atypical processes and stages in children's development
2. Ability to recognize symptoms of specific handicapping conditions
3. Skill in observing and recording behavior of individual children
4. Ability to employ informal procedures in diagnosing educational problems
5. Ability to prepare long-term goals and short-term objectives developmentally appropriate and consistent with each child's style of learning and observed strengths and weaknesses
6. Ability to structure the environment to adapt to specific needs
7. Understanding of the philosophy that underlies the curriculum model in use
8. Ability to develop a trusting relationship

with children through effective communication

9. Skill in techniques to enhance positive interactions between children of varying levels of skills and abilities
10. Familiarity with and ability to use appropriate resource persons in the school and community
11. Skill in recruiting, training, and working cooperatively with paraprofessionals
12. Ability to listen reflectively to parents and to develop a viable program of parent involvement
13. Ability to recognize one's own limitations and to seek assistance when necessary

CONDITIONS NECESSARY FOR EFFECTIVE MAINSTREAMING

One consistent theme runs throughout studies that have evaluated the effectiveness of efforts to teach handicapped and nonhandicapped children in the same classroom. Even though research efforts have been limited, specialists agree that just putting children together physically does not create the desired results. "In other words, if you want developmental growth, you must train developmental tasks by modifying the learning environment, reinforce the desired behaviors when they occur, and work out a system for maintaining desired behaviors over time" (Raver, 1979, p. 23). Ideally, children can grow progressively from a natural need for firm structure toward self-guided discovery.

Systematic planning

Well-planned, structured practices that facilitate cross-peer interaction appear necessary to optimal development in a mainstreamed program. Directly training handicapped children to imitate nonhandicapped peers has shown promising results (Apolloni, Cooke, and Cooke, 1977). Positive results occur when teachers "set up" socially integrative play situations and then systematically reinforce both handicapped and

nonhandicapped children for playing together cooperatively. (Techniques to facilitate cooperative behavior are discussed in Chapter 8.)

The ratio of handicapped to nonhandicapped children. Experience has not specified a certain number of children that should be integrated into any one classroom. However, specialists find that when only one or two are included, isolation is more likely to occur. Three to six seem to be a realistic number of handicapped children to integrate into the regular classroom. Decisions of how many must be based on the needs of the children being integrated, characteristics of the nonhandicapped children, the attitudes and training of the staff, support services available, and the ratio of adults to children.

Developmental levels rather than age. Consideration should be given to integrating special children with normal children of a lower chronological age to decrease the developmental differences (Peck, Apolloni, Cooke, and Raver, 1978). Children tend to more readily imitate those who are only slightly more advanced. To group children according to developmental levels rather than ages, teachers must carefully observe and assess individual differences. (These important skills are discussed in Chapter 4.)

Individualized, structured learning experiences. Tawney (1981, p. 29) credits Dunn (1968) with correct identification of the key element in any program of early education: "individualized, structured learning experiences." Such an approach is natural to teachers with a developmental orientation, allowing them to identify each child's strengths and weaknesses. Children are not expected to move as a group from level to level. Instead, a child's weakness becomes the basis for a teaching objective. The child's strengths are incorporated into instructional strategies matched to specific objectives. Progress is then determined by individual rather than group accomplishment. Within small groups, adaptations are made in materials used, questions posed, and directions given. The same basic task can be presented with modifications for a number of children during the same lesson period. (Examples of such individualized instruction are found throughout this book.)

Partnership with parents

Evidence is building to suggest that parental involvement is critical to the success of mainstreaming (Allen, 1981). Educators have moved from a position of only limited parent involvement to extensive participation of parents in educational planning for their children (Marion, 1981). Researchers continue to find one of the major elements of a quality preschool is significant involvement of parents (Schweinhart, 1981). Teachers are urged to recognize that parents are the primary teachers of their children. No one else knows their child as well or, hopefully, spends as much time with them. Parents can become extended hands of the teacher, increasing the opportunities for individualization (Techniques for encouraging meaningful parent involvement are thoroughly discussed in Chapter 9.)

Supportive personnel and services

To feel confident and effective, teachers need to learn about the handicapping conditions of children they serve. They must seek specialists in their area who can assist them in acquiring needed knowledge and in programming for individual student requirements. The ability to work with and efficiently incorporate the expertise of other disciplines is a critical link in the development of a viable mainstreamed program.

Support from colleagues can be essential to the morale and overall attitude of teachers (Meisels, 1977). Administrators must be willing and able to encourage teachers to innovate, realizing that not everything will be successful or always met with enthusiasm. Teachers' efforts deserve appreciation and recognition. Support of teacher's aides and volunteers must be acknowledged and provided whenever possible. Consultative help to teachers or direct assistance to children needs to be arranged when handicaps require the skill of specialists. Everyone, including the bus driver who delivers the children and the custodian who cleans up after them, influences the effectiveness of the program and the morale of all who are involved.

Continued search for new ways and means

No one can list all of the considerations necessary to ensure successful integration of handicapped preschoolers. Each child is different, each program is unique, and circumstances change. Therefore educators must constantly search for new ways and means to serve their children. They must be flexible and open to change. Each day may bring a new challenge that must be turned into an opportunity. The patience and skills of even the most experienced teacher may not seem to be sufficient at times. Even very mildly impaired children may show what seems to be extremely slow progress. Teachers and parents may have to adjust and readjust their expectations. Sights must be set far ahead while satisfaction comes bit by bit.

Recognition of when mainstreaming is not the best alternative

Remember, the inclusion of a handicapped child within a program with nonhandicapped children is only one placement alternative. (Other placement alternatives are illustrated in Chapter 3.) Several reasons have been given, suggesting that it is the best or most appropriate alternative for many children. It has also been noted that each child must be considered as an individual with very unique needs. Some children with more severe handicaps need more specialized services than can be provided in some preschool centers. In other cases the program cannot be adapted suitably to accommodate children with certain needs. In still others some of the conditions just discussed cannot be achieved. Teachers and administrators are encouraged to study each situation carefully before placement and continuously throughout placement. Any child should be kept in a placement only as long as that placement is the most appropriate alternative for him or her. Teachers who find many of the adaptations suggested in this book to be impossible or difficult should wait to include handicapped children until adequate preparations can be made.

SUGGESTIONS FOR INCLUDING CHILDREN WITH SPECIAL NEEDS

The suggestions that follow are based on the belief that teachers play the central role in the development of programs that successfully integrate handicapped children. The tone of the classroom is set through the teacher's attitudes and actions. Therefore teachers are strongly encouraged to acknowledge their own fears and apprehensions before initiating a mainstreamed program. It helps to remember that every child is more like others than different from them. Understanding that all children can have adjustment problems because of their stage of development makes it possible for teachers to recognize that some deviant behavior is just plain normal. Learning something about each specific handicap will alleviate many fears and help one to feel less helpless. The following suggestions are general and can be considered only in light of each specific situation:

1. Meet with the child's parents before including him or her in the program. Besides seeking vital parental support, special interests, specific problems, and solutions can be explored. Unpleasant times may be avoided

through preventative advice. Some teachers find it helpful to have the child visit the classroom either as a guest for a short time during the day or after the other children have departed. Arranging such a visit before a regular day of enrollment relieves the fears of many children.

2. After the brief visit just described, phase children in slowly. A parent may need to be present in the beginning. Adding only one handicapped child at a time will allow you the opportunity to give as much individual attention as necessary.

3. Be positive. Focus on the attitudes and behaviors you wish to see in children. Be what you want to see expressed.

4. Be realistic. Do not expect too much or too little. Go slowly. Get to know the child very well. By thoroughly understanding the child's educational strengths and weaknesses, it will be possible to be realistic.

5. Do not be afraid to be structured. Young children need clear, firm guidelines for behavior. Before school begins, identify specific safety rules. Tell and show the children what to do from the first day where safety and cleanliness are involved.

6. Develop guidelines for classroom behavior *with* the children. Keep the rules simple and few in number. Do not expect the handicapped child to understand and follow all rules immediately. Tell other children that they must help the new child to learn by showing him or her how to behave.

7. Focus on each child's strengths. Each child does have strengths. By pointing these out, children will realize their own strengths as well as those of others.

8. Avoid negative expectations. Remember, if you think Johnny will misbehave, the chances are that he will misbehave.

9. Respect each child. Show your respect by listening thoughtfully to what each one says. Encourage the children to suggest ideas, help to solve problems, and take care of the things in the room.

10. Avoid doing for children what they can do for themselves. Try not to be overly solicitous if help is needed. Provide what is necessary in a matter-of-fact way. Be alert to withdraw assistance as soon as possible.

11. Express enthusiasm and pleasure as each milestone (no matter how small) is achieved. Be genuine. Do not exaggerate.

12. Be honest in dealing with children's questions. Give short, truthful answers. Avoid making a big production about introducing the child or explaining his or her differences. Remember, children are more alike than different. To the child who asks "Why does Susie talk so funny?" you can reply "Susie had an operation so that she can learn to talk just like you. Perhaps you will be able to help her make new words while you are playing with the puppets today."

13. Give parents support and encouragement. They will need it. They especially want to be kept informed of their child's progress. Be positive and encourage them to participate as much as possible.

14. Most of all, do not expect too much of yourself or of the situation. Progress takes time. Innovation takes courage.

SUMMARY

Young children with developmental lags or special handicaps require individualized educational experiences to promote attainment of their unique potential. Within the preschool this involves sensitive adaptation of curriculum, materials, space, instruction, and adult expectations to stimulate a nurturing environment.

The question of how to provide learning opportunities best for young special needs children has sparked controversy and differing philosophies among educators for generations. Currently the scales are tipped in favor of integrating preschool handicapped and nonhandicapped children within the same classroom.

Naturally some severely and profoundly handicapped children may not receive maximum benefit from such a placement. But there are educational advantages that make integration or mainstreaming especially workable for many young handicapped children at the preschool level.

In an integrated classroom, nonhandicapped children serve as role models to stimulate developmental imitation. Imitative learning is especially strengthened when three or more handicapped children are grouped with normally functioning children who may be slightly younger. Matching children by developmental levels rather than ages appears to be showing positive results.

During the preschool years, the educational focus is more on the process of exploration, manipulation, expression, sharing, and active involvement than on the content or products of learning. Such processes, when modified for the child with special needs, enhance growth and development within the context of the regular preschool experience.

The early placement of handicapped children into the educational mainstream carries certain cautions and challenges that are not commonly encountered in preschools without special needs children. Diagnostic labels, which categorize the type of handicap, may accentuate the effects of the handicap (leading to self-fulfilling prophecies) rather than help the search for appropriate teaching strategies.

The ability and attitude of the teacher are key factors in successful mainstreaming. Knowledge of how to individualize instruction within a regular curriculum becomes a requisite skill. The ability to individualize instruction is built on a series of skills beginning with an understanding of normal and atypical stages of child development. These teacher skills range from recording observed behaviors to preparing appropriate developmental goals and objectives; to task analytical sequencing of lessons; to working directly with parents, paraprofessionals, and specialists.

Mainstreaming is not the only, and at times not the best, alternative for educating handicapped preschoolers. The value of early integration of handicapped and nonhandicapped children achieved national importance with the passage of P.L. 94-142. This law mandated that special needs children be placed in the *least restrictive environment* appropriate to their needs. Over time the extent of federal funding or preschool special education may be questionable because of shifts in political ideologies and governmental needs. Nevertheless, even if publicly supported education of handicapped preschool age children is severely cut, the spirit (if not the mechanism) for their integration into regular classrooms remains a viable educational ideal.

REFERENCES

Allen, K.E. Curriculum models for successful mainstreaming. *Topics in Early Childhood Special Education*, 1981, *1*, 45-55.

Apolloni, T., Cooke, S., and Cooke, T. Establishing a normal peer as behavior model for developmentally delayed toddlers. *Perceptual and Motor Skills*, 1977, *44*, 231-241.

Bijou, S.W. Practical implications of an interaction model of child development. *Exceptional Children*, 1977, *44*, 6-14.

Bricker, D.D. A rationale for the integration of handicapped and nonhandicapped preschool children. In M.J. Guralnick (Ed.), *Early intervention and the integration of handicapped and nonhandicapped children*. Baltimore: University Park Press, 1978.

Cooke, T., Ruskus, J., Apolloni, T., and Peck, C. Handicapped preschool children in the mainstream: Background, outcomes, and clinical suggestions. *Topics in Early Childhood Special Education*, 1981, *1*, 73-83.

Dunlop, K., Stoneman, Z., and Cantrell, M. Social interaction of exceptional and other children in a mainstreamed preschool classroom. *Exceptional Children*, 1980, *47*, 132-141.

Dunn, L.M. Special education for the mildly retarded—Is much of it justifiable? *Exceptional Children*, 1968, *35*, 371-379.

Kronick, D. The pros and cons of labeling. *Academic Therapy*, 1977, *13*, 101-114.

Marion, R.L. *Educators, parents, and exceptional children.* Rockville, Md.: Aspen Systems Corp., 1981.

Meisels. S.J. First steps in mainstreaming. *Young Children,* 1977, *33,* 4-13.

Peck, C., Apolloni, T., Cooke, T., and Raver, S. Teaching retarded preschoolers to imitate the free play behavior of nonretarded classmates: Trained and generalized effects. *The Journal of Special Education,* 1978, *12,* 195-207.

Raver, S.A. Preschool integration: Experiences from the classroom. *Teaching Exceptional Children,* 1979, *12,* 22-26.

Safford, P.L. *Teaching young children with special needs.* St. Louis: The C.V. Mosby Co., 1978.

Safford, P., and Rosen, L.A. Mainstreaming: Application of a philosophical perspective in an integrated kindergarten program. *Topics in Early Childhood Special Education,* 1981, *1,* 1-10.

Schweinhart, L.J. What makes a quality preschool? *Keys to Early Childhood Education,* 1981, 2(4), 7.

Siegel, G.M., and Spradlin, J.E. Programming for language and communication therapy. In R.L. Schiefelbusch (Ed.), *Language intervention strategies.* Baltimore: University Park Press, 1978.

Tawney, J.W. A cautious view of mainstreaming in early education. *Topics in Early Childhood Special Education,* 1981, *1,* 25-36.

Vincent, L., Brown, L., and Getz-Sheftel, M. Integrating handicapped and typical children during the preschool years: The definition of best educational practice. *Topics in Early Childhood Special Education,* 1981, *1,* 17-24.

Wynne, S., Ulfelder, L., and Dakof, G. *Mainstreaming and early childhood education for handicapped children: Review and implications of research.* Washington, D.C.: Division of Innovation and Development, Bureau of Education for the Handicapped—United States Office of Education, 1975.

2

Providing for special needs in the preschool: the challenge

The attitudes toward young children have changed dramatically in the last 100 years. In the nineteenth century children were required to work on farms and in factories at a very early age. In the initial part of the present century large numbers of children under age 10 worked 12 hours a day 6 days a week for a total wage of 75¢ a week! Going to school at all was a luxury. Children were "to be seen and not heard."

In an environment that encouraged child labor, the weak, the infirm, and the handicapped presented an intolerable burden to all but the wealthiest of families. Imagine you are the parent of a child with a handicap about 100 years ago.

You've just become a parent. You are so excited, but you look at John and he doesn't look right. Your child grows, but he is different. He doesn't walk as early as your other children or as early as your neighbor's child. He falls a lot. His speech is very difficult to understand. It is 1880. There is little you can do to help John. No one seems to care about him. As time goes on, you will be able to send him away to an institution and you will be advised to forget him.

Continue to imagine. Times have changed. You are parents halfway through the twentieth century. It is 1945. People do care. Your child, Jimmy, will be tested, labeled, and put into a special program. That special program will be in a separate school. It may be far from your home. He will not bother anyone. He certainly won't get in the way of the normal children. You are encouraged to accept him and to take advantage of the special facilities provided. If you have means, you have the option of sending him away to a private school.

Imagine again. Now it is 1978. Experts are eager to identify your child, Mary, as soon as possible. They want to help both of you. In fact, you are even being told that she will receive part of her education in the classroom with normal children. They are going to do something for her called mainstreaming. You will be asked to help decide what education will be the most appropriate for Mary. You have some choices, be-

cause a range of special services are available. You are excited but somewhat apprehensive.

Being the parent of a special child, one who is different, has never been easy. It is not easy in the 1980's either. But times are changing, and help is more readily available. Parents are able to choose from a variety of placement alternatives. Specialists work with parents in choosing the placement and array of special services that are most *appropriate*. Although some children may still receive the most appropriate education in a residential or institutional setting, others can be educated appropriately with nonhandicapped peers. In fact, legislation passed in the form of P.L. 94-142 requires children to be educated in the *least restrictive environment*. That means that to the maximum extent appropriate, children should be placed with nonhandicapped peers. This mandate presents a challenge, both legally and professionally: the challenge of providing for special needs in the preschool. To meet this challenge educators from early childhood education and special education are combining forces to create a new field of early childhood special education.

HISTORICAL PERSPECTIVES ON EARLY CHILDHOOD SPECIAL EDUCATION

Bettye Caldwell reminded us just how new this field of early childhood special education really is. Speaking at the Invisible College Conference on Early Childhood Education and the Exceptional Child held in 1972 in San Antonio, Texas, she characterized the period before the 1950's as a period of "forget and hide." The next two decades were a time to "screen and segregate." The most recent decade she described as a time to "identify and help." Caldwell (1973) accentuated the rapid progress that is continuing to unfold in early childhood special education.

The 1980's open with concern for the rights of handicapped individuals. Educational advances

1600 —— 1700 —— 1800 —— 1850 —— 1900 →

HUMANISTIC ADVOCACY

+ John Locke's "blank tablet" (1600's)

+ Rousseau's "Emile" (1762)

+ Pestalozzi (1800's)

CONSIDERATION FOR HANDICAPPED

+ Itard (1799)

+ Sequin (1840's)

+ Montessori (1907)

+ Binet (1904)

EARLY PROGRAMS FOR YOUNG CHILDREN

+ Froebel (1830's)

+ Schurz (first U.S. kindergarten) (1856)

+ Peabody (first English speaking kindergarten) (1860)

+ First public kindergarten (1873)

SPECIAL HANDICAPPED PROGRAMS

+ Gallaudet (deaf) (1817)

+ Howe (blind) (1830's)

+ NEA Division (for handicapped) (1897)

+ 100 plus public classes for handicapped (1911)

+ International Conference for Exceptional Children (1922)

+ White House Conference (1930)

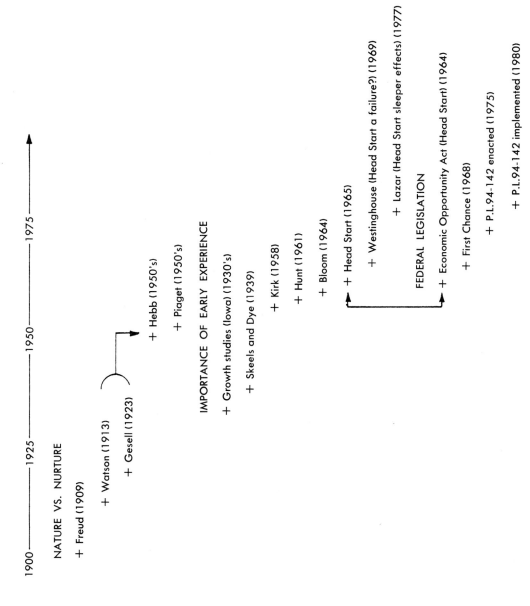

FIG. 2-1. Contributions to early childhood special education.

should be even more astonishing in the next few years. The following historical perspectives, summarized in Fig. 2-1, are included to help you visualize some of the achievements that have given birth to the new subfield of early childhood special education. This table presents only highlights of the forces that have contributed to the development of this new field—those that combine the thinking of authorities in early childhood education and special education.

Pioneering influences on early childhood education

The field of early childhood education is one that is relatively new. So new, in fact, that a number of states have not developed certification programs. Despite this, however, there are historical roots. As early as the late 1600's, voices cried out in search of special consideration for the individuality and innate goodness of young children. John Locke, concerned about the harsh discipline of his time, cultivated the "blank tablet" concept of the newborn's mind to overcome the popular belief that a child was born full of evil ideas. He advocated that children be given empathic understanding.

In his book *Emile*, Jean Jacques Rousseau (1762/1911) stressed the importance of beginning the child's education at birth. He believed that strong discipline and strict lessons were inappropriate conditions for optimal learning. Children should be treated with sympathy and compassion as humans in their own right.

Johann Pestalozzi's writings in the early 1800's indicated his belief in children's ability to learn through self-discovery. He felt that education should be based on the natural development of children. Mothers were believed to be the best teachers. He felt that the home served as the basic model for learning. It was the expression of humane attitudes such as these that served as the original source of an attitude of caring for the unique needs of special children.

The first kindergartens. During the 1830's the first kindergarten was developed in Germany. Friedrich Froebel created this kindergarten in his native homeland because of his concern for the social and emotional development of the "whole child." He sought to make the education of young children different from that of older children. Indeed, certain modern methods of preschool education such as block building, clay modeling, and painting were originally a part of the early training program developed by Froebel.

Influenced by Froebel's philosophy, Margarethe Schurz immigrated to America and established a kindergarten for German-speaking children in 1856 in Watertown, Wisconsin.

Elizabeth Palmer Peabody was so impressed with the work of Schurz that 4 years later she opened the first English-speaking American kindergarten in Boston. Peabody was instrumental in getting William Harris, then superintendent of schools in St. Louis, Missouri, to open the first public school kindergarten in the United States. And so, in 1873, early childhood education was established within the public schools to become a part of the American educational tradition.

The beginnings of special education

Jean-Marc Itard undertook one of the first documented efforts to work with a special child. In 1799 a child approximately 12 years old was found living in the forest near Aveyron, France. The boy, named Victor, was thought to have been raised by animals and was described as "an incurable idiot." Itard refused to accept the idea that Victor's condition was incurable and irreversible. He undertook to humanize Victor through a series of carefully planned lessons stimulating the senses.

Itard (1962) recounts his feelings of optimism, frustration, anger, hope, and despair in *The Wild Boy of Aveyron*. Teachers today who work with extremely handicapped children may easily recognize these feelings. Although Itard did not achieve the success he visualized, his efforts had a significant impact on the future of special education. Itard was one of the first to demonstrate and record an attempt to understand empathically the needs of a special child.

In addition, Itard developed unique teaching techniques and provided much encouragement to one of his students, Edouard Seguin. Seguin profoundly influenced international progress in the treatment of the mentally retarded. He brought his pioneering work in the systematic training of the mentally retarded to the United States, where he is credited with founding the American Association on Mental Deficiency.

The first attempt to identify children in need of special instruction. Public attention was given to the identification of handicapped children as early as 1904. Alfred Binet was commissioned by France's minister of public instruction to design a test to determine which children

could succeed in the public schools and which children needed special attention. It is interesting to note that the French had as a major consideration the retention of special children in regular classrooms. Just as we are concerned today with what is known as mainstreaming, they wanted to keep handicapped children with normal peers. They sought to create a method of identification that would avoid the problem of prejudice. Imagine the chagrin of the French commissioners if they could witness the need for legal trials to reduce the labeling and discrimination of handicapped children in the 1980's!

Casa dei Bambini. While France was developing special public school programs for children who were found by Binet and co-worker Theophile Simon to be in need of such services; Maria Montessori was busy in Italy creating a nursery school, Casa dei Bambini. Montessori revolutionized the notion of early education

with her establishment of the "Children's House" in the Roman slums in 1907. She began her career as a physician and spent her earliest professional years working with mentally retarded children. Because of her training, early interests, and the nature of the school she was asked to develop, Montessori stressed cleanliness, order, and housekeeping skills as well as reading, writing, and arithmetic. Aspects of both the discovery approach to learning and programmed instruction can be found in the techniques developed by Montessori. She suggested that teachers observe the natural, spontaneous behavior of children and then arrange learning experiences to encourage their development. Her nursery school included children as young as 2½ years of age at a time when American educators were considering the use of her ideas in programs for 4- and 5-year old children.

Like Edouard Seguin, Montessori believed in developing the child's natural curiosity through systematic training of the senses. Both proceeded with optimism and determination to train those who some might believe to be beyond hope. Even so, Montessori's approach was out of favor in the United States for some time. The 1960's brought a resurgence of interest in Montessori techniques. Montessori's "sensorial" materials are advocated for use with handicapped children, because they are manipulable, three-dimensional, and concrete. Advocates cite the emphasis on task analysis, sequencing, and individualization evident in the Montessori approach as worthy for use with children who have limited abilities as well as those who are gifted.

Nature v. nurture controversy

With a faith in the influence of genetically predetermined patterns, Arnold Gesell established the Yale Clinic of Child development, which was a center for research on children for over three decades. Historically, Gesell is the most articulate spokesman for maturation as the central concept of child development. Although Gesell acknowledged the role of the environment as the setting for growth, he simply contended that children would grow as their genes directed.

Gesell's normative stages. In *The Preschool Child*, Gesell (1923) emphasized the importance of the early years. He stated: (The preschool period) "is biologically the most important period in the development of an individual for the simple but sufficient reason that it comes first in a dynamic sequence; it inevitably influences all subsequent development" (p. 2).

Gesell's influence on early childhood special education came from his interest in abnormal children and his clinical goal—diagnosis of developmental deviance. To this end he created the normative approach based on keen observation of children at various ages. To Gesell age was unquestionably a convenient line along which to show the orderliness of development. However, Gesell warned that the "ages and stages" concept could be interpreted too literally. He did not feel that norms were rigid but rather indices of types of behavior likely to occur at a particular age. Gesell's warning is still appropriate, because current preschool screening efforts often use the Gesell scales as convenient measures of what is or is not considered to be normal development.

Watson's environmental behaviorism. At the same time Gesell was continuing his work on measurement and diagnosis, John Watson sought to study behavior by more objective methods. In 1913, he made the leap from a theory that emphasized the influence of heredity in the development of children to one that emphasized the contribution of specific environmental influences.

His most lasting contribution to our knowledge of children is derived from his studies of infants and his surprising proposal that parents could make of their children what they wished. Parents were warned that the most sensible way to treat children was to be objective and kindly firm. Children were not to be coddled. Indeed, this more rigid disciplinary approach was reflected in the articles from popular women's magazines analyzed by Stendler (1950). Present-day curriculum for children with behavior disorders that stresses the use of behavior modification might be said to have its roots in the behaviorism espoused by Watson as well as such famous scientists as Ivan Pavlov and B.F. Skinner.

Freud's affective development. While Gesell was espousing maturation and Watson emphasized the role of classical conditioning in the development of the child, Sigmund Freud added yet another dimension to the understanding of the child. Concentrating on affective development, Freud brought back a pessimistic, demonic view of the child long forgotten. Childhood, as depicted by Freud, was ambiguous, incoherent, and filled with conflict (Freud, 1953; Kessen, 1965). He espoused a subtle form of maturationalism. Permissiveness was advocated to free the child of conflict and neurosis. Present-day treatment of children with emotional disturbances that uses free expression in such therapeutic techniques as play therapy originated in Freud's psychoanalytical approach.

Hebb's interaction model. In the late 1950's D.O. Hebb insisted that child development was not the result of either heredity or environment alone. The heredity v. environment–nature v. nurture controversy began to gain the perspective that is present today. Hebb proposed that behavior is produced by the interaction between genetic and environmental variables. It is this interaction model of child development that is espoused currently as the most realistic approach to the education of young handicapped children. In fact, the keynote address given at the Council for Exceptional Children's first series of training institutes on early childhood education (held in February, 1977) was entitled

"Practical Implications of an Interaction Model of Child Development" (Bijou, 1977).

It is fortunate for the handicapped child that educators are realizing the need to consider both the developmental characteristics of children and the present as well as the predicted future characteristics of the society. Either extreme position would be to the detriment of young handicapped children. For example, individuals who see one's heredity or nature as the prime determinant of development may question the need for individualized instructional techniques. After all, what can the early childhood teacher provide that will not be provided as a result of maturation anyway? The very concept of labeling implies an irrevocable condition that must be internally controlled.

On the other hand, teachers who feel the environment to be the primary determiner of development may take on an unrealistic burden, leaving them defeated and feeling much the same as Itard. Even though the environmentalist position is the more optimistic of the two, extreme advocacy could lead to unrealistic rather than appropriate educational experiences for children. Educators would have to be infallible in their ability to regulate contingencies with the special child's environment.

As a result, some theorists who consider the interactional model to be too static turn to a more dynamic theory to explain developmental deviations. This theory, the transactional model, considers both the organism and the environment to be plastic in nature. A continual and progressive interrelationship is fostered with the organism functioning as an active participant in its own growth. "From this position the child's response is thought to be more than a simple reaction to his environment. Instead, he is thought to be actively engaged in attempts to organize and structure his world" (Sameroff and Chandler, 1975, p. 235).

Piaget's spontaneous cognition. Although published in the early 1900's, it wasn't until the

1950's that Jean Piaget's elaborate descriptions of the development of children's thinking began to be accepted by American psychologists. Piaget proposed an inborn tendency toward adaptation that, in its encounter with the environment, results in categories of knowledge that are remarkably similar among all human beings. Piaget's concept of child development and his stages of cognitive development will again be considered in Chapter 7. His prolific writings and those of followers continue to remind us of the need to be aware of the unfolding internal mental capacities of children.

According to Piaget, the purpose of education is to provide opportunities that allow a child to combine experiences into coherent systems (schemes) that constitute the child's knowledge. "Knowledge" then is constructed from within rather than acquired from without (Furth, 1970). Therefore each child's capacity to learn is thought to be uniquely experientially based. Piaget's concept of the child as an active learner stimulated by inborn curiosity has prompted the development of preschool programs designed to allow the child to become an active initiator of learning experiences. From a developmental point of view, a child's strengths rather than deficits receive emphasis. Most notable of the Piagetian-based programs is the Perry Preschool Project developed in the late 1950's in Ypsilanti, Michigan. An extension known as the High/Scope First Chance Preschool serves as a model program for those desiring to integrate handicapped preschoolers into programs with nonhandicapped preschoolers (Banet, 1979).

EDUCATIONAL PROGRAMS FOR CHILDREN WITH SPECIAL NEEDS

In 1817 the first residential school for the deaf was organized in Connecticut by Thomas Hopkins Gallaudet. Using the terminology of the time, it was known as the Asylum for the Education and Instruction of the Deaf and Dumb. Samuel Howe directed the opening of the New England Asylum for the Blind in Boston in the 1830's. Over 100 large city school systems had established special schools or special classes for the handicapped by 1911.

Before World War II parents were inclined to hide their more severely handicapped children in institutions or were unwilling to admit their children needed special services. The mildly handicapped child usually received no services before placement in a regular classroom where he was unsuccessful, frustrated, humiliated, and usually a "dropout."

After World War II the public began to feel some awareness of and guilt over the numbers of formerly healthy young men who returned in a maimed condition. Parent organizations developed and directed political pressure toward improvement of services for the handicapped, including children. Success of the programs for the sensory impaired (which had provided stimulation to children from nonstimulating, possibly overprotective environments) were certainly a boost to the efforts of advocates of special education. Between the years of 1953 and 1958 the increase in enrollment in special classes was 260% (Love, 1972).

Project Head Start

The creation of Project Head Start is thought to have evolved through a series of influences. One of the earliest attempts to demonstrate the close relationship between nurturing, environmental stimulation, and mental growth processes grew out of the Iowa growth studies in the late 1930's. Skeels and Dye transferred 12 children under 3 years of age from an orphanage to an institution for the retarded. In the institution the children were cared for with great affection by adolescent girls who were considered to be retarded. A comparison group of children remained in the orphanage where they received no specialized attention. Follow-up testing demonstrated that those placed in the stimulating environment increased their intelligence test scores while those who remained in the orphanage decreased their intelligence test scores (Skeels, 1942). Twenty-one years later Skeels (1966) found dramatic differences between those who had been placed in the enriching environment and those who had not. The 12 children in the experimental group were found to be self-supporting. Of the comparison group, four had been institutionalized and one had died. Educationally speaking, four of those who had been in the enriching environment completed college, and the others had a median high school education. On the other hand, the median education for the comparison group was only at the third grade level.

Samuel Kirk (1958) also conducted experiments on the influence of early education on the development of young, mentally handicapped children. In his textbook, Kirk's suggestion that inadequate cultural environment might be a cause of mental retardation helped to convince politicians of the need for compensatory educational programs for young children. Perhaps more convincing was the conclusion reached by Benjamin Bloom (1964) that claimed that about "50% of the (intellectual) development takes place between conception and age 4, about 30% between ages 4 and 8, and 20% between ages 8 and 17" (p. 88).

Bloom's argument was advanced by J. McVicker Hunt's popular book *Intelligence and Experience* (1961), which so eloquently argued against the notion of fixed intelligence. Attempting to lay to rest the heredity v. environment controversy, Hunt supported well his contention that heredity sets the limits, whereas environment determines the extent to which the limits will be achieved. And so, under the belief that children's intelligence develops early and rapidly and that enrichment early in life can have profound influences on the child's development, federal funding for Project Head Start was provided in 1965.

A breakthrough. The primary purpose in passing the Economic Opportunity Act of 1964 was to break the cycle of poverty by providing educational and social opportunities for children from low-income families. The result was the implementation of Head Start during the summer of 1965 with approximately 550,000 children in 2,500 child development centers. Parent involvement both within the Head Start classroom and on policy committees set a precedent. This has, no doubt, influenced legislators to require parent involvement in current decisions involving handicapped children.

The Head Start Program had a significant impact on the development of early childhood special education. It was the first major public exposure to the importance of early educational experiences. As Caldwell (1973) points out, "the implicit strategy of early Head Start was to devise a program that fits the children as they are found and that institutes remedial procedures to correct whatever deficiencies they have, whether they are nutritional, experiential, or medical" (p. 5).

Legislation enacted in 1972 required Head Start programs to include handicapped children to the extent of at least 10% of their enrollment. Mainstreaming handicapped children into classrooms with nonhandicapped children has become a major activity of Head Start. In fact, the 1978 Head Start enrollment of handicapped preschoolers exceeded 40,000.

A success. After the extreme optimism that accompanied the establishment of Head Start, it came as a shock to those who worked daily with the children and their parents that the program failed to produce notable gains. The Westinghouse report of 1969 cited data suggesting that measured gains made by Head Starters faded rapidly. By the end of first grade there often were no significant differences between the overall academic performance of children who had attended Head Start programs and those from the same kinds of homes who had not. Doubting the validity of this investigation, influential people fought for a stay of execution (Gotts, 1973). Among them was Edward Zigler, who was a member of the original planning committee that conceptualized Head Start and later director of the Office of Child Development. Zigler (1978) retorted: "I ask my colleagues in the research community to forgo the temptation of delivering definitive pronouncements concerning the fade-out issue and await instead the collection and analyses of more data" (p. 73).

Indeed, Zigler was to be rewarded for his faith. A consortium of researchers under the direction of Irving Lazar conducted longitudinal investigations into the persistence of the effects of a number of preschool programs located throughout the United States (Lazar and Darlington, 1979). The evidence from the projects studied clearly indicated that there are long-lasting positive effects from early intervention programs. Tracing children who had been involved in preschool programs into their teens or early twenties, Lazar and his colleagues found that children who had been exposed to some form of preschool education were far less likely to require special education or to be left back a grade. Achievement and intelligence quotient (IQ) gains that were found immediately after preschool and then seemed to fade out reappeared later in the children's academic careers. Just the economic implications of decreasing the need for retention or special education alone should convince legislators of the value of early childhood special education.

The First Chance Program

In 1968 Congress recognized the need for model programs to spur on the development of services for handicapped children from birth through age 8. Legislation was enacted to establish the Handicapped Children's Early Education Program, better known as the First Chance program. These projects were required to include parents in their activities, run in-service training, evaluate the progress of both the children and the program, coordinate activities with public schools, and disseminate information on the project to professionals and the public. In 1980 the total number of funded projects was 177, with 111 including infants in their population (Swan, 1981). These projects serve two basic purposes: (1) to provide models of exemplary services for young handicapped children that can be replicated and (2) to disseminate information that will encourage this replication.

Delivery systems. The concept of delivery systems applies to how, when, and where services are delivered to children and their families. Karnes and Zehrbach (1977) summarized the unique approaches of 120 First Chance programs. The majority of these fell under the following delivery system headings: (1) home, (2) home followed by center, (3) home and center, (4) center, and (5) technical assistance and consultative services.

Most projects that deliver services only within the home view the parents as the primary teachers of their children. Such programs are especially useful in rural areas or where parents are reluctant to have their children leave home. Many of the children originally served only at home enter a center program when they become 3 years old. Some receive services in both a center and at home. Staff members model appropriate teaching techniques in their homes. A number of the center-based programs are not only cross-categorical but also include normal children. Finally, those centers that use technical assistance do so for help with diagnosis and in-service training. It should be remembered that the programs vary considerably in the population served, the geographical location, and the theoretical basis as well as in the delivery systems. Karnes and Zehrbach (1977) and Swan (1980) provide more details on these fascinating projects.

SOCIETAL PRESSURES: THE IMPACT OF LITIGATION AND LEGISLATION

As illustrated in the historical overview, it was not until the mid-1900's that the public school really began to make provisions for children with varying degrees of handicaps. Concerned citizens and active parent and professional associations have played a vital role in society's changing attitude toward the exceptional child.

Development of professional groups

It has been said that Alexander Graham Bell, inventor of the telephone and a strong advocate of oral education of the deaf, should be given credit for organizing professional advocates of special education. He petitioned the Nation Education Association (NEA) to establish a division to be concerned about the needs of the handicapped. In 1897 the NEA established such a division and named it the Department of Education of the Deaf, Blind, and the Feebleminded. As attitudes and knowledge of the handicapped changed, this name was later changed to the Department of Special Education.

The formation of the International Council for Exceptional Children in 1922 provided the impetus for what some believe to be the most influential advocacy group continuing to provide national leadership in behalf of exceptional children. The 1930 White House Conference on Child Health and Protection was a milestone in marking the first time that special education had received national recognition.

The power of private citizens

Several factors came together after World War II that gave rise to the development of strong parent organizations in the late 1940's. Professional knowledge was expanding, the country felt responsible to aid its wounded, and prominent people such as Pearl Buck, Roy Rogers and Dale Evans, and the Kennedy family were visibly calling for better education of the handicapped. Parents no longer felt the need to hide their handicapped child. Pressure groups like the United Cerebral Palsy Association, the National Association for Retarded Citizens, and the American Foundation for the Blind began to demand alternatives, other than institutionalization, for the education of their handicapped children.

Professional groups joined parent groups in capitalizing on the historic Supreme Court decision in *Brown v. Board of Education of Topeka* (1954). Although primarily an integration initiative, the Court ruled that state laws that permitted segregated public schools were in violation of the Fourteenth Amendment's "equal protection under the law" clause. Realizing that decisions applicable to one minority group must be applicable to another, pressure groups sought to secure legislation that would create significant educational changes in behalf of exceptional children. However, little actually occurred until after the publication of an article by Dunn (1968) that provided a blueprint for changes that recognized the rights of handicapped students. The boxes on pp. 24 and 25 summarize some of the landmark court cases and legislative milestones in the development of free and appropriate education for all children.

Public Law 94-142—Education of All Handicapped Children Act

It is the intent of P.L. 94-142 that a free, appropriate public education is made available to all handicapped children when they reach 3 years of age. The law states that such services will be available no later than September 1, 1980, in all states where the requirement is not inconsistent with state law or practice or the order of any court (P.L. 94-142 Sec. 612 [2] [B]). Incentives have been designed to encourage all states to implement P.L. 94-142. The federal government has provided special grants to encourage the provision of services for early childhood special education. Only time will tell how effective these incentive grants become. In the meantime it is imperative that teachers understand the basic principles of the law if they are to be influential as child advocates (public supporters of children's rights) as well as professionals in early childhood special education.

SIGNIFICANT LITIGATION

Litigation	Description
A. The right to free education	
Pennsylvania Association for Retarded Children v. the Commonwealth of Pennsylvania (1971).	The court ruled through a consent agreement that the state must provide free public education to all retarded children, regardless of the degree of their handicap. It is interesting to note that the court also intended that placement be in the most integrated environment (Gargiulo, 1980). The PARC case established the right of parents to participate in major decisions affecting their children.
Mills v. Board of Education of the District of Columbia (1971).	The court specifically established the constitutional right of all exceptional children, regardless of the degree of severity of their handicap, to a public education.
B. The right to appropriate education	
Diana v. State Board of Education of California (1970).	Through a court-approved stipulation it was agreed that Mexican-American and Chinese-American children enrolled in classes for the educable mentally retarded (EMR) would be reevaluated using their primary language, test items would be revised to be suitable to the minority culture, and misplaced children would be returned to the regular programs.
Larry P. v. Riles (1972).	The court ruled that no black student could be placed in an educable mentally retarded class on the basis of criteria that rely primarily on the results of intelligence tests. It further required school officials to demonstrate the rationality of test-based classification procedures. In a subsequent ruling the court prohibited the public schools "from utilizing, permitting the use of, or approving the use of any standardized intelligence tests . . . for the identification of black E.M.R. children or their replacement into E.M.R. classes, without securing prior approval by his court" (*P. v. Riles*, 1979, p. 104). This decision was based on the court's finding that standardized intelligence tests are racially and culturally biased and therefore have a discriminatory impact on black children.

SIGNIFICANT LEGISLATION

Public Law 85-926 (1958) Training of Professional Personnel	Established training grants to universities and state educational agencies to train special education leadership personnel
Public Law 88-164 (1963) Training of Professional Personnel	Expanded authority to train personnel for handicapping areas not previously covered
Public Law 95-568 (1964) Economic Opportunity Act	Created the Office of Economic Opportunity that developed and began administration of Project Head Start during the summer of 1965
Public Law 89-10 (1965) Elementary and Secondary Education Act (ESEA)	Provided a $1.33 billion commitment to improve elementary and secondary education; expanded special programs
Public Law 89-750 (1966) Education for Handicapped Children	Expanded P.L. 89-10, authorizing funds to initiate, improve, and expand services for the handicapped; established a National Advisory Committee on Handicapped Children and created the Bureau of Education for the Handicapped (BEH).
Public Law 90-538 (1968) Handicapped Children's Early Education Assistance Act	Significant to the education of handicapped preschool children; established experimental early education programs throughout the country
Public Law 91-230 (1969) ESEA	Extended P.L. 89-10 by authorizing the establishment of model education centers for children with learning disabilities; included a provision for gifted and talented youth
Public Law 92-424 (1972) Economic Opportunity Act Amendments	Established a preschool mandate that required that not less than 10% of the total number of Head Start placements be reserved for handicapped children
Public Law 93-380 (1974) Education Amendments	Preceded P.L. 94-142 and established a total federal commitment to the education of handicapped children, concerns included education within the least restrictive environment, nondiscriminatory testing, and privacy rights (Title V., "Buckley Amendment")
Public Law 94-142 (1975) Education of All Handicapped Children Act	Revised and expanded P.L. 93-380; provides a free, appropriate public education with related services to all handicapped children between ages 3 and 21; details of this act will be discussed in the following section

Purpose. The purpose of P.L. 94-142 is:

To insure that all handicapped children have available to them . . . a free, appropriate public education which includes special education and related services designed to meet their unique needs, to insure that the rights of handicapped children and their parents or guardians are protected, to assist States and localities to provide for the education of all handicapped children and to assess and insure the effectiveness of efforts to educate handicapped children (Sec. 601 [c]).

Appropriate public education. The law requires that a qualified school representative, teacher, the parents or guardian, and whenever possible the child join together in the development of an Individualized Educational Plan (IEP). This written statement must include (1) a statement of the child's present level of academic functioning, (2) a declaration of annual goals complete with appropriate short-term instructional objectives, (3) a description of specific educational services to be provided to the child and the degree to which the child will participate in regular educational programs, (4) the proposed date for initiation and estimation of the required length of services, and (5) annual evaluation procedures specifying objective criteria designed to determine if the short-term instructional objectives have been met (Sec. 602, 19).

Procedural safeguards. The law requires that handicapped children be served in the least restrictive environment appropriate to their educational needs. Children can be placed in separate classes or schools only when their handicap is so severe that regular school placement is considered inappropriate. The act also requires nondiscriminatory testing and the use of multiple criteria in the determination of placement (Sec. 612, 5, C). This requirement implies the need for all teachers to become skilled in the education of children who exhibit a variety of educational needs.

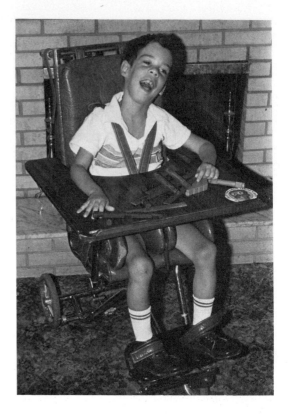

P.L. 94-142 provides the right for parents or guardians to examine all records, obtain independent evaluation, and require written notification in their native language of plans to change a child's educational program. The intent is to ensure that a child's rights are legally protected. Parents or guardians are entitled to a hearing before termination, exclusion, or classification of a student into a special program.

The current challenge

With the documented success of experimental preschool intervention programs (Lazar, 1979) and the implementation of P.L. 94-142, educators are optimistic about the future of both special and general education. In the provision of an analysis of public policies, Gilhool (1976, p. 13) stated:

Thus special education may become general and general education, special. We are approaching the day when for each child, handicapped or not, the law will require that the schooling fit the child, his needs, his capacities, and his wishes; not that the child fit the school.

It is this need to fit the schooling to the child that is the heart of this textbook. The following sections review strategies and models appropriate for the integration of handicapped children into the mainstream. Additionally we explain (1) implications of research for the future education of young handicapped children and (2) a view of the trends and most promising practices in the education of special-needs children. It is intended that this review will help to support our thesis that teachers must be trained and willing to engage in educational practices that fit schooling to the child rather than requiring the child to fit the school.

EDUCATIONAL STRATEGIES FOR THE INCLUSION OF HANDICAPPED PRESCHOOL CHILDREN

With the focus on public-supported preschool education created by the 1964 funding of Head Start came the need for development of model centers. Preschool education had been almost exclusively the domain of the middle and upper classes within settings that did not provide for the inclusion of children who were different in culture or ability. Programs primarily followed what has become known as the "child-development" or "normal-development model" (Anastasiow, 1978; Mayer, 1971). The concept of "readiness" has been associated with this model. Children were thought to develop at their own rate if encouraged by a warm, nurturing, and organized environment.

Educators were highly influenced by developmental age enthusiasts such as Gesell and prepared curricula experiences according to the developmental scales available. Children were

seen as active learners capable of choosing activities from a variety of activity centers. Social-emotional development, large group involvement, self-concept enhancement, and child-to-child interaction were high priorities. Teacher-oriented activities were prepared for groups of children. By all appearances these programs, which really did not have to accommodate significant differences in behavior or ability, were successful. But nothing really noteworthy had been done in the way of program evaluation or the development of model programs that could readily be replicated.

Faced with a lack of program models, directors of the newly funded programs for children of low-income families began to experiment with ideas and techniques. Out of their efforts came the development of programs based on (1) behavioristic principles as purported by Watson, Skinner, and others; (2) the cognitively oriented strategies of Piaget; and (3) the resurgence of techniques developed by Montessori. These programs, in turn, served as the bases for the development of the model programs funded by the Bureau of Education for the Handicapped in the late 1960's and 1970's. These First Chance programs have been and continue to be evaluated. The intent is to determine those instructional elements most critical in the development of the potential of preschool handicapped children.

The integration of early childhood education and special education

Programs that adapt curricula to meet the needs of children with a wide range of differences in skills, learning styles, background, and potential require deliberate integration of facets from both early childhood education and special education. Early childhood specialists promote awareness of needs of the "whole child," whereas special educators promote awareness of unique needs within the total child. These unique needs are considered in relation to tasks being taught and the environment in which they are taught. Learning characteristics of the child as well as the tasks are analyzed. The focus of this book is definitely one of combining the best of both fields.

Very recently Anastasiow (1981) challenged teacher preparation departments to recognize that handicapped children are more like normal children than different. He is especially concerned with basic needs such as emotional development and creative play. Future coursework in the area of early childhood special education needs to encompass widely what is known in child development and learning theory. Anastasiow (1981) envisions the development of early childhood programs in which "behaviorism (task analysis or applied behavioral analysis) will be used as a technology of program construction and implementation while cognitive theories will be used as the theoretical basis to account for and describe human behavior" (p. 277).

Probable dimensions of effective intervention programs

Even though evaluation studies have failed to determine that any one model of early childhood education is the most effective, these studies point the way to some probable dimensions of effective programs. In brief, teachers are urged to consider the following 10 elements when initiating or evaluating a program (Anastasiow, 1978; Karnes, 1973; Lazar, 1979; Safford, 1978; Vopava and Royce, 1978; Weikart, 1972):

1. High adult-to-child ratio (1 adult to 4 or 5 children)
2. Commitment of the staff to the approach being implemented
3. Extensive and cooperative planning for instruction
4. High level of parent involvement
5. Implementation of definite plans to improve parenting

6. Individualized instructional objectives with continuous evaluation and revision, when necessary
7. Experimentation and evaluation of a variety of techniques to determine those most effective in meeting the individualized objectives
8. Strong emphasis on language development
9. Provision for positive reinforcement and effective use of principles of behavior management, task analysis, and modeling
10. Continuous in-service training and program evaluation

The importance of developmental guidelines

Most educators readily agree that there is an incredible similarity in the sequential patterns of children regardless of their place of origin. Of course, there is also an equally incredible amount of variance or individuality within the sequential patterns of development. Cognizant of the necessity of understanding unique needs within an overall pattern of growth, educators continue to rely on the use of normal developmental scales and checklists for guidance. (Appendix A provides sample guidelines.)

Traditionally, children whose behavior was too deviant from what was determined to be "normal" were excluded from most day-care centers and nursery schools. Increasingly, children who function reasonably within the 2- to 5-year span of "normalcy" are being included. Teachers are using developmental guidelines, not as a criterion for exclusion but as a source of information on which to base instructional objectives.

The need for informed eclecticism

In reviewing the literature that evaluates programs for disadvantaged children, Mayer concludes that "other than the inclusion of an emphasis on language, curriculum components are less crucial to a program's effectiveness than the planning component" (1971, p. 312). After analyzing data evaluating five intervention models, Karnes (1973) stated, "As simple as it may seem, the major guideline derived from these data is that when you want a child to learn something, a deliberate effort has to be made to teach him what you want him to learn" (p. 56). More recently in a discussion of strategies and models for mainstreamed early childhood programs, Anastasiow (1978) emphasized the realization "that there is no one set of techniques and strategies available for facilitating development of all children" (p. 95). He further states that teachers must use planned experimentation to discover effective remedial techniques.

This planned experimentation to discover effective techniques required knowledge of specific features of various instructional approaches and their influences on the behavior of individual children (Lillie, 1975). Such knowledge is prerequisite to eclecticism (choosing methods from various sources), which is informed and, thus, more likely to be effective.

Options within early childhood education

Theoretical approaches within early childhood education have been categorized in a number of ways. For clarity, the categorical approach selected here is in keeping with the historical overview presented earlier. It should be remembered that these approaches overlap in a variety of ways and that there are almost no "pure" programs. Therefore this description may be somewhat unlike that of others who set about to relate the same basic information.

The child-development, maturationist or normal-development approach. The child-development, maturationist, or normal-development approach was discussed briefly earlier in this chapter, because it has been typical of traditionally oriented nursery schools or kindergartens. Curriculum experiences are organized around units and themes such as community helpers, the family, and the zoo. Unique abilities are developed within a relatively unrestrictive environment where the teacher facilitates each child's natural rate of development. Early compensatory Head Start programs turned to this model in their quest to provide "enrichment" for children thought to be deprived of experiences received by children of better means. Activities are often carried on in groups using activity centers. Field trips are a highly valued part of the curriculum. Play is considered to be essential to both cognitive and emotional development. Gesell, of course, is considered to be the originator of this maturationist viewpoint.

The behaviorist approach. In contrast to the compensatory programs that provided enriching theories through the somewhat nondirected approach of the child-development model, the behaviorist approach concentrates on direct teaching of skills. Although the child developmentalists view the child as a very active participant in learning, the behaviorists perceive the child as passive. Behavior is to be shaped through manipulation of environmental circumstances that produce specific responses to be rewarded. Academic skills receive high priority. Skills are analyzed, and component skills are sequenced. This sequence then directs the curriculum content. Direct Instruction Systems for Teaching Arithmetic and Reading (DISTAR), which originated with a program begun by Bereiter and Englemann (1966), is considered characteristic of this approach.

The psychoanalytical-psychosocial approach. The psychoanalytical-psychosocial approach originated with Freud but is recognized most easily through the writings of Erikson (1963). It emphasizes the emotional, affective nature of a child's development. The child is seen as evolving through a series of psychosexual stages, which are discussed in detail in Chapter 8. Proponent curricula focus on attitudes, values, and promotion of positive interaction with others. Children explore and actively interact with their environment under the watchful eyes of teachers who encourage autonomy and mastery. The Bank Street model (Biber, 1970) is characteristic of this approach.

The cognitive-interactional approach. Programs within the cognitive-interactional approach envision active learners who seek interaction through which cognitive development occurs. Although different in structure, programs developed according to the teachings of both Piaget and Montessori stress this basic view. Reference is made to the cognitive curriculum developed during the course of the Perry Preschool Project by Weikart (1971). Children are encouraged to become actively involved and to engage in "discovery learning" designed toward movement through the Piagetian stages of cognitive development. Teachers set up opportunities for experiences in classification, seriation, temporal relations, and spatial relations that are facilitated through observation and questioning.

Within a Montessori program children learn through active discovery but rely more on highly sequenced, specialized materials. The importance of sensory-motor learning is again paramount. Children's learning can be self-directed because the materials permit self-correction. Learning is highly individualized with little opportunity for group teaching. Specific skill development is ensured through this highly structured approach.

The contribution of special education

The contribution of special education is derived primarily from emphasis on the need to consider individual differences when selecting curriculum approaches and planning activities. A diagnostic-prescriptive program is often the result. Such an approach has roots in the medical model, where the individual's condition is diagnosed, and treatment is prescribed. Ysseldyke and Salvia (1974) discuss two basic models within the diagnostic-prescriptive teaching approach. Descriptions follow.

The ability training approach. The ability

training approach seeks to identify the processes or abilities that create observed interindividual and intraindividual differences. Profiles of an individual's strengths and weaknesses in perceptual, cognitive, psycholinguistic, and psychomotor development are constructed from information obtained from testing. Activities based on the test constructs are then prescribed. The GOAL kit developed and used by Karnes in the Precise Early Education for Children with Handicaps (PEECH) project (Karnes and Zehrbach, 1977) contains characteristic activities.

Although the ability training approach as a total approach is under criticism (Hammill and Larsen, 1978), a worthy contribution has been made. Understanding an individual child's strengths and weaknesses, both in terms of his or her individual profile and in comparison to others of the same age, allows teachers to adapt the curriculum accordingly. For example, children who have better auditory processing skills (see Chapter 6 for definitions) will perform better when something is verbally explained as well as visually demonstrated. This combination allows the weaker visual skills to be strengthened with the help of the stronger auditory skills.

The task analysis approach. While the ability training approach analyzes the process or ability strengths and weaknesses within a child, the task analysis approach looks at the subcomponents of a task. The ability training approach may look at the child's performance in terms of visual, auditory, and tactile performance. This approach examines the requirements of the task. What is the child expected to learn, and how is he or she expected to learn it? Terminal behaviors (skills) are broken into en route behaviors that are sequenced from the easiest to the most difficult. This approach, which is essentially behavioral, is well described in Chapter 4.

The need for both ability training and task analysis. The direction taken in this book is in agreement with Smead (1977) in which both ap-

proaches; used in combination, provide the most appropriate education for children with unique needs. Analysis of individual strengths and weaknesses in abilities or processes allows teachers to select the most appropriate mode of instruction. Analysis of the task, when combined with analysis of what the child can and cannot do, allows the teacher to begin where the child is and then progress in a step-by-step direction to a realistic goal.

The move toward noncategorical instruction. For years special education has focused on diagnosing children and teaching them according to categories such as mental retardation, emotional disturbance, and learning disability. The detrimental effects of labels (Algozzine, Mercer, and Countermine, 1977) and the difficulty of making a differential diagnosis of young children (Lerner, Mardell-Czudnowski, and Goldenberg, 1981) strengthen the arguments for noncategorical placement. Such placement also recognizes the needs of multihandicapped children. However, the instructional techniques developed for

use within various handicapping categories should not be overlooked. These have evolved through much effort, and their use has often been evaluated. They are a contribution from the field of special education. Although we do not advocate labeling and categorizing children, definitions of current categories are included in Appendix C. The literature devoted to these categories serves as a rich resource from which to choose instructional strategies. Many of these have been incorporated throughout this book.

A successful eclectic approach

Notable is the extensive program developed by Bricker and Bricker (1976) that integrates a variety of theoretical bases. This experimental program includes an equal number of nondelayed children who are matched by developmental level with delayed children. Therefore, this program serves not only as a model of informed eclecticism but also as a model that educates handicapped and nonhandicapped children together.

TABLE 1
Comparison of program models

Variables	Approaches				
	Child-development	Behavioral	Piagetian	Montessori	Developmental-prescriptive
View of child					
Active	X		X	X	X
Passive		X			
Stage determined			X	X	X
Age determined	X				
Focus-emphasis					
Sensory-motor			X	X	X
Language		X			X
Thought processes			X		X
Social-emotional	X				X
Self-help	X			X	X
School readiness	X	X			X
Self-concept	X				
Approach					
Skill assessment		X		X	X
Sequenced, small steps		X		X	X
Modeling-reinforcement		X			X
Repetition-drill		X			X
Prescriptive training		X		X	X
Inquiry			X	X	
Play highly valued	X		X		
Planned language learning		X			X
Incidental language learning	X		X	X	
Self-correction		X		X	
Self-paced		X	X	X	X
Activity centers	X		X	X	
Creative activities	X		X	X	X
Direct instruction		X			X
Teacher as facilitator	X		X	X	
Inquiry encouraged			X	X	

Based on interpretations of Anastasiow, 1978; Anastasiow and Mansergh, 1975; Safford, 1978; Stevens and King, 1976.

After careful consideration these researchers felt that adherence to either a traditional maturational orientation or a behavioristic learning theory approach could not adequately account for the complexities of human behavior they would encounter. Therefore they combined several key Piagetian concepts into a position they refer to as the "constructive interaction-adaptive" position. Believing that the sensori-motor period is critical to subsequent language development and that infants learn from active interaction, they insisted on beginning intervention in the first year of life.

The parent training program became an integral part of the project, because these developers believe strongly that parents and teachers must avoid working at cross purposes. Parents were trained in the use of behavioral management techniques. A task analysis orientation, characteristic of special education and called "developmental programming" by the Brickers, was used to organize an educational curriculum covering language, sensorimotor, social, and motor development. Lessons were planned in small steps, and positive reinforcment (rewarding appropriate behavior) was used. Psycholinguistic and perceptual theory, again drawn from the field of special education, provided needed contributions to critical language training. And the teachings of social learning theory were used when promoting positive peer modeling.

Some attempt has been made to discuss this program at length to encourage the development of eclecticism that is based on an understanding of basic theoretical orientations and their consequences. Table 1 illustrates a brief comparison of some of the models that are presently described in the literature. Readers must recognize this is an effort to summarize some very involved theories and therefore does not do any of them justice. This interpretation is also open to question and perhaps rebuttal. We are taking the risk of including it here in hopes of generating student-instructor discussion and investigation that will lead to greater understanding of possible theoretical underpinnings. Annotated references are included at the end of the chapter to facilitate such inquiry.

Model similarities. Generally all programs, perhaps with the exception of the strictest of behavioral approaches, see the child as an active explorer intrinsically involved in learning. White (1959) refers to the child's tendency toward playful exploration as competence or effectance motivation. It is this capacity to interact effectively with the environment that is thought to result in cumulative learning that paves the way to maturity.

Most programs thus emphasize the role of sensory-motor involvement in the development of curricula for young children. They recognize the importance of stimulation in the development of normal children. Handicapped children may have a natural lack of stimulating opportunities by virtue of being deprived of sensory or motor experiences. Educators therefore are faced with the necessity of searching continuously to find techniques or approaches that might make effectance motivation possible for the child who lacks the capacity to explore or investigate on his or her own.

Model differences. Although most models of early childhood education would agree that instructional goals must include all aspects of development, they differ in their presentation of how one aspect of development relates to another. For example, there is disagreement as to whether social maturity is the result of cognitive development or whether both develop simultaneously. The strict behaviorist stresses that academic accomplishments will lead to self-esteem. On the other hand, child developmentalists see intellectual growth developing out of feelings of self-worth and social competence.

Role of the teacher

The role of the teacher and the methods of instruction differ considerably among the models illustrated. The teacher in the traditional child development model sets up an environment conducive to activity both in small and large groups. This teacher nurtures the children's interests and waits to observe their needs unfold. Opportunity to experiment in a stimulating environment where the teacher uses a questioning approach to guide hypotheses generation characterizes a Piagetian approach. In a Montessori school a director or directress would encourage individual involvement with concrete materials designed to achieve self-paced sequential learning with little verbal interchange. Children attending a strict behavioral program would receive considerable direct instruction planned to prompt, model, and shape observable behavior toward clearly defined academically oriented goals. Finally, a developmental-prescriptive model would promote the analysis of tasks and the assessment of individual children's strengths and weaknesses in relation to the task sequence. Instruction would then begin at each child's level of entry and proceed in developmental sequence. A variety of techniques might be used to proceed from step to step.

Individualization encourages adaptive innovation. P.L. 94-142 requires an individualized educational program developed by an interdisciplinary team for each child with identified special needs. Therefore it is reasonable to expect a variety of approaches to be used in meeting the great diversity of needs encountered. For example, children who need help controlling aggressive tendencies may profit from the consistent, systematic approach of the behaviorists. Shaping behavior through prompting and reinforcement helps some children develop self-control. Children who need opportunities to manipulate concrete materials at their own pace with immediate feedback and repetition will benefit from the Montessori orientation. The multisensory discovery approach advocated by Piaget may be the best way to meet the needs of highly talented children as well as those who lack appropriate sensory stimulation.

Safford (1978, pp. 19-20) sums up the similarities and differences in theoretical approaches to early childhood special education by identifying two "streams." The first stream is characteristic of privately operated nursery schools, parent cooperatives, and laboratory schools that are identified with the "traditional" or "child-development" model. Spontaneity and social cooperation are highly valued. The second stream involves a high degree of structure and teacher-directed activities. The Montessori approach is used as an example. Safford further states:

In practice, there are probably very few early childhood educators who adhere to a "pure" approach. Most are eclectic, drawing from various theories, adapting what others have found to be successful, and modifying their program on the basis of their own experience (p. 24).

Teacher preparation is critical. Yes, teachers do adapt and modify on the basis of their own experience. Therefore any approach will be only as good as the teacher who implements it. According to a research report discussed in the seventh annual report on Head Start published by the Department of Health, Education, and Welfare (HEW), one of the primary reasons for Head Start's success in mainstreaming is in the implementation of training programs. The most important factor cited for success was the teacher's experience in working with handicapped children.

To develop and implement the Individualized Educational Programs (IEP) required by law, teachers must be able to plan lessons that incorporate techniques from the variety of remediation and enrichment strategies available. They must be able to choose those most appropriate for each child. To do so, teachers should have the ability to assess the educational needs of each child, to implement step-by-step programming, and to evaluate the effectiveness of techniques used. Teachers need to involve parents and other professionals. Their inclusion in extensive planning is vital to the success of the program and to the development of each child's potential. Therefore subsequent chapters demonstrate how special educational needs can be translated into educational practices that truly create a school experience that fits the child.

SUMMARY

This chapter reviews the field of early childhood special education historically and theoretically. Over the past 100 years, the lot of special needs children has shifted from "hide and forget" to "identify and help." Pioneering ventures into formal early education in the United States began with the establishment of kindergartens during the 1850's. With the testing performed by Binet soon after the turn of the century, the identification of handicapped children progressed toward a formal societal concern.

Controversy over the influence of nature (genetics) v. nurture (environmental experiences) has spawned numerous theoretical and empirical approaches. Gesell stressed biological importance and developed normative "ages and stages" indices. Watson and Skinner emphasized the importance of environmental contingencies as forerunners to current behavior modification approaches. Between the extremes, in the late 1950's Hebb proposed that behavior is an interaction between genetic and environmental variables. Meanwhile Piaget emphasized the role of the child as active learner with inborn tendencies toward patterned stages of cognitive development that are experientially based.

Results of several research studies led to greater acceptance by the mid-1960's of the belief that intelligence develops rapidly in the primary years of life, and early stimulation can influence this development. Head Start began as a federally funded project in 1965 to provide enrichment opportunities for young children in poverty families and was subsequently extended to include at least 10% handicapped children. Initial research indicated that the immediate educational gains for Head Start children quickly faded. But longitudinal studies by Lazar and colleagues substantiate long-term persistence of this early intervention. Handicapped children between birth and 8 years of age were given a boost in 1968 through legislation that created the First Chance program. The resulting model programs emphasized inclusion of parents in their child's educational activities.

P.L. 94-142 intends that appropriate public education is made available to all handicapped children as early as possible. One significant provision of this law is that each child should have a written IEP. Handicapped children also are to be served in the "least restrictive" environment that meets their needs. This law mandates inclusion in a regular classroom unless the child is too severely handicapped. In effect, the thrust is to fit the schooling to the child rather than fit the child to the school. Such an aim provides the major impetus of this book. This aim is pursued through informed selection of teaching strategies, with teacher preparation as the critical foundation.

Strategies for inclusion of handicapped children into the preschool curriculum have several possible theoretical origins. Traditionally, nursery schools and kindergartens are designed around the child-development or normal-development model, organizing enriching experiences around theme units and play. The behaviorist approach involves a more deliberate manipulation of the environment to reward desired behavioral responses, which typically are structured around sequences of skills. Others draw heavily from the affective nature of child development, as an outgrowth of Erikson's theory, or from the cognitive-interactional approach to learning through discovery, as advocated by Piaget. However, as special education has entered more actively into the preschool realm, ability training (comparing a child's strengths and weaknesses to peers) and task analysis (sequencing of en route to terminal skill behaviors) combine to individualize education based on data about what the child can and cannot do. Adaptation of early childhood curricula to accommodate varying needs does require informed incorporation of techniques originating from a variety of viewpoints.

DISCUSSION TOPICS AND ACTIVITIES

1. Characterize the impact on a teacher's behavior of the belief that a child's growth is determined primarily by heredity-nature or the belief that growth is determined primarily by the environment. What is your belief and your opinion? How do or how will your beliefs influence your behavior as a teacher?
2. Choose at least six articles about child rearing or education that have appeared in leading popular magazines

during the past year. Discuss these in light of the beliefs espoused. How can these beliefs influence behavior of parents and teachers? Do you see any relationship between these beliefs and historical developments? In what way might these be setting precedents?

3. Read the summary or complete report from Lazar and colleagues. Discuss the full implications of the research results with class members. What aspects should be translated into classroom practice or program development and how?

4. Research one of the First Chance programs. Send for literature or visit a program. Share what you have learned with classmates.

5. Discuss specific criteria an evaluator might use to determine if a program encompasses the critical dimensions of effective intervention programs listed in the chapter.

ANNOTATED REFERENCES

Historical perspectives on early childhood special education

Kessen, W. *The child.* New York: John Wiley & Sons, Inc., 1965.

This interesting paperback traces the development of ideas about children from the 1700's through the thinking of Piaget in the early 1960's. Kessen thoughtfully comments on theoretical excerpts from a variety of writers selected to illustrate our changing attitudes toward the child.

Lazar, I., and Darlington, R.B. *Lasting effects after preschool* (OHDS 79-30179). Washington, D.C.: Administration for Children, Youth, and Families, OHDS—Department of Health, Education, and Welfare, 1979.

This report is the result of a collaborative effort of 12 research groups conducting longitudinal studies of low-income children who participated in experimental infant and preschool programs initiated in the 1960's. It is essential reading for anyone who doubts or wishes to secure evidence for the value of early childhood education.

Stevens, J.H., and King, E.W. *Administering early childhood education programs.* Boston: Little, Brown & Co., 1976.

Chapter 1 of this book presents a very readable discussion of perspectives on early childhood education from history and philosophy. The intent is to clarify present issues by reviewing similar issues with which others have struggled. Advances through the 1970's are highlighted along with predictions for the future.

Educational programs for young children with special needs

Jordan, J.B. (Ed.). The exceptional child's early years. *Exceptional Children*, 1971, *37*, 626-712.

This specially prepared journal issue provides a capsule

view of the status of early childhood special education in the early 1970's. It offers insight into the beliefs and struggles of early implementation of the Handicapped Children's Early Education Assistance Act (1968) and the developing model programs. Summaries of the research to date on prevention of learning problems are provided along with a directory of resources and an annotated bibliography.

Jordan, J.B., and Dailey, R.F. *Not all little wagons are red: The exceptional child's early years.* Reston, Va.: Council for Exceptional Children, 1973.

This book is a product from the Invisible College Conference on Early Childhood Education and the Exceptional Child. Each chapter is the basic presentation of one of the participants. The purpose of the document was to present the thinking of the time in intervention research, curriculum and materials development, personnel training, and program evaluation.

Jordan, J.B., Hayden, A.H., Karnes, M.B., and Wood, M.M. (Eds.). *Early childhood education for exceptional children.* Reston, Va.: Council for Exceptional Children, 1977.

This book focuses on the First Chance programs and presents exemplary practices in such areas as identification, record keeping, curriculum, physical environments, parent involvement, staffing patterns, and evaluation. Included is a directory of the BEH First Chance programs along with a list of standardized tests used by these programs. This is a valuable resource, because it offers insight into the legislation that established the First Chance programs as well as provides an excellent overview of the variety and unique contributions of these programs.

Educational strategies for the inclusion of handicapped preschool children

Allen, K.E. Curriculum models for successful mainstreaming. *Topics in Early Childhood Special Education*, 1981, *1*, 45-55.

Curriculum models described as behavioral, language-based, open-education, Piagetian cognitive, Montessori, and developmental-interaction are analyzed according to their use as mainstreamed approaches. The role of the teacher, program structure, physical arrangements, learning through imitation, and interdisciplinary programming merit discussion as important components of a successful mainstreaming program.

Anastasiow, N.J. Strategies and models for early childhood intervention programs in integrate settings. In M.J. Guralnick (Ed.), *Early integration of handicapped and non-handicapped children.* Baltimore: University Park Press, 1978.

This chapter clearly describes and analyzes four basic preschool model programs: behavioral, normal-developmental, cognitive-developmental, and cognitive learning. The author concludes that the cognitive-developmental and cognitive learning models may be the most adaptable to the environmental changes necessary to successful mainstreaming of handicapped children. This assumption is made because these two models are thought to pay considerable attention to individual differences.

Anastasiow, N.J., and Mansergh, G.P. Teaching skills in early childhood programs. *Exceptional Children*, 1975, *42*, 309-317.

This article explores behavior modification, normal-developmental, and cognitive-developmental models as potential sources for the construction of preschool programs for handicapped children. The similarities among the programs are discussed, and the necessary steps to implementation of each approach are outlined.

Franklin, M.B., and Biber, B. Psychological perspectives and education: Some relations between theory and practice. In L.G. Katz (Ed.), *Current topics in early childhood education* (Vol. 1). Norwood, N.J.: Ablex Publishing Corp., 1977.

This chapter represents a thoughtful analysis of the behavioristic-learning theory perspective, the Piagetian cognitive-developmental perspective, and the developmental-interaction approach to education as exemplified in the Bank Street model. Basic issues involved in the application of psychological theory of the educational domain are discussed.

Hare, B.A., and Hare, J.M. *Teaching young handicapped children: A guide for preschool and primary grades.* New York: Grune & Stratton, Inc., 1977.

This text is described by its authors as a "how-to" book written to provide practical direction and strategies for programming handicapped children. In addition to discussing the various handicapping conditions, it provides descriptions of common assessment devices and techniques for behavior management. A chapter is devoted to the importance of play with suggestions offered for the encouragment of playful behavior.

Hendrick, J. *The whole child.* St. Louis: The C.V. Mosby Co., 1980.

This is a very comprehensive, well-written book designed to equip beginning teachers with the attitudes and specific skills necessary to function effectively. An entire chapter is devoted to working with handicapped children within the ordinary nursery school. Special attention is given to the teacher as a screening agent and to specific guidelines for including exceptional children in heterogeneous programs.

Mayer, R.S. A comparative analysis of preschool curriculum models. In R.H. Anderson and H.G. Shane (Eds.), *As the twig is bent.* Boston: Houghton Mifflin Co., 1971.

Four approaches to early education are examined with emphasis on how and why they differ. These models, the child-development, sensory-cognitive, verbal-didactic, and the verbal-cognitive, are compared according to their effectiveness. This clearly written, thorough review allows the reader the opportunity to understand how theoretical differences relate to the choice of teaching strategies and the design of curriculum materials. Students should consider this to be essential reading.

Project Head Start. *Head Start, mainstreaming preschoolers series.* Washington, D.C.: U.S. Department of Health, Education, and Welfare, OHD—OCD, 1978.

This series of eight guides may be ordered at low cost from the U.S. Government Printing Office. There is one for each traditional category of exceptionality. Although originally intended for teachers, parents, and volunteers who work in the Head Start program, anyone working with young handicapped children will find this series to be extremely practical, well organized, and easy to understand.

Safford, P.L. *Teaching young children with special needs.* St. Louis: The C.V. Mosby Co., 1978.

This extremely comprehensive text organized around identified areas of exceptionality, including giftedness, focuses on the child from birth to 8 years of age. It is a highly recommended resource, because it provides the basic information necessary to understanding handicapping conditions that affect young children along with realistic teaching suggestions.

Spodek, B. (Ed.). *Early childhood education.* Englewood Cliffs, N.J.: Prentice-Hall, Inc., 1973.

This book encompasses a very readable presentation of the primary philosophical bases of early childhood education with indepth discussion of several model programs. It is an excellent resource for those wishing to understand how theory is translated into practice.

Webster, L., and Schroeder, R.M. *Early childhood education.* Princeton, N.J.: Princeton Book Co., Publishers, 1979.

This brief paperback book provides a useful overview of the history, basic theories, experimental efforts, and contributors to the field of early childhood education.

Societal pressures: the impact of litigation and legislation

Cohen, S., Semmes, M., and Guralnick, M.J. Public Law 94-142 and the education of preschool handicapped children. *Exceptional Children*, 1979, *45*, 279-284.

This article provides a concise historical perspective and explanation of P.L. 94-142, including its limitations in the area of education for handicapped preschoolers. The status of mandated programs within the United States is described along with the role of Head Start and continuing concerns related to the implementation of P.L. 94-142.

LaVor, M.L. Federal legislation for exceptional children: Implications and view of the future. In R.D. Kneedler and S.G. Tarver (Eds.), *Changing perspectives in special education.* Columbus, Ohio: Charles E. Merrill Publishing Co., 1977.

    Historical perspective of the significant legislation leading up to P.L. 94-142 is presented. The essential requirements of P.L. 94-142 and its relationship to section 504 of the Vocational Rehabilitation Act are discussed. Finally, basic issues and unresolved questions receive much needed attention.

Melcher, J.W. Law, litigation, and handicapped children. *Exceptional Children,* 1976, *43,* 126-130.

    This brief article is the eighth in a series commemorating the American Bicentennial. The author relates an overview of America's history in special education and predicts the future in law and litigation.

Weintraub, F.J., Abeson, A., Ballard, J., and LaVor, M.L. *Public policy and the education of exceptional children.* Reston, Va.: The Council for Exceptional Children, 1976.

    This book serves as an excellent resource for those wanting a more advanced understanding of public policies for exceptional children. It examines the rights that advocacy groups have won for handicapped children; explores what is happening at the federal, state, and local levels; discusses avenues of change; presents techniques necessary to effect change; and considers professional rights and responsibilities.

REFERENCES

Algozzine, B., Mercer, C.D., and Countermine, T. The effects of labels and behavior of teacher expectations. *Exceptional Children,* 1977, *44,* 131-132.

Anastasiow, N.J. Strategies and models for early childhood intervention programs in integrated settings. In M.J. Guralnick (Ed.), *Early intervention and the integration of handicapped and nonhandicapped children.* Baltimore: University Park Press, 1978.

Anastasiow, N.J. Early childhood education for the handicapped in the 1980's: Recommendations. *Exceptional Children,* 1981, *47,* 276-282.

Anastasiow, N.J., and Mansergh, G.P. Teaching skills in early childhood programs. *Exceptional Children,* 1975, *42,* 309-317.

Banet, B.A. A developmental approach for preschool children with special needs. In S.J. Meisels (Ed.), *Special education and development.* Baltimore: University Park Press, 1979.

Bereiter, C., and Engelmann, S. *Teaching disadvantaged children in the preschool.* Englewood Cliffs, N.J.: Prentice-Hall, Inc., 1966.

Biber, B. Goals and methods in a preschool program for disadvantaged children. *Children,* 1970, *17,* 15-20.

Bijou, S.W. Practical implications of an interactional model

of child development. *Exceptional Children,* 1977, *44,* 6-14.

Bloom, B.S. *Stability and change in human characteristics.* New York: John Wiley & Sons, Inc., 1964.

Bricker, W.A., and Bricker, D.D. The infant, toddler and preschool research and intervention project. In T.D. Tjossem (Ed.), *Intervention strategies for high risk infants and young children.* Baltimore: University Park Press, 1976.

Brown v. Board of Education. 347 U.S. 483, 1954.

Caldwell, B.M. The importance of beginning early. In J.B. Jordan and R.F. Dailey (Eds.), *Not all little wagons are red: The exceptional child's early years.* Reston, Va.: Council for Exceptional Children, 1973.

Cohen, S. Service for young handicapped children—A position paper of the division for early childhood council for exceptional children. *The Communicator,* 1981, Spring, 7(2), 21-25.

Cohen, S., Semmes, M., and Guralnick, M.J. Public Law 94-142 and the education of preschool handicapped children. *Exceptional Children,* 1979, *45,* 279-284.

Diana v. State Board of Education. Civil No. C-70-37 RFP (ND, Cal, January 7, 1970 and June 18, 1973).

Dunn, L.M. Special education for the mildly retarded—Is much of it justifiable? *Exceptional Children,* 1968, *35,* 5-22.

Erikson, E.H. *Childhood and society.* New York: W.W. Norton & Co., Inc., 1963.

Freud, S. Three essays on sexuality. In *Standard edition,* (Vol. 7). London: Hogarth Press, 1953.

Furth, H. *Piaget for teachers.* Englewood Cliffs, N.J.: Prentice-Hall, Inc., 1970.

Gargiulo, R.M. Litigation and legislation for exceptional children: An historical perspective. *Illinois Council for Exceptional Children Quarterly,* 1980, *29,* 2-24.

Gearheart, B.R. *Special education for the 80's.* St. Louis: The C.V. Mosby Co., 1980.

Gesell. A.L. *The preschool child.* New York: Macmillan, Inc., 1923.

Gilhool, T.K. Changing public policies: Roots and forces. In M.C. Reynolds (Ed.), *Mainstreaming: Origins and implications.* Reston, Va.: Council for Exceptional Children, 1976.

Gotts, E.E. Headstart research, development and evaluation. In J.L. Frost (Ed.), *Revisiting early childhood education.* New York: Holt, Rinehart & Winston, Inc., 1973.

Hammill, D., and Larsen, S. The effectiveness of psycholinguistic training: A reaffirmation of position. *Exceptional Children,* 1978, *44,* 402-414.

Hohmann, M., Banet, B., and Weikart, D.P. *Young children in action.* Ypsilanti, Mich.: The High/Scope Press, 1979.

Hunt, J.M. *Intelligence and experience.* New York: Ronald Press, 1961.

Itard, J.M.G. *The wild boy of Aveyron.* New York: Appleton-Century-Crofts, 1962.

Jordan, J.B., and Dailey, R.F (Eds.). *Not all little wagons are red: The exceptional child's early years.* Reston, Va.: Council for Exceptional Children, 1973.

Karnes, M.B., and Zehrbach, R.R. Alternative models for children for early intervention with the handicapped. In J.B. Jordan and R.F. Dailey (Eds.), *Not all little wagons are red: The exceptional child's early years.* Reston, Va.: Council for Exceptional Children, 1973.

Karnes, M.B., and Zehrbach, R.R. Alternative models for delivering services to young handicapped children. In J.B. Jordan, A.H. Hayden, M.B. Karnes, and M.M. Wood (Eds.), *Early childhood education for exceptional children.* Reston, Va.: Council for Exceptional Children, 1977.

Kessen, W. *The child.* New York: John Wiley & Sons, Inc., 1965.

Kirk, S. *Early education of the mentally retarded.* Urbana, Ill.: University of Illinois Press, 1958.

Larry P. vs. Riles, 343 F Supp 1306 (ND, Cal, 1972).

Lazar, I. Does prevention pay off? *The Communicator,* 1979, Fall, 1-7.

Lazar, I., and Darlington, R. *Lasting effects after preschool* (OHDS 79-30179). Washington, D.C.: Administration for Children, Youth and Families, Office of Human Development Services—Department of Health, Education, and Welfare, 1979.

Lerner, J., Mardell-Czudnowski, C., and Goldenberg, D. *Special education for the early childhood years.* Englewood Cliffs, N.J.: Prentice-Hall, Inc., 1981.

Lillie, D.L. *Early childhood education.* Chicago: Science Research Associates, Inc., 1975.

Love, H.D. *Educating exceptional children in regular classrooms.* Springfield, Ill.: Charles C Thomas, 1972.

Mayer, R.S. A comparative analysis of preschool curriculum models. In R.H. Anderson and H.G. Shane (Eds.), *As the twig is bent.* Boston: Houghton Mifflin Co., 1971, 286-314.

Mills v. Board of Education of the District of Columbia, 348 F Supp 866 (D.C. 1972).

P. v. Riles, No. C-71-2270, RFP slip op. (Oct. 16, 1979).

Pennsylvania Association for Retarded Children v. Commonwealth of Pennsylvania, 334, F Supp 1257 (ED, Pa, 1971).

Public Laws 85-926, 88-164, 89-10, 89-750, 90-538, 91-230, 92-424, 93-380, 94-142, 95-568. Washington, D.C.: U.S. Government Printing Office.

Rousseau, J.J. [*Emile.*] (B. Foxley, trans.). London: Dent, 1911. (Originally published, 1762.)

Safford, P. *Teaching young children with special needs.* St. Louis: The C.V. Mosby Co., 1978.

Sameroff, A., and Chandler, M. Reproductive risk and the continuum of caretaking casualty. In F.D. Horowitz (Ed.), *Review of child development research* (Vol. 4). Chicago: University of Chicago Press, 1975, 187-245.

Skeels, H. A study of the effects of differential stimulation on mentally retarded children: A follow-up study. *American Journal of Mental Deficiency,* 1942, *46,* 340-350.

Skeels, H. Adult status of children with contrasting early life experiences. *Monographs of the Society for Research in Child Development,* 1966, *32*(2).

Skeels, H., and Dye, H.A. A study of the effects of differential stimulation on mentally retarded children. *Proceedings of the American Association on Mental Deficiency,* 1939, *44,* 114-136.

Smead, V. Ability training and task analysis in diagnostical prescriptive teaching. *The Journal of Special Education,* 1977, *11,* 113-125.

Stendler, C. Six years of child training practices. *The Journal of Pediatrics,* 1950, *36,* 122-134.

Stevens, J.H., and King, E.W. *Administering early childhood education programs.* Boston: Little, Brown & Co., 1976.

Swan, W. The handicapped children's early education program, *Exceptional Children,* 1980, *47,* 12-16.

Swan, W. Programs for handicapped infants and their families supported by the office of special education. *The Communicator,* 1981, Spring, *7*(2), 1-15.

Vopava, J., and Royce, J. *Comparison of the long-term effects of infant and preschool programs on academic performance.* Paper presented at the annual meeting of the American Educational Research Association, Toronto, March 1978.

Weikart, D. *The cognitively oriented curriculum: A framework for preschool teachers.* Washington, D.C.: National Association for the Education of Young Children, 1971.

Weikart, D. Relationship of curriculum, teaching, and learning in preschool education. In J.C. Stanley (Ed.), *Preschool programs for the disadvantaged: Five experimental approaches to early childhood education.* Baltimore: The Johns Hopkins University Press, 1972.

Westinghouse Learning Corporation, Ohio University. *The impact of Head Start: An evaluation of the head start experience on children's cognitive and affective development.* Washington, D.C.: Department of Health, Education, and Welfare, 1969.

White, R. Motivation reconsidered: The concept of competence. *Psychology Review,* 1959, *66,* 297-333.

Ysseldyke, J.E., and Salvia, J. Diagnostic-prescriptive teaching: Two models. *Exceptional Children,* 1974, *41,* 181-186.

Zigler, E. The effectiveness of Head Start: Another look. *Educational Psychologist,* 1978, *13,* 71-77.

CHAPTER

3

Recognizing special educational needs: identification and assessment

Mr. Curtis is a third-year teacher at Happy Hours Day Care Center. He especially enjoys the 3-year-olds. But Vicky has him worried. She is always "on the go." From the moment she arrives she flits from one toy to the other. And en route she bumps into everything and everyone! Today he has arranged for his aide and two mothers to supervise the free choice session. He plans to observe Vicky, and write down what he sees. He is using a form developed to help him observe objectively.

Where: Happy Hours Day Care Center
Time: 10 AM—10:15 AM
Activity: Free Choice Time
Others present: 15 boys and girls, aide, and two mothers

Child: Vicky R.
CA: 3-8
Date: 3-23-81
Observer: Mr. Curtis

Preceding activity	*Child's behavior*
Vicky bumped into Sara, knocking Sara flat.	Vicky kept right on going, ignoring Sara's yell.
Vicky picked up form board from shelf.	Dumped pieces of board on floor and put in two pieces. Got up and wandered away.
Vicky walked to doll corner and grabbed Tina's doll.	Vicky tugged at the doll until she got it, then ran to corner of room and sat on the doll.
Tina ran after Vicky and began to push her.	Vicky screamed and kicked until Miss J. walked over to her.
Andy painting at the easel; Vicky grabbed his brush.	Vicky painted three long strokes over Andy's picture and giggled, running away when he reached for the brush.
Four children in the kitchen individually "cooking and stirring."	Vicky ran into the kitchen, yelled "Me cook too" and grabbed a bowl, knocking the artificial vegetables to the floor. Other children just stared. Tim began to cry.

Follow-up: Contact Mr. Jones, the psychologist, to work out a plan to help Vicky control her behavior. Maybe Vicky's vision should be checked. She seems to bump into so many things.

Traditionally young children have been considered "too young for formal schooling" until age 5 or 6. Children who were "slow" were expected to be "late bloomers." "Don't be a worried mother. Johnny (or Susie) will outgrow it" was the advice most often received by alert and concerned parents. "Children learn at different rates; you can't hurry them" was also a frequently heard comment.

When concerned parents sought to enroll their late bloomers in kindergarten, they were often told to wait a year, because their children were "immature" and needed an extra year of growing time. It was not unusual for such children who repeated a grade to become "failures." Finally, by third grade these children were considered "old enough to test."

By this time failure had convinced everyone, most of all the child, that something was wrong "in the child." Testing, done by one examiner, was brief and often inappropriate. Labels were attached, for example, retarded and emotionally disturbed. Special education then was offered in a state or county facility, often away from children's homes. Lives of both parents and children were disrupted. Potential was ignored. The label predicted the outcome to be expected! Usually, those who predicted useless lives in care facilities were right. Failure was assured.

CHANGING PHILOSOPHIES AND PRACTICES

Practices in identification, assessment, and evaluation are changing rapidly. New systems for describing special education services and the children who need them are evolving. It should be recognized that practices in some communities may vary somewhat from those described here.

The trend is away from categorical descriptions (for example, retarded and learning disabled) toward descriptions that convey an understanding of the educational needs of children (Hoffman, 1980). The emphasis is shifting from diagnosis of a problem to be found in the child to (1) analysis of the specific instructional needs of a child, (2) determination of services required to meet these needs, and (3) avoidance of the stigma that can accompany traditional labeling. Both the kinds of tests used and the interpretations made of resulting information are changing. Greater care is given to recognizing the effect of ethnic background, previous experiences, daily environment, and the stress placed on children during testing. For example, traditionally Vicky (p. 40) would have been described as hyperactive, without consideration of previous experience and daily environment.

Perhaps most apparent is the earlier ages at which testing and remediation begin. Many programs provide diagnosis and assessment from birth. In fact, P.L. 94-142 actually specifies that birth is the point at which "child-find" should begin. Additional adaptations include the following:

1. A multidisciplinary team conducts the diagnostic study.

2. Parents and teachers are included in programmatic decisions and planning.

3. Labeling is avoided whenever possible.

4. Education is provided in the homes or at nearby facilities within the local public schools.

5. When appropriate, education is provided in mainstream day-care centers and preschools with assistance from special education personnel.

From child-find to program evaluation

The very nature of teaching requires teachers to be primary observers of children. Therefore teachers must assume responsibility for continuous involvement in the processes of identification, diagnosis, assessment, and evaluation. The flow chart provided in Fig. 3-1 provides an overall picture of the relationship and sequencing of the observational processes to be dis-

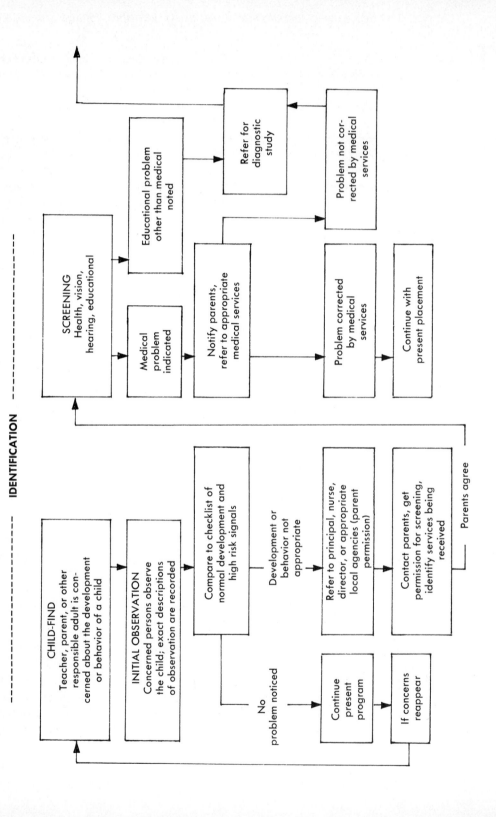

IDENTIFICATION

CHILD-FIND
Teacher, parent, or other responsible adult is concerned about the development or behavior of a child

INITIAL OBSERVATION
Concerned persons observe the child; exact descriptions of observation are recorded

Compare to checklist of normal development and high risk signals

Development or behavior not appropriate

Refer to principal, nurse, director, or appropriate local agencies (parent permission)

Contact parents, get permission for screening, identify services being received

Parents agree

No problem noticed

Continue present program

If concerns reappear

SCREENING
Health, vision, hearing, educational

Medical problem indicated

Educational problem other than medical noted

Notify parents, refer to appropriate medical services

Refer for diagnostic study

Problem not corrected by medical services

Problem corrected by medical services

Continue with present placement

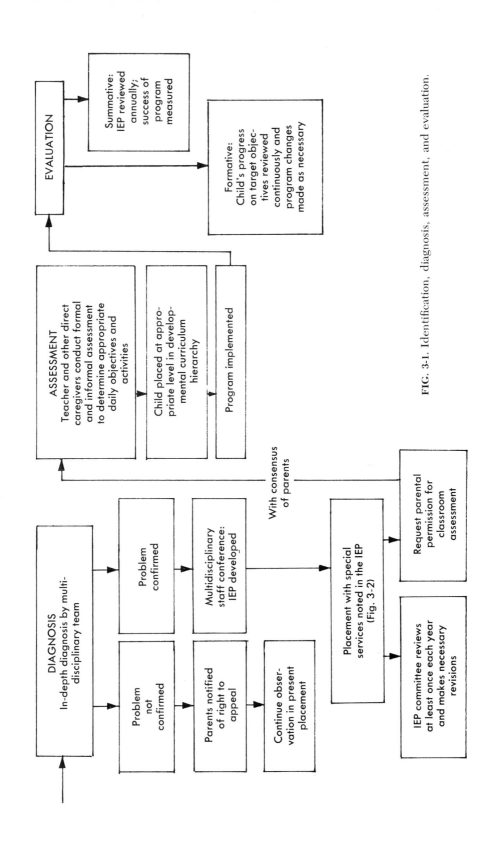

FIG. 3-1. Identification, diagnosis, assessment, and evaluation.

cussed in this chapter. The complete sequence of observational opportunities is presented within the chapter. Outlined also are the processes from the teacher or parent's initial concern about a particular child to the point at which the young child is receiving appropriate special services. NOTE: Because the terms *diagnosis, assessment,* and *evaluation* are used in a variety of ways in the literature, there may be disagreement with the manner in which these terms are used in this chapter. Considerable study went into the decision to separate the identification, diagnostic, assessment, and evaluation procedures as we have. It was our goal to achieve clear communication of actual practices regardless of the terms used to describe them.

WHAT IS THE PROCESS OF IDENTIFICATION?

P.L. 94-142 mandates free, appropriate public education for *all* children ages 3 to 21 except in states where existing laws or practices are inconsistent with this requirement. To receive services children with special needs must be found and identified. Identification involves both the child-find and screening activities that locate and identify handicapping conditions in children who are either not receiving an education or who are receiving inadequate educational services.

Child-find. The process of child-find includes the finding and identifying of children with handicapping conditions. Educational regions within states often hire child-find "teams" that are usually interdisciplinary in nature. These teams are responsible for planning and conducting a public awareness campaign to inform and educate community members concerning the right to a free and appropriate education for all children. A primary goal of the public awareness campaign is to generate referrals for screening.

Screening. Screening is the initial step in the assessment and intervention process intended to assist children in receiving an appropriate

education. "The purpose of screening is to find potential deviance" (Salvia and Ysseldyke, 1978, p. 460). Screening is a limited procedure. The process of screening is to identify those children who *might* have a problem that should be investigated thoroughly. Children with obvious or severe handicapping conditions who have been located through child-find procedures should not be involved in the screening process. These children should be referred directly to the local department or agency responsible for thorough diagnosis of the child's handicapping condition(s).

The role of the teacher in the processes of identification

Traditionally teachers "referred" children for testing and "received reports" of the diagnosis. Currently the role of the teacher in the processes of child-find and screening varies with local areas and teacher expertise. In some areas teachers of young children have been asked to assist in public awareness activities and in conducting massive screening programs, sometimes called "roundups." At the very least, all teachers of young children are expected to be able to recognize high risk or danger signals of handicapping conditions in the children within their classes (Fig. 3-3).

Teachers who consent to participate in screening young children should do so realizing the responsibilities involved in the process. Even though great efforts are usually taken to ensure that the screening process is fun for children, it is, nevertheless, a time of anxiety. Parents, especially, need support and encouragement to realize that screening is only a preliminary step and does not determine the definite existence of a handicapping condition. Care must be taken to avoid labeling children. As Frankenburg (1973) states: "It is important to explain to parents that results of a screening test do not make a diagnosis, and the results of screening should not be interpreted to parents as indicating that a child has a particular problem" (p. 33).

The selection of a screening test is an important decision. Numerous tests have entered the market in the last several years. The selection committee must keep the following considerations in mind when selecting a screening instrument:

1. Qualifications of individuals who will use the test
2. Reliability (consistency or stability) of the test
3. Validity (extent to which the test screens what it is suppose to screen) of the test
4. Provision of items that cover the major functional areas, including language skills, cognitive skills, fine and gross motor skills, and social-emotional development
5. Similarity of the children used to establish the norms to those being screened
6. Degree to which the screening instrument discriminates against minority groups
7. Cost and time factors

The annotated references at the end of the chapter can be used as guides to prepare teachers for involvement in the process of test selection. In addition, brief descriptions of some of the most used tests are included in Appendix D.

Regardless of the instrument or test to be used, participating teachers assume responsibility for preparedness to administer whatever section of the instrument is assigned to them. Reading the manual of directions the night before is not enough. Practice is essential. Teachers must also recognize their own limitations. They should only agree to administer those sections of a test that are within their areas of expertise. For example, only trained ears really hear and differentiate articulation errors. Teachers who do not have this skill should not give speech and language sections that require this skill. In Danny's case (see Chapter 4) Ms. McLynn would not feel qualified to evaluate his speech and language.

The goal of diagnosis

Diagnosis is considered by Cross and Goin (1977, p. 25) to be "a process designed: (a) to confirm or disconfirm the existence of a problem, serious enough to require remediation, in those children identified in a screening effort and (b) to clarify the nature of the problem (is it organic, environmental, or both?)." The goal of diagnosis is thorough, multidisciplinary investigation yielding information comprehensive enough to generate an intelligent decision on the appropriate educational placement for the child. The process of diagnosis determines the type or kind of intervention appropriate for the child. The type of intervention can range from placement in a regular preschool program, on the least restrictive side of the continuum, to placement in residential programs that represent the most restrictive placement possible. Mainstreaming or placement in the regular preschool classroom is an alternative provided by P.L. 94-142. However, it is critical to remember that this is an option only when it is deemed appropriate for the child. After considering the child's needs, the age of the child, and the quality of services available, a decision must be made as to which alternative would most appropriately serve the child. If mainstreaming is considered, attention must be given to such factors as teachers' attitudes and training, special assistance available, and facilities. Fig. 3-2 presents a possible continuum of services presently available. These will differ with geographical regions and as more options become available.

The role of the teacher. Traditionally teachers were not seen as active participants in decision making about children with problems. Increasingly teachers are expected to be astute observers and communicators of their observations. Teachers are included as part of the multidisciplinary diagnostic team. Their careful observations are helpful in corroborating or refuting formal test results. Current practice requires that teachers understand what each spe-

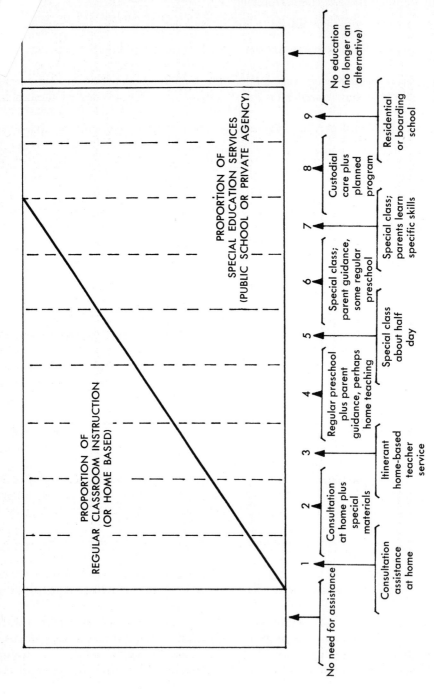

FIG. 3-2. Some appropriate placement alternatives that are determined by the nature of the child's handicap and available services.

SPECIAL CONSIDERATIONS WHEN TESTING HANDICAPPED CHILDREN

Before testing, examiners should try to determine what impairments the child has and how these might influence the administration of the test or the test results. Are there any special problems that might occur during testing, such as a seizure? How long and in what position can the child work effectively? Should some parts of the test be omitted? Do the directions or materials used have to be adapted? What is the child's most efficient mode of communication? Does the child respond better to auditory or to visual cues? What form of reinforcement does the child respond to?

During the testing, examiners must be continually alert to such factors as fatigue and frustration. Without giving the answers to a child, they should do everything possible to find out what a child's actual capabilities are? If formal tests are used, notes can be made of the adaptions needed. Examiners should be positive and encouraging.

Tests should be interpreted in light of the child's handicaps. The examiner should seek observational information from others before any conclusions are made from test results and be willing to disregard test results if observations to the contrary can be documented. The child should be given the benefit of the doubt.

cialist is saying and recommending. Teachers today must be alert to recognize conflicting advice, the failure of a specialist to use tests that take into account multiple problems, or the need to coordinate conflicting opinions and directions. It is critical that *all* information, whether derived from formal testing, parental interviews, or informal observations, be integrated and synthesized. It is often the teacher who must assume this responsibility in an effort to see that a comprehensive picture of the child's level of functioning is obtained.

Recently a child with a mild hearing problem was judged as retarded by a psychologist who used norm-referenced IQ tests that required understanding and use of language. Because of the hearing loss language was limited, scores were low, and an inappropriate diagnosis was made. This same child, tested by another psychologist who based decisions on performance testing (nonverbal IQ tests) was again described as retarded. However, both parents and the teacher were unconvinced that this child was indeed retarded. The second diagnosis was ap-

propriate for a hearing impaired child; however, the second psychologist noted: Vision should be checked.

A thorough visual examination revealed severe myopia (nearsightedness)! Provided with glasses and teaching adapted to both vision and hearing problems, this 3 year old began to learn. In this case if the teacher had not observed that specialists were not communicating, and if the teacher had not persisted in encouraging the parents to see that all of the team members had all of the information, the diagnosis of retardation might have been accepted. The child's precious early learning years might have been lost.

Teachers will be expected to be completely familiar with the environmental aspects of his or her own classroom. If asked whether or not a child would benefit from placement in their particular classroom, teachers should be able to answer with confidence. Thus, for example, if Mr. Curtis has 20 children in his group, and the IEP for Vicky notes that she will need small group activities, he may say his classroom is inappropriate for her. If she needs to be in a group of three or four children to modify her behavior effectively, a special education class in a public school may be the preferred alternative.

Teachers can develop understanding of their own personal teaching styles and the atmospheres they develop only through willingness to be honest and to seek feedback from others who observe them. They should initiate dialogue with principals, school psychologists, speech therapists, and nurses to help gain as objective a picture as possible of the characteristics of the classroom in which they teach. Use of audiotapes and videotapes may help teachers (1) to determine if they seem to have greater patience with one type of disability than with another, (2) to see if they seem to reinforce children differentially by age or sex, (3) to assess the degree of structure they impose in a classroom, and (4) to discover their most effective techniques of child management. Just as children differ, so do teachers and parents. Honesty and objective observation will help to create the learner-environment match that is increasingly being encouraged in the literature (Buktenica, 1980).

The purpose of assessment

"The purpose of assessment is to identify the child's skills, behaviors, and repertoires. Assessment allows the teacher to know where the child should be placed in the curriculum and exactly what behaviors should be taught. When skillfully performed, assessment results in a set of specific goals and instructional objectives for each individual student in the classroom" (Van Etten, Arkell, and Van Etten, 1980, p. 82). Assessment is an *ongoing* process. Initially it is necessary to use various informal and formal techniques to carry out in-depth observation in an effort to pinpoint each child's skills and deficits. What the child can do as well as can not do must be determined to select appropriate behavioral objectives and effective instructional strategies. As the instructional year progresses,

ongoing assessment data need to be collected to update educational objectives and educational programming.

The role of the teacher. Traditionally teachers followed an adopted curriculum and lesson plans. Although good teachers have always individualized lessons to some extent, current practice requires much more thorough initial assessment, increased ongoing assessment, and continuous adaptation of planned lessons. "We feel strongly that regular classroom teachers, resource personnel, and other special classroom teachers should play an important role in the assessment of children with learning difficulties" (Wallace and Larsen, 1979, p. 9).

Assessment is essentially the first task of the teacher in developing the individualized instructional program required for each handicapped child. Assessment requires frequent observation of children in a variety of situations. Observation may be done with the help of standardized (formal) or informal teacher-made techniques of measurement. This observation helps to confirm or refute screening results at the same time weaknesses are pinpointed and a basis for individualized planning is developed. For example, Ms. McLynn would observe Danny regularly to see if the planned adaptations are achieving the objectives.

Assessment procedures must be directly related to program objectives. Hayden and Edgar (1977, p. 79) summarize the uses of ongoing assessment information:

. . . By collecting ongoing data on child performance, the teacher can know exactly what skills each child has mastered, what skills the child is currently engaged in learning, and whether the child is in fact acquiring new skills. By using explicit behavioral objectives and measuring child performance in relation to them, the teacher has a daily record to tell him which programs are not facilitating child growth. When this occurs, he can use his collected data to alter the educational activity appropriately in order to individualize instruction of improved child performance.

Evaluation

"Evaluation differs from other purposes of testing in the sense that the educational program rather than the student is being evaluated" (Salvia and Ysseldyke, 1978, p. 16). Although the term *evaluation* is sometimes used interchangeably with *assessment* and *diagnosis*, evaluation is considered here as a separate but vital process. There are generally two purposes for evaluation: (1) to collect evaluative information that is used as the basis for ongoing program decision making and (2) to provide evaluative information for external support agencies such as the Office of Special Education and The Danforth Foundation.

Evaluative information is used in making value judgments as to whether or not an instructional program produced the desired results. Evaluators discuss two types of evaluation: formative and summative. With formative evaluation, data on the progress of children are collected periodically and used to make ongoing program changes. Summative evaluation is concerned with the overall effectiveness of a program. It is a final accounting of program success. Testing typically is done at the beginning of an instructional program and at the end to determine if desirable learning changes have occurred.

The role of the teacher. Often teachers in public school preschool programs have had little input into curriculum planning and program evaluation. Present practice, demanding teacher accountability, makes their participation in these areas a necessity. Teachers may or may not be directly involved in the process of gathering information to determine the effectiveness of a program. Some programs choose to acquire assistance from an outside agency to conduct the evaluation. These evaluations are usually summative in nature.

However, procedures of evaluation must be planned at the beginning of a program to ensure ease of information gathering and to avoid the hazard of gathering data that are not relevant to the instructional program. Information gathered during the formative or ongoing assessment of a child's progress is usually appropriate in making summative program evaluations. Whenever ongoing assessment information is used to make value judgments about a program's effectiveness, teachers are most certainly involved. Therefore the more organized, objective, and thorough a teacher is when observing and recording, the easier program evaluation will be.

THE TEACHER'S RESPONSIBILITY AS A PRIMARY OBSERVER OF CHILDREN

Recognizing children's special needs is often the primary responsibility of the teacher. Observing children and measuring their progress in accomplishing stated objectives are two critical components of a teacher's job. Without systematically collecting and recording information about children's educational strengths and weaknesses (what they can do as well as cannot do), the preschool experience will not be truly individualized to meet each child's particular needs.

Teachers who teach classes in which handicapped children are included have a three-fold responsibility: (1) the obligation to be able to recognize the existence of or potential for special needs that were not identified previously, (2) the continuous assessment of each child's strengths and weaknesses to establish appropriate objectives and to provide developmental and/or remedial instruction, and (3) the determination of the adequacy of each child's progress. The teacher's skills in observing and hypothesis making are thus critical to the success of any program of early childhood special education.

Knowledge of normal development is critical

Recognition of special educational needs requires that an observer be keenly aware of the behavior normally exhibited by children. This awareness makes it possible for an observer to identify unique behaviors that may signal the need for special instruction. It is important to know the ages at which specific development is expected. Developmental delays as well as unusual behaviors are significant "warning signs" that special help may be needed. For example, Danny's misunderstanding of Tim's request for the truck is a warning sign of possible hearing loss, and Vicky's constant flitting from one thing to another is not typical of children her age.

Developmental scales are included in Appendix A as an aid in becoming thoroughly familiar with normal-developmental milestones. Annotated references are provided to further encourage in-depth understanding of basic sequences of growth and development.

Watch for the unusual

With the exception of the most seriously impaired, handicapped children are more like their normal peers than unlike them. Therefore we must be ever cognizant of the basic developmental changes through which all children pass. However, developmental deviations in cognitive, language, social, and motor skill development should alert caregivers to the possible existence of special needs.

Although these developmental domains are the traditional areas of concern, other unusual behaviors should also attract attention. Children who overreact to failure or who resist new experiences may need help. Learning styles that are ineffective, apparent lack of motivation to learn, and failure to exhibit enjoyment of problem solving are warning signals. Lack of willingness to accept direction and correction as well as

lack of age-appropriate self-discipline are signs that help is necessary.

Fig. 3-3 represents a composite of the most obvious signs that should signal referral to specialized personnel or agencies for complete diagnosis. The teacher should not be reluctant to seek additional evaluations if observation suggests undetected or incorrectly diagnosed problems. If a problem goes unnoticed, the child's special needs cannot be met.

Making a referral

If a problem is suspected, the observer must be able to list the specific signs or behaviors that suggest a special need. A checklist such as the one illustrated in Fig. 3-3 is a convenient way to record the information needed. This information is then given to the appropriate professionals, as outlined in the school's procedures for referral. Suspected speech, language, or hearing problems are usually referred to the speech clinician, the audiologist, or a regional diagnostic facility. Physical or vision problems are reviewed by the school or public health nurse. Probable learning or behavior problems can be referred to the school counselor, psychologist, or local community agencies. The list on p. 56 gives brief descriptions of the roles various specialists play in the diagnostic process.* A list of helpful agencies is included in Appendix G.

---

*Adapted from Project Head Start, *Head Start: Mainstreaming Preschoolers Series*, Washington, D.C.: U.S. Department of Health, Education and Welfare, Office of Human Development Services, Administration for Children, Youth and Families, 1978.

Text continued on p. 56.

FIG. 3-3. Referral signals checklist. NOTE: One or two symptoms do not a problem make. Tables of normal development found in Appendix A should be checked carefully because preschoolers naturally exhibit some degree of many of these behaviors. Patterns should be noted and observation continued when there is a question. Language signals can be found in Chapter 6. (Adapted from Garwood et al. [1979]; Gearheart and Weishahn [1980]; Safford [1978].)

AUMITORY SIGNALS *Observable signs, symptoms, or complaints*	Some- *times*	*Yes*	*No*
Fluid running from ears	[ ]	[ ]	[ ]
Frequent earaches	[ ]	[ ]	[ ]
Frequent colds or sore throats	[ ]	[ ]	[ ]
Recurring tonsillitis	[ ]	[ ]	[ ]
Breathes through mouth	[ ]	[ ]	[ ]
Complains of noises in head	[ ]	[ ]	[ ]
Voice too loud or too soft	[ ]	[ ]	[ ]
Delayed or abnormal speech, excessive articulation errors	[ ]	[ ]	[ ]
Seems to "hear what he wants to hear"	[ ]	[ ]	[ ]
Seems to be daydreaming	[ ]	[ ]	[ ]
Often looks puzzled, frowns, or strains when addressed	[ ]	[ ]	[ ]
Appears uninterested in things others find interesting	[ ]	[ ]	[ ]

Observable behaviors

Turns or cocks head to hear speaker	[ ]	[ ]	[ ]
Scans when called rather than turning to source	[ ]	[ ]	[ ]
Lack of "paying attention"	[ ]	[ ]	[ ]
Especially inattentive in large groups	[ ]	[ ]	[ ]
Extreme shyness in speaking	[ ]	[ ]	[ ]
Difficulty in following oral directions (and records)	[ ]	[ ]	[ ]
Acts out, appears stubborn, shy, or withdrawn	[ ]	[ ]	[ ]
Marked discrepancy between abilities in verbal and performance test items	[ ]	[ ]	[ ]
Watches classmates to see what they are doing before beginning to participate	[ ]	[ ]	[ ]

FIG. 3-3. For legend see opposite page.

	Some-times	Yes	No
Often does not finish work	[ ]	[ ]	[ ]
Hears teacher only when he sees him or her	[ ]	[ ]	[ ]
Hears some days but not others	[ ]	[ ]	[ ]
Gives answers totally unrelated to question asked	[ ]	[ ]	[ ]
Frequently requests repetition or says "huh"	[ ]	[ ]	[ ]

VISUAL SIGNALS
Observable signs, symptoms, or complaints

	Some-times	Yes	No
Red eyelids	[ ]	[ ]	[ ]
Pupils turn in, out, up, or down (perhaps independent of each other)	[ ]	[ ]	[ ]
Watery eyes or discharges	[ ]	[ ]	[ ]
Crusts on lids or among the lashes	[ ]	[ ]	[ ]
Recurring styes or swollen lids	[ ]	[ ]	[ ]
Pupils of uneven size	[ ]	[ ]	[ ]
Excessive movement of pupils	[ ]	[ ]	[ ]
Drooping eyelids	[ ]	[ ]	[ ]
Excessive rubbing of eyes (seems to brush away blurs)	[ ]	[ ]	[ ]
Shutting or covering one eye	[ ]	[ ]	[ ]
Tracking or focusing difficulties	[ ]	[ ]	[ ]
Headaches or nausea after close work	[ ]	[ ]	[ ]
Tenses up during visual tasks	[ ]	[ ]	[ ]
Squints, blinks, frowns, and distorts face while doing close work	[ ]	[ ]	[ ]

Observable behaviors

	Some-times	Yes	No
Tilts head (possibly to use one eye) or thrusts forward	[ ]	[ ]	[ ]
Trys to avoid or complains about light	[ ]	[ ]	[ ]

FIG. 3-3, cont'd. Referral signals checklist.

	Some-times	Yes	No
Complains of pain or ache in eyes	[ ]	[ ]	[ ]
Holds objects close to face	[ ]	[ ]	[ ]
Complains of itchy, scratchy, or stinging eyes	[ ]	[ ]	[ ]
Avoids or is irritable when doing close work	[ ]	[ ]	[ ]
Moves head rather than eyes to look at object	[ ]	[ ]	[ ]
Tires easily after visual tasks	[ ]	[ ]	[ ]
Frequent confusion of similarly shaped letters, numbers, or designs	[ ]	[ ]	[ ]
Unusually clumsy or awkward, trips over small objects	[ ]	[ ]	[ ]
Poor eye-hand coordination	[ ]	[ ]	[ ]
Cannot follow a moving target held 10 to 12 inches in front of him	[ ]	[ ]	[ ]

HEALTH OR PHYSICAL SIGNALS
Observable signs, symptoms, or complaints

	Some-times	Yes	No
Flushes easily or has slightly bluish color to cheeks, lips, or fingertips	[ ]	[ ]	[ ]
Excessive low-grade fevers or colds	[ ]	[ ]	[ ]
Frequent dry coughs or complains of chest pains after physical exertion	[ ]	[ ]	[ ]
Unusually breathless after exercise	[ ]	[ ]	[ ]
Is extremely slow or sluggish	[ ]	[ ]	[ ]
Is abnormal in size	[ ]	[ ]	[ ]
Is excessively hungry or thirsty	[ ]	[ ]	[ ]
Complains of pains in arms, legs, or joints	[ ]	[ ]	[ ]
Has poor motor control or coordination	[ ]	[ ]	[ ]
Walks awkwardly or with a limp	[ ]	[ ]	[ ]

FIG. 3-3, cont'd. Referral signals checklist.

	Some-times	Yes	No
Shows signs of pain during exercise	[ ]	[ ]	[ ]
Moves in a jerky or shaky manner	[ ]	[ ]	[ ]
Walks on tiptoe, feet turn in	[ ]	[ ]	[ ]
Hives or rashes are evident	[ ]	[ ]	[ ]
Loses weight without dieting	[ ]	[ ]	[ ]
Appears to be easily fatigued	[ ]	[ ]	[ ]

Observable behaviors

	Some-times	Yes	No
Moves extremely slowly or in a sluggish manner	[ ]	[ ]	[ ]
Is excessively hungry or thirsty	[ ]	[ ]	[ ]
Complains of pains in arms, legs, or joints	[ ]	[ ]	[ ]
Is excessively restless or overactive	[ ]	[ ]	[ ]
Is extremely inactive, avoids physical exercise	[ ]	[ ]	[ ]
Faints easily	[ ]	[ ]	[ ]
Is extremely inattentive	[ ]	[ ]	[ ]
Is unable to chew and swallow well	[ ]	[ ]	[ ]
Exhibits difficulty with motor tasks, including balance	[ ]	[ ]	[ ]

LEARNING SIGNALS
Observable signs, symptoms, or complaints

	Some-times	Yes	No
Cries easily, is very easily frustrated	[ ]	[ ]	[ ]
Clumsy, awkward, visual motor difficulties (for example, unusual difficulty with coloring, puzzles, or cutting)	[ ]	[ ]	[ ]
Exhibits visual or auditory perceptual difficulties	[ ]	[ ]	[ ]
Appears easily disturbed by loud noises	[ ]	[ ]	[ ]
Often seems confused or unsure of self	[ ]	[ ]	[ ]

FIG. 3-3, cont'd. Referral signals checklist.

	Some-times	Yes	No
Observable behaviors			
Works very slowly or rushes through everything	[ ]	[ ]	[ ]
Has difficulty working independently	[ ]	[ ]	[ ]
Is highly distractible, impulsive	[ ]	[ ]	[ ]
Extremely short attention span	[ ]	[ ]	[ ]
Unable to follow directions	[ ]	[ ]	[ ]
Excessively active or excessively inactive	[ ]	[ ]	[ ]
Perseverates (repeats activity over and over)	[ ]	[ ]	[ ]
Seems to catch on quickly in some areas but not in others	[ ]	[ ]	[ ]
Extremely inconsistent in performance	[ ]	[ ]	[ ]
Does not transfer what is learned in one area to another	[ ]	[ ]	[ ]
Actively resists change	[ ]	[ ]	[ ]
Constantly disrupts class	[ ]	[ ]	[ ]
Does not remember classroom routine, other memory problems	[ ]	[ ]	[ ]
Has difficulty making choices	[ ]	[ ]	[ ]
Lacks inventiveness, interests below age level	[ ]	[ ]	[ ]
Learns so very slowly that cannot participate well with others	[ ]	[ ]	[ ]

FIG. 3-3, cont'd. Referral signals checklist.

Specialist	Description	Specialist	Description
Audiologist	Conducts screening and diagnosis of hearing problems and may recommend a hearing aid or suggest training approaches for children with hearing handicaps	Otolaryngologist	Conducts screening, diagnosis, and treatment of ear, nose, and throat disorders; is sometimes known as an E.N.T. (ear, nose, and throat) physician
Dentist	Conducts screening, diagnosis, and treatment of the teeth and gums	Pediatrician	Specializes in the diseases, problems, and health care of children
Neurologist	Conducts screening, diagnosis, and treatment of brain and central nervous system disorders	Physical therapist	Conducts an evaluation of a child's muscle tone, posture, range of motion, and locomotion abilities; plans physical therapy programs aimed at promoting self-sufficiency primarily related to gross motor skills such as walking, sitting, and shifting position; helps with special equipment such as wheelchairs, braces, and crutches
Nutritionist	Conducts an evaluation of a child's eating habits and nutritional status; provides advice about normal and therapeutic nutrition and information about special feeding equipment and techniques to increase a child's self-feeding skills		
Occupational therapist	Conducts evaluation of children who may have difficulty performing self-help or other preschool activities that use arms, head, hand, and mouth movements; suggests activities to promote self-sufficiency and independence	Psychologist	Conducts screening, diagnosis, and treatment of children with emotional, behavioral, or developmental problems; is primarily concerned with cognitive and emotional development
Ophthalmologist	Conducts screening, diagnosis, and treatment of diseases, injuries, or birth defects that limit vision	Psychiatrist	Conducts screening, diagnosis, and treatment of psychological, emotional, developmental, or organic problems; prescribes medication; is alert to physical problems that may cause nervous disorders
Optician	Advises in the selection of frames and fits the lenses prescribed by the optometrist or ophthalmologist to the frames	Social worker	Provides counseling or consultative services to individuals or families who may be experiencing problems
Optometrist	Conducts an examination of the eyes and related structures to determine the presence of visual problems and/or eye diseases and to evaluate a child's visual development	Special education teacher	Conducts screening and diagnosis to plan individualized programs for children with special needs; is specially trained to work with specific types of disabilities
Orthopedist	Conducts screening, diagnosis, and treatment of diseases and injuries to muscles, joints, and bones	Speech-language pathologist	Conducts screening, diagnosis, and treatment of children with communication disorders; may also be called a speech clinician or speech therapist

If appropriate professionals are not available, the referral is made to the school principal, director, or directly to the parents. A list of local referral resources should be given to the parents at this time. The teacher should always seek a conference with the principal or director to determine the established referral policy. It is important to remember that written permission to release information about a child must be obtained from the parents or guardians before information about any child can be released to an outside agency. For example, it would be inappropriate for Mr. Curtis to discuss Vicky's behavior with others before the written permission is available.

Guidelines for successful observation

Observation is the skill of deliberately listening to and watching children's behaviors. They can be observed alone or in a group, at any time of the day, and under a variety of circumstances. While observing, the teacher notes aspects of appearance or behavior. Specific behaviors to be observed are determined by the purpose of the observation. Observers differ considerably in the process of recording information. Teachers often just make mental notes of what they see or hear. But use of a standardized checklist results in more systematic recording procedures. If the purpose of the observation is to assess the child's progress in an individualized program, systematic recording is essential to ensure objective, comprehensive data collection. The following guidelines help prepare teachers to become systematic, objective observers:

1. Focus on observing exactly what the child does. Record special, detailed observations of precisely what the child *does* and *says*. Use action verbs. Note the date, time, setting, what preceded the child's action or reaction, and what followed the behavior. *Do not* record inferences or opinions. Write down what is actually seen or heard. Both Ms. McLynn and Mr. Curtis were careful to do this.

2. Record the observational details as soon after the observation as possible. With practice, teachers develop the ability simultaneously to participate and observe by making mental notes. However, it is important to plan schedules so that recording of details can be done as quickly as possible. Details are important and are easily forgotten. That is why both Mr. Curtis and Ms. McLynn planned ahead to make observation time available.

3. Observe in a variety of settings and at different times within the child's school day. Changes in time and in setting will often provide clues about children's interests. For example, children who are not comfortable on the playground may seek the solitude they never seek when in the classroom. Or they may become bullies on the playground, whereas they are self-controlled within the classroom. Children may be overly active when playing with other children but not so when playing alone. There may be a certain time of day, perhaps just before lunch, when some children are especially irritable. Identifying these times and circumstances makes it possible to plan needed changes that create a smoothly run day. Watching for patterns often leads to an explanation of behavior. It was Danny's pattern of misunderstanding the children that helped to convince Ms. McLynn that his hearing must be checked more thoroughly.

4. Be realistic in scheduling observations. When the purpose of the observation is to determine the developmental level at which a child is functioning, it is critical to be able to observe and make notes as often and in as many situations as necessary to get a complete record of the developmental areas under concern. Observations that are haphazard or incomplete jeopardize the correctness of any diagnosis. Be realistic when planning observation time. Be certain that there is a chance the observation will actually occur. On some days the only available observation time might be free-choice time.

5. Begin by focusing on one child at a time. Focusing on one child at a time and using checklists or rating scales will help to develop observational skills without running the risk of missing or forgetting information.

6. Avoid being obvious. Avoid calling attention to the child being observed or the fact that the observation is taking place. Interact as naturally as possible. Be seated in a place normal for the teacher to be during the activity that is being observed. For example, when observing playground activities, teachers usually post themselves in a spot providing optimal visibility. Stand or sit in the usual position when observing any activity. Mr. Curtis made all the needed arrangements before the children were present.

7. At all times, ensure confidentiality. Notes must *never* be left around; a system of coding names should be developed to ensure privacy. *Never* discuss observations in front of other children or parents of other children. Read and become familiar with The Family Educational Rights and Privacy Act of 1974 (P. L. 93-380) because it is important to be aware of the parents' rights to read the records created. Never send or give data collected from observation or test scores to outside agencies or individuals without written parental permission.

8. Choose a workable recording system. Teachers often need to experiment with file cards, notebooks, and three-ring binders to determine exactly what process is most convenient for them. Of course, the system used depends on the purpose and method of the observation. Well-organized, easy-to-review notes will facilitate the detection of patterns of behavior that may be extremely vital to real understanding of the child. Mr. Curtis preferred using a 8½ × 11 page format, whereas Ms. McLynn chose 6 × 9 file cards.

TYPES OF OBSERVATION TECHNIQUES

Teachers should observe children in a variety of situations with as many purposes as they have objectives for the children. The particular technique chosen should relate directly to the purpose established. Listed below are some of the more common types of observation. As the list progresses, the techniques become more standardized (formal), requiring greater systematic planning and structure from the observer.

1. *Photographs.* Photographs provide a quick, easy method of obtaining children's reactions to various lessons. They provide an automatic record of involvement. These pictures can be taken at planned intervals to demonstrate sequential development. A dual purpose is served when the snapshots are used to stimulate language development, as discussed in Chapter 6. Using photographs in bulletin board displays offers repeated chances to encourage the development of self-esteem.

2. *Motion pictures and videotape and cassette recordings.* With the advancement of instructional technology, more and more classrooms commonly employ the use of videotape and cassette recorders. Teachers have the advantage of participating directly in the activities and can later review the children's responses to their own unique teaching style. However, care must be taken to prevent the presence of recording equipment from distorting the observation. Children thoroughly enjoy observing and listening to themselves. Again, such techniques provide ideal opportunities for language stimulation as well as allow the teacher to collect language samples. Moving pictures have often been used to provide evidence for development in such areas as motor coordination and social interaction. Local service clubs are often willing to make donations to help with film and processing costs.

3. *Collection of children's work.* Although early childhood education is hopefully process oriented rather than product oriented, there are opportunities to collect children's work. Collecting samples of such things as paintings, tracings, cuttings, and attempts to print one's name

allows the teacher to analyze progress and to make this obvious to parents. Vicky's paintings also demonstrated a lack of coordination.

4. *Activity lists.* Programs that provide activity centers with some degree of free-choice time may post lists of children's names to be dated or checked off at each center area. By listing each child's name and the length of participation, the child's interests and level of involvement can be determined. The teacher will need to decide whether choices should be limited or children should be encouraged to broaden their participation. Mr. Curtis identified Vicky's short participation span this way.

5. *Anecdotal records, diaries, and logs.* Teachers record specific details of their observation, including exact behavior, precisely what precedes the behavior, any reactions to the behavior, time, setting, and individuals involved. Care is taken to avoid making judgments, choosing isolated events, or overgeneralizing from atypical incidents. Systematic and regular recording allows the teacher to study patterns of behavior.

6. *Passports.* The passport (Runge, Walker, and Shea, 1975) is an ordinary spiral notebook that the child carries with him daily to and from home and the classroom. All adults who work with the child are encouraged to make observational notations in the passport. Records are required to be brief, positive, honest, and consistent. The objective of the passport is to promote positive parent-teacher communication and cooperation. A passport might help Vicky by creating consistency in behavioral expectations at home and at school.

7. *Timed running records.* Timed running records contain the same basic information as anecdotal records but are more systematic. A recording is made at predetermined time intervals. Emerging or prevalent behavior patterns that are described accurately and precisely can be extremely valuable when planning for individualized instruction.

8. *Checklists and rating scales.* Checklists and rating scales help specify exactly what the observer is to be observing. Use of such instruments makes it possible to vary the observer and still maintain consistency in the behavior that is observed. Illustrations of checklists and developmental scales are included throughout this text and in most texts in the field of early childhood special education. However, teachers are encouraged to design their own to ensure that the behavior observed is related to the goals and objectives of their program. (Ms. McLynn may have different priorities for her program than Mr. Curtis does for his.)

9. *Criterion-referenced tests.* Criterion-referenced devices or tests are designed to compare a child to a set of standards rather than to other children. Commercial tools usually establish the set of standards by selecting and sequencing items from several standardized developmental scales such as those developed by Bayley (1968) and Gesell (1940). The use of a criterion-referenced scale is illustrated and discussed in Chapter 4.

10. *Norm-referenced tests.* Norm-referenced tests provide the most standardized information gathering opportunities for observation. The intent of norm-referenced measurement is to compare a child's performance to the performance of other children who are the same chronological age, "CA." Few norm-referenced instruments are useful in planning individualized programs for children (Meeker, 1974). These tests tend to be less reliable with young children. The main value in using them is to identify the existence of developmental lags. However, funding agencies sometimes do require norm-referenced tests to complete program evaluations. Cautions when using such tests are discussed later in this chapter. Annotated references at the end of the chapter supply sources for brief descriptions of the tests that are available commercially and listed selectively in Appendix D.

DETERMINING THE FOCUS OF AN OBSERVATION

As previously stated, the target, setting, time, and conditions should be determined by the purpose of the observation. Informal observations help provide a more comprehensive view of the child than the observations obtained solely with the aid of structured inventories, checklists, rating scales, and tests. The focus of the observation is limited only by the imagination and time of the observer. It is important to observe a variety of situations during different times of the day. The focus should be more general when teachers are assessing the overall development of a child.

On the other hand, if teachers are trying to determine if a child has accomplished a particular objective, they will narrow their observation to very specific behavior under specified conditions. (Mr. Curtis looked for the number of things Vicky did as well as exactly what she did.) Most teachers will refer to a written objective to guide their observation. For example, if the IEP requires the child to learn to button a coat, the observer will watch specifically to see if the child can button a coat, under what conditions, and with what degree of skill.

Observing how children perform a task

The primary purpose of most teacher observation is to determine the strengths and weaknesses in children's learning repertoires in order to develop instructional goals and strategies. The teacher should not be concerned with etiology (investigation of causative factors) or assignment of diagnostic labels. The teacher must instead be concerned with exactly what children can (and cannot) do and how they do it. In closely analyzing task performances the teacher observes children's processes or styles of performance, in addition to determining whether or not children can perform specific tasks.

For example, when asked to describe what is happening in a picture, does a child impulsively respond? Or does he or she give a more deliberate or reflective response, taking time to note details while carefully scanning the picture? When copying a figure does the child seem to study the picture and plan? Or does he or she start drawing with only a brief reference to the drawing presented? Research on problem-solving style indicates that differences in cognitive styles may influence individual differences in performance in a variety of school-related tasks (Keogh, 1977).

Considering motivational factors

Children's performance is also greatly influenced by motivational factors. Children who are afraid to try new tasks or to take risks obviously miss out on learning opportunities and may not be able to exhibit the breadth of their capabilities. Some children appear to be highly dependent and are unable to work well alone. These children depend on the assurance or reinforcement from adults or other children to give them confidence to perform. Investigators have found that as early as first grade, children who are autonomous standard setters tend to read better than children who constantly turn to teachers or parents for feedback of whether their efforts have been good enough (Dreyer and Haupt, 1966).

Realizing environmental influences

Earlier in this chapter the importance of environmental or situational influences on task performance was mentioned. Various researchers have discussed the importance of focusing on the interaction of the child with the environment rather than focusing on either the child or the environment independently (Bortner and Birch, 1970). Stoneman and Gibson (1978) found the assessment performance of developmentally disabled preschool children improved when tested by familiar figures and when tested away from classroom distraction. The influence of situational factors again suggests that the teacher must vary the conditions of observation to get the most comprehensive view of a child's learning strengths and weaknesses.

Recognizing the interrelationship of skills

Finally, observers must be aware of and attuned to the interrelationship of skills. Children who are concentrating on the development of a motor skill may or may not exhibit what might be considered to be normal verbal or social interaction with other children during that period. On the other hand, children who are skilled in the motor activity may exhibit greater verbal fluency because of their confidence in their motor skills and lack of verbal inhibition.

Young children do not develop skills in isolation. The most obvious example of the interdependence and interrelationship of and between skill development is noted by psycholinguists in their study of language development. Chapter 6 elaborates on the importance of realizing that the potential for language development is present during every waking moment, assuming the child is not severely impaired and is in a relatively stimulating environment. The teacher then must be aware of a child's total performance even when focusing on a single aspect of behavior.

In summary, observation is a complex, critical skill that can only be developed through systematic practice. The importance of becoming skilled in objective, systematic observation is made clearly evident by a recent study conducted by the Illinois State Board of Education (1980). The study found that the most frequently used technique for child performance evaluation by teachers of young handicapped children was observation of the child's behavior. In addition, national model programs also reported making frequent use of observational data. Therefore it is imperative that teachers strive to incorporate the following six abilities into their observational repertoire:

1. In-depth understanding of what is considered to be normal behavior
2. Skill in recognizing high risk behavior or danger signals
3. Ability to follow the guidelines for responsible observation
4. Ability to choose types of observational techniques appropriate to the purpose of the observation
5. Awareness of the influence of performance styles, motivational factors, environmental variables, and extraneous behaviors on the judgments to be made about children's educational strength and weaknesses
6. Continuous practice of professionalism through respect for confidentiality, restraint from labeling, and attempts to counteract any tendencies toward placing stereotyped expectations on children

USE OF STANDARDIZED TESTS WITH YOUNG CHILDREN

In recent years emphasis has been given to a shift away from the use of standardized or formal tests to assess learning strengths and weaknesses. Increasing emphasis is given to the logical match between instructional goals and assessment procedures. Standardized instruments continue to be used, however, during initial processes of screening and diagnosis. They also continue to be used for summative evaluation of learning progress. But increasingly, teacher-developed informal techniques are seen as the mainstay of assessment and evaluation.

Contributing to this move away from routine standardized testing are (1) the lack of reliability and validity of standardized tests for use with young children, (2) the need to obtain information that can easily be transformed into educational plans, (3) the cultural biases built into many standardized instruments, (4) the influence of situational factors on test performance, and (5) the increased recognition of the teacher as the individual most responsible for any child's progress.

Cautious use of norm-referenced tests

Standardized tests are instruments designed to be administered by a trained examiner after specified procedures. Depending on the purpose, standardized tests or assessments could be completed by psychologists; psychometrists; speech, language, and hearing clinicians; pediatricians; or social workers. Typically these examiners report test scores and norm-referenced information. (*Norm-referenced* refers to tests that report a particular child's performance in relation to other children of the same CA.)

Norm-referenced test scores reflect comparison of the performance of the child being tested with performance of other children of the same age who took the test when norms were being established. Thus a child with a mental age, "MA," of 3 years and 6 months (3-6) is said to have performed on the norm-referenced tests, such as the Stanford-Binet test, in the way that most children do at CA 3½. If that child were, in fact, age 2½, his or her IQ would be 132. This child would be identified as superior in intellectual functioning. On the other hand, a child with a CA of 5 years with the same MA of 3-6 would have an IQ of 67 and would be considered to be mildly retarded if deficits in adaptive behavior were also evident.

Instruments such as those that assess MA are of little value when assessing the performance of handicapped children or those from a minority culture if the normative standards do not take into account the influence of the children's unique conditions or the nature of their development. Children who have developed in a different manner by virtue of being handicapped, bilingual, or deprived cannot be compared logically to children who have been raised in what society considers to be normal circumstances. Only when used with caution by a skilled examiner can standardized, norm-referenced tests provide information worthy of consideration for planning individualized instruction programs.

For example, norm-referenced tables typically are used by speech, language, and hearing clinicians as a comparison for a child's receptive and expressive language skills. Usually children have internalized most of the rules of grammar and syntax by age 4. Those who do not speak distinctly and in grammatically correct ways by that age are described as having "delayed speech and language development." Useful information can be gained about the specific nature of a child's delay by analyzing performance on individual items of standardized, norm-referenced tests. Practitioners who are skilled in analyzing performances on individual test items will note patterns in development and behavior that can serve as the basis for instructional goals and objectives.

For example, when Mr. Curtis looked closely at Vicky's Peabody Picture Vocabulary Test results (Dunn, 1970), he noted that she consistently missed items that included verbs. Recorded observations also revealed less than average vocabulary and sentences that were immature for her age. These patterns prompted Mr. Curtis to seek advice from the speech and language clinician to plan lessons that would enrich Vicky's receptive and expressive language skills.

Awareness of specific task performance can also be helpful to the teacher who has an understanding of the thinking and acting processes involved in test items missed. Knowledge of weaknesses will allow the teacher to use informal observational techniques to observe the child doing similar tasks. This observation will create increased understanding of how or why the child missed the items. The opportunity to refute or collaborate the original test results is thus provided by observation.

When observing Danny, Ms. McLynn continued to have the uneasy feeling that Danny could not hear well, even though he had passed the auditory screening test. She decided to play games with Danny such as asking him to point to the source of sound when blindfolded and to repeat simple sentences. Danny had much more difficulty with these tasks than the other 4 year olds in the room. Ms. McLynn became even more convinced that Danny must have a complete audiological examination. She spoke to Danny's parents who agreed to take Danny to the speech and hearing clinic at the nearby university.

The above illustrations emphasize that it is the responsibility of the teacher to determine if a child's test scores are an accurate reflection of abilities. Only observation on a day-to-day basis can confirm or refute examiner conclusions based on test performance. In this regard, Hare and Hare (1977, p. 31) offer valuable advice to teachers of young children:

A critical factor for the teacher to remember is that test scores should not determine an educational program; they are contributing bits of information. All standardized tests provide only a sample of the child's behavior at a specific point in time. . . . The teacher also should be aware that traits are not immutable, and even what we call intelligence varies during the life of an individual.

Considerations for interpreting standardized test results

P.L. 94-142 specifies that placement decisions cannot be based on the results of any single test. The norm-referenced or ability training approach is being criticized partly because of the tendency of some educators to make generalizations based on low performance on one process test. For example, poor performance on the repetition of digits designed to measure short-term memory does not necessarily reveal a weakness in all aspects of the auditory memory process. The skill of repeating back digits or nonsense syllables may be very different from remembering meaningful auditory directions. Yet some educators have tended to generalize from this and initiate training in all aspects of auditory memory. Summative program evaluations of such training have yielded disappointing results. This suggests that educators need to

rethink and redesign programs that have been based on such generalizations (Ysseldyke and Salvia, 1974).

Furthermore educators need to be alert to hidden penalties that may understate test results of handicapped and culturally different children. What amounts to impossible response requirements for some children distorts even further the inappropriateness of single-test normative samples. A recent example comes to mind. Consider the validity of a norm-referenced IQ on a severely visually handicapped child who was given a Stanford-Binet test with no accommodations for the visual defect. What is even more disturbing is the fact that the child's mental capacity was classified and reported according to the score received.

It is the teacher who may need to confirm or refute the face validity of test results. Do scores seem reasonable when reality tested against the teacher's observational experiences with the child? To provide assistance to teachers who will be expected to interpret the results of tests or reports filed by diagnostic specialists, the Glossary of Selected Measurement Terms on p. 64 defines the essential terms attached to test results. A clear understanding of these terms helps teachers to explain the results of assessment procedures to parents and/or instructional aides, just as they help in the use of test information for the development of instructional strategies.

But even before becoming involved in the assessment process, teachers should talk with the school psychologist, the speech and language clinician, and other specialists. They should discuss the instruments used by these specialists and techniques for interpretation and translation of diagnosis into instructional goals. Such a discussion helps the teacher to understand the situational factors that may influence the performance of children tested by these specialists. Teachers will also be able to determine the referral information most useful to the specialists.

GLOSSARY OF SELECTED MEASUREMENT TERMS

age and grade equivalent scores—Reflect the average performances of the average X-year-old and average Xth grader, respectively. Average is determined by those children included in the normative sample.

mental age (MA)—Level of mental function. An MA of 4-0 suggests that the child is functioning mentally as an average child who is chronologically 4-0 years old.

norms—Scores on performance of the standardization group of children against which a child's score is being compared (normative sample).

percentile rank—Indicates how a child's score compares to other children who took the test as part of the normative population and the percentage of children tested who made scores equal to or lower than the specified score.

reliability—Extent to which the test measures a given performance consistently; its dependability, stability, and relative freedom from errors of measurement.

standard error of measurement—Helps to determine the reliability of a test; how much an individual's score is likely to fluctuate if the test is administered repeatedly or by another examiner. The greater the standard error of a test, the less reliable is that test.

stanine—A score ranging from one to nine with a mean of five derived from dividing the normal curve into a "standard nine-point scale."

validity—Extent to which a test measures what it is supposed to measure; how well it measures what you want it to measure; how well a test does the job for which it is used; the extent to which it measures exactly what you want it to measure, no more or no less. One must have a clear understanding of what is to be measured to determine if a test is a valid measurement device.

Providing useful referral data enables teachers to establish themselves as necessary members of the team.

Selection of formal (standardized) assessment instruments

To date no single assessment instrument appears to be the instrument of universal choice. Indeed the rapidly growing market of standardized tests for use with young children only serves to confuse, even further, the educator who is conscientiously trying to select the best battery of assessment techniques. Hare and Hare reported in 1977 over 3,000 testing devices in print, if research instruments were included. Teachers or specialists must then establish a logical list of criteria for selection of any standardized tests to use with young children.

The instruments selected should complement but not necessarily duplicate information more quickly obtained from informal assessment. The overall process of assessment explained in this chapter uses formal testing only to collaborate or refute information previously gained through informal (observational) techniques. The following 10 concerns readily serve as the basis for the development of test selection criteria:

1. Information obtained from the assessment instruments should be readily transformed into educational goals and strategies. The test should contribute information useful to the development of individualized instructional programs, or it should not be given. Educators must continually ask "What am I measuring? Why am I measuring it? What do I do with the results?"

2. The test items should be adaptable across

all suspected handicapping conditions. That is, the test should be suitable for use with all of the children being tested. The test should not contain items that would bias the performance of minority group members. Of course, this concern does not apply to the use of specialized tests with the population for which they were designed.

3. The items should provide the opportunity of direct observation of children's behavior rather than rely on memory or inferences on the part of others.

4. The items should provide for objective observation of skills appropriate to the level of the children being tested.

5. For the very young or for severely handicapped children, items should allow for a choice in manner of response. For example, nonverbal children should be able to use gestures or other manipulative responses to avoid being penalized for their nonverbal nature in areas where their verbal ability is not the focus of assessment.

6. Young children should not be penalized for lack of speed. Speed in complying to adult requests is not considered to be a normal characteristic of preschoolers.

7. The instruments should possess adequate validity and reliability.

8. The tests should be economical in cost and time required for administration.

9. The instructions should provide for assessment in a setting that would allow for the least number of situational influences.

10. The instruments selected must require administration and interpretation skills within the expertise and training potential of those who are designated to use them.

In addition to the above considerations, anyone involved in the selection of standardized instruments for use with young children should carefully review the test manuals and technical reports for information on the basis for establishing norms, reliability, validity, stan-

dard error of measurements, sampling procedures, and any other information that may influence a child's performance. The Buros (1978) *Mental Measurements Yearbook* contains review information on validity, reliability, and other factors that is invaluable in the selection of tests. Other guides are described in the annotated bibliography at the end of the chapter.

Because no one test meets all the criteria just listed, teachers are encouraged to review thoroughly any standardized instrument being considered. The listing of 10 selection criteria hopefully challenges reviewers to become aware of the responsibility that goes with test selection and use. Mishandling of assessment instruments and procedures, as well as the tendency to label children according to test results, contributes to the trend away from standardized assessment. Educators can be encouraged that practice seems to be turning toward the development of teacher-administered, criterion-referenced assessment and away from the norm-referenced techniques that have been so difficult to translate into educational practice.

ASSESSMENT WITHIN THE CLASSROOM

The purpose of assessment within the classroom is to set up situations whereby each child can be observed systematically in an effort to pinpoint his or her educational skills and deficits. This observation is prerequisite to implementation of an effective instructional program. In an effort to select the most appropriate procedures, teachers usually choose a combination of informal and formal assessment techniques.

Anytime the teacher is observing the child with an eye toward what the child can or cannot do and making hypotheses about his or her learning style, progress, and behaviors, informal assessment is occurring. Because informal assessment is ongoing, is not expensive, and is less time consuming than formal assessment, it typically becomes the basic mode of assessment and formative evaluation. Informal testing is usually preferred by teachers because they can use instructional materials to develop testing items similar to the desired outcome or criterion behavior.

The development of ongoing classroom assessment

Unless existing diagnostic information suggests immediate usage of more structured formal or informal techniques, the first place to begin is with observation of the child in the classroom and/or at home. Selection of a developmental checklist or rating scale such as the one illustrated in Chapter 4 will facilitate ob-

jective recording of the teacher's observation. Teachers should select checklists or scales that contain individual items similar to or that match behavioral objectives within the classroom curriculum.

Preschool curricula are generally developmentally based and divided into such areas as sensory-motor, language, cognitive, social-emotional, and self-help skill development. Many curriculum guides presently in use were developed from existing or specially designed developmental scales that are also divided into the areas just mentioned. The teacher can readily see that by sequencing behavioral objectives developmentally, successful completion of one

objective will prepare the child to begin work on the next objective in the behavioral hierarchy of skills. Each time a task is completed, a check may be put in the appropriate box on the checklist. Ongoing, informal assessment is thus underway.

Of course any of the types of observation discussed earlier in the chapter can be used to determine if a child is achieving established objectives. Integration and synthesis of information obtained from sources such as anecdotal records, children's work, activity lists, photographs, and recordings provide analytical clues of whether further diagnostic work is needed or if a child is progressing as planned. Analysis of these records helps detect when additional, more formal norm-referenced tests or informal criterion-referenced measurement is needed.

Neisworth, Willoughby-Herb, Bagnato, Cartwright, and Laub (1980, p. 43) suggest that informal assessment is useful for the following:

1. Identifying absent, inconsistent, poorly developed, and excessive behavior patterns across multiple areas
2. Identifying different settings, events, materials, and activities that appear to control both desirable and undesirable behaviors
3. Identifying materials, activities, and rewards that stimulate desirable behavior by children
4. Identifying prerequisite goals for children
5. Identifying functional handicaps that will affect performance and learning and therefore require adaptive procedures and materials

Using criterion-referenced devices in the classroom

Comparing a child's performance to that of other children the same age is the traditional norm-referenced assessment. By contrast, criterion-referenced assessment compares the child's performance to a standard or expected mastery of a skill. A few criterion-referenced instruments that provide information directly transferable to program objectives are the Carolina Developmental Profile, Boehm Test of Basic Concepts, Portage Guide to Early Education, and the Valett Developmental Survey of Basic Learning Abilities (Cross and Goin, 1977). Some others are listed in Appendix D. However, directors and teachers of preschools often choose to develop their own criterion-referenced measurement instruments. They have the advantage of being able to tie the assessment devices to the program objectives.

Criterion-referenced measurement allows the test to become the task and vice versa. This approach is the crux of what is referred to currently as *prescriptive* or *diagnostic teaching*. This process of determining instructional content employs *task analysis*. As described by Larsen (1977, p. 128), such a program consists of the following:

a. Delineating the sequence of skills that needs to be mastered to perform a given task, b. determining a precise profile of the student's ability to perform these skills, c. devising an instructional program to teach the skills that have not yet been mastered, and d. evaluating the effectiveness of the educational program and initiating modifications when necessary.

A program employing this process is described as a *criterion-referenced program*.

It should be readily apparent that criterion-referenced devices facilitate daily planning for children. Appropriate tasks are sequenced, and the child is requested to perform each item, beginning with the most difficult. Instruction begins with the first item a child cannot complete in a sequence. It is said that we assess from the top down, or the hardest to the easiest, and teach from bottom up, from the easiest to the hardest. When assessing, concern is not with how well a child did in comparison to other children but with determining the next appropriate skill for a child to master.

Cross and Goin (1977) discuss the strengths and weaknesses of criterion-referenced tools. As strengths they cite (1) the measurement of intraindividual progress, (2) the ease in developing program objectives as a result of sequentially developed devices, (3) the fact that such devices usually cover many developmental areas and often have more items than norm-referenced techniques, and (4) the greater flexibility of administration necessary for use with handicapped children. Weaknesses of criterion-referenced devices include (1) the tendency to design techniques for specific groups of children, (2) the inclination to test very specific skills that may not give a picture of the total child, and (3) the characteristic of measuring skills in acquisition rather than generalization. For example, there is a big developmental difference between a child who happens to place items correctly on a form board through trial and error and one who places the items correctly with obvious ease.

In summary, Cross and Goin (1977, p. 44) conclude that (1) criterion-referenced measures provide more information to facilitate programming than do norm-referenced devices and (2) to give the teacher the most complete understanding of the child, criterion-referenced assessments should be used in combination with careful behavioral observation.

SITUATIONAL FACTORS TO CONSIDER DURING ASSESSMENT

Increasing attention is being given to consideration of the importance of situation factors in determining a child's performance on specified tasks (Stoneman and Gibson, 1978). To do so, teachers consider such variables as the setting of the assessment, the timing of the assessment, and the individuals involved in the assessment as well as the actual techniques of measurement used when implementing any type of evaluative process. Fig. 3-4 emphasizes the dynamic, interactive nature of five primary variables.

One rule of thumb to remember is that a child is capable of doing as well as his performance

demonstrates, but we are never certain of how much better he or she might do given optimal circumstances. Unfortunately, many school districts lock assessment into the calendar rather than into the child. That is, testing is scheduled for the first 3 days of school and is to be completed within that time. Sometimes little attention is given to establishing rapport or the fact that a child might be nervous in a new situation, sick, or drained by the heat of September. Federal agencies are guilty of establishing time lines for preassessment and postassessment that may not consider the critical influence of situational factors on assessment performance.

Rapport is critical

Before beginning any type of assessment or even observation, the teacher or other examiner has the responsibility of working to establish rapport with the child. Establishing rapport involves the development of a climate or an atmosphere in which the child feels comfortable enough to perform as well as possible. Rapport is evidenced when the child does not feel anxious, threatened, sad, or angry or experience any feeling that might lead to lack of cooperation. Preschool children often feel shy, uneasy around strangers, generally afraid, or even indifferent. Examiners may provide interesting toys and cooperative playtime before testing to gain the child's trust and confidence.

The need to establish rapport is another reason why teachers should not allow assessment procedures to be determined by the calendar. Several days may be needed to help the child feel comfortable and secure when interacting with the teacher. Needless to say, results from some team diagnostic interviews may be suspect if examiners have not taken sufficient time and effort to establish rapport. Again, we see the need to confirm or deny conclusions from initial diagnosis through continual and ongoing assessment.

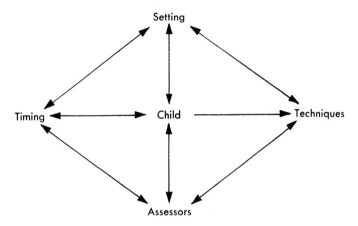

FIG. 3-4. Situational factors that influence assessment.

Allowing sufficient time

Young children with handicaps may need several days to complete what normal children may do within one setting. The length of time devoted must be very short to ensure the necessary "on task" behavior. Young children cannot be expected to concentrate for much longer than 10 to 20 minutes, depending on how demanding the task is. Handicapped children often fatigue more quickly than normal children. Teachers should observe the child before assessment to determine how much concentration time can be expected of the child before testing begins. Informal testing as accomplished by observing a child in play and checking a simple rating scale often capitalizes on the child's natural display of motivation and concentration. Both Ms. Mc-Lynn and Mr. Curtis would need to do more of this kind of observation.

The setting is important

Children's performance can be influenced by the setting in which the assessment occurs. Young children are usually very distractible and cannot concentrate when surrounded by activity. The table being used should be cleared of all objects when the child enters the testing space. Then items should be brought out for use one at a time. Children should be comfortable, using child-size tables and chairs whenever possible. The temperature of the testing area can be important. Young or insecure children may need to have their mothers or other familiar adults sitting nearby to ensure the best possible performance. Most parents can be cooperative and will not interfere if they have been advised ahead of time of what is to occur. Recent research is suggesting that the presence of parents may indeed make a significant positive difference in a young child's performance (Stoneman and Gibson, 1978).

Selecting the most appropriate time

Timing as well as length of assessment can influence results. Some children are slow starters in the morning and may need to ease into the day's routine. Other children are eager beginners and become increasingly tired as the day wears on. Generally young children and handicapped children tire more easily than older or nonhandicapped children. Nutritional factors can influence optimal timing of assessment. Care should be taken not to remove a child from his favorite activity of the day.

Children who have been playing outside may need time before they can be expected to concentrate on a demanding quiet task. Visual or auditory concentration should be interspersed with active periods for most children. However, some children might be "set off" by activity, and a different type of relaxing approach such as closing the eyes or music would be in order. An often forgotten feature of timing is toileting. Many examiners have realized too late just why a child was squirming in his or her seat rather than concentrating as desired. The examiner should always suggest the child drink water and use the bathroom before sitting him or her down to concentrate. In any case the individual behavioral characteristics of each child should be observed before the assessment procedure is initiated.

Considering the appropriateness of directions

One of the major reasons why testing of young children is often unreliable is due to the difficulty of directions involved in some formal testing procedures. If an examiner chooses to use a standardized test, he or she is compelled to follow the directions explicitly. However, it is not unusual to find that the formal test must become an informal one because of the need to alter directions. Cues frequently need to be offered for a young or handicapped child to understand directions. There is more to be gained from altering directions so that a child can respond than from declaring the child untestable because he could not comprehend the task.

If the examiner must alter procedure in any way, this should be noted and generalizations made accordingly. Again, observation ahead of time will help the examiner to know what can reasonably be expected of the child to be tested. It should be remembered that it is critical to establish eye contact and to get the child's at-

tention before ever beginning to elicit a testing response. Sometimes gentle cues of touching or holding the child's hand are necessary to help gain attention. This would definitely hold true for both Danny and Vicky. Each time a new item is presented, attention must be regained. Even if the teacher chooses to do only informal testing, time could be well spent reading standardized test manuals to acquire some of the testing skills required.

Focus on what the child can do

Examiners must be very careful observers. If a child fails an item, they must try to determine why. Did the child actually lack the knowledge or thinking ability to respond? Or is his or her performance penalized by an inability to respond as directed? For example, a child may not be able to make a cross on the Boehm Test of Basic Concepts, but he or she may be able to demonstrate understanding of the concept by touching the picture named. There is a vast difference between a child who stands limp and gazing off into space when a bean bag is thrown to him or her and one who coordinates eye and hand in reaching for, but missing, the bag. However, both responses might be counted as failures on some standardized tests. From the teacher's point of view, the process involved in the catching attempt is more important than the product of catching or not catching the object.

Young children and disturbed children have the tendency to perseverate when being tested. They get a "set" with one task and cannot switch to the requirements of the next task. If the correct picture is in the upper right hand corner of the Peabody Picture Vocabulary Test plate, the child might point to the upper right hand corner time after time. The examiner then should discontinue the task until the child is able to cooperate more adequately. The same procedure would be necessary if obvious random guessing is occurring. All of these influences combine to make it extremely important that the examiner carefully observe the child. It is always better to record "test incomplete" on a folder than to enter results that are known to be invalid.

PROBLEMS ASSOCIATED WITH EARLY IDENTIFICATION, ASSESSMENT, AND EVALUATION

Educators continue to raise questions, discuss concerns, and encourage caution in attempts to diagnose young children or to attach labels to them. The necessity of early identification of readily apparent physical, sensory, or gross developmental problems is not questioned. However, as Keogh and Becker (1973) so convincingly argue, extreme care must be taken in hypothesizing about the potential for learning failures that actually have not occurred. Hypothesizing future learning problems may indeed create an expectancy phenomenon. Keogh and Becker emphasize the need to be more concerned with what is necessary for success in the present or very near future. In other words, the teacher of 3 year olds should be more concerned with acquisition of motor skills that influence the ability of children to dress themselves than with how well the children will be able to print their names.

Labels are not for children

Another caution that has led some states to establish noncategorical preschool classrooms is a concern over the possible negative effects of labeling children. Research is suggesting that categorizing and labeling children, for example, emotionally disturbed, hearing impaired, or learning disabled, may be responsible for the development of negative expectations on the part of classroom teachers and others. These negative expectations in turn may further the child's existing difficulties (Algozzine, Mercer, and Countermine, 1977; Kronick, 1977). For example, if a child is described as retarded, the lowered expectations of parents and other caregivers may lead to delayed development. Failure to stimulate, reward, and expect normal mental growth may result from the labeling. This failure to nurture, rather than an innate limitation, may exaggerate the developmental delay.

Importance of reliable and valid tests

Tests developed for young children usually lack rigor in terms of reliability and validity. Therefore it is difficult to use norm-referenced tests in developing educational plans with any confidence (Ysseldyke and Salvia, 1974). The term *reliability* refers to the consistency or dependability of a testing procedure. It is the degree to which a child's score is a true score. That is, little or no error in measurement is present. The reliability of a test is often determined by comparing results from repeated administrations of the test (test-retest), by giving equivalent forms of the test, by comparing the results of each half (split-half), and by noting the consistency in rating between two or more scorers (interscorer). Even though it is essential to be certain that results do not reflect considerable error, many test manuals do not report results from efforts to determine the reliability. Consistency in any performance is not characteristic of young children, but attempts must continue to be made to ensure as much reliability as possible when assessments are made.

When a test is reliable, it may not necessarily be valid. *Validity* refers to what a test measures and how well it does so (Anastasi, 1976). Does it measure what it is suppose to measure? For example, if a teacher wishes to determine a child's level of problem solving, then he or she must require a child to solve problems. Asking a child to identify pictures by pointing to those named and recording a resulting MA score does not tell a child's potential for solving problems. A valid problem-solving test has not been given. Instead a valid test for assessing a child's level of receptive language and ability to associate a verbal symbol with a visual symbol has been given.

Three types of validity are usually discussed: construct validity, content validity, and predictive validity. Of the three, construct validity, or the ability to determine how well a test measures the conceptual idea behind its construction, is the most difficult to determine. Today many question whether or not intelligence tests actually measure the abstract quality called intelligence. Content validity assumes that the test has a representative sample of the behaviors it is supposed to measure. Tests of eye-motor coordination that omit eye-foot tasks do not include a truly representative sample of test items. Predictive or criterion-related validity is concerned with whether or not performance on the test items can predict actual achievement on another test that is supposed to measure related skills or future performance in related life skills.

Predictive validity is an issue of considerable concern to developers of screening or readiness tests. The very attempt to predict difficulties that have not occurred is risky (Keogh and Becker, 1973). Furthermore ethical considerations interfere with attempts to determine validity. Children are not expendable! If we know how to help children, it is unthinkable to withhold the help. Researchers would like to conduct rigid studies to determine how valid (effective) a test is in predicting future learning problems. If they do so, parents and educators of those children who take tests will not be given the test results.

Once concerned adults learn of a child's potential learning problems through the diagnostic interpretation of testing, they feel compelled ethically to implement remedial or preventative actions as soon as possible. Therefore the researchers are prevented from conducting long-term studies to find out if the predicted problems actually did occur. That is, if the remedial program has been successful, then children suspected of having learning problems would not be expected to continue to exhibit the predicted problems. As a result, the ability of tests to predict the actual existence of future problems is questionable. Rather than prevent children from obtaining the services they need, educators are choosing to rely less on test results and more on teacher and parent observation and judgment.

Growing interest in task analysis approach to early education

The task analysis or criterion-referenced approach would not hypothesize poor auditory memory to be the cause of a learning problem. It would instead analyze the component skills that children are expected to perform. By breaking tasks into their component parts and sequencing these parts from the simplest to the most difficult levels of performance, a criterion-referenced scale is developed. Children would be observed to determine their current levels of functioning. The instructional program would focus on the next step in the hierarchy of skills to be acquired for each individual.

For example, a teacher may detect a weakness in a particular processing ability such as the ability to visually discriminate between colors. Next, the teacher could do a task analysis and possibly find that the child may be able to learn to match colored objects before he or she can sort or visually discriminate between differences in colors. The teacher would then be actively combining the ability training and the task analysis approaches to the education of young children.

SUMMARY

Today there is a movement away from categorical descriptions of the handicapped child toward an analysis of specific instructional needs of the child. Typically a multistage process is involved that consists of (1) initial identification of children with problems, perhaps involving observational comparisons against a develop-

mental checklist and screening for medically related problems; (2) diagnosis resulting in multidisciplinary staff development of an IEP; (3) teacher assessment, determining appropriate daily objectives and activities based on a developmental curriculum; and (4) evaluation on a continuous basis of the child's progress for the purpose of updating the child's program and periodically to review success of the overall program.

Several phases in the process of recognizing and accommodating a child's special needs require assistance of numerous specialists. But the preschool teacher plays an instrumental role in the continuous success of the child's efforts. To be successful at this, part of the teacher's role is to know what constitutes normal behaviors. Armed with such knowledge, the teacher can then systematically observe for high risk signals

that might indicate the need for referral to specialized personnel or agencies. Guidelines and suggestions are given for how to strengthen this observational process.

Preschool teachers should be particularly cautious when using standardized tests as part of the assessment process. Norm-referenced tests which compare a child's scores with norms established by groups of children of the same age, may distort a child's capabilities if handicaps or unique needs are not considered. Criterion-referenced assessment compares a child's performance to a developmental standard or sequence of skills to be mastered. But increasingly, informal teacher-developed techniques serve as the basis for assessment and evaluation.

Finally, it was emphasized that the ultimate responsibility for assessment, choice of daily objectives, and effective teaching remains with the teacher. This is a responsibility for which few teachers feel prepared. To become skilled in the techniques of observation, formal and informal testing, and programming, practice and patience are essential. This chapter has attempted to clarify some of the ambiguities in the whole arena of evaluation, to bring to light some of the critical concerns surrounding evaluative procedures, and to encourage study and practice. The next chapter presents a workable method of turning information gained from assessment into realistic instructional strategies while providing for necessary program evaluation.

DISCUSSION TOPICS AND ACTIVITIES

1. Differentiate identification, diagnosis, assessment, and evaluation. Give the purposes of each process.
2. Select or construct your own developmental rating scale. Observe at least two children. If possible, observe a child suspected of having a handicap and a child with no known deficits. Check and compare their performances according to your rating scale. Write a summary of the educational strengths and weaknesses you observed. Be certain you have parental permission, and observe all aspects of confidentiality.
3. Design a few informal assessment procedures that you can use to determine a young handicapped child's educational strengths and weaknesses. Note the behaviors you would look for in order for the procedure to be useful to you in writing plans for the child being assessed.
4. Differentiate norm-referenced and criterion-referenced tests, and give the advantages and disadvantages of each type of test.
5. Use the Buros Mental Measurements Yearbook to thoroughly research a commonly used assessment instrument such as the Peabody Picture Vocabulary Test or the Developmental Test of Visual-Motor Integration (VMI). Present a critique to your classmates. Be certain to research such important factors as reliability, validity, and the characteristics of the normative sample.
6. Role play techniques for developing rapport with a young handicapped child.

ANNOTATED REFERENCES

Buros, O.K. (Ed.). *Eighth mental measurements yearbook.* Lincoln: University of Nebraska Press, 1978.
The purpose of these yearbooks is to present comprehensive reviews of a large variety of assessment instruments. Critical reviews from professionals both question and support claims made by test authors and publishers. Before using any instrument, these yearbooks should be consulted. Recent publications may not be included, whereas older tests may be found in previous editions of the yearbook.

Coordinating Office for Regional Resource Centers (CORRC). *Preschool test matrix: Individual test descriptions.* Lexington: University of Kentucky Press, 1976.
Detailed information about specific tests that can be used for screening, diagnosis, and assessment of young children is given on a series of test descriptor forms. This book, which is available through the Educational Resources Information Center (ERIC) (ED 129 041), serves as a very useful, quick reference to such data as publisher, price, time of administration, qualifications of examiner, basic content, reliability, and validity.

Cross, L., and Goin, K. (Eds.). *Identifying handicapped children: A guide to casefinding, screening, diagnosis, assessment and evaluation.* New York: Walker & Co., 1977.
This book was developed in an effort to define the scope of an identification program and to examine the five basic elements of casefinding, screening, diagnosis, assessment, and evaluation. An overview of the whole process of identifying handicapped children is offered along with definitions and discussion of the basic elements. A rather thorough annotated bibliography of screening, diagnosis, and assessment devices is included.

Divoky, D. Screening: The grand delusion. *Learning Magazine,* 1977, 5, 28-34.
This article clearly addresses the controversies involved in the process of screening. It identifies and discusses a number of potential abuses. The author is concerned with the excuses for not teaching that can result from labeling. Although no attention is given to possible benefits of screening, the point is rightfully made that a screening tool is only as good as the user's understanding of the behavior of young children.

Garwood, S.G., et al. (Eds.). *Educating young handicapped children: A developmental approach.* Germantown, Md.: Aspen Systems Corp., 1979.
In addition to the provision of a strong theoretical background for the understanding of the relationship between normal developmental progress and the educational implications of handicapping conditions, this book provides an annotated listing of many of the assessment measures currently in general use.

Hare, B.A., and Hare, J.M. *Teaching young handicapped children: A guide for preschool and the primary grades.* New York: Grune & Stratton, Inc., 1977.
With emphasis on educational intervention during the preschool years, practical direction and strategies for programming handicapped children are provided. Chapter 2 is devoted to the discussion of skills and techniques of assessment, diagnosis, and remediation. Concern over the use of standardized tests and the importance of careful

observation receive attention. Annotations of frequently used norm-referenced and criterion-referenced tools of measurement are included.

Hennon, M.L. *Identifying handicapped children for child development programs.* Atlanta: Humanics Press, 1977.

This publication is intended to serve as a manual to educators who wish to mainstream handicapped preschool children. Issues such as why should they attend preschool classes with other children, how do they differ from other children, identification of differences, and available resources are presented and discussed. Names and addresses of service agencies are listed.

Joiner, L.M. *Identifying children with special needs: A practical guide to developmental screening.* Holmes Beach, Fla.: Learning Publications, Inc., 1978.

This volume focuses on what is believed to be the first step in an effective program for detecting and meeting the special needs of young children: developmental screening. Such topics as planning a screening program, building community awareness, and evaluating instruments are discussed. Finally, an instrument profile of over 100 screening instruments as well as names and addresses of publishers is made available.

Meisels, S.J. *Developmental screening in early childhood: A guide.* Washington, D.C.: National Association for the Education of Young Children, 1978.

The purpose of this book is to clarify some of the issues and practical components necessary for the design of an effective developmental screening program for young children. Critical decisions involved in planning the screening program, selecting instruments, and involving parents and the community are discussed. Included is an annotated bibliography of appropriate readings.

Salvia, J., and Ysseldyke, J.E. *Assessment in special and remedial education.* Boston: Houghton Mifflin Co., 1978.

This text is an introduction to psychoeducational assessment in special and remedial education. It is an excellent resource for those who wish to gain a deeper understanding of testing in the broader context of assessment. Most of the major tests in use are objectively described. For each test, the general format, kinds of behaviors sampled, kinds of scores provided, nature of the standardization sample, and evidence of validity and reliability are described. Technical adequacy of various tests is evaluated.

Assessment within the classroom

Bell, D.R., and Low, R.M. *Observing and recording children's behavior.* Richland, Wash. Performance Associates, 1977.

The major goal of this book is to teach those skills necessary to conduct accurate and systematic observations. These authors have managed to present the essential elements of objective observation in a clear, concise manner while offering useful practical examples.

Cohen, D.H., and Stern, V. *Observing and recording the behavior of young children* (2nd ed.). New York: Teachers College Press, 1978.

This book carefully presents and discusses the details of observing and recording while maintaining the quality of interaction. The reader is treated to a multitude of examples of what to look for and how to look for it throughout daily activities.

Quanty, C., and Davis, A. *Observing children.* Sherman Oaks, Calif.: Alfred Publishing Co., Inc., 1974.

This is a workbook designed to provide guidelines for observing the behavior of preschool children. Each section discusses an area of child development and recommends a method for students to employ in observing that particular behavior.

Lindberg, L., and Swedlow, R. *Early childhood education—A guide for observation and participation.* Boston: Allyn & Bacon, Inc., 1976.

Numerous worksheets are provided to focus attention on the specific components of an early childhood program. The content is arranged according to both the activities of a program and the curriculum areas of social studies, communication arts, mathematics, and science. Each section includes objectives, pretests, posttests, worksheets, and resource materials that give theoretical and practical background.

McCormack, J.E. The assessment tool that meets your needs: The one you construct. *Teaching Exceptional Children*, 1976, *8*, 106-109.

This article presents a step-by-step process, beginning with the identification of skills to be taught and ending with a pupil analysis sheet that allows the teacher to determine appropriate objectives for each child. An excellent example of an effective classroom assessment process is described and illustrated.

Problems associated with early identification, diagnosis, and assessment

Keogh, B.K., and Becker, L.D. Early detection of learning problems: Questions, cautions and guidelines. *Exceptional Children*, 1973, *40*, 5-11.

This article is essential reading for anyone involved in the processes of early identification and diagnosis. The questions raised and cautions discussed are critical to the development of programs with integrity. The proposed guidelines have the interests of children at heart.

REFERENCES

Algozzine, B., Mercer, C., and Countermine, T. The effects of labels and behavior on teacher expectations. *Exceptional Children*, 1977, *44*, 131-132.

Anastasi, A. *Psychological testing* (4th ed.). New York: Macmillan, Inc., 1976.

Bayley, N. *Bayley infant scales of development*. New York: Psychological Corporation, 1968.

Bortner, M., and Birch, H.C. Cognitive capacity and cognitive competency. *American Journal of Mental Deficiency*, 1970, *74*, 735-744.

Buktenica, N.A. Special education and school psychology: Whither the relationship? *School Psychology Review*, 1980, *9*, 228-233.

Buros, O.K. (Ed.). *Eighth mental measurements yearbook*. Lincoln: University of Nebraska Press, 1978.

Cross, L., and Goin, K.W. (Eds.). *Identifying handicapped children: A guide to casefinding, screening, diagnosis, assessment and evaluation*. New York: Walker & Co., 1977.

Dreyer, A.S., and Haupt, D. Self-evaluation in young children. *Journal of Genetic Psychology*, 1966, *2*, 185-197.

Dunn, L.M. *Peabody Picture Vocabulary Test*. Circle Pines, Minn. American Guidance Association, 1970.

Frankenburg, W. Increasing the lead time for the preschool aged handicapped child. In J.B. Jordan and R.F. Dailey (Eds), *Not all little wagons are red*. Arlington, Va.: Council for Exceptional Children, 1973.

Garwood, S.G. et al. (Eds.). *Educating young handicapped children*. Germantown, Md.: Aspen Systems Corp., 1979.

Gearheart, B.R., and Weishahn, M.W. *The handicapped student in the regular classroom*. St. Louis: The C.V. Mosby Co., 1980.

Gesell, A. *The first five years of life*. New York: Harper & Row, Publishers Inc., 1940

Hammill, D.D., and Larsen, S. The effectiveness of psycholinguistic training. *Exceptional Children*, 1974, *41*, 5-16.

Hare, B.A., and Hare, J.M. *Teaching young handicapped children: A guide for preschool and the primary grades*. New York: Grune & Stratton Inc., 1977.

Hayden, A., and Edgar, E.B. Identification, assessment, and screening. In J.B. Jordan, A.H. Hayden, M.B. Karnes, and W.W. Wood (Eds.). *Early childhood education for exceptional children*. Reston, Va.: Council for Exceptional Children, 1977.

Hoffman, G. Special education categories and educational needs. *ICEC Quarterly*, 1980, *29*, 19-21.

Illinois State Board of Education. *Early childhood education for the handicapped: Special study*. Springfield: Illinois State Board of Education, 1980.

Jordan, J.B., Hayden, A.H., Karnes, M.B., and Wood, M.M. (Eds.). *Early childhood education for exceptional children*. Reston, Va.: Council for Exceptional Children, 1977.

Keogh, B. Research on cognitive styles. In R.D. Kneedler and S.G. Tarver (Eds.), *Changing perspectives in special education*. Columbus, Ohio: Charles E Merrill Publishing Co., 1977.

Keogh, B., and Becker, L.D. Early detection of learning problems: Questions, cautions, and guidelines. *Exceptional Children*, 1973, *40*, 5-11.

Kronick, D. The pros and cons of labeling. *Academic Therapy*, 1977, *13*, 101-104.

Larsen, S.C. The educational evaluation of handicapped students. In R.D. Kneedler and S.G. Tarver (Eds.), *Changing perspectives in special education*. Columbus, Ohio: Charles E Merrill Publishing Co., 1977.

Logan, D.R. Diagnosis: Current and changing considerations. In R.D. Kneedler and S.G. Tarver (Eds.), *Changing perspectives in special education*. Columbus, Ohio: Charles E Merrill Publishing Co., 1977.

Meeker, M. Intelligence in the classroom: Individualized curriculum based on intelligence patterns. In R. Coop and K. White (Eds.), *Psychological concepts in the classroom*. New York: Harper & Row, Publishers, Inc., 1974.

Neisworth, J.T., Willoughby-Herb, S.J., Bagnato, S.J., Cartwright, C.A., and Laub, K.W. *Individualized Education for Preschool Exceptional Children*. Germantown, Md.: Aspen Systems Corp., 1980.

Public Law 93-380. Washington, D.C.: U.S. Government Printing Office, 1974.

Rosenthal, R., and Jacobson, L. *Pygmalion in the classroom*. New York: Holt, Rinehart & Winston, 1968.

Runge, A., Walker, J., and Shea, T. A passport to positive parent-teacher communications. *Teaching Exceptional Children*, 1975, *7*, 91-92.

Safford, P.L. *Teaching young children with special needs*. St. Louis: The C.V. Mosby Co., 1978.

Salvia, J., and Ysseldyke, J.E. *Assessment in special and remedial education*. Boston: Houghton Mifflin Co., 1978.

Stoneman, Z., and Gibson, S. Situational influences on assessment performance. *Exceptional Children*, 1978, *45*, 166-169.

Van Etten, G., Arkell, C., and Van Etten, C. *The severely and profoundly handicapped*. St. Louis: The C.V. Mosby Co., 1980.

Wallace, G., and Larsen, S.C. *Educational assessment of learning problems: Testing for teaching*. Boston: Allyn & Bacon, Inc., 1979.

Ysseldyke, J., and Salvia, J. Diagnostic-prescriptive teaching: Two models. *Exceptional Children*, 1974, *41*, 181-185.

CHAPTER

4

Developing instructional strategies

77

The previous chapter introduced some of the major issues surrounding the processes of identification, diagnosis, assessment, and evaluation. Attention was given to preparing teachers for their primary role as astute observers of children's behavior. The options available for assessment within the classroom were discussed. This chapter suggests practical instructional strategies. Focus is on the choice of goals to meet individual needs, correct writing of instructional objectives, and use of these objectives in the development of instructional plans. Emphasis is placed on using a clearly stated sequence of objectives to individualize teaching while working with a group of children.

The overall plan presented in this chapter makes it possible to include handicapped children or children with developmental lags in a regular preschool. By using sets of sequentially planned objectives, effective lessons can be taught to children who learn quickly as well as to those who learn more slowly. The least restrictive environment for developmentally delayed children can be an exciting and challenging environment also for normal and gifted children. Teacher planning time can be decreased. Record keeping (accountability) is simplified.

BEFORE LESSON PLANNING CAN BEGIN: THE IEP

Current federal guidelines require children who will receive any special education services to be seen for a diagnostic study by members of a multidisciplinary team before services can begin. They do not specify the professionals to be included. It is expected that choice of the members for a specific team will be determined by the characteristics and suspected handicaps of a particular child. For example, in all cases of suspected speech and/or language delays, the child must be seen by a speech-language pathologist. This pathologist must also be present at the subsequent meeting or "staffing," at

which time the IEP is determined, and a written statement is developed. Other people who attend this meeting include the following:

1. Any member of the school staff, other than the child's teacher, who is "qualified to provide or supervise the provision of, specially designed instruction to meet the unique needs of handicapped children" (P.L. 94-142, Sec. 602[19])

2. At least one teacher, special or regular, who will implement the child's IEP

3. One or both of the child's parents

4. The child, when appropriate

5. Other individuals whose expertise may be desired by the parent or school

6. A member of the diagnostic team or a representative who is knowledgeable of the evaluation procedures used with the child and is familiar with the results of the evaluation

For example, Danny's IEP conference members would include his preschool teacher and the speech-language pathologist who had evaluated him (pp. 87 to 90). His parents and another member of the school staff, qualified to provide or supervise needed services, would be present. If a nurse had done part of the evaluation, he or she would also be present.

The multidisciplinary diagnostic team

The multidisciplinary diagnostic team, including the parents as valid members, considers the child's current educational needs. Priorities are chosen. Goals are specified and behavioral objectives written for each goal.

The referring teacher's preparation. In preparation for the multidisciplinary staffing, Ms. McLynn would write observations of Danny in several different settings and circumstances. She would summarize any information gained from informal or formal classroom assessment and gather relevant samples of Danny's work. She must be prepared to give evidence of Danny's present level of classroom functioning. A copy of the referral form she had completed earlier on Danny would be included in her

Miss McLynn teaches a preschool class of 4-year-olds. For several weeks she has been puzzled about Danny. He just won't pay attention. Sometimes when she calls him he comes right away. Other times he pays no attention until she raises her voice and speaks firmly. Often he acts as if he hears her call, but then he looks for her in the wrong direction. Or when she tells him to do something he does something else. Then he just gives her a blank look when she explains all over again what she wants him to do. (At first Miss McLynn had wondered if he had a hearing problem, but the nurse said he had passed the hearing screening.) Today she has decided to observe him carefully and take notes. Her aide, Mrs. Cain, is playing a game with four children, while 10 others, including Danny, are playing with various toys and games. Here is what she wrote.

Danny is playing in the corner with some toy animals. Another child called him but he didn't turn, so Susan poked him. He turned, surprised. Tim said, "Danny, I want that little duck." When Danny gave him the dog, Tim said, "Not dog, you silly. I want the duck." Danny obligingly gave him the toy truck! So Tim went over and picked up the duck.

Danny walked over to the clay table and began to pound the clay. He hit it with all his 4-year-old's vigor.

Remember to ask Danny's mother about allergies. His nose always seems to be dripping. Even though he passed our screening, he just doesn't seem to be hearing.

preparation file. Questions, based on her concerns, should be prepared. These might include the following:

1. "Sometimes he seems to hear us and at other times we get the feeling he doesn't want to pay attention. Does his hearing change from time to time?"

2. "He seems to pay more attention to a man's voice than to a woman's. Why is this?"

3. "It is very difficult to understand Danny. He can't be deaf. He loves to sing, and he keeps on pitch as well as the others do. But his speech is nearly unintelligible. Why is this?"

4. "If we show him how to do something, he is quick to learn. Why is he so slow when we tell him what to do?"

Ms. McLynn would be ready to present any information she has about Danny, and she would be prepared to answer any questions other team members would have. Of course, she would have obtained a signed "release of information" from Danny's parents. She would also plan to report any intervention she has already tried with Danny, including any special materials or methods. For example, when Ms. McLynn worked with Danny alone, he seemed to do much better. She also found that Danny had difficulty following musical records with directions. He could, however, follow the same directions when she sang them.

Finally, Ms. McLynn would be prepared to state as clearly as possible exactly what she needs to know to instruct Danny appropriately. Her prepared questions will help her to gain the information she needs. Having her questions and concerns written down ahead of time will help her to be certain that no important consideration is overlooked. Teachers must actively seek all the information they feel necessary for the planning and implementation of the services listed on the IEP form. The teacher's responsibility in this role cannot be overemphasized.

The specialists' preparation. Whenever possible the specialists who evaluate young children ask to see observations made by others, including teachers and parents. Many use a questionnaire to elicit information relevant to their particular field before they begin formal testing. Often a screening test is used as a preliminary to in-depth evaluations.

Each specialist will choose test instruments judged to be relevant to the suspected problems. During the diagnosis it may become apparent that additional tests are needed. If one specialist obtains information that suggests that additional specialists need to be included in the multidisciplinary diagnostic team, it is his or her responsibility to request the necessary additional diagnosis. The chairperson of the staffing in which the IEP is developed is the person referred to in the law as "representative of the local educational agency . . . who shall be qualified to provide, or supervise the provision of, specially designed instruction" (P.L. 94-142, Sec. 602[19]). This person may be responsible for collecting all assessment information and being certain that no important aspect of the diagnostic process is overlooked. Specialists must be prepared to relate test results, their level of confidence in the child's performance, and recommendations for placement and services to the chairperson. They should make every possible effort to translate their findings into information directly useful to program and lesson planning.

When participating in the multidisciplinary staffing, professionals should be prepared to speak in language that parents understand. They must remember that parents as well as professionals are to be included as active, vital members of the team.

The parents' preparation. Parents will be expected to organize any information they have received from previous examiners. They have the responsibility of honestly and accurately sharing information about their child's behavior and perceived educational strengths and weaknesses. Parents serve as the child's advocate.

A DAY-CARE CENTER WHERE CHILDREN WITH SPECIAL NEEDS ARE WELCOMED AND EDUCATED

Until recently many public and private day-care centers were reluctant to accept children with special needs. They said that they were neither trained nor equipped to help them. Other centers accepted handicapped children but simply took care of their physical needs.

Ms. Johnson and Ms. McLynn want to provide the best possible services for the handicapped children who come to their center. They begin by listening carefully to the parents' requests and descriptions of their children. Then they observe the children in their preschool environment.

These teachers find the following sequence helpful:

1. Before a child is enrolled, parents meet with the director and the teacher. Information, parent concerns, and available services are considered. The enrollment form includes questions about previous experiences as well as a health history. The child's developmental level is discussed.
2. For the first few weeks the child is observed throughout the day. Special needs are identified. Ms. McLynn and Ms. Johnson discuss these with the parents at a second conference.
3. During this second conference recommendations are made to the parents about where and how to find special educators and other trained personnel to evaluate the child's needs, if this seems to be needed.
4. After a child has been evaluated and recommendations for special education services and procedures have been received at an IEP conference, Ms. McLynn and Ms. Johnson incorporate the suggestions and activities into the child's daily program.
5. Regular contact with parents and others working with the special children is maintained through telephone conversations, conferences, and written reports.

This day-care center includes several handicapped children during each session. If the special children require a great deal of extra time and attention, an additional teacher aide is provided. In some cases parents are required to pay for this service in addition to the tuition. Where federal and state money provide for the education of very young children, parents are not expected to pay.

This day-care center and others in the 1980's accept the challenge of including children who are in need of special education. However, they expect the children to receive these services through public or private agencies. Wise teachers refuse to merely "love and take care of children." They are aware that the most critical years for learning occur before the traditional school entrance age of 5 or 6. As a result, they cooperate with parents and special educators by including handicapped children in their centers. They are careful to meet individual needs appropriately.

Teachers can be very helpful in assisting parents to prepare information they wish to share as well as in developing a list of questions to be asked of professionals. Parents should be given any assistance necessary to help them fully understand the program and services being proposed. In some cases translators or multilingual specialists will have to be included as part of the multidisciplinary team. Initial understanding and genuine acceptance of services to be offered can save many hours of discussion or even the necessity of changes later on.

THE CASE OF DANNY

The following narrative gives insight into the background and proceedings of one child's multidisciplinary conference.

Background information

Danny's parents are worried. Twice they have been asked to withdraw him from day-care centers. Now the private preschool that he has been attending has called them in for a conference. Both parents work, and they want the best possible placement for Danny. Several friends have told them that they know he would not be accepted in the public school kindergarten next year. He rarely talks, and when he does, it is very difficult to understand him. He is also bullheaded. Many times when they tell him to do something, he acts as if he does not hear them unless they yell at him. They have heard that he would be placed in a special education class if they took him to a public school. They are frightened.

December 10, 1981. Danny has now been enrolled in the private preschool for 3 weeks. Ms. McLynn and Ms. Johnson are anxious to discuss their observations with Danny's parents.

Ms. Johnson: Thank you for coming. We are enjoying Danny and hope he is enjoying us. We have observed Danny in a variety of situations and would like to discuss our observations with you.

Mrs. Dickson: We are so pleased that Danny is coming to your school. We are grateful for the help you have given Danny and are anxious to hear about how he is doing.

Ms. Johnson: Well, as you know, it is sometimes difficult for us to understand what Danny is saying, and it seems that often he doesn't understand us. When we try to tell him something to do, he just seems so confused. We can get him to pay attention by standing in front of him and talking directly to him. He also seems to have trouble with the names of things like colors and body parts.

Mrs. Dickson: We have also noticed some of the things you are talking about. His pediatrician examined him, as you suggested, and he said he is fine. He told us that many children don't learn to speak clearly until they are in school. He said that we could take him to the public school and they might give him speech therapy. However, he had heard that they don't begin therapy until second grade, because most children outgrow their baby talk.

Mr. Dickson: Our friends the Joneses have a little girl who the psychologist said is very slow. She doesn't talk clearly either, and they put her in a special class. We really don't want Danny put in a class with children who have problems or can't learn. Danny isn't dumb.

Ms. McLynn: I agree with you, Mr. Dickson. Danny isn't dumb. But something is wrong. He misunderstands us most of the time, and we can't understand him. He doesn't know the names of lots of things the others know.

Ms. Johnson: We feel that we aren't helping Danny enough. He needs special kinds of help that we aren't trained to provide. We are hoping that you will agree to have specialists test Danny to help us find the best ways to teach him. There is a new law that requires the public schools to give children special tests and to provide a free, appropriate education for any child who needs specialized help. Danny could attend the local public school. Or, if you would like, he could also come to our school for part of the day. Transportation is provided. We will be happy to work with his teacher at the public school and with you in any way that we can. Before any decisions are made about how best to educate Danny, you will receive the test results and can ask questions. In fact, you are supposed to be totally involved in any decisions that are made. In other words, agreeing to let Danny be tested doesn't mean he will have to be in a special class. What do you think?

Mr. Dickson: I'm not sure. Are you sure that Danny needs all of this help? We can understand him.

Ms. Johnson: Yes, I believe you can understand Danny. He does the most difficult puzzles easily and builds wonderful towns with blocks. We would just like to find out what is causing Danny's problems and how we should be teaching him. Why don't you think about finding out what educational possibilities are available. You can visit any classrooms that might be suitable. You will get to make any final decisions.

Mr. Dickson: Okay. Who do we call?

As Mr. and Mrs. Dickson left the preschool, they still felt somewhat frightened. Mrs. Dickson remembered that one preschool teacher had said her son had a "dull expression" and another said that he seemed "bewildered." But when they spoke to friends and relatives, they all reassured them that Danny was just a late bloomer. In spite of their fears, they did call their local public school office, and an appointment for a diagnostic interview was made. They had to sign papers to release information from the preschool and to confirm that they agreed to the testing.

January 15, 1982. A multidisciplinary team staffing conference is in progress at the Special Education Office. In addition to Danny's teacher from the private preschool and his parents, a school psychologist, nurse, social worker, speech-language pathologist, and supervisor of special education are present. The supervisor has reviewed the background information.

Supervisor: So, you see, on the basis of these tests, it appears that Danny would be eligible for placement in our Early Childhood Special Education Class.

Mrs. Dickson: What kinds of children are in this special education class?

Supervisor: Well, lots of kinds. They are all between the ages of 3 and 5. One wears very thick glasses, another walks with a brace, and two don't talk very well. The little boy with the brace is already reading. Why don't you come to visit the class? I think

you will be surprised at how friendly the children are and how much they are learning. Some even spend part of their day in the kindergarten.

Mr. Dickson: I am eager to hear what the psychologist has to say.

Psychologist: Danny worked very hard and seemed to want to try everything. Because Danny seemed to understand so little speech and language, and I had a hard time understanding him, I gave him two kinds of tests. Well, really three. First, I tried a vocabulary test. For that test, I show pictures and name them. All Danny had to do was point to the picture that I named. There are four pictures on each page, and only one is correct. On that test, Danny responded by naming or pointing to a few pictures correctly. He often seemed confused. He couldn't identify as many pictures as most children his age.

Then, I attempted to use a standardized intelligence test that requires Danny to listen to me and answer questions and point to things, too. Again, he was unable to do most of the items that other 4 year olds can do. So, next I used a nonverbal performance test. On this test, Danny had to listen to only a few directions and did not have to talk to me. He did have to watch me carefully, and then imitate some of the things I did. And here he was more successful. He seemed to enjoy these activities. His confused expression disappeared and he looked more interested. Danny was able to match the colors very well. He could do difficult puzzles, complete copying designs, and put pattern pieces together. When he finished, he grinned at me and seemed to want to do more.

Ms. McLynn: That's the way he is at school, too. He can color and draw better than most of the other children. He is quick to learn how to make things.

Speech-language pathologist: When I evaluated his speech and language, I observed that he has all of the "music of speech" when he talks but few of the right speech sounds.

Mr. Dickson: What is music of speech?

Speech-language pathologist: One of the first things babies learn to do as they are learning to talk is to imitate the way we raise and lower our voices to signal statements or questions. At first, if you listen to a baby about 9 or 10 months old, it almost sounds as if they are talking, but there are no words. You can hear the rising pitch at the end of their "sentences," and it really sounds like questions some of the time. We call those pitch changes *suprasegmental aspects* or *prosodic features.*

Mr. Dickson: Now that you mention it, I've noticed that music too. But you can't understand what he's saying when he is making those sounds.

Speech-language pathologist: Right. By themselves, those pitch changes aren't enough. My tests indicate that Danny says most of the vowels correctly, although the short vowels as in p*i*n, p*a*n, p*e*n, and p*u*n aren't distinct. He can imitate the voiced consonants, for example, /b/, /d/, /g/, /m/, and /n/, and he uses them in some words but he often omits them on the ends of words. He says ba*w* for ba*ll* and d*aw* for d*og*, for example. When he tries to make sentences, he leaves off /s/, /t/, and /z/ at the ends of words, so he cannot "signal" past tense as in hopp*ed* and look*ed*. He doesn't use plurals, as in car*s* and truck*s*. Notice when you say hopped you are putting a /t/ sound on the end, even though we write the letter *d*. When you say balls you are using a /z/, even though we spell it with an *s*. He doesn't say /p/, /t/, or /k/ in any words, so of course, it is impossible to understand him.

When I asked him to listen to me say a sentence and point to the picture that showed what I had said, he was really confused. One picture page has a little boy looking into a mirror seeing himself and another picture where he is looking at a shelf. Danny had no idea what I wanted him to do. When I said "He sees himself," he pointed to both pictures. Also, I recorded more than 50 things that he said while we played with some cars and trucks and a toy garage. He really enjoyed that. When I analyzed what he said, I found that he is using three- and four-word sentences, although the words are not clear. He tried to ask me for things, too.

Nurse: Danny responded very quickly and accurately to my vision screening test. I showed him just once what I wanted him to do. He was all business, paid close attention, and quickly demonstrated that he has good eyesight. But the hearing testing was another story! He wiggled and giggled. He said he heard the tones when the audiometer was off. At 25 decibels, the loudness level used for hearing screening, he heard 500 and 1000 Hertz in one ear, but he did not respond to the same loudness at higher frequencies. In the other ear, he did not answer correctly at all at 25 decibels. So, I referred him to our Speech and Hearing Center for a complete hearing evaluation with more sophisticated equipment. The audiologist, a specialist in evaluating hearing and recommending needed remediation, reported that Danny exhibited a precipitous high frequency sensory-neural hearing loss in one ear and a mild, conductive loss in the other ear. The audiologist said that Danny's problems understanding speech and learning to talk could be explained on the basis of his hearing problems alone. He recommended that Danny be seen by an otologist, an ear specialist, to determine the causes of the hearing loss. He said that it was possible that Danny might benefit from a hearing aid. Efforts to correct the hearing loss should be made first.

Speech-language pathologist: Danny has problems hearing the difference between the high frequency sounds in particular. He had trouble with other auditory processing tasks, too.

Mr. Dickson: But if he can't hear, how come he can hear us when he wants to? He can be sitting in front of the TV and just pay no attention when I tell him something. But if I get angry, he jumps right away.

Speech-language pathologist: When you get angry, you probably speak louder, and your tone of voice changes.

Mr. Dickson: You bet it does.

Speech-language pathologist: He can hear those changes, because the vowels are in the lower frequencies, and he hears them almost as you and I do. He can hear the change in your tone of voice for the same reason. What he cannot hear is the consonants. All these years he must have been hearing things with the most important parts missing. For instance, with the reported hearing loss he hears "Come to supper" as "um oo u er."

Mrs. Dickson: Why, that is exactly what he says when he tells someone it is time to eat!

Speech-language pathologist: So, you see, he has been saying what he has been hearing.

Mrs. Dickson: But he has only had one earache, and it didn't last long. His nose "runs" a lot, but he is never sick. He does have lots of allergies, though.

Nurse: Often children don't complain about mild earaches. You will want to check with your pediatrician to be sure that his ears are okay now.

Speech-language pathologist: But even if his ears are perfect now, his speech won't be cleared up right away. You see, it is as if he has been looking through smeary glasses that really were not right for his eyes. Everything he has heard has been distorted and incorrect. Now, he has learned to say many things the wrong way, and he will have to learn to talk all over again in the right way.

Mr. Dickson: So what do we do now?

Ms. McLynn: Is there someone who can help us to teach him what he needs to know? We really want to help Danny.

Speech-language pathologist: My suggestion would be that he attend the special education class in our school each day for 2½ hours. During that time I can work with him regularly. I'll give his teacher many special activities to help him to learn in spite of his hearing loss. He can learn to use his hearing better, and he can learn to supplement what he hears through lipreading.

Mrs. Dickson: But we both work. We need to have him in the right place all day.

Psychologist: Could he attend the special class in the morning and go to your preschool in the afternoon, Ms. McLynn?

Ms. McLynn: Could someone teach us, too?

Supervisor: Yes, we could arrange for you to visit the special class and talk with his teacher and the speech pathologist. They could suggest special ways of helping him while he is at your school. We can include that in his IEP if you wish.

Mrs. Dickson: That would be a great help to us. We really do think Danny can learn.

Psychologist: You are right, even though all of his test scores that include understanding or using language are very low. The important clue is that when the tests did not require him to understand what I *said* or to talk to me, he was able to score well within the normal range.

Mr. Dickson: I'm ashamed for all of the times I've spanked him for not listening. But he always heard his brother's motorcycle when he was half a block away. And he was always the first to run outside to look for jet planes. He loves the hi-fi and sings right along with the tunes. You are telling me he can hear all that but not hear the speech sounds like /p/ and /t/?

Speech-language pathologist: Right. And I can teach him how to make those sounds and to recognize them when he sees them on people's lips, even if his hearing doesn't improve. Of course, we will expect that it will.

Psychologist: You may be disappointed with yourselves, but remember, very few parents discover this kind of problem themselves. That is why the federal law encourages local school districts to test *all* children by age 3.

Ms. McLynn: We've noticed he seems to hear a man's voice best. Should he be placed in a man's class?

Speech-language pathologist: Not necessarily. But it will be helpful if you speak more slowly and in shorter sentences. Be close to Danny, and be sure that you have his attention before you tell him something. Avoid having sources of bright light such as a window behind you when you talk to him. He will need to see your lips and mouth. Even though he is not dependent on lipreading, he will be taught to use visual as well as auditory clues. If the light is in his eyes, it is harder to see your lip movements.

Ms. McLynn: What about the singing times?

Speech-language pathologist: By all means include him, but if you use records, be sure you sing along with them. He needs to see your lips as well as hear the sounds.

Ms. McLynn: What should we do when we don't understand Danny?

Speech-language pathologist: Use all the situational cues available. Sometimes tell him to tell you again. If you still don't understand, ask him to show you. Encourage him to use gestures. When you do understand, let your face show your pleasure. Then, say what Danny was trying to say. Look expectant. Be pleased if he repeats your model, but don't insist. Make no corrections of his articulation at this time. You are striving to motivate him to talk more and to keep trying.

After the discussion, the members of the multidisciplinary team wrote the IEP that is illustrated in Fig. 4-1. His parents agreed that it was an excellent plan. They were grateful for the care with which everyone had evaluated Danny. They felt that the specific suggestions met his needs very well.

Some weeks later Danny's parents were happy to report that the runny nose and the fluid in Danny's middle ear that had apparently caused much of his hearing problem had been taken care of, although the high frequency hearing loss in one ear had been described to them as a sensory-neural loss. The otologist (a physician who specializes in problems with ears) and the audiologist (a specialist trained to evaluate hearing and assist with the choice of hearing aids) had explained to them that Danny would benefit from wearing a hearing aid in the ear with the high frequency loss. Mr. Jones, the audiologist, explained that unless people can hear with both ears, they cannot tell where sounds are coming from until they see the source. In addition conversations or the teacher's voice would be distorted and difficult to understand unless Danny had his "good ear" toward the speaker. People need two ears for effective listening. This is particularly important for young children. These specialists told them that until recently they could not have suggested amplification for a high frequency loss, but in the 1970's technical improvements in hearing aid design as well as new techniques for making ear molds have made it possible to fit children like Danny with hearing aids.

The audiologist had explained that Danny would not suddenly begin to speak distinctly nor would he respond to everything that he heard. That would take time, patience, and special education. He also showed Danny's parents how to care for the hearing aid, test its functioning, and adjust it properly. Then, he talked about helping Danny learn to use and enjoy his new aid. He explained that they should begin gradually, letting him wear it in quiet places and for a short time at first. However, Mr. and Mrs. Dickson laughed as they told Ms. McLynn that once Danny had his new hearing aid, he did not want to take it off. They were grateful, because some children find the adjustment difficult.

The required contents of the IEP

The IEP is a written plan that must contain the following:

1. A statement of the child's present levels of educational performance (based on results of norm-referenced and criterion-referenced tests)

2. A statement of annual goals and related short-term behavioral objectives

3. A statement of the specific special education and related services to be provided to the child

4. The extent to which the child will be able to participate in regular education programs

5. The supporting services needed within the regular program

6. The projected dates for initiation of services and the anticipated duration of services

7. The appropriate objective criteria and evaluation procedures

8. The schedules for determining whether the short-term instructional objectives are being achieved (each child's program must be evaluated at least once each year)

Although the precise written format may differ from area to area, the required content must be included. Fig. 4-1 is an example of a typical IEP report form.

The purposes and limitations of the IEP

The annual goals included in the IEP describe what a handicapped child can be expected to accomplish within a specified period. Usually the allotted time in one school year. However, the scheduled period may be as little as a few weeks or months.

There must be a direct relationship between the child's present level of educational performance and the goals, objectives, and services to be provided. However, the IEP is *not* intended to be detailed enough to be used as a complete instructional plan. The written goals and objectives are expected to state skills that are most needed based on assessment of a child's level of

Text continued on p. 91.

INDIVIDUALIZED EDUCATIONAL PROGRAM

I. STUDENT INFORMATION   *Date*   Jan. 15, 1982

    Student name Dickson   Danny   R. _____ *Sex*   M
                    Last   First   Initial   *Grade placement*   M-F

    Birth date June 6, 1977   *Parents* John and Mary Dickson   *Phone* 463-9546
                  Mo Day Yr

    Address   61 Lakeside Road   Lincoln   *Zip* 69745
                  Street   City

    District of residence Lincoln   *Receiving school/agency* Lincoln

II. MEDICAL INFORMATION

    A. *Vision screening* Nov. 5, 1981   Ms. Land, R.N.   Passed
                            Mo Day Yr   Examiner   Results

    B. *Hearing screening* Nov. 5, 1981   Ms. Land, R.N.   Failed
                             Mo Day Yr   Examiner   Results

        Comments   Failed screening at 25 db. Referred to Speech & Hearing Center

III. LEVEL OF CURRENT PERFORMANCE
     (Based on achievement, diagnostic, and criterion-referenced testing and teacher observation.)

    A. *Achievement*

        Spelling level   Pretest   Posttest   *Date*

        Math level   not appropriate   Posttest   *Date*
                                Pretest

        Reading level   Pretest   Posttest   *Date*

    B. *Mental ability*   *Test*   *Date*
        MA 3-0   IQ 65   (CA 4-6)   Stanford-Binet   Nov. 25, 1981
        Perf.   IQ 92   Wechsler Preschool and Primary Scale

    C. *Psychomotor*   *Test*   *Date*
        VMI age 4-4   Beery-Buktenicka Test of Visual   Nov. 25, 1981
                                             Motor Integration (VMI)

    D. *Social behavior*   *Test*   *Date*
        As reported by parents,   Vineland Social Maturity Scale   Nov. 5, 1981
        age appropriate, except
        for severe tantrums

    E. *Speech-language*   *Test*   *Date*
        Articulation—multiple omis-   Goldman-Fristoe Articulation   Nov. 13, 1981
        sions and substitutions
        Language age—approximately   Environmental Language Inventory
        30 mo.

    F. *Other (Self-help, vocational, etc.)*
        Self-help—superior for age

IV. PROGRAM ELIGIBILITY   *(Check appropriate item[s].)*

    [ ] A. EMH   [X] E. *Speech impaired (SI)*   [ ] J. *Deaf-blind (DB)*
    [ ] B. TMH   [ ] F. *Visually impaired (VI)*   [ ] K. *Physical handicap (PH)*
    [ ] C. BD   [ ] G. *Autistic (AUT)*   [ ] L. *Educational handicap (EH)*
    [ ] D. LD   [ ] H. *Deaf (D)*   [X] M. *Early childhood (EC)*
                      [X] I. *Hard of hearing (HH)*   [ ] N. *Other (specify)*

FIG. 4-1. An example of an IEP.

Student name Dickson, Danny K.
              Last   First Initial

V. PROGRAM PLACEMENT *(Enter information in columns following listing.)*

		Date	Duration	Extent of participation in percentages
A.	Waiting list			
B.	Regular class			
C.	Regular class with consulting	12/1	90 days	50% (2½ hours daily)
D.	Regular class with supplementary teaching treatment			
E.	Regular class with rest room			
F.	Part-time special class	12/1	90 days	50% (2½ hours daily)
G.	Full-time special class			
H.	Residential school			
I.	Special day school			
J.	Hospital school			
K.	Hospital-treatment center			
L.	Alternative school			
M.	Homebound			

VI. SUPPORTIVE SERVICES *(Enter item[s] in columns following listing.)*

		Date	Duration	Extent of participation in percentages
A.	Counseling	12/1	90 days	Weekly — 1 hour
B.	Individual psychological counseling			
C.	Group psychological counseling			
D.	Speech therapy	12/1	90 days	Consulting and individual
E.	Occupational therapy			
F.	Hearing aid evaluation			
G.	Adaptive physical education			
H.	Regular physical education			
I.	Parent-infant education			
J.	Remedial reading			
K.	Social work			
L.	Braille-large print			
M.	Orientation-mobility			
N.	Adaptive equipment			
O.	Barrier-free environment			
P.	Diagnostics			
Q.	Physical therapy			
R.	Audiological therapy	12/1	90 days	Consulting — evaluation only
S.	Hearing therapy	12/1	90 days	Consulting — twice weekly
T.	Vision therapy			
U.	Physically handicapped-mentally handicapped			
V.	Behavior therapy			
W.	Supportive materials			
X.	Other (specify)			

FIG. 4-1, cont'd. An example of an IEP.

p. 3

Student name Dickson, Danny   R.
$\overline{\text{Last} \quad \text{First} \quad \text{Initial}}$

Primary language English

VII. PLACEMENT COMMITTEE

> Mrs. L. Wilson, Supervisor
>
> Ms. N. Hess, Speech-language pathologist
>
> Ms. A. Neff, Social worker
>
> Ms. C. Land, Nurse
>
> Mr. B. Decker, School psychologist
>
> Ms. McLynn, Preschool teacher

VIII. REVIEW SCHEDULE

> [ ] A. *30 days*   [X] C. *90 days* 1st review
>
> [ ] B. *60 days*   [X] D. *Annual*

IX. ASSESSMENT CRITERIA

> Review for appropriateness of plan after 90 days. Review again after 1 year.

X. ANNUAL GOALS

> A. To encourage Danny to listen carefully and follow directions
>
> B. To improve Danny's expressive language skills
>
> C. To encourage Danny to listen to the teacher's spoken model and imitate her with improved articulation
>
> D. To increase Danny's vocabulary of everyday words
>
> E. To improve Danny's articulation of phonemes and syllables
>
> F. To reduce temper tantrums

XI. PARENT INVOLVEMENT

> *I have been involved in the preparation of this individualized plan and*
>
> [X] *I am in agreement with it.*
>
> [ ] *I disagree with its contents.*
>
> *I realize that this is an educational plan and not a binding legal contract.*
>
> John Dickson   Mary Dickson
> $\overline{\text{Signature of parent(s)/guardian(s)}}$

FIG. 4-1, cont'd. An example of an IEP.

XII. SUMMARY OF SERVICES RECOMMENDED BY THE MULTIDISCIPLINARY
      TEAM AT THE IEP CONFERENCE, JAN. 15, 1982

> Because Danny's parents both work, they need him to be cared for throughout the day. The
> Early Childhood Special Education Class maintains a daily program for $2\frac{1}{2}$ hours each day.
> As a result, it was decided to plan Danny's day as follows:
>
> AM: The school bus will pick Danny up at his home at 8:50 and take him to the public
>   school near his home for a $2\frac{1}{2}$-hour session. His program will include all of the
>   planned curriculum, appropriate to his present level of performance, as well as the
>   specific goals and objectives in his IEP. Each week he will receive two 20-minute
>   speech and language lessons with three other children. In addition, the speech-
>   language pathologist will plan and monitor a developmental speech and language pro-
>   gram at both his day-care center and the special education class. This pathologist
>   will also provide guidance to his teachers and parents with regard to his special
>   needs as a mildly hearing impaired child.
>
> PM: The day-care center will pick Danny up at his public school at 11:30 each day. He
>   will be served luncheon at that center. After a nap time, he will participate in
>   the activities at the center. The speech-language pathologist will be available for
>   consultation with Danny's teachers there. Twice each month Danny's special educa-
>   tion teacher will contact the day-care center for consultation. Teachers from the
>   day-care center will visit the special education class to observe Danny after 1 month.

XIII. INSTRUCTIONAL OBJECTIVES FOR ANNUAL GOALS INCLUDING EVALUATION CRITERIA AND DATE

> A. Given a three-stage direction in one long utterance, Danny will (1) attend to the
>   speaker, (2) wait until directions are completed, and (3) do the activities in the
>   order presented within 1 minute.
> B. During a 30-minute activity period Danny will converse with the teacher or another
>   child at least five times. He will use three- or four-word sentences. The "con-
>   versation" will fit the situation and be spontaneous, not directed.
> C. When the teacher models a sentence for Danny, he will imitate her, using the same
>   number of syllables (up to four syllables) and with partially intelligible articu-
>   lation.
> D. When shown five pictures in each of the categories, (1) clothing, (2) toys,
>   (3) foods, (4) transportation, and (5) furniture, Danny will name them correctly,
>   with no more than one error within each category.
> E. During a structured speech lesson, Danny will imitate the teacher's production of
>   all vowels and these consonants in isolation and syllables: /p/, /t/, /k/, /f/,
>   /m/, /b/, /d/, and /g/.
> F. During a 30-minute play period, Danny will not have any temper tantrums. During
>   the complete school day, he will have no more than one outburst of anger.

FIG. 4-1, cont'd. An example of an IEP.

achievement. They are designed to target remediation of particular developmental lags or to accelerate learning. The intent is to focus attention and teaching effort on critical areas that are listed by priority and area of need.

The IEP is intended to serve as a basis for the subsequent development of a detailed, individualized instructional plan that encompasses the complete curriculum. For example, although Danny's IEP focuses on his goals and objectives in speech and language, his complete instructional plan would include social development, gross and fine motor skills, cognitive development, and school readiness activities. In all of these areas Danny would be expected to participate and learn. Adaptations to meet his needs would be made in the process of instruction.

In Vicky's case (Chapter 3) her IEP would state specific goals and objectives related to her behavior and her motor skills. Her complete instructional plan would include her participation with the other children in language and cognitive development as well as readiness skills. Of course, the activities throughout the day would become one of the vehicles for nurturing her improved behavior. Behavior management techniques would be used during the complete class day.

Considerations beyond the IEP

Interpreters of the law recognize that special education teachers have primary responsibility for implementation of the IEP. These teachers are expected to monitor each child's progress. If at any time they feel the plan is no longer appropriate, they are expected to request another meeting to review the IEP. Parents may also request a review of the individual program.

When children with special needs attend regular classes, even part time, their mainstream teachers should have copies of their IEPs. The special education teacher should explain the contents of each plan. This teacher should be available to serve as consultant to the classroom teacher. Consultations should include a mutual sharing of concerns and information, suggestions for behavior management, materials, and teaching strategies.

WHEN LESSON PLANNING IS READY TO BEGIN: FROM ANNUAL GOALS TO DAILY LESSONS

Because a child's education is not to be limited to goals pinpointed in the IEP, the complete curriculum needs to be included in the teaching efforts. A match between the program's or classroom's curriculum objectives and the child's educational strengths and weaknesses should be created. Fig. 4-2 conceptualizes a workable process designed to create a match between the child's skills and deficits and the instructional plan.

Planning the curriculum

To develop a match between what a child needs to learn and what he is taught, teachers must determine where a child is on the continuum of developmental skills within the curriculum. Some preschools and day-care centers have written curricula, checklists, and/or reporting systems. Many do not. Often teachers find themselves faced with the need to design the curriculum, the recording and reporting systems, and the daily plans. The most efficient method of creating a match between the child and the curriculum is to develop or adopt an appropriate developmental checklist to use as a guide for curriculum development. The checklist should specify the skills and behaviors expected to be developed by the children during their tenure in the particular program to which they have been assigned.

When choosing or developing a checklist, preschool and day-care teachers need to consider the unique needs of children entering the kindergartens in their community. Items considered basic to successful entrance into the kindergartens in the local area should appear as target behaviors on the checklist. For example,

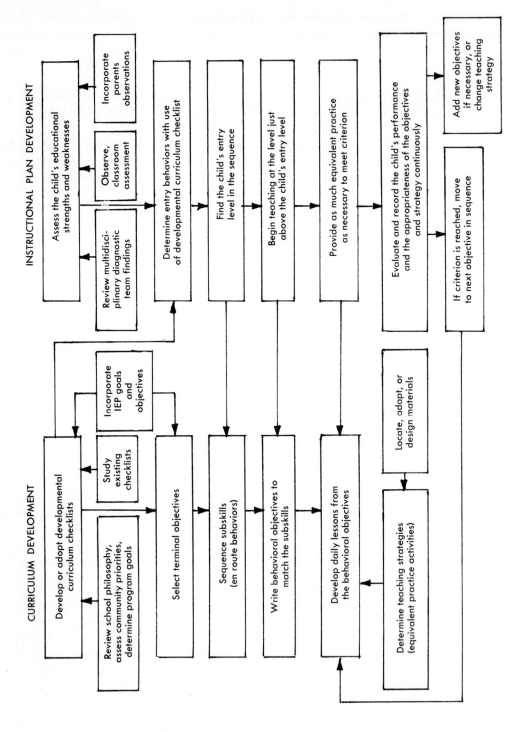

FIG. 4-2. Matching the attributes of the child with the instructional process.

if a community has a kindergarten that uses a highly structured reading readiness program, the prerequisite skills should appear on the preschool checklist.

This does not suggest that the preschool should teach kindergarten and first grade skills, unless that particular preschool encompasses 5 and 6 year olds. But the skills children must demonstrate when they enter kindergarten should be on the preschool checklist. These skills are important target behaviors and their development should not be left to chance.

In the past there has been much discussion about readiness. The inference has been that in some mysterious way some children were ready for kindergarten, while others were not. But it really is not mysterious! Some children had been nurtured and taught in the home in ways that developed the skills needed for success in kindergarten. Others had not. Some had obvious or hidden handicaps that interfered with normal development. In spite of caring and nurturing parents, these children were not ready.

If the intent of early childhood special education is to accelerate growth and development and remediate deficits, then readiness must be planned for. The skills and behaviors deemed essential for success in kindergarten must be identified, specified, and carefully taught.

Most checklists used as a basis for curriculum planning include items chosen from norm-referenced tests. Typically those preparing the checklist use a range of standardized tests that are appropriate for use with young children. Duplicate items are deleted. The remaining items are arranged in a sequence of behaviors. Appendix D and the annotations at the end of this chapter provide references to checklists and rating scales that are available commercially. These range from those that emphasize comparison with age mates, such as the Gesell Developmental Schedules (Knobloch and Pasamanick, 1974), to those that focus on skills mastery, such as the Carolina Developmental Profile (Lillie, 1975).

Many of the newly developed scales have been constructed primarily for teacher use and are linked directly to the curriculum. One well known example was developed by the Portage Preschool Project (1969). The Portage Guide to Early Education is a checklist that like most, offers specific statements about expected skills at various age levels. Before using any of these commercially available checklists, they should be examined and evaluated to determine if the skills listed appropriately match the program's curriculum goals and objectives. Few are "just right" for total adoption, but all provide helpful guidelines.

Deciding on the arrangement of checklist items

Most checklists are arranged sequentially according to the ages at which particular skills and behaviors are expected to emerge. (Checklists are based on norm-referenced or standardized tests.) Typically these sequences of behaviors are grouped according to four or five major categories. The divisions usually include motor, cognitive, language, social-emotional, and self-help skills. Since there is always overlapping from one division to the other, the segregation is somewhat arbitrary. For example, self-help skills require motor skills, and language and cognitive skills interrelate and overlap.

There is a major disadvantage in arranging the checklist according to age levels. In effect, each skill that children are expected to have established by age 5 (the usual age for entering kindergarten) has many prerequisite skills. If listed, these prerequisite skills are scattered throughout the checklist by age levels. The subskills develop gradually through the years from birth to age 5 in the nonhandicapped child. For example, cutting with scissors is preceded by gradually increasing control of finger movements. But for the handicapped child the prerequisite skills may be totally lacking by age 3 or 4. To identify the sequence of prerequisite skills, when the checklist is arranged according

CHECKLIST: Fine motor area

Goal: To learn cutting skills

Key: + = Skill already established

☐ = Current target behavior

▨ = Date achieved

	Meg A.	Mary C.	Danny D.	Bobby J.	Vicky M.	Eric R.
Tongs and cotton balls	+	+	+	+	+	+
1-inch snipping	10/81	9/81	10/81	+	☐	+
1-inch snipping on heavy line	☐	10/81	10/81	+		+
3-inch cutting on heavy straight line		☐	☐	10/81		+
3-inch cutting on heavy curved line				☐		10/81
Cutting out 3-inch in diameter circle, heavy line						☐

FIG. 4-3. For legend see opposite page.

to age levels, it is necessary to find the skill described at a number of different places in the list. It is difficult to get a clear picture of the sequence and the nature of the prerequisite skills.

For example, under motor skills one widely used checklist listed the following skills one after the other (Portage Preschool Project, 1969, p. 30):

Cuts with scissors.
Walks upstairs, one foot on each step.
Throws a ball with direction.
Stands on one foot without aid.
Pedals tricycle.

All of these behaviors, expected to emerge at the 3- to 4-year level, have many subskills. To find them it is necessary to go back to the younger age levels and search for the related skills.

In practice, if children enter the program lacking skills expected of other children their age, the teacher's first task is to identify each child's *entry behavior* or the skill each child is demonstrating at that time. Having identified the entry behavior, the next step is to plan a sequence of objectives that will make it possible for the children to learn all of the subskills quickly. The more precisely this sequence of objectives is arranged, the more effective the teaching will be.

These objectives should relate directly to the checklist for simplicity in assessing and maintaining accurate records. If the checklist is arranged according to prerequisite skills, the task of the teacher is greatly simplified. Fig. 4-3 is an example of the checklist for one area of fine motor skills.

In effect, although the checklist was originally developed from norm-referenced (standardized) tests, it is most useful if it is arranged by curriculum area in a *criterion-referenced sequence.* Reference to the ages when the subskills should have developed is irrelevant to the teacher who is planning an individual's program. If the child is 4 years old, knowing that he or she should have developed a particular skill at age 18 months is not germane to the teacher's task. What is important is discovering what the child can do *(entry behavior)* and planning the shortest journey *(the en route behaviors)* to the destination *(the terminal objective* or the most difficult related item on the checklist).

By matching the checklist to the curriculum objectives, a quick and easy way to keep track of the progress of individual children is provided. By placing the items on the checklist in a column down the left side of the page and the names of the children across the top, it is easy to record progress and to identify each child's current en route behavior. The teacher (or aide) simply records the date and level of accomplishment for each item. Some prefer to include only the date of achievement. Then, the next item on the list becomes the current en route behavior to be practiced. The parent's checklist (Fig. 4-4) provides a combination curriculum guide, overall plan, and reporting system. Unlike "report cards," it informs in a useful way. By helping parents to keep their checklist up to date with the teachers, they have a consistent picture of

---

FIG. 4-3. Developmental curriculum checklist. For children with physical coordination problems special scissors with four finger holes can be used. This allows the teacher to assist with needed control and pressure. For some children the use of squeeze scissors may be best. These enable the child to squeeze a loop rather than control individual fingers. For visually impaired children a line of glue sprinkled with sand provides a guide for cutting. Many children with vision problems will be able to see a heavy brown line on buff-colored paper. Whenever possible, this should be used. However, tactile clues are useful with those who cannot see the heavy line.

FIG. 4-4. Example of parent's checklist. Learning to cut is a difficult task, with many skills that must be previously learned. Parents should keep in close touch with their child's teacher, and help their child to practice on the same skills at home that are being learned at school. As the child is able to demonstrate doing each of the things suggested, parents will know that he or she is ready for the next step.

	Date achieved
1. When I give my child tongs, a bowl, five cotton balls, and help by showing and guidance, my child can pick up the balls with the tongs and drop them into the bowl.	
2. When I give my child blunt-tipped scissors and a strip of paper 1-inch wide, my child can snip the paper into little pieces.	
3. When I give my child a strip of paper 1-inch wide with heavy, black lines on it, my child can cut on the line, cutting through the paper.	
4. When I draw a straight line 3 inches long on a strip of paper, my child can cut on the line.	

FIG. 4-4. For legend see opposite page.

what their child's education includes. They are better able to understand the teacher's objectives as well as things they can do to be supportive.

The example of the parent's checklist includes pictures. We have found that parents appreciate these, and they tell us that they can understand what is wanted more easily. Other suggestions for including parents as effective partners in fostering their child's growth will be discussed in Chapter 9.

Using the developmental curriculum checklist to plan daily lessons

After skills on the checklist have been grouped according to the curriculum, philosophy, and goals of the preschool program, the skills must be listed in sequential order and translated into behavioral objectives. By reviewing the missed items from the formal tests given during the diagnostic stage and by carefully observing the child, the teacher can check those items that the child has already achieved, those that appear to be emerging, and those that show no evidence of development at that time. Most teachers develop a code like that illustrated in Fig. 4-3 to designate these different levels of accomplishment.

Initially teachers identify developmental levels in each area of the curriculum. After identifying these entry behaviors, teachers are ready to plan daily lessons.

A recording system that provides opportunity for continuous assessment is automatically provided by the checklist. In addition, those children who are either on the same step or on steps close to each other can be grouped for instruction. Children who are significantly ahead in one or more areas of the developmental curriculum scale may assist those who have not yet reached their level of development. The age of the child becomes irrelevant when behavioral objectives are linked to developmental levels. The child is not compared to others and thus does not have to experience the feelings of fail-

ure that can come from such comparison. Instead, the child's successes are recognized, recorded, and emphasized as he or she progresses from step to step.

Individualizing daily lessons

Children whose skills have been carefully assessed are apt to be more efficiently taught. Teachers who have a clear picture of individual needs can be more effective in planning as well as teaching. However, teaching one child at a time is neither suggested nor inferred by the special education rules and regulations. The intent is to provide an education in the least restrictive environment. To do this, it is inevitable that children will be learning in the same class with others who have a range of skills. If they are to learn *from* those more advanced, they must be able to watch them, interact with them, and participate in mutually satisfying ways.

Each child can be both teacher and learner at some time during the day. A spirit of mutual caring can be established in a class of very young children. Learning to give and receive help develops naturally.

Occasionally a teacher may prefer to work with one or two children at a time. However, if goals and appropriately sequenced objectives are available, it is possible to teach a group of five or more children at the same time. This is true, even if each child is working toward a different behavioral objective. The *goal* and *terminal objective* will be the same for all of the children even though each one is receiving *equivalent practice* on a different en route behavior. For example, consider the small group lesson outlined in Tables 2 and 3. Note the two different ways of writing the same goals and objectives.

By writing the goal and objectives for cutting with scissors on one page, the teacher has a helpful one-page reference to guide planning the lesson to be useful to a group of children with widely varying skills. The terminal objective is an appropriate skill for a 5 year old,

TABLE 2
Example of using goals and objectives to individualize a lesson

Given (the teacher will provide or restrict)	The child will	Criterion
Goal		
To learn cutting skills		
Terminal objective		
Blunt-tip scissors; paper with a 3-inch straight line, 3-inch curved line, and a 3-inch (diameter) circle; and directions to cut on the line and cut out the circle	Cut as directed	Cut within ¼ inch of lines within 5 minutes
En route objectives *(least to most)*		
1. Tongs, 5 cotton balls, 4-inch bowl, teacher's guidance in placing fingers and thumb and forefinger in cutting position, and help in opening and closing tongs	Open and close tongs around cotton ball, lift it to bowl, and release it into bowl, accepting teacher's assistance as needed	Keep fingers in correct position and accept help
2. Same as above, except restrict teacher's help to verbal directions, encouragement, and reminders	Same as above	Keep fingers in correct position and complete action (no time limit and no penalty for "dropped" cotton)
3. Same as above	Same as above	Maintain correct position, lift and drop cotton into bowl (no more than one ball outside bowl within 2 minutes)
4. Blunt-tip scissors and strips of construction paper 1 inch wide and 11 inches long	Cut paper	Cut at least 10 pieces within 5 minutes
5. Same as above, with heavy black lines marked on paper at 1-inch intervals	Cut paper on lines	Cut within ¼ inch of lines, one cut per line (no time limit)
6. Blunt-tip scissors and construction paper 3 inches wide and 11 inches long, with heavy black lines at 1-inch intervals the width of the paper	Make three cuts per line	Cut within ¼ inch of lines, severing each piece within 10 minutes
7. Same as terminal objective (except longer time criterion)	Cut as directed	Cut within ¼ inch of lines within 10 minutes
8. Same as terminal objective		

whereas lifting cotton balls with the tongs can be accomplished by most 3 year olds.

However, some 5 year olds with developmental delays may find it difficult to learn to use the tongs. They may require help and physical guidance as well as encouragement and verbal guidance for many days or weeks before they can proceed to the second objective. However, by being included in the activity with children who can do the more difficult tasks, they observe and discover that they also can learn.

It is critical to remember that one of the reasons for the sequence of carefully planned en route behaviors is to provide *each* child with a

TABLE 3

Example of how a series of en route behaviors can be used to individualize a lesson

---

Goal: To teach children to cut with scissors

Terminal objective: Given blunt-tip scissors, a piece of paper on which are drawn a 3-inch straight line, a 3-inch curved line, and a 3-inch (diameter) circle, and the directions to cut on the line and cut out the circle, the children will cut as directed, staying within ¼ inch of the line. They will complete the total task within 5 minutes.

En route behavior (*least to most skilled*): Prerequisite skills: pincer grasp, holding paper between fingers

1. Given tongs (similar to those used in cooking), 5 cotton balls, and a 4-inch bowl, a child will allow the teacher to place his or her thumb through one finger hole, the forefinger on the outside of the bar, and the remaining fingers into the other hole. With the teacher's help, child will open and close the tongs on a cotton ball, lift it to the bowl, and release it into the bowl. Criterion includes keeping fingers in the correct position and accepting teacher's help.

2. Given the same circumstances as above, the child will perform the same actions without teacher's physical help but with encouragement and any needed reminders.

3. Given the above materials, a child will (a) maintain correct finger positions, (b) lift cotton balls with tongs and drop them into the bowl, (c) drop no more than one cotton ball outside the bowl, and (d) complete the task within 2 minutes.

4. Given strips of construction paper 1 inch wide and 11 inches long, and blunt-tip scissors, the child will snip the strip of paper into at least 10 pieces within 5 minutes.

5. Given strips of construction paper 1 inch wide and 11 inches long with heavy black lines at 1-inch intervals, and blunt-tip scissors, the child will snip within ¼ inch of the line, cutting with one snip for each line through the paper.

6. Given strips of construction paper 3 inches wide and 11 inches long, and heavy black lines at 1-inch intervals, using blunt-tip scissors the child will make 3 cuts on each line within ¼ inch of the line, severing each piece within 10 minutes.

7. Given a piece of construction paper or paper of similar weight on which are drawn a 3-inch straight line, a 3-inch curved line, and a 3-inch (diameter) circle, using blunt-tip scissors the child will cut on the straight line and curved line and cut out the circle, staying within ¼ inch of the lines within 10 minutes.

8. Same as terminal objective.

Adaptations for children with physical handicaps include a squeeze scissors instead of traditional scissors. For some children scissors with four finger holes may be useful because they allow the teacher to cut with the child. Visually impaired children should be provided buff-colored paper with a heavy brown line for necessary contrast.

---

task until criterion is reached. It is possible to develop difficult skills gradually and without the pain of failure. Beginning by expecting each child to "cut on the line" is to guarantee failure for many of them.

To teach five or more children to cut on the line, it is necessary to provide each one with the materials needed, demonstration at his or her level of performance, and continued encouragement. In this way, no one fails. Rather, each child *succeeds*. Most will recognize the challenge of the next step and be eager to try it.

In addition to the usefulness of the clearly written behavioral objectives to the teacher, as the lesson is planned and conducted, these same objectives help in pinpointing necessary *branching* or smaller steps.

The basic set of goals and objectives should be designed to be useful guides in teaching the majority of the children. But some children will need even smaller steps. By analyzing the existing objectives, the teacher can identify what these more precise steps should be.

The format of the page of objectives is a help in analyzing the task. If the child is not succeeding, where is the breakdown? Should a change be made in what the teacher is providing or restricting? Or is the quantity of work or time allowed inappropriate? Sometimes the en route behaviors become more difficult because the task changes. At other times only the time limitations changed. By evaluating the task, the criterion, and "what the teacher does or does not do," it is possible to establish a much better sense of successful teaching for the teacher as well as the children.

Throughout all of the teaching activities, teachers attempt to help children to establish independence, accuracy, patience, and persistence. These qualities can be nurtured more successfully when en route behaviors are clearly stated.

WHEN THE DEVELOPMENTAL CHECKLIST IS THE CURRICULUM BASE: WRITING GOALS AND OBJECTIVES

The obvious reason for writing goals and objectives is that the law requires them to be included in educational plans for children with special needs. However, there are even more compelling reasons. These reasons are contained in the following characteristics of objectives:

1. What is to be taught is described precisely and accurately. Anyone reading the objective knows what to do and the conditions in which it is to be done.

2. What the children will be doing when the objective has been achieved is defined and described.

3. The time allowed to complete the task is stated. How well the child must perform (the criterion) is clearly identified.

4. Because the task, the performance expected, and the criterion for success are clearly stated, accountability is facilitated.

In addition to these advantages are the following two less obvious but equally important benefits:

1. After writing objectives and working with them, teachers often discover that they are able to analyze learning problems more efficiently. They recognize the critical importance of small changes in what they are doing. These seemingly small changes, sometimes referred to as branching, can make enormous differences in teaching success. In effect, practice in *thinking* in the manner required to write behavioral objectives enhances teaching skills.

2. Once a series of performance (behavioral) objectives has been developed, they can be used to teach other children with similar needs. A well-written file of objectives can be a tremendous time-saver in lesson planning.

Basics of writing behavioral objectives

Mager (1962, p. 1) states "you cannot concern yourself with the problem of selecting the most efficient route to your destination until you know what your destination is."

Behavioral (or performance or instructional) objectives require that the teacher state the destination precisely. "Fuzzy" terms are appropriate in goals. They are not allowed in behavioral objectives. For example, a correctly written *goal* might read "To teach the colors red, yellow, and blue." But the *objective* related to the goal must contain the following three components:

1. What the teacher will *provide*, *restrict*, and *do*.

2. What will the learner be doing or saying when the objective has been achieved (a behavior that can be seen or heard)

3. How well or how often the learner must perform in this manner to convince the teacher that the task has been "learned" (within what time frame this performance must occur)

An example of a correctly written objective related to the goal "To teach the colors red, yellow, and blue" might be "When the teacher points to any one of 15 different items (five of each color red, yellow, or blue) and asks 'What color is this?' the children will answer within 20 seconds, stating the color correctly on 80% of the trials." The box below illustrates terms useful in writing goals and objectives.

"Eighty percent of the trials" is the standard that must be achieved to accomplish this objective. This standard is referred to as the *criterion*. Eight of ten (or 80%) correct performances are usually described as "proficiency" on the task. Ten of ten or (100% accuracy) are defined as "mastery level." (The level required must vary with the needs of individual children. Some cannot be expected to reach 100%.)

The following is an example of an objective and goal related to a motor skill:

Goal: To teach children to draw circles
Objective: Given a pencil and paper the children will watch as the teacher draws a 2-inch circle (counterclockwise) and then imitate the teacher's model, using the same directionality, holding the pencil in the same manner, and completing a circle between 2 and 3 inches in diameter. The circle will be no more than ½ inch out of round.
Criterion: Four of five trials correctly.

In some cases a time limit becomes part of the criterion for judging successful performance, for example, within 2 minutes.

Guidelines for choosing and writing behavioral objectives

Teachers will want to write objectives to meet particular needs. Norm-referenced tests and preschool curriculum guides suggest similar goals for all early childhood classes. However, each class and each program are unique and special.

The following procedure has been useful in

APPROPRIATE VERBS FOR WRITING BEHAVIORAL OBJECTIVES

1. **Goals**
   The verbs suggested in this category are useful for writing *goals* but are *not appropriate* for writing behavioral objectives:

To consider	To discover	To improve	To practice
To develop	To encourage	To introduce	To understand

2. **Behavioral objectives**
   The verbs suggested in this category are useful for writing *behavioral objectives* and can be used to describe *observable behaviors*:

To answer	To follow	To name	To recall
To color	To hold (as directed)	To pick up	To say
To complete	To imitate	To place together	To sort
To cut	To list	To point to	To use
To draw	To look at		

writing objectives for preschool children. Each objective must contain the basic components, but the manner in which they are recorded may vary. Several different forms are suggested, but the process of choosing them and sequencing them remains the same.

1. *Identify a particular goal.* Goals should state in general what you want to teach. Examples of goals include "to teach children to count," "to teach colors," and "to teach the children to copy a square." Goals are not specific. They do not describe what teacher or child will do.

2. *Decide what you want the children to learn in relation to the goal.* Choose the most difficult task you want them to be able to do. Visualize exactly what they will be doing when you look at them "doing it" and say "Now, they *know* that." Write a description of what you have visualized in your mind's eye. This will be the observable behavior.

3. *Think about what you will give them and tell them when you want them to perform this observable behavior.* This will become the part of the objective that identifies what the teacher will do, provide, or restrict. Often this section begins with "Given" or "When the teacher."

4. *Write what you have visualized in the form you have chosen.* At first, it seems helpful to write the objective in one long sentence that includes all of the components. Later, you may prefer the shorter versions. Each must be complete. If you do not state a criterion or standard within each objective, you must state it someplace and indicate that it applies to all of them. For example, you may say "All objectives to be achieved at proficiency level (80%)."

5. *Begin task analysis.* So far you have chosen a goal, decided on the most difficult of the objectives you want to achieve in relation to the goal, and written all of this in the form you have chosen. What you have written is the terminal objective. Next, think about what you would need to do if the children could not do this objective in the way you have written it. Assume that it was too difficult for any of them. But you

do want all of them to achieve it at least by the end of their experience in your preschool. How could you make it a little bit easier? Write this slightly easier en route behavior (one of the objectives on the route to the terminal objective). Sometimes it is helpful to actually do the task yourself or carefully watch another do it to determine the en route objectives.

6. *Continue task analysis as suggested above.* Write en route behaviors that are simple and include so many prompts (cues) that you are certain every child you teach will be able to do at least the easiest one.

7. *Do not try to write every possible step.* Choose steps between objectives that you feel the majority of the children will be able to take. (Analyze the samples offered with this consideration in mind.) If you have a child who can do a specific objective but seems unable to do any part of the next one in your sequence, you may need to plan another *branch*. That is, for an occasional child it may be necessary to insert additional objectives. Usually these need not be added to your sequence but rather recorded separately on the child's record. If you discover that you need this particular branch for a number of the children, add it to your sequence. (As noted earlier, keeping each en route behavior on a separate card makes it easier to add or delete objectives.)

8. *Assemble your objectives.* At first, putting the en route behaviors on individual cards makes it easier to arrange them in sequential order. Later, as your skill in task analysis grows, it becomes less necessary. However, if the en route behaviors are on separate cards, it is easier to insert additional steps for children who need tasks broken into very tiny steps. After assembling the en route behaviors (objectives), it is helpful to actually do the task as outlined to verify the initial sequence and detect any missing steps.

Write the goal at the top of the form you have chosen. Beginning with the simplest one, write the objectives in sequence from the easiest to the most difficult. Remember, the most difficult one is your terminal objective. All of the others are called en route behaviors. They are similar to en route destinations on a trip. The terminal objective is your final destination, and the other objectives are specific places you will proceed through on your way to this destination. When you are headed toward a particular place on a trip, it may be your "target" for that day or week. In the same way, you may refer to a particular objective for a certain child as the target behavior. This process of analyzing terminal objectives and discovering and sequencing en route behaviors is referred to as the process of *task analysis.*

9. *Identify the entry behaviors of each child.* Each of the children will enter your preschool or class with some awareness of the information or behavior you have chosen to teach. A few will be able to demonstrate the skills described in some of your terminal objectives the very first day. Others will be completely unaware of any facet of that particular target behavior. This is why you must analyze the terminal objective, and write the en route behaviors. Attempts are then made to determine which of the en route behaviors each child can do (assessment). Dates must be recorded. When this is done, each child's entry behavior has been identified. Now you know where to begin.

10. *Provide a variety of equivalent practice.* Use many different materials and toys until you feel your criterion has been achieved. Don't rush. At first, some children will progress very slowly. When you feel confident that an individual has achieved criterion on the entry behavior (the objective this child was able to do when entering your class), record the date by the name, and begin working on the next objective in the sequence.

11. *Provide as much equivalent practice as necessary.* The sequence of the objectives is intended to be useful to you in planning for all of the children. Some of them may learn very

quickly. Do not be surprised if some children move through a whole series of en route behaviors and right through the terminal objective in a very short time. Others may take days or weeks on each en route behavior. For accelerated children a range of different activities and materials should be provided. Maintain the same level of difficulty your written objective states as you provide this equivalent practice.

Your written objective describes particular materials to be used in checking for criterion performance (at least in some instances). But you should *feel completely free to use any materials you choose in lessons, games, or spontaneous play.* The intent is to provide each child with many successful experiences (equivalent practice) on each level. The critical feature is to *maintain the appropriate level of challenge.* A well-planned sequence of behavioral objectives serves as a very helpful frame of reference for working effectively and efficiently with individual children.

12. *Sometimes use Montessori's "periods" as a guide in planning.* Although Montessori (1972, p. 126) did not know the terminology of behavioral objectives, she used a guide that is helpful in planning and sequencing objectives. She referred to the following periods:

Period 1. Naming ("This is ____.")

Period 2. Recognition ("Show me the ____" or "Give me the ____.")

Period 3. Recall (Montessori referred to this as *"The Pronunciation of the Word."* She asked "What is this?")

This outline is helpful in thinking about the sequence of objectives. First activities require that the teacher provide experiences or activities that involve *naming* things in an explicit way. Recognition is easier than recall, but practice in recognition makes recall possible.

13. *Use the objectives you have written as the basis for daily lessons.* As soon as you have written your first goals and objectives, use them. Experiment with them. Use them as the basis

for lessons with individual children. Try using them with a small group of children who are working on adjacent en route behaviors. Next, attempt working with a larger group, all of whom are working on two or three adjacent objectives. Gradually, as you feel comfortable with this new way of planning lessons, attempt to include one or two children who are working toward the same terminal objective but who are working on widely separated en route behaviors.

14. *Evaluate your objectives continuously as you use them.* Writing a series of objectives becomes easier with practice. Trial and error can be an efficient teacher. However, failure by the children must be interpreted as information to the teacher to change the objectives in some way. Asking the following questions can be helpful, if problems occur:

 a. Could the children do any part of the task?
 b. Did they listen and look, or were the directions too long?
 c. What modality or modalities were involved in the teacher's directions, that is, visual, auditory, tactile-kinesthetic, or combinations of these?
 d. Which modalities were required in the response?
 e. What distractors interfered?
 f. What additional cues might have helped?
 g. Did both the teacher presentation and the expected response allow for individual adaptations because of handicapping conditions? For example, if the child was visually impaired, were auditory and tactile-kinesthetic clues provided? If the child was hearing impaired, were visual and tactile-kinesthetic clues available?
 h. Was the time allotted adequate?
 i. Was the content limited and specific to avoid misunderstanding?
 j. Were the related subskills well learned before the presentation?

In practice, children should be able to demonstrate proficiency performance or 80% accuracy on one objective before proceeding to the next. The new objective should be partially achievable on the first try. That is, if the next en route behavioral objective is a total mystery to the children (or to any one child), more branches or tinier steps are needed. A well-written sequence allows for continued success experiences. A limited amount of failure can be instructive. It can lead the children to use their mistakes as clues in the discovery of what they need to do differently. But for children who have experienced a great deal of it, failure must be kept to a minimum for a long time.

15. *Add new goals and objectives to the curriculum as the need for them appears.* Remember, your goals and objectives are your curriculum. You will want to add to them regularly. You will also want to delete or remove some from time to time. As you become accustomed to thinking in terms of what the children will be observed saying and doing (or not doing) as a result of your teaching, you will feel more effective as a teacher. Planning will be simplified. Individualizing lessons, based on the en route behaviors you have written, will be much easier. En route behaviors that don't work can be deleted. More steps can be inserted, if needed, for some children. Many children will be able to achieve each en route objective very rapidly. When the steps are small enough for the slowest to "climb," many children will achieve each level within a very brief time.

PROVIDING A WIDE RANGE AND VARIETY OF ACTIVITIES AND EXPERIENCES FOR EACH EN ROUTE BEHAVIOR
Choosing appropriate activities

Choosing appropriate activities or "equivalent behaviors" for each en route behavior requires the following two factors:

1. What the teacher does and what the child is expected to do are equivalent or at the same level of difficulty as the written objective.

2. Any difficulties encountered will be corrected by a smooth return to a simpler objective.

When these two factors are considered, the appropriate activities and experiences to be provided are limited only by the teacher's imagination and creativity. For example, the following objectives might be chosen to achieve the goal "To teach the children the names of their body parts":

Terminal objective: When the teacher points to any body parts (eyes, ears, nose, mouth, arms, hands, or feet) and says "Tell me what this is called," a child will name them correctly with no more than two errors in ten trials. Each body part will be checked on a doll, the child, and another child.

En route behaviors *(all criteria equal eight of ten):*

1. When the teacher points to any of the body parts listed and says "This is a _____," the children will imitate the teacher's spoken model.
2. When the teacher points to any of the body parts listed and says, "Is this the _____?" the children will name the part.
3. When the teacher says "Show me your _____," the children will point to their own named body part.
4. When the teacher asks "What is this?" as she or he points to her or his own, another child's, or a doll's features, the children will name the features correctly.

The following list of activities could be used to provide equivalent practice on any of the objectives just described. It should be remembered that each activity will be accompanied with as many verbal labels as possible.

1. Bathing a doll
2. Dressing a doll
3. Washing hands and faces
4. Doing a puzzle (that includes body parts)
5. Drawing at the chalkboard
6. Drawing on paper
7. Making a jack-o'-lantern
8. Pasting features on a teddy bear made of construction paper
9. Singing a song ("Made up" charts are fun, for example, "I touch my nose and blink my eyes. I clap my hands and say 'Surprise!'")
10. Making a gingerbread man
11. Telling stories, and encouraging the children to "act them out"
12. Puppet plays

As illustrated in the following dialogue, these activities will allow children to work on different en route behaviors while participating in an activity together.

The lesson: Bathing a doll

EQUIPMENT: Aprons, warm water, soap, wash cloths, towels, a doll bathtub, and a dirty doll

Teacher: Sally, will you help me wash our doll? She is so dirty. Look at those hands and feet. (pointing)

Sally: I get the water and soap.

Danny: Wa-er (water).

Teacher: Get the towel, Danny.

Vicky: Where? (grabbing the doll)

Teacher: Hold her carefully, Vicky. Be gentle. (pointing to the arm) See, her arm is all wet.

Danny: Dere no (nose). (pointing)

Teacher: Right Danny, that's her nose.

Danny: Wha da? (what's that?)

Teacher: That's her ear. (pointing) Show me her arms, Danny.

Danny: Dere. (there)

Teacher: Is this her hand, Sally?

Sally: Yep.

Using the objectives, the teacher can individualize any lesson by applying the expected level of performance (criterion) requirements to the activity.

Evaluating effectiveness of each activity

The usefulness of any activity is determined largely by its appeal to children. In addition, the activity should lend itself to repetition with minor variations. (Children enjoy a meaningful amount of repetition.) Each activity should be chosen to develop skills in ways that are a challenge but do not overwhelm the least capable

child in the group. Participation is a prerequisite for effective learning with young children. "Just watching" is a useful beginning for some very shy or young children. With gentle encouragement these children can be helped to become full participants.

Using an activity to achieve more than one objective

Most activities can be used to achieve several objectives at the same time. For example, learning to follow two- and three-stage directions is an important skill. Counting and learning colors and other concepts are goals included in every preschool curriculum.

In bathing the doll teachers might say "Get the blue towel. It is under the sink" (emphasizing color and the preposition *under*). She might say "Take off both socks. See one sock is on her foot, and the other is on the floor" (emphasizing one-to-one correspondence, foot, and the preposition *on*).

Of course, most preschool teachers do many of these things spontaneously and without much conscious planning. However, when the program includes children with special needs, this important emphasis on specific skills cannot be left to chance. These children require explicit examples, meaningful repetition, and a variety of related experiences. One experience is inadequate. The ability to generalize from one experience to the next must be conscientiously nurtured.

KEEPING RECORDS

Each preschool and day-care center has unique needs for record keeping. Some require a great deal of detailed information to be recorded about each child each day. Others rely on occasional notes to parents and brief comments in the children's files. Individual preferences often determine both the kinds of records kept and the frequency with which they are updated. However, if children with special needs are included in the class, certain information must be recorded, kept up to date, and available for those responsible for the children's education. Doing this in the simplest manner possible is important. Unwieldy systems are time consuming, difficult to understand, and ineffective.

Choosing a system

During the first years of early childhood special education classes, many federal grants were available. Schools, universities, and private facilities developed model programs. Many of these model programs became available for replication in other schools. Most of these subsidized programs provided time for teachers to plan, analyze problems, write objectives, experiment, and revise at each step. Volumes of objectives were recorded in each domain. As a result of this, very bulky "Curriculum Guides" filled many shelves.

The intent to be thorough sometimes resulted in record keeping systems that required a computer or many hours of the teacher's time each day. This luxury is rarely available to most preschool and day-care teachers today. At least, if many hours are required for record keeping, these are hours that the teacher would prefer to be doing other things. The best system is the simplest and easiest to maintain. But it must be effective and complete.

Factors to consider. The first consideration should be the purpose of the records. Will they be used with special children as the basis for lesson planning, or will they be used primarily to report to parents at the end of specified times? As preschool teachers discover the advantages of using the developmental checklist as a basis for curriculum planning, it is probable that this system will be used for all children. Thus the record keeping purposes expand for all

those attending the preschool and not just those needing IEPs.

Deciding who will maintain the records is important. If a secretary is available, perhaps records can be more elaborate. But if the teacher is expected to keep all of the records up to date, the process must be streamlined.

For some children quarterly reports to parents are adequate. For others a number of people may need to be continuously informed. Thus determining who will need to be regularly informed is a deciding factor in style and method of record keeping.

It is important to ask "How will the information be distributed?" Will a phone call suffice or must written reports be made? Is it enough to have the information available in the classroom for those who need to review it regularly?

Although the teachers will want to be able to check the children's skill levels daily, it is useful to consider how often others will need to be informed of progress. Teachers must ask "How frequently should this information be reported?"

Other important questions to ask and factors to consider when planning a record keeping system include (1) Where will the records be kept? (2) What provisions for privacy of records must be made? and (3) Can the record keeping system be used to enhance teaching and planning for all members of the group?

Suggestions for record keeping

Usually a readily available checklist that includes a brief statement about each objective and the names of all of the children is adequate for daily use. The more available it is, the more useful it is. Some teachers prefer to keep this checklist in a notebook. Others find it useful to have it on a bulletin board beside the teacher's desk.

By itself the checklist is inadequate for record keeping for children with special needs. It *is* adequate for daily recording. But unless it is written in behavioral objectives, it is not acceptable for children who need IEPs. And if the checklist includes a complete set of objectives, it is too long and bulky!

A workable solution to the problem just described is to (1) have the checklist, as described, and (2) have the correctly written behavioral objectives associated with each item on the checklist filed in an accessible cabinet. For example, the checklist might simply read "Recognizes colors." The complete objective, filed under the cognitive domain might read: "Given five items of each of the primary colors mixed together and the teacher's direction 'Give me the/a (color name) (item name).' The children will do as directed eight out of ten trials for each color."

In addition to the checklist and the behavioral objectives, some form of report designed especially for the parents is useful. Some schools prefer an abbreviated version of the checklist. The form and the arrangement of the items usually parallel the longer checklist used in the classroom.

Although it is important to keep accurate records of each child's skills as they develop, it is inappropriate to "grade" them in the usual sense of that word. An "A" in "learning colors" is meaningless. The only relevant information is whether or not the child can perform in the manner and under the circumstances described in the objective. As a result, there should be no place for a letter grade on the report.

One type of report to parents (Fig. 4-4) that has been particularly useful can serve in three very different ways. Designed to be useful as long as the child is attending preschool, this report form includes all of the items on the curriculum checklist. However, each is written in a simplified objective form and illustrated with a cartoon drawing. First, this report form serves to acquaint the parents with all of the goals and objectives of the curiculum. Second, with a minimum explanation it enables the parents to identify their child's entry behavior. Third, it allows them to keep track of their child's prog-ress as it occurs. By using this form, parents feel they understand the curriculum.

Developing daily and weekly lesson plans

Traditionally, preschool lesson plans have identified the activities to be included, the songs to be sung, the games to be played, and the snack to be eaten. Although it was expected that the children would develop cognitive, language, motor, and social skills, it was not considered necessary to individualize the lessons in any structured or formal way. The children were expected to grow and develop normally. Children with special problems were rarely included, and if they were, each teacher was on his or her "own" to figure out how to deal with the unusual ones.

With the advent of P.L. 94-142 many preschools and day-care centers as well as the early childhood special education classes have found it necessary to plan their daily lessons in a highly structured manner. Individualizing each activity has become the necessity.

Teachers planning weekly and daily lessons for a group of preschoolers rarely have the luxury of hours "on school time" for planning. Teaching young children is demanding work at best. It is important to develop efficient, effective ways to plan. To do this requires a well-organized developmental curriculum checklist and a set of related goals and objectives. These have been described and defined throughout this chapter.

The suggestions for preparing and writing lesson plans that follow are based on experience. At first, each day's plan required several hours to complete! Gradually, greater efficiency developed. Finally, each weekly lesson plan required only a few minutes to complete.

The first step in planning is to ask the following questions:

1. How will the day be divided into the various activities?
2. How much time will be allowed for each activity?

PLANNING A WEEK'S ACTIVITIES AND INDIVIDUALIZED LESSONS

Ms. McLynn plans the activities and lessons a week in advance. She is careful to choose things that the children are able to do and will enjoy.

Each week she chooses a theme. Vocabulary, concepts to be emphasized, and gross and fine motor activities as well as music and stories are chosen in relation to the theme. For example, if the theme is "See signs of spring and learn about them," she will plan a walk to look at buds and spring flowers, plant seeds, do a craft (fine motor) activity such as make crepe paper flowers, and learn a song about spring.

Many of the objectives for each child require practice over time. Each day Ms. McLynn chooses materials and games that promote these skills. This equivalent practice makes it possible for the children to do many different things at essentially the same skill level. They are not bored, even though they are practicing the same skills daily. The needed repetition never becomes meaningless drill.

Ms. McLynn found it difficult to include each child's individual objectives on the weekly lesson plan. She prefers to list the activity, such as "block patterns" or "numerals and counting," on the plan. Then, she uses her checklist and objectives to provide individualized lesson targets for each child. This does not mean that she works with them one at a time. She conforms her directions and questions to each child on the basis of individual skills during the group activity. Experience has taught her that she can match the appropriate en route behavior to each child without writing each objective on her weekly plan.

Ms. McLynn's friend Ms. Watts has less experience in teaching young children with different individual needs. She prefers to have a separate page for each child. She writes the specific objective for each part of the weekly lessons on the individual child's lesson plan. Then, she writes a comment each afternoon about the effectiveness of her planning. In this way she is learning to evaluate and adjust her planning. Each of these teachers chooses a theme and plans individualized activities within group lessons. However, they prefer a different system for organizing and record keeping.

3. What routines and activities will be repeated daily (for example, greeting the children as they arrive, bathroom routines, playtime, and outdoor time)?
4. Will a theme be used to provide focus for the activities each week?
5. What use will be made of small and large groups for specific teaching?
6. Which activities must be repeated frequently over time to allow for increasingly complex skill development? (Examples include most motor skills, many cognitive skills, and all language and social skills.)
7. Who will have to follow these lesson plans?

By answering these seven questions, a system appropriate for the classroom will emerge. First, consider question 7. *WHO* will have to interpret and follow your lesson plans? Of course, the teacher will. But so will substitutes when the teacher is away. Teacher aides and volunteers will need to understand what is being done and why. The supervisor or principal will want to know what the teacher is planning. So while writing plans, the answer to question 7 should be considered continuously.

Next, how the day will be divided and how much time will be spent on each activity (questions 1 and 2) should be considered. To avoid having to fill in a blank space each week with repetitive comments such as "Greet children individually" or "Take care of bathroom needs" or even "Sing the Clean-Up Time Song," it is helpful to write a time-use plan that can be used for many weeks. Any activities that are repeated daily should be included. Enough detail should be included so that a substitute will be able to have a clear picture of what is expected during each time segment. The box on pp. 113-114 is an example of this kind of a plan.

In addition to the time-use plan, a form with blanks, including places to write specific activities, themes, or vocabulary, is needed. It is

helpful to focus on particular cognitive and motor skill areas each day. These also can be printed on the form. For example, note "Colors" on the sample plan (Fig. 4-5). This is a helpful reminder to plan an activity that focuses on colors at that time each week. However, whatever the teacher does during that lesson must reflect individualization of the lesson. Here, reference to the checklist and the related behavioral objectives will serve as a guide.

Regardless of the materials used or specific activities, teaching will be guided by the hierarchy of the en route behaviors that have been developed. For instance, if the teacher chooses to teach colors this week by baking cookies and icing them with the colors he or she has chosen to teach, he or she will conform to the objectives by asking some children to "Show me the blue icing" or "Use the yellow icing." For children who have demonstrated that they can *recognize* colors (for example, "Show me") the teacher will be ready to ask "What color did Joe use on his cookie?" This, of course, reflects individualizing because Joe is asked to *recall* the color, a more difficult objective than to merely recognize it when the color is named. By planning in this way, it becomes unnecessary to write objectives for each different lesson because the teacher is providing *equivalent practice*. That is, the teacher is expecting each child to perform on the level identified on his or her column of the checklist.

However, some lessons will involve cooking, whereas others involve dressing the doll, sorting different colored toys, or choosing paper for a fine motor project. While teaching, the teacher is continually assessing the individual performances. He or she can be very creative in the activities chosen but will not need to write each one in detail. The checklist with its related objectives saves time and repetitive effort. The weekly lesson plan identifies the activities and the themes.

Activities for week of: __Feb. 8-12__   Teacher: __Mc Lynn__

Theme for this week: __Valentines - "Caring"__   Teacher aide: __Cain__

Vocabulary to be emphasized: __valentine, heart, love, caring, love, sharing, kind__

Concepts to be emphasized: __match, doesn't match, corner, center, middle, edge__

Please note: All work is individualized, even during group activities. See the checklist and the sequenced behavioral objectives.

	Daily activities	Monday	Tuesday	Wednesday	Thursday	Friday
8:30 AM 12:15 PM	Shelf choice and greetings-open choices	play doh	easel painting	large blocks	puzzles	cutting pasting
8:45 AM 12:30 PM	Circle time (All together)	The "DAILIES": weather, day of the week, calendar of who's here, who's absent, and show and tell				
		(Colors)	*(Shapes)*	*(Numbers)*	*(Listening)*	*(Feelings)*
	Special emphasis: (for example, holiday, field trip, or visitor)	pink red white	"heart shape"	addresses	post office	happy, fear, love, sharing
9:00 AM 12:45 PM	Small, group-choice time	match colored valentines	crawl-through shapes	addressing valentines	field trip	long mfg story post office
9:30 AM 1:15 PM	Snack time	raspberry yogurt	toast shapes milk	fruit	making rom-teaming	mothers' treat
	(Note: This is an important teaching time. In addition to learning to prepare and eat a wide variety of foods, spontaneous and directed conversations are used to teach concepts [above], math readiness, colors, textures, shapes, and categories of foods.)					
9:50 AM 1:35 PM	Story time	Peek #50	"I'm glad I'm me"	"Jennie's Val. Party"	Peek #90	"What Color is Love?"
10:10 AM 1:55 PM	Movement time	tunnel	parachute	balance beams	free play	dancing
10:30 AM 2:15 PM	Music and art time	band	coloring valentines	cutting/pasting valentines	records	"Love Somebody"
10:50 AM 2:35 PM	Dismissal preparation	self-help		zippers, buttons	→	→
11:00 AM 2:45 PM	Dismissal	buses		wait for bus in front hall		

FIG. 4-5. Example of weekly activity plan.

EXAMPLE OF A DAILY TIME-USE PLAN

Time-use plan and description of daily routines for both morning and afternoon classes*

8:30 AM
or
12:15 PM

Greeting. Children are individually greeted as they arrive. Welcome by name, encourage to respond with eye contact and use a smile and "hello" or "good morning." Help only as much as necessary to hang up coats and get ready for their special work. Ask if they have brought a note from home. Some (as needed) go to the bathroom.

Active conversation with them about everything they are doing is a must, since their primary need is to develop social, language, and cognitive skills about their everyday experiences. Encourage them to look into the mirror to see if they are "neat" and ready for school. During the first 30 minutes children will appear to be playing, some alone and some in small groups of *their choice.* This open classroom is an important teaching time, because they choose "lessons," games, or toys. Teachers, aides, and parents may play or work with them, but it is the child's option to choose what to do. Encourage children to choose carefully, complete an activity, then return toys and games to the shelves. They are not required to share what they have chosen and may play alone if they prefer. It is important to enjoy conversation with childen about what they are doing, although this will be a bit one-sided at first. Interactive conversation (which includes the adult listening) is the optimum way to teach speech and language skills.

Concepts to be emphasized are listed on the weekly theme page and on the *concept board* behind the teacher's desk. The intent of the concept board is to provide a "prompt sheet" for adults in the classroom to use these words continually in appropriate ways throughout the day. Contrive occasions for children to use these concepts correctly. Spontaneity is important. Repeated use is requisite.

8:45 AM
or
12:30 PM

Clean-up time. Children take turns ringing the bell to announce the end of "play time." Sing the "clean up" song. All participate in cleaning up and moving chairs to form a semicircle facing the bulletin board. Reward with praise those who arrive first with their work completed.

Circle time. Sometimes children sit on "their own" carpet square on the floor or under a tree to allow for variety. The purpose of this period is to give children practice in participating, listening, and controlling themselves in a large group. This takes time. "Dailies" include a review of the weather, days of the week, the calendar, learning names, recognizing who is absent, and "show and tell." These activities not only help children become socially aware but also they help develop language expression, memory, and just plain everyday knowledge.

9:00 AM
or
12:45 PM

Small group time. Children choose from activities previously set up by the teacher. These usually include a fine motor activity, language activity, problem-solving activity, and combination activity such as cooking which builds fine motor skills, language, and concepts. Some children may work individually with the teacher, aide, or therapist at this time. For children with special needs, their choices may be narrowed to develop target behaviors such as cleaning up, toileting, and washing hands.

*NOTE: Times suggested are approximate. Little children should not be rushed. Flexibility is necessary to capture "teachable moments" and to accommodate special events such as field trips.

Continued.

EXAMPLE OF A DAILY TIME-USE PLAN—cont'd

9:30 AM
or
1:15 PM

Snack time. A wide variety of nutritious foods are eaten to encourage conversation and understanding of differences, for example, in color, texture, taste, and shape. As children finish, they brush their teeth and select a book from the shelf.

9:50 AM
or
1:35 PM

Story time. Sometimes all children "read" to themselves. At other times, some read to themselves while others join an adult to listen to a story. When enough adults are available, several stories may be listened to in small groups around the room.

10:10 AM
or
1:55 PM

Movement time. Depending on the weather, movement activities may be inside the room the gym, or outside. Music may accompany such activities. The physical therapist may work with some children, as noted on the physical therapy list.

10:30 AM
or
2:15 PM

Music and art time. Music and fingerplay activities may be done in the group circle. Art activities are usually done in small groups. Sometimes parents will share special interests with children at this time. Choice is given, when possible.

10:50 AM
or
2:35 PM

Dismissal preparation. Children clean up and then join others in the circle. One at a time children get belongings, put on coats while others exchange feelings about the day, and sing the closing song.

11:00 AM
or
2:45 PM

Dismissal. Children are released to parents or bus drivers.

SUMMARY

The expanding need for early childhood teachers to plan programs for children of varied developmental levels requires these teachers to design effective curricula. One way to do this is to base the content of the curricula on a developmental checklist. That is, those skills identified as usually developing at specific ages become the target skills stated in the curricula. Once these target skills have been identified, they can be arranged in a checklist for ready reference. Usually the skills are grouped into "domains" or skill areas.

By themselves, checklists do not provide precise statements about the skills to be learned. They do not identify specific behaviors to be taught nor do they describe how well the children must perform and under what circumstances. Because it is important to describe ex-

actly what is meant when the teacher says the children know something, behavioral (or performance) objectives should be written for each item on the checklist. Objectives specify what the teacher will do (or refrain from doing) and what behavior the teacher will observe when the children know or have learned what was taught. Objectives also include a criterion for performance and are precise and graduated.

After the checklist has been developed, goals and objectives written, and a parent report form devised, it becomes a simple matter to link assessment with individualized lesson planning. Grading becomes irrelevant. The only important questions become, first, can this child perform this behavior, and second, if he or she cannot, what related simpler objective can be identified as the entry behavior.

By using a set of well-planned objectives,

groups of children at different developmental levels can be taught together. In both small and large groups it is possible to individualize lessons. Children with developmental lags in one or more areas can be successfully included in classes with children who are more advanced. By making it possible for the teacher to pinpoint what needs to be taught, teaching is greatly simplified.

Using the checklist and the objectives to link assessment to teaching targets, the individual child, regardless of capabilities, is taught what he or she needs to learn. Although only those children identified as having special needs *must* have an IEP, it is possible to provide *each* child with an individualized program with a minimum of effort. By using the checklist for both assessment and as a curriculum guide, teaching is more successful. Daily and weekly lesson planning are simplified. Record keeping is easier and more quickly accomplished. The records maintained on the checklist serve as both formative (everyday progress) and summative (final achievement at the end of the year) evaluation criteria.

DISCUSSION TOPICS AND ACTIVITIES

1. Consider the following problem. The IEP conference for David has concluded. The parents are pleased with the suggestions made by the multidisciplinary team. These include continued placement in your preschool class for 3 year olds. An early childhood special education teacher has been assigned to help you plan activities for David. Test results indicated that David is lagging in all developmental areas. What questions will you want to ask the special education teacher when he or she visits you the first time?

2. Choose something about which you know a great deal. Consider activities such as baking a cake, playing a simple tune on a musical instrument, roller skating, or coloring in a coloring book. Write an appropriate goal and a terminal objective. Then, write five en route behaviors. Remember to work backward from your terminal objective. Then, arrange your en route behaviors in sequence from the easiest step to the final, terminal objective. Try to teach someone, using your sequence of objectives. Identify any missing steps, look for incomplete objectives,

and be aware of the appropriateness of the sequence.

3. Describe the difficulties you encounter in your attempt to write and sequence the objectives for the activity you chose.

4. Now consider this problem. You have a mildly hearing impaired girl assigned to your class of typical 4 year olds. You can understand some of what she says but most of her efforts to communicate result in confusion for you. Describe three things you could do if she runs from the doll corner to tell you something in a happy, enthusiastic manner, but you are unable to understand her. Write an objective for her that reflects your desire to teach her first how to attempt to tell you something. Then, if you do not understand, assume that you want her to show you what she is trying to say. Last, you want her to attempt to imitate your spoken model of what she was trying to say.

5. You are a teacher in a newly established preschool. You have been asked to help design a system for record keeping. You must consider the following: who will maintain the records, who will read the records and maintain confidentiality, how the information will be distributed, how frequently the information must be gathered, and how often it must be reported. Develop a system for record keeping and discuss it with other class members.

ANNOTATED REFERENCES
Before lesson planning can begin: the IEP

Hayden, A.H., and Edgar, E. Developing individualized education programs for young handicapped children. *Teaching Exceptional Children*, 1978, *10*, 67-73.
The authors outline what they consider to be the five major steps in the educational process for handicapped children: assessment-diagnosis, goal setting, planning for instruction, implementation, and evaluation. Vital considerations are explored and questions are asked that are often ignored. This is a brief but very worthwhile article.

Levitt, T. *Writing and implementing an IEP.* Belmont, Calif.: Fearon Pitman Publishers, Inc., 1979.
This paperback book presents a step-by-step analysis of how to prepare the contents of an IEP. Included is a model form that can be adapted for specific uses. Lists of goals and objectives, record keeping techniques, and sequences of skills also can be found.

Lowenthal, B. IEP purposes and implications. *Young Children*, 1979, *34*, 28-32.
This brief article explains the purposes of P.L. 94-142, the requirements of the IEP, how goals and objectives are determined, how the IEP planning meeting is to be conducted, and the author's view of the impact of P.L. 94-142. Parents and teachers are viewed as absolutely crucial to effective implementation of the intent of the law.

Maher, C.A., and Barbrack, C.R. A framework for comprehensive evaluation of the individualized education program (IEP). *Learning Disability Quarterly*, 1980, 3, 49-55.

This article describes a process for the comprehensive evaluation of the IEP. It provides for collection of a range of evaluation information about the design, implementation, practicality, and effectiveness of the program. Useful suggestions are made to those who are charged with evaluating the appropriateness of services provided to handicapped children.

Torres, S. (Ed.). *A primer on individualized education programs for handicapped children*, Reston, Va.: The Foundation for Exceptional Children, 1977.

This primer is intended to serve as a practical guide to the implementation of IEPs for handicapped children. Sections are arranged sequentially to help the reader to develop, implement, and evaluate an IEP for all handicapped children who require special services. A sample program form is provided, and essential elements of the law are discussed. This brief paperback book serves its purpose well.

When lesson planning is ready to begin: from annual goals to daily lessons

Anderson, R.C., and Faust, G.W. *Educational psychology*. New York: Dodd, Mead & Co., 1973.

This educational psychology text book contains a self-paced instructional program on how to write behavioral objectives. Students who have used this program have found it to be extremely helpful.

Charles, C.M. *Individualizing instruction*. St. Louis: The C.V. Mosby Co., 1976.

Although this book was not planned for use with preschoolers, it includes many relevant and useful ideas. The purpose of this book is to present instructional strategies appropriate to student differences that influence learning. Topics covered include approaches for enhancing students' self-concepts, cognitive styles, diagnostic-prescriptive teaching, learning centers, and management of individualized programs.

Fredericks, H.D., Baldwin, F.L., Grove, D.N., and Moore, W.G. Record keeping. In J.B. Jordan, A.H. Hayden, M.B. Karnes, and M.M. Wood (Eds.), *Early childhood education for exceptional children*. Reston, Va.: The Council for Exceptional Children, 1977.

This chapter presents records and record keeping systems used by the First Chance Network projects. Numerous examples are included to illustrate various approaches to the documentation of children's progress. Review of this chapter is useful to anyone setting up a record keeping system.

Howell, K.W., Kaplan, J.S., and O'Connell, C.Y. *Evaluating exceptional children: A task analysis approach*. Columbus, Ohio: Charles E. Merrill Publishing Co., 1979.

This text was written for use in a course on evaluation of exceptional children. Of particular value are the chapters on task analysis and the clear, concise instructional program on the basics of writing good behavioral objectives.

Kemp, J.E. *Instructional design*. Belmont, Calif.: Fearon Pitman Publishers, Inc., 1971.

Precise directions for writing objectives are given. Included are verbs that are useful in making expected behaviors explicit. The author discusses The Instructional Objectives Exchange Center that is designed to form a national depository where teachers can send their ideas or ask to receive objectives written by others. It is housed at the University of California at Los Angeles.

Lillie, D.L. *Early childhood education*. Chicago, Ill.: Science Research Associates, Inc., 1975.

The focus of this book is on a specific individualized approach to developmental instruction. The Carolina Developmental Profile is included as a base from which to organize educational activities. This book is an excellent resource for anyone wishing to individualize curriculum for young children.

Mager, R.F. *Goal analysis*. Belmont, Calif.: Fearon Pitman Publishers, Inc., 1972.

The goal analysis procedure described in this book is useful in the development of relevant and achievable objectives. Focus is placed on the understanding of the meaning of goals. Goals are thought to be outgrowths of attitudes, appreciations, and understandings. The author believes that by understanding the meaning of one's goals, better decisions about their attainment can be made.

Mager, R.F. *Preparing instructional objectives*. Belmont, Calif.: Fearon Pitman Publishers, Inc., 1975.

This small paperback is a "must." The author has provided much needed specific instruction in how to select goals and clearly state objectives. It answers questions about "what" as well as "how" to write. Included is a "self-test" to assist readers in determining if they have met acceptable criterion in the preparation of instructional objectives.

Mori, A.A., and Olive, J.E. *Handbook of preschool special education*. Rockville, Md.: Aspen Systems Corp., 1980.

The authors focus on the need for early intervention with infants and toddlers. Presented are the essential steps involved in effective use of the developmental checklist and curriculum lesson plans they have devised for use with children from birth to 26 months of age.

Neisworth, J.T., Willoughby-Herb, S.J., Bagnato, S.J., Cartwright, C.A., and Laub, K.W. *Individualized education for preschool exceptional children*. Germantown, Md.: Aspen Systems Corp., 1980.

These authors stress the importance of linking developmental diagnosis with curriculum planning. Half of the book is comprised of a curriculum of developmentally sequenced objectives for children from birth to 5 years of age. This curriculum is organized into four domains: communication, personal and interpersonal skills, motor development, and problem solving.

REFERENCES

Bloom, B.S. (Ed.). *Taxonomy of education objectives, Handbook I: Cognitive domain.* New York: David McKay Co., Inc., 1956.

Bruner, J., Goodnow, J., and Austin, G. *A study of thinking.* New York: John Wiley & Sons, Inc., 1956.

Charles, C.M. *Individualizing instruction.* St. Louis: The C.V. Mosby Co., 1976.

Kemp, J.E. *Instructional design.* Belmont, Calif.: Fearon Pitman Publishers, Inc., 1971.

Knobloch, H. and Pasamanick, B. (Eds.). *Developmental diagnosis.* Hagerstown, Md.: Harper & Row Publishers, Inc., 1974.

Krathwohl, D.R., Bloom, B.S., and Masia, B. *Taxonomy of educational objectives, Handbook II: affective domain.* New York: Harper & Row Publishers, Inc., 1974.

Lillie, D.L. *Early childhood education.* Chicago: Science Research Associates, Inc., 1975.

Mager, R.F. *Goal analysis*, Belmont, Calif.: Fearon Pitman Publishers, Inc., 1972.

Mager, R.F. *Preparing instructional objectives.* Belmont, Calif.: Fearon Pitman Publishers, Inc., 1962.

Mager. R.F., and Pipe, P. *Analyzing performance problems or 'you really oughta wanna.'* Belmont, Calif.: Fearon Pitman Publishers, Inc., 1970.

Montessori, M. *Dr. Montessori's own handbook.* New York: Schocken Books, Inc., 1972.

Piaget, J. *The psychology of intelligence.* Paterson, N.J. Littlefield, Adams & Co., 1960.

Popham, W., and Baker, E.I. *Establishing instructional objectives.* Englewood Cliffs, N.J.: Prentice-Hall, Inc., 1970. (a)

Popham, W., and Baker, E.I. *Planning an instructional sequence.* Englewood Cliffs, N.J.: Prentice-Hall, Inc., 1970. (b)

Portage Preschool Project. *The Portage guide to early education.* Portage, Wis.: Portage Preschool Project, 1969.

Public Law 94-142. Washington, D.C.: U.S. Government Printing office, 1975.

Stellern, J., Vasa, S.F., and Little, J. *Introduction to diagnostic-prescriptive teaching and programming.* Glen Ridge, N.J.: Exceptional Press, 1976.

Torres, S. (Ed.). *A primer on individualized education programs for handicapped children.* Reston, Va.: The Foundation for Exceptional Children, 1977.

Vargas, J.S. *Writing worthwhile behavioral objectives.* New York: Harper & Row Publishers, Inc., 1972.

Ward, M., Cartwright, G.P., Cartwright, C.A., and Campbell, J. *Diagnostic teaching of preschool and primary children.* University Park: The Pennsylvania State University Press, 1973.

CHAPTER

5

Helping preschool children to develop motor skills

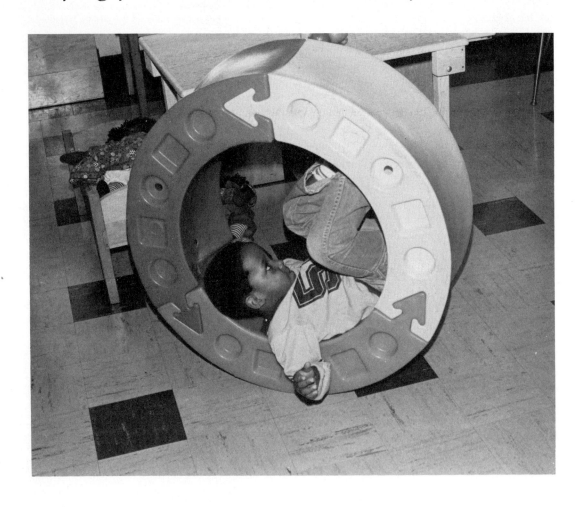

Working with young children to develop motor skills requires a special kind of planning. Competition and "winners," often associated with physical education in schools, are inappropriate. Young children need to learn about their bodies. They need to develop balance and coordination. It is important for them to discover themselves in relationship to space. Care must be taken to help children develop an inner awareness of the difference between the two sides of the body, since moving through space requires both sides of the body to act as a team. Coordination of movement skills contributes to the development of confidence and trust in themselves and their bodies. This sense of bodily trust is considered to be important to the emergence of healthy personalities (Erikson, 1963). These are just some of the reasons that sensory-motor integration activities have held a dominate place in preschool curricula.

Motor skills are usually divided into at least two general categories. *Gross motor skills* refer to activities that involve the use of the large muscles of the neck, trunk, arms, and legs. Included are basic body movements such as lifting the head, rolling, crawling, creeping, walking, running, leaping, jumping, hopping, galloping, and skipping. Large muscle strength and endurance are also important in climbing, pushing, pulling, hanging, and lifting.

Fine motor skills involve more precise movements of the small muscles, especially those of the eyes, speech musculature, hands, fingers, feet, and toes. Movements such as blinking, focusing, sucking, grasping, releasing, pinching, and writing are considered to be fine motor activities. Many fine motor skills, including, cutting, copying, stringing beads, and pasting, require the eyes to direct the hands. These activities are referred to variously as those that require perceptual-motor, visual-motor, sensory-motor, ocular-motor, or eye-hand coordination.

This chapter discusses some of the important concepts and activities associated with the development of motor skills. The sequence of development is outlined, and atypical development is discussed. Specific suggestions for teaching lessons and modifying activities are made. Special efforts are taken to encourage the integration of movement skills with other areas of the curriculum.

IMPORTANCE OF MOTOR SKILL DEVELOPMENT IN THE PRESCHOOL

Few activities in the preschool curriculum give children the joy and satisfaction provided by learning to control their bodies. Learning to run without falling, bouncing, throwing, and catching a ball are exciting experiences. Discovering how it feels to move in different ways and how to avoid bumping into things are immediately helpful to preschool children. The awareness that they can consciously control their bodies is critical to their developing self-image. Children who have physical disabilities learn that they also can do things previously considered impossible. This beginning of self-mastery is motivating in and of itself.

When presenting a workshop on the teaching of movement skills, Frostig (1974) described the following 10 purposes of movement education:

1. *Health and fitness.* Blood circulation and resistance to disease are thought to be related to physical fitness. Children from crowded environments or who have difficulty moving as a result of a disability need special encouragement to move as vigorously as permissable.

2. *Development of motor ability.* Movement exploration using natural movements needs to be fostered. Simultaneous use of sense modalities and movements develops cognition and mastery in space.

3. *Development of movement attributes.* The attributes include coordination (which is difficult to define), rhythm, flexibility, speed, agility, balance, strength, and endurance.

4. *Establish use of laterality and directionality.* The concept of laterality is likened to the "map of inner space" and directionality to the "map of outer space" by Hunter (1968). Consideration is given to the development of muscles in each side of the body as well as verbal labeling (e.g., "right-hand side").

5. *Development of body awareness.* All goal-directed movement is thought to contribute to body awareness. Body awareness is the growing understanding of what one's body parts are and can do. It is critical to the development of the concept of "I" or "me." Dubose (1979) relates the visually impaired child's delayed use of the pronouns *me* and *I* to lack of sensory-motor integration experiences. Children with the con-

cept of body awareness can realize that they are independent beings separate from the world around.

6. *Mastery of space.* Time and space awareness develop slowly in children. It is not until they are between 8 and 11 years of age that most children can handle successfully spatial relations (Hohmann, Banet, and Weikart, 1979). However, mastery of space is related to body awareness as the child perceives time, causality, and number in relation to himself or herself through such thoughts as "How fast did I run?" "How far did I go?" "How high did I jump?" and "How can I jump higher?"

7. *Development of social consciousness.* When children share space and equipment,

they must become aware of one another. They are required to take turns and cooperate. Social feelings arise from working in small groups and pairs. Games require leaders as well as followers. Trust develops when two must work together to solve a problem. One movement activity that develops trust and cooperation requires two children to kneel facing the same direction on a large piece of sheet or a large towel. Then, ask the children to move themselves and the sheet across the floor. Unison of bodily movement is required.

8. *Development of integrative functions and thought processes.* Throughout the preschool years children are learning to integrate perceptions of the various senses into appropriate responses. Movement assists in this critical aspect of development. When given the verbal direction to "fly like an airplane" until the "stop sign" is raised, children must integrate visual and auditory perceptions into requested bodily movements.

9. *Development of attention and concentration skills.* The ability to control one's motions is believed by some to be more a matter of the ability to attend and concentrate than a developmental phenomenon (Wolff, 1979). Of course, fine muscle movements are made possible by the ability to control large muscle movements. Anyone involved in a very intricate fine motor task is aware of the concentration necessary for accomplishment.

Teachers are often surprised at how quickly overactive children can exhibit self-control when crossing the room with an egg balanced on a spoon. Movement activities can actually help children to become consciously aware of what paying attention really means in terms of bodily response. Balance beam exercises, "freezing" on command, being alert to signals to change directions, and exercising in slow motion all require practice in concentration and body control.

Later work in academics is enhanced because children have learned to follow directions and control their bodies. Listening until a three-stage direction given in one long sentence is complete and then doing as directed in the correct sequence is an important attending exercise. In elementary school, children will be expected to do this both in physical education classes as they learn to play organized games and in the classroom as they complete academic assignments.

10. *Development of visualization and imagery.* The ability to visualize or use imagery is critical to the development of young children. Through the storage and manipulation of mental representations, children develop the ability to "think about their thinking" (Voyat, 1980). Movement planning involves the use of imagery. By translating images into plans that are carried out through movement, a child can receive immediate reinforcement through his or her own bodily feelings as well as through acknowledgement by others. Consider the visualization and imagery involved in pretending to be a small, hungry kitten lost from its mother in the middle of a strange neighborhood. Creative solutions to the problem are amazing.

It should be noted that while Frostig did enumerate these 10 purposes of movement education, the elaborative comments reflect the authors' research and experience in the field. For more in-depth study of Frostig's program in movement education that includes specific activities, refer to the annotated bibliography at the end of the chapter.

PERCEPTUAL-MOTOR INTEGRATION

Much has been written about the integral relationship between developing motor and perceptual skills (perceptual-motor skills) as well as visual and auditory perception. To comprehend the dynamic role of sensory-motor and perceptual skills in a child's development and in typical preschool curricula, it is necessary to have a basic understanding of perception.

Perception

Lerner, Mardell-Czudnowski, and Goldenberg (1981, p. 127) explain perception in the following words:

> Perception is an interpretive function of the brain. It is the translation of sensory impressions into some representational level that is easily stored and recalled. In reality, the functions of sensation, motor activity and perception are so closely related that it is difficult to separate one from the other.

Perceptual disorders can occur in any of the sensory areas. Visual perception involves the translation of sensory impressions from the eyes, whereas auditory perception includes translating what has been heard into something easily stored and recalled. If children do not learn how to interpret sense impressions in expected ways, they are described as having perceptual disorders. Disorders of touch (tactile) or "muscle memory" (kinesthetic) can interfere with learning and recalling as do disorders of seeing and listening.

Perception is a learned cognitive process. Encountering sensory stimulation of a particular kind for the first time, children *receive* (sense) the stimulation. Subsequent encounters usually result in their *perceiving* (interpreting) the stimulus. If any of the senses are impaired, even slightly, children may not be able to sense the initial stimulus accurately. If they do not receive an accurate first impression, later interpretations of that stimulus will be wrong or confusing to them.

Failure to develop accurate perceptions has been observed in children described as learning disabled. The early works of Strauss and Werner (1942) and Strauss and Lehtinen (1947) emphasize that perceptual deficits interfere seriously with all learning. Cruickshank (1967) also

believed this. Of course, not all perceptual skills involve motor skills. Hearing and recognizing or discriminating among speech sounds is a perceptual skill but not a perceptual-motor skill, for example. Other perceptual skills that do not involve motor skills are defined in Table 5 and discussed throughout Chapter 6.

Perceptual-motor skills

In an effort to remediate *perceptual-motor* (coordination of what is perceived with movements of body parts) deficits, specific teaching systems and techniques have been devised. Proponents of these include the following:

1. Kephart (1964, 1971) believed that motor development must come before and is basic to perceptual development.

2. Getman (1965) developed a visuomotor model of learning based on a pyramid of skills. These skills, which contain a strong visual perception emphasis, are considered to be the path of learning characteristic of the majority of children in our highly visually oriented society.

3. Barsch (1967, 1968) originated the "Movigenic Theory" based on his belief that the acquisition of spatial movement patterns leads to more efficient learning.

4. Cratty (1967, 1969) believes that there is a definite, although possibly indirect, relationship between motor skills and academic success. He does not claim that movement is the basis of a child's mental development. However, lack of motor ability is thought to lead to lowered self-esteem and decreased peer acceptance. These in turn are thought to reduce academic performance.

5. Frostig (1970) in association with Maslow wrote that movement education would "enhance the total development of young children—their physical and their psychological abilities, their ability to learn, their ability to get along with one another, their feelings about

themselves, and their relationship to the environment" (p. 13).

6. Ayres (1972), an occupational therapist, believes that some children experience tactile defensiveness (interpreting touch as a sign of danger) that interferes with learning and requires sensory integrative intervention to prevent social isolation.

In summarizing his review of the research to date on perceptual-motor training programs, Mercer (1979, p. 278) warns:

> Many of the perceptual-motor training programs commonly used, then, do not directly improve academic achievement or perceptual-motor development. Until further research, the inclusion of academic content in motor activities is desirable.

After considering more than 60 studies, Larsen and Hammill (1975) concluded that the relationship between visual, perceptual, and academic performance is not significant. Therefore Hammill and Bartel (1975, p. 230) urge teachers "to implement perceptual-motor training on a remedial basis in only those few cases where improvement in perception is the goal." They further suggest that such training is more acceptable for preschoolers than for kindergarten or school-aged children.

Or, as Piazza (1979, p. 47) suggests, "If perceptual, motor, or psycholinguistic skills are to be trained they should be done for their own sake and not for some projected transfer to an academic area. Children do need to be taught the difference between the left and right sides of their bodies, and . . . such tasks as cutting." It is for these reasons that we encourage the development of perceptual-motor skills as tasks, in and of themselves, but in association with language and concept development.

THE DEVELOPMENT OF MOTOR SKILLS

"In general, the development of motor skills proceeds according to the laws which govern the physiological maturation of the child, with the development of movement patterns progressing from simple arm or leg actions to highly integrated total body coordinations" (Espenschade and Eckert, 1967, p. 135). The rate of development is thought to depend not only on the quality of environmental stimulus but also on the stage of brain development (Wolff, 1979). No distinction is usually made in the motor abilities of boys and girls in infancy and early childhood because the differences are not very great. During the late preschool years girls appear to perform better on tasks requiring manual dexterity, whereas boys are more adept when using large (gross) muscles. The extent to which this difference may be culturally determined is still being questioned (Herkowitz, 1978).

Environmental factors such as amount of sleep, exercise, medical care, and adequacy of nutrition also influence the rate and ultimate degree of physical and thus motor development. Individuals from the upper socioeconomic classes tend to be larger in body size (Tanner, 1970). In general, a child's potential for motor skill development is considered to be the result of his genetic origin and the specific environmental factors that affect him or her.

Sequential trends of motor development

O'Donnell (1969) discusses seven basic principles that govern the sequence of motor development. These are outlined in the following sequence:

1. *Cephalocaudal pattern.* Muscular development proceeds from the head to the foot. For example, infants have voluntary control over their heads before lower parts of their body. Similarly, children can usually throw before they can catch.

2. *Proximo-distal pattern.* Growth and development tend to proceed from the spine (proximo) to the outer extremities (distal). That is, voluntary movement begins in the shoulder, then

TABLE 4
Typical motor skills activities

Gross motor development

Eye-foot coordination	*Eye-hand coordination*	*Body awareness*	*Balance*
Kicking	Climbing	Crawling in and out of things	Standing on tiptoe
Climbing	Hanging	Crawling through and around things	Walking the balance beam
Jumping	Striking balloons		Riding wheeled toys
Hopping	Throwing	Moving like an animal	Walking around tire edges or sandbox rails
Dancing	Catching	Mirroring activities	
Walking the balance beam	Using tools	Playing "Simon Says"	Moving and carrying something without spilling it
Jumping over ropes	Block building	Steering wheeled toys	
	Rolling balls		Walking with bean bag on head or shoulder
	Pounding		
	Stirring		

Fine motor development

Eye-hand coordination

Cutting	Lacing	Outlining with stencils or templates
Coloring	Geoboards	Copying
Drawing	Tracing	Pasting
Sewing	Painting	Building block towers
Puzzle building	Paper folding	Stacking
Bead stringing	Copying designs	

Self-help skills

Dressing (buttoning, zipping, snapping, buckling)
Eating
Personal hygiene (brushing teeth, washing hands)
Toileting

moves on to the elbow area, wrist, and finally, the fingers.

3. *Mass to specific pattern.* Body movement of young infants is undifferentiated involving the total body. Later specific patterns of movement develop out of these generalized mass movements. When learning new skills, it takes time for children to inhibit the unwanted, extraneous movements.

4. *Gross motor to fine motor pattern.* Children usually gain control over large muscle activity before fine or small muscle activity. In addition, a child must gain differential control. That is, movement of muscles on one side of the body should occur without similar movement on the other side of the body, unless desired.

5. *Maximum to minimum muscle involvement pattern.* Like the mass to specific pattern, body movement becomes increasingly more efficient. With practice, children learn to eliminate unnecessary expenditures of energy. Where it once took a whole bodily effort to catch a ball, children learn to catch with the use of just one arm and hand.

6. *Bilateral-to-unilateral pattern.* Children progress from undifferentiated use of both sides of the body to unilateral preference referred to as the *establishment of laterality.*

7. *Orderly development pattern.* Children differ in the rate of their development but do tend to follow a similar pattern if environmental conditions are adequate and no organic deficits are present.

These broad trends are outlined here to encourage the understanding of children's need to practice a variety of skills during their preschool years to move from mass, undifferentiated activity to efficient, voluntary motor control. Children's development can be delayed for a number of reasons. Many of these are out of the control of either a teacher or the child.

There are, however, some children who are delayed from lack of opportunity or fear of failure. Familiar is the child who fails to alternate feet when descending stairs and thus fails a preschool screening. Consideration may or may not be given to whether or not the child has ever been around stairs. The same example can be used readily with the fine motor skill of cutting. Practice in motor skills, for their own sake, is prerequisite to an appropriate preschool curriculum. A sample list of skills to be practiced is found in Table 4. A chart of normative expectations can be found in Appendix A.

Developing gross motor skills

Gross motor skills refer to the involvement of the large muscles of the neck, trunk of the body, arms, and legs. Most children enter preschool with well-developed large muscle skills. That is, they run well, climb readily, and are learning to catch and skip. Early childhood affords the time and practice for emerging skills to become accomplished before rapid bodily changes begin to occur. Children learn to walk the balance beam with ease, catch with elbows at the side of their body, throw with greater accuracy, and jump with relative skill. The extent to which children become proficient in these skills is dependent on muscle development as well as opportunity for muscle use. However, it must be remembered that even in the most optimal situations, large and uneven growth spurts do occur. To provide the stimulation needed, safe environments free from obstacles and full of encouragement are needed. References at the end of the chapter suggest how to facilitate the development of growth-producing play areas.

Proficiency in gross motor skills is influenced by changes in body proportions. The 2 year old's head accounts for about one fourth of the child's height. By the time the child is 5 years old, it accounts for only about one sixth of the total height (Cratty, 1970). As children become less top-heavy, their ability to balance themselves develops. Children entering kindergarten have

usually experienced an increase in muscle tissue, creating a larger potential of muscle energy available for movement (Espenschade and Eckert, 1967).

Atypical development. Atypical motor development or motor differences can occur for a variety of reasons. Lerner, Mardell-Czudnowski, and Goldenberg (1981) discuss the following three deviations in muscle development that require consideration when programs are planned:

1. *Deficits in muscle tone.* Two types of muscle tone deviation are noted. The first, *hypotonicity*, describes limp muscles that do not exhibit resistance to a stretch. This difficulty is reflected in the child's inability to maintain postural control without extreme effort. *Hypertonicity* refers to a condition in which muscles are stretched and constantly excited. Extreme force is required to move muscles in this condition. *Spasticity* and *rigidity* are the two types of hypertonicity encountered. Rigid muscles resist

any movement. Erratic movement can result when muscles are spastic.

2. *Deficits in muscle control.* The term *tremors* is used to describe rapid, jerky, involuntary movements of muscles. These involuntary movements disturb balance and coordination.

3. *Deficits in muscle strength.* There may be differences in muscle strength among and within children. One side of the body may exhibit more strength than the other. A muscle weakness is termed *paresis*, whereas complete inability to move is termed *plegia*.

Adapting classroom and equipment. Astute observation can detect those who are experiencing less than normal muscle tone, control, or strength. Children whose movement is restricted for any reason need special considerations in planning movement experiences. Many of these children will have a prescription from a physician that is implemented by an *occupational therapist* or a *physical therapist*. Physical therapists work with large muscle movement and gross motor activities, whereas occupational therapists are concerned with the evaluation and treatment of perceptual-motor (fine motor) functioning.

These specialists may both work with some children, whereas in other cases only one of them is needed. Each will have useful suggestions for living and working with children with motor impairments. However, helping children who cannot coordinate their movements readily, are confined to a wheelchair, or use special braces requires knowledge of the individual child.

The physical therapist should be called upon to assist teachers in obtaining and using adaptive equipment, in understanding proper positioning techniques, and in increasing the child's range and efficiency of motion. The physical therapist will also assist parents in developing therapeutic techniques for home use. Practical suggestions such as removing clothing from nonaffected limbs first and dressing the impaired limb first will be offered.

The occupational therapist uses a multisensory approach to encourage adaptive responses. This specialist will assist teachers to adapt materials and equipment to use with children who have difficulty with fine motor control. For example, pencils are placed through rubber balls or pieces of Styrofoam to provide a larger object to grasp. Paper is taped to tabletops to prevent undesired movement, pencils and crayons are fastened to the child's chair with a piece of string for retrieval, and Velcro or magnets are attached to blocks for easier manipulation. Catalogs illustrate a large variety of equipment available to assist children develop critical self-help skills. Teachers have been very successful in getting adaptive equipment built inexpensively with the help of parents and school custodians. Not only is this approach less expensive, but also the item is usually suited to the child's individual needs. Plans for constructing adaptive equipment are available from national advocacy

groups, Finnie (1975) and Copeland, Ford, and Solon (1976). An introductory special education text should be consulted for more in-depth understanding of the effects of various handicapping conditions on motor skill development and special equipment needed.

Developing fine motor skills

Fine motor skills involve small muscles. Most fine motor skills, as far as preparation for school is concerned, involve hands and fingers. Coordination of hands and fingers is often described as requiring strength, flexibility, and dexterity. The coordination of eye-hand movement is referred to as a visual-perceptual skill.

Handedness. When observing children engaged in fine motor activities, the question of "handedness" or hand preference usually arises. Preschool teachers can relax. Research indicates that it is usual to find children frequently interchanging the use of either hand or both through early childhood. Hand dominance is often not achieved until the age of 6. Even then, some children develop functional ambidexterity (Espenschade and Eckert, 1967; Westphal, 1975). The fact that children tend to use their right hand more often in taught activities such as cutting and throwing suggests the influence of our cultural bias.

Practice payoff. Long before a baby can walk, mothers often report "Sally picked up a raisin today." Surprised that their child could pick up something so tiny, mothers become more alert about leaving beads and other nonedibles around. Later, this ability to see small things and pick them up will become the foundation for grasping and holding crayons, pencils, and other small objects.

Although merely having things available to pick up is all that is necessary for most young children to learn important fine motor skills, they must have opportunities to practice. Building with small blocks, manipulating small toys,

OCCUPATIONAL THERAPY INITIAL EVALUATION
September 7, 1981

NAME: Tim Jent   BD: 8-4-76   SCHOOL: Avondate Cross   TEACHER: Mr. Lontelle

I. Introduction
Tim is a 5-year-old boy who attends a preschool 3 hours each day. He was referred by his teacher, and his parents agreed that he appeared to have more trouble than his brothers and sisters with all physical activities. The evaluation revealed problems in the areas of fine motor skills, reflex integration, and self-help skills as well as perceptual abilities.

II. Range of motion and muscle strength
Tim had full passive range of motion in the upper extremities. Muscle strength was adequate for function.

III. Reflex integration
Tim was unable to cooperate in a number of the tests. However, protective extension was present and head righting reflexes were well developed. Additional testing is indicated.

IV. Gross motor skills
These skills were age appropriate.

V. Fine motor skills
Tim has good grasp and release, crossed the midline easily, and used a tip pinch for picking up small objects. He had difficulty with tasks that required use of pencil and scissors. He was unable to fold a paper.

VI. Perceptual abilities
Tim has trouble with interpretation of tactile, auditory, and visual sensation. He appeared to be fearful when equilibrium responses were tested. His parents report that he seems clumsy to them. He bumps into things and falls more often than his peers.

VII. Self-help skills
Tim's parents completed the self-help checklist. They said that he is independent in feeding himself and can cut some meats. However, he is very dependent on them for help with dressing himself, often getting things on upside down and backward if he tries this alone. He can pull his pants up but cannot zip or snap them without some help. He is unable to button large buttons or to tie his shoes.

VIII. Education area affected by handicap
Many areas of education will be interfered with by Tim's problems. Learning through visual channels, learning to write, manipulation of small objects, and participation in games and sports will be difficult.

IX. Recommendations
Tim would benefit from occupational therapy. The therapist should plan to work with him directly once each week and direct his teachers and parents in daily activities at home and at school.

Submitted by,

Zelda Torens

Zelda Torens, O.T.R.

and using crayons, chalk, and scissors all lead to the improvement of essential skills.

Snap-together beads, geoboards, puzzles, beads for stringing, button and lacing boards, and large nuts and screws offer interesting and challenging fine motor practice for young children. Even cooking activities help children to develop skills such as stirring, cutting, pounding, and rolling, while learning a variety of concepts.

Self-help skills

Self-help skills include both fine and gross motor skills. Children entering kindergarten can usually take care of most of their personal needs. They can put coats and sweaters on and take them off. Some children continue to need help with getting zippers started and small buttons buttoned. Many need help tying shoes.

Parents should be encouraged to provide clothes that are easy for their children to manage. Some parents will need encouragement to allow their children to do things for themselves. This may be especially true if the child has a physical problem of any kind. It is helpful to show parents where to begin with a child who has special needs. For example, long before children can put socks on, they can take them off. Show parents how to pull the sock part way off, and then put the child's hand on the toe and pull. Smiles and praise for success, combined with "You pulled your sock off," encourage self-help and build language. The Portage Preschool Project (1969) offers a series of steps to teach a number of self-help skills.

Reverse chaining. The most complete curricula developed for the teaching of self-help skills has been contributed by those who work with the moderately and severely handicapped. A sample of this is found in the annotated bibliography at the end of the chapter. These guides are especially helpful to teachers of young children as they present complete sets of task analyses directly useful in preschool classrooms.

Task analyses in the areas of dressing, eating, and personal hygiene are usually offered. Sometimes toileting is included. The teaching of self-help skills is usually done through the process known as *reverse chaining*. As pointed out in the example of taking socks off, the last part of the task is done first. Consider the following steps outlined by Fredericks, Riggs, Furey, Grove, Moore, McDonnell, Jordan, Hanson, Baldwin, and Wadlow (1976, p. 36):

1. Child puts on sock when just above heel
2. Child puts on sock when just below heel
3. Child puts on sock when toes started in
4. Child puts on sock when handed to him with heel in correct position
5. Child puts on sock (heel in correct position)

In addition, this resource suggests that oversized clothing be used when children are having considerable difficulty. They further question the use of dressing form boards because it is difficult to transfer to clothing which is on one's body. Some preschool teachers have had success with the placement of form board fronts on pillows that can be held by the child in front of himself or herself. A piece of elastic around the child and attached to either side of the pillow is also helpful.

Think back to the steps outlined for putting on socks. Reverse chaining means that the child would initially be helped at step one and reinforced for success. When this step has been accomplished, then teaching would begin at step two the next time socks needed to be put on. Of course, astute observation allows the teacher or parent to know with which step to begin the process of reverse chaining.

ASSESSMENT OF MOTOR SKILLS

Careful observation with the use of a checklist of developmental expectations may enable the teacher to detect fine or gross motor difficulties which have previously gone undetected. If a teacher suspects a problem, the parents should be notified. They then should be encouraged to seek the advice of a physician who will request the assistance of physical and occupational therapists, if necessary. In some cases the "unusual" motor behavior may be the result of health problems that can be corrected through diet control or a change in environmental conditions.

Focus on individual task approach

Effective observation of motor skills requires teachers to keep in mind that the process or approach to motor tasks is significant. How a child goes about trying to catch a ball is much more revealing than whether or not the ball is caught. There is a great difference in ability between (1) the child whose eyes are following the path of the ball and whose hands are working together to attempt a catch and (2) the child who seems not to be looking at the ball and whose hands hang loose or do not seem to work together. Although each may not actually catch the ball, their differences in attempts must be carefully noted and considered. They are clearly at different levels developmentally. Furthermore a child's lack of experiences in such activities as climbing stairs or using scissors influences performance. The child's level of excitement or fear of strangers and/or new tasks could be further inhibitors to motor processes.

As the quality of performance is dependent on physiological maturation and experience, assessment for the purpose of developing instructional objectives must depend on individually referenced criteria. Although comparison with group norms can provide the teacher with a general frame of reference, it cannot determine if individual progress is adequate in light of changes that take place within that individual. For example, a 3 year old who has the body height and weight of a 2 year old cannot be expected to perform balance tasks with the ease of most 3 year olds. Considering lack of balance to be a weakness and including objectives to teach balance would be inappropriate until a shift in bodily proportion takes place. In short, teachers are expected to "combine data from normative tests with her (their) knowledge of individual differences in her (their) class and develop a set of *criterion-referenced* objectives" (O'Donnell, p. 53).

Developmental task analysis. Once a teacher has used a developmental checklist derived from normative expectations and has observed very carefully while considering individual levels of maturation, interests, and experiences, teaching objectives can be determined. Using each individual's profile of needs, strengths, and weaknesses, behavioral objectives can be recorded on the developmental curriculum checklist discussed in Chapter 4. This checklist may include only broad curriculum objectives that may be stated more as goals, or it may contain more specific task analysis that analyze each broader goal into teaching steps. An example of both levels of a developmental curriculum checklist is illustrated in Fig. 5-1. This checklist then becomes a teaching as well as testing or assessment tool.

Normative tests. A number of instruments are available for screening and assessment of motor problems. Many specialists suggest that there is nothing better than in-depth understanding of developmental milestones (Taft, 1979). Among the instruments often used by teachers is the Denver Developmental Screening Test (Frankenberg, Dodds, Fandal, Kazuk, and Cohrs, 1975), which assesses both fine and gross motor development from birth to 6 years of age. Developmental schedules such as those produced by Gesell and associates (Knobloch and Pasamanick, 1974) are available to assist in general assessment of motor performance. Descriptions and critiques of assessment techniques can be found in the *Buros Mental Measurements Year-*

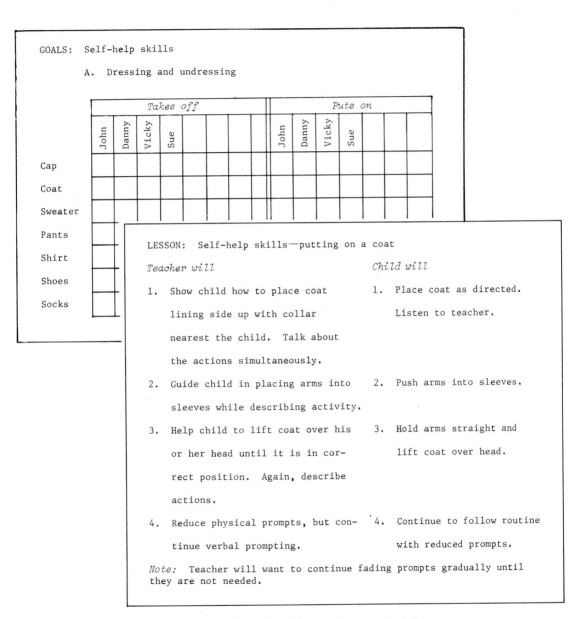

GOALS: Self-help skills

A. Dressing and undressing

	Takes off							Puts on						
	John	Danny	Vicky	Sue				John	Danny	Vicky	Sue			
Cap														
Coat														
Sweater														
Pants														
Shirt														
Shoes														
Socks														

LESSON: Self-help skills—putting on a coat

Teacher will	*Child will*
1. Show child how to place coat lining side up with collar nearest the child. Talk about the actions simultaneously.	1. Place coat as directed. Listen to teacher.
2. Guide child in placing arms into sleeves while describing activity.	2. Push arms into sleeves.
3. Help child to lift coat over his or her head until it is in correct position. Again, describe actions.	3. Hold arms straight and lift coat over head.
4. Reduce physical prompts, but continue verbal prompting.	4. Continue to follow routine with reduced prompts.

Note: Teacher will want to continue fading prompts gradually until they are not needed.

FIG. 5-1. Sample goals and lesson for self-help skills.

books, available in most libraries. Appendix D also lists some of the most used assessment techniques.

MOVEMENT EDUCATION

The practical suggestions for planning a program of movement education and teaching specific motor skills offered throughout the remainder of this chapter must be taken in light of children's total needs. Sensitivity is important. All movement activities do not need to include conscious attempts to develop cognitive and language skills. Large amounts of teacher direction are not necessary to all lessons. The opportunity for choice and just plain "fun" is important to a successful program.

Variety in movement education

To help ensure variety, teachers can check to see that activities involve all or most of the following attributes of movement identified by Frostig and Maslow (1970): (1) coordination and rhythm, (2) speed and agility, (3) flexibility, (4) strength, (5) endurance, and (6) balance. Of these, comments will be made on balance and coordination, which seem particularly important to early childhood curricula.

Balance. Balance is a state of bodily equilibrium maintained by the vestibular system within the inner ear. It is the ability to maintain a position against the force of gravity. Static balance occurs when the child is able to maintain a steady position in such activities as standing on tiptoe or on one leg on a stable surface. Dynamic balance "involves the ability to maintain a position on a moving surface, as a rolling ship or while moving the body with minimal support" (Frostig, 1974). The child's weight distribution or center of gravity must be adjusted to maintain balance. Practice walking a balance beam is a familiar preschool activity giving practice in dynamic balance. Children soon discover how to accomplish this activity when left alone to practice. Spinning, twirling, somersaults, bend-ing, leaning, tiptoeing, scooter boards, and twist boards provide ample opportunities to develop balance. Such practice may be especially important for children with disturbances in inner ear functioning.

Coordination. It is difficult to find an agreed on definition of coordination. Most writers speak of it as a "working together" of various body parts, for example, hands or feet following direction from the eyes or ears or both sides of the body working reciprocally. Familiar activities were listed in Table 4. A word needs to be said about the importance of *ocular-motor* skills in the development of coordination, whether of fine or gross motor skills. Children who are experiencing difficulty in attanding or concentrating in activities of coordination should have a thorough ophthalmological examination at once. Lack of attention during movement activities should be suspect because most children really wish to attend when movement is involved.

Problems can occur in the ability of the eyes to *accommodate* or change focus from near to far objects and vice versa. Sometimes both eyes do not look at an object simultaneously creating problems in *fixation*. *Pursuit* problems result when eyes cannot follow a target. Later reading problems can be the result of the inability of eyes to *track* or move smoothly across lines of print. Once the problems are diagnosed, the vision specialists can assist teachers in implementing eye coordination exercises such as suspending a ball from the ceiling and having a child visually pursue the moving ball without moving any other body part.

Adaptations in movement education

Popovich (1977) suggests the use of prompts (cues) when assisting children who are having difficulty developing motor skills that should be within their behavioral repertoire. If a child does not respond to normal verbal directions and modeling of desired responses, the verbal direction is repeated and accompanied by gestures. If there is still no response or an inadequate response, the verbal request can be accompanied by physically helping the child to perform the act. Positive reinforcement is given at whatever level the act is attempted. Of course, physical or gestural prompts are removed (faded) as soon as possible. Other adaptations are included below. Some of these guidelines are patterned after those offered by Frostig (1974).

1. Carefully plan lessons consistent with classroom guidelines for behavior.

2. Incorporate some degree of movement education into each day's plan.

3. Alternate vigorous activities with more relaxing ones.

4. Give attention to all attributes of movement. None should be left out in the total week's plan.

5. Body positions should be varied in on-the-floor activities as well as during activities that involve locomotion.

6. Intersperse activities in a group with activities alone or with a partner. This variation creates opportunities for cooperation without too much repetition.

7. Equipment and music allow for creative variations but should not be a part of every lesson. Children need time to concentrate on their own bodily actions.

8. Conscious teaching of concepts does not need to be included in every activity. Instead, concepts should integrate logically into the day's schedule.

9. Care must be taken to allow for repetition in and modeling when giving directions to children who may be delayed perceptually or linguistically. Move from the known to the unknown and from the simple to the complex. Do not expect transfer from one activity to another.

10. Use physical, tactile, and verbal prompting as needed. Break tasks into simple, sequential steps. Give positive reinforcement with each step of progress. Be patient with those who are slow or reluctant. Vocabulary must be kept within the children's level. Do not expect understanding of the verbal labels "left" and "right."

11. All young children, especially those with handicaps, need adequate rest periods. Do not try to cover too much at once or continue an activity for too long.

12. Children who have difficulty paying attention and/or controlling bodily movements should experience varied but structured activities. Activities should be simple and free from distractions. Eye contact should be maintained. Be gentle but firm. Do not give the child a choice if a choice is not intended. For example, saying, "Do you want to ____" allows the child to say "No."

13. If a child is visually impaired, be certain to use his or her name when verbally directing activities. Minimize eyestrain by not standing where the child must look into a glare. Give these children an extra dose of body awareness activities.

14. Visual cues such as "stop" and "go" signs in red and green are not only attention getters but also assist those with hearing impairments. Also be certain hearing impaired children can read your lips when giving directions. Be certain that shadows are not in your face and stand relatively still. Be certain to get the child's attention before beginning an activity. Withdrawal or hyperactivity can be the result of not being able to distinguish words.

15. Physically handicapped children should be included whenever possible. For example, when running under a parachute, children can be pushed under. When possible, substitute a sitting or lying position for a standing position.

16. Most important of all is the need for lessons to be enjoyed by everyone. Teachers should not attempt activities that involve movement and noise if they are not in a mood to tolerate what they create.

LESSON PLAN 5-1: A GROSS MOTOR LESSON

Goal: To develop body image; to increase awareness of moving in different directions (directionality)

Objectives: Given directions to move forward, backward, and "sideward," the children will do the following:
1. Individually do as directed when the teacher prompts (physically, gestural, or with additional words, as needed).
2. As a member of a group, follow the teacher's spoken and gestured signal.
3. As a member of a group, follow spoken directions (no gestures).
4. Throughout this lesson, individually will stop and remain still in the exact position they were in at that moment, when asked to "freeze." (this condition helps children learn to inhibit unnecessary movements.)

Procedure: Begin with children sitting in a line facing the teacher. Then the lesson may proceed according to the following steps (of course, variations will be determined by the individual needs of the children):
1. "Susie, come stand here" (point to a masking tape **X** on the floor).
2. "Good, now walk forward" (physically prompting and gesturing to Susie).
3. "Right, you walked forward. Thank you. You may sit down. Tommy, it's your turn. Come stand on the **X**."
4. "Tommy, can you walk backwards?" (Gesturing—but because Tommy begins to move backwards, no physical prompting is needed.)
5. "Tommy, you did that just the right way. You walked backwards."

Procedural notes: The teacher's enthusiasm and encouragement are of critical importance. The lessons will be individualized as each child's movements are observed. Physical prompts, gestures, and demonstrations will be faded as quickly as possible. Children will be encouraged to verbalize their understanding of their body movements through natural conversation as the activity progresses. Other considerations include the following:
1. Initially each child should be given a brief, individual turn. Children will learn from watching. Begin with the child who is most likely to succeed with little or no help. This child serves as a model for the others to follow.
2. Next, pair two children at a time to follow the directions. The children may be given the same or two different directions, depending on their stage of development. (Keep the activity moving.)

3. As soon as possible (but for some children this may take several days), have groups of 3 to 5 children moving at the same time.
4. To add variety, a 4/4 march or dance rhythm can be introduced with records, a drum, or by singing. A square dance "calling" format can be included with the help of another adult. Guide children as needed using modeling or prompting as well as calling the directions.
5. New directions should be introduced following this same sequence, before incorporating them into the "dance."

Lesson adaptions:
1. For the hearing impaired child:
   a. Be sure he/she can see your face and gestures.
   b. Place a child with normal hearing on either side.
   c. Let this child feel the drum or other musical instrument as the rhythm is played. It sometimes helps to set record players on the floor and let the child perform with bare or "stocking" feet.
2. For the visually impaired child:
   a. Use physical prompts until the verbal prompts can be followed. (Fade physical assists as soon as possible.)
   b. Assign a sighted partner. Holding hands will be helpful.
   c. Be certain the space used in free from "trip and fall" hazards.
3. For the physically impair ' child:
   a. Encourage as much participation as possible.
   b. Use supports (for example, walkers and crutches) as needed.
   c. Have an adult push a wheelchair, if necessary.
   d. Assign the child to be caller or drum beater.
4. For the slow learner:
   a. Continue the prompting as needed.
   b. Place excellent models beside the child.
   c. Give directions slowly and one at a time.
   d. Repeat directions as often as necessary (with kind enthusiasm).
   e. Demonstrate patience if the child cannot do what he or she could do the day before.
   f. Socially reward each small step of progress.

Movement skills and the self-image

It would be difficult to argue with the proposition that there is a relationship between the development of a positive self-image (self-esteem) and the development of competencies (Garwood, 1979). As the child develops physical competencies, general feelings of self-competency tend to result in increased social interaction, as well (Herkowitz, 1977; Johnson, Fretz, and Johnson, 1968).

What one thinks of oneself is partially based on one's concept of one's body or body-image that is a subpart of total self-image. Movement activities not only create awareness of bodily parts but also of how they function in relation to one another and what they can or cannot do. Helping children to understand their body and to feel good about it develops both competence and a positive self-image. Lesson Plan 5-1 is included as an illustration of an activity that develops awareness of one's body as it moves in space.

Movement skills and concept development

First encounters with the *use* of the right word with the associated activity are important. Conceptualization is a cognitive skill but having the concept is relatively useless unless the word

is associated with it. Knowing a concept involves grasping the associated ideas and connecting or pairing them with the correct words. For example, as a child crawls *through* a tunnel or puts the string *through* a bead, both visual-motor and knowledge-conceptual skills can be taught simultaneously. If the teacher repeatedly talks about what the child is doing as the event occurs, learning will result.

Time awareness. Learning to understand time concepts is difficult for young children. Yesterday is eons away, and tomorrow can be expected any minute. But the awareness of shorter time intervals can be taught. "Wait until you hear the bell" or "Hop to the desk" when combined with a concept phrase such as "After you hear the bell" can be effective. Listening to a specific number of claps before moving, combined with the teacher's use of "Before you move, listen for two claps" is both fun and important learning. Discovering the meaning of "first" as well as "last" happens most easily in the context of lining up, taking turns, and watching who is first and last. The sequence of events is an important discovery. Although there are many other interesting ways to teach children the order in which things occur, movement activities, games, and gross motor skill development lessons provide a natural high interest springboard from which to teach time awareness.

Space awareness. Becoming aware of space includes learning how to stay in one's own space and out of someone else's space. Many little children need to learn this. Teachers of young children often refer to "bumping behavior." Children bump into each other as well as the furniture and the walls. Recognition of themselves in relation to other people and objects is critical information. All of the prepositions can be taught as they jump *over*, crawl *through*, walk *around*, and skip *beside*. Movement within and around Hula-Hoops or on carpet squares provides opportunities to learn to understand "body space" with the help of concrete aids.

Shape and sizes. Outlining a shape on the floor with ropes and then standing around the edge helps children to understand the concept "circle" and "square" in more than one dimension. Most children enjoy crawling through large pipes. Discovering that these are cylinders and that each end is a big circle leads to a wider concept of shapes. Large plastic shapes on the floor can be used in a variety of ways. "Sit on the circle" and "Walk backwards to the little square" are much more interesting directions than "Point to the circle." By combining two or three directions, auditory sequential memory can be improved. "Walk to the circle, then hop to the little triangle and walk sideways to the square" can be enjoyed by children who are ready for longer directions.

Number awareness. Number names and numerals must be encountered in a great variety of ways before they become meaningful. Learning to count the number of children in an activity, to count equipment, and then match these one to one is basic to later arithmetic readiness. Movement games allow for many opportunities to count and see number relationships.

Standing in groups of two and then in groups of three helps children to recognize the meaning of those numbers. Jumping a specific number of times, clapping, rolling over, and crawling when the directions include a number are useful ways to practice numbers that are enjoyable.

Movement skills and language development

Teaching receptive language through movement is a way to combine the children's need for active play with following directions. The discussion about teaching concepts through movement included a number of ideas for receptive language teaching. As children learn to listen to the teacher, wait for a signal to begin to move, and to stop on signal, they are also learning attending skills. One of the most important skills young children need in early elementary school is careful listening. Children who have learned to wait and then listen before moving are more apt to be able to follow directions. Directions must be kept well within the listening capacity of the children. Although some of the time the directions will be given to a group of children, occasions for giving directions of different length and complexity to individual children should be provided.

Teaching expressive language skills during active lessons can take many forms. Children enjoy chanting games, where one group calls a direction and the other group responds. Classes enjoy a routine where first the children choose an action and then, together move about using the activity they have chosen while they sing "We are hopping, watch us hopping, slowly, slowly, quickly, quickly—Stop." Immediately, the child chosen as "question asker" says "What did we do?" with a strong accent on *we*. The hoppers respond "We hopped." As the children practice asking and answering questions during this activity, expressive language skills are improved. Their freedom to shout and chant as they move affords opportunities for the shy children to enter in without feeling conspicuous.

Auditory memory requires careful listening to what is said. Remembering statements long enough to repeat them is a part of many readiness activities. Children enjoy playing "messenger." This can be done in a small space, but it is much more fun out of doors. The teacher may tell the direction to one child who in turn moves as directed to the next child and repeats (delivers) the message. Some favorites include the following:

1. Roll up into a little ball, and roll on the grass.
2. Jump two times, then walk backwards to the tree.
3. Bounce the biggest ball two times, then throw it to _____.
4. Run through the tunnel, then go up the slide.
5. Jump three times.

For younger messengers and receivers of the message the directions should include just one statement, and adjectives should be kept to a minimum, for example, simply "Jump" or "Bounce the ball" rather than "Jump three times, and then bounce the ball." The directions must be something the messenger can remember and the listener can recall long enough to do what the messenger said.

Visual memory can be developed through procedures similar to those described under auditory memory. Stick figures showing various body positions can be used instead of spoken directions. Learning to look and imitate the positions of the figures is a big challenge at first. Pictures should be kept simple and demonstrate just one position. Children can also be taught the actions of various animals. Then, when they are shown the picture of the animal, it can be the signal to combine recall of the movement with recognition of the animal. Learning to look at the pictures and then recall the name of the action or the animal or both provides another opportunity to use movement experiences to nurture language.

Movement skills and music

Dancing, marching, imitating, and imagining are often more enjoyable with music. Most of the commercially prepared records and tapes move a bit too fast for preschoolers, at least at first. If so, sing the songs without the records, and say the directions first. Gradually, as their ability to listen and move quickly grows, the recording can be used. Some children feel lost with the recorded voice. Particularly young children with mild hearing losses or perceptual problems find recorded voices difficult to understand.

Rhythm bands, whether they include real instruments or pans with spoons, are exciting to children. Banging on something is really an excellent way to develop awareness of body movement. The music may not be concert hall quality, but it certainly pleases the performers. Learning to make different kinds of noises by stamping feet loudly and then tip-toeing quietly lead to other kinds of body awareness.

Nelson (1977, 1978) has published a number of books to assist teachers in movement skills learning with the accompaniment of music. She cautions that because it is difficult to define

---

LOCOMOTOR AND NONLOCOMOTOR CHALLENGES

The following locomotor and nonlocomotor movements may require some direct teaching of the various skills before using the skill in the movement challenge.

Locomotor challenges
1. Move about the room using any movement you wish. On signal, freeze.
2. Be a giant, dwarf, or a witch as you move.
3. Move about the room using different swimming movements.
4. Move so one foot is always off the ground.
5. Run with fast tiny steps.
6. Move like popcorn popping.
7. As you run, bounce as high as you can.
8. Cross your feet over each other as you walk.
9. It has just rained. Leap over the mud puddles you see.

Nonlocomotor challenges
1. Make yourself big and on signal make yourself small.
2. Make shapes using arms and legs.
3. Make angels in the snow
4. Make different kinds of bridges with your body.
5. Show different ways to twist your body.
6. Alternate curling and stretching movements.

Combinations of locomotor and nonlocomotor challenges
1. Run, leap, and roll.
2. Run, collapse, and roll.
3. Twist and lift.
4. Twist and smile.
5. Lift and grin.
6. Hop, turn around, and shake.
7. Run, change direction, and collapse.
8. Hop, make a shape, and balance.
9. Rock, jump high, and sit down.
10. Rock and twist.
11. Curl, roll, and jump.
12. Twirl and make a statue.
13. Show us how waves come in on the beach.
14. Kneel and balance.
15. Kneel and sway.
16. Stretch like a rubber band. Snap back.
17. Blow up like a balloon. Let the air out.
18. Blow up like a balloon. Let the balloon burst.
19. Twist and untwist, slow one way and fast the other.
20. Click your heels in different ways.

Reprinted with permission of Karin Adams, LeClaire School, Edwardsville, Illinois.

dances or other rhythmic activities in terms of age, teachers must carefully think through their children's developmental characteristics. Even the most appealing jingle can frustrate children if the accompanying movements are too difficult. For children with special needs, she suggests beginning with the most simple and gradually working up to the more difficult songs or games. Reluctant children may need a personal invitation to join by offering them your hand. If they do not accept, they should not be forced to join. Rather, she suggests the use of song games that invite children to join by name.

Movement skills and imagination

Children often need help in imaging things as some have had little opportunity to pretend. Pretending while sitting still is not very satisfactory for them. See *Locomotor and Nonlocomotor Challenges* on p. 139 for a list of several imagination stimulating locomotor and nonlocomotor challenges. Children also enjoy pretending to be engineers on trains, drivers of buses, animals, and robots. Dress clothes add to the fun but are not really necessary. Films and film strips can start an idea. Stories and flannel board materials can lead to stimulating ideas. Pretending to put out a fire with an imaginary hose is almost as exciting as the real thing, and much safer.

A series of pictures can be used that show firemen, pilots, farmers, and policemen at work. Children discover the motions these people make through a combination of seeing real people, films, and pictures. Then, they take turns "pretending." Gradually, they become more creative. The fireman has to put out a fire on the roof, so he stretches up high. Next, the fire is in the basement, so he aims the hose down low. A robot, walking with stiff legs, may move very slowly. Then as someone "turns the controls" he moves faster or even more slowly. Although the teacher may need to suggest ways to move at first, imagination improves quickly.

Because so many teachers think they cannot encourage imagination and creativity through movement without being musicians, they sometimes do not try. Cherry (1971) offers step-by-step assistance to teachers who are "nonmusicians." She gives specific guidelines to assist children to originate their own ways of moving and exploring body capabilities. Motor and movement activities combine with imagination to enrich learning of self and space.

SUMMARY

Gross and fine motor skills, self-help skills, and movement activity deserve conscious inclusion in the preschool curriculum. Motor skill development helps promote a child's self-image while stimulating mastery and self-control. Thus growth of motor skills should not be taken for granted or overlooked as a possible contributor to certain components of perceptual, concept, language, and social development.

Preschool teachers need to be alert to the sequential trends in motor development. Knowing a child's level of sequential development enables concentrated instruction and practice to relate to individual needs. For the learning disabled child, concentrated effort on motor skill development helps remediate some forms of perceptual deficits. Although not all perception is motor-related, perceptual-motor tasks form some bridges with language and concept development.

Special attention should be given to differentiating between performance outcomes and behavioral attempts. Although two children may both fail to catch a ball when tossed to them, differences in their attempts may reveal that they are at different stages in their acquisition of motor skills. For self-help skills teachers and parents are encouraged to consider reverse chaining and perhaps oversized clothing when children need more than the usual help. Developmental checklists combined with task analysis help focus on motor skill levels and needs of individual children. Children who seem to be resisting experimentation with normal motor skills can be physically prompted and positively reinforced whenever an attempt is made. Several suggestions are offered to link motor skill development to development of concepts, language, and imagination.

DISCUSSION TOPICS AND ACTIVITIES

1. Thoroughly review at least three developmental checklists. Pay special attention to the sequential order of the motor skills. Adopt a checklist that seems to be complete or compile your own. Observe a normal child and a handicapped child or children of two different ages. Were you able to detect differences in skill development? If not, your checklist needs to be broken into smaller steps.

2. Now take a major skill like throwing, and break it into subskills as directed in Chapter 4. Sequence these skills. After your task analysis is complete, try to teach the skill to a friend or a child. What subskills did you leave out? Did the order of your skills need to be changed? With adults, skipping is a good skill to analyze.

3. Interview or ask a physical and occupational therapist to visit class. Ask for information, for example, of positioning techniques, adaptive equipment, and special teaching procedures. Be certain to ask them to explain their view of motor development.

4. Investigate the relationship between motor skills and body awareness. Begin a file of activities especially designed to teach body awareness and contribute to self-esteem.

5. There are several suggestions in the literature that training in perceptual skills may not be defensible. Research this matter. Discuss and debate the issue with classmates.

6. Try to explain the sequential trends of motor development to another person, deriving and using specific examples. If you can explain them clearly to another, then you probably understand them well.

7. Research and discuss the various handicapping conditions, such as cerebral palsy, muscular dystrophy, and visual impairment, that have an impact on motor skill development. If possible, invite a member of the community who has experienced difficulties from such an impairment to discuss ways teachers can be of assistance.

8. Plan a motor lesson. Be creative. Consider parachutes, isometric exercises, and dances. Teach this lesson to your classmates. Discover the fun some movement activities really are. Do your lesson with children.

9. Design a playground that would be suitable for children

with a variety of handicaps. The annotated reference by Jones can help you to begin.

ANNOTATED REFERENCES

Arnheim, D. D., and Sinclair, W. A. *The clumsy child: A program of motor therapy.* St. Louis: The C.V. Mosby Co., 1979.
This book was developed to assist practitioners in their efforts to help children who are physically awkward, to achieve and enjoy motor skills. Teachers will find the analysis of skills called "activity progressions" to be extremely useful in the construction of a developmental curriculum checklist and corresponding lesson plans.

Cherry, C. *Creative movement for the developing child: A nursery school handbook for non-musicians.* Belmont, Calif.: Fearon Pitman Publishers, Inc., 1971.
Indeed, a nonmusician can effectively orchestrate the creative movement exercises described in this useful handbook. Guidelines are offered on how to arrange the environment and the day to promote creativity, to help the nonparticipant, and to encourage the usual developmental skills. Nursery songs, with or without accompanying music, set the stage for the variety of movement activities presented.

Espenschade, A. S., and Eckert, H. M. *Motor development.* Columbus, Ohio: Charles E. Merrill Publishing Co., 1973.
This paperback text serves as an excellent, well-documented resource for those wishing to understand the processes of physical growth and the interrelationships of structure and function. A chapter is devoted to the development of motor behavior during the early childhood years from ages 2 to 6.

Frost, J. L., and Klein, B. L. *Children's play and playgrounds.* Boston: Allyn & Bacon, Inc., 1979.
Coming from the child development point of view, these authors give instructions for planning and constructing playgrounds to encourage activities. Photographs, diagrams, lists of materials, and tools assist in the design of playgrounds that are sensitive to the needs of children. Of great value is the chapter on play and playgrounds for handicapped children.

Frostig, M., and Maslow, P. *Movement education: Theory and practice.* Chicago: Follett Publishing Corp., 1970.
Even though this book is becoming dated, it remains an excellent resource for teachers who wish to develop programs of movement education that truly consider individualized development. Research current to the time is well summarized. Teachers will be pleased with the ideas for specific activities designed to promote coordination, rhythm, flexibility, speed, agility, balance, strength, and endurance without fear of failure or competition. A handy file of cards that contains some of these and other activities can also be obtained through the same publishing company. They are called *Move, Grow, Learn.*

Geddes, D. *Physical activities for individuals with handicapping conditions.* St. Louis: The C.V. Mosby Co., 1974. This book is a relatively inexpensive, excellent resource for anyone needing to adapt motor activities to individuals with special needs. A practical approach is adopted and the contents can be applied to physical activities in a variety of settings. Specific suggestions are given for children with intellectual, visual, hearing, orthopedic, and emotional problems. This book is "chuck full" of the helpful hints that make the difference between a good lesson and a super one. A list of equipment, supplies, and resources is included in the Appendix.

Jones, M. Physical facilities and environments. In J. Jordan, A. Hayden, M. Karnes, and M. Wood (Eds.), *Early childhood education for exceptional children.* Reston, Va.: Council for Exceptional Children, 1977. This chapter presents a clear analysis and description of several well-planned First Chance and other programs' playgrounds and equipment. The requirements for suitable environments for handicapped children are discussed along with detailed illustrations. Resources for more in-depth information are included.

Ridenour, M.V. (Ed.). *Motor development: Issues and applications.* Princeton, N.J.: Princeton Book Co., Publishers, 1978. This book, intended for college students, is presented in three parts: a theoretical model of growth and development, discussion of contemporary issues such as sex-role expectations and memory processes, and practical applications of research. It is a theory-based resource with a developmental approach to application. Separate chapters are devoted to the design and evaluation of play spaces and developmental task analysis. A method for locating motor development literature is included in the Appendix.

Sinclair, C. *Movement of the young child: Ages two to six:* Columbus, Ohio: Charles E Merrill Publishing Co., 1973. This brief paperback provides helpful suggestions on how to assess children's developmental levels through observation and how to select and use equipment. Case studies and photographs illustrate the differences in children's movement characteristics. Ways to integrate a program of movement into daily experiences are discussed.

Skinner, L. *Motor development in the preschool years.* Springfield, Ill.: Charles C Thomas, Publishers, 1979. The material contained in this guide will definitely assist teachers to include motor activities in any preschool curriculum with a minimum of effort. The attributes of motor development are explained clearly and concisely. Numerous absolutely delightful games and songs are included. Of particular interest is the analysis of cutting and the inclusion of skills labeled "preball skills."

Ward, M., Cartwright, G.P., Cartwright, C.A., and Campbell, J. *Diagnostic teaching of preschool and primary children.* University Park: The Pennsylvania State University Press, 1973. This handbook was designed to be used in college level computer-assisted instruction. A number of broad topics related to the prescriptive process are covered. Of particular interest is the section that applies their diagnostic teaching model to motor development. Unique movement pattern checklists complete with clear illustrations and offered for standing, walking, running, kicking, jumping, hopping, and skipping. Use of these checklists encourages novice observers to focus on motor skill pattern elements. These serve as excellent devices to train astute observation skills and task analysis. Activity suggestions are also included.

REFERENCES

Ayres, J. *Sensory integration and learning disorders.* Los Angeles: Western Psychological Services, 1972

Barsch, R. *Achieving perceptual-motor efficiency.* Seattle: Special Child Publications, 1967.

Barsch, R. *Enriching perception and cognition.* Seattle: Special Child Publications, 1968.

Cherry, C. *Creative movement for the developing child.* Belmont, Calif.: Lear Siegler, Inc./Fearon Pitman Publishers, Inc., 1971.

Copeland, M., Ford, L., and Solon, N. *Occupational therapy for cerebral palsied children.* Baltimore: University Park Press, 1976.

Cratty, B. *Developmental sequences of perceptual-motor tasks.* Freeport, N.Y.: Educational Activities, 1967.

Cratty B. *Perceptual-motor behavior and educational processes.* Springfield, Ill.: Charles C Thomas, Publisher, 1969.

Cratty, B. *Perceptual and motor development in infants and children.* New York: Macmillan, Inc., 1970.

Cratty, B. *Active learning: Games to enhance academic abilities.* Englewood Cliffs, N.J.: Prentice-Hall, Inc., 1971.

Cruickshank, W. *The brain-injured child in home, school, and community.* Syracuse, N.Y.: Syracuse University Press, 1967.

Dubose, R. Working with sensorily impaired children, Part I: Visual impairments. In S. Garwood (Ed.), *Educating young handicapped children.* Germantown, Md.: Aspen Systems Corp., 1979.

Erikson, E. *Childhood and society.* New York: W.W. Norton & Co., Inc., 1963.

Espenschade, A., and Eckert, H. *Motor development.* Columbus, Ohio: Charles E Merrill Publishing Co., 1967.

Finnie, N. *Handling the young cerebral palsied child at home.* New York: E.P. Dutton and Co., 1975.

Fredericks, H., Riggs, C., Furey, T., Grove, D., Moore, W., McDonnell, J., Jordan, E., Hanson, W., Baldwin, V., and Wadlow, M. *The teaching research curriculum for moderately and severely handicapped.* Springfield, Ill.: Charles C Thomas, Publishers, 1976.

Frankenburg, W., Dodds, J., Fandal, A., Kazuk, E., and Cohrs, M. *Denver Developmental Screening Test.* Denver: University of Colorado Medical Center, 1975.

Frostig, M., and Maslow, P. *Movement education: Theory and practice.* Chicago: Follett Publishing Co., 1970.

Frostig, M. *Movement education, Its theory and practice.* Workshop presented at The Marianne Frostig Center of Educational Therapy, Los Angeles, May 1974.

Garwood, S. (Ed.). *Educating young handicapped children.* Rockville, Md.: Aspen Systems Corp., 1979.

Garhardt, L. *Moving and knowing.* Englewood Cliffs, N.J.: Prentice-Hall, Inc., 1973.

Getman, G. The visuomoter complex in the acquisition of language skills. In J. Hellmoth (Ed.), *Learning disorders* (Vol. 1). Seattle: Special Child Publications, 1965.

Getman, G., Kane, E., and McKee, G. *Developing learning readiness* program. Manchester, Mo.: McGraw-Hill, Inc., 1968.

Hammill, D., and Bartel, N. *Teaching children with learning and behavior problems.* Boston: Allyn & Bacon, Inc., 1975.

Hammill, D., and Larsen, S.C. The relationship of selected auditory perceptual skills and reading ability. *Journal of Learning Disabilities,* 1974, 7, 429-435.

Herkowitz, J. Movement experiences for preschool children. *Journal of Physical Education and Recreation,* 1977, 48, 15-16.

Herkowitz, J. Sex-role expectations and motor behavior of the young child. In M. Ridenour (Ed.), *Motor development: Issues and applications.* Princeton, N.J.: Princeton Book Co., Publishers, 1978.

Hohmann, M., Banet, B., and Weikart, D. *Young children in action.* Ypsilanti, Mich.: The High/Scope Press, 1979.

Hunter, M. The role of physical education in child development and learning. *Journal of Health, Physical Education, and Recreation,* 1968, 39, 56-58.

Johnson, W., Fretz, B., and Johnson, J. Changes in self-concepts during a physical development program. *The Research Quarterly,* 1968, 39, 560-565.

Kephart, N. Perceptual-motor aspects of learning disabilities. *Exceptional Children,* 1964, 31, 201-206.

Kephart, N. *The slow learner in the classroom.* Columbus, Ohio: Charles C Merrill Publishing Co., 1971.

Knobloch, H., and Pasamanick, B. *Gesell and Amatruda's Developmental Diagnosis.* Hagerstown, Md.: Harper & Row, Publishers, Inc. 1974.

Larsen, S., and Hammill, D. The relationship of selected visual perceptual skills to academic abilities. *Journal of Special Education,* 1975, 9, 281-291.

Lerner, J., Mardell-Czudnowski, C., and Goldenberg, D. *Special education for the early childhood years.* Englewood Cliffs, N.J.: Prentice-Hall, Inc., 1981.

Mercer, C. *Children and adolescents with learning disabilities.* Columbus, Ohio: Charles E Merrill Publishing Co., 1979.

Nelson, E. *Movement games for children of all ages.* New York: Sterling Publishing Co., Inc., 1977.

Nelson, E. *Dancing games for children of all ages.* New York: Sterling Publishing Co., Inc., 1978.

O'Donnell, P. *Motor and haptic learning.* Sioux Falls, S.D.: Adapt Pres, Inc., 1969.

Piazza, R. *Three models of learning disabilities.* Guilford, Conn.: Special Learning Corp., 1979.

Popovich, D. *A prescriptive behavioral checklist for the severely and profoundly retarded.* Baltimore: University Park Press, 1977.

Portage Preschool Project. *The Portage guide to early education.* Portage, Wis.: Portage Preschool Project, 1969.

Strauss, A., and Lehtinen, L. *Psychopathology and education of the brain-injured child.* New York: Grune & Stratton, Inc., 1947.

Strauss, A., and Werner, H. Disorders of conceptual thinking in the brain-injured child. *Journal of Nervous and Mental Disease,* 1942, 96, 153-172.

Taft, L. Clinical appraisal of motor functions. In L. Taft and M. Lewis (Eds.), *Developmental disabilities in the preschool child.* Symposium presented by Rutgers Medical School, Educational Testing Service, and Johnson and Johnson Baby Products, Chicago 1979.

Tanner, J. Physical growth. In P. Mussen (Ed.), *Carmichael's manual of child psychology.* New York: John Wiley & Sons, Inc., 1970.

Voyat, G. *Piaget on development and learning.* Workshop presented through Southern Illinois University at Edwardsville, 1980.

Westphal, R. (Ed.). *Human development: 2½ to 6 years.* Costa Mesa, Calif.: Concept Media, 1975.

Wolff, P. Theoretical issues in the development of motor skills. In L. Taft and M. Lewis (Eds.), *Developmental disabilities in the preschool child.* Symposium presented by Rutgers Medical School, Educational Testing Service, and Johnson and Johnson Baby Products, Chicago 1979.

Nurturing speech, language, and conceptual skills

Throughout history man has puzzled over the origins of language. In some cultures, language is thought to have magical properties. Repetition of certain words and phrases is used to ward off demons and prevent disasters. Myths, often similar, abound across cultures. Many cultures in widely separated parts of the world have some version of the Tower of Babel to explain that there are different languages.

Where and how did speech and language begin? Historically, belief in the divine origin of language finds similar explanations all over the world and in nearly every culture. Judeo-Christian belief has it that Adam chose the names for things. Egyptians believe that their god, Thoth, gave man speech. Hindus and Brahmans give the credit to women. Perhaps they were the first to notice that in a number of cultures girls often begin to talk at an earlier age than their brothers.

Even so, no one really knows how each infant rapidly discovers the power and uses of language and then proceeds to learn how to talk and understand what is said. This chapter will be concerned with the ways in which theorists believe speech and language are acquired, explanation of the various elements of speech and language, and descriptions of the environmental and personal conditions most conducive to the enhancement of these skills. Specific techniques for the development of speech, language, and conceptual skills are offered. Finally, attention is given to some special problems. To begin, *Definitions of Some Language-Related Terms,* which appears on p. 146, provides an introduction to some of the frequently used terms within this area of interest.

HOW IS LANGUAGE LEARNED?

Learning to talk and understand language happens quickly and with little direct evidence of a teaching-learning process. But it does not just happen. Professionals who study both psychology and language (psycholinguists) do not agree about how communication skills develop. Some feel very strongly that language learning is biologically inherent or innate within the human infant. Others believe that imitation plays the major role, while some suggest language is a natural outgrowth of expanding thinking skills.

Nativists say that babies are born preconditioned to learn language universals (Chomsky, 1957; Lenneberg, 1967; McNeill, 1966). They emphasize that all over the world, no matter what language they are learning, children learn similar features in essentially the same manner.

Behaviorists or associationists insist that stimulus-reinforcement and imitation-practice explain how language and speech are acquired. Skinner (1957) is the best known advocate of this position.

Cognitivists constitute a third major group of students of language acquisition. They propose a process theory of language development. In part, this theory is a reaction to the extreme positions taken by either nativists or behaviorists. This third position explains language learning on the basis of underlying cognitive abilities rather than an innate ability related solely to language learning. Cognitivists such as Bloom (1973), Bowerman (1976), Brown, (1973), and Slobin (1979), agree that children do learn language. But they feel that cognitive processing interacts with the stimulation of the environment and that observing, experiencing, and discovering rules enable children to learn language. They disagree with the nativist position, which attributes little significance to the influence of the language learning environment.

Dale (1976) underscores the fragmented theoretical bases that explain how children learn language in the following statement:

> The child's language gradually unfolds in an ever more elaborate system. How does she do it? We do not have any complete theories that can be seriously considered as explanations for syntactic development

DEFINITIONS OF SOME LANGUAGE-RELATED TERMS

language—"A language is a code whereby ideas about the world are represented through a conventional system of arbitrary signals for communication" (Bloom and Lahey, 1978).

speech—A vehicle for conveying language. Normal speech is characterized by the correct production (articulation) of speech sounds, the maintenance of appropriate speech rhythm (fluency), and the control of the voice (vocal production).

cognition—The process or act of "knowing." Perception, memory, conceptualization, and problem solving are all involved in cognition. Theorists disagree about the relationship between language learning and cognitive development. Language is a prerequisite to efficient communication of what one is cognizant of (knows) to others.

concept—An expression of a rule that organizes the stimuli in one's experiences (Siegel, 1975). Verbal concepts or symbolic labels enable individuals to classify and retrieve information.

grammar—The linguistic rules that make it possible for those who share a knowledge of those rules to communicate. A finite set of rules in each language makes it possible to understand (receive communication) as well as to create (express) an infinite number of utterances.

receptive language ability—The ability to understand the intent and meaning of someone's effort to communicate.

expressive language ability—The ability to send a communication according to a system of rules and in a manner that can be understood by others who know the rules.

prescriptive grammar—The accepted rules of a language that determine how people who speak that language should speak and write to be "correct."

descriptive grammar—The delineation or explanation of what speakers of a language must know to use that language.

auditory discrimination—The ability to differentiate between and among various sounds and to hear likenesses and differences.

auditory memory—The ability to recognize and/or recall stimuli presented orally; demonstrated by being able to follow reasonable directions.

auditory figure ground—The ability to distinguish sound in the foreground from sounds in the background.

auditory association—The ability to draw relationships or make associations from what is heard to what is seen or can be said.

auditory closure—The ability to identify a word from an incomplete word presented orally.

visual discrimination—The ability to differentiate between and among various shapes, sizes, colors, numbers, and/or letters.

visual memory—The ability to retain and recall symbols or information that has been presented visually.

linguistic performance—Refers to both understanding what is said and to talking. Performance can be observed, tested, and measured.

linguistic competence—Refers to everything one knows about language. It is the undergirding knowledge that enables one to "perform," but it cannot be measured directly.

in toto. Instead we have a mixed bag of mechanisms, processes and strategies that may each play a role (p. 137).

WHEN DO SPEECH AND LANGUAGE DEVELOP?

"Speech and language develop systematically, beginning with the birth cry" (Weiss and Lillywhite, 1976, p. 42). Infants a few days old detect differences in speech sounds (Eimas, Sigueland, Jusczyk, and Vigorito, 1971). By the time they are a few months old they are soothed by mother's voice. At age 6 months they imitate their own noises, and at age 12 months most babies understand at least 10 words and say 2 or 3 words (Appendix B).

Traditionally it was believed that the period between the production of first words and the use of two- and three-word sentences was rather a dormant time for language learning. More recent studies describe this brief period as one where major cognitive and linguistic development occurs (Slobin, 1979). By the time they are age 4, normally developing children have acquired the basic knowledge of all of the subskills of language. They use grammar much like that of adults, and their articulation of speech sounds is accurate enough for everyone to understand them.

Failure to develop all of these interrelated skills on schedule can be expected to interfere seriously with later success in school. As Weiss and Lillywhite (1976) say in the introduction to their book, parents and professionals need to help children when help is needed "so that some day there will not be over twenty million people in this country who have communication disorders" (p. 3).

WHAT ARE THE SUBSKILLS OF LANGUAGE?

It is important to keep in mind that the separation of language into subskills is arbitrary. As more attention is given to the study of the way in which children learn communication skills,

the complexity of the skills involved becomes increasingly impressive. Presented in the box on p. 148 are definitions of the speech and language subskills that should be developing during the preschool years.

Pragmatics

Learning how language functions in social situations (pragmatic functions) is essential. Saying the wrong thing at the right time can be troublesome to young children as well as adults. Children can be heard saying things differently to their preschool peers than they do to their mothers. Not only the manner in which they speak but also what they talk about differs.

Speakers and listeners follow a set of unconscious guidelines as they talk to each other. These include such behaviors as looking at each other and looking away and waiting for the speaker to pause before beginning to speak. These behaviors require attention to subtle cues. Facial expressions and body language appropriate to particular circumstances must be learned. Because of this nonverbal communication, children are often quick to perceive insincerity.

The situation, the specific topic, the relation of listener to speaker, and many other variables determine *what* is said as well as *how* it is said. Children who have not acquired these pragmatic skills stand out as "different" in preschool groups almost as much as those whose speech is unintelligible. But it is more difficult for parents and teachers to pinpoint how and why they are different.

Hopper and Naremore (1978, p. 63) present a useful introduction to pragmatics. They list the following five ways in which the situational context influences how a person communicates:

1. The people present
2. What was just previously said
3. The topic of conversation
4. The task that communication is being used to accomplish
5. The times and places in which the communication occurs

SUBSKILLS OF LANGUAGE—KEY CONCEPTS

pragmatics—The gamut or whole range of functions language serves in social contexts. Anthropologists as well as psycholinguists and sociologists study the way in which people use language in their efforts to communicate. Factors such as the situation, the relations of speaker to hearer, and the speaker's intent influence the manner of communication. Learning to take turns in conversation as well as recognizing what is appropriate or inappropriate in specific situations involves the development of pragmatic language (communication) skills.

semantics—The meanings of words. Meaning is influenced by use and the place in the utterance where the word is used.

syntax—The rules that organize morphemes. Without the rules, utterances would be unintelligible. *Grammar* and *syntax* are terms usually used interchangeably in traditional language ("grammar") teaching in English classes. Current theories define three major divisions of syntax: morphological rules, phrase structural rules, and transformational operations. The study of *syntax* is the study of sentence structure.

morphology—Morphology is one aspect of syntax. It is the facet that enables speakers to create words from morphemes, for example, S is a morpheme when it is used with another word to indicate "more than one." Psycholinguists disagree on a definition of morpheme. One frequently used description of a morpheme is "a minimal unit of meaning." Thus *boy* is one morpheme, and *boys* is composed of two "minimal units of meaning." Morphemes provide inflectional information as well as content information.

phonology—The sound patterns of a language. In all languages song patterns can be found that convey meaning. For example, in English a rising tone at the end of an utterance indicates a question has been asked. Pitch changes that convey meaning are referred to as prosodic features (prosody) or suprasegmentals. Speech sounds or phonemes are the smallest discernable segments of speech. English has approximately **44** phonemes (varied by regional differences). Prosody (song patterns) and phonemes (individual speech sound) are two facets of phonology.

Observation suggests that young children readily use these contextual clues to enable themselves to understand much more than words alone.

Semantics

Learning the meanings of words (semantics) is very dependent on interactions with adults who use words in a way that makes their meaning clear. For example, talking about the ocean to a child who has never seen one will result in little understanding of "ocean." Young children do not learn word meanings through vicarious experiences. Things they see must be named while they are looking at them and touching them. Activities must be described while they are happening. And then, they must have the opportunity to experiment with the words to discover if they have learned what each word really means.

Since most words have more than one referent, children have quite a task. They must discover that the other words in the sentence (or even the sentences said before or after the particular sentence containing the new word) may also change the meanings. The following sentences are some of the contexts in which a child hears his or her mother use the word *run:* (1) "I have a run in this stocking." (2) "Let's run to the store." (3) "Run fast and catch Daddy." The child who distinguishes these different meanings is learning some of the complexities of semantic rules.

In spite of the many things to be learned, children progress rapidly. By the time they are age 3, some recognize nearly 1,000 words. By age 5 they understand at least twice that many. They use words creatively to express ideas and ask questions. They invent delightful variations adults would never think of, and they do it all with considerable skill.

Syntax

Learning the rules for correct word order in sentences in one aspect of syntax. Syntax includes knowing that it is correct to say "We are going to the ball game" rather than "Game ball to going we the are." Of course, children learning to utter syntactically correct sentences are really just trying to communicate. They are not consciously practicing the rules they are learning.

But as they learn, children everywhere develop in essentially the same manner. Somewhere between ages 9 and 14 months most of them use single words to communicate. By age 2, they string two or three words together, and by age 4 they are creating grammatically correct sentences that follow the rules of the native language they have been hearing and practicing. Their word order is not different from the adults with whom they have been living. They rearrange word orders to ask questions. They may ramble on, just as adults do. But the word order is obviously rule governed.

Morphology

Learning the rules for changing the form of individual words (rules of morphology or accidence) makes it possible for children to understand and communicate singular and plural meaning. They discover when to "add s," when

to "add es," and when to change the word "man to men." They discover how to form possessives, and how to use number and tense in verbs (for example, he walks, they walk, he walked, he is walking, or we walked). Children learn comparatives (long, longer, longest) and how to add prefixes and suffixes to alter meaning. They use pronouns as possessives (his or hers), as subjects (I, he, or they), and as objects (him or her).

As they learn these rules of morphology, children make many interesting mistakes. They overgeneralize, saying "We wented" and "The mans." However, their errors are logical and confirm that they are not just imitating what they are hearing. They are learning rules. Exceptions to the rules, such as irregular verbs and irregular plurals will be learned also but a bit later. Often very young children can be heard using irregular verbs correctly (men, ran, or fell). As they begin to internalize language rules, they may change to rule-governed forms (mans, runned, or falled). Then the adult models around them must help them to discover these exceptions to the rules all over again.

Phonology

Learning the rules of the sound systems of speech and language (phonology) involves discovering that pitch changes and rhythm changes make a difference along with the individual speech sounds or phonemes. The song patterns (prosodic features or suprasegmentals) are learned very early. Babies just a few months old babble in ways that sound almost like the patterns adults use. A conscientious listener can hear questions and statements in the intonation patterns of babies long before words can be heard. Careful listening will also detect exclamations! They sound much like a radio that is too soft to understand but transmits the rhythm and pitch changes.

As they near 6 months of age, many babies begin to babble in syllables that include some of the phonemes (speech sounds) of the adult system. Their production is usually somewhat wide of the mark. By age 1, they have learned to use some sounds accurately some of the time, and first words begin to appear. Skill in producing speech sounds accelerates rapidly during the preschool years.

However, accuracy or production is highly dependent on being able to hear the targets they are trying to produce clearly, accurately, and often. They do not need to hear the sounds in isolation or even in syllables. Hearing them in words and connected speech (phrases and sentences) appears to be enough. But they do need to hear the phonemes, and they do need lots of opportunity to practice them. Most children learn to produce nearly all of the 44 phonemes of English by the time they are 4 years old.

LANGUAGE LEARNING IS RULE LEARNING

Recall that each of the subskills involves learning rules. Although children must learn to imitate and recall the production of phonemes (speech sounds), they rarely imitate whole sentences. From the beginning, they generate their own meaningful utterances. And from the beginning, psycholinguists can identify rules they are using. Slobin (1979, p. 99) summarizes this in the following way:

> We can be fairly sure that a child has some rule system if his production is regular, if he extends these regularities to new instances, and if he can detect deviations from regularity in his own speech and the speech of others.

Slobin emphasizes that this does not suggest that children can state the explicit rules they are unconsciously using to understand and talk to others. Even after years of formal lessons in grammar, most people still find it difficult to recognize the rules they use, even though they spoke in grammatically correct ways before they were 4 years old.

How do young linguists work?

When linguists study a new language in an attempt to discover the rules that govern it, they look for regularities and basic structures. Apparently, children also do this. Muma (1978, p. 148) observes, "Verbal imitation does play a role in language learning, but not the central role as had been previously thought. Induction of latent structure is considerably more important." He notes that the induction of latent structure appears almost to be a mystical ability.

This inductive structuring is evidenced in the fact that few people try to make the rules obvious and explicit for children. Rather, children figure out the rules and how to use them from brief, spontaneous contacts with them. Just as adult linguists form hypotheses and test them, children seem to formalize their hunches, try them out, and change them when they do not work. This manner of learning language appears to be universal, regardless of the language being learned (Dale, 1976).

NECESSARY CONDITIONS FOR LANGUAGE LEARNING

Basic to all learning is the ability to receive a stimulus, attend to it, recognize it when it recurs, and recall it over time. Identifying, matching, and associating stimuli with specific events are requisite to early learning. Within the first month babies quiet when light levels or sound levels change. Soon, they will stop crying at the sound of familiar footsteps.

Reception is basic to perception. Unless the baby can receive (hear) sounds, it is not possible to recognize (perceive) them when they recur. It is for this reason that early detection of hearing problems is essential.

Stimulation plays a critical role. From babies' earliest weeks, native speakers of the language must provide something for them to listen to, and the environmental noise level must be low to enable them to hear soft sounds. Television, radio, stereo, and family conversations need to be quieted at least some of the time. If there is constant background noise, young learners may not hear the minute differences between and among speech sounds. They may miss the suprasegmentals (song patterns). The habit of attending to important stimuli may not develop as it should. Later, unless it is quiet enough for them to hear the difference between unvoiced consonants (for example, /t/ as in "hot" and /p/ as in "hop"), they may be unaware that those phonemes are present, let alone that they are different.

Practice, practice, practice. In a sense, during the early months, babies are practicing the musical features of speech. These reveal the first evidence of speechlike learning. If babies have an interested audience who play with the speech sounds with them (imitating and enjoying the interaction), learning will proceed more quickly. The complicated muscle movements that allow sound to be molded into some of the more than 40 English phonemes are strengthened through the practice of babbling.

This kind of practice usually is not planned. Just having a gurgling, cooing baby around prompts most adults to play the role of imitator and modeler without any conscious effort. But if they do not, or if vision or hearing problems interfere, development may lag.

Importance of a nurturing language environment. The importance of a nurturing language environment is sometimes underestimated. Chomsky (1980, p. 241) notes: "As for development, language grows in the child through mere exposure to an unorganized linguistic environment, without training or even any particular language-specific care." However, when Broen (1972) studied the way mothers talk to young children, she detected a unique style that was different from the way in which they spoke to older children and adults. She found the mothers' speech to be slower with pauses located at the end of sentences. A smaller range of vocabulary was used and often

repeated. The repetitions were linguistically meaningful and broken sentences were seldom spoken.

Broen stated, "Mothers' sentences seemed to fall into two major sentence patterns. One pattern is built on the imperative sentence and in general expands that sentence form in a variety of ways. The other sentence pattern includes variations and permutations of a 'be' sentence with that, this, it, there, or here. Mothers also used single-word grammatically incomplete responses in talking with their younger children" (p. 63).

Qualifications for these observations were provided. The study was conducted in a laboratory setting with mothers who had above average educations. This makes it impossible to generalize freely to the typical home environment of young children. But the consistent changes made by mothers when speaking to young children suggests that, at least in these circumstances, the child's language competency influenced both the style and complexity of the mother's input.

Other influences on language. Even though a child (1) may have excellent capacity for hearing, (2) is stimulated, (3) can practice, and (4) is nurtured, other factors may still influence speech and language learning. Remember, some theorists believe humans have an innate capacity for language learning. When young children appear to have language learning problems, it is thought that the predisposition to learn is still there and usually can be nurtured.

Cognitive processes undergird what is learned as well as when it is learned. Language learning involves communicating what is being thought. Piaget (1960) relates the acquisition of cognitive skills to biological stages of readiness. As a result, developmental stages are thought to remain the same, although the rate at which the stages succeed each other may vary.

In summarizing a chapter on language acquisition, Muma (1978, p. 208) emphasizes the interrelationship between the development of cognitive and language skills:

The literature on language learning has challenged several misconceptions. The notion of age norms is no longer acceptable as a way of indexing development. Developmental sequences *within* systems are more appropriate. The recent literature is showing an intimate relationship between cognitive-linguistic-communicative systems and processes in language learning. Moreover, it is revealing individual strategies of language learning.

CHARACTERISTICS AND CIRCUMSTANCES THAT INTERFERE WITH LANGUAGE LEARNING

The learning of language for some children is delayed or blocked because of one or more sequences of interference. The process of diagnosis and the effects of diagnostic labeling on parents can also interfere with learning (Fig. 6-1).

Characteristics that interfere

Hearing impairments. No matter how mild or how infrequent, hearing impairments interfere with the learning of speech and language. Deaf children can be taught to speak and to understand language, but the task is not an easy one. For children who do not hear normally to acquire oral communication skills, the help of highly trained parents and teachers is required. Deaf children are usually identified, although not as soon as one would hope. In the case of children with mild hearing losses, the cause of their lack of language development is often not recognized (Davis, 1977).

Children with mild hearing losses cannot hear all of the phonemes with equal clarity. The distorted speech pattern they hear is inconsistent and incorrect. As a result, their speech may include the song patterns of language, many of the vowels and some of the consonents, but it is unintelligible. Downs (1977) and Bess and McConnell (1981) discuss the effects of mild, intermittent hearing loss and the long-term negative interference with language development.

tive interference with language development.

If children fail to develop normal communication skills at expected ages, regardless of what other factors seem to be involved, their hearing should be checked and regularly rechecked by audiologists competent to use a variety of test equipment. If any hearing deficit is detected, the causes should be discovered and removed. If this is not possible, parents should receive guidance, and the child's language development should be monitored and directed by a speech-language pathologist or a trained teacher of the deaf. Children who are unable to hear normally during the first years of life are handicapped in all aspects of language and speech development. Davis (1977) says,

The effects of hearing loss are such that the longer the hearing impairment is undetected and untreated the more serious is the problem and the less likely it is to be remediated optimally (p. 27).

Chapter 3 pinpoints some high risk signals that all teachers should review often.

Auditory-perceptual impairments. Auditory-perceptual impairments are presumed to be the cause of specific language disorders in some children. A review of the literature on this topic (Lubert, 1981) notes that a diversity of labels and assessment instruments has led to some confusion. This article reports that these disorders have been studied by several disciplines, including neurology, psychiatry, psychology, speech pathology, audiology, and linguistics. Terms used include "developmental aphasia, congenital aphasia, aphasoid children, developmental dysphasia, language deficit, language delay, learning disability, verbal auditory agnosia, and central auditory dysfunction."

The perceptions and observations of the various specialists have led to different conclusions, theories, and remediation approaches. Lubert (1981, p. 7) reports, "The above research suggests that language-disordered children may be characterized by an impaired rate of processing

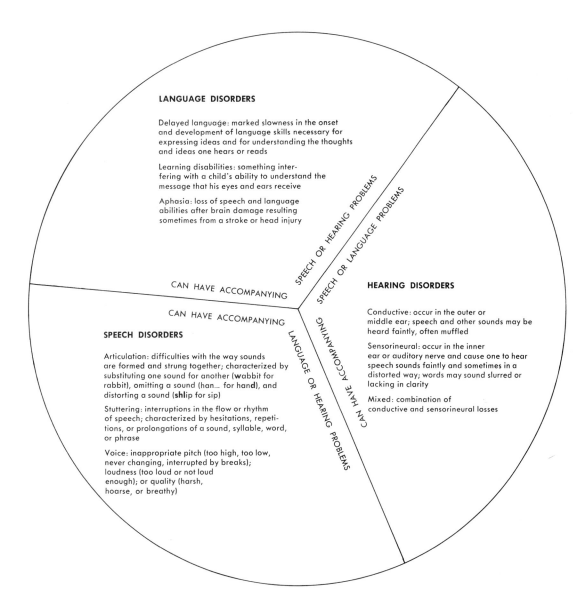

LANGUAGE DISORDERS

Delayed language: marked slowness in the onset and development of language skills necessary for expressing ideas and for understanding the thoughts and ideas one hears or reads

Learning disabilities: something interfering with a child's ability to understand the message that his eyes and ears receive

Aphasia: loss of speech and language abilities after brain damage resulting sometimes from a stroke or head injury

CAN HAVE ACCOMPANYING SPEECH OR HEARING PROBLEMS

SPEECH OR LANGUAGE PROBLEMS

CAN HAVE ACCOMPANYING

SPEECH DISORDERS

Articulation: difficulties with the way sounds are formed and strung together; characterized by substituting one sound for another (**w**abbit for rabbit), omitting a sound (han_ for han**d**), and distorting a sound (**shl**ip for sip)

Stuttering: interruptions in the flow or rhythm of speech; characterized by hesitations, repetitions, or prolongations of a sound, syllable, word, or phrase

Voice: inappropriate pitch (too high, too low, never changing, interrupted by breaks); loudness (too loud or not loud enough); or quality (harsh, hoarse, or breathy)

LANGUAGE OR HEARING PROBLEMS

CAN HAVE ACCOMPANYING

HEARING DISORDERS

Conductive: occur in the outer or middle ear; speech and other sounds may be heard faintly, often muffled

Sensorineural: occur in the inner ear or auditory nerve and cause one to hear speech sounds faintly and sometimes in a distorted way; words may sound slurred or lacking in clarity

Mixed: combination of conductive and sensorineural losses

FIG. 6-1. Characteristics of common communication disorders. (From public information materials of the American Speech-Language-Hearing Association. Reproduced with permission.)

for rapidly changing acoustic information. . . . An obvious treatment implication is that the signal should be slowed down to facilitate its perception by the language-disordered child."

Vision impairments. If the child cannot see clearly, it is difficult to recognize the things and events that are being talked about. Because blind children, by virtue of their handicap, have a deprived experiential base, special help must be given to encourage acquisition of speech and language. Partially sighted children have special needs just as partially hearing children do. These needs often go unnoticed. Fraiberg (1977) offers specific and useful information to aid early identification of children with vision impairment.

Identification and remediation of the visual problems is the first and most important step. For those children who continue to have difficulty seeing, many special adaptations should be made from the earliest possible time, such as the following:

1. Expand tactile-auditory experiences in every way possible. Associate everything the child touches with words.
2. During vocalizations, touch the child to let him or her know you are there and listening. "Converse" or interact with the child verbally, just as you would with any youngster of the same language developmental level.
3. Play interaction games, for example, rhythm games and hand clapping activities, that allow the child to feel the motion of an adult's hands as well as his or her own.
4. Talk about what you are doing and what the child is doing as it happens. Label actions as well as things.
5. Be certain the child uses vision to the maximum extent possible and then combine looking with touching and talking.
6. Be certain that visually impaired children see and feel all parts of an object and

understand the relationship of parts to the whole.
7. Spatial relations are difficult to demonstrate. Place the child in various positions and encourage touching and manipulating. Sometimes use toys to demonstrate concepts like "on-off," "up-down," and "in-out."
8. Train the auditory modality with great care. Lengthen auditory memory through sequenced instructions, games that require memory for place, and the teaching of phone numbers and addresses.
9. Associate words with textures, surfaces, positions, and temperature.
10. Teach the child to localize sounds and recognize their source.

Chapter 3 also includes a list of high risk signals of possible visual impairments. Such a checklist should be readily available and studied frequently.

Structural abnormalities. Craniofacial deformities of any kind interfere with speech skill development. If the child cannot imitate and reproduce the speech sounds of the language, the skill in using language as well as speech will be reduced. For example, if deviant mouth structure precludes placing tongue and teeth in the correct relation to pronounce the /s/, as in boys and shoes, the child cannot use the language rule "Add /s/ to form plurals."

Hypernasality, often associated with cleft palate, also interferes with learning speech. Only three English speech sounds are intended to have this characteristic nasal quality: /m/, /n/, and /ng/ (as in ring). When most of the sounds of speech are nasalized, listeners usually characterize the speech as unintelligible. Conditions other than cleft palate can cause this. If a child sounds as if he or she is "talking through his or her nose," the causes should be discovered and corrected.

Children who have abnormal mouth and vocal structures need help as soon as the condition is detected. If the first signs of trouble are abnormal speech sound productions, then that should be the signal for a thorough evaluation of causes and solutions to the problem. Dental abnormalities as well as palatal abnormalities must be corrected. Ignoring care for teeth that have been knocked out or lost interferes with speech.

Motor problems. Normal control of the muscles necessary for speech is needed for correct articulation. This develops so spontaneously in most children that the tremendous accomplishment is not recognized. Playing the violin skillfully is far less complex than pronouncing a word correctly. One way to discover this is to watch radiographs of a speaker at half speed. You will get some clue if you shut your lips lightly and pay attention to your tongue as you say, "Look at Larry's new green coat." (Shutting your lips helps to focus on the tongue activity.)

Cerebral palsy interferes with muscle coordination. Injury, other physical problems, and certain drugs also interfere. Teachers will want to work closely with other therapists when children have problems of this kind.

Voice problems. The effect of a cleft palate and/or lip may result in a nasal voice, even if a surgical repair was completed early in the child's life. Children who have frequent respiratory infections may lack nasal resonance. Children who scream a lot may be hoarse. All of these problems need skillful attention and remediation. Teachers and parents should seek professional help for these children.

Mental impairments. Mental retardation is presumed to be the cause of delayed speech and language in some children. Since many tests of intelligence rely heavily on verbal interactions between examiner and child, it is difficult to decide which is cause and which is effect. Qualified examiners should be able to make this distinction but many find it difficult. Thus a young child without speech and language may be judged developmentally delayed and the as-

sumption made that the delay is the cause of the lack of communication skills. Davis (1977) cautions that tests containing verbal items reflect the child's linguistic age and not necessarily the intellectual status.

Children with slower than typical cognitive development need thoughtfully planned and tenderly provided individualized opportunities and challenges. But for the most part, they are able to learn to talk and understand speech and language in the expected sequences, although at a slower pace. It is especially important to provide these children with a language-nurturing environment that matches their linguistic age, rather than their chronological age. Thus if they are just beginning to use two words, they should be talked to, listened to, and played with in a manner appropriate to that language development. Teachers will want to be more concerned about fostering continued development than about test scores, although with young children, tests can provide goood clues to the kinds of things that need to be fostered.

Children who have been described as retarded may need special help in the pragmatic skills of language, as well as vocabulary, grammar, and articulation. Helping them to understand when to talk as well as what to say that is appropriate should be part of the planning for them.

Stuttering. Stuttering is speech with disturbed rhythm. When a speaker repeats a sound or syllable, prolongs it more than is typical of other speakers, or blocks (a complete halting of the speech flow), many people describe this as stuttering. Some stutterers develop patterns of grimaces and gestures in an effort to avoid disturbing their flow of speech. These behaviors are sometimes described as secondary characteristics. They are often thought of as habits that reflect the speaker's anxiety. They are seen as an effort to break tension.

Research has neither been able to pinpoint organic or hereditary causes for stuttering nor support the belief that forcing a left-handed child to use the right hand causes a problem with fluency. Imitation of one stutterer by another rarely occurs. That is, there is no evidence to suggest that a child will begin to stutter just because he or she is around a child who stutters.

No single factor has been identified as a "cause" for stuttering, and no single treatment can guarantee that the stutterer will improve. Andrews, Guitar, and Howie (1980, p. 287) examined 42 studies that covered treatment of 756 stutterers. They concluded that "despite the many reports of stuttering treatment, there is little consensus either on the long term effectiveness of treatment or on which treatments are the most effective."

Stuttering usually begins between the ages of 2 and 4, although it may begin much later. Normally all speakers repeat, hesitate, and sometimes prolong sounds. This is especially true of young children. They are in a hurry. Finding the right word is difficult for little children. This alone is reason enough for them to hesitate and to repeat.

Some speech-language pathologists believe that calling attention to the perfectly normal disfluencies of young children may result in more repetitions. Telling children to slow down or to think before they speak may cause them to stumble even more. Then, already anxious parents become more anxious and so do their children.

Requiring children to strive for goals they cannot achieve increases anxiety. Physical and emotional shocks have been followed by increasing stuttering. Most pathologists feel that a key guide to prevent stuttering is to avoid an atmosphere of tension and pressure. The following suggestions are useful to both parents and teachers of young children who are beginning to stutter:

1. Be sure the home and school are happy and pleasant places to be. Avoid rigid rules and overly perfect surroundings.

2. Be consistent. Be sure the children understand what is expected of them. Be kind but firm in working with them.

3. Avoid watching the children's effort to speak in obvious ways.

4. Avoid reacting with anger, shock, or distaste to speech blocks or repetitions.

5. Avoid suggesting by word or touch that you "know he or she has a problem, but you love him or her anyway."

6. Do not tell stuttering children to "stop and start over" or other similar comments.

7. Do not train or suggest that they use "starters" such as snapping fingers, tapping a foot, or any similar physical act.

8. Breathing and relaxation exercises are not generally believed to be useful and may serve to make children feel something is "wrong" with them.

9. If the stutterer is so disturbed by the disfluency that a reaction from you is expected, say something like "That was a hard word" or "Sometimes my words get stuck, too."

10. Refuse to feel anxious yourself. It won't help.

Additional suggestions useful for teachers as well as parents can be found in the publications of Speech Foundation of America (1977). Publication number 11, "If your Child Stutters: A Guide for Parents," is especially useful.

Circumstances that interfere

Emotional problems. Deviant language development or the refusal to communicate at all often result from emotional problems. Although these problems require the skillful and caring therapy of persons especially trained to help children and their parents, much can be done to support mental health in a preschool environment. Recognition of emotional disturbances in young children, like recognition of all of the other conditions that interfere with speech and language learning, should result in carefully planned supports. Chapter 8 offers a number of classroom support strategies for children with emotional or social problems. Cooperation between and among therapists, parents, and teachers is especially critical in this area.

Lack of stimulation. Lack of appropriate stimulation limits communication development. Recent studies in many areas support the importance of loving, emotionally satisfying stimulation from birth. Experience during many years of working with parents of young children suggests that many of them simply do not know how to talk to their young children. It is not uncommon to have them say, "What can you say to a baby?" or "My friends will think I'm crazy if I talk to a 2 year old."

It is usually assumed that people who speak a language, children as well as adults, instinctively know how to talk to children. This is not always true. Later, suggestions for teaching parents and others how to talk to their children will be given. In any case, when a child is "not talking," be alert to help parents create a language nurturing environment from that time on.

Regardless of other causes for the lack of oral communication skills, the lack of stimulation should be considered as an ongoing contributor to the delay. This may be especially true if the child has physical problems, including hearing and vision deficits that have delayed normal language acquisition. Once language development is "off schedule," parents may feel helpless and fail to provide the stimulation that would have come naturally and intuitively to them otherwise. Kleffner (1973) reports that a child's lack of communication ability, when added to their fears and anxiety, can result in parents changing their family life-style. They may become over solicitous, do fewer things together, and talk less or differently.

Parents who find themselves distracted and fearful will need tender and kindly guidance. They will not be able to change all at once. They may benefit by observing the teacher demon-

strate many times before they are willing to try to do similar things, even at home. Ideally the parents will be willing to practice their new teaching skills while the teacher observes and makes suggestions. For many, this will not be easy or accomplished without pain and embarrassment. It is a goal worth pursuing, however.

Some schools have developed home demonstration teams, or teachers may arrange a room at school to be homelike. Both mothers and fathers need to learn how to use everyday experiences to teach communication skills. Cooking, cleaning, and gardening are excellent experiences for children. Conversation during these activities becomes an excellent language teaching time. Washing the car or working with tools provides additional excellent opportunities to foster speech and language learning. But parents will need encouragement, effective examples, and thoughtful reminders if they are to make their child's language learning environment stimulating.

Diagnosis. Chapter 3 discusses many of the difficulties involved in testing young children, particularly children with handicapping conditions. Comments in this chapter have also underlined this important consideration. One of the major reasons for avoiding categorical special education classes for young children is that identifying the correct category is so difficult and often impossible until diagnostic teaching has been carefully done. Placing a child on the basis of low test scores alone is unthinkable in the 1980's.

Test scores of young children lack predictive validity (predicting later levels of functioning). When scores are low, this is sometimes overlooked. If children with learning or language impairments are given tests that rely on verbal understanding or performance, the scores will be misleading.

Low test scores, a diagnosis of mental retardation, or "possible brain damage" are devastating diagnoses for parents. This has been mentioned earlier in this chapter, but it is repeated here to underscore that the diagnosis, in and of itself, often becomes one of the circumstances that interfere with the child's development. Encouragement, guidance in specific things to do, and the support of professionals and other parents must become a regular part of any of our efforts to diagnose.

Cole and Dunn (1977, p. 5) say "decisions should be made on the basis of observations of and experience with each student rather than merely on the results of diagnosis." They further state that standardized tests yield inaccurate information when used with children under stress or who have vision or hearing problems. They believe these children need a multisensory approach during diagnosis.

RECOGNIZING CHILDREN WHO NEED PROFESSIONAL EVALUATION

Speech and language disabilities or developmental lags are usually identified by comparing a particular child to the expected skills demonstrated by most children. Bloom and Lahey (1978, p. 290) summarize the different behaviors that are most often noticed to include "little or no talking, little or no understanding of instructions, any unusual use of words or phrases, or grammatical mistakes in sentences that interfere with communication." They describe language disorders as "a broad term to describe certain behaviors, or the lack of certain other behaviors, in a child that are different from the behaviors that might be expected considering the child's chronological age."

High risk signals

The following are high risk signals of speech and language disabilities or developmental lags of which parents and teachers should be aware:

1. Failure to understand what other children of the same age understand

2. Failure to speak as intelligibly as others the same chronological age (This includes articulatory errors.)

3. Speech that is not fluent (Normally, young children hesitate and repeat themselves to some extent, but tension, strain, and constant repetition are not to be expected.)

4. Voice quality that is strained or pitched too high or too low for the expected communication

5. The use of sentences that are too short or incomplete for the age of the child (For example, the 3 year old who is using only one or two words to form little sentences is lagging in language development.)

6. Failure to demonstrate the social skills of language (Children who refuse to speak or who are never quiet do need help. They may not need the services of a speech-language pathologist, but attention to developing the pragmatic skills is important.)

7. Any sudden change in the quantity or the quality of the child's efforts to communicate (Although children sometimes appear to remain at the same developmental level for a few months, failure to continue to improve communication skills in the expected way should not be overlooked.)

Normative comparison

A child who manifests any of the high risk signals should be evaluated through a more structured series of observations. Whenever a developmental checklist is used to compare the child's speech and language behaviors to the age-appropriate norms, more than one observation should be made. (Table 5 is an example of such a checklist.) It is helpful to record a number of conversations with different people, including children and adults. Watching the child playing with peers and during class sessions is useful.

If tape recording is not practical, one teacher or aide should write down a number of conversations as they occur. Although it is useful to write simple descriptions of what happened and what was said, it is also helpful to record what the child was attempting to accomplish by what was said. For example, an entry might appropriately read: "Tony wanted the big blocks. He pulled on teacher's skirt and pointed, saying 'Me wan dem.' "

Observing communication intent (pragmatics) requires more than just noting that the child asks for things. Some of the qualities to be observed are subtle. The following should be observed, recorded, and developed:

1. Does he or she try to satisfy own needs by asking for things?

2. Does this child try to direct what others do by speaking to them and telling them what to do and how to do it?

3. Is an effort made to establish and maintain social contact through speech and language?

4. Do the communication efforts include a normal range of other people, including both children and adults?

Recording observations should be done with great care to discover if the child is indeed lagging in developing receptive and expressive language skills.

1. Observe over a period and under a variety of circumstances. Does this child understand what is said? Does this child talk sometimes?

2. Ask parents to listen and report their observations to you. Does the child communicate differently at school and home?

3. Be specific. Does the child understand sometimes? When?

4. Consider each subskill separately, as well as the overall success of the child's communication efforts. Include accuracy of speech sound production, grammar (morphology and syntax), vocabulary and concepts, and communicative intents observed.

Preventing learning disabilities

The definition of learning disability includes the statement that it "means a disorder in one or more of the basic psychological processes involved in understanding or in using language, spoken or written—" It emphasizes that "the term does not include children who have learning problems which are primarily the result of visual, hearing, or motor handicaps, of mental retardation, of emotional disturbance, or of environmental, cultural, or economic disadvantage" (PL 94-142, U.S. Office of Education, 1977).

In this definition the central role of language disorder in learning disabilities is emphasized.

A word of caution. Although the definition of learning disabilities excludes learning problems that result from sensory or environmental causes, it does not take into account the possibly pervasive effect of the existence of these problems at a very early age. If a child has been deprived of normal reception through the eyes or ears at some time (or all of the time) during the first 3 or 4 years of age, this deprivation can be expected to cause developmental delays that do not disappear quickly. This will be true even if it is possible to correct the physical problems as soon as they are discovered (Bess and McConnell, 1981).

Interested readers will want to read the position statement on language and learning disabilities of the American Speech-Language-Hearing Association (American Speech-Language-Hearing Association, 1980, pp. 628-636).

One cannot help but wonder how many children entering school with learning problems at age 6 have been the victims of sensory deprivation (vision and hearing impairments) during their early years. But at the time of school enrollment, the original interference with normal reception has been corrected. Hearing and vision tests made then do not reveal impairments. With glasses, the child sees well enough to pass the tests, even though the glasses may have been worn only for a few weeks or months. The hearing may well be within normal limits, although earlier an intermittent hearing loss havocked efforts to learn language and speech. But the evidence is gone. The symptoms and the observable behaviors that suggest sensory impairments are no longer present. Seeking a cause for the clearly evident learning disorders may lead to inappropriate speculations.

Early detection and correction of sensory deprivation are crucial. Equally important is effective remediation of the developmental delays during the preschool years.

Working with the speech-language pathologist

A child who performs below the range of minimal expectations according to the teacher's observations relative to developmental norms should be referred to a speech-language pathologist. When special therapy is prescribed, it is important for the teacher to maintain an ongoing involvement with the therapist. Regular conferences with the parents and the speech-language pathologist should be a part of every therapy session. These may be brief. After a program is functioning smoothly, some of them may be by telephone.

When possible, parents and teachers should observe therapy sessions regularly, and the pathologist should observe the child in a variety of situations. These observations may be more or less frequent, depending on the progress the child is making. If there appears to be little or no improvement in the skills that are lagging, observation in structured activities as well as free play is desirable. Little improvement will be noted unless the language-nurturing environment is consistent in every possible way.

Each child is unique. Specific remediation and the activities designed by the speech-language pathologist will be adapted to accelerate skills in the areas where lags or deficits have been observed. If either teachers or parents do not understand exactly what they are to do, they should ask to find out what is expected of them (Schiefelbusch, 1978).

NURTURING SPEECH, LANGUAGE, AND CONCEPTUAL SKILLS: GENERAL CONSIDERATIONS

Throughout the sections that follow, it is important to remember that teacher and parent attitudes will be reflected by a child in subtle as well as obvious ways. The child who desperately needs speech-language nurturing may remain quiet for a long time. Although he cannot be forced to talk, he can be encouraged to want to talk. Furthermore alert teachers provide more verbal children with conversation appropriate to their advanced language age. This is particularly important if language skills are far ahead of chronological age.

As a rule for language nurturing, avoid thinking in terms of children's chronological ages when talking to them. Rather, adapt langauge usage, vocabulary, and topics to their skills and interest. Individualizing language stimulation in this way assumes teachers and aides as well as parents conscientiously interact with children while they are playing, during snacks and meals, and even during baths. Language nurturing truly is a continuous process.

Begin where the child is

It seems obvious that children's awareness of the environment must precede their reaction to it. But research suggests that although environmental differences can alter the rate of development in young children, it does not alter the inevitability of the order of the development (Uzgiris and Hunt, 1975).

If we apply this observation to the development of communication skills with speech and language, our practices in nurturing receptive and expressive language suggest that teachers attend to children's *levels* of development. Having identified this, planning should be based on doing what is appropriate for children at their level. Thus if 4-year-old Sean does not yet try to tell adults something, one of the things that should be nurtured is the "telling" of things in the sense that very young children do this. If Susie cannot produce any speech sounds distinctly, she may need to be encouraged in simple vocal play and babbling. If Tommy does not try to ask for things, perhaps he needs to be expected to make some kind of sound before he is given what he wants.

Developmental scales of speech and language should be used in two very different ways. Initially they can be checked to determine if a child has a developmental lag, as previously outlined. But then, they can be used to help in planning the activities and the kinds of things to be done to accelerate language growth. Speech and language pathologists can assist as questions arise. Table 5 illustrates one type of speech, language, and hearing checklist.

TABLE 5
Normal language development—expected sequence and approximate age norms*

Age (approximate)	Pragmatics	Phonology	Grammar Morphology-syntax	Semantics
1 month	Gazing, crying, "comfort sounds"	Begins to play with pitch change		
3 months	Laughs, smiles when played with; looks at speaker; *Sometimes responds to a speaker by vocalizing*	Vocalizes two or more syllables		
6 months	Babbles and smiles at a speaker; stops (begins turn taking) when someone speaks	Babbles four or more syllables at one time; plays at making noises; labial (/p/, /b/, /m/) consonants emerge; vowels		
8 months	Plays "peek-a-boo" and "pat-a-cake"; listens to adult conversations; turns toward speaker; understands gesture	Intonation patterns for questions and commands; jargon includes vowels and consonants (five or more of each)	(No *real* words, but vocalizing sounds as if it is a sentence or question)	*Recognizes* names of some common objects
10 months	Follows simple commands; enjoys clapping to music; begins to "send message" by pointing	Uses a varied jargon, with pitch and rhythm		Says "first" words; tries to imitate words

*From Brown (1973), Bzoch and League (1970), Dale (1976), Hopper and Naremore (1978), Prutting (1979), Wilkinson (1979).

Continued.

TABLE 5

Normal language development—expected sequence and approximate age norms—cont'd

Age (approximate)	Pragmatics	Phonology	Grammar Morphology-syntax	Semantics
12 months	Responds to manner and attitude of speaker (for example, joy, anger, or hurry)	Consonant-vowel and consonant-vowel-consonant jargon	"Holophrastic speech" (one word stands for a whole sentence)	Uses two or more words; learns new words every few days
12 to 18 months	Follows one- and two-step directions	Imitates noises and speech sounds	Some begin to use two-word sentences	Recognizes and points to many familiar objects; learns new words almost daily
18 to 24 months	Jargon and some echolalia; "dialogue" uses speech to get attention; "asks" for help	Uses /p/, /b/, /m/, /h/, /t/ and vowels	Two- to three- word sentences but omits articles and most modifiers; begins to use personal pronouns; "telegraphic speech"	Says 10 to 20 words at 18 months, but some say as many as 200 words by 24 months; understands many more
24 to 36 months	At 2, speech is not used for social control, but at 2½, demands and attempts control	Many begin to use additional consonants; add /f/, /k/, /d/, /w/, /g/; vowels 90% intelligible	Uses word order only until 2½. Then, inflections begin to appear in this order: -ing (present progressive) -s and es (plurals) -ed (past tense) A, an, the (articles) My and 's (possessives) Auxiliary verbs	Recognizes names and pictures of most common objects; understands 500 words. Prepositions

By age 3, 70% of speech is intelligible, although articulation errors are still common. Short sentences (three to four words) are common. All vowels are correct, but /r/, /s/, /ch/, /j/, /v/, /l/, /x/ are often incorrectly spoken. Vocabulary ranges to as many as 1,000 words. Sentence types include agent-action, action-object, and agent-object.

TABLE 5

Normal language development—expected sequence and approximate age norms—cont'd

Age (approximate)	Pragmatics	Phonology	Grammar Morphology-syntax	Semantics
36 to 48 months	Social control; whispers; tells name; "explains" what happened; asks questions, sustains topic; systematic changes in speech depend on the listener; some role playing; metalinguistic awareness (ability to think about language and comment on it); "hints" at things through smiles and gestures as well as words	All vowels correct; although many children articulate most consonants accurately, articulation errors on the following are still within "normal range": /l/, /r/, /s/, /z/, /sh/, /ch/, /j/, /th/; pitch and rhythm variations similar to adults, but this age enjoys extremes—yells and whispers	Expands noun phrases with tense, gender, and number; conjugates "to be" correctly; uses pronouns, adjectives, and plurals; near age 4, begins using longer and more compound and complex sentences; begins to interrelate clauses (uses and, because, when, and then)	Vocabulary grows rapidly; actively seeks to learn new words; likes to "experiment" and makes many charming errors; continues process of differentiating lexical types; knows between 900 and 1,000 words
48 to 60 months	Seeks information constantly; "why" is a favorite; becomes aware of behavior listeners attend to; begins to grasp relevance	Begins to use stress contours, pitch changes purposefully; articulation errors still common, but diminishing; nonfluency not unusual; blends difficult	Uses comparatives (big, biggest); uses all sentence types, including relative clauses; grammar approximates that of adults	Size of vocabulary varies widely with experiences; many know 2,000 or more words

The importance of conversations

Conversations about familiar things that interest young children are a critical tool in helping them to learn communication skills. Nelson (1974) reported that children's first verbal labels or names are of objects they know and can associate with. Unless they are truly interested and can make associations, they will not attend. And attention is a prerequisite for learning anything.

At first, playing with them with toys they have chosen is helpful. Talking about what they are doing, describing what they are doing with the toys and naming parts of the toys is a beginning. Pausing at the end of each short sentence and waiting for their response is a prerequisite for their responding. And it may not happen right away. One often wonders if anyone has listened to them before, they seem so surprised.

For many children, the presence of an interested adult is the key that unlocks the door of beginning communication efforts.

The strategies suggested so far and some of those that follow take normal first language learning processes as the model. Experience has taught us that children of preschool age who have not developed expected communication skills benefit from intensive efforts to surround them with the language nurturance usually provided for first language learners. We cannot overlook the possibility that at least some of their delayed language learning may have resulted from lack of appropriate stimulation. We agree with Kleffner (1973) who reports that limited development of verbal skills in young children often shapes both the quality and the quantity of the efforts the family makes to communicate with them. The cause and the effect of the delayed language may be interlaced in ways that are difficult to identify in clinic office or classroom.

In practice, finding the optimum level of language stimulation and use for each child is critical. We have found it helpful to think in terms of synchronizing what is said and what is expected of the child in terms of what a relaxed, language-nurturing family would do for a normally developing child of the same linguistic age. There are no precise assessment procedures to pinpoint exactly what should be taught. Helping children to communicate is a loving art as well as an attempt to use current theoretical models as a base for teaching.

Teachers and parents as well as clinicians should not rely on any one intervention strategy, however (Muma, 1978). Art requires creativity, skill, and knowledge in every effort made.

Choosing what to talk about. For the really reluctant talker, food is a good place to begin. It is something they can experience directly. Sitting around a table with other children while the teacher cuts an apple into pieces can be a powerful stimulator. Conversation about the smooth, red skin and small, black seeds, the sharp knife, and how the apple will taste comes naturally to most children as well as adults. Pragmatic skills also can be nurtured in this "social situation."

Any game, any dollhouse, play kitchen, or toy barn can be used as the conversational focal point. At first, the teacher should join the children in an ongoing activity with toys they have chosen. Later, when rapport has been well established, the teacher may choose the activity. Introducing variety is important. But at first, joining into the children's choice of things to do is best.

For adults who find it difficult to converse with young children, the following suggestions may prove useful:

1. Listen attentively. Even if the things children are saying are unintelligible, look at them with interest and listen.

2. Speak slowly and distinctly but in the natural song patterns of speech (the prosodic features). Don't sound like a robot without inflections.

3. Keep sentences short, no more than three or four words. Sometimes use single words. Repeat frequently.

4. Unless you really want to learn something you do not know, *do not ask questions*. Of course, do ask questions if you are seeking information. But avoid asking "What color is your shoe?" or "Where is the ball?" when both of you can see the answer. Questions asked one after another do not constitute conversation. In fact, just as with adults, too many questions result in no conversation. Good questions lead to problem solving and planning, however.

5. Talk about the here and now. Vicarious experiences are not useful as conversation starters with young children.

6. Use a calm and pleasant tone of voice. Bring fun to every conversation.

7. Use words the children are interested in

because they can see or understand what they refer to as you talk. Tell them the names of actions as well as things.

8. Pause between sentences. Don't be in a hurry.

9. As the children understand and speak more, gradually make your sentences longer, and use a larger vocabulary and less repetition.

Listening. Adults should listen to children "with great interest." This is especially true if the children have not developed speech and language skills at the expected rate. If they are unable to talk, every effort on their part requires more than the usual amount of trying. The reward most apt to accelerate the growth of speech and language is *not* an M&M. It is an interested listener. Facial expression, remaining quiet, not moving about as if in a hurry, and merely looking at them are important considerations.

Developing pragmatic skills. Pragmatic skills are the social skills of language. Turn taking during a conversation, not interrupting a speaker,

and conforming what is said to the appropriate thing in that time and place cannot be learned in isolation. Children require social experiences and are dependent on social interaction. Probably these skills cannot be taught directly to young children. But by modeling correct pragmatic skills, attention can be directed to courteous ways of conversing.

Expanding skills. Ideally children's language skills are expanded through increasingly complex conversations with them. As sentences grow longer and vocabulary more complex, the process results in an improved product. If children have the opportunity, the process expands their skills. If their development has been delayed, the rate may continue to be slower than is expected, but the developmental sequence probably will not differ. The following box suggests ways to promote children's syntactic development.

An interesting observation of a young child learning to talk involved a boy named Jimmy. He had a moderate to severe hearing impair-

---

SOME WAYS TO PROMOTE SYNTACTIC DEVELOPMENT

Tony uses many two- and some three-word sentences. And he loves to talk. Both his parents and his teachers have many conversations with him throughout the day. They *listen* to him with obvious interest. Some of the time they *expand* what he has said. When he says "Falled down," they may say "Your big tower fell down. That was noisy." They do this in a way that suggests "You're right, it fell down," never in a manner that indicates "Now, say it the right way."

As the adults do things while Tony is present, they may use *self-talk*. They talk about what they are feeling and doing, as they do it. "Time for supper. I'll take the plates to the table, now. The meat and the green beans are almost ready, and it's time to make the salad. I'll cut the carrots, first." Of course, the speaker pauses after each sentence, and *listens* if Tony starts to say something.

Sometimes his teachers and parents use *parallel talk*. They talk about what Tony is doing. "Tony, you put the toys on the shelf just the right way. I like the way you are picking up those blocks. You put the biggest ones on the bottom."

When Tony says something incorrectly, they rarely correct him directly, but they do use *corrective echoing*. If he says "Her frew dat ball," they might say "You saw Susie. She *th*rew the ball." And although they may exaggerate the "She" and the "th" slightly by saying them slowly, they are really just confirming that they understood.

ment and had not learned to understand or use language by age 3½. Jimmy had just been fitted with a hearing aid, and he was delighted. Of course, he did not begin to talk right away, any more than we would begin to speak French immediately if we heard French for the first time.

His parents were eager to help, but they had been in the habit of gesturing and exaggerating everything they said to him. Thus the speech-language pathologist's assignment was to teach them how to talk to Jimmy.

Jimmy had a 2-year-old brother named Jeff. The difference in the manner in which the parents talked to Jeff was dramatic. They followed the intuitive pattern of most parents as they talk to little children. Jeff was developing right on schedule, and the parents were just doing what came naturally to parents of most 2 year olds. Both boys were essentially the same "language age." So, the speech-language pathologist advised the parents to help each other to talk to Jimmy in exactly the same manner that they spoke to Jeff.

At first, both parents reported that this was very difficult. Jeff chattered back at them, but Jimmy did not. The feedback from Jeff prompted them to continue talking to him, whereas Jimmy's silent state made them want to stop talking. But they persisted. Within a few weeks, Jimmy was saying single words. Then, he began to use two words to make little sentences. He pointed to everything and wanted them to tell him the names of things over and over again. When he played alone, he murmured and rambled on and on. When he played with Jeff, he quickly took the lead. By the time he was 5 years old, his sentences and the things he talked about were almost age appropriate. His articulation was almost too precise. The models his parents had given him as they spoke were precise and exact, and so he followed their lead. For several more years, his vocabulary lagged behind other children his age, but his parents took special care to teach him new words and

concepts. By third grade, a new teacher could not believe that there had ever been a language delay. His communication skills were judged "superior."

Jimmy demonstrated that he understood many concepts before he could talk about them. Throughout his early years he had seemed "bright" even though his speech was delayed. (In spite of this, several examiners suggested he was autistic or retarded because he did not understand or speak at the expected ages.)

Although providing language learning environments appropriate to the child's linguistic age is important, continuing to challenge the child to solve problems, group things into categories, and discover new ideas must not be forgotten. Cognitive development should not be stifled because language skills lag.

Not all young children make the rapid and continued progress that Jimmy made as soon as his language environment changed. However, many do. Because it seems so simple, it is easy to overlook the importance of conscientiously communicating with young children about what interests them. This seems very difficult to do if they seem to lack interest in communicating. Stimulating their need to communicate, accepting any attempts they make without trying to "make them say it right," and listening with enthusiasm to their first feeble efforts are crucial. Speaking in short, meaningful sentences and using vocabulary they understand are also basic. Formal language "lessons" in a speech therapy room are not very effective. To focus on perfect articulation can convince some children that they just cannot talk at all. So, they do not.

CLASSROOM STRATEGIES FOR NURTURING COMMUNICATION SKILLS

The suggestions that follow are derived from many years of experience working with young children whose communication skills were limited when they entered preschool. The ideas have been developed through trial and error and success and failure, as well as constant study of the literature to find out what others were doing that "worked." Young children do have the desire to learn. Their world should be arranged in such a way that they can discover and use new information effectively.

Children need to be helped to discover the rules of language. Very young children do this quickly and effortlessly during what appears to be an optimum language learning time (Slobin, 1979). However, if children of age 3 or 4 are lagging far behind in speech and language development, just being around speakers of the language is not enough. Kleffner (1973) believes that they should be "led directly into deductive instruction designed to produce some specific linguistic performance both receptively and expressively." He emphasizes the following:

Instruction must make the rules and principles of language as explicit as possible since the child probably has passed the point of discovering many of them on his own (p. 43).

To make the rules and principles of language explicit the teacher will need to choose a particular principle and then design interesting, repetitive practice. Examples of playing ball with children and using the activity to make rules about pronouns and verb use explicit are given later in dialogues. Other rules should be made obvious in similar activities.

Regardless of the specific teaching objective, remember the following:

1. All language teaching should be associated first with what young children are doing as they are doing it.
2. Later, pictures may be used to recall experiences and provide additional practice.
3. Choose activities and experiences the children enjoy, but be alert to expand their interests.
4. Adapt what is said to them and what is expected of them to each individual's unique language skills.

For some children who make little or no effort to communicate, carefully planned behavior modification can be a useful strategy. Muma (1978, p. 246) reports "behavior modification is one of the most effective strategies in dealing with nonverbal children. Clinical reports of its effectiveness with nonverbal autistic and retarded children are impressive." But he adds, "Once minimal labeling is obtained, behavior modification seems to be less effective than other strategies."

Kleffner explains it this way (1973, pp. 46 and 47), In the long run, the child's motivation and interest for communication will be advanced more by his own perception of communicative success than by any amount of external reinforcement.

Look for examples of these different approaches and strategies throughout this chapter. Principles of first language learning are basic to most of the activities. But alone, these are not enough for some children. Regardless of the strategy chosen, creating an interesting and happy environment in which efforts to communicate are rewarded by success is basic.

Arrival time to build language and conceptual skills

As the children arrive, each one should be greeted individually. Eye contact and a smile encourage social skills as well as a feeling of welcome and belonging. The box on p. 168 provides an example of conversation as the children arrive.

Circle time, language drill, and expanding horizons

Formal drill that sounds and looks like drill to little children is inappropriate. There are many things that are fun and gamelike that can be used to make language rules explicit and provide needed repetition. No attempt to correct articulation or pronunciation directly by comment or frown is appropriate. Modeling, ex-

---

ARRIVAL TIME TO BUILD LANGUAGE SKILLS

THE SCENE: Children are arriving and the teacher and aide are greeting them individually.

THE TEACHING STRATEGY: A warm greeting and a brief conversation with each child are designed to make each child feel welcome and expected. Modeling, expanding what the children say, and listening to them are some of the strategies to be used to promote communication skills. Direct correction of articulation errors or grammatical mistakes will be avoided.

Ms. McLynn: Good morning, Sally. I am so glad you brought your doll. Do you want to take her coat off?

Sally: Me do it. Her coat dirty.

Ms. McLynn: I know you can take her coat off. We can brush the dirt off.

Sally: Me got new wed shoes.

Ms. McLynn: I like those new red shoes. They are shiny.

Timmy: Hey, looka dat! Dat nose wiggles.

Ms. McLynn: I see our rabbit. I think she is hungry.

Nancy: Ms. McLynn, my mommie said that she couldn't come today but she will call you afterwhile. She has to go to the supermarket 'cause we're having company tonight.

Ms. McLynn: I'm glad you told me she couldn't come. Would you like to pretend that you are at the supermarket, too? We have lots of things in our store, too.

---

panding, and encouraging imitation are good strategies.

During circle time (usually a large group activity), finger plays, poems, songs, and chants can be used to provide repeated practice on specific language targets. Rote practice on counting, days of the week, and similar things in a group chant encourage reluctant children to chime in. Individual speech sounds associated

with clocks, tires going flat, and animals have been used by speech clinicians for years to encourage efforts to practice. Stories that include pauses for the children to add sound effects can be delightful. For those who cannot or will not use their speech mechanisms to make sounds, a bell or other noisemaker can be woven into the story. But usually children enjoy learning to hum like a motor, hiss like a snake, buzz like a bee, growl like a bear, or make the /th/ sound (the final sound in "moth"). As they imitate these phonemes, they are also learning to listen carefully. This *auditory discrimination* (recognizing the difference between and among sounds) practice is basic to later reading readiness as well as to correct articulation.

Young children need to be active at regular intervals. If they appear to be restless (or preferably, just *before* they become restless), an opportunity to jump, hop, fall, or skip is needed. If this is teacher directed, two purposes are served. The need for activity is met in positive ways, and vocabulary and language practice are achieved.

Chanting the direction in a happy tune, "Jump, jump, jump together; jump, jump up and down; jump, jump, jump together, and, then, sit down," appeals to most children. If teacher asks "What did we do?" immediately after they sit down, and then immediately models "We jumped" for the children, they will soon join in the chant, the question, and the answer. Any other active motion is equally useful. Occasionally interspersing blinking, hand clapping, and foot stamping provide variety.

As soon as a few of the children are regularly joining in the chant, one of them may be chosen to lead the activity. Children love to be "teacher." Of course, the adult teacher will remain close by. Occasionally a reluctant child may be helped if the teacher or aide gently moves the arms and legs. But this should never be done in a way that suggests the child is being "made" to participate. Encouragement, not force is the needed attitude.

Pictures of the children themselves as they jump, hop, or clap; stick figure sketches; or commercial pictures made to depict action verbs can be associated with the activity in two different ways. These visual aids are especially helpful to children with auditory weaknesses.

1. As soon as the children stop moving, show them a picture of the action they have just completed. Pointing to the picture, say "We _____," inserting the appropriate verb. If the picture is of a particular child, teacher may choose to have that child act, than ask "Who _____?" and model the answer, as needed.

2. Show the children the picture. Based on what they see, expect them to demonstrate the action. Then, ask and answer the questions that are appropriate. Model as needed, reducing this modeling or prompting as soon as the children can do the action and talk about it.

Children enjoy daily repetition of many things. What is done is readily adapted to focusing on specific language teaching. Choosing to focus on the use of pronouns, for example, might lead to this lesson. (This activity will be used later to demonstrate teaching other language targets.)

Ms. McLynn: I have some pictures of *you.* Let's see if *you* can tell *me* what *you* did. Here is Susie. Susie threw the ball. What did Susie do?

Susie: Me frew ball.

Nancy: She threw the ball. *I* bounced *it.*

Danny: Aw i (caught it)

Ms. McLynn: Danny caught the ball. *I* rolled *it* to him. Danny, what did *you* do?

Danny: I aw ball. (I caught ball)

Ms. McLynn: Right, *you* caught the ball.

Of course, this same activity could take place as the ball game proceeds, but it is also fun with snapshots of the children as conversation starters. Later, pictures of other children or pictures from books can be used to serve the same purpose. Children enjoy talking about what they have done. Since helping them to discover an awareness of verb tense is important, it is useful to use the same activity as a base for teaching different tenses.

In practice, the teacher's intended purpose determines the emphasis placed on various phases of the activity. For example, if the intent is to provide practice on future, present progressive, and past tense of verbs instead of pronouns, the activity could proceed this way.

First, the teacher should decide on the verbs to be used. If a ball or other toys are needed, they should be assembled, with an instant picture camera ready. If someone is able to sketch or draw stick figures, as the activity occurs, children will be delighted. Cardboard about 6 × 8 inches in size and of a light color should be used.

For this lesson, the objective could be stated in the following way: Given the opportunity to bounce a ball, throw it, and catch it, and the teacher's spoken model of future, present progressive, and past tense at appropriate times, the children will listen, imitate the spoken model, act as directed, and return to their places.

Teacher: Danny, say "I *will bounce* the ball."

Danny: I i *boun* a baw. (Danny bounces the ball)

Teacher: Danny *bounced* the ball.

Children: (Imitating in whatever way they can) Danny *bounced* the ball.

Teacher: Danny, you say "I *bounced* the ball."

Danny: I *boun* a baw.

Teacher: Now, let's do that again. Watch me. (bouncing the ball) I *am bouncing* the ball. (continuing to bounce it) What *am* I *doing?*

Children: You *are bouncing* the ball. (Modeled again by teacher as needed)

The intent is to give the children examples of the use of verb tense in a way that enables them to discover the rules and practice them. Language learning is rule learning. Normally, children induce the rules from the spontaneous conversations around them. If they have failed to do this for any reason, it becomes necessary to make the rules very obvious and very explicit. Obviously, "telling them the rule" will not work.

Of course, they will not learn the rules in 1 or 2 days. But most of them will begin to demonstrate that they understand the rules within a few weeks. Then, with continued opportunity to drill in this way, the use of the targeted rule of grammar will be developed.

Sketches or photos can also be used in a lesson. They can be placed along the edge of a chalkboard or on the floor. The teacher should attempt first to elicit the spontaneous sentences about the pictures. No direct corrections should be made of articulation or language. Rather, what the child says should be accepted with a smile of approval and then the corrected sentence modeled without comment. Next, the teacher may describe one of the pictures, "Danny bounced the ball," and indicate that one child should find the picture. If Danny is chosen to find his own picture, his response should include the correct pronoun "*I* bounced the ball," as he points to the picture.

Receptive language skills (the ability to understand what is said and in this case find the picture) as well as *expressive language* (saying the sentence) can be practiced in this way. It is important to remember that very young children just learning to speak cannot remember a four- or five-word sentence. We expect this short sentence with a child age 2 or even 3. The repetition of only two words should be accepted if that is all the child can do. For instance, if teacher says "Danny bounced the ball" and the child says "Danny ball," this may be appropriate for this child's language age. Through practice and many opportunities to imitate a four-word sentence without criticism, learning will occur.

Sometimes it is useful to follow this sequence to increase the child's *auditory memory* and complexity of sentences expressed.

Teacher: Danny bounced the ball.
Jane: Danny ball.
Teacher: (Without other comment) Danny bounced. (Then pause and wait expectantly for the child to say that much)
Jane: Danny bounced. (Remember, she can recall two words)
Teacher: The ball. (And again, the expectant look)
Jane: Danny bounced ball.

Keep the activity moving, enthusiastic, and brief. Five to ten minutes of this kind of practice is useful but longer can be boring. Interestingly, because they are talking about themselves, they enjoy using the same pictures over and over.

Remember, the intent is to provide them with explicit examples of correct articulation and in this instance verb tense. Young children usually learn the present progressive tense first, shortly after they are 20 months old. However, past tense may not be used until after they are 2 or 2½ years old. It is not unusual for children approaching age 3 to just begin to use tense markers. The idea of "future" and "finished" as well as "now" is enhanced when they use tense markers correctly.

Some teachers are uncomfortable using the pictures for practice of past tense since stories and children's books often use the present progressive tense. However, in this case the children are looking at pictures of themselves and remembering what they did. It is not useful to labor this point because the children will not. The teacher should continue to read stories that include present progressive tense, talk about pictures, using past tense, and practice the verbs at the time of the action. Most children begin to use tense easily and correctly within a short time.

Experience stories foster language and cognitive growth

Kindergarten and primary grade teachers often use language stories to develop reading readiness. Preschool teachers can also use this strategy to good advantage. Language develops naturally from interest in real experiences.

1. Plan an interesting experience with the children. Talk about what you will do, the things you will need, and what each will do. Use the future tense for the discussion but keep the conversation natural and informal.

2. Collect the things for the experience. Let the children see you making notes on the board about what each will do and when. This helps them to grasp the idea of sequence and ordering of events.

3. During the experience converse about what is happening, name the items used, describe them, and talk about what each of the children is doing as he or she does it. Use concept vocabulary at appropriate moments.

4. As soon as the activity is finished, talk about what *was* done. Be sure to include how each of the children felt about it. That is, if they noticed something was hot or cold, squishy or sticky, or "yukky," this should be discussed.

5. If pictures were made, the children should look at them and immediately try to remember what was done in sequence, for example, first and second. In this manner sequence can be included in the lesson.

SUSIE'S BUTTON

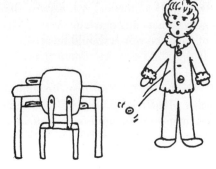

Susie's button popped off.

That button rolled under the desk.

Danny found the button.

He picked it up.

Ms. McLynn sewed the button
   on Susie's coat again.

FIG. 6-2. An example of a story chart. (Courtesy Lori Harshbarger, Godfrey, Ill.)

6. Before the next day the teacher will want to make a story chart (Fig. 6-2) large enough for all to see. Illustrations that will help to recall the activity should be included. If preferred, the photographs may be included on the chart. However, if these are mounted on small cardboard and held together with a ring, they become a book. Later, the photos can be matched to the sketches on the chart. They can be used as "talk starters" for story times and arranged in the right order to practice sequence.

7. An informal "reading lesson" using the story chart becomes another language lesson. If the teacher moves her hand from left to right under the sentence as she reads it and then encourages the children to read it, useful language practice occurs. Follow the same format suggested for the sentence practice with pictures. The teacher should read the whole sentence in a natural way, then encourage a child to imitate what was said. Avoid reading one word at a time, with the child parroting each word. The intent is to encourage the use of natural intonation and inflections. Precise articulation will come later. These activities provide the occasion for repetition and review. Just as children love to hear their favorite stories over and over, so will they love to help teacher read their favorite stories. Of course, avoid any hint of criticism of their efforts to read.

8. Continue to review the story charts regularly. Groups of three or four children at a time enjoy this. Again, keep the activity brief (5 to 10 minutes) and happy. No hint of insistence on perfect speech or direct correction of language errors should intrude. Recall that the intent is to provide the children with language stimulation appropriate to their language ages. In addition, the goal is enjoyment.

9. Avoid beginning sentences with *we*. Rather, use the name of a particular child at the beginning of each sentence, if at all possible. One *we* or *everyone* per story is enough. Keep most of the sentences short. One longer sentence and one two-word sentence add variety.

10. Use the "old" story chart as a hint to review and repeat the same activity. If the chart has been used regularly for a few weeks, several of the children will be capable of helping the teacher plan. In this way spontaneous talking can be elicited easily. A child who speaks very little often becomes more verbal when the situation is contrived in this way.

Design snack time to teach concepts and language

Most preschool and day-care centers focus on teaching children how to enjoy a wide variety of foods. Good nutrition is stressed. Pleasant social manners are encouraged. Snack time provides a unique opportunity for teaching concepts. The routine remains essentially the same each day. Although different foods are eaten, the need to arrange the table, decide how much food is needed, and discuss the qualities of the food remain constant. Eating is a multisensory experience that should not be taken for granted.

Unlike nouns, concept words cannot be taught directly. It is not possible to associate an object with the name. Rather, through many experiences that express examples of the concept, combined with the use of the concept word, the concept can be taught. For example, the concept of *big* can be realized only through numerous comparisons with *not big*.

Boehm (1971) developed the Boehm Test of Basic Concepts to probe conceptual understanding of preschool and primary grade children. Concepts included in the test are those used by teachers in the first years in school. But words such as *nearest, full, empty, before,* and *after* cannot be learned in one short lesson. Understanding of these develop over time and as a result of many experiences. Preparing and eating food each day provide an optimum occasion for needed practice in learning concepts through experiences.

Number concepts develop rapidly when the teacher does not have enough of a favorite food. How many do we need? How many more do we need? How many children are here? These become meaningful questions. Discussing what to do leads to use of concepts *more* and *less*. Discovering that one child needs a straw helps children to understand the purpose of counting.

Size concepts are particularly meaningful if one child has a slightly larger piece than another. For the child who does not like a particular food, the need to say "I want a little piece" leads to understanding concepts *big* and *little*. Comparatives (big, bigger, biggest) are learned quickly in the context of pieces of an orange.

Of course, this does not suggest that snack time is the only time to focus on the teaching of concepts. It is just one of the best and often overlooked times. The ability to attend is greatly enhanced when touchable favorite foods can be smelled, are in sight, and will be tasted. Even those children called hyperactive can learn to sit quietly if there are good things to eat nearby.

Snack time also provides many opportunities to use language to facilitate social interactions. "Please" and "thank you" are important to most parents, and they help to make the social amenities obvious to little children. Thoughtfulness grows through practicing being kind to one another. Passing the celery sticks and remembering to offer the cottage cheese dip made as part of the snack lesson teach more than the vocabulary involved. Expressing their own ideas about what they are doing should be encouraged, again, through attentive listening on the part of the teachers as well the children. As the children learn to take turns in talking, add to the topic begun by another, and contribute their own original ideas to a discussion, many skills are expanded.

Establishing and maintaining this language-nurturing environment take practice. Teachers will want to observe carefully to discover what facilitates and what interferes with using language to express ideas, to enjoy talking, and to speak fluently.

Use story time variations

Most children enjoy being read to by an adult. They like to see the pictures. Many of them enjoy hearing and seeing the same story over and over.

Children with delayed speech and language development may be restless during story time. If they cannot understand what is said, it is not much fun. Of course, they should not be excluded from the regular story times if they can sit quietly and not interfere with others' enjoyment. However, some special adaptations may be needed. For example, hearing impaired children should be seated where they can see your lips.

Flannel boards enhance interest. The visual representation and the changes are attractive to most children and can be felt by a visually impaired child. If a teacher allows them to change the figures, interest and attention are increased. During the story, if children are encouraged to provide the sound effects, many speech sounds can be practiced. Clocks say /t/, /t/, /t/ or whisper /t/, /k/, whereas the "bong" of a chime adds fun. Animals can be assigned specific sounds or syllables. Of course, cows say "moo" and cats "meow," but each animal can have its special sound.

An old television with the picture tube removed becomes a puppet stage. Children love to "tell" the story with puppets. For those who are unable to say much, any role that allows them to make a sound or say a single word is tremendously useful. Although just listening is a skill that little children must learn, first experiences may need to include a wide range of "hands-on" supporting materials. Dolls, trucks, trains, and dollhouses can be used to tell stories.

Often the best stories are those the teacher makes up on the spot. If the teacher can capture enthusiasm about something the children have just done, they will enjoy hearing a story about other children who did the same thing. One of the favorite stories of a preschool group was

based on washing the furniture. They had cleaned their furniture the day before. A big spill of water was an exciting event. They mopped and cleaned for a long while. The next day they sat enchanted for 10 minutes while the teacher told about some "other children" who also spilled water.

Picture books can be cut up and individual pages mounted. Many children enjoy holding one page and then telling about that when it is their turn. If the story is clearly shown in the pictures, the children may be able to shuffle the pictures and then arrange them in the right order. Again, this helps to reinforce concept words such as first, last, before, and after.

Commercial language kits, sequence story cards, and homemade pictures of events help to focus attention during story time. All of these adaptations are useful in helping the child with language deficits to "catch up."

Provide opportunities for following directions

Throughout the day children need to learn to develop their memories to follow directions. At first, these must be very simple, one-stage (for example, "Stand up") directions. By the time they are 3 years old, most children can listen to three simple directions given in one long sentence. Then, they can do the things in the right sequence. But children with developmental delays find this very difficult.

Following multistage directions can be taught, and a good place to begin is during play time. The teacher should talk about what their dolls are doing, then give directions to the doll to "Push the buggy, open the door, then shut it" or "Put Big Bird into the truck, push it slowly, then have him jump out," and watch the children's responses. If they do only the first or last thing, the teacher should provide them a great deal of practice with two-stage directions. The teacher can discover what they can do and very gradually increase the length and complexity of directions. Visual aids may help some. As soon as they can follow two-stage directions, three-stage directions can be offered. But again, this should not be forced. A lot of practice doing two-stage directions will be much more efficient than trying to force them to follow three-stage directions.

Use of modifiers should be avoided at first, for example, "Push the chair" or "Roll the ball" instead of "Push the big chair over by my desk" or "Roll the little red ball with the green stripe." Auditory attention will not allow for that, at first. However, when simple directions are followed readily, more modifiers can be added. Usually it is unwise to increase the number of directions and the number of modifiers at the same time. One or the other should be done.

When the group is ready to move to other centers, or different activities, this is a natural opportunity to practice following directions. Direct the children one at a time. Give each one a direction you know he or she can follow. Don't be surprised if some of the children do what they *saw* the previous child do, rather than what you said. This is evidence that, so far, that child understands what is seen better than what is heard.

Encourage questions

Some children seem never to stop asking questions. However, if you watch and listen you will discover that others never ask a real question. They may say "going home now" or "cookies" with a rising inflection, and it sounds like a question, but the word order is not appropriate. Helping these children to learn to use questions appropriately is important.

To encourage the use of questions, create the need for the children to ask, as well as answer, questions. Each question form suggests its own kind of activities. For example, "Where?" questions grow out of games where something or someone is hidden. One child becomes the questioner, and others the answerers. "What did *(child's name)* do?" can be easily encouraged during activity periods. "Who?" is useful during many games, especially if one child is chosen to ask the question after being out of the room while the activity occurred.

Perhaps the most important rule of all to remember is that speech and language are tools of communication. To the degree that the rules of language can be learned in real situations with real people, language learning is normal at any age. Contriving occasions to use particular language is often necessary. But the contriving should not be obvious to the children. It should be designed to help them discover the rules. The more natural and spontaneous the opportunities for communication are, the more effective the learning will be.

INCLUDING CHILDREN WITH LITTLE OR NO LANGUAGE

Children who do not speak at all or appear to understand very little need special help. The speech-language pathologist should plan the program, monitor the progress, and consult regularly with all of the children's caregivers. However, all of the suggestions made throughout this chapter are essential when working with these children.

Avoid criticism for not talking. It is often said "Johnny could talk if he wanted to. He's just stubborn" or "The other children talk for her. That's why she won't talk." However, we have rarely found any of these statements to be true. Rather, these are the children discovered to have hearing losses, vision problems, or emotional disturbances. Trying to "make" them talk is not only useless, it is cruel. In one case a mother was told not to give the child anything to eat until he said something. She persisted for several days. A badly dehydrated child barely escaped serious illness when a concerned neighbor alerted the mother to the seriousness of the child's condition.

Create the need to talk. Many examples of ways to create the need to talk have been suggested throughout the chapter. They are all appropriate for the severely handicapped child. But the teacher should be very patient and es-

pecially alert to continue parallel talk, conversational monologues about things that interest the child, and warm, tender encouragement for any attempt to pay attention (eye contact or looking toward the speaker) or to say something—anything. Even a grunt or a murmur may be where *that* child has to begin. Of course, this does not suggest that other things cannot also be done. At home and at school, children who are motivated to speak to satisfy the need to communicate learn more efficiently. It is helpful to think about the way children can be encouraged to *use* language. Setting the stage so they have a reason to say something is the best way. The box on pp. 177-178 provides a series of suggestions for identifying and promoting reasons for talking.

Horstmeier and MacDonald (1978) offer a very useful book, *Ready, Set, Go Talk to Me*, to parents and teachers. It is an excellent guide-

---

PROMOTING SPECIFIC REASONS FOR TALKING

Using language for finding out about things
Curiosity is expected of young children. Hide something in a box or bag, and then encourage them to "guess what is in here?" Ask "Is it round?" "Can it swim?" This offers the opportunity to teach how asking questions leads to answers. If "Why?" and "How?" questions are not being used by some children, games and experiments with different toys can initiate them.

Using language for getting involved
As young children often play beside each other rather than with each other, sand, water, and block play encourage "getting involved." As they learn to express intentions, tell others what to do (directing), and report what has happened, new language is learned quickly. Combining verbal children and those who speak less well provides a natural language learning opportunity.

Using language for getting help
Wanting something that is put away or too high to reach provides the need to ask for it. Zippers that stick and shoes that come untied create the need to ask for help. This becomes the opportunity for the adult to act as if gestures, helpless looks, and even tears do not communicate. However, any attempt to say something should be rewarded.

Modeling "Tie my shoe" and accepting the child's "Tie oo" at first encourages greater effort. Gradually, if the teacher is absolutely certain that the child is able to say it better, it is possible to appear to be puzzled until the child makes a better attempt.

Continued.

PROMOTING SPECIFIC REASONS FOR TALKING—cont'd

Using language to get attention or approval

Some children poke and pull at adults as well as children. Children need something to take the place of a habit that needs to be changed. The words "Look" or "Watch me" can be used in many situations. Each time they attempt to get attention in other ways, avoid responding immediately. Turning away, ask "Do you want me to look?" (pause) "Tell me (pause) look." Then, refuse to watch unless they say *something*.

Using language to tell something

If there are interested listeners, most children want to tell them something. Asking parents to write a note to let teachers know about interesting events at home is helpful. Then, teachers can initiate the discussion. Sometimes a picture or a favorite toy from home serves this purpose. Formal show and tell is not usually effective with young children, but informal telling teacher or a friend is popular.

Using language to defend themselves

"Stop that" needs to be learned early. "Move, please" is better than shoving. Teaching children how to defend themselves verbally instead of with a push or shove results in more pleasant homes and classrooms. They will need examples, models, and teachers' insistence that saying something is better than just shoving.

Using language to learn new things

Children who know how to express themselves in one way are quicker to learn other ways to talk about things. By providing a wide range of new experiences throughout the year, new ideas and new words are learned. The vocabulary of taking care of the science corner is not the same as the vocabulary for music time. For children with very limited speech and language, the initial focus should be on things they need to know and say in the classroom and at home, then expand the horizon.

Using any utterance to begin communication

For some children with severe disabilities any attempt to make a sound will need to be rewarded with instant encouragement. If it appears that the child wants something and is attempting to ask for it, give it to the child immediately. If you know what word was attempted, model (say) it to confirm that you understood. First efforts should never be the occasion for an attempt to improve the child's production. That comes *much* later. But letting the child know that he or she has in fact communicated is rewarding in itself. Tangible rewards (such as bits of food) should be used with caution and only if a planned behavior modification program is in operation. Used indiscriminately they can interfere more than enhance the child's awareness of the need to communicate orally.

book for working with severely delayed children. Throughout they are explicit in providing detailed suggestions that work. Their basic message is "Remember, your child can be trained to communicate better than he or she is doing now." They proceed to tell parents and teachers how to achieve this.

WORKING WITH THE HEARING IMPAIRED

Preschool teachers whose class includes a hearing impaired child find that a trained teacher of the hearing impaired is vital to assist in planning the child's overall education. Although special training and experience are necessary in training the most severely handicapped, the regular classroom teacher can learn to work with different types of hearing impaired children. The following list identifies several considerations-techniques that teachers can use to help communicate with children who have hearing losses:

1. Be sure that windows or other light sources are not behind you or shining into the eyes of the children. To read lips or to interpret signs the light must be on the speaker or signer, not in the children's eyes.

2. Speak at your normal rate and loudness, unless you typically speak too quickly to be appropriate for any language teaching-learning situation. Your rate of speaking and/or signing should consider the age and skills of the children. But don't speak so slowly that the normal rhythm and stress of speech are lost.

3. Stand or sit still! It is very difficult to focus eyes on a moving target.

4. Don't ask "Do you understand?" (Children will say "yes" regardless.) Rather, discover how much has been understood by asking questions or giving directions that will let you know how much and how well you have been understood by what the children do.

5. Do not exaggerate lip movements or pause between each word. This makes lipreading more difficult. It also establishes poor expecta-

tions. Rather, speak carefully. Articulate clearly. Your lips must move to allow for "speechreading."

6. If the children appear to be puzzled, add clues in the following order:

a. Repeat what you said.

b. Then, if more clues are needed, say the same thing in a slightly different way.

c. If confusion continues, combine "telling and showing" if at all possible.

d. If you are attempting to teach something, make a mental note to use this particular communication frequently until it is usually understood. Be explicit.

7. Remember to follow the suggestions made for nurturing the learning of speech and language among children who are not hearing impaired.

The deaf

Profoundly deaf children can be taught to speak and to understand what is said to them. There is, however, much controversy about the way in which this should be done. It is not appropriate here to consider the controversy about oral v. manual communication v. "total communication." Within each of these communication styles there are complex divisions and subdivisions and methods and variations on the methods. (The bibliography includes a number of suggested additional readings, if you find it useful to pursue this study.)

For practical purposes, spoken or oral communication is necessary if the hearing impaired are to achieve their full potential as human beings. Although manual communication serves many purposes, the person limited to its use cannot experience the same opportunities he or she would have if spoken communication were the modus operandi. The suggestion that signing or finger spelling expedites language learning in the young child has been debated for more than 200 years. For purposes of working with a young hearing impaired child in a preschool setting, the decision about signing or speaking must be made by the parents. The teacher should accept their decision and work with them and the trained teacher of the deaf.

The mildly hearing impaired

Perhaps the most misunderstood and confusing handicapping condition is the one referred to as a mild hearing loss. For the young child attempting to learn to speak and understand language, there is no other condition so apt to cause misery.

The child may turn toward a speaker and so appear to hear. But critical speech sounds are missing. He or she cannot learn language rules or normal articulation. The child may be thought to be retarded.

Auditory closure. Auditory closure is the ability to hear part of a word or a sentence and be able to guess the whole thing because you know what it is probably going to be. For example, if a child hears someone say "-ets go ge- -um i-- ream," he or she may be able to guess the speaker is saying "Let's go get some ice cream." But if that child had never heard it clearly, he or she could not fill in the missing pieces or perform auditory closure.

Because young children learning language do not already know what the words and sentences are, they cannot "close" or fill in the missing parts. To begin with, the unvoiced consonants are high pitched (or high frequency phonemes) as well as very soft sounds. If there is a fan or blower on, chances are that even children with normal hearing will not hear these phonemes, unless they are very close to the speaker. With the slightest of hearing losses, those critical sounds are lost altogether. Imagine trying to learn to say "cat" if all you heard was the short /ă/!

Intermittent hearing losses

Often young children have hearing losses that "come and go." Fluid in the middle ear, wax in the ear canal, and frequent colds, no matter how mild, may result in a hearing loss that comes and remains awhile. Usually physicians are unaware of this condition unless parents report it to them. And parents are unaware because the child is not complaining. However, they often report that "Johnny has been so stubborn this week. He doesn't come and do what I tell him unless I yell at him." Or they may say "Sandy has been so grumpy all week. She won't listen. She just pretends not to hear me.

All hearing losses are serious

In addition, there is growing evidence that children with losses of 10 to 15 decibels, which are not even considered as loss by many examiners, show academic retardation, limited vocabulary, and less well-developed language skills. Typical hearing screening tests sweep the frequencies (check the child's ability to hear the frequencies) at 20 to 25 decibels. An alert child may have a mild loss and yet respond at this level. Downs (1977) believes that mild fluctuating hearing loss in the region of 15 to 26 decibels can cause delays in both language and educational achievement. Bess and McConnell (1981) and Naremore (1979) believe much more should be known about mild hearing losses before their negative effects are considered "mild." Naremore (1979) states, "The consequences of hearing loss in these early years can be striking. Roughly 60% of the children who come through our clinic with language problems, many labeled "learning disabled," have some degree of hearing loss, and most of these have histories of chronic otitis media." These observations indicate that screening tests are missing many children who do indeed have problems hearing.

WORKING WITH THE LANGUAGE-DIFFERENT CHILD

The English spoken by the majority of people in the United States is usually called "Standard American English." Realistically, there is little question that people who speak standard English have advantages in school and in the job market. Awareness of this has led many who speak a dialect to want their children to learn both the dialect and standard English. The same concern applies to families for whom English is a second language.

Dialectal variations

Through the years, delineating which dialect speakers are speech and language handicapped and which are merely "different" has become a recognized necessity (Adler, 1979; Baratz and Baratz, 1970). Teachers are being encouraged to consult with speech-language pathologists to separate language deficiencies from language differences before initiating a program of language development. In turn, the speech-language pathologist is expected to be aware of the limitations of culturally biased tests currently used in determining whether or not a child has a language deficiency.

The Ann Arbor decision. During the latter part of the summer of 1979, a United States District Judge in Michigan's Eastern District Court ruled that the Ann Arbor School District develop a plan for teaching standard English to dialect speakers while respecting differences in dialect (Bountress, 1980). This decision was in response to black parents' contention that their children were experiencing academic difficulties as a result of teacher insensitivity to the students' native dialects. "The best recommendation appears to be that the teacher should respect the black child's dialect just as she respects the Mexican or Puerto Rican child's Spanish, yet while doing this, also make it possible for him (or her) to learn standard English" (Hendrick, 1980, p. 239).

There is a growing acceptance of various social dialects, and attempts are being made to assist children in the development of both their native dialect and standard English. Adler (1979) is an avid proponent of *bidialectalism,* which is an approach to the teaching of standard

English while maintaining the native dialect. He states that "the espoused goal of such programs is to increase language skills *in general—* to teach children to use standard English in appropriate contexts while respecting and maintaining the native dialect" (p. 125). The intent is to teach children to be competent in any social situation by being able to use whatever form of language is appropriate to the participants and the setting.

English as a second language

The same degree of respect is necessary for children who are learning English as a second language. In addition to learning the vocabulary, grammar, and syntax of the new language, these children must discover acceptable social behaviors in the new culture. Learning two sets of social-language interactions as well as two sets of grammar can result in confusion and discomfort, unless the transitions are tenderly developed.

More and more programs are expecting either the teacher or an assistant to be bilingual. When this is not possible, teachers should study the basic social differences. Conferences with parents as well as others who can explain the cultural expectations are needed. For example, one difference often noticed is the degree to which speakers of different languages expect or avoid eye contact. Teachers who do not understand social differences may accuse the Indian or Puerto Rican child of not paying attention when he or she is avoiding eye contact in an effort to show respect to adults. This is only one of many pragmatic functions of language that influence a child's desire and ability to learn.

Learning a new language

The most efficient way to help children learn a second language is through conversations about the things they are interested in throughout the day. Tough (1977) contends that the same principles that undergird the fostering of language in all children should be the basis of teaching. She emphasizes that the dialogue between teacher and child should be in situations that maintain the child's interest and attention. However, she points out some important differences in the way the teacher might use the same situation with a first and a second language learner. The teacher may help the child who is already using the language (first language learners) to think and speak beyond and away from the immediate situation. Such children can be reminded of similar past events or can be helped to anticipate future similar situations. On the other hand, children learning a new language may need to focus only on present situational clues to understand what is being said. The teacher needs to use language that makes the meaning clear for each specific time and place.

As we have emphasized throughout this chapter, consideration of each child's unique needs is necessary whether children are first or second language learners. Likewise, "other conditions that help the child learn his first language seem likely also to help a child learning a second language" (Tough, 1977, p. 84). The conditions referred to by Tough include giving the child ample opportunity to hear the same phrases again and again, encouraging practice of well-formed phrases at appropriate times, modeling and expanding, and concentrating on a small number of phrases at first and then extending the variety and precision of what the child is able to say and understand.

THEORY INTO PRACTICE

Although a number of theories about how language is learned have been discussed in this chapter, it has been emphasized that no single comprehensive theory has been agreed on. Neither is there any one method or procedure guaranteed to accelerate language and speech development. This should not become the basis for an excuse to ignore the implications of

theories for practice. Rather, teachers will want to understand the application of theoretical concepts to daily practice in their classrooms.

Throughout this chapter the suggestions for fostering speech and language have been adapted from many different sources. Methods for teaching deaf children, aphasic children, the visually impaired, and the retarded have been considered and assimilated. The bases for these teaching procedures were developed painstakingly through trial and error by talented and dedicated teachers long ago. It would be impossible to trace the sources for particular teaching strategies. However, it is important to recognize that these intuitive, effective teaching methods continue to influence what is done in the 1980's. Although theory continues to change, and teaching plans must reflect this, effective practices should not be discredited or discarded until better ways are available.

Because this book is about teaching young children, most of the suggestions are in harmony with what is known about first language learning today. No matter what the etiology is presumed to be, children should be given the opportunity to demonstrate that their innate capacity to learn language is present. Providing children with the opportunity to make use of this innate capacity demands that physical disabilities and environmental limitations be corrected whenever possible and at the earliest possible time. Language teaching must reflect awareness of the interferences imposed by the disabilities, even if it has been possible to correct them. A hearing or vision problem or structural abnormality corrected by age 4 does not in and of itself make up for lost time. Anything that interferes with reception interferes with perception. The effects of such interference can be reduced by skillful teaching, synchronized and matched to the individual child's language age.

It is useful to consider Uzgiris and Hunt's observations (1975, p. 26) that ". . . the nature of the circumstances encountered can influence the rate of other developmental achievements commonly attributed to maturation." Much of the development observed in most children is influenced by "the circumstances encountered," not by just growing older.

It is important to attend to much more than test scores when planning for children. Low scores do not necessarily reflect limited capacity. Siegel and Spradlin (1978, p. 379) tell us the following:

For most of the children seen in educational programs or speech and language programs, the condition exists as the expression of some unknown mixture of biological and environmental influences, and the best predictions concerning the child's developmental potential can be derived by analyzing the child's previous accomplishments and his response to therapy.

It is suggested that good teaching can and will make a difference.

SUMMARY

This chapter considers how speech and language are learned as well as what is learned during the development of communication skills. Each of the subskills of language is considered. It is emphasized that although each is distinct in its contribution to communication, all of the subskills are interrelated and inseparable.

Language as a process of rule learning is discussed. For most children this process appears to happen quickly and with little evidence that anyone makes an effort to teach the rules. However, for children with language learning problems, making the rules explicit through planned experiences is useful. A range of ways of helping children to discover the rules is presented. Dialogues to demonstrate the ideas suggested are given.

The characteristics of environments conducive to speech and language learning are described. Conditions that foster growth of language as well as those that interfere with it are identified. Throughout, special attention is

given to helping children with developmental lags. Examples of specific activities include working with the hearing impaired as well as children with other presumed conditions and deficits.

An eclectic approach to the education of young children with speech and language delays is suggested. The purpose is to provide tested, practical information for teachers and parents who live and work with young children. Opportunities for repetition, highly sequenced practice, and reinforcement, characteristic of a behaviorist approach, are described. However, it is emphasized that the most effective teaching of communication skills will occur throughout the day as adults and children talk together about what is happening. These verbal exchanges are typical of a traditional preschool center.

Snack time is discussed as just one example of a time to promote problem solving, conceptual development, and social skills simultaneously. These and other examples are typical of the cognitively oriented programs.

Finally, the importance of finding the child's level of strengths and weaknesses indicates a diagnostic-prescriptive orientation that seeks to match the curriculum to the individual child. This approach is in keeping with the interactionist view, which stresses understanding the way in which a child's developmental characteristics interact with those of the environment.

Throughout, the intent is to provide practical information based on both research and successful teaching experience.

DISCUSSION TOPICS AND ACTIVITIES

1. Using a good quality tape recorder, record "conversations" of mothers and young children. Look for mothers who have more than one preschool age child. Record the verbal interactions with each child, alone. How are they similar? How do the conversations differ?
2. Analyze the children's responses to mother's speaking pattern. Consider length, grammar, and syntax, using tapes made for Activity #1.
3. Record your own conversations with children of these ages: 1 year, 2, 2½, 3, and 4 years of age. Attempt to

interact intuitively with these children. Then, analyze what you have done in response to the feedback from the children.

4. Bring the tapes to class. Listen to them, and critique the appropriateness of the adult's utterances with the children. Consider vocabulary, length of sentences, speed, pauses, interest to the children, and the effect on the children's vocalizations.

5. Record a 15-minute conversation with one 4 year old and an adult as they make cookies or do something similar. Play the tape for the class. What *new* concepts were introduced?

6. Record the conversations of several 4 year olds as they play together. Analyze the speech and language used from the frame of reference of each of the subskills of language.

7. Write dialogues to demonstrate appropriate conversations with children from ages 2 through 5.

ANNOTATED REFERENCES

Adler, S. *Poverty children and their language: Implications for teaching and treating.* New York: Grune & Stratton, Inc., 1979.

This textbook is designed to provide a strategy for working with children whose language processes are different from those who speak standard English. A bidialectal or bicultural approach to be used along with conventional "enrichment" programs is described in detail. Of particular interest is the linguistic description of social dialects found in the Appendix.

Bess, F.H., and McConnell, F.E. *Audiology, education, and the hearing impaired child.* St. Louis: The C.V. Mosby Co., 1981.

This book fulfills a need to combine critical information about the hearing impaired with descriptions and discussions that will be useful to parents and teachers as well as physicians and audiologists. The authors identify effective procedures to implement services for hearing impaired children. Throughout the book vignettes provide clear and concise examples of the topics discussed.

The organization of this textbook includes a description of normal hearing, the major causes of hearing impairment, and factors that relate to classifying hearing loss. The first part of the book includes a useful description of the interrelationships between the development of audition and the establishment of language skills. Later chapters emphasize ways of meeting the challenges of identification, management of varied services, and appropriate educational planning.

Brackett, D., and Henniges, M. Communicative interaction of preschool hearing impaired children in an integrated setting. *The Volta Review*, 1976, 78, 276-284.

This study considers the types of communications that occurred in a preschool setting that included children with normal hearing as well as the hearing impaired. Implications for preschool programing are included.

Calvert, D.R., and Silverman, S.R. *Speech and deafness: A textbook for learning and teaching.* Washington, D.C.: Alexander Graham Bell Association for the Deaf, 1975.

This book is designed to improve the skills of parents and teachers who want to teach the deaf and hearing impaired to speak and understand spoken language. It provides descriptions of the way speech sounds are made and includes suggestions for teaching speech and language to young children. Major current methodologies of teaching speech to the deaf are examined. Teachers and parents who want to understand how to help children produce or correct speech will find this book useful, regardless of the degree of hearing impairment.

Cazden, C.B. (Ed.). *Language in early childhood education.* Washington, D.C.: National Association for the Education of Young Children, 1972.

This is an excellent reference for anyone who works and plays with young children. The various authors cover nearly every facet of language development and suggest numerous ways to promote oral communication. A section about day-care programs includes useful ideas for working with children whose language style or dialect is different.

Clezy, G. *Modification of the mother-child interchange in language, speech, and hearing.* Baltimore: University Park Press, 1979.

Clezy emphasizes that the primary caregiver must be the best speech-language therapist. However, often these caregivers, whether mothers or others, need encouragement, guidance, and specific suggestions. Throughout the book the author takes a firm stand that language therapy cannot be isolated from social and natural learning environments. Although the text is written in a way that is easy to understand, the rationale for the suggestions is based on carefully articulated theories.

Dale, P.S. *Language development: Structure and function* (2nd ed.). New York: Holt, Rinehart & Winston, 1976.

This is a widely used textbook for students of speech and language. Both theory and practice are provided. The section on dialect differences and language development includes a discussion about the important shift from a "deficiency model" to a "differences model" in current thinking about working with children who speak a nonstandard dialect.

Dubard, E. *Teaching aphasics and other language deficient children: Theory and application of the association method.* Jackson: University Press of Mississippi, 1974.

Instructing university students about the theories, principles, and purposes as well as techniques of implementing The Association Method developed by Mildred Mc-Ginnis led Dubard to develop this volume. She explains the ideas that work, as well as the kinds of language-delayed children for whom these special techniques are useful. Practical, clearly written lessons are provided.

Egerer, M.M. *Enrich you child's speech and language development*. Danville, Ill.: The Interstate Printers and Publishers, Inc., 1975.

Designed to help clinicians, teachers, and parents, this small pamphlet is useful as a guide for those who have had little or no contact with speech-language problems. Terms are defined and specific suggestions for "how to" are included.

Eisenson, J. *Is your child's speech normal?* Reading, Mass.: Addison-Wesley Publishing Co., 1976.

Written for parents this small paperback is a practical introduction to evaluating their children's speech and language as well as promoting the development of communication skills. It is also a useful book for teachers' bookshelves.

Eliason, C.F., and Jenkins, L.T. *A practical guide to early childhood curriculum* (2nd ed.). St. Louis: The C.V. Mosby Co., 1981.

This is not a book about speech and language development. However, it is included here for the excellence of the activities suggested for an early childhood curriculum. It is suggested that following the directions given throughout for activities and combining these with appropriate language stimulation will result in children who have a broad experiential base for their conversations. Language cannot be learned in a vacuum or in brief speech lessons. The suggestions made in this curriculum guide offer a wealth of activities that will make children want to talk.

Fraiberg, S. *Insights from the blind: Comparative studies of blind and sighted infants*. New York: Basic Books, 1977.

Careful research, thoroughly described, forms the basis for a very useful book. The effects of visual deficits on the child's organization of early experience and on ego development are reported. Specific suggestions for promoting the mental and physical development of infants and young children are explicit. The section on language acquisition is a must for anyone working with the visually impaired.

Gordon, I.J. *Baby learning through baby play: A parent's guide for the first two years*. New York: St. Martin's Press, Inc., 1970.

This delightfully illustrated paperback is not primarily a book about speech-language learning or about children of typical preschool age. But it is an invaluable guide to parents and teachers who may discover that a child over 2 years old is not talking. The suggestions for encouraging children to talk about what they are doing are also interesting and appropriate for the older child.

Hatten, J.T., and Hatten, P.W. *Natural language: A clinician-guided program for parents of language-delayed children* (rev. ed.). Tucson, Ariz.: Communication Skill Builders, Inc., 1975.

Designed to be given to parents, this small book suggests that the clinician choose and direct the way parents use it. The authors point out that when children have not internalized language rules in the expected way and at the expected age, it is necessary to "make the various language rules more visible and understandable" (p. 60). Their suggestions for doing this will be useful to teachers as well as parents.

Hendrick, J. *Total learning for the whole child*. St. Louis: The C.V. Mosby Co., 1980.

Part six, "developing language skills and mental ability," includes a section on "building cognitive competence by encouraging the development of verbal fluency." In addition to offering many useful ideas, specific lesson plans are provided. Resources, including books, music, and poetry, are abundantly presented. Ways to use the materials suggested are creative and exciting. Reasons for selection of the resources are given.

Horstmeier, D.S., and MacDonald, J.D. *Ready, set, go talk to me: Individualized programs for use in therapy, home, and classroom*. Columbus, Ohio: Charles E Merrill Publishing Co., 1978.

In the introduction the authors state "*Ready, Set, Go Talk to Me* is a series of prescriptive training programs for establishing prelanguage skills and initial verbal communication in individuals who have yet to develop socially useful language. The programs have been developed and tested with over 200 developmentally delayed children ranging in age from 1 to 30 years." Detailed directions for teaching the nonverbal child are useful to both parents and teachers.

Kirk, S.A., and Kirk, W.D. *Psycholinguistic learning disabilities: Diagnosis and remediation*. Urbana: University of Illinois Press, 1971.

Chapter 9 offers many suggestions for developing the skills identified by *The Illinois Test of Psycholinguistic Abilities* by the same authors. The ideas are presented in a way that makes them adaptable to children of different ages. Teachers will find the examples useful.

Ling, D. *Speech and the hearing impaired child: Theory and practice*. Washington, D.C.: The Alexander Graham Bell Association for the Deaf, 1976.

"A systematic approach to the teaching of speech and a challenge to all involved in the development of spoken language skills in hearing-impaired children," this text is included here because it impels those who work with children who need help in learning to talk to be innovative. It will be useful to teachers who want more in-depth information on this subject and to speech-language pathologists.

McGinnis, M.A. *Aphasic children: Identification and education by the association method.* Washington, D.C.: The Alexander Graham Bell Association for the Deaf, 1963.

Although this method was developed to teach speech and language to the severely impaired, many of the activities and the basic techniques are useful in developing attention, communication, and reading readiness skills in children with less severe language deficits. Children who have been described as having "auditory perceptual impairments" or as "learning disabled" benefit from these procedures.

Readers will want to remember that some of the ways of talking about language disorders have changed since this book was written. Beliefs about etiology as well as descriptive labels change regularly. As a result, the first part of the book may be useful primarily as a glance at the past. But the descriptions of the children's behavior and effective ways of dealing with them have changed little.

Nix, G.W. *Mainstream education for hearing-impaired children and youth.* New York: Grune & Stratton, Inc., 1976.

The chapter by Northcott provides a great deal of useful information about practices, progress, and problems, including the preprimary hearing impaired child in the regular classroom.

Pushaw, D.R. *Teach your child to talk: A parent guide* (rev. ed.). Fairfield, N.J.: Cebco Standard Publishing, 1976.

Filled with practical suggestions for monitoring and promoting speech and language development in young children, as well as delightful cartoon illustrations, this small paperback is invaluable to teachers as well as parents. Slides, cassettes, films, and a Workshop Outline and Guide can be purchased. An Appendix includes guidelines for identifying problems, as well as a Glossary. Good descriptions of the production of consonants and vowels are included.

Simmons-Martin, A., and Calvert, D.R. (ed.). *Parent-infant intervention: Communication disorders.* New York: Grune & Stratton, Inc., 1979.

Well-known specialists tell about current theory and practice. References and discussions include nearly every area of normal and disordered language development. In Chapter 6 "Myth—Communication" Richardson states, "The task of the adult is to develop flexible methods of instruction that will meet each child's needs rather than to search for ways to make the child fit a particular method or curriculum—like putting him into a Procrustean bed and chopping off his feet if he's too long." Richardson has much to say about labels and presumed brain damage as a cause for developmental deviations.

Tough J. *Talking and learning: A guide to fostering communication skills in nursery and infant schools.* London: School Council Publications, 1977.

Through dialogues, discussions, and examples this book emphasizes fostering communication skills for all young children. In addition, it includes chapters on children with special needs and an excellent section on children learning English as a second language. Curriculum planning and classroom practice are explained. Based on practices in British nursery and infant schools, the information is directly useful to anyone working with little children. Useful chapters on the nurturing of reading, writing, and math readiness skills are included.

REFERENCES

Adler, S. *Poverty childen and their language: Implications for teaching and treating.* New York: Grune & Stratton, Inc., 1979.

Andrews, G., Guitar, B., and Howie, P. Meta-analysis of the effects of stuttering treatment. *Journal of Speech and Hearing Disorders,* 1980, *45,* 287-307.

American Speech-Language-Hearing Association Ad Hoc Committee on Language/Learning Disabilities. Language and learning disabilities ad hoc develops position statement. *American Speech-Language-Hearing Association,* 1980, *22,* 628-636.

Baratz, S.S., and Baratz, J.C. Early childhood intervention: The social science base of institutional racism. *Harvard Educational Review,* 1970, *40,* 29-50.

Bess, F.H., and McConnell F.E. *Audiology, education and the hearing impaired child.* St. Louis: The C.V. Mosby Co., 1981.

Bloom, L. *One word at a time: The use of single-word utterances before syntax.* The Hague: Mouton Publishers, 1973.

Bloom, L., and Lahey, M. *Language development and language disorders.* New York: John Wiley & Sons, Inc., 1978.

Boehm, A.E. *Boehm Test of Basic Concepts.* New York: Psychological Corp., 1971.

Bountress, N.G. The Ann Arbor decision: Implications for the speech-language pathologist. American Speech-Language-Hearing Association, 1980, *22,* 543-545.

Bowerman, M. Semantic factors in the acquisition of rules for word use and sentence construction. In D. Morehead and R. Morehead (Eds), *Normal and deficient child language.* Baltimore: University Park Press, 1976.

Broen, P. The verbal environment of the language-learning child. American Speech-Language-Hearing Association *Monographs,* 1972, *17.*

Brown, R. *A first language: The early stages.* Cambridge, Mass.: Harvard University Press, 1973.

Bzoch, L.R., and League, R. *The Bzoch-League Receptive-Expressive Emergent Language Scale.* Gainesville, Fla.: The Tree of Life Press, 1970.

Charles, C.M., and Malian, I.M. *The special student: Practical help for the classroom teacher.* St. Louis: The C.V. Mosby Co., 1980.

Chomsky, N. *Syntactic structures.* The Hague: Mouton Publishers, 1957.

Chomsky, N. *Rules and representations.* New York: Columbia University Press, 1980.

Cole, R.W., and Dunn, R. A new lease on life for education of the handicapped: Ohio copes with 94-142. *Phi Delta Kappan,* 1977, *59,* 3-101.

Dale, P. *Language development: Structure and function.* New York: Holt, Rinehart & Winston, 1976.

Davis, J. *Our forgotton children: Hard of hearing pupils in the schools.* Minneapolis: University of Minnesota Press, 1977.

Downs, M.P. The expanding imperatives of early identification. In F.H. Bess (Ed.), *Childhood deafness: Causation, assessment and management.* New York: Grune & Stratton, Inc., 1977.

Eimas, P., Sigueland, E., Jusczyk, P., and Vigorito, J. Speech perception in infants. *Science,* 1971, *171,* 303-306.

Fraiberg, S. *Insights from the blind.* New York: Basic Books, Publishing Inc., 1977.

Hendrick, J. *The whole child: New trends in early education.* St. Louis: The C.V. Mosby, Co., 1980.

Hopper, R., and Naremore, R.J. *Children's speech: A practical introduction to communication development.* New York: Harper & Row, Publishers, Inc., 1978.

Horstmeier, D.S., and MacDonald, J.D. *Ready, set, go: Talk to me: Individualized programs for use in therapy, home and classroom.* Columbus, Ohio: Charles E Merrill Publishing Co., 1978.

Kleffner, F.R. *Language disorders in children.* Indianapolis: The Bobbs-Merrill Co., Inc., 1973.

Lenneberg, E. *Biological foundation of language.* New York: John Wiley & Sons, Inc., 1967.

Lubert, N. Auditory perceptual impairments in children with specific language disorders: A review of the literature. *Journal of Speech and Hearing Disorders,* 1981, *46,* 3-9.

McNeill, D. The capacity for language acquisition. *The Volta Review,* 1966, *68,* 17-33.

Muma, J.R. *Language handbook: Concepts, assessment, intervention.* Englewood Cliffs, N.J.: Prentice-Hall, Inc., 1978.

Naremore, R.C. Influences of hearing impairment on early language development. In D.G. Hanson and R.F. Ulvestad (Eds.), Otitis media and child development: Speech, language and education. *The Annals of Otology, Rhinology and Laryngology,* 1979, *88,* 54-63.

Nelson, K. Concept, word and sentence: Interrelations in acquisition and development. *Psychological Review,* 1974, *81,* 267-285.

Piaget, J. *Psychology of intelligence.* Paterson, N.J.: Littlefield, Adams, & Co., 1960.

Prutting, C. Process: The action of moving forward progressively from one point to another on the way to completion. *Journal of Speech and Hearing Disorders,* 1979, *44,* 3-23.

Schiefelbusch, R. (Ed.). *Language intervention strategies.* Baltimore: University Park Press, 1978.

Siegel, I. Concept formation, In J.J. Gallagher (Ed.), *The application of child development research to special education.* Reston, Va.: Council for Exceptional Children, 1975.

Siegel, G.M., and Spradlin, J.E. Programming for language and communication therapy. In R.L. Schiefelbusch (Ed.), *Language intervention strategies.* Baltimore: University Park Press, 1978.

Skinner, B.F. *Verbal behavior.* New York: Appleton-Century-Crofts, 1957.

Slobin, D.I. *Psycholinguistics.* Glenview, Ill.: Scott-Foresman & Co., 1979.

Speech Foundation of America. *If your child stutters: A guide for parents.* 1977, No. 11.

Tough, J. *Talking and learning: A guide to fostering communication skills in nursery and infant schools.* London: School Council Publications, 1977.

U.S. Office of Education. Assistance to states: Procedure for evaluating specific learning disabilities. *Federal Register,* 1977, *42,* 65082-65085.

Uzgiris, L.C., and Hunt, J. McV. *Assessment in infancy: Ordinal scales of psychological development.* Chicago: University of Illinois Press, 1975.

Weiss, C.E., and Lillywhite, H.S. *A handbook for prevention and early intervention in communication disorders.* St. Louis: The C.V. Mosby Co., 1976.

Wilkinson, L.C. Theoretical bases of language and communication development in preschool children. In L. Taft and M. Lewis (Eds.), *Developmental disabilities in the preschool child.* Symposium presented by Rutgers Medical School, Educational Testing Service, and Johnson and Johnson Baby Products, Chicago, 1979.

Encouraging problem solving and academic readiness: cognitive skills reconsidered

Cognitive behavior involves the ability to use what one knows to solve new problems. It requires that new information be taken in and related to what was known earlier, adapting both new and old knowledge to solve problems more efficiently. Or, as Kodera and Garwood (1979) explain, "Acts of cognition are thought to represent an individual's attempts to make sense of experience. This 'sense' is accomplished whenever some subjective relationship is recognized between prior and present experiences, providing structure for interpreting present and future experiences" (p. 153).

This chapter presents an introduction to theories of cognitive development, necessary conditions for nurturing problem-solving behaviors, and techniques for teaching reasoning and pre-academic readiness skills. Although this chapter concentrates on the learning and application of conceptual skills, one must remember that the child is evolving physically, verbally, conceptually, and socially; one cannot be separated from the others.

ALTERNATIVE VIEWS OF HUMAN LEARNING

Opinions of how an individual learns or develops the ability to "make sense out of experience" depend highly on one's view of the nature of man.

Cognitive developmentalists

Cognitive developmentalists believe children have an innate potential for growth that develops through active interchange with the environment. Perhaps the most notable spokesman of this process-oriented view has been Piaget (1960). Development is seen by Piaget to be neither a series of learned "acquisitions in which the child is systematically dependent on environmental stimuli; nor is development synonymous with the unfolding or maturation of internal or inborn sources of knowledge. Rather,

development refers to reorganization of psychological structures that results from interaction between the organism and the environment" (Meisels, 1979, p. 3).

Inherent in this conception of the child as active learner is the premise that through exploring, questioning, manipulating, and, in general, interacting, children pass through qualitatively different sequences of cognitive development. The sequential stages represent changes in the underlying organization of thoughts. Although theorists have attached ages to the sequential stages, they generally acknowledge that children progress at different rates (Furth, 1970). A review of the literature suggests that educators are turning to cognitive theories that do not expect children to develop in the same way at the same time (Anastasiow, 1981; Meisels, 1979).

Stages of cognitive growth. Piaget describes the first stage that begins with birth and goes through the first 2 years of life as the *sensorimotor period*. During this time the young child is preoccupied with his or her senses and motor activities. The child begins with only basic reflexes but builds toward coordinating a sensorimotor "schema." For example, a child may develop the visual or looking schema, the reaching schema, and the touching schema, which become coordinated into seeing, reaching for, and holding an object. This initial trial-and-error experimentation in which the object is obtained develops the notion of object permanence. Along with this comes learning about space, location, and the beginnings of causality.

Although children develop at different rates, most children enter the *preconceptual thought period* somewhere around 2 years of age. During this time the child develops the ability to form mental symbols of objects based on the properties learned during the previous stage. The child is freed from having to have the object in hand in order to think about it. Language develops and progresses from being focused on

TABLE 6
Hierarchical sequences of Piaget and Bruner

Piaget	Bruner
Sensorimotor period (birth to 2 years): Child moves from uncoordinated and undifferentiated sensory impressions to the ability to perceive and manipulate objects in time and space with some understanding of cause and effect. **Preconceptual period (2 to 4 years):** Words serve as symbols. Child is perceptually dominated, usually concentrates on one feature of an object at a time, is capable of imaginative play, and often does not separate fantasy from reality. **Intuitive period (4 to 7 years):** Symbols can be manipulated. Child begins to consider more than one feature of an object at a time, moves from envisioning objects in their absence to symbolizing them and relations between them, and attempts to think about thinking.	**Enactive mode:** Reality of an object is dependent on direct interaction between the child and the object. **Iconic mode:** Images are used to represent action. Direct experiences are translated into visual imagery.

things in the immediate environment to the words that stand for things not present. This capability allows the child to engage in imaginative play. The child's thinking, however, is still basically dominated by what is perceived through direct seeing, hearing, or tasting.

Children approximately 4 years of age move into the *intuitive thought period,* which comprises the remaining early childhood years (through age 7). Language becomes more complex and is used for socialization. Beginning by focusing on one attribute at a time, children can group objects into classes. After considerable experience, they begin to give attention to more than one quality at a time.

Assimilation and accommodation. Two basic mental operations are thought to be involved in the progressive changes in mental structure that comprise cognitive development. *Assimilation* in which incoming information is perceived and interpreted according to existing structures cannot be taught directly. But providing many

similar (although not identical) experiences allows this skill to grow. Through a variety of similar experiences children learn to recognize the similarities in what is done, how it is done, and what the results are.

It is also useful sometimes to repeat identical experiences. For example, doing the same routine over and over makes it possible for children to grasp a particular sequence firmly. If the activity is then varied only slightly, they can recognize the changes. If nothing is repeated, however, and each lesson is completely different, children do not observe enough to assimilate different procedures.

Accommodation occurs when the new information restructures mental processes. Adaptation or accommodation skills grow only if many genuine opportunities to adapt are available. One interesting experience grew out of a teacher washing the box used to store some doll furniture when it was not in use. The teacher forgot to replace it on the shelf when clean-up time came. Missing the box that they were used to, the children just left the toy furniture scattered around. When the teacher noticed the mess, she did not immediately provide the expected box but suggested the children put the furniture away. They stood there looking helpless and puzzled. Finally, one creative boy said, "We could put 'em in a pile on the shelf."

Bruner (1966) also believes that cognitive development occurs in recognizable stages, but he believes that the rate of development is more dependent on environmental experiences. Piaget believes it is unwise to try to speed up development, whereas Bruner suggests that readiness experiences be created through an environmental arrangement designed to enhance the child's own discovery process. Table 6 briefly outlines the hierarchical sequences of Piaget and Bruner as they are applied to young children.

Learning theorists

Learning theorists see the development of cognitive skills as resulting primarily from response to stimulation rather than through the maturing of innate capacities. This product-oriented view can be traced to such early advocates as Locke (Chapter 2) who rejected the notion of innate capacity in his conception of the *tabula rasa* or blank slate description of the mind. Skinner (1953) most readily comes to mind as the chief proponent of those who concentrate on the influence of environmental manipulation. Although Skinner believes that children can initiate behavior, he stresses the role of systematic reinforcement in determining the rate and direction of behavior. Without this reinforcement, the initiating behavior that may be essentially trial and error is thought to fade. This behavioristic view suggests that readiness experiences be planned to instigate specific responses that can be reinforced systematically rather than rely on the child's discovery process.

Social-learning orientation

Social-learning theorists agree with the importance of reinforcement in furthering the acquisition of a number of skills but find some behaviors to be the result of identification, imitation, or modeling. Theorists such as Bandura and Walters (1963) have been strong advocates of this position. Children are thought to imitate readily the actions of those with whom they identify.

Social-learning theorists differ from the behavioristic theorists in that they attribute more importance to the individual's conscious control of his or her own behavior. The role of the teacher as a model of appropriate behavior is stressed along with the manipulation of the environment so that others can model what is expected. This view leads many to argue for including handicapped children in classrooms with nonhandicapped children. Researchers have had positive results when attempting to develop language and social behaviors that are attributed to imitation and modeling (Guralnick, 1978). The following box contains some of the terms characteristic of the behavioral and social-learning orientation.

Cumulative learning hierarchy

Gagné (1970), although a behaviorist in that he believes the development of cognitive capabilities is exclusively the result of learning, also proposes a cumulative hierarchical development of skills. The child begins by acquiring reflexive habits that are the foundation for the acquisition of motor and verbal responses followed by simple discriminations, concepts, simple rules, and later, complex rules. Cognitive development is the result of learning a progressively more complex set of rules.

Gagné postulates a cumulative-learning model that is related to age. It is related to age only because learning takes time and society determines when specific information is "taught." A child's readiness in the Gagné hierarchy does

TERMS CHARACTERISTIC OF THE BEHAVIORAL AND
SOCIAL-LEARNING ORIENTATIONS

target behavior—The behavior you wish to change. The target behavior must be analyzed in terms of its frequency, its intensity, and its duration, as well as what precedes it and follows it.

reinforcement—An event that follows a behavior. Reinforcement may increase, decrease, or maintain behavior.

positive reinforcement—A rewarding event that increases or maintains a specific behavior. Food, stars, and tokens are *tangible (concrete) reinforcers*, while smiles, hugs and approving comments are *social reinforcers*.

negative reinforcement—An existing aversive and ongoing event that is removed or eliminated. If a child has been ridiculed, teased, or constantly corrected for unusual speech patterns, he or she may stop talking. Eliminating the teasing, ridicule, and constant corrections helps to increase the speaking behavior by removing the negative consequences of earlier attempts to talk.

punishment—Adding an aversive event as a consequence of a behavior, or taking away something the child perceives as desirable. A child may suppress the behavior that is punished, but it is rarely eliminated.

extinction—The removal of the events that follow a behavior that previously sustained or increased the target behavior. Ignoring unwanted behavior can effectively decrease the behavior and possibly eliminate it.

identification—Manifesting the characteristics of others with whom the individual has been in close and intimate contact over time.

imitation—Modeling the attitudes, actions or behavior of another. The learner observes and attempts to duplicate what he or she has seen or heard.

modeling—Demonstrating a new behavior to be copied by another or or imitating (copying) another's behavior.

shaping—Systematic reinforcement of successive approximations of a desired behavior. Initially, the behavior may be only slightly related to the desired behavior! Through rewarding each successive attempt (even though it is only an approximation) behavior is shaped or changed gradually.

prompting—Giving cues to assist another in learning a skill or new way of behaving. Initially, prompting may combine physical manipulation of the child's body with spoken cues. Later, gestures or spoken cues may be sufficient prompting.

fading—The gradual step by step removal of prompts. Usually physical prompts are reduced and then eliminated first; then gestures and spoken (verbal) cues are systematically decreased or attenuated.

feedback—Immediate or nearly immediate knowledge of the results of a behavior. Self-correcting materials (puzzle pieces that fit only one way, for example) or the response of an observer provide feedback. Feedback that is meaningful to the learner is necessary for increasing, decreasing, or maintaining a behavior.

not depend on internal, biological factors but on the mastery of prerequisite skills. This view is similar to a task analysis approach in which academic readiness is taught by identifying and sequencing prerequisite skills. The child's level is determined and the next prerequisite skill taught. Such an approach is basic to the process of curriculum development outlined in this book.

Lerner, Mardell-Czudnowski, and Goldenberg (1981, p. 162) succinctly list Gagné's eight phases in the process of learning that can be applied to the teaching of most skills as follows:

1. Presenting the stimulus or information. This is the motivation or incentive to learn.
2. Directing the child's attention to what is to be learned.
3. Providing a model of the performance that is expected.
4. Furnishing external prompts.
5. Guiding the direction of thinking.
6. Inducing transfer of knowledge.
7. Assessing learning attainment.
8. Providing feedback.

The McGinnis Method (1963) presented later in this chapter is one example of an effective approach to academic readiness. This method incorporates all of Gagné's phases plus the addition of decreasing or fading the prompting as the child progresses through the use of more than one modality.

CURRICULUM STRATEGIES

The views of the developmentalists just mentioned and others have been reflected in the variety of curricula successfully implemented with both handicapped children and nonhandicapped children. The longitudinal study of early intervention programs supports long-lasting effectiveness of preschool involvement, regardless of the theoretical orientation applied (Lazar, 1979) (Chapter 2). A comparison of models also indicates that no one model is superior (Miller and Dyer, 1975).

Considering various early childhood curric-

ulum models, Lillie (1975) suggests that specific curriculum features and their effects on individual children's responses should be studied. In the meantime, preschool teachers should "try as many techniques as necessary until they find one that works."

For example, children who have been deprived of sufficient background experiences are thought to need the stimulation of a multisensory environment open to experimentation. Children who have difficulty controlling their behavior or who feel too insecure to participate may need experiences provided in a highly structured environment. A carefully planned sequence and an emphasis on modeling like that found in a behavioristic program has helped disadvantaged children learn the skills necessary to survive in middle-class schools (Bereiter and Engelmann, 1968). Conversely, children with sensory or perceptual deficiencies may progress rapidly in a cognitively oriented program that stresses experience, action, and problem solving, using concrete, multisensory materials (Hohmann, Banet, and Weikart, 1979; Orem, 1969).

This chapter suggests methods for developing cognitive skills that result in problem solving and academic readiness. Ideas are drawn from all of the major developmental theories and their curriculum models. Teachers should study existing models in greater depth to understand more fully why these and other ideas "work." In general, nonhandicapped children and handicapped children are thought to need a multitude of multisensory, hands-on experiences, environments rich in language stimulation, opportunities to explore and ask questions, tasks that fit their level and are sequenced appropriately, positive models, and a structure sufficient to ensure safety and security.

Teaching observation skills

Seeing. Seeing what happens is largely a matter of learning to attend. Failure to pay attention is a serious interference to learning anything. One of the ways we have found to encourage active looking and thinking is cooking. For example, children love to crack eggs. This is a learned skill; it is messy but worth the effort.

Properly attired with an apron, and after protecting the table and floor with paper, each child is allowed to go to the refrigerator (one at a time) to get an egg. First, the teacher "shows how," and then each child is encouraged to describe what he or she will do, and later, what was done. "Tap the egg on the edge of the bowl. Put your thumbs in the broken place. Pull it apart." Demonstrated and talked about, egg breaking is a fine motor lesson, a language lesson, and a sequence lesson all rolled into one.

Other cooking lessons teach many things. One class has a yellow bowl, a purple spoon, a green measuring cup, a red-handled scraper, and a shiny beater. Before the cooking lesson these implements are lined up about 10 feet away from the cooking table. Ten children at a time sit around the rectangular table. The teacher asks "What do we need first?" and at least one child says "The bowl." That child is directed to "Get the yellow bowl." This process is continued until the needed items are on the table. Each child has a particular part to play in making the simplest food. Making muffins is a good place to begin.

All of the concept words on the bulletin board are included in some way in the cooking lesson (see p. 208). Each child does at least one thing, although all should have a turn at stirring and beating. Putting the mix into the oven is part of the project, and of course eating the finished product is the reward. Using the experience as the basis for an Experience Story Chart (Chapter 6) also makes it possible to combine reading and math readiness into the lesson.

Hearing. Hearing what happens is far more difficult for most children, even if they have perfectly normal hearing. The activity just described is also an excellent way to teach children to listen. If they fail to attend to the directions,

they may lose their turn to do something they really wanted to do. Of course, one must be careful to avoid punishing children who truly cannot understand.

For the hearing impaired child or for the child with limited language comprehension, this lesson offers the teacher the opportunity to give the directions first and then lead the child through the activity. As the child completes what he or she was told to do, the teacher should say "Good work. You brought the green measuring cup" or "You broke the egg just the right way." The teacher should be alert to model and expand whatever the child says unless language usage is correct. But do not stop the activity to insist on "good speech." Rather, use the activity simultaneously to develop thinking skills and listening skills.

Critical observation. Critical observation can be taught. Even very young children know when they have been fooled. Learning to listen, see, touch, taste, smell, and observe carefully are preludes to thinking critically. Understanding that some things are "safe" and others "dangerous" involves observation and critical thinking. Conversation that nurtures this awareness is needed. Asking "Do you think we should _____?" and "Is everything ready?" help children to begin to solve problems. The teacher should avoid doing things for them whenever the opportunity to think and make choices is a possibility.

Imaginative observation. Imaginative observation is basic to nurturing creativity. Just lying on one's back seeing animals in the clouds is a good place to begin. Seeing funny things in the shape of puddles after the rain and noticing the way a crumpled piece of paper looks are not expensive activities. But doing this consistently teaches children to observe imaginatively.

Often, we are very careful to show children pictures as we read to them. But sometimes it is fun to offer them crayons and paper and see if they can draw something about what has just been read. Perhaps they can look at a squashed tennis ball and with a little help see a mountain or a spaceship. Then, as they show and talk about their creations with friends, they will develop additional observations. Observation through the senses of smell, touch, and taste also enliven the products of children's imaginations.

THE CHILD'S WORLD OF PROBLEM SOLVING

It is all too easy to structure activities with young children so carefully that they never have the opportunity to solve problems or to realize the relationship between cause and effect. Alert parents and teachers often prevent problems so consistently that young children seldom have the chance to recognize a problem, let alone solve it. Yet everyday activities at home and at school can offer many opportunities to teach children these important skills.

Conditions necessary for cognitive skills acquisition

Young children are curious and want to know. They are explorers, but their skills in navigating are limited. Ideally the teacher of young children prepares a voyage with fascinating things to discover, appropriate to the ages and interests of the children, and encourages them to become fearless explorers. The teacher assists in helping the children to be efficient navigators, keeps the ship from getting into dangerous waters, and steadies the boat when storms occur.

Maintaining a steady course is more difficult when children come from many different backgrounds and when they have a wide range of skills. Children with disabilities require adaptations in certain routines. All young children need the opportunity, however, to discover the same information, to explore their own abilities with caring support, and to be free of the fear of failing.

Freedom from fear of failure. Freedom from fear of failure is the most essential condition basic to learning new things. Failure should be interpreted as a clue to try another way, according to Bruner (1960, p. 65), who writes, "Yet it seems likely that effective intuitive thinking is fostered by the development of self-confidence and courage in the student. . . . One who is insecure, who lacks confidence in himself, may be unwilling to run such risks."

Taking risks is natural to young children. That is why they must be watched so carefully. But taking risks in trying new things requires courage for some children. This is especially true if their early explorations resulted in pain and punishment. Sometimes the punishment has been a part of their disability.

A young hearing impaired child who cannot understand what is said fails when trying to talk. Unless one understands the reasons for this and offers adaptations, that child may be severely frustrated. The visually impaired child who bumps into things but whose disability was not detected and understood may also resist exploring. Physically handicapped children may be overprotected or abused children may be afraid. Children who have had limited opportunities to play, to use a variety of different toys and materials, and to discover need help in freeing their natural talents and curiosity.

Opportunities to experience cause and effect. Young children readily learn the relationship between cause and effect through inquiry and experimentation. One must eagerly receive, listen to, and act on children's questions. Safe conditions, inside and out, should allow for experimentation. Noise and mess often accompany inquiry. Children learn when they can dig and pile up things. Pouring and stirring with sand and water teach new concepts. The opportunity to discover is controlled in part by what there is to discover. Clearly marked areas allow spatial ordering. But the freedom to "do it myself" must be taught to some. Merely standing back and letting children "try" is an important teaching skill central to encouraging them to understand cause and effect.

Encouragement and reinforcement. Encouragement and reinforcement are also necessary for cognitive learning. Cognitive learning is interfered with if children fear punishment. The natural consequences of making a mess should be cleaning it up; never scolding or saying "I warned you not to do that." Encouraging experimentation may merely require making the materials available. But some children need to be told repeatedly that is is all right to play with particular things that were (and perhaps are) forbidden at home. Both these children and their parents need to understand that some things are appropriate at school and not at home.

Teachers need to be alert to provide social and tangible rewards for progress in expressions of curiosity and resilience and for the learning achievement. Just as structured, sequential lessons are needed for children to learn to recognize shapes and colors, so prompting and supporting are needed for children to learn qualities such as curiosity, experimentation, and problem solving (Zimmerman and Pike, 1972).

Problem-solving skills to be nurtured

The problem-solving strategies discussed here are the result of a successful problem-solving skills curriculum developed and tested in a preschool classroom. Note the similarity to the sequence identified by Merrifield, Guilford, Christensen, and Frick (1962) and reported by Kodera and Garwood (1979, p. 224). This sequence includes "preparation for problem-solving; analysis of the problem; production of a possible solution; verification, evaluation, or judgment of the solution; and reapplication of problem solving activities when a solution is judged to be unsuccessful."

Recognizing problems. Recognizing problems in everyday situations as they occur is the first step in nurturing problem-solving skills. The

child who stands helplessly waiting for someone to hang up a coat needs help in thinking about alternatives. The child who cries when the milk is spilled has a basic problem-solving opportunity misinterpreted as a threatening-punitive situation. If the teacher uses the words "We have a problem. What shall we do?" and then encourages the children to define the problem and to clean up the mess, progress can be rapid. Children basically enjoy solving problems.

Deciding where to have a snack or the best place for playing with clay presents opportunities to talk about why one place is better than another. This is the beginning of problem solving. "Staging" or contriving problems to solve is a useful addition to those problems that occur spontaneously. Having too few cartons of milk at snack time creates the need to count the children before going to get the milk. Losing pieces of puzzles can become the occasion to talk about how this problem could be avoided in the future. Children can then be helped to see that puzzles should not be put away unless they are finished and complete. Discovering that the taller children can reach things whereas others cannot leads to problem solving, an arithmetic lesson, and a lesson on concept comparatives. (For example, who is tallest? John is tall, but Timmy is taller. Bill is the tallest child in the class.")

Although problem solving itself is considered to be a cognitive (thinking) skill, it involves language learning, social awareness, and motor activities. The alert teacher sees the distinct opportunities to develop many skills from the simplest situations.

Defining the problem. Defining the problem is a skill that precedes effective problem solving. One afternoon in a classroom the children complained of being hot. They were sitting around a table near a large west window playing with clay. It would have been easy for the teacher simply to say "Oh, you are sitting in the sun. That's why you are hot. Here, I'll move the table into a shady spot." Instead she asked

"Why are we uncomfortable? I'm hot, too." (Note that she used the long word "uncomfortable" but coupled it with the word they knew, "hot.")

One of the boys responded "That old window is stuck," but he did not add that it was bitter cold outside and energy conservation forbade opening windows. A little girl made the good suggestion that the heater should be turned off. But after the thermostat was turned down they were still uncomfortable. Finally, one announced, "We got too much solar energy in here." Earlier the teacher had told them about how the sun could be used to provide energy. She had explained that the sun heats water and other things. It was not long before the children were agreeing that solar energy was the reason (cause) they were hot (effect). They had defined the problem. They were ready to think of ways to solve it.

Attending to critical features and conditions. Facilitating attending to critical features and conditions of the problem is the teacher's role. In the case just mentioned she suggested that one boy feel the table where the sun was hitting it. Before she could suggest it, another boy decided to feel the floor where the sun was not hitting it. He reported it was cold. Then three children at once saw the solution. "Move the table into a spot where the sun wouldn't hit the table," they offered. But the little boy who had made the first comment about solar energy had another idea. "Let's sit under the table. It's cool down there." And they did.

Sitting under the table would not have occurred to the teacher. It was a temporary solution but a good one. The children were very pleased they had "thought it up" themselves.

Considering alternative solutions. Children can consider alternative solutions as soon as they have learned how to recognize and state a problem. Creative thinking is a result of thinking about alternatives.

Raudsepp (1980, p. 73) says, "The importance of creativity to professional and personal success cannot be overestimated. Professionally, creativity plays a fundamental role in the problem-solving and decision-making that are intrinsic to technical and managerial activities. Personally, creativity supplies the insight and variety that help make life interesting and meaningful." Raudsepp was not talking about preschool! He was describing the importance of nurturing creativity in business managers and engineers. He points out the need to overcome personal and environmental factors that inhibit the development of creativity.

1. *Creativity.* If creativity is so essential, it should be systematically cultivated from earliest experiences. Raudsepp suggests playing games that develop the ability to discover principles linking different situations and things. He emphasizes that recognizing simple solutions (such as sitting under the table to avoid the sun) is a skill that can be learned.

One of the games Raudsepp suggests is Tangram, which originated in China around 1800. The game consists of a seven-piece set of "tans." With these seven pieces over 1,600 designs can be arranged! Very young children enjoy doing this, and with encouragement they create fascinating figures. After a few experiences with Tangrams, they begin to play more creatively with blocks, clay, and all other "manipulables." The mere awareness that the same pieces can be put together in different ways creates a mental set that establishes the habit of thinking creatively.

2. *Divergent thinking.* Seeking divergent solutions is important in developing problem-solving skills. Divergent thinking (Guilford, 1967) is a form of creative thinking involving an opportunity to go off in different directions exploring various strategies to solve problems. After one group of 4 year olds had the knack of divergent thinking, a whole carton of milk spilled on the floor. One creative thinker quickly suggested the best solution was to find a hungry cat! Another used the concept of osmosis and suggested placing a terry cloth towel in a

pan with one corner placed into the puddle. She had previously noticed that when her towel had just one corner in the bathtub the water "climbed up the towel" and made a mess on the floor. She translated this observation into a way to clean up the spilled milk.

3. *Brainstorming*. Brainstorming in preschool is exciting. As soon as children understand that the teacher really respects their ideas and will adopt them, they express unbelievable creativity. We find it useful to let them watch us write their suggestions on the chalkboard in a column. After they have made a number of suggestions, we read them together to see if one is better than the others. If all of the suggested solutions to a problem are similar, the teacher may offer a very different idea, even an obviously silly one.

Choosing the best alternative. Discussing the suggested alternative solutions to a particular problem provides opportunities for developing language, vocabulary, and cognitive skills. As children talk about the different ways of meeting a particular need, they become engrossed in what they are thinking about and add new ideas. But one alternative must be chosen and given a fair trial. Reasons for the choice should be discussed. Verbal children usually take the lead in telling their ideas. Even nonverbal children, however, can be encouraged to suggest different ways to solve a problem.

One teacher who contrived a problem placed the tumbling mats beside a shelf so that to get around them everyone had to walk several feet out of the way. The teacher even pretended to stumble over them several times. Then she announced "Boys and girls, we have a problem." Fifteen pairs of feet marched over to see what was happening. The teacher explained, "These mats are in the way, and we don't have any place to put them away. What shall we do?"

Silence. Then, one very small boy announced, "We could open 'em up and walk on them."

"No," said another child. "They'd get dirty."

Another boy said, "Let's just frow [throw] them away." (He did not enjoy tumbling.)

A little girl who could speak very little pointed up and said, "Up dere." She had noticed that the top shelf had some space. Everyone quickly agreed that "up dere" was indeed an effective answer.

Evaluating results. Evaluating the "up dere" solution did not take long. When they tried to get the unwieldy mats to the top shelf, they discovered it would not work. Just as adult engineers go back to the drawing board, so did the children. They reviewed all of their ideas. None seemed useful. So they decided to think about it some more. The next day one little girl came bouncing into the room. "I'se got sootion [solution]," she said. "Puts dem over dere by da books. Den we can sit soft while we read." And they did.

Developing flexibility and independence. Teaching effective problem solving requires teachers to accept some solutions that do not seem appropriate to adults. Surprisingly, children quickly develop a sense of things that will work and things that will not. But at first they must be encouraged to try the things that occur to them. The boy who suggested that the cat should clean up the milk forgot one thing: the school did not have a cat! When this was remembered he suggested more conventional means of mopping up spilled milk. But if she had had any way of anticipating his suggestion, the teacher vowed that she would have brought a cat to school that day. Rewarding creative thinking causes it to blossom. The reward is as simple as seriously accepting the suggestions and trying them.

Avoiding critical attitudes and fault finding. If a teacher does not laugh at or ridicule a suggestion, neither will the children. If one child observes "That's a dumb idea, the teacher may quickly respond, "There are no dumb ideas around here. Remember, we're brainstorming." If the teacher uses this term for a few days, the children will add it to their vocabularies, but more important, they will add it to their way of thinking. They will learn to withhold critical judgment until several ideas are expressed.

Nurturing affective development through solving conflicts. If children are accustomed to thinking in terms of alternative solutions, they will transfer this learned skill to the task of solving personal problems. If two children are determined to play with the same toy, problem-solving skills should be brought to bear on the resolution of this "problem." If they are used to thinking in terms of alternatives, it will not be long before you will hear them calmly suggesting that they can "take turns," play together, or find something else to do for awhile.

Nurturing language and reasoning through problem solving. Nurturing language and reasoning through problem solving is as simple as encouraging a great deal of discussion about "what to do." At first the discussions will of course be brief, simple, and monopolized by a few children. The teacher can prevent this, however, by insisting that everyone have the chance to "say something" or to "help solve our problem." New vocabulary, new concepts, and new ways of looking at old problems grow out of the process. The product (the solution) may be less than the best for awhile, but with patience and continued encouragement, young children can become excellent evaluators. They can also become a genuine help in keeping things running smoothly.

The ability to judge and reason wisely is a skill that can be developed very early. Consistent management by persons important to the children is basic. Teachers must recognize that problem solving in the best sense facilitates both cognitive learning and language development. Expecting young children to use good judgment, setting the stage for it in thoughtful planning, and then allowing them to experiment and evaluate what they do helps develop intelligent behavior.

IDENTIFYING ESSENTIAL PREACADEMIC SKILLS

Teachers must be able to identify essential preacademic skills. A recent research report produced by the Illinois Board of Education (Gill, 1980) summarized interviews with eight nationally recognized experts in early childhood special education. It indicated national concern about the effectiveness of the transition from school to school or program to program. The first recommendation reads: "Prior to placement of a child into a new program, a determination of the skills necessary for the program must be made. Some teaching toward those skills needs to occur" (p. 9).

Communication with kindergarten teachers

For the preschool teacher, determining which skills are prerequisite for a successful entrance into kindergarten usually means communicating with kindergarten teachers. The literature does offer some ideas, however, about what readiness skills might be expected or desired. Adelman and Feshbach (1971) spent many years working with disabled readers. They found the skills listed in the box on p. 201 to be essential to academic achievement. Practice in these skills or habits can and should begin during the preschool years. Even so, teachers should remember that neither excessively emphasizing academic readiness nor conscientiously avoiding readiness skills is appropriate. Preschool teachers must use their own good judgment when developing a curriculum and objectives for young children.

Obviously such a list can only be used to supplement the ongoing preschool curriculum and must be considered in relation to each child's unique needs and abilities. One could hardly justify spending time trying to get a child to answer questions about a simple story if the prerequisite listening and language skills were missing. A verbal survey has consistently found that kindergarten teachers place high priority on the skills of "paying attention" and "following directions." Therefore these skills receive considerable practice in the suggestions offered throughout this book. Perhaps the most useful thing to be gained by opening communication with kindergarten teachers is the possibility for more understanding and tolerance when children with problems reach the kindergarten classroom.

Typical cognitive activities

Whatever the theoretical orientation of and the skills expected by kindergarten teachers, nearly every preschool curriculum has similar preacademic (or cognitive) goals. In one way or another activities are included related to classification (grouping) including sorting and matching, categorization, and seriation (ordering), and the development of concepts related to color, shape, space, time, number, opposites, and letters. In general, expectations move from the concrete to the abstract, from the simple to the complex, and from the here and now to the remote in time and space (Hohmann, Banet, and Weikart, 1979).

Matching (a form of discrimination) and then putting things together that are the same or alike is among the first of the expected skills. Identical things are matched, whereas things that are alike in some way are *grouped*. *Sorting* is also a form of discrimination followed by separating according to differences. Both matching and sorting activities are described within the broader context of *classification* (distinguishing characteristics of things; then sorting, matching, or otherwise grouping them). Note that the ability to understand the concepts of "same" and "different" is essential to performing on tests and following directions. Teachers should carefully teach the verbal labels of "same and alike" and "different, not the same and not alike." Children cannot understand these concepts without using the verbal labels unless prompted to do so.

As children learn to classify, they are en-

couraged to begin with concrete, multisensory objects. Attention must be called to the various *attributes* (features or characteristics) of the objects. It is a pleasure to watch children as they move from the concrete to the abstract or from the simple to the complex in their thinking. For example, very young children are dominated by what they see, hear, smell, or touch. We call this being "perceptually dominated." They will describe an orange as something that is orange in color, round, or rough (depending on the words within their vocabulary). Later they be interested in its function and will classify it as "something to eat." Finally, it will become part of a whole class labeled "fruit." This cognitive hierarchy is reflected on intelligence tests that award a greater number of points to the answer "It's a fruit" than are awarded to "It's orange."

Seriation (ordering according to relative differences) is thought to be preliminary to understanding number concepts. Practice in serialization helps children to coordinate relationships as they begin to understand size, position, and time comparisons. Teachers begin with highly dissimilar objects and move gradually toward the discrimination of finer and finer differences.

Making comparisons seeing what "goes together" and what does not, enhances thinking skills. *Grouping* and regrouping in many different ways requires flexibility of thought. This flexibility is basic to successful reasoning, judging, and of course problem solving.

DEVELOPING PREACADEMIC SKILLS

Once critical preacademic skills are identified as preschool objectives, the next step is to translate these into a workable curriculum. The following sections present pragmatic suggestions for teaching and developing necessary preacademic skills in young children. The box at the bottom of p. 201 is offered to help teachers implement their curriculum with children who need extra time and spaced practice.

BEHAVIORS NEEDED FOR SCHOOL ACHIEVEMENT*

1. Can follow directions
2. Can concentrate long enough to complete a task
3. Can observe and remember
4. Answers questions about a simple story
5. Contributes to conversations
6. Directs and pays attention
7. Solves simple problems
8. Tolerates failure sufficiently to persist with a task
9. Makes transitions easily
10. Works on a task over a reasonable period
11. Accepts adult direction without objection or resentment
12. Works without constant supervision
13. Accepts classroom routine
14. Suppresses tendencies to interrupt others

*Adapted from Adelman, H.S., and Feshbach, S.: *Exceptional Children*, 1971, 37, 349-354.

PROBLEM SOLVING IN A PIAGETIAN CLASSROOM

Children in a Piagetian-based preschool would be encouraged to select from a variety of multisensory materials and activities. The teacher is an active observer who helps the child plan his or her daily involvement. Active, key experiences provide movement from the concrete to the abstract, from the simple to the complex, and from the here and now to the there and then. Teachers extend the key experiences through open-ended questions that stimulate thought. They assure ample time for response. Children are encouraged to learn from their mistakes and to solve as many of their own problems as possible.

SPECIAL CONSIDERATIONS FOR CHILDREN WHO NEED EXTRA TIME AND SPACED PRACTICE

1. *Concrete, multisensory tasks.* Preschool-aged children naturally learn more easily when tasks are straightforward and concrete rather than abstract.
2. *Find the child's most efficient mode of learning.* Observe carefully to determine each child's strongest mode of learning. If it is visual, then use visual cues to assist auditory directions. If auditory, then accompany visual tasks with auditory assists. If motoric, then use movement as much as possible to teach language and cognitive skills.
3. *Pacing.* Children who must work extra hard to concentrate or to process information usually tire easily. The amount of effort exerted should be varied to allow for occasional rest times, quiet activities, or soft music. Children who process information more slowly should receive less information or should receive it over a longer time.
4. *Repetition.* Some children need to try things again and again or need to have something repeated several times before it can be grasped. Intermittent practice helps children to remember skills they have learned.
5. *Plan for modeling and imitation.* Some children do not acquire information incidentally. If a specific response is desired, plan experiences where the behavior is demonstrated and positively reinforced. Once the child imitates the desired behavior, be certain to give the expected reinforcement.
6. *Task analysis.* Tasks must be broken into simple, short steps that can be sequenced from the easiest to the most difficult.
7. *Directions.* For some children it is necessary to give nearly all directions slowly and in small steps. One step can be completed before giving the next direction.

Teaching classification

Classification is basic to making analogies. Teaching classification should stress teaching children to organize (group or sort) the same information in different ways. Most preschool curricula emphasize teaching colors, shapes, and sizes. Initial classification of things by these attributes should include a wide range of items. As children become adept at sorting things by color, they should be introduced to colored shapes. As they learn to sort by shapes, they should be provided with shapes of different sizes and thicknesses.

Sorting activities should never be limited to one set or one kind of materials. Matching socks of different colors and sizes is as useful as more elaborate teaching materials. Sorting colored balls into two boxes can be both a learning experience and a useful clean-up activity. The teacher should encourage children to think of *their own* criteria for grouping. In this way the teacher can reward their tendencies toward divergent or creative thinking.

Attribute blocks. A good set of Attribute Blocks includes red, yellow, and blue circles, squares, rectangles, and triangles. Each shape is provided in two sizes and two thicknesses. Children can sort them into several identical plastic boxes with low sides (to make it easy to see them). At first the children are taught to put all the red shapes together, mixing all the shapes in the same container but keeping the color constant. The blocks are mixed together on the floor in a pile, in equal amounts of red, yellow, and blue. The teacher begins by saying "Let's put all the red ones here," and then picks up three or four red blocks one at a time, saying "This one is red" each time. Next, a child is directed to "Find another red one" and place it into the correct box. The process is continued until all of the blocks have been sorted according to color.

After a few days of doing this, circles and squares are contrasted. Again, blocks of all three colors and both shapes are mixed in a pile on the floor. The teacher sets the stage in the manner just described, except that now *shape* (square or circle) is the criterion (rule or principle).

As soon as the children are secure in this classification, multiple criteria can be introduced. Using the identical materials (and boxes), they sort the blocks according to color *and* shape.

Blue squares can be placed in one box and yellow circles in another. Later, big blue squares and little blue squares may be segregated. Yellow circles and yellow triangles should be sorted before thin yellow circles are segregated from thick yellow circles. We stress beginning with the attribute of color because research suggests that children focus on this attribute earlier than they focus on shape and other attributes (Pick, Frankel, and Hess, 1975).

Individualizing behavioral objectives. Individualizing behavioral objectives is important, because as in all teaching activities, the teacher's skill in making the activity interesting and enjoyable is important. There should never be a sense of solemnity or serious importance with games. It is critical for the teacher to be alert to support each child at his or her success level. If the lesson includes children of more than one skill level (and it should), all of the suggestions made for *individualizing* within the group should be followed.

A well-organized set of performance objectives enables the teacher to move forward or backward in providing the appropriate challenge while avoiding the overwhelming obstacle of failure. For example, the teacher may hand a red circle to Willie and say "Let's put this big red circle with the other big red circles here," as she points and literally guides Willie's hand to the right box.

But she may say to Susie, sitting next to Willie, "Susie, what should go into this box?" (as she points to the box with big red circles). Susie likely will respond "Big red circles." In this way, each child is challenged but no child fails. They also learn from each other. Groups of 4 or

VIGNETTE 7-3: GIFTED CHILDREN NEED SPECIAL ENCOURAGEMENT

These children are usually curious about everything. They want to experiment all of the time. They are persistent in problem solving. They have a large fund of information, often more than the teacher does about things that particularly interest them. They are not easily distracted, and want to remain at a particular task until they have mastered it. Their ability to attend and concentrate is usually greater than that of others.

If their insatiable curiosity is not rewarded, their unique abilities may be limited. If the messes they create as they "experiment" are the occasion for punishment, they may stop experimenting.

Young gifted children need expanded opportunities. The materials they can enjoy, the books they like to have read to them, and the conversations they will seek should be appropriate to their level of development. Often these children are particularly sensitive to the feelings of adults. They can be skillful manipulators. Be alert to help them to use their special gifts, but not abuse them.

Almost any material can be adapted to meet the needs of children who are capable of creative or divergent thinking. The attribute blocks discussed earlier are an obvious example. For example, most children will quickly learn to sort by color, shape, and size. Advanced children can learn to sort the differences among more than one attribute. Making an alternating chain of one and two differences does challenge the mind of most preschoolers.

TABLE 7

Example of en route objectives leading to a terminal objective

Sequential steps	Descriptions

Area: Cognitive

Goal: To teach children to identify shapes in the environment

Terminal objective: The child will name shapes (circle, square, triangle, and rectangle) in his or her environment with 100% accuracy, no matter what size or color the shapes take

1. Matches shapes	Given an assortment of 10 objects of 2 different shapes and the teacher's statements "This (object) is (shape name)" and "Put all of the (shape's name) in this box," the child will place all of the items of the designated shape together.
2. Sorts shapes with verbal directions	Given 10 items of each of 2 shapes and the same relative size, and the teacher's request "Give me a (shape name)," the child will choose an item of the shape named and give it to the teacher. The teacher will randomize his or her requests to reduce the chances of successful guessing.
3. Imitates shape name	Given the teacher's spoken word model, "This shape is (shape name)" and the request for the child to "Tell me about this shape," the child will imitate what has been said.
4. Recalls shape name	When asked "What shape is this?" as the teacher shows one of the shapes, the child will respond correctly, naming the shape.
5. Recognizing shapes of toys	When told to "show me something that is (shape name)," the child will respond by pointing to a toy, furniture, or any item he or she can see of the shapes named.
6. Recalls shape names	When asked, "What shape is the (any environmental item)?" the child will respond correctly by saying the appropriate shape name.

TABLE 8
Checklist for teaching terminal objectives

Objective: The child will name with 100% accuracy shapes in the environment, no matter what size or color the shapes

NOTE: Completion date for this child in boxes beside the shape named and below the performance specified.

Child's name _____
Teacher _____
Date begun _____

List shapes to be practiced here	(1) Matches shapes	(2) Sorts shapes with verbal directions	(3) Imitates shape name	(4) Recalls shape name	(5) Recognizes shapes of toys	(6) Recalls shape names

5 are optimum, but as many as 10 can enjoy this kind of classification lesson. Tables 7 and 8 suggest the sequencing of the development of shape concepts that makes individualization possible.

Attending to relevant features

"Knowledge of the rule enables attention to be directed to the appropriate information" (Pick, Frankel, and Hess, 1975, p. 356). Using the Attribute Blocks to develop the understanding of rules has been useful. During the beginning sorting activities the teacher can say "My rule (criterion) in this box is everything yellow" or "My rule in this box is only circles." After several sessions using the term *rule* the teacher may ask, "What is my rule in this box?" as she points to a box with blocks of one characteristic. If the children seem puzzled, the teacher can simply answer the question "My rule in this box is ____," and then call one child to "follow the rule" and choose a block to add to the box.

The teacher should continue to use the term *rule* and to assist any child who does not grasp the idea. Usually several children will begin to understand and use the word correctly. They provide continued practice for the others. For those who grasp the idea quickly a new dimension can be added. By providing them with an assortment of blocks and boxes, the teacher can encourage the children to "make up a rule" and make the teacher figure out their rule. But this is very difficult for many children long after they can quickly identify the teacher's rules. The teacher should be patient. Continuing to play with the blocks in this manner leads to a firm grasp of a very important principle. The same things can be sorted (categorized or classified) in different ways.

Grouping the same things using different rules. Awareness of grouping the same things using different rules is necessary for reading. After all, the same letters can be grouped in many different ways. Children must recognize

that they can group things according to one category, such as animals, food, things that go (transportation), and toys, and then that these things can be grouped in other ways. But as soon as children grasp the idea of primary categories, they should be introduced to sorting each category into subclassifications. Foods divide into fruit, meat, and vegetables. Animals can be classified as farm and zoo, tame and wild, or pets and nonpets. Clothing can be sorted into things for the head, things for the feet, things to wear outdoors, and things to wear inside. Each of these cognitive skills requires knowing the names of things, the uses of things, and the way in which they can be sorted. Remember these are readiness activities for true hierarchical grouping that occurs later.

Encouraging flexibility in thinking. Teachers need to encourage flexibility in thinking. Sorting toys into different storage containers at different times is one useful way of doing this. For example, a class had been keeping toy animals in a box with pictures of animals on it and Lincoln Logs in their special box. One day two boys insisted that Lincoln Logs belonged with the animals. Their reasoning: "We plan to use the logs to make a fence in our zoo tomorrow." Because teaching children to think in flexible, creative ways is a major goal, the logs stayed with the animals. That is, until someone else decided they were just right for the farm. Then, they sorted the zoo animals and the farm animals separately with no direction from the teacher. The logs moved to the farm.

Building a bridge to kindergarten. Children enjoy the challenge of sorting anything, if the teacher is enthusiastic and excited when they grasp new ideas. For example, a teacher laminated a large piece of cardboard and divided it into four sections. Pictures were chosen from categories the children had been studying. At first, the cardboard merely took the place of the boxes used in the first lessons. (For some children, it is useful actually to place the boxes on the cardboard at first.) Then, when they recognized that the task was the same (sorting according to categories), the boxes were removed. The teacher continued to refer to the divisions on the cardboard as boxes.

Later, the children will need to know that rectangles and squares in their kindergarten workbooks are called boxes. These earlier experiences help them to bridge the gap between real boxes and boxes on paper. Children who learn less quickly than some of their peers will benefit from a larger variety of materials. Not only does this help them to see more relationships, but it also avoids boredom in doing the same thing in the same way over a longer period.

Teaching seriation

Introducing children to serial ideas such as first and last should be done in the context of everyday activities, especially those that involve whole body movement. First and last may refer to place in line or when one does something. These concepts are critical for young children entering kindergarten. Most of the problems involved in lining up or being allowed to do something are caused by children's lack of understanding and experience with these terms. Understanding the concept (cognition) and using the correct label (language) cannot be separated. Without the concept words, one cannot talk about the concept. Without the idea, the word is useless.

Montessori cylinders and "nesting" toys are typical seriation materials. Hardware stores often provide sample paint cards that can be used to seriate from dark to light. The teacher should not overlook using household measuring cups or variously sized nails.

Teaching concepts

Providing children sufficient experiences with the many concepts they must learn and the association with the words is a challenge. Merely

keeping track of the concepts requires a system. A system for teaching concepts includes the following features:

1. Identify the concepts to be taught.
2. Plan a large number of activities and experiences that make explicit the idea of the concept.
3. Use the associated concept word throughout many class sessions as the need for the word occurs. That is, grasp the moment most likely to demonstrate the concept meaning to the child, and use the word at that moment.
4. Provide many experiences involving a particular concept close together, but in natural, spontaneous ways.
5. When half the children seem to grasp the idea, plan a structured drill-like activity. The intent is to emphasize the common features associated with the different activities, but to concentrate on one target concept. For example, if grasping the idea of "first" is the target, play many different games requiring lining up in serial order. Focus on "first" in moving from one activ-

**PROBLEM SOLVING IN A
MONTESSORI CLASSROOM**

A visit to a Montessori classroom would reveal an array of attractive materials. Each would emphasize teaching one dimension. Each would be "self-correcting" in that the material would reveal the error, allowing the child to correct himself or herself by further experimentation. For example, the knobbed cylinders shown in the picture on p. 206 fit snugly in only one corresponding hole. Focus between the ages of 3 and 6 would be on self-directed concentration.

ity to another in the room. Lining toy animals in a row, identifying the animal that is "first," and then turning all the animals around to discover that the one that was first is last helps to make the concept clear.

6. Provide for contrived uses of the concept word by the children. That is, create the occasions when spontaneously using the target word throughout the day is appropriate.

7. When most of the children use the word some of the time and most of them appear to understand it, one should have a system for regular review. Of course, if the concept words are used frequently because they are needed and useful, the review is spontaneous and effortless.

Each playgroup or classroom will want to focus on many of the same concept words. Needs are quite universal. An examination of teacher's manuals for kindergarten and first grade reading and arithmetic yields a large number of necessary concept words. These should be introduced through real life and play

activities at least 2 years before the children encounter them in school. "Put your finger at the top of the page" is a much harder direction to understand if children have not learned about "the top shelf" or "the top of the page" in a book as someone read a story. A review of the Boehm Test of Basic Concepts (Boehm, 1971) or the work of Bangs (1968) will be most helpful in selecting "target concepts."

Record the concepts being taught. The system for recording the concepts being taught that we have found useful is described as follows:

1. Identify the concepts to be taught, and print each one large enough to be seen across the room. Write the words on individual pieces of cardboard. (We use pieces about 1 × 5 inches.)

2. Choose a bulletin board that is high and not of particular interest to the children. Divide it vertically into four sections.

3. The first section (on the left) may be labeled "Provide experiences." The second section can be called "Fun drills." The third column might say "Contrived experiences" and the last row "Monitor children's use."

4. Place the target concept words in the first column, "Provide experiences." Alert parents, teachers, and aides to use these words at appropriate times throughout the day both at home and at school. Begin with only two or three simple concepts.

5. When half the children demonstrate that they understand a concept, move the card with that concept word to the next column. Add a new concept to the first column.

6. Continue moving each concept from left to right, allowing it to remain in the columns as long as necessary. If a concept is not used by the children when it is in the "Monitor use" column, simply move it back to the left to the "Contrived experiences" column.

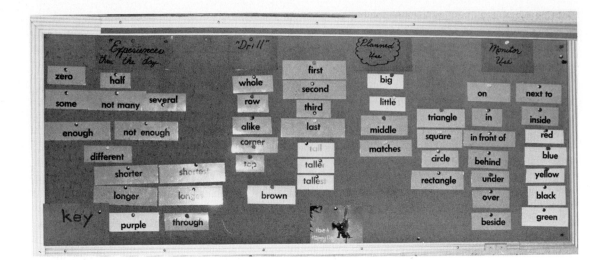

Avoid stereotyped, labored teaching of concepts. Teachers should provide opportunities for children to learn the concepts through experiences appropriate to a particular setting. They should not leave the learning of important concepts to chance.

Identify the concepts.
Use them.
Make meanings clear.
Monitor use over time.

McGINNIS REVISITED—AND ADAPTED

Mildred McGinnis was a teacher of the deaf at the Central Institute for the Deaf in St. Louis during the First World War. Most of the time she taught children. But part of her responsibility was to work with men who had lost their ability to communicate using speech and language because of brain injuries suffered in the war.

The men appeared to be unable to talk and understand speech, although they were usually normally intelligent in other ways. Through trial and error, creative attempts, and determination, McGinnis (1963) developed a system that worked in teaching many of these men to talk again. Basically she taught them how to make one sound at a time, associate these phonemes with the written letters (phoneme-grapheme correspondence), combine them into words, and later combine the words into sentences.

The McGinnis method and children

Because McGinnis' primary responsibility continued to be teaching children, she naturally adapted the method that worked with the soldiers to children who appeared to be unable to learn in the expected way. Hearing aids were very inadequate at that time. It is therefore not surprising that McGinnis opposed using hearing aids for those children who were having difficulty learning. She felt that the natural voice spoken near the children's ears provided a better speech model. By careful observations and trial and error, she discovered a successful method of teaching hearing impaired children, as well as those who had been diagnosed as aphasic.

In recent years we have found the McGinnis method a very useful tool for children with severe language delays, with mild hearing losses, and for children who have been described as learning disabled or pre-learning disabled. It would be inappropriate for teachers who are not trained in teaching the deaf or as speech-language pathologists to attempt to use the complete McGinnis method (1963). Many of her strategies and ideas, however, are very effective in working with a wide range of language delayed children.

The following adaptations have proven to be simple to use, effective, and of great interest to children. They also are a significant help in developing readiness skills in children whose overall developmental lags may interfere seriously with their attempts to get ready for kindergarten. Even if these children do not appear to have a language learning deficit, their achievement of early reading readiness skills demands preliminary language subskills too often overlooked.

We suggest that this adaptation of the McGinnis method with 3 to 5 year olds can reduce kindergarten failure and learning disability for many young children. In and of itself, it cannot develop all of the readiness skills, but it is one of many useful tools and techniques.

McGinnis—"attention exercises"

Just as learning disabled children today are often described as hyperactive, so were children in earlier years identified as aphasic and considered to be too active. Their attention spans and memories appeared to be brief and fleeting. Accordingly, McGinnis designed the first steps to deal with the need to teach children to pay attention. She was aware that often they did not pay attention because they did not understand what they were expected to do. Hearing impaired and language delayed children move around frequently in their efforts to avoid the uncomfortableness of not understanding what is said to them.

To teach these children how to pay attention, McGinnis used controlled commands designed to develop attention habits. Children were allowed to perform only after a command or direction had been given. Initially all activities followed a consistent pattern:

A child is called, and he is given a command. He performs the requested task and awaits the order to return to his seat before the next child is called. . . . To develop further attention the command is given to the group, and then one child is called on to perform (McGinnis, 1963, p. 80).

These first activities should be designed to develop looking, listening, waiting, and acting on command. Deliberate, quiet, and slow motions are important. The goal and objective could be written as illustrated in Lesson Plan 7-1. Note the similarities in the focus on attending skills characteristic of Montessori (Orem, 1969), Zeaman and House (1963), and others who have developed teaching strategies for individuals who have difficulty learning. Apparently the role of attention or concentration in acquiring the ability to learn cannot be overestimated.

If the teacher is enthusiastic and warmly approves each child's attempts with smiles and words, the goal will be achieved quickly. In practice, it is useful to do these exercises with all of the children. Children who do not have problems paying attention may need to do them only once. By doing the exercise with all the children, however, they establish the habit of waiting for a signal. (Usually the child's spoken name is enough, but it may be necessary to point or even physically assist the child.)

For children who are able to understand spoken directions, this same model or teaching procedure is useful in helping them to develop skill in following multistep spoken directions. Unless they have had practice before they are 5 years old, the task is overwhelming for many elementary school children.

It is important always to discover each individual child's "entry behavior" (see Chapter 4 about writing objectives). Then provide "equiv-

---

LESSON PLAN 7-1: SAMPLE McGINNIS-BASED LESSON PLAN

Goal: To teach the children to recognize the teacher as a model to be imitated when they are directed to do so (designed to help hyperactive or inattentive children to develop attending skills).

Objective: When the teacher performs a simple action, the children will watch, wait for the teacher's signal that it is their turn to perform, and then (one at a time) imitate the teacher's action when directed to do so. CRITERION: Children should perform 8 of 10 actions.

Procedure: Begin with three or four children, a teacher, and an aide. Place the children in a semicircle on chairs, facing the teacher. (If one or more of the children need to be helped to remain quiet, the aide may sit behind them and touch them gently. The proximity of an adult does wonders for hyperactive children!)

The teacher should call one child to stand up to focus that child's attention. Then the teacher should do a simple physical action that previous observation of the children convinces her they are able to do. Stepping slowly and deliberately over a block, placing a block on another block, or clapping hands are good first activities. (Do just one.)

Next, say the child's name: "Danny, you do it." If Danny needs further help, the aide may gently put him through the motions. Any help of this kind should be eliminated as quickly as possible. As soon as the action has been completed, the teacher should smile and say "Good work, (pause) sit down."

Each child should have two or three turns. The activity should not drag on. It should not last more than 10 minutes. Then, a free play period is in order.

---

alent practice" until the child is able to meet the criterion. If the objectives are sequenced correctly, the next step will be easy for each young student.

McGinnis adapted—first steps to reading readiness

Recall that 4-year-old Danny has had a hearing loss during critical language learning years. He continues to omit unvoiced consonants in spontaneous speech and his language development is delayed. Although with his improved hearing he may be able to hear many of the speech sounds he formerly missed, he has not learned to attend to them. Unlike children learning to attend to phonemes during the optimum years for learning to talk, Danny will need to have them brought to his attention. Be-

cause he could not hear them, he did not know they were there. Now, speech and listening habits need to be changed through thoughtful, skillful teaching.

Children who are very active or who have limited attending skills need structured transitions. After they can attend to the teacher's model of a gross motor action (for example, jump or clap hands) and can imitate it on signal, they can be taught to attend to speech sounds. The same teaching format described earlier should be used. Simply substitute the teacher's model of a phoneme for the physical actions.

It is now necessary to build a bridge between the *process* of modeling physical actions and the *process* of modeling speech sounds. The teacher should build that bridge by doing some of each

---

DESCRIPTION OF THE PRODUCTION OF SOME CONSONANT SOUNDS*

NOTE: Each consonant has three distinctive features: the place in which it is made, the manner of production, and whether it is voiced or unvoiced (breath only). For the exercise described here, it is desirable to use consonants that differ from each other as much as possible. /F/, /m/, and /t/ are suggested for the first activities. Later, additional consonants may be introduced.

Sound—/m/
Production: /m/ *is a bilabial nasal resonant.* Lips are shut, lightly touching. The nasopharyngeal port is open. The voice moves through the nasal cavity and out through the nostrils. The resulting sound is often described as "humming." For this exercise, associate the letter *m* with a slightly prolonged hum.

Sound—/t/
Production: /t/ *is a lingua-alveolar breath stop.* The tongue touches the alveolar ridge (just behind the upper front teeth) and the edges of the molars on both sides of the mouth. Air is retained in the oral cavity until it is "exploded" gently between the teeth and lips. For this exercise, associate the letter *t* with a whispered "ti-," (the first two sounds, or consonant-vowel [CV] of the word *tip*).

Sound—/f/
Production: /f/ *is a labio-dental breath fricative.* The lower lip lightly touches the upper front teeth while breath is emitted between the teeth and lip. No voice is used. The nasopharyngeal port is closed. For this exercise, associate the letter *f* with a slight prolongation of the /f/ at the end of the word "half." (Avoid biting the lip. Teeth should lightly touch the lip as the air flows.)

*For a more technical description of correct sound production refer to Calvert and Silverman (1975).

---

during the same lesson. For example, the teacher could model stepping over a block for Susie. Then, when it is Danny's turn, the teacher could pronounce /f/. At first he might need to see the air blow a bit of tissue off the teacher's hand. Later, he could be expected to see the lips move and recognize /f/ and imitate it. (The box shown above describes the way to produce /f/, /t/, and /m/ correctly.)

Introducing speech sound books. As soon as the children learned to attend, McGinnis introduced them to speech sounds and associated them with the related graphemes in an individual book for each child (Fig. 7-1). The first page always included a sketch of the child, and the child's name under it. Then, the next pages included the written letters for the speech sounds, as each was taught. Each page had only

one sound represented by the letter written four or five times in different colors.

McGinnis used letters about the same size. Recent experience has found it useful to write the same letter in different sizes. It is a simple and meaningful way to communicate to children that size and color are not the keys to the phoneme to be spoken. Rather, the shape of the letter is the key. Children often fail to understand this, and many first graders are puzzled when they must associate the big letter on the chalkboard with the little one in their primers. By writing the lower case letters in different sizes on one page, this difficult concept can be taught effortlessly.

Making a book for each child is time consuming but very rewarding. They treasure their books and expend great effort in learning every-

FIG. 7-1. Sample pages from a speech book. (Courtesy Lori Harshbarger.)

thing in them. The teacher is not expecting to teach the children to read but rather to develop the ability to hear and produce speech sounds and to recognize the associated letters. The resulting readiness skills justify the time involved.

McGinnis adapted—next steps to reading readiness

Thus far attending skills have been developed and speech sounds introduced after the ability to watch, wait for a signal, and imitate a non-speech action. The children have then been introduced to individual speech sound books.

These preliminary activities are background for the development of the following two very different things.

1. Prereading readiness skills for all young children, including two critical speech-language skills: the ability to distinguish between and among the sounds in words, and the ability to associate written letters with referent speech sounds

2. The visual and auditory skills needed by all children, but in particular by young children with speech-language delays

Speech-language pathologists long have known that if a child can imitate a speech sound in isolation or in a syllable, even if he or she is not "using it in words," that sound is "emerging." Because the child has demonstrated that he or she knows the sound exists, one can expect that it will soon "emerge" in connected speech. Often these children were not assigned to speech therapy because experience had taught the pathologist that the missing sounds would soon appear in the child's spontaneous speech. In effect, by teaching the "Dannys" in the class to recognize and produce the individual phonemes, they are placed in the advantageous position of "knowing the sound is there."

The list that follows is designed to allow the teacher to use as much or as little of the adapted McGinnis method as he or she judges is useful to individuals or to all members of the class. Usually these activities are best achieved with groups of no more than five children at a time. Each lesson should last no longer than 15 minutes. There should be no sense of pressure or rush. All of the activities should be managed in a way that the children recognize as interesting and rewarding. If the teacher maintains enthusiasm for each small step of progress, the children also will.

1. Establish attending skills.
2. Introduce individual books.
3. When the children can produce a correct speech sound, associate it with the written letter, and write a page of a child's book as he or she watches.
4. As soon as the children know three phonemes, copy them from their books onto a card as described earlier. Be sure that they observe this copying. Each phoneme should be written once on a separate card. (If possible, laminate them or cover them with plastic because they will receive hard use.)
5. The lesson form may now include the following:
   a. Each child pointing to the letter in his or her own book, and recalling the speech sound (saying it). The teacher should help by saying the speech sound whenever needed.
   b. The teacher may then have the children close their books but continue to hold them. Then the teacher should show the children one of the letter cards, and have them find the same letter in their books. (Repeat until each letter is found once or twice.)
   c. The teacher may hold the cards so that the children cannot see the letter as he or she looks at it and reads the letter (says it). The children should then find the letter in their books. If some cannot do this, the letter may be turned for them to see as the teacher repeats it.

   d. Place three or four letter cards on the floor. The teacher may say one of the phonemes, and have a child pick up the letter for the sound spoken. (This is of course auditory and visual discrimination.) Children like Danny, however, should be encouraged to watch the teacher's lips also at first. Later, and only if it is easy for the "Dannys" in the class, they may be encouraged to "just listen" and find the card.
   e. Listening to a direction may be combined with listening for a phoneme. For example, say "Vicky, put both hands on /t/," "Danny, hop to /m/," or "Susie, stand on /f/."

Later, for the 5 year olds, beginning auditory discrimination activities similar to those in the kindergarten readiness books may be used. The teacher should choose two very different sounding phonemes and place their graphemes on the floor (/m/ and /f/ are good choices). Maintaining an appropriate level of attending, waiting, and performing on signal, the teacher should do the following:

1. Say one of the phonemes, and call a child to point to it. Then tell the children to listen carefully while the teacher says some words that begin with that sound. A set of cards with pictures that begin with the target speech sound should be used. The teacher should look at the picture, say the word with a slight exaggeration of the beginning consonant, and then have the children in turn repeat the word. One of them should place the picture on or just beside the target sound. (Sometimes it is useful to have a container for the pictures. The letter may be attached to it. Coffee cans, small boxes, or plastic buckets are appropriate.) Continue until five or six pictures beginning with the same consonant have been placed correctly.
2. Repeat the procedure, as just described, with a contrasting phoneme. (At first,

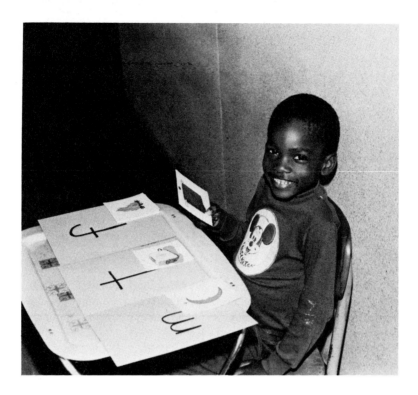

avoid using consonants that have two features the same. For example, do not use /p/ and /b/, or /t/ and /k/. Good first choices include /m/ and /f/, /m/ and /t/, or /t/ and /f/.

3. Third, shuffle the cards that begin with the two different consonants. Repeat the activity, alternating the two sounds randomly.

Later, more consonants may be added to the activity. Those that are more similar may be contrasted when the children have demonstrated that they understand what they are expected to do.

For variety, children enjoy adding more vigorous physical activity to the lesson. Hanging the letter cards from the ceiling (usually an available light fixture) and forming teams to see who can listen to the teacher's spoken word and hop, jump, or walk backwards (on signal, of course) to the correct letter adds variety. The intent is to provide needed practice in listening for beginning sounds in words, a much needed skill for success in most kindergarten readiness programs.

Any children with developmental lags will find these discrimination activities difficult. Many readiness programs provide very little practice or appropriate introduction to these listening lessons. For this reason they have been included in some detail here. Children who have had articulatory problems earlier can be expected to need more practice and more carefully structured practice than their peers. Unless this is provided effectively in preschool, kindergarten and first grade can be a disaster.

We have emphasized that each community is different in its educational practices. The expectations of kindergarten and primary grade teachers for entering students vary widely. The trend, however, is to expect well-developed visual and auditory perceptual skills, as well as good language and appropriate social behaviors.

SUMMARY

Developing conceptual and problem-solving skills together with reading and arithmetic readiness in young children is a responsibility all preschool and day-care teachers share. This task is especially important for teachers of children with developmental delays or handicaps. This chapter has focused on practical ways to identify and teach these skills.

Enhancing cognitive skills in preschoolers can occur readily within a seemingly natural environment of play and curiosity. Elements from all of the major theories of child development help in devising strategies to stimulate problem-solving skills and academic readiness. The theories presented in this chapter ranged from Piaget's belief in the gradual unfolding of innate capacities to Skinner's view that cognitive skills result from response to environmental stimulation. Linking elements of these extreme models of human learning, Gagné's cumulative-learning model is presented as a sequencing of prerequisite skills similar to the process of task analysis.

When given the freedom to explore and the opportunities to learn from failure free from anxiety, one can easily incorporate problem-solving skill development into a curriculum. Examples and rationales are provided to illustrate how children can develop the skill to identify and define problems, to consider alternative solutions, to choose among alternatives, and to evaluate results with flexible judgment. The relationship between problem solving and academic readiness becomes apparent as concepts and abstract images are translated into words that facilitate movement through the stages of problem solving.

If a preschool is to be successful in preparing children for the transition to kindergarten and beyond, it must identify the preacademic skills relevant to any local school district. In addition

to "pays attention" and "follows directions," the curricula of most early childhood classrooms provide readiness activities involving classification (including sorting, matching, categorization, and serialization), colors, shapes, space, time, numbers, opposites, and letters. Suggestions for promoting a child's awareness of various attributes or relevant features necessary for generating and following "rules" used to manipulate concepts are included.

The McGinnis Method for teaching aphasic and hearing impaired children was adapted for use with a variety of children who need special considerations. The method as presented is particularly useful for cognitively preparing a child for early reading experiences. As with the other instructional activities suggested throughout this chapter, the emphasis was on a way to work individually with children at different developmental levels within a group learning situation.

DISCUSSION TOPICS AND ACTIVITIES

1. With classmates, role play a debate between theorists who emphasize the development of innate abilities and those who stress the role of the environment in developing cognitive abilities.
2. Outline a lesson plan from at least two different viewpoints: the behaviorist or skill-oriented model, the cognitive (Piaget or Montessori) model, the child-development or enrichment model, and the task analysis model. Discuss the applicability of your outlines to children who have special needs.
3. Try to recall the last problem you were conscious of solving. Review your actions. Which skills did you employ and why? If you had it to do over again, would you select another alternative or seek additional data? You may wish to exchange experiences with classmates.
4. Design some preschool lessons that will encourage children to experience cause and effect relationships. If possible, carry these out with children. What improvement could be made in your lesson design? Did you get the results you desired? Discuss the children's involvement with classmates. Perhaps a recording of the children's responses will help you to analyze the children's reactions in greater detail.
5. Why is it important to maintain a balance between social-emotional and intellectual activities in the preschool? This is a critical issue that is receiving attention national-

ly and should be thought through periodically. Recognize your own philosophy and investigate its implications for young children.

6. Role play your answer to a parent who insists that reading per se should be taught in preschool. Ask colleagues for constructive criticism.

7. Go on a "trust walk" to help develop your observation skills. Children also enjoy this exercise.

ANNOTATED REFERENCES
Alternative views of human learning

Beard, R. *An outline of Piaget's developmental psychology for students and teachers.* New York: The New American Library, Inc., 1972.

The author of this concise, well-written outline of Piaget's chronological stages took great care in presenting difficult material in an easy-to-read manner. A glossary of the significant vocabulary and an extensive bibliography are included. Direct implications for preschool teachers are discussed.

Biber, B., Shapiro, E., and Wickens, D. *Promoting cognitive growth: A developmental-interaction point of view.* Washington, D.C.: National Association for the Education of Young Children, 1971.

This is another standard work. This paperback manual illustrates how a preschool teacher can strengthen cognitive development. A series of descriptive incidents depict the Bank Street approach that builds cognitive abilities through daily activities. The teaching-learning events that were taken from observational records and interviews with teachers create a realistic picture of spontaneous growth experiences.

Brearley, M., and Hitchfield, E. *A guide to reading Piaget.* New York: Schocken Books, Inc., 1972.

The authors have presented a method of understanding excerpts from Piaget's major works covering a broad array of subjects including number, measurement, moral judgment, and floating and sinking. Practical classroom implications are discussed following each presentation. The book ends with a very concise summary of Piaget's developmental stages.

Hohmann, M., Banet, B., and Weikart, D.P. *Young children in action.* Ypsilanti, Mich.: The High/Scope Press, 1979.

This comprehensive volume is designed as a manual to present the Cognitively Oriented Preschool Curriculum, which is organized around a set of "key experiences." These key experiences are derived from Piaget's theory and are thought to be the primary cognitive characteristics of children in the "preoperational" stage of development. They are the guidelines for the development and evaluation of the Cognitively Oriented Preschool Curriculum. All related classroom activities are built on concrete, active experience.

The child's world of problem solving

Bradbard, M.R., and Endsley, R.C. How can teachers develop young children's curiosity? *Young Children,* 1980, 35, 21-32.

This excellent article reviews the implications of current research for the development of curiosity in young children. Specific suggestions are made about how teachers can foster the growth of this important attribute. The tone of this article makes it perfectly clear that teachers can actively influence the expression of exploratory types of behavior. Such behaviors are not necessarily a result of intellectual capacities.

Copple, C., Sigel, I.E., and Saunders, R. *Educating the young thinker: Classroom strategies for cognitive growth.* New York: D. Van Nostrand Co., 1979.

This supplementary text combines a theoretical perspective with a practical approach. It demonstrates strategies to foster thinking and problem-solving skills. With a Piagetian orientation it integrates problem-solving skills into daily activities including art, music, imaginative play, and science.

Estvan, F.J. Teaching the very young: Procedures for developing inquiry skills. In R.H. Anderson and H.G. Shane (Eds.), *As the twig is bent.* Boston: Houghton Mifflin Co., 1971, 267-274.

Practical suggestions are offered to assist the teacher in setting up a stimulating environment and guiding a child toward inquiry through thought provoking questions. Especially helpful are the four levels of abilities necessary to participate in a cognitive investigation (experiment) described by the author. "The teacher's questioning is the basic technique for guiding the very young child through the inquiry process" (p. 271).

Pick, A.D., Frankel, D.G., and Hess, V.L. Children's attention: The development of selectivity. In E.M. Hetherington (Ed.), *Review of child development research.* Chicago: University of Chicago Press, 1975.

This excellent chapter allows the more advanced student to obtain a view of what is known about the process of attention and its importance to problem solving and learning in general. The developmental changes revealed through research are directly applicable to curriculum design. Of note is the importance of deliberate attempts to accentuate relevant features when specific concepts are being taught.

Sharp, E. *Thinking is child's play.* New York: E.P. Dutton & Co., Inc., 1969.

This brief paperback book clearly outlines Piaget's philosophy. Simple games using homemade materials are then described that teach various classification and serialization skills. Numerous usable ideas are provided by a mathematics teacher.

Valett, R.E. *Developing cognitive abilities: Teaching children to think.* St. Louis: The C.V. Mosby Co., 1978.

The author states that "the purpose of this book is to help teachers and psychoeducational therapists develop the cognitive abilities of learning-handicapped children" (p. vii). Brief reviews on the effects of education on mental growth are included along with descriptive classroom activities that foster cognitive development. Although this book focuses on primary and elementary approaches, it offers invaluable insights into the evaluation and development of thinking, processing, and problem-solving skills.

Identifying essential preacademic skills

Calvert, D.R., and Silverman, S.R. *Speech and deafness.* Washington, D.C.: The Alexander Graham Bell Association for the Deaf, Inc., 1975.
An objective discussion of major current methods for teaching deaf and hearing impaired children. Practical suggestions and useful statements about relevant theory combine to make this a readable, easily understood book. The descriptions of the production of speech sounds are useful to teachers interested in developing auditory discrimination skills in young children. For many of them, learning to hear sounds in words (a basic reading readiness skill) must be preceded by learning to hear the phonemes in isolation. Teachers must understand how to produce the speech sounds in isolation to introduce some children to "hearing the sounds of speech."

Carew, J.V., Chan, I., and Halfar, C. *Observing intelligence in young children.* Englewood Cliffs, N.J.: Prentice-Hall, Inc., 1976.
This unique, relatively brief book affords the reader the opportunity to observe in the homes of eight young children. Following verbatim descriptions of adult-child interaction, the authors offer interpretations of the intellectual value of the interchanges. The authors do not claim that the correctness of their interpretations is undisputed. Their concern is to convey what can be learned by carefully observing behavioral interactions over time. The episodes described are conducive to lively classroom interaction.

Orem, R.C. *Montessori and the special child.* New York: Capricorn Books, 1970.
Although numerous books are available that review the Montessori approach to the education of young children, this one is particularly helpful because it clearly describes various ways of applying Montessori techniques to the education of children with special needs. A very useful table lists Montessori methods and materials to be used with children who exhibit physical, perceptual, language, cognitive, and behavioral deficiencies. The lessons covered are applicable to all young children.

McGinnis, M.A. *Aphasic children: Identification and education by the association method.* Washington, D.C.: The Alexander Graham Bell Association for the Deaf, Inc., 1963, 1977.

Although the method described in this book was developed to teach speech and language to severely impaired people, many of the activities and the basic techniques are useful in developing communication and reading readiness skills in children with less severe handicaps. Often such children have been described as having auditory perceptual problems. Others have been identified as learning disabled. Early childhood teachers and speech-language pathologists will find this small book useful because of the detailed teaching procedures outlined. Perhaps a second look at this 60-year-old method may even save us from reinventing the wheel.

REFERENCES

Adelman, H., and Feshbach, S. Predicting reading failure: Beyond a readiness model. *Exceptional Children*, 1971, 37, 349-354.
Anastasiow, N.J. Early childhood education for the handicapped in the 1980's: Recommendations. *Exceptional Children*, 1981, 47, 276-282.
Bandura, A., and Walters, R.H. *Social learning and personality development.* New York: Holt, Rinehart & Winston, 1963.
Bangs, T. *Language and learning disorders of the pre-academic child.* Englewood Cliffs, N.J.: Prentice-Hall, Inc., 1968.
Bereiter, C., and Engelmann, S. *Teaching disadvantaged children in the preschool.* Englewood Cliffs, N.J.: Prentice-Hall, Inc., 1968.
Biehler, R.F. *Psychology applied to teaching.* Boston: Houghton Mifflin Co., 1978.
Boehm, A.E. *Boehm test of basic concepts.* New York: Psychological Corporation, 1971.
Bruner, J. *The process of education.* New York: Alfred A. Knopf, Inc., 1960.
Bruner, J. *Toward a theory of instruction.* Cambridge, Mass.: Belknap Press of Harvard University, 1966.
Calvert, D.R., and Silverman, S.R. *Speech and deafness.* Washington, D.C.: The Alexander Graham Bell Association for the Deaf, Inc., 1975.
Furth, H. *Piaget for teachers.* Englewood Cliffs, N.J.: Prentice-Hall, Inc., 1970.
Gagné, R. *The conditions of learning.* New York: Holt, Rinehart & Winston, 1970.
Gill, D.G. *Early childhood education for the handicapped: Special study.* Springfield: Illinois Board of Education, August 1980.
Guilford, J.P. *The nature of intelligence.* New York: McGraw-Hill, Inc., 1967.
Guralnick, M.J. (Ed.). *Early intervention and the integration of handicapped and nonhandicapped children.* Baltimore: University Park Press, 1978.
Hohmann, M., Banet, B., and Weikart, D.P. *Young children in action.* Ypsilanti, Mich.: High/Scope Educational Research Foundation, 1979.

Kodera, T.L., and Garwood, S.G. The acquisition of cognitive competence. In S.G. Garwood and colleagues (Eds.), *Educating young handicapped children.* Rockville, Md.: Aspen Systems Corp. 1979.

Lazar, I. Does prevention pay off? *The Communicator.* Reston, Va.: Council for Exceptional Children, Division of Early Childhood, 1979.

Lerner, J., Mardell-Czudnowski, C., and Goldenberg, D. *Special education for the early childhood years.* Englewood Cliffs, N.J.: Prentice-Hall, Inc., 1981.

Lillie, D.L. *Early childhood education.* Chicago: Science Research Associates, Inc., 1975.

McGinnis, M.A. *Aphasic children: Identification and education by the association method.* Washington, D.C.: Alexander Graham Bell Association for the Deaf, Inc., 1963.

Meisels, S.J. (Ed.). *Special education and development.* Baltimore: University Park Press, 1979.

Merrifield, P.R., Guilford, J.P., Christensen, P.R., and Frick, J.W. The role of intellectual factors in problem solving. *Psychological Monographs,* 1962, 76 (No. 529).

Miller, L., and Dyer, J. Four preschool programs: Their dimensions and effects. *Monographs of the Society for Research in Child Development.* 1975, 56.

Orem, R.C. *Montessori and the special child.* New York: Capricorn Books, 1970.

Piaget, J. *The psychology of intelligence.* Paterson, N.J.: Littlefield, Adams & Co., 1960.

Pick, A.D., Frankel, D.G., and Hess, V.L. Children's attention: The development of selectivity. In E.M. Hetherington (Ed.), *Review of child development research.* Chicago: University of Chicago Press, 1975.

Raudsepp, E. Creativity games: A little imagination goes a long way. *Machine Design,* July, 1980, 73-77.

Sears, R.R., Rau, L., and Alpert, R. *Identification and child rearing.* Stanford, Calif.: Stanford University Press, 1965.

Skinner, B.F. *Science and human behavior.* New York: Macmillan, Inc., 1953.

Valett, R.E. *Developing cognitive abilities.* St. Louis: The C.V. Mosby Co., 1978.

Wepman, J.M. *Wepman auditory discrimination test.* Chicago: Language Research Associates, 1973.

Zeaman, D., and House, B.J. The role of attention in retardate discrimination learning. In N.R. Ellis (Ed.), *Handbook of mental deficiency.* New York: McGraw-Hill, Inc., 1963.

Zimmerman, B.J., and Pike, E.C. Effects of modeling and reinforcement on the acquisition and generalization of question-asking behavior. *Child Development,* 1972, 45, 892-907.

8

Promoting social and emotional development

Helping children to be happy means helping children to develop a healthy personality. Numerous attempts have been made to describe the attributes of a healthy personality. Even so, a review of the literature reveals that many educators turn to the work of Erikson (1963, 1971) for an explanation of the development of personality.

Although Erikson (1971) uses the same eight stages to describe the emotional development of all individuals, he acknowledges the uniqueness of each individual within a range of healthy behavior:

> It is not all or nothing: trust or mistrust, autonomy or doubt. . . . Instead, each individual has some of each. His health of personality is determined by the preponderance of the favorable over the unfavorable, as well as by what manner of compensations he develops to cope with his disabilities" (p. 122).

A teacher's acceptance of the uniqueness of each child's response to the daily environment fosters the development of a healthy and happy personality. Teachers who work with young children must be prepared to accept those "unpleasant" behaviors exhibited by all preschool children. Each child will have some emotional and behavioral problems from time to time. For many children preschool is their first experience in a group setting. They may need assistance in handling this new experience. All children are in the process of learning to recognize and to cope with their feelings.

This chapter aims to help teachers and parents understand how adults can help children to be emotionally and socially well adjusted. We present techniques for dealing effectively with emotional and behavioral needs. We emphasize the importance of play in the creation of a secure, growth-producing preschool experience.

DEVELOPING A HEALTHY PERSONALITY

In his developmental outline, Erikson discusses three stages of psychosocial development thought to be characteristic of the young child. Each stage includes the solution of a problem involving conflicting feelings and desires. The resolution of the central problem of each stage creates a favorable disposition for adjustment at the next developmental stage. Table 9 presents Erikson's stages of personality development along with adult behaviors that can help children come to a healthy solution of each stage's problems of conflicting desires and feelings.

Sense of trust v. mistrust

The first year of life is considered by Erikson (1963) to be the crucial time for the development of a sense of trust. During this time, an environment characterized by consistency and dependability fosters the development of trust in those responsible for the child's care. The quality of caregiving is more important than the quantity of food or love given. Caregiving that is basically consistent and sensitive to an infant's needs promotes a view of the world as dependable and safe. Negative, inconsistent, or insensitive caregiving, by contrast, stimulates a fearful, suspicious view of the world.

The child's development of a sense of trust (or mistrust) in the world is only one of the personality attributes developed during infancy. Erikson also discusses the importance of children's perceptions of their ability to control their own body movements. Through such actions as continuous repetition of grasping and holding objects, children learn that they can depend on their bodies to do their bidding. It is not difficult to imagine the frustration experienced by children with physical disabilities during their quest to develop a sense of trust in their own bodies. A curriculum that incor-

TABLE 9
Adult behaviors to promote child's personality growth

Erikson's stage	Appropriate adult behaviors
1. To promote sense of *trust*	Be consistent and sensitive in caretaking
	Play trust-building games (playful repetition, such as peek-a-boo)
	Provide prompt relief of discomfort
	Provide genuine affection
	Establish climate of stability and predictability
	Avoid showing favoritism (teachers)
	Provide for choice making
2. To promote sense of *autonomy*	Allow opportunities to explore
	Forbid only what really matters
	Couple firmness with tolerance
	Avoid shaming
	Let child set pace, try developing skills
	Be accepting of individuality
3. To promote sense of *initiative*	Provide leeway for imagination
	Encourage role playing
	Serve as an appropriate model
	Hold punishment to a minimum
	Talk about feelings and dreams
	Answer questions

porates specialized body movement activities encourages even handicapped children to become more trusting in their body-control.

Teachers who provide an atmosphere of consistent, sensitive caring help to further a young child's development of trust in the environment. Conversely, helter-skelter experiences in the classroom can make a fearful child even more fearful or a basically secure child question his or her relationship to others. A trustful atmosphere is easily developed through establishing reasonable, enforceable rules of conduct, the regularity of a basic schedule of activities, and sensitive, immediate responses to children's needs.

Sense of autonomy v. shame and doubt

From the end of the first year of life through the second and third year of life most children are busy exploring their environment and trying to establish some independence. Children who are primarily trustful usually do not hesitate to join "the terrible twos" if encouraged to develop skills at their own pace. Children of this age who are given opportunities to make simple choices, to exercise their expanding sensory-motor abilities, and to experiment with their new found verbal skills will become confident enough to assert themselves appropriately.

Children who are shamed (for example, being called a "bad boy") or told "no" continuously will begin to doubt themselves and their abilities. They may react by defiance or act ignorant of authority. Children who are not allowed to make choices when they are young may become over dependent and fearful when they need to make major life-choices. Some children may withdraw into their feelings of worthlessness whereas others may strike out aggressively.

Teachers can assist children in developing

autonomy with a reasonable degree of self-control by creating opportunities for young children to explore, to make decisions, to ask questions, and to exercise appropriate self-restraint. Curricula and room arrangements that provide centers with materials to manipulate and activities from which a child can choose ideally promote autonomous, confident behavior. Establishing firm, reasonable guidelines for classroom exploration and conduct encourages autonomy while not letting children become overwhelmed by their need for independence and by their lack of mature judgment. Children of this age who are readily propelled by their more mature large muscles may be easily frustrated when their smaller muscles do not react so efficiently. Teachers must lend assistance that does not create conditions for loss of self-esteem. Handicapped children may need special incentives to venture into the activities so easily enjoyed by unencumbered children.

Although controls and gentle firmness are essential protections for young children, these controls must have meaning. In this regard, Erikson (1971) suggests that the most constructive rule an adult can follow is "to forbid only what really matters and, in such forbidding, to be clear and consistent" (p. 126).

Sense of initiative v. guilt

Children who have developed a basic trust in their environment and in themselves and who have experienced a growing self-confidence in their ability to explore and experiment are ready to develop a sense of initiative. Around 4 or 5 years of age, children experience a heightened period of imagination and fantasy. It is a time for reaching out and intruding both physically and verbally. Children with healthy personalities and healthy bodies vigorously try out their developing ideas of themselves. They are great imitators as evidenced by their "super hero" play and their use of any and all four letter words.

Children of this age are also beginning to develop what is termed a conscience. As they often have difficulty separating fantasy from reality, they may feel guilty about merely thinking unkind thoughts. Teachers who are aware of this tendency try to avoid overreacting to a child's characteristic statement of "I hate you." When difficulties occur in the home such as a death or a divorce, children need to be helped to realize that their actions or thoughts did not cause the unpleasant to happen. This is also an age of nightmares and dreams. These children need extra comfort and reassurance in separating fantasy from reality.

Teachers who allow leeway within secure guidelines for children's developing sense of initiative can contribute significantly to their motivation to achieve (Cook and Cook, 1981). This motivation is important to the next stage of industry v. inferiority, and is necessary to the development of self-esteem and the desire to try out the freedom to explore, to imagine, to question, to help plan, to make choices, to participate in meaningful activities, to create, and to engage in role playing behavior. Teachers of young handicapped children must be aware of the need to teach some children to explore, to play, and to attempt what may be difficult. Children whose abilities or environments are limited may have to be directly helped if they are to develop feelings of trust, autonomy, and initiative. Usually these qualities develop spontaneously in nonhandicapped children through nurturing environments.

BUILDING A HEALTHY ENVIRONMENT

Helping children and teachers to be happy means creating an atmosphere conducive to preventing emotional or behavioral problems. Such a climate can not only prevent the occurrence of problems, but it can also be the major factor in resolving conflicts that develop between children and their environment. The following sections discuss characteristics that most researchers consider essential to optimum

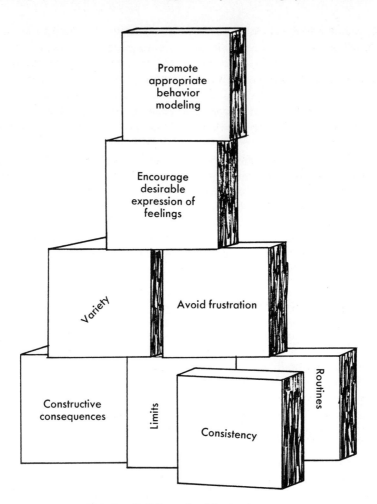

FIG. 8-1. Building a healthy environment.

growth during the early childhood years. These are highlighted in Fig. 8-1.

Consistency

Blackham (1968) points out why reasonable consistency is an absolute prerequisite to effective teaching: "nothing upsets a child more than not knowing what is expected of him and what he can expect from his teacher" (p. 109). Consistency means predictability. In instructing parents and teachers in techniques for effective child management, Smith and Smith (1976)

equate predictability with the feeling of being safe. Like Maslow (1968), they see the expectation for safety as a basic bodily need. When we cannot predict what will happen next, we are usually constantly ready to defend ourselves. "If our predictions come true, we feel safe. If they don't come true, it is upsetting—we become angry. If we can't make any successful predictions at all, we are in a constant state of turmoil" (Maslow, 1968, p. 7).

From a practical point of view, caregivers must be consistent for children to learn the rules of conduct for social acceptance. They are as baffled by inconsistent rules as we would be if we were trying to learn the rules of baseball and the batter sometimes ran to third base instead of first base after a hit. If it is sometimes all right for a child to jump up and down on the sofa, and if other times a spanking results, the rule the child learns is to "try and see."

Instead of the "terrible twos" we should call toddlers the "testing twos." Given consistent responses to their testing, they learn the rules and usually try to function within them.

Routines

To develop Erikson's sense of trust or the feelings of being safe, teachers must plan carefully. Routines or schedules that allow children to predict within reason what will happen next helps them to relax and to handle transitions from one activity to another with relative ease. Although schedules should not be so rigid that teachers cannot take advantage of "teachable moments," children can be prepared for changes in routine and for the times between activities when movement, a change of pace, or grouping is required.

Misbehavior often results when children do not know when or how to change to the next activity. Children should be given a signal such as a flick of the lights or a soft word that they will soon need to stop the activity in which they are engaged. Young children need time to become uninvolved just as they need time to become involved. Teachers should discuss obvious changes in the daily schedule with children so that they can develop the understanding that change can be predictable.

Limits

Reasonable limits or rules help provide consistency. Rules or limits not only contribute to children's emotional needs for security, but also create conditions for bodily safety. Whereas children have a strong need to be autonomous, they lack the cognitive judgment to control their own behavior enough to avoid harming themselves or others at times. Behavioral limits offer children guidelines they can imitate and internalize in their development of appropriate self-control. As pointed out earlier, teachers must establish a delicate balance between necessary limits and the freedom to explore.

Only rules that are absolutely necessary to a positive learning environment for both children and teachers should be established. Too often teachers and parents establish so many rules that none can be learned or enforced consistently. Teachers should remember that if children are to follow a rule or a direction and have no choice, they should not be given a choice. Inadvertently, adults sometimes make the mistake of saying something such as "it is time to go home, wouldn't you like to put your coat on?" What if the child replies "No"?

Smith and Smith (1976) suggest that a good rule should fulfill the following three requirements:

1. *Rules must be definable.* Rules have to be at the developmental level of the children both in vocabulary and expectations. They must state specific behaviors that are expected or not allowed. For example, we often hear parents or teachers tell children to "be good." What does "be good" mean to the child or to the adult? To the child it may mean not running in the building because that is what he or she got into trouble for yesterday. To the parent it may mean eating all his or her lunch because the parent has noticed many leftovers in the lunch pail. Rules or expectations must be clearly stated in behavioral terms. If teachers want children to stay within a certain area while sitting on the carpet, then they should mark the area with a piece of tape so the child knows exactly what the limits are. Concrete, visual aids help young children learn rules of conduct just as they help them develop cognitive skills.

2. *Rules must be reasonable.* Teachers must judge the developmental level of children before rules can be established. It is not reason-

able to expect many 2½ year olds to "share" to the extent that many parents and teachers would like them to. A constant reference to developmental norms is necessary. It must be remembered that developmentally delayed children require extra patience as they learn to adapt to limits that others may adapt to more easily. For example, some children may only be able to listen to a story for 5 minutes, whereas other children may still be engrossed 20 minutes later.

3. *Rules must be enforceable.* Teachers and parents must assume that not all children can or will adhere to all limits. Some rules will be broken. For limits or rules to help children feel safe and trustful, any established rule must be enforceable. When children observe that teachers cannot or will not do anything about a broken rule, they cannot predict what will happen and become anxious. Children seek and enjoy limits. Some will break a rule just to see if they can indeed predict what will happen. This is generally called "testing the limits" and happens in any and all classrooms. As suggested earlier, teachers should see a certain amount of this as normal in children's establishing predictability. Teachers should react firmly, consistently, and calmly. This reaction will define for children the consequences of their behavior. It will tell them what will happen if rules are broken. Seeking to avoid the consequences will motivate them to control their behavior. They feel security when others are helping them to develop self-restraint. Of course, only developmentally appropriate rules can be enforced. If a special circumstance causes a teacher to change the rules or limits, a discussion with the children will help them to understand the need for flexibility within consistency.

Constructive consequences

Dreikurs (1964) advocates using natural and logical consequences as very effective means of helping children to develop social responsibility. *Natural consequences* occur when an adult does not interfere at all and a child learns from what naturally happens in a situation. For example, children who do not cooperate when games are played soon learn that other children avoid playing with them. If a child does not eat the prepared snack, becoming hungry may help him or her to learn to eat when food is available.

Logical consequences, conversely, are those developed by adults who find that natural consequences either are not readily available or are harmful. These usually help to keep or to restore order and avoid chaos. For example, children who insist on throwing sand must be removed from the sandbox. Consequences that help children to learn to control their own behaviors must be both logical and immediate. If a consequence does not bear any logical relationship to the misbehavior, then it will be difficult for the child to learn the logical relationship between cause and effect. A consequence that occurs long after the misbehavior will not be associated with it by the child. If the child cannot remember what it was that caused the consequence, then he or she will not make the link between cause and effect. This is of course one of the reasons why the threat, "Father will punish you after he gets home," does not work.

Logical connections. A logical connection between an act and its consequences has a number of advantages to establishing and maintaining a healthy relationship between children and their environment. Children who are denied the use of materials after being careless with them are less likely to see the teacher as arbitrary than when they are told to sit in the corner for being careless. Children will only feel "picked on" if ordered to sit in the corner. Removing the materials, however, can be seen as necessary to the protection of the other children. A logical connection also helps children to focus on the behavior to be changed, making it easier to interpret the misbehavior as the cause of the consequence.

A child who is also given some control over the extent of the consequence will be more likely to feel the ability to do something about terminating or preventing such consequences in the future. For example, children who are asked to remove themselves from the group for being disruptive, and told they may return when they feel they can control themselves, have an opportunity to take part in their own rehabilitation. They can learn not only that disruptive behavior will cause removal but that self-control can create return. Conversely, children who are told to sit in the "time-out" area for 20 minutes or until the teacher comes for them feel that immediate self-control will not help and that only passage of time changes events.

Variety

Careful planning to include a change of pace during the day is essential to motivating children to learn. A variety of both individual and group activities consistent with the children's development level should be included. Young children need to have active involvement interspersed with quiet activities. Handicapped children whose senses or physical mobility are limited will fatigue more quickly and need an opportunity for rest. Others may need additional opportunities to move freely to release inner tension.

By nature, young children generally have short attention spans. (Of course, there are exceptions). This needs to be considered carefully when planning the daily schedule. If children's attentions wander and they are bored or frustrated, they become restless. This restlessness can become contagious, influencing the behavior of a number of children. This is one of the reasons why learning theorists recommend that practice of any kind be distributed over time.

Carlson (1980) reminds us that novelty, newness, and change enhance motivation. It has been found that young children are more likely to explore novel objects than familiar objects

(Henderson and Moore, 1980). Some mothers are surprised to find the usually unwanted vegetables disappear when served in a special dish or arranged to resemble a happy face.

Finally, a change of pace also means including activities that are just plain fun and full of laughter. Most adults are guilty of being in too much of a hurry or so intense that they miss the occasional opportunities to laugh with children or to turn a mistake into a learning experience. Even shoes on the wrong feet often appear funny enough for a chuckle and for encouragement to try again rather than the usual response of "Your shoes are on the wrong feet."

Avoid frustration

Teachers who are astute observers of children are able to plan and implement a therapeutic environment. They are alert to individual signs of frustration and stress. Understanding the developmental level of each child makes it possible to plan appropriate activities. Even the best matched activities, however, can produce frustration in a tired, hungry, or sick child. Teachers should quickly recognize such warning signs as fussing, crying nail-biting, sighing, fidgeting, thumb-sucking, and tantrums. Usually a prompt change of activity will reduce the frustration and thus *prevent* disruptive behavior.

Frustration can be avoided by teachers reducing clutter and noise, keeping directions simple, providing meaningful activities that are relatively short, and being available if the child needs help. They should analyze tasks and break them into manageable subskills that are appropriately sequenced. Efforts, regardless of outcomes, should receive recognition. Competition should be avoided. Activities that guarantee success can not only make a child's day but can also make the day of the teacher.

Transition times can be periods of frustration for children if not smoothly organized. Distractable children can become unruly if left to wander or wonder. Withdrawn children may become fearful. Routines for transition times must be explicitly taught. As discussed earlier, signals such as flickering the lights help children to wind down from one activity to get ready for the next. Hurrying young children only frustrates the teacher who forgets that preschoolers have not developed the inner time clocks that often become the bosses of adults. Scheduling major activities to end at natural breaks during the day makes transitions smoother. For example, it is easier to gain children's cooperation in cleaning up art materials if they know lunch will follow.

Encourage desirable expression of feelings

In spite of an appropriately planned schedule of activities, consistency, and well-defined limits, unpredictable things do happen. Children need to learn to cope constructively with feelings that arise from interpersonal situations. Anger, jealousy, depression, fear, and other unpleasant feelings are common interpersonal emotions. Teachers choose either to provide an opportunity for helpful expression or insist on at least temporary suppression. The success and choice of teachers' approaches often depend on how well they can handle unpleasant feelings within themselves. Teachers who have confidence in their own abilities to handle negative feelings, and who have carefully created a trustful relationship with their children can handle stressful situations in ways that promote emotional growth (Biehler, 1978).

The sensitive teacher finds many opportunities to help children accept and express their feelings appropriately. Practically any unpleasant experience in the classroom can be the source of discussion. Young children cannot assimilate long lectures explaining feelings or behavior. Short statements or a warm physical touch will help a child to know that having feelings is all right. The active listening process discussed in Chapter 9 is an ideal way to help children acquire verbal labels for their feelings

while the teacher's acceptance of these feelings is demonstrated. A simple acknowledgment and inquiry about coping behaviors will help a child understand and express emotions appropriately while feeling accepted. For example, the teacher might say "It is okay to be mad when Johnny rips your paper, but I can't let you hit him. Can you think of another way to let Johnny know how angry you are?"

Numerous well-written books are available that help children learn to cope effectively with their developing feelings. Even difficult topics such as death and divorce are the recent subjects of sensitive presentation. A sample of children's books and commercial materials concerned with emotions is included in Appendix E. Puppets, role playing activities, art activities, punching bags, and imaginative, unstructured play also give children opportunities to work through their feelings acceptably. Fig. 8-2 and the boxed material "Teaching Thoughtfulness" illustrate some lessons that can be planned to help children learn to understand, label, and constructively express their feelings.

Promote appropriate behavior modeling

Young handicapped children often learn new and more adaptive behavior through imitating their nonhandicapped peers. The modeling effect is a strong current argument for integrating handicapped children and nonhandicapped children in early education programs. Bricker (1978) emphasizes: "Children can acquire new responses from observing and modeling others' behavior; however, the opportunity for watching and imitating more complex behavior must be available" (p. 19).

The teacher's responsibility is to understand the dynamics of learning through imitation and to ensure that appropriate models of desired behavior are available. A number of variables help determine whether or not a child will reproduce the observed behavior. A number of researchers have found that simply placing

Animal friends
Some children find it easier to talk about relationships between animals rather than between people. Copy pictures of animals "being friends" to poster size and display them in the room. Use coloring books, magazines, and story books for ideas. You may want to read stories about animals and then make posters about them.

Monster day
Plan a monster day. Have each person (including yourself) create a monster. Hang them and discuss them. Include a discussion of fears and nightmares as well as those unexplained monsters (UFO's and Loch Ness) and the friendly ones (Cookie Monster and monster books).

Happy-sad face
To help a child identify and label the way he or others may be feeling, make happy-sad faces. Draw eyes on a paper plate, attach a smile-frown with a paper fastener, and rotate the mouth to express feelings. This may work well with children who have trouble verbalizing their feelings.

Give them a hand
If a child has trouble remembering to raise his hand, give him a hand. Let him trace his hand, cut it out and write his name on it. It will provide a physical reminder for him to indicate when he wants to speak.

Personality mirrors
Cut an oval shape from poster board and cover it with foil. Have the child put his name on it with letters cut from construction paper. Then let him find magazine pictures of things that he likes to do or eat. Display them for all students to see.

Apartment windows
Make an apartment, house, or store from poster board. Attach "windows" using pictures cut from magazines or newspapers. Discuss what rooms the occupants are in or what they are doing or feeling.

Slides
Make a slide presentation of people's faces that are expressing feelings, communication signals, or different ways of handling situations.

FIG. 8-2. Affective domain activities. (Reprinted with permission of Cathi Effinger Steinmann, St. Louis.)

TEACHING THOUGHTFULNESS

Goal: To create daily opportunities to nurture thoughtfulness in children.

How to begin:
1. *Be* what you wish to see children express. If you want them to be thoughtful, be thoughtful yourself.
2. Notice nearly every expression of *that* quality. Call attention to the child who expresses it in a spontaneous way. Do not make a major production of it. Rather, touch the child gently, or hug lightly. Say "That was thoughtful. You helped Susie with her coat," or "That was thoughtful." You may think that the other children are not paying attention, but they are. In no time they will try to figure out ways to get you to tell them how they are being thoughtful. And of course they will be learning the subtle meanings of "thoughtful."
3. Avoid calling attention to thoughtlessness. Ignore it.

After a few days:
1. Reduce the frequency with which you call attention to the target quality. Continue to do all of the things suggested above, just less often.
2. Make up short stories about children who are thoughtful. Use puppets, flannel boards, or Polaroid pictures. Catch a child expressing thoughtfulness. Paste the picture on one page and write a brief story below it telling what happened:

> "Susie couldn't get by. Tommy moved his chair. Then she could get through. That was thoughtful."

3. Read stories and comment about the examples of thoughtfulness as you read. ("Little Red Riding Hood was thoughtful. She shared her cookies with her Grandma.")
4. Occasionally, with puppets and stories, mention lack of thoughtfulness (or whatever quality you are focusing on at the time). Then ask the children to suggest a "thoughtful" thing to do. Be careful. At this point, do not lecture. Do not try to relate it to something they should have done.
NOTE: Remember, you are not only nurturing thoughtfulness, but you are also helping the children to learn the names of their feelings and actions. All too often adults tell children to "be thoughtful," or "That was a thoughtless thing to do." Children may not have the slightest idea what they are talking about. Labeling the good behaviors makes it easier for children to express them spontaneously and purposefully.

From then on:
1. Continue to call attention to examples of the qualities you wish to see expressed. Of course, as these qualities increase in number, it becomes impossible to call attention to each of them constantly. It also becomes unnecessary. There seems to be a special magic to the expression of positive qualities. If a once established quality seems to be diminishing, however, merely begin to call attention to it again, and do so on a regular basis.
2. Introduce new targets regularly. Watch them expand. You may discover quickly that even some of the naughtiest children express some of the target qualities from the first day. You may not have noticed before.

handicapped children with nonhandicapped children does not necessarily result in the desired peer imitation (Raver, 1979). In fact, program evaluation studies are demonstrating that teachers who directly reinforce children for imitating appropriate behavior and who manipulate the environment to ensure desired peer interaction increase the chances for positive social behavior (Peck, Apolloni, Cooke, and Raver, 1978).

FACILITATING POSITIVE BEHAVIOR

To be most effective, teachers should study the literature related to social learning theory or imitation. Some principles, however, can be kept in mind as beginning teachers set out to provide classroom experiences that promote the development of positive behavior. These are discussed in the following.

1. Group children for playful interaction who are functioning at a similar developmental level. When imitation is desired, however, children of slightly higher skill or social development should be included in the group (Apolloni and Cooke, 1978).

2. Group children who are socially compatible. Not only is the social interaction more likely to be positive, but also children have been found to be more likely to model the behavior of those with whom they can empathize (Gewirtz and Stingle, 1968).

3. If imitation is definitely a goal, group children by sex. Research suggests a tendency for children to be more likely to model the behavior of others of the same sex (Bandura, Ross, and Ross, 1963).

4. Keep the groups relatively small (from two to four children) when structured learning activ-

ities are involved. Small groups make it possible for teachers to facilitate ongoing positive social interactions without interrupting them.

5. Provide materials appropriate to the skills or interaction desired. Children must learn to use play materials before they can be expected to play with them in cooperative situations. Children who become frustrated because they do not have the skill to use a material may become disruptive or withdrawn. Research has also revealed that some materials are more conducive to positive social interaction than others. For example, simple table games such as Lotto or Candyland with specific rules may be more conducive to cooperative play than more unstructured play materials such as sand. Handicapped children who have not developed imaginative play may need to move gradually from structured to unstructured play when positive interpersonal relationships are a high priority goal. Teachers will need to observe carefully to determine which materials are most conducive to the behavior desired.

6. Make sufficient materials available to promote cooperation and imitation. When children outnumber the materials available, cooperative play obviously is dependent on children's willingness to share. If sharing is not one of the priorities for the play activity, then abundant materials should be available. Imitation is also not immediately possible and cannot be reinforced if children must wait to use the materials.

7. Plan definite activities. Hewett and Taylor (1980) describe a number of tasks that require at least two children to communicate and cooperate to reach a mutual goal. Each one's actions are indispensable to the other. For example, the pan sorting task requires one child to sit on each side of a screen. Each has three different colored pans and a number of objects. One child is the dispatcher who describes what he or she is doing as objects are placed in the pans. (for example, "I am putting the yellow car in the red pan."). The other child attempts to follow these directions to imitate the actions of the dispatcher. Such an activity is particularly helpful to children who have difficulty cooperating and paying attention long enough to follow directions. Of course, the more verbal the children, the easier the task. Remember some children must be taught how to imitate or to model the behavior of others.

8. Quickly reinforce specific desired behavior. The role of positive reinforcement or reward in guiding and directing children's behavior is well-documented. Behavior is thought to be a function of its consequences (Ross, 1977). Behavior that brings positive reinforcement to children directly or vicariously is likely to be strengthened, whereas behavior that goes unnoticed or is punished is likely to be weakened or possibly not repeated again or as often. Teachers must therefore be prepared to reinforce the behavior of those children modeling a desired behavior whether this behavior occurs spontaneously or is programmed by the teacher. Merely being in the presence of a good model does not ensure imitation.

When children exhibit desired behaviors, teachers must act quickly to give attention to this behavior by saying or doing something that will help the child to feel better about himself or herself and to see that he or she is capable of worthwhile behavior. This reward or reinforcement must be done as soon as possible and should include specific verbal statements. Words should clearly tell children exactly what behavior the teacher wishes to see repeated. A statement such as "Vicky, you may be the first to choose your free-play toy because you cleaned up, and then sat still and waited so nicely" is useful because it tells the children exactly what Vicky did that was helpful. Consider this statement: "Vicky, you may be first to choose your free-play toy because you were so helpful." The other children, and even Vicky, may not know exactly what behavior the teacher considered helpful.

9. Identify potential reinforcers. To do this teachers need to observe children carefully to determine their interests, desires, and dislikes. Most young children thoroughly enjoy physical reinforcement such as a hug or a pat on the shoulder, but some find this to be aversive. Children usually respond to smiles and words of praise. Tangible reinforcement such as raisins or peanuts usually are not necessary and should not be used without accompanying social rewards (smiles and words of praise). Tangible rewards, however, especially food, may be the only thing that some children will work for at first. Each child and each situation are different. The following boxed material lists some of the many effective reinforcers for young children along with useful, specific rewarding statements.

PROMOTING SELF-ESTEEM

Research is accumulating suggesting that lack of achievement may be related to children failing to link acceptable performance with their own efforts or abilities. They may instead attribute their successes to chance, task ease, or powerful others (Cook and Cook, 1981). Given this tendency of some children to attribute performance to external causes, teachers must be extremely careful in phrasing their praise.

Give credit where credit is due

The praise must describe in specific terms the behavior that the teacher wishes to have repeated either by the child being praised or by those who are watching at the time. Furthermore, the praise must give the child credit for his or her efforts or abilities. Consider these statements: "Danny, you should feel happy. You listened carefully to my directions and then tried to do exactly what you were asked to do." Such statements point out to others what behavior is expected at the same time Danny is helped to realize that his efforts are important. Note that effort rather than outcome was emphasized.

Young children, and especially young handicapped children, must be encouraged to focus on effort rather than on outcome. After all, they

---

A SAMPLE OF REINFORCERS

Social activity	Concrete activity	Rewarding statements
Verbal praise	Food or special treat	"You are really trying hard. I I like that."
Physical praise: hug, pat, smile	Toys	
Showing and telling	Stamping smiling face on hand	"Thank you very much."
Helping the teacher with special task or errand	Giving gold stars	"Wow!"
	Playing with special puppet or game	"That's right. Good for you."
Clapping by others		"You should be proud of your good work today."
Going to head of the line	Giving badges of honor or recognition	
Displaying child's art work or photo	Giving a special hat or cloak to wear	"I appreciate your help."
		"Give yourself a smiling face for being so helpful."
Choosing songs to sing or play	Going on a special field trip	
Phoning parents	Giving parties	"Thank you for using an inside voice."
Inviting parents to class.	Sending happy note to parents	"I like the way Johnny is sitting."
	Playing records	

may be able to control their efforts even though successful outcomes are sometimes out of reach. Consider these statements: "Danny, I'm so glad you have a new hearing aid. You were able to follow my directions." Danny now feels that he could succeed because of the hearing aid, not necessarily because of his effort. He may or may not put forth effort in the future, especially once his hearing aid is no longer a novelty.

Control the reward to punishment ratio

To minimize negative side effects of any form of punishment, teachers and parents must make careful efforts to control each child's reward to punishment (R-P) ratio. Rewards are considered to be any action or statement that builds a child's self-esteem or anything that makes the child feel good about himself or herself. Punishment may refer to any action or statement that decreases a child's self-esteem or makes him or her feel less worthy.

Kirkhart and Kirkhart (1972) clearly point out the importance of the reward to punishment ratio in the development of a healthy personality: "A reward to punishment ratio of five rewards for every one punishment is about optimal in guiding and directing a child's behavior. However, when the R-P ratio falls down to only two rewards for every one punishment, neurotic symptoms begin to develop, especially those of inferiority and inadequacy and a generalized fear of failure" (p. 152). They further state that predelinquent behavior is often observed in children whose reward to punishment ratio falls to one-to-one or below.

Observations of classrooms readily suggest that many teachers are unaware of the reward to punishment ratio they are using. This is especially a problem when a child does very little that merits reward and functions as if negative attention is better than none at all. To control the reward to punishment ratio, teachers must plan carefully to ensure that such children are attempting tasks for which their efforts can be rewarded.

Preventative observation is essential. When teachers see children begin to lose control or interest because of frustration, fatigue, or hunger, they must quickly change the child's activity. The reward to punishment ratios can approach optimal levels by preventing punishment and by increasing reward. Teachers can develop special nonverbal signals such as a nod or a wink to be given as reminders to children who seem about to misbehave. Then immediate reward or reinforcement can be given when a child increases the effort to control his or her behavior.

Ignore truly nondisruptive behaviors

Some irritating behaviors will disappear if they receive no attention or reward from anyone. Teachers must be astute observers. Even though a teacher may ignore a behavior that does not mean that other children are not giving attention to it. Simply ignoring the behavior will not work in such a situation. The child is getting attention of some kind and is possibly modeling inappropriate behavior for other children.

Some children will use troublesome four letter words, stick out their tongues, or tap their tables, merely to get a reaction from the teacher. Observant teachers usually guess when this is the case. Ignoring behavior can be effective as long as the teacher realizes that the child may go on until some kind of attention is given. The answer is to find a way to give the child positive attention. This can be done by directing the child into an activity while simultaneously ignoring the undesired behavior. Depending on the child, ignoring alone may just bring on more disruptive behavior.

Keep punishment to a minimum

As discussed earlier punishment needs to be kept to a minimum to assure a satisfactory reward to punishment ratio. Punishment is thought only to decrease the rate at which inappropriate behaviors occur and can also produce negative side effects such as fear, tenseness, and withdrawal (Clarizio and Yelon, 1967). Any aggressive acts by an adult also provide undesirable models for children to imitate.

Punishment in the form of logical and natural consequences can have an informative effect if used wisely. Punishment that is part of rule setting in the classroom can be a natural consequence predicted by those who do not follow classroom rules. When linked directly to their behavior, they can see the relationship between their causative act and the resulting effect.

If children know that hitting others or otherwise fooling around during circle time will cause them to be asked to go to the time-out seat, then they will see the punishment as justified and directly caused by their behavior. They will not see the teacher as arbitrary or themselves as unresponsible for the outcome. They will know how to prevent the punishment in the future if the teacher has said specifically exactly why they were punished. The teacher might say, "Vicky, you must take time-out. You have hit Susie and we cannot hurt others."

Walker and Shea (1980, p. 89) offer the following guidelines to those who find it absolutely necessary to use punishment:

1. Specify and communicate the punishable behavior to the children by means of classroom rules for behavior.
2. Post the rules where the children can see them, and review them with the group frequently.
3. Provide models of acceptable behavior.
4. Apply the punishment immediately.
5. Apply the punishment consistently, not whimsically.
6. Be fair in using the punishment (what is good for Peter is good for Paul).

Of course, these rules have to be adapted for use with very young children. Picture symbols might be used instead of words when listing the rules. Walker and Shea also list 14 reasons why teachers should avoid using either physical (spankings) or psychological (derogatory statements) punishment. Basically other forms of behavior management are more effective and

TABLE 10
"Logical consequences" v. punishment

The behavior (what happened)	Logical and natural consequence	Punishing the personality
Child spills milk	Child cleans up spill	"You are so clumsy." "Don't you ever watch what you're doing?" "You messed up again."
Child grabs another child's toy	Returns the toy	"You're a brat again." "Must you be so bad?" "You're always the selfish bully."
Child "forgot" to hang up coat	Hangs up coat	"Can't you remember anything?" "You're such a slob." "How many times have I told you. . . ?"
Child yells loudly at supermarket	Softly say, "Let's practice soft noises" Return to market and practice being quiet	"Shut up; you're a bad girl." "Good girls are quiet in public." "I'll never take you to the store again."

avoid damaging effects. More importantly, punishment bruises the already fragile developing self-images of children.

Punishment that is in any way derogatory or demeaning should be avoided at all costs. Only punishments that are logical, natural, and unattached to the child's person or personality should be used. Table 10 illustrates the importance of this suggestion. Acceptable punishments when kept to a minimum and used as a last resort include deprivation of privileges (including time-out) and compensation for intentional wrong-doing such as picking up deliberately spilled puzzle pieces. It should be remembered, however, that any form of punishment should be administered with firm kindness to avoid becoming derogatory or demeaning.

HELPING CHILDREN WITH PARTICULAR SOCIAL AND EMOTIONAL PROBLEMS

No matter how consistent and positive a teacher and the environment are, there will be children who continue to need additional help as they strive to develop a healthy, happy personality. Some children have developed strong habits that make it difficult for them to become involved in positive interpersonal relationships. Others are fearful, frightened, or withdrawn for reasons that may never be known or understood. The following sections suggest some practical methods of giving additional assistance to those children whose behavior interferes with learning or that can be described as disruptive or harmful.

Children who lack sufficient self-control

Children who lack sufficient self-control are usually thought of as aggressive, hostile, overactive, impulsive, or hyperactive. Such children find it difficult to follow the classroom rules of conduct. Some, such as hostile and aggressive children, may deliberately strike out at others or damage equipment. Others, such as hyperac-

tive or impulsive children, may merely be unable to control extraneous movements. The basic problem for the classroom teacher or parent is the same—helping the child to control his or her own behavior. Many of the same techniques for behavior control can be used effectively with all children who have these problems. Some, however, will need individualized help. We will begin with those techniques that will be useful with a number of children and then follow with special considerations.

Do not permit aggressive behavior. Not permitting aggressive behavior should be the first rule toward helping children control the expression of unacceptable, possibly harmful behavior. From the very beginning, adults must make it perfectly clear that "hitting, kicking, pushing, and shoving will not be allowed." Then teachers and parents must act swiftly in the face of the expression of such behavior to demonstrate consistently and firmly what the consequences of such actions will be. Children thus learn that such acts will not be tolerated, as they lead to nonpunitive but effective consequences. Firm consistency helps children develop trust in themselves and in others.

Despite the teacher's best efforts toward preventative discipline, aggressive acts do occur and must be dealt with immediately. The key to dealing with aggressive children is to be nonaggressive oneself. Nonhurtful discipline such as a time out is considered to be effective (Marion, 1981). Children learn that aggressive behavior will not be tolerated of anyone, not even of the teacher. They also learn that the teacher can be trusted to be nonhurtful. If teachers are to give attention, they should give it to nonaggressors. That is, the teacher should give attention to the victim rather than to the aggressor. Throughout this chapter, other examples of nonaggressive methods of behavior control are discussed. These merit consideration.

Prepare the child's environment. Teachers need to prepare the child's environment. Children who are hyperactive, anxious, or angry often find it almost impossible to sit still, to take turns, or to wait for explanations. They may constantly squirm, turn, or wiggle. Such children may be easily overstimulated if they have difficulty filtering out extraneous sounds or sights (Cruickshank, Bentzen, Ratzeburg, and Tannhousser, 1961). Teachers must take care to limit the noise level in their classrooms and the visual stimuli surrounding these children. Some children's inabilities to filter out extraneous stimuli and to control impulses may be the reason some of these children can be so difficult for parents to handle when shopping in department or grocery stores. Conversely, Zentall (1977) finds that some hyperactive children may actually need more stimulation. He hypothesizes that some children produce their own stimulation through activity because they are understimulated. Such different views again require that teachers be astute observers to consider each child's needs when preparing the environment.

Concentration can be improved by providing a quiet place to work free from distraction. Ample equipment and materials should be available so that these children do not have to do too much waiting or sharing. Teachers should limit the use of toys or games with many small pieces to manipulate that can create frustration. They must space tables or desks far enough apart so that extraneous movements will not bother others. They should eliminate toys such as guns and soldiers that elicit aggressive behavior. They should place impatient children in a position to receive snacks or working materials relatively early in the waiting time. As these children show signs of increasing their capacities for self-control, waiting time can be increased.

Carefully consider curriculum implementation. Teachers must carefully consider curriculum implementation. Children who find it difficult to concentrate may fall behind in developing preacademic skills and may be labeled as learning disabled later on. Sometimes their speech is so fast that words and thoughts become a jumble. This may result in excessively using gestures. Children's frustrations may develop into aggressive behavior and a loss of self-esteem from being ashamed of their lack of self-control. To avoid these frustrations, directions need to be extremely clear and given one by one. Teachers should analyze tasks and present them in sequential steps so they can reinforce success intermittently and frequently. Using the child's name often while working with a group helps the child to focus his or her attention. A calm voice is a must. A raised voice will only create anxiety and heighten the child's level of activity.

Unstructured free play times or transition times can be especially difficult for impulsive children. Choices for these children may have to be limited. It helps to establish definite procedures for transition times, such as those suggested in the boxed material appearing on p. 239. A teacher or paraprofessional will need to stay with the most impulsive children until they have become involved in their new activities. Hewett and Taylor (1980, p. 189) describe "order tasks" that can be especially useful in "helping children learn to adapt to routines, follow directions, complete assignments, and control their behavior." These are tasks that usually involve eye-hand coordination and are simple enough to complete so that they can readily realize success. Examples include picture puzzles, pegboard designs, bead stringing, and most of the activities included in *Workjobs* (Lorton, 1973). When children are losing control during either free play or worktime, they can be directed to these order tasks to help them gain composure acceptably and nonpunitively.

Using loud, lively records during music time can be upsetting for children who have difficulty with control. Some activity records require children to be able to process auditory information quickly to participate. For children who lack self-control, these records may be inappropriate or can be used for only a very short time.

Teachers must remember that many behavior problems are simply children's responses to overstimulation or frustration. Why create or accentuate such problems?

Teachers can use visual aids to help children control themselves. Carpet squares or tape on the floor gives them a definite, visual, and tactile space in which they are to keep themselves. Having a definite location for their belongings is also important to all children. It helps them to control their things and themselves. While on field trips, overactive children should be in small groups and close to adults. If they are verbally engaged, they usually have better body control. Identical name tags for groups of two or three help these children to feel a manageable sense of belonging to be with just these two or three.

Deescalate play behavior. Caldwell (1977) offers several useful suggestions for working with children who lack sufficient self-control, espe-

cially those who are aggressive or hostile. She outlines a number of reasons why ignoring or physically punishing aggressive behavior is ineffective. Generally, ignoring may imply approval and physical punishment certainly models aggressive behavior while producing unwanted side effects. Caldwell instead suggests that teachers work closely with parents to develop cooperative, consistent efforts toward behavior control, because otherwise parents may be encouraging the very behavior teachers are trying to stop. Activities that involve altruism (helping and cooperating) also should be systematically planned and reinforced.

Children need to be helped through active adult participation to deescalate their play when it gets out of hand. To illustrate the need to help children refocus their play when they become too involved, Caldwell describes the all too familiar sandbox scene. Children begin innocently making sand pies and then one child steps on or

---

TRANSITION TECHNIQUES

A. When children are playing (free-play or free-choice activities)
1. *Five minutes before "clean-up time,"* the teacher should quietly say "It's almost clean-up time." Speak to small groups and individuals—do *not* make a group announcement.
2. Have a child ring a bell to signal "Clean-up time, *now.*"
3. Sing a "Clean-up song."
4. The teacher may move among the children, helping them find containers and properly sorting and replacing toys. As children learn where things belong, the teacher's assistance should be reduced.

   SUGGESTIONS: Early in the year have a limited number of toys and games available. As the children learn to replace those correctly, add new ones and remove some things. Avoid clutter. Provide variety, that is, puzzles, games, blocks, beads, or coloring materials. Have a specific container for each kind of toy. Provide a particular place to which each container is returned as they "clean up."
B. Transition from circle time or a group activity to another directed activity—such as a small group lesson, snack time, or individual lessons
1. As the activity in progress draws to a close, tell the children "It's almost time for _____."
2. Establish brief eye contact with each—a look and a smile at the same time. Then say "Listen for the directions. It is _____'s turn."
3. Give each child in turn specific directions for moving to the next lesson or activity location. For example:

   Teacher: "Matt, clap your hands two times, touch your ear, and walk backwards to the table for a snack."
   (Others watch as Matt follows the directions. The directions are given in one long sentence. Matt must wait until the teacher finishes speaking before he begins.)

   Teacher: "Danny, jump two times, then push your chair to the table."
   (Danny's directions are shorter—two stage—and spoken more slowly.)

   By using specific directions for going to the table or the next activity location, children learn to listen to and follow directions while being able to "let off a little steam." The transition occurs in an orderly way and enhances a sense of appropriate behavior.

---

otherwise destroys a child's product. Then hostility erupts and aggression occurs. Caldwell suggests that involved adults should not only catch the behavior before it escalates but should return children to positive playfulness by not making judgments and reading intent into every aggressive act.

Use time-out effectively. Marion (1981) discusses a number of steps that should be considered when developing effective time-out procedures. These include the following: (1) Simply explaining to the child that he or she will be placed in a time-out every time the unacceptable behavior occurs; (2) designating a non-frightening time-out area away from activity but within view of the teacher; (3) calmly insisting that the child take a time-out if resistance is shown; (4) praising the child who participates in a time-out as planned; (5) keep the time-out short; and (6) reward positive behavior when the child returns to an activity after a time-out.

Several conditions increase the success of this approach: teachers are cautioned to warn the child only once, to describe the child's probable

VIGNETTE 8-1: PARENTS AND TEACHERS WORKING TOGETHER

Most often it is the mother who comes to the preschool to talk about behavior problems. Sometimes she has carefully avoided letting the teacher know that "her Tommy" is prone to temper tantrums, and it is necessary to ask her to come. For this Vignette let us assume that Tommy's mother has been asked to come because Tommy has some temper tantrums each day. He is disrupting the class. The tantrums must be stopped.

SCENE: It is 11 AM. Mrs. Jones has agreed to come for a conference about Tommy. Over the phone she noted that Tommy is "all boy." She described him as "just like Uncle Joe. When he doesn't get his way he blows his top." She said that he has tantrums at home, too, and it really upsets everyone. She said that the worst times are at the supermarket. If she doesn't buy everything he wants, he kicks her and yells right in the store. She has "done everything" and "nothing works." Tommy is 4 years old and strong for his age.

Mrs. Jones: "Tommy really is a darling boy, you know. He just can't help it. He has a short fuse. Things make him so mad."

Ms. McLynn: "What kinds of things make him angry at home?"

Mrs. Jones: "Oh, just everything. If his little sister touches his toys he screams and hits her. If his big brother won't let him play with his train, he knocks it on the floor. They just fight all the time."

Ms. McLynn: "This really makes you angry, doesn't it."

Mrs. Jones: "It sure does. But he doesn't act that way when his daddy is home. My husband really can settle him."

Ms. McLynn: "Oh? What does Mr. Jones do that stops the tantrums?"

Mrs. Jones: "It really makes me nervous. He uses his slipper, and really spanks him hard. Then, I get all upset and cry, and he stomps out of the house."

Ms. McLynn: "This whole thing really makes you miserable, doesn't it?"

Mrs. Jones: "Yes, and its getting worse. I just don't know what to do."

Ms. McLynn: "Well, Tommy has been having tantrums here, too. We can't let him disrupt classes several times a day. We have some ideas about teaching Tommy to control himself, but we need your help."

Mrs. Jones: "You have my permission to spank him. It's the only thing that works. Just don't hit him too hard."

Ms. McLynn: "On, no. We never hit children."

Mrs. Jones: "Well, you must really have a mess. If you never spank you must have tantrums all the time."

Ms. McLynn (laughing): "Oh, no. In fact, tantrums here at preschool are actually rare and do not last very long. We just make it very unprofitable to act that way."

Mrs. Jones: "Well, what do you do?"

Ms. McLynn: "First, we never let a tantrum 'work' for a child. The minute one begins, we move the child to our time-out room. One of us stays with the child, but we give him no attention. Usually we read a book or write a note until things quiet down. Then, we may say 'Are you ready to go back to the room, now?' Sometimes, they begin to scream again, and if that happens, we just go back to our reading. After a while, when the child is in control, we explain quietly and in a very few words, 'You may not act that way around here. We just don't do that.' "

Mrs. Jones: "How can I stop Tommy's tantrums?"

Ms. McLynn: "Let's plan a series of trips to the supermarket designed to limit the tantrums there. First, plan to purchase only two or three items of interest to Tommy. Before you go, make a shopping list. Use pictures to show Tommy what you will buy, and talk about those things. Using can labels provides an opportunity for a matching lesson. He can look for the same label on a can at the store. When you arrive at the store, park as near to the door as you can. Sit quietly in the car for a few minutes, and tell Tommy what you will do in the store. Say something like this:

'Tommy, we need to find three red apples, a can of green beans, and a can of peaches. You will walk beside me. We will look for things together.'

Avoid saying anything about being good or bad. Rather, tell him exactly what to do. Walk into the store, and show him (as you tell him) to 'walk beside me.' Talk about everything you see. Try *not* to hold his hand, but do hold it if you must. *Converse* with him as you look for the three things on your list together. Then, go immediately to the checkout line. Again, talk about what you are doing. Leave as soon as you have checked out. Tell Tommy what a good helper he was, but don't call attention to any misbehaviors. The intent is to have a happy shopping trip together. Be certain to tell Tommy's father how helpful Tommy was. You may wish to let Tommy choose what you will have for dinner or in some other way reward him.

Of course, if he misbehaves at the store, pick him up. Move quickly. Say nothing, but go directly to the car. Behave very quietly—even if he screams. Go directly home and put him in the 'time out' spot. Do not get into a discussion or scold. Just act.

Several days later, try again."

feelings with kindness, to restate clearly the broken rule, to make the child responsible for knowing when he or she is once again in control, and to assist actively the child's return by helping him or her become involved in the ongoing activities. Hewett and Taylor (1980) add the importance of allowing the child to return without lecturing or attempting to obtain promises to be good in the future. They also suggest that when the child returns the teacher should make an effort to engage him or her in a task in which the child is interested and can be successful.

Maintain physical proximity and touch control. Physical proximity or a gentle touch will help some children maintain control over their behavior. This is especially useful when young children are placed in situations that require extra efforts at control. Many public-supported early childhood programs are placed within elementary schools. As a result, children may be expected to stand and walk in lines and to control their behavior in ways that usually are not expected until they reach kindergarten age. Teachers may even need to take the hands of some children to help them maintain the needed control. This should not be done as a punishment for misbehavior, but should be done before problems arise as a help to the child. If the teacher uses handholding as a punishment, the teacher might become an aversive stimulus and the child might feel less worthy.

Signal interference to prevent loss of self-control. Signal interference can be very effective with impulsive children if teachers have observed carefully to see what usually "sets off such children." Sometimes patterns in behavior are obvious, such as excessive frustration or activity just before a snack, during circle time, or near the time to go home. Environmental factors such as overstimulation, lack of sufficient movement space, or lack of time to complete a task might be a part of the patterns. Nonverbal (and sometimes verbal) signals such as a nod or a wink can be especially effective if used in the

beginning stages of misbehavior and with children who are capable of understanding them and can remember why the signal is being given.

Signals must be used before a child becomes so emotional that he or she is unable to stop the behavior. A warm relationship between the teacher and the child contributes to the effectiveness of this approach. As children mature, they can be taught to understand their own signs of impending loss of control. They can then be encouraged to signal the teacher that they need a time-out or a change in activities.

Deal consistently with temper tantrums. Temper tantrums that are only bids for attention may go away when they are consistently ignored. If the tantrums persist, then the child becomes a candidate for the five-step time-out process just outlined. Nonthreatening statements are preferred such as "It seems that you are unable to play with us right now. I hope you will be able to work with us after some time in the 'thinking corner'." Once the child is back and participating appropriately, reinforcement should be given for the constructive behavior in progress.

Mutual cooperation with the parents is essential to establishing firm, consistent guidelines. Above all, adults must be certain that a tantrum does not result in the child getting his or her way if that way is inappropriate. The child's day should be programmed so that numerous opportunities exist for the child to get attention in constructive ways. Vignette 8-1 reveals how one teacher and parent worked together to improve behavior at home and at school.

Help overactive children to feel good about themselves. Many children who overact are angry underneath and expend energy covering up feelings of inferiority or fears of being vulnerable. Possibly the primary objective for such children is to help them see themselves as worthwhile people capable of developing self-control. Experience has shown that once these children begin to feel like responsible individuals, their need for negative behavior is diminished (Glasser, 1969).

Healthy, young children enjoy pleasing adults whom they can trust. When these children misbehave, teachers should ask themselves if something they are doing or not doing is causing the problem. Have the children been allowed to change activities frequently enough? Is too much being demanded? Are children being allowed to express constructively their feelings verbally and physically by pounding clay or knocking down tenpins? Is the reward to punishment ratio at an optimum level? The teacher's responsibility is to prevent children from losing control of their behavior. Loss of control creates shame, guilt, and lowered self-esteem.

The curriculum needs to be reviewed periodically to assure realistic expectations. During a recent meeting of the National Association for the Education of Young Children, leading experts cautioned educators to beware of stressing academics to the detriment of social and emotional development. Elkind suggested that teachers "avoid emphasizing academics during the preschool years. Instead they should concentrate on certain prerequisites like listening, being able to relate past experiences to present activities and using and respecting the tools of learning." Nimnicht encouraged education to "promote positive self-concepts for children and help them solve their problems." He further urged that children's self-confidence be the object of "loving, tender care" (Harris, 1980, p. 10).

Finally, helpful teachers will (1) express their acceptance of children's feelings, negative and positive; (2) reassure overactive children that one of the teacher's jobs is to protect children from harming others or themselves; (3) exhibit confidence in children's abilities to improve self-control; and (4) demonstrate that children will be allowed greater opportunities to control their own behavior as they exhibit increased self-restraint and appropriate expressions of feelings.

A word about medication and nutrition

Medication. Perhaps the most controversial method of handling children who lack sufficient self-control involves using psychotropic drugs. Stimulants such as methylphenidate hydrochloride (Ritalin) and dextroamphetamine sulfate (Dexedrine) seem to have a paradoxical effect on children who are overactive. Such drugs do not actually act as a sedative because they do not slow down or suppress a child's initiative. Instead they "may inhibit production of substances that interfere with the normal work of neurotransmitters" (Swanson and Reinert, 1979, p. 110). The child is then able to focus on meaningful stimuli and organize bodily movement. Possible side effects include insomnia, stomach upset, dizziness, and nervousness.

Tranquilizers such as chlorpromazine hydrochloride (Thorazine) and thioridazine hydrochloride (Mellaril) are used with some children. These drugs seem to decrease aggressive and destructive behavior, but can create drowsiness (Swanson and Reinert, 1979). Response to medication is specific to each individual child. Because one of the primary purposes of medication is to help children to respond appropriately within their classroom, teachers become the primary observers of the effects of the medication. The systematic physician depends on the teacher to observe and to record changes in the child's behavior. The dosage level must be monitored regularly because effects are different at different dosage levels. Teachers must be alert to possible side effects and report their occurrence.

When school opens, teachers need to request that parents keep them informed of any child's medication and its possible effects. If teachers are expected to administer any medication, the proper procedures must be followed. Nurses, principals, and directors can help teachers be certain that parent consent forms are on file and that policies are followed. A recording system should be developed. The teacher must be certain that objective communication of observed behavior is maintained among the teacher, the parents, and the doctor.

Remember: drugs do not teach. Teachers ought to be certain to prepare the environment carefully, to look for positive behavior to reward, and to treat the child as one who is learning to develop self-control. Beware of the self-fulfilling prophecy: "Oh, you forgot to take your pill this morning. I guess this will be a bad day." Too many children and parents come to believe that the child's improved concentration is totally the result of medication. Teachers should remember that without the child's effort, improvement would not be possible. More than ever, credit must be given where credit is due. It is essential to help children believe in themselves so that the medication can be withdrawn as soon as possible. Each time the child feels he or she is responsible for the improved behavior, the more likely he or she is to work toward self-control (Cook and Cook, 1981).

Nutrition. A number of efforts are being made to determine the significance of the relationship between foods consumed and behaviors produced. Possibly the most well-known attempt to regulate behavior through diet control is the Feingold diet (Feingold, 1974). The basic premise of those who monitor the reactions of children to various foods is that difficult behavior such as hyperactivity, fatigue, irritability, and nervousness may be the result of adverse reactions to various food substances. Eliminating food colors, additives, sugar, and milk products is found to help relieve and control the symptomatic behavior in some children (Crook, 1975).

Although the relationship between nutrition and behavior or learning problems currently is a matter of controversy, results of diet control do seem to be dramatic. Teachers are encouraged to pay close attention to the research as it is reported and to encourage parents to talk to their doctors about the possibility of allergic reactions to food. In the meantime, teachers will want to choose carefully the snacks offered in the classroom. Most teachers are convinced that sugar promotes tooth decay, if not hyperactivity. This alone is a good enough reason to eliminate sugar from snacks. A local director of a nursery school eliminated milk, sugar, and red dye from the snack list altogether. The children quickly adjusted to the variety of fruits, vegetables, juices, and other nutritious snacks (Lansky, 1978). Most parents were delighted to find their children being introduced to new foods and that they were building better eating habits. Some even found themselves trying something new at the request of their child. Anyone who doubts the wisdom of reducing the intake of sugar should visit an elementary school the day after Halloween.

Involve parents. Many parents would gladly improve their child's nutrition if they knew how to. One effective way to gain parents' interest and cooperation is to sponsor a tasting party. Begin by obtaining a book from the local library that lists the basic food nutrients such as protein, minerals, vitamins, and carbohydrates, and the important food sources of each. Then make charts with pictures of the food sources included under each nutrient; for example, iron: liver, dried beans and peas, and green leafy vegetables. Ask each parent to bring a food source to be set on a table under the appropriate chart and to be sampled by children and parents together. Of course the larger the number of samples the more the parents will realize how much they need to increase their understanding of nutrition. This experience is even more effective when teachers are able to conduct a diet analysis of each child through cooperation with area doctors or universities. Such an analysis is obtained by asking parents to record what a child eats over a specific period of time. A computer responds by printing out the child's abundance or lack of certain nutrients. For example, it is surprising to find the number of children deficient in iron (Pipes, 1977). With an analysis in hand, parents are encouraged to pay closer attention to the foods they are sampling. They may then encourage their child to try foods containing nutrients found to be deficient in the child's diet.

Children who are reluctant to participate

Children who are reluctant to participate are rarely a bother to teachers and classmates. Shy children and timid children are easily overlooked. Special attention is important for children whose behavior ranges from timid and inhibited to completely withdrawn. Otherwise their needs may go unnoticed. Such children usually separate themselves physically, avoid group activities and verbal interaction, seem afraid to try new tasks, sometimes appear disinterested, and may seek comfort through self-stimulation (rocking, twisting their hair, or thumb-sucking). Kauffman (1977) describes these children as those who lack the very behaviors that bring them into social contact such as looking, talking, playing with, and touching. He sees them as "lacking in responsiveness to others' initiations of social contact" (p. 207). Teachers then find themselves responsible for helping these children to develop approach behaviors and responsiveness behaviors.

In addition to lacking social contact behavior, some of these children may be preoccupied with self-stimulation or with daydreaming and fantasy. By being so absorbed in their imaginations or their repetitive acts of sensory stimulation, they miss social cues. This lack of attention prevents them from the social learning available to children who are not isolated either physically or emotionally. Children who also experience language delays are at an even greater disadvantage. Even if they are paying attention, they may not be able to understand directions or to

ask necessary questions. They have or take few opportunities to demonstrate what they know and understand. Skill and patience are absolutely necessary to help these children develop the trust they so desperately need.

Prepare the child's environment. Swap (1974) seeks to explain the tasks of teachers working with these overly controlled children to prepare their environment by combining the theoretical approaches of Hewett (1968) and Erikson (1963). This combination encourages teachers to help children develop trust in themselves and their environment at the same time they are being taught how to listen and respond. "On the one hand, the teacher needs to establish a climate of safety, predictability, and consistency. . . . On the other hand, the teacher needs to extend . . . an acceptance of his [the child's] responses, however limited, and provide nurturance, nourishment, and individual attention regardless of the quality or quantity of the child's initial output" (Swap, 1974, p. 165).

Children who are reluctant to participate will appreciate a small, safe place into which they can retreat. The place must not be like the time-out area. The child should be able to view the classroom activities from the safe place. Many inhibited children learn a great deal from watching others. Through watching they may develop the confidence necessary to attempt a new or different task.

As the child becomes more trustful, the "watching chair" can be moved closer to the ongoing activity. At an intermediate point, identical play materials can be placed within the child's reach. The teacher should not coax the child. No attention should be given to the child unless he or she attempts the activity either alone or with the others. If this occurs, then positive reinforcement should be given quietly and inconspicuously. The teacher must know what the child enjoys. A smile rather than a public announcement of the child's participation would probably be more appropriate.

These children will feel more secure if materials are kept in the same place day to day. They want a definite place for their own objects, including crayons and coats. The teacher should not force them to share until they are ready to do so. Consistency in routines and procedures helps them to predict and therefore feel more comfortable. The child must be prepared in advance for any new or strange situations such as visitors, field trips, or tornado drills.

Promote peer assistance. Seating nonparticipating children near relatively quiet but competent children can do wonders in promoting peer assistance. Experience has shown that extremely shy children often respond to another child much more quickly than to an adult. Caring, concerned children who do not move too loudly or quickly are excellent models and they do not threaten the insecure child. Such children can be prompted to invite the reluctant child to participate without begging for involvement. Sometimes the best approach is for the child or maybe the teacher to ask for help. For example, "Johnny, will you please help me clean up this paint," or "Please hold the picture." Help can begin with an independent activity such as passing snacks and can graduate to a cooperative activity such as two children going to get the juice. Helping others gives the child an easy basis to establish relationships; at the same time self-esteem can be enhanced.

Consider curriculum adaptations. Like most children, inhibited children need a predictable schedule that includes both group time and individual time. Group size can be increased as the child builds confidence. Some children who are unwilling to express themselves in conversation will join in a song because they feel less conspicuous. They may sit on the edge initially. The teacher should not rush them. In the beginning, peripheral involvement such as holding pictures rather then naming them can be encouraged. Many of these children will participate physically before they will participate verbally. If a story is being read and followed by questions, call on the reluctant child last and then do not coax. Teachers must remember that the child must set the pace.

Many young children will interact with pets before they will interact with people. Letting such children take care of pets helps them to feel they are contributing to the welfare of the pets and to the classrooms. Their involvement also gives them a chance to receive the approval they seek.

Research suggests that socially isolated children respond to the social learning principles of modeling and imitation (Kauffman, 1977). Teachers should therefore seriously plan opportunities for these children to observe positive, pleasant social interaction as discussed earlier.

Individual attention is sometimes the key to getting reluctant children to participate in instructional activities. Teachers should approach them calmly, speaking slowly and clearly, and state exactly what they expect. They should present activities that they are reasonably certain are interesting to the child. Teachers must try to couple their attention to the child with something pleasant. They should help children to be reminded of good things when they see or think of their teacher. If the child refuses to become involved, then the teacher should merely place the materials nearby and let the child watch. This procedure should be followed at snack time as well. The teacher should not become anxious if the child does not eat. The more uncomfortable attention the child receives, the less he or she is likely to eat.

Walsh (1980) offers the following suggestion for helping isolated children become a part of the group: begin by standing close to the isolated child. Then suggest that "he or she join a group: 'Tim and Laura could use someone to help build a bridge. . . . —why not give them a hand, Bob?' At this point, the teacher should move away, returning to give more attention only if the child acts on the suggestions" (p. 11).

Teachers then may wish to give additional suggestions if they seem to facilitate involvement.

Provide opportunities for expressing feelings. Inhibited, withdrawn children typically experience many unexpressed emotions. Special encouragement thus must be given to self-expression. Drawing, painting, puppetry, clay, water play, fingerpainting, and music can provide opportunities for this expression. Of course these children must not be forced and their efforts must be rewarded without regard to their products. As trust develops, teachers can gradually encourage verbal expression by asking such questions as "Is the girl in your picture very upset or unhappy today?" Like "active listening" (Gordon, 1975), this approach helps children to feel understood and accepted. They can attribute their unpleasant feelings to the object in the drawing and thus find these feelings to be less threatening.

Pictures, especially photographs of the children themselves, are especially useful when talking about feelings. Pictures that show clear facial expressions, definite gestures, or obvious effects of the child's actions on others should be chosen. Such pictures help the child to perceive how another may feel and to discover cause and effect relationships. Guided discussion should focus on describing what is happening, what will happen, and how those in the picture might feel.

Help reluctant children feel good about themselves. Above all, teachers must be conscious of the need to help reluctant children feel good about themselves so that they may find the courage to develop the social contact and attention skills critical to healthy social involvement. The teacher should begin with step by step presentations of noncompetitive tasks that can be achieved by the child. Nonthreatening rewards for effort coupled with a trusting relationship developed through dependability are essential. When children participate little, it is extremely difficult to manipulate the environment to en-

sure an optimal reward to punishment ratio. Avoiding punishment may be the most efficient means toward helping the child build confidence and trust in the beginning. Reinert (1976, p. 137) lists the following five methods as methods that *do not work* with reluctant children:

1. Forcing the child to become involved
2. Embarrassing the child
3. Ignoring the behavior
4. Asking the child why he or she does not want to take part
5. Comparing the child to other children

As a child's inhibited, withdrawal pattern can be a developmental pattern later associated with serious disturbance, it is imperative that teachers work closely with parents, counselors, and psychologists. When a child's severe reluctance persists after a couple of months of consciously structuring the environment and creating nonthreatening opportunities for involvement, the teacher should not hesitate to seek help. After giving the child a reasonable time to become adjusted, considering the child's age and previous experiences (or lack of them), the teacher takes careful observational notes. The teacher should study these carefully to see if any progress is being made, and he or she should discuss minimal progress with the school psychologist or with some other mental health worker to determine if additional evaluation or a change in programming is necessary.

ENCOURAGING DEVELOPMENTAL PLAY BEHAVIOR

"When a child solves a problem in play, his sense of adequacy and self-esteem grows" (Berger, 1974, p. 32). Although relatively little systematic research has been done on play development per se, it is generally accepted that play contributes significantly to the development of happy, healthy personalities. "Through sensory-motor and symbolic play, the young child learns to deal effectively with the objects and people in his environment, to master his emotions, and to prepare himself cognitively, socially and emotionally, for the next stage in his life—the school years" (Smith, 1975, p. 147).

The importance of play

The importance of play has been noted in the early literature as far back as Plato and Aristotle (Cherry, 1976). Freudians view the repetition of experiences in play as a means of gaining mastery over painful events. Eriksonians consider play to be a method by which children organize and integrate life experiences. Piagetians see play as an essential means of mastering one's environment. Sutton-Smith emphasizes the role of play in developing creativity and in increasing the child's repertoire of responses (Bergstrom and Margosian, 1977; Cherry, 1976; Smith, 1975).

The value of play in fostering cognitive development and motor skills is being publicized increasingly. Local newspapers and popular magazines often advise parents, especially at Christmas time, on how to select toys that match their child's interests and level of development. It is becoming easier for teachers to convince parents that although their child looks as if he or she is "just playing" he or she is actually "working." The idea that painting and coloring develop eye-hand coordination, that puppet play enhances verbal skills, and that cooperation can be taught in the block corner is being accepted. Researchers have found a decrease in self-stimulatory behavior, self-inflicted aggression, and social isolation through the development of play behavior (Wehman, 1978).

The importance of creating an environment that promotes spontaneous and appropriately directed play cannot be underestimated. Early childhood educators have long realized the need for play activities within all preschool curricula. The issue of accountability, however, has jeopardized the role of spontaneous play in some classrooms. Teachers feel pushed to judge the value of a play activity by what is learned. Perhaps the challenge now is to create a three-way balance among less structured creative activities, freedom of choice, and directed tasks designed to remedy developmental deficits.

The nature of play

Piaget (1963) placed play into three broad categories. First, *practice play* accompanies the sensory-motor stage of cognitive development. Practice play is characterized by the exploration and repetition involved in mastering an activity. The game of "taking things out and putting things in" is typical practice play.

Symbolic play describes the second type of play that occurs during the preoperational stage of cognitive development. Preschool children involved in symbolic play can be seen using one object to represent or symbolize another. A child might attribute the qualities of a camera to a small wooden block and go around "taking pictures." The child's increased verbal ability allows imitating and reenacting experiences. Social play flourishes along with interaction with specific toys.

The third kind of play is referred to as *games with rules*, which requires more complex communication and cooperation. Whereas some may engage in rule-oriented play during preschool, interest in this behavior is thought to heighten during the concrete operational stage of cognitive development near 7 years of age.

The development of play

Education usually emphasizes structured, teacher-directed play because some children do not appear to learn readily through spontaneous play. Wehman (1978) suggests that inappropriate toys and play materials may contribute to handicapped children's limited play behavior. Toys that are not durable fail to withstand rough treatment and toys such as dolls designed for symbolic play are not developmentally appropriate for some children. Children who still need to engage in practice play must be provided with toys strong enough to accommodate repeated use. Children who lack attending skills, imitation skills, or communication skills cannot be expected to share or take turns. Developing these abilities takes time and is taught deliberately through modeling and reinforcement. Teachers need to assess a child's developmental strengths and weaknesses to encourage the most appropriate play activities.

Once the teacher notes that a child has begun to explore the environment and effectively uses a variety of different toy objects, Wehman (1978) encourages the development of "(a) more sophisticated and sustained toy play and (b) greater frequency of social interaction patterns" (p. 284). The boxed material appearing on pp. 249-250 suggests some guidelines to enhance productive free-choice play.

Imagining and pretending may be difficult for many children. This freedom to be somebody else or something else is often a good way to lead the withdrawn child out of his or her shell. Dress-up clothes, an assortment of hats (fireman, cowboy, train conductor, or nurse), and old costumes left from Halloween are appealing. Pretending to be animals during story times and participating in musical activities allow many children to romp and move freely. With freedom of movement comes greater ease in being around other children.

A large box with holes for windows provides a sense of protection. As the children crawl in and out they discover new ways of looking at things. Looking through the window in the box restricts the view in unexpected ways. Moving becomes purposeful. Seeing what is inside intrigues some

---

SETTING THE STAGE FOR PRODUCTIVE FREE-PLAY TIMES

A. *Arrange the play area thoughtfully*
  1. Provide adequate space indoors and out. Avoid crowding.
  2. Arrange small play spaces, separated by shelves or other dividers. Puzzles, books, and other things to do alone should be available.
  3. Prepare larger spaces for cooperative play with blocks and other building materials.
  4. A play kitchen in a corner encourages group play. Provide some full-sized pans and spoons and child-sized equipment.
  5. Maintain the same basic room arrangement over time, but vary the play materials available. Have a storage area where toys may "rest." Sometimes allow the children to choose what will be stored and what will be available.
  6. Include clay and easels but monitor their use.
  7. Puppets, dolls and doll houses, and barns and animals should be regularly available. These imagination stimulators require set-up space, whether used alone or with a group.
  8. Remove toys that appear to encourage an activity or noise level incompatible with the best interests of all the children. In small areas, large cars and trucks usually generate too high an activity level for safety.
  9. Plan to alternate indoor and outdoor play whenever possible. Outdoor areas should provide safe climbing and running spaces, as well as tricycles and structures for crawling in, over, and under.
  10. Be alert for special needs. Provide special equipment for children with physical disabilities.

Continued.

SETTING THE STAGE FOR PRODUCTIVE FREE-PLAY TIMES—cont'd

B. *Establish rules or guidelines from the beginning*
1. Keep the rules simple and limited in number.
2. Telling children rules is important, but not very effective. They will need to learn the guidelines by observation and experience. But the teacher should have the rules firmly in mind.
3. Rules should be designed to establish thoughtful, kind, and courteous behavior. The following are some we have found useful:
   a. The child who chooses a toy first may decide if he or she wants to play alone or with others. The child's decision will be respected.
   b. Sharing is not required especially if the item to be shared belongs to a particular child. Sharing is, however, encouraged.
   c. Children wanting to join an established group must be invited to join. The newcomer may ask to play, but cannot move in without a welcome.
   d. Good manners are modeled and expected. "May I," "please," and "thank you" are routinely used by teachers. Children absorb these courtesies quickly.
   e. When a child or a group is finished with an item, the item must be returned to its place on the shelf before a different toy or game is chosen.
   f. Sometimes children like to just watch for awhile. This wish is respected. A rocker and a beanbag chair are often used by watchers.
   g. Just as child newcomers may not barge into an established group, so adult (teacher or parent) newcomers must ask permission and be accepted.
C. *Some attitudes for teachers and parents during free play*
1. Respect the children's ability to choose an activity suited to their present learning needs. By providing a range of materials and possible activities, the self-knowledge of each child is allowed to function.
2. Trust each child to use good judgment. Interfere only if real danger or unkindness is imminent. Anticipate and prevent trouble rather than punish it after the fact.
3. Be aware of what is happening throughout the room. Even when attending to a particular child, the teacher must be alert to everyone and everything. Evidence of this awareness from the beginning leads children to follow the rules consistently.
4. Avoid overprotecting the child who lacks assertiveness. By "making" more aggressive children share, the child who fails to assert himslf or herself is rewarded for this lack of assertiveness. Rather, suggest to the quiet ones that they ask for a turn. If they begin fussing, remove the object of the argument for a time. Explain that they will have to find a way to resolve the problem.
5. If an unacceptable behavior persists, reevaluate the whole situation. If things are being thrown in the wrong place, find a place where it is appropriate to throw, and move the throwers there. If loud noises inside are a problem, be outside more often.
6. Avoid making children self-conscious. Calling everyone's attention to a mistake or a mess is unkind.
7. Avoid comparisons. Respect uniqueness consistently.

children. If the box is large enough, a small carpet and a place for a snack will encourage some children to enter.

Teachers may want to tell short stories using a flannel board or pictures. Then as the teacher provides simple props and withdraws from the center of the activity, children usually accept the suggestion to "play the story."

Role playing is a form of pretending and imagining. An apron and play kitchen equipment makes it possible for children to be Mom or Dad. A plastic hammer or wrench enable a child to be a carpenter or a garage mechanic.

Some children pretend to be their big broth-

ers and sisters. Much insight into fears and frustrations can be gained by encouraging role playing without evaluating it. Of course the insights gained may not be pleasant. Judgment about the use made of what is learned requires compassion, understanding, and wisdom.

Puppets are therapeutic and fun for most children. A box with a "stage" cut out, an old television (with the insides removed), or a table with a curtain becomes the puppet theater. Of course a real puppet stage can be constructed by a willing parent. The puppets can be made from socks or sewn from a simple pattern. Commercial puppets are enchanting, although most are expensive. Children enjoy merely playing with the puppets, but if a teacher puts on the first show, they will have a better idea of how to be puppeteers.

It is not unusual for withdrawn children to say their first words with a puppet on their hands. Often they will find it necessary to use the puppet for days whenever they want to talk. Offering a change of puppets should be done with care. If a particular puppet is effective, the teacher should not rush into expecting the child to assume many roles with other puppets. Some children require prolonged encouragement before they can venture out.

Peers and play often draw children out of their shells. Suggesting that one child help another by picking up a spilled puzzle leads to later spontaneous kindnesses. Some children notice the needs of other youngsters more completely than most adults believe. Consider this experience of Lance and Carla.

Lance was enrolled in kindergarten, but over a period of several months he stood quietly but firmly in one corner of the room. The kindergarten teacher was patient and experienced; but with 32 other children, the situation was overwhelming to Lance. Because of Lance's continued withdrawn behavior his parents placed him in a preschool. On entering school his eyes were unsmiling and his lips were taut. For several days the other children played around him. He refused snacks, special treats, and all efforts to involve him in play. Then Carla took over. She was 4 years old. She walked right up to Lance and said, "I like blocks. Play with me." Without further ado she pulled Lance abruptly to the floor, pushed the blocks to him, and began to build. Smiling and chatting away (definitely a monologue) she told him all about the wonderful house she was building. Lance stared emotionless, but Carla was not disturbed. After awhile Carla said, "Help put the blocks back. We'll do a puzzle." Lance did not move. A few minutes later Carla announced. "Lance likes grapes." The teacher did not discover how Carla knew of Lance's liking for grapes, but promised to bring the fruit the next day.

The following day, Carla asked for some grapes "for Lance." Carrying the grapes with one hand and dragging Lance with the other, she moved to the puzzle corner. She said, "We'll do a puzzle first." With the grapes plainly in sight, but out of Lance's reach, they began a puzzle. "When we finish we eat grapes," said Carla. Lance smiled and slowly pushed a puzzle piece to Carla. He also ate grapes with Carla.

Carla's mothering continued for weeks as she ignored Lance's rebuffs. She regularly told everyone, "Lance is my friend," and busily planned things to do with him. Alternately she insisted and cajoled. Frequently, when Lance ignored her she walked away, only to return as if nothing had happened a few minutes later. Carla literally planned and executed therapy for Lance.

SUMMARY

This chapter provided an overview of the essential elements of a home and school climate conducive to developing healthy personalities. Some of Erikson's (1963) growth stages were reviewed to emphasize the interaction between forces within the child and conditions from without. These necessitate early warmth and consistency in caregiving, encouraging autonomy within reasonable guidelines, and developing initiative tempered with gentle direction.

The essential blocks that build a growth-producing environment were illustrated and described. Teachers were urged to prevent inappropriate behaviors by building security through the use of a number of behavioristically oriented principles including establishing limits, routines, variety, constructive consequences, avoidance of frustration, behavior modeling, and opportunities for appropriately expressing feelings.

Some children arrive at preschools and day-care centers with attitudes and behaviors that interfere with learning. They may be too active or too withdrawn. They may lack self-discipline. Some are overly dependent on adults for direction, whereas others refuse all directions from their teachers. Techniques for working with unique ways of behaving were suggested. These range from effectively using a time-out in an engineered classroom to using puppets and play found in the traditional child development program. Throughout, the role of positive reinforcement and appropriate modeling of behavior was emphasized. Enhancing self-esteem is an ever-present goal.

Finally, guidelines were offered to assist teachers in creating an environment that fosters the development of spontaneous play behavior considered to be essential in the development of emotional well-being. We believe that young children are happiest when they know someone cares enough to allow them to be unique, while preventing them from behaving in selfish, thoughtless ways.

DISCUSSION TOPICS AND ACTIVITIES

1. Make a list of necessary classroom limits or rules. Be certain to see that each is definable, reasonable, and enforceable. Role play the explanation of these limits to determine if they are indeed definable.
2. List and discuss any special adaptations that will have to be made in classroom structure and management for children with handicaps.
3. Develop a workable classroom schedule that provides a balance between active and passive involvement, experiences that require visual attention, those that necessitate auditory attention, and group and individual activities. Exchange constructive criticism with classmates.
4. Make a chart of as many natural and logical consequences for behavioral difficulties as possible. Use Table 10 on p. 235 to help you begin. Keep the chart handy. Observations in classrooms should help you expand your list. A review of one of Dreikurs' excellent books will convince you of the importance of these alternatives to punishment.
5. Role play how you would deal with a parent who insists his or her child should settle arguments by fighting.

6. Try to identify toys that might be frustrating to some children. Make a list of these toys and the types of children who might have difficulty with them.
7. Develop a repertoire of techniques to effect smooth transitions. Role play some of these with classmates.
8. Study one of the many excellent texts on behavior modification techniques. Conduct a behavior modification project to increase or decrease a designated behavior. Report the results of your project in graphic form to your classmates.

ANNOTATED REFERENCES
Developing a healthy personality

Dinkmyer, D., and Dreikurs, R. *Encouraging children to learn: The encouragement process.* Englewood Cliffs, N.J.: Prentice-Hall, Inc., 1963.
In introducing the book the authors state, "Most people consider encouragement as a supplementary aspect of their correctional efforts and do not recognize its pivotal significance; nor do they fathom the complexity of the process called encouragement." They then go on to explain how and why encouragement is so critical to all of us. Through specific guidelines, helpful examples, and thought provoking discussion, the authors provide parents and teachers with essential ideas for facilitating "the encouragement process."

Dinkmeyer, D., and Losoncy, L.E. *The encouragement book: Becoming a positive person.* Englewood Cliffs, N.J.: Prentice-Hall, Inc., 1980.
This book is designed to "show you how to be there when someone needs your emotional support." It provides exercises and examples designed to "bring out the encouraging person in you." Parents and teachers will find the ideas useful as they work with young children, although the book was not written specifically for this purpose.

Erikson, E.H. A healthy personality for every child. In R.H. Anderson and H.G. Shane (Eds.), *As the twig is bent.* Boston: Houghton Mifflin, 1971.
This extremely well-written, fascinating paper is a digest of the report to the Midcentury White House Conference on Children and Youth, 1951. It offers the reader a glimpse of the eight stages of man that are considered to be the impetus of much of today's lifespan research. If one has a "must" list, this should be included.

Samuels, S.C. *Enhancing self-concept in early childhood.* New York: Human Sciences Press, 1977.
The author has effected well-organized integration and relationship between empirical knowledge and practical classroom situations related to the development of self-concept. Various means of understanding a child's self-concept and suggestions for creating a healthful classroom climate are presented. The easy reading style makes the book useful for paraprofessionals, parents, and of course teachers.

Simon, S.B., and O'Rourke, R.D. *Developing values with exceptional children.* Englewood Cliffs, N.J.: Prentice-Hall, Inc., 1977.

In the introduction the authors say, "We want each of our children at Boxelder School to feel important, cared for, listened to, and loved as people who are learning to extend themselves in loving ways." Although the book is about working with older children, the philosophy and practical suggestions for developing values will be thought provoking for teachers of children of all ages.

Yamamoto, K. (Ed.) *The child and his image.* Boston: Houghton Mifflin, 1972.

Although this book has been on the shelves for a number of years, its value is evidenced by its tattered pages. The focus is on children between the ages of 3 and 10. It is designed for teachers who are or who will be in the position to nurture the self. Concrete, useful, practical suggestions are included to assist in the development of healthy self-concepts.

Promoting positive social and emotional development

Baker, B.L., Brightman, A.J., Heifetz, L.J., and Murphy, D.M. *Behavior problems.* Champaign, Ill.: Research Press, 1978.

This concise, well-organized manual was written primarily to assist parents in using principles of behavior modification. Its format is clear and to the point. Teachers can obtain useful ideas that will transfer to the classroom.

Blackham, G.J. *The deviant child in the classroom.* Belmont, Calif.: Wadsworth Publishing Co., 1968.

Although this book was published in the 1960's, the problems and the solution have not changed. The purpose of this book was to provide an understanding of the bases of deviant behavior, to describe classroom dynamics contributing to deviant behavior, and to provide practical methods for working with such behavior. The role of basic defense mechanisms including rationalization, repression, and denial are well explained.

Buckley, N.K., and Walker, H.M. *Modifying classroom behavior.* Champaign, Ill.: Research Press, 1978.

A semiprogrammed format is used to present the procedures and amplifications of behavior modification. It is brief and nontechnical. Classroom examples increase the reality of the suggestions made. Teachers will find it worthwhile to have one such book on their shelves.

Halperin, M. *Helping maltreated children: School and community involvement.* St. Louis: The C.V. Mosby Co., 1979.

In a brief, useful format the author defines maltreatment, describes ways of recognizing it, and offers practical suggestions for dealing with it. The author also includes strategies for preventing maltreatment.

Hewett, F.M., and Taylor, F.D. *The emotionally disturbed child in the classroom.* Boston: Allyn and Bacon, Inc., 1980.

The authors provide a behavioral-educational approach to the management of any child whose behavior stands in the way of receiving an effective education. Teachers in early childhood programs may find it beneficial to consider designing centers that correspond to the attention, response, order, explorations, and social hierarchy discussed and illustrated in this book.

Kauffman, J.M. *Characteristics of children's behavior disorders.* Columbus: Charles E. Merrill Publishing Co., 1977.

This text is designed to provide insight into the problems and characteristics of emotionally disturbed children. It is intended for the student who wishes to be introduced to the theory and research related to behavioral disorders. It is not, however, designed to be a "how-to-do-it" methods book. Even so, there are examples of how to control disruptive behavior throughout the book.

Marion, M. *Guidance of young children.* St. Louis: The C.V. Mosby Co., 1981.

At last, this much needed text has arrived. This well-written brief paperback is based on the assumptions that adults want to help children learn to control themselves, to like and value themselves, to be humane, caring, competent, independent, assertive, cooperative, and helpful. The child, the adults in his or her life, and the environment are considered the essential components in the guidance system. The book is enormously helpful to anyone involved in early childhood education. It is soundly based in theory and research while offering a great variety of well-received practical suggestions for guiding young children.

Shea, T.M. *Teaching children and youth with behavior disorders.* St. Louis: The C.V. Mosby Co., 1978.

This very readable text focuses on prescriptive teaching methods applicable to children, youth behavior difficulties, and their parents. It is thorough in its presentation of problems and characteristics, diagnostic procedures, parent education, and teaching and management strategies. Numerous examples help one apply the content.

Smith, C.A. *Promoting the social development of young children, Strategies and activities.* Palo Alto, Calif.: Mayfield Publishing Co., 1982

This practical text is a much needed resource of over 100 strategies and activities designed to encourage the development of body and sensory awareness, emotional awareness, empathy for others, friendship, conflict resolution, cooperation, and the expression of kindness.

Swanson, H.L., and Reinert, H.R. *Teaching strategies for children in conflict:* Curriculum, methods, and materials. St. Louis: The C.V. Mosby Co., 1979.

The authors discuss various alternatives to meet the individual needs of children with emotional and social problems. They draw methods from a variety of conceptual approaches, and intend a match between the child and the most appropriate intervention. This is an excellent text for those who wish to obtain an excellent overview of the theory and practice relevant to children with social and emotional problems.

Walker, J.E., and Shea, T.M. *Behavior modification: A practical approach for education.* St. Louis: The C.V. Mosby Co., 1980.

The specific purpose of this text "was to provide experienced teachers, teachers-in-training, and paraprofessionals with a guide for the application of behavior modification techniques in special and general educational settings" (p. ix). The authors have managed to translate the often misunderstood principles of behavior modification into classroom practices readily usable by practitioners. This is a handy tool for those wishing to become more effective managers of behavior.

Walsh, H.M. *Introducing the young child to the social world.* New York: Macmillan, Inc., 1980.

This well-written book offers theoretical ideas and practical suggestions for facilitating young children's social competence. Walsh believes that, "A major goal of early childhood is to help young children grow beyond considerations of themselves only toward a concern for the welfare of others and a knowledge of the social world around them" (p. vi). It is a refreshing change from the emphasis on the development of cognitive and preacademic skills.

Wolfgang, C.H. *Helping aggressive and passive preschoolers through play.* Columbus: Charles E. Merrill Publishing Co., 1977.

This inexpensive book suggests a number of schemes for general environmental design, classroom strategies, and organization of time. These ideas can be helpful to the teacher who has time to implement one-to-one interactions. The strategies outlined give teachers options to try even though the theoretical basis is somewhat unclear and possibly too simplified.

REFERENCES

Apolloni, T., and Cooke, T. Integrated programming at the infant, toddler, and preschool levels. In M.J. Guralnick (Ed.), *Early intervention and the integration of handicapped and nonhandicapped children.* Baltimore: University Park Press, 1978, 147-165.

Bandura, A., Ross, D., and Ross, S.A. Imitation of film-mediated aggressive models. *Journal of Abnormal and Social Psychology*, 1963, *66*, 3-11.

Berger, A.S. Choosing toys for the amazing work of play. *Day Care and Early Education*, 1974, *1*, 21, 32.

Bergstrom, J.M., and Margosian, R.K. *Teaching young chil-dren.* Columbus: Charles E. Merrill Publishing Co., 1977.

Biehler, R.F. *Psychology applied to teaching.* Boston: Houghton Mifflin, 1978.

Blackham, G.J. *The deviant child in the classroom.* Belmont, Calif.: Wadsworth Publishing Company, Inc., 1968.

Bricker, D.D. A rationale for the integration of handicapped and nonhandicapped preschool children. In M.J. Guralnick (Ed.), *Early intervention and the integration of handicapped and nonhandicapped children.* Baltimore: University Park Press, 1978, 3-26.

Caldwell, B.M. Aggression and hostility in young children *Young Children*, 1977, *32*, 4-13.

Carlson, N.A. General principles of learning and motivation, *Teaching Exceptional Children*, 1980, *12*, 60-62.

Cherry, C. *Creative play for the developing child.* Belmont, Calif.: Fearon Publishers, Inc., 1976.

Clarizio, H.F., and Yelon, S.L. Learning theory approaches to classroom management: Rationale and intervention techniques. *The Journal of Special Education*, 1967, *1*, 267-274.

Cook, R.E., and Cook, C.W. *Evaluative feedback: Reward or punishment?* Manuscript submitted for publication, 1981.

Crook, W.G. *Can your child read? Is he hyperactive?* Jackson, Tenn.: Pedicenter Press, 1975.

Cruickshank, W.M., Bentzen, F., Ratzeburg, F., and Tannhousser, M.A. *A teaching method for brain-injured and hyperactive children.* Syracuse, N.Y.: Syracuse University Press, 1961.

Dreikurs, R., *Children: The challenge.* New York: Hawthorn Books, Inc., 1964.

Erikson, E.H. *Childhood and society.* New York: Norton, 1963.

Erikson, E.H. A healthy personality for every child. In R.H. Anderson and H.G. Shane (Eds.), *As the twig is bent.* Boston: Houghton Mifflin, 1971.

Feingold, B. *Why is your child hyperactive?* New York: Random House, 1974.

Gewirtz, J.L., and Stingle, K.G. Learning of generalized imitation as the basis for identification. *Psychology Review*, 1968, *75*, 374-397.

Glasser, W. *Schools without failure.* New York: Harper and Row Publishers, 1969.

Gordon, T. *Parent effectiveness training.* New York: New American Library, 1975.

Harris, E.C. (Ed.) *Report on education research.* Washington, D.C.: Capitol Publications, 1980.

Henderson, B., and Moore, S.G. Children's responses to objects differing in novelty in relation to level of curiosity and adult behavior. *Child Development*, 1980, *51*, 457-465.

Hendrick, J. *The whole child*. St. Louis: The C.V. Mosby Co., 1980.

Hewett, F.M. *The emotionally disturbed child in the classroom*. Boston: Allyn and Bacon, Inc., 1968.

Hewett, F.M., and Taylor, F.D. *The emotionally disturbed child in the classroom*. Boston: Allyn and Bacon, Inc., 1980.

Kauffman, J.M. *Characteristics of children's behavior disorders*. Columbus: Charles E. Merrill Publishing Co., 1977.

Kirkhart, R., and Kirkhart, E. The bruised self: Mending in early years. In Yamamoto, K. (Ed.), *The child and his image*. Boston: Houghton Mifflin, 1972, 121-177.

Lansky, V. *The taming of the C.A.N.D.Y. monster*. Wayzata, N.Y.: Meadowbrook Press, 1978.

Lorton, M. *Workjobs*. Atlanta: Addison-Wesley Publishing, Co., 1973.

Marion, M. *Guidance of young children*. St. Louis: The C.V. Mosby Co., 1981.

Maslow, A.H. *Toward a psychology of being*. New York: Van Nostrand Reinhold, 1968.

Peck, C., Apolloni, T., Cooke, T., and Raver, S. Teaching retarded preschoolers to imitate the free play behavior of nonretarded classmates: Trained and generalized effects. *The Journal of Special Education*, 1978, *12*, 195-207.

Piaget, J. *Play, dreams and imitation in childhood*. New York: Norton, 1963.

Pipes, P.L. *Nutrition in infancy and childhood*. St. Louis: The C.V. Mosby Co., 1977.

Raver, S.A. Preschool integration: Experiences from the classroom. *Teaching Exceptional Children*, 1979, *12*, 22-26.

Reinert, H.R. *Children in conflict*. St. Louis: The C.V. Mosby Co., 1976.

Ross, A.O. The application of behavior principles in therapeutic education. *The Journal of Special Education*, 1977, *1*, 275-286.

Smith, J.M., and Smith, D.E. *Child management*. Champaign, Ill.: Research Press, 1976.

Smith, L. (Ed.) *Human development: 2½ to 6 years*. Costa Mesa, Calif.: Concept Media, Inc., 1975.

Swanson, H.L., and Reinert, H.R. *Teaching strategies for children in conflict*. St. Louis: The C.V. Mosby Co., 1979.

Swap, S.M. Disturbing classroom behaviors: A developmental and ecological view. *Exceptional Children*, 1974, *41*, 163-172.

Walker, J., and Shea, T.M. *Behavior modification*. St. Louis: The C.V. Mosby Co., 1980.

Walsh, H.M. *Introducing the young child to the social world*. New York: Macmillan, Inc. 1980.

Wehman, P. Play skill development. In N.H. Fallen and J.E. McGovern, (Eds.), *Young children with special needs*. Columbus: Charles E. Merrill Publishing Co., 1978, 277-303.

Zentall, S. Environmental stimulation model. *Exceptional Children*, 1977, *43*, 502-511.

9

In partnership with parents

People are increasingly recognizing the importance of parent involvement in the education of young children. Teachers are being called on to develop comprehensive programs of parent education. Many teachers are not prepared to understand the unique needs of parents of young handicapped children.

Parents of handicapped children often report that they are confused. They say that even the experts disagree. Diagnoses differ, and the directions parents receive are conflicting. Some of those to whom they have turned for help have made them feel guilty and inadequate. Others have failed to tell them anything helpful.

Other parents, however, say that they have received immediate and useful guidance. They were told the nature of their children's problems, and were given practical suggestions for living and playing with their children. Most important of all, they were led to perceive themselves as capable of successful parenting. These parents were guided to understand their role as the primary and most effective teachers of their children.

A parent-professional partnership

The successful education of handicapped children demands an effective partnership between the professionals and the parents. Meier (1978, p. 36) in fact relates evidence that "indicates that knowledgeable and skillful parenting is the most effective and economical means for fostering the optimum development of the child." This is why Public Law 94-142 requires parents to be involved in planning and implementing programs for children with special needs. This partnership should begin as soon as possible—certainly as soon as parents seek opinions about their fears. Although they may begin the conversation with an examiner by saying, "Of course, I know nothing serious is really wrong," they may really be saying, "Please tell me that I am worrying needlessly."

Until recently, concerned parents were not recognized as partners in all aspects of their children's lives. Because of this, few teacher training programs have offered any specific guidelines for working with parents. Of course some teachers instinctively did helpful things. Often these were individuals who had raised children with special problems. Through their own experiences they had developed sensitivity and insight into the needs of other parents of children with special needs. But for many teachers, parents were perceived of as part of the problem rather than as active agents working out solutions.

This chapter provides teachers with guidelines for working with parents of young children. Whereas special attention will be given to the needs of parents of handicapped children, the guidelines will increase a teacher's effectiveness for working with parents of all children. Readers are encouraged to seek more in-depth understanding through studying the many good books written about parent education. The annotated bibliography at the end of the chapter provides an overview of some of these.

EMOTIONAL NEEDS OF FAMILIES WITH HANDICAPPED CHILDREN

As with every aspect of human relations, "everything is the cause of anything," (Davis, 1962). It is possible for people's emotional strength and stability to grow rapidly when they are faced with severe problems. For some, however, minor difficulties may result in breakdown and disaster. Just as each child needs an Individual Educational Plan (IEP), so each family needs an individual set of supports and guidance.

Basic needs

Certain needs are basic to all parents who seek professional help. First, they want to be assured that they are receiving the best and most up-to-date information possible. They want to have confidence in those who profess to know how to help their child. Second, parents want to be recognized as caring, intelligent people. They need to be viewed as individuals capable of effective parenting, and they want to know that they are seen in this way. Third, they want and urgently need guidance in what to do in the immediate *now*. Although they want positive opinions about what the future holds, they need to have useful suggestions immediately (Stigen, 1976).

Failure to consider basic needs. Many of the emotional reactions attributed to parents may be heightened by the failure of those to whom the parents have turned for help to consider their basic needs. Of course some parents are hostile, unrealistic, and unable to cope no matter how helpful others have tried to be. Professional mishandling of parents' needs, however, is a serious problem. Roos (1975) identifies eight categories of mishandling, as follows:

1. Professional ignorance. Professionals fail to recognize a handicapping condition. They tend either to predict that the child will outgrow the problem or that the child's condition is hopeless.
2. Professional hopelessness. Professionals generate self-fulfilling and self-limiting prophecies. They convey defeatist or negative attitudes.
3. Referral ad infinitum. Perhaps, because of a lack of expertise, some professionals refer parents from professional to professional. Although it is true that some parents shop around hoping for more positive diagnoses, numerous occasions of unneeded referrals do occur.
4. Veil of secrecy. Despite the encouragement of Public Law 94-142 to include parents in making decisions involving their children, some medical and mental health professionals still attempt to withhold information necessary to effective decision making.
5. Deaf ear syndrome. Many parents still experience the frustration of having their requests ignored or their opinions seemingly unheard.
6. Professional omniscience. Whereas most parents can accept the honesty of a professional who readily admits that he or she does not have all of the answers, it is difficult for parents to cope with one who wishes to claim that he or she knows everything.
7. Professional omnipotence. Many parents still believe that only professionals have enough wisdom to determine what is best for a child. Adherence to the requirements of Public Law 94-142 will ideally stop the practice of professionals informing parents *after* they have made important decisions about a child's educational program.
8. Parents as patients. As some professionals still continue to see the parents as having a problem (a handicapped child), they have the tendency to confuse a need for information with a need for "therapy."

Even if teachers do not mishandle the needs of parents in any of these ways, they should realize that some parents may have experienced such treatment by someone. This realization will help teachers to sustain the patience and understanding so necessary when working with parents who are anxious, angry, or troubled.

The need for emotional support. Parents need emotional support. Assuming that parents are seen as partners by all of the professionals with whom they come into contact, their ability to cope effectively with their problems will influence what they do and how well they are able to do it (Weikart, 1980).

Many of the parents who seek to enroll their children in regular daycare centers and preschools have youngsters whose problems are not severe. These parents will be less distressed than parents of a deaf child, a blind child, a severely retarded child, or a physically handicapped child. They will, however, also require understanding and thoughtful guidance. Some of these parents may need to be led to recognize the importance of working with their children at home. Because the child's handicap is not severe, these parents may expect their child to "outgrow it" without their active participation as the primary teachers of their child.

For all parents, regardless of the nature or the severity of their children's problems, professionals must learn to provide emotional support and educational programming. Parents of young handicapped children need to feel the warmth and caring support of people who know how to teach their children. Professional knowledge is useless if it does not include kindness. Before families can be professionally helped, they must be convinced that the teacher cares about them and their children.

STAGES OF PARENTAL REACTION

A number of writers, both parents and professionals, have described various phases of adjustment in parents' acceptance of their child and his or her handicapping condition. Boyd (1950) discussed three levels of adaptation: the need to pull back and focus solely on one's own needs, a gradual turning toward the needs of one's immediate family, and a desire to aid others with similar problems. More recently, writers are turning to the grieving process described by Kübler-Ross (1969) for an understanding of the possible emotional reactions of some parents to the perceived "death" of a normal child (Tanner, 1980).

Fig. 9-1 illustrates the phases of emotional reactions that may be experienced by families with handicapped children. One must remember, however, that parental reactions are unique. Some parents take issue with the whole concept of stages or phases of emotional adjustment (Searl, 1978). Teachers must therefore cautiously apply the concept of stages realizing that the sequence and completeness of each phase of adjustment may differ with each indi-

vidual. Individual family members may differ from each other in developing an accepting attitude. Some may never fully accept their child and his or her condition.

Shock, disbelief, and denial

Parents and professionals alike describe the first stage of parental reaction as one of shock and disbelief on learning of a child's disability or disfigurement. This shock and possible disbelief may be accompanied by feelings of shame, guilt, and unworthiness. As the reality of the child's condition is slowly assimilated, parents may try to deny the existing problems. Often, first attempts to find out what is wrong are really attempts to find someone who will say that "nothing is wrong." For this reason, some parents go from doctor to doctor and from clinic to clinic seeking opinions. Some parents do this, however, because each professional recommends that they should seek additional opinions. Diagnosis of problems in young children is far from an exact science. Rather, it is a piecing together of diverse observations, bits of information, and confusing evidence. Cause and effect interact to the point that it is difficult to decide which is which.

Some parents refuse to seek any guidance. They can be heard telling relatives and friends "Oh, he's just like Uncle Joe. He didn't talk until he was seven," or "Aunt Susie never did learn how to do puzzles, and our Sally is just like her."

Other parents may deprive the rest of their family while working diligently to prove diagnosticians wrong. They hope that intensive training will eliminate whatever developmental lag exists. But their nagging suspicions continue to grow. Unless parents can and will accept available guidance, precious time is lost. Fear that is allowed to grow undermines effective solutions to the simplest of problems.

Teachers can help. The teacher can help if he or she suspects that a parent is feeling fearful, guilty, or anxious while experiencing shock,

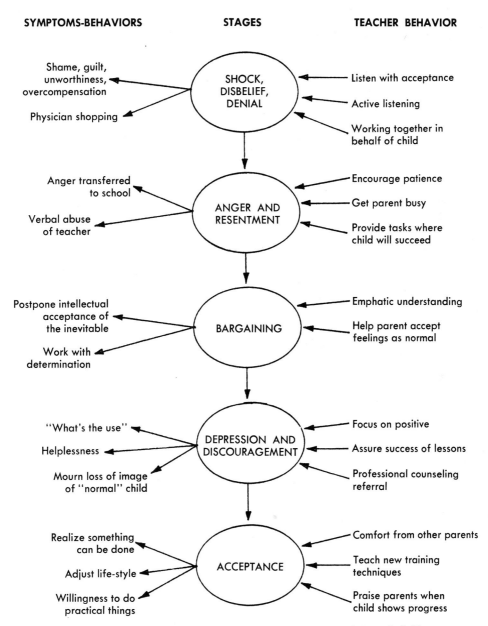

FIG. 9-1. Possible parental stages of reaction to the handicapped child.

disbelief, or denial. A teacher can help such a parent to understand that these feelings and experiences are appropriate. It is normal and acceptable for parents temporarily to blame, reject, or even hate the child or themselves (Lepler, 1978). Teachers should listen with acceptance. Pushing parents to "face the child's limitations" will only create defensiveness (Seligman, 1979). Teachers should try to help parents focus on ways the teacher and parents can work together on behalf of the child. Teachers can become effective "active listeners" (Gordon, 1970) through patience and practice.

Teachers must remember that anxiety creates problems, and that lack of knowing what to do creates anxiety. This is why parent-infant programs are needed. Initial fear and grief can be minimized if parents can be taught to do constructive things from the beginning. Energy is wasted by grief and anger. Energy used to play and work with children in useful ways minimizes grieving time. Time *is* important. Learning begins at birth; children do not wait.

Anger and resentment

When parents can no longer deny the existence of their child or his or her condition, they may feel anger, resentment, rage, or envy. Even though they may have intellectually accepted the child's problems, they may be so caught up in their emotions that they cannot focus on positive approaches to their concerns. They may even direct their anger at the very professionals who are trying to help the most. Suspicions about a teacher's motives may explode in angry accusations. Other parents try to prove that the teacher is "wrong." Verbal abuse is common. At this stage teachers need to demonstrate true professionalism. They need to be understanding, compassionate, and gently caring during this time.

Getting parents busy. The anger will pass, and will pass more quickly if the parents are given tasks to do with their children at which they absolutely cannot fail. This is not the time to try to make rapid progress with either children or their parents. Rather, the parents need to have constant reminders that they do indeed make a difference to their children. They must discover and rediscover that they have resources within themselves that they did not know were there. They must be provided with supports that match their individual weaknesses. All of this must be done with a kindness that refuses to blame or to react to the unreasonable demands that accompany the grief of parents.

Bargaining

Some parents may try to resolve their anger and resentment by going through what Kübler-Ross (1969) describes as a process of bargaining. It resembles an attempt to postpone complete intellectual and emotional acceptance of the inevitable. During this time, parents and other family members may work with great diligence and determination. It is as if they are saying "If I do everything you tell me to do, then surely this problem will go away." If progress is not as rapid or as great as they expect, bargaining is sometimes followed by the gray-black world of depression.

Empathy is essential. To be helpful, teachers must display empathetic understanding by recognizing and accepting the natural feelings of the parents. Helping parents to realize that their feelings and states of mind are normal can convey an attitude of interest and caring. A simple statement reflecting active listening such as "It must be very frustrating to have the constant care of a child with special needs" can be very comforting (Lichter, 1976).

Depression and discouragement

"What's the use?" and "Why bother?" can become the reaction of some parents to all teaching and behavior management suggestions. An oppressive weight of hopelessness can add new dimensions to the problems. For some, this very feeling of helplessness may make them more amenable to being helped. Because of feeling helpless, they may be more likely to ask for assistance. Roos (1979, p. 104) contends that "the absence of such feelings [depression], particularly when realization of the child's retardation is recent, is unusual enough to raise suspicions regarding the possibility of atypical techniques of handling emotions (e.g., repression and isolation of affect)." A parent of a handicapped child, Kirk (1979), describes the need at this point to mourn as if to say good-bye to a disappearing image of one's missing, "normal" child. He feels that once this mourning occurs, the parent can begin to accept the child as she or he is. Parents can begin to focus on productive solutions to their problems.

Focus on the positive. Teachers must focus on the positive and avoid adding to parents' depression by their own eagerness to get on with the task of teaching the child. During this time, lessons must be planned for the parents in a way that assures their success. Teachers must halt the growth of seeds of self-doubt about being a good parent. They should avoid all indirect and direct criticism. Teachers must also avoid giving excessive, unwarranted praise because parents interpret it as insincere.

Parents who continue to suffer deep depression may need professional counseling. Teachers should not hesitate to find some tactful way to suggest this. Often the simplest way is to listen carefully to the cry of "What's the use?" and then to suggest that they may find help in many ways. Some parents will want and need the counsel of psychologists and psychiatrists. Others may find great comfort from other parents who have passed through depression and who have moved on to practical solutions to their problems. An informal gathering of classroom parents may help some parents to find comfort from one another. Many might benefit from an opportunity to look through a carefully developed file of local resources including churches, synagogues, mental health agencies, and parenting groups. All parents need to know someone cares.

Acceptance

Acceptance, the final stage in parents' emotional recognition of the need to modify their lives or their kinds of interactions with the handicapped child, means parents having an increasing willingness to do practical, useful things. Acceptance means that today's needs are recognized, not denied. Acceptance at its best means parents firmly deny that a tragedy has occurred and that nothing can be done about it. It means they have a willingness to learn and to apply new knowledge to meet day-to-day needs. It means they have a deep conviction that each human being is unique, special, and worthy of love and affection.

Acceptance should not mean that the handicapping condition is accepted as unalterable. Rather parents accept the need to learn skillful ways to alter the negative effects of the perceived condition. True acceptance includes the conviction that much needs to be done, and that what is done will make a difference.

Consider this mother's definition of acceptance:

To me acceptance means finding whatever pleasure I can in caring for Benjamin day to day. It means looking at other children without always wishing that he were like them. It means looking at the situation not in terms of what Benjamin can do for me, but what I can do to enhance his potential (Lepler, 1978, p. 33).

Encourage patience. Teachers must encourage patience when parents have begun to accept their children as they are, because most can achieve realistic expectations and give appropriate help. They will quickly and often eagerly learn new training techniques. There will be occasions, however, when they will feel stupid and confused. They must be helped to understand that the disability they are dealing with is a new experience and they will need time to grow accustomed to it. As teachers, parents may be clumsy at first, but the tasks will become easier after many trials under patient guidance. Teachers must give the parents much praise for their child's progress and for the parents' participation. All parents feel better when they are able to see themselves as vital contributors to their child's progress. Parents who focus on positive training techniques will provide constructive options for interacting with their child.

A father's perspective

Commenting to a group of educators on his own experience as a father, Kirk (1979) states:

If you help us to recognize the normality of our "abnormality," the appropriateness of our strange and sometimes frightening feelings, we will more quickly and smoothly graduate to acceptance. We need your nurturance and acceptance, your sharing of the commitment that has drawn you to this work. I believe that with you we can more fully realize that we can grow stronger and stand taller as a result of our pain and frustration—that we can mend our shattered egos and evolve into more sensitive, more tolerant and wiser parents (p. 6).

Crisis periods

Crisis periods can occur at any point in the adjustment process. Teachers cannot predict accurately the exact moment when the impact of the long-term implications of the presumed handicap will hit. Some parents conceal these crises from professionals; other parents do not. Nevertheless, an atmosphere that communicates kindness and affection helps. Parents are comforted when they know someone understands the need to cry, yell, or scream.

Even though parents may have basically accepted their child and the handicapping condition, adaptation may never be complete for some (Searl, 1978). Parents report that tears come even as the child grows into adulthood. Sometimes a crisis brings out the incompleteness of a parent's adaptation. Teachers can avoid judging or comparing parents' coping skills. The reassurance that someone who understands is available to listen may make the difference between a productive reaction to a crisis and a debilitating one. Teachers will remember that the emotional needs of families are as unique as the needs of the child. Reactions to the shattering of parental expectations and to the real concerns of daily care and worry about the future must be coped with adequately before parents can fully participate in whatever parent involvement opportunities are available.

SIBLING AND EXTENDED FAMILY NEEDS AND REACTIONS

Siblings and the extended family of the child also have needs and reactions. Grandparents grieve deeply, too. Theirs is often a double hurt because they not only experience pain for their grandchild, but they also grieve for their own children. Seeing a loved son or daughter try to cope with long-term problems is disheartening. One grandfather arrived at a diagnostic clinic with a blank check. "Just tell me what it costs," he said, "I'll find the money somehow."

Denial, blame, and anger may run rampant among grandparents. They may say "It's because she smoked while she was pregnant," or "His family never was any good," or "If only they hadn't. . . ." There is no doubt to whom the angry grandparents are referring.

Most grandparents and other close relatives, however, can be helped to provide needed moral, mental, and emotional support (Susser, 1974). Often relatives are the major source of babysitting relief for parents. All of those who spend much time caring for a handicapped child will find it helpful to be included in conferences and planning and teaching demonstrations. Often involved grandparents feel left out and deeply confused about what they should do.

Professionals must be sensitive to this, and with the parents' approval include these extended family members.

Chinn, Drew, and Logan (1979) discuss the needs of nonhandicapped siblings. Among these are (1) the need to be included in discussions about decisions concerning the handicapped child, (2) the need to have opportunities to express their feelings about the reactions of peers and to acknowledge their own feelings of guilt, (3) the need for an adequate amount of attention from parents, and (4) the need for honesty in general. Even with their own unique needs, nonhandicapped siblings usually adopt their parents' attitudes toward their handicapped sibling (Klein, 1972; Grossman, 1972).

Parents and teachers can help siblings cope with their needs. One effective way is to provide siblings with opportunities to participate in working with their handicapped brother or sister. Even very young children can learn to be effective teachers. In fact, young children who have just learned how to do something themselves may be superior teachers. It is imperative, however, that parents be sensitive in their requests of nonhandicapped siblings. Farber (1960) warned that siblings who assume too much responsibility for the care of their handicapped sibling can create their own inadequate personal adjustment. Along these same lines, it is essential that parents refrain from expecting too much from siblings. Sometimes the siblings are expected to make up for what the handicapped son or daughter cannot do.

Regardless of the age or the relationship of the extended family members, the teacher must be tactful, open, and honest. The parents' feelings and attitudes must always be given careful consideration and top priority. Everyone in the family interacts in some way with everyone else. Insofar as the teacher can influence these interactions in positive ways, the children will gain. Having faith that one can be a positive help to a handicapped child buoys young siblings and

mature grandparents. Specific tasks at which success is guaranteed are the place to begin. Then everyone benefits.

HELPING PARENTS TO UNDERSTAND THE EDUCATIONAL NEEDS OF THEIR CHILDREN

In helping parents to understand the educational needs of their children, those who evaluate children's skills and developmental levels are expected to communicate the result of their testing to parents meaningfully. If parents are to understand the educational needs of their children, they need first to understand what the examiners are talking about. This means that information must not be given in professional jargon. Educators can translate test results and implications into layman's language. For example, telling parents that their child may have a visual perceptual problem is meaningless to many of them. Conversely, parents can grasp readily the types of problems their child has when you talk in terms of tasks such as using the eyes and the hands at the same time when copying, stringing beads, doing puzzles, or stacking blocks.

Using a developmental curriculum checklist

It may be helpful to use a developmental curriculum checklist, because in spite of the best efforts of examiners to explain test results and the implications of these to parents, many parents find it very difficult to understand them. Few parents are in the habit of thinking about developmental levels. They may be well aware that something is wrong but find it difficult to grasp how the child's problem relates to normal development. By creating a developmental curriculum checklist that can be completed by the teacher and the parents together, as described and illustrated in Chapter 4, parents can grasp more readily the educational needs of their child.

Teachers can direct parents' attention to the

Learning to stack blocks is an important skill. Any size will do at first. At school we use several sizes. We like colored 1-inch cubes for this activity.

You should	*Your child should*	*Date completed*
1. Give your child three 1-inch cubes. Say "Watch me." You build ▯ with three other blocks in front of you.	Watch you. Pick up cubes between thumb and forefinger and make the same pattern, in front of him or her.	
2. Same as above, ▯ except use 5 blocks.	Same as above.	
3. Same as above, ▯ except use 8 blocks.	Same as above.	
4. Same as above, except ▯	Same as above.	

Comments: (Do you feel the lessons were successful? What would you do to make them even better?) _____

_____

_____

FIG. 9-2. Sample page from a checklist for parents.

sequence of tasks as they translate the strengths and weaknesses found during testing into what the child can and cannot do as listed on the developmental checklist, Ideally, this checklist will include some things that every child is able to do at the beginning of the program. For example, Fig. 9-2 illustrates a parent checklist that might result from a child's inability to stack blocks as expected in the Denver Developmental Screening Test (Frankenburg, Dodds, and Fandal, 1970).

The developmental curriculum checklist can be especially helpful when parents find it difficult to "hear" or to remember because they may be in the denial stage. These parents are encouraged when they see by using the "check off" exactly what their child can do. They can then be helped to begin instruction on the next, small step when achievement is expected in a reasonable time. By focusing on the positive and by not forcing parents to be overwhelmed with what their child cannot do, teachers may be able to help parents give up denial more quickly. This does not mean that teachers should shy away from helping parents to see that a developmental delay does not simply mean that a child will "catch up" if someone merely teaches him or her to learn faster.

The task of helping distressed parents to understand the implications of test results is not easy. It must be done with kindness and gentleness. It is not necessary for parents to understand all of the implications of test scores and evaluator's observations. But they must know what the child can do and what is planned for the next learning objective.

Establishing goals and objectives

Public Law 94-142 requires parents to be included in planning a child's Individual Educational Program (IEP). During the initial planning conference, parents should be encouraged to express their feelings about what they believe is important for their child to learn. Even though they may not understand that a lack of a particular skill identifies a "developmental delay," they are aware that the child cannot do certain things. Psychologists and teachers will need to identify what the child is ready to learn next, and how these things can be taught most effectively.

Parents may have strong feelings, however, that should be considered when skills are sequenced in order of importance. Teachers should listen to parents with care. For example, a particular parent might consider it more urgent for a child to learn to zip his or her coat than to button his or her shirt. Whenever possible parents should be encouraged to identify goals that are critical to them. These goals can then become the basis for appropriate short-term behavioral objectives. Each child's developmental curriculum checklist will therefore be somewhat different. Parents who have participated in choosing goals and objectives are much more apt to become effective partners in achieving them.

It is important to tell parents that an objective describes what a child will be doing and how well he or she will be doing it when everyone agrees that the objective has been achieved. Parents are then ready to understand that the first step toward achieving the objective is to do a related activity that is simpler. Helping parents to think in terms of modifying what they do or the materials they use when teaching their child is an effective first step toward successfully working with the child at home.

Parents can become effective teachers of their children

When assisting parents to become effective teachers of their children, teachers must expect mature, constructive behavior and should model the behavior they expect. Willing and open minds are essential. Parents grow along with their children when they cooperate in following directions, asking questions, and listen-

ing to suggestions. It is helpful when parents can generalize from specific directions in one activity by adapting those directions to a variety of activities. Failures should be interpreted as clues that there must be a better way. The better way should be actively sought through intelligent experimentation and more insightful observations of demonstration lessons. Parents will ideally support each other's efforts. They must strive to build up each other and to avoid destructive criticism.

By expecting constructive behavior, professionals are more apt to view parents as effective partners. They will less often talk down to parents or use professional jargon. Professionals who fail to anticipate mature, intelligent responses from parents may waste their time and efforts. Teachers who do not expect a constructive response often miss it when it does occur. Many if not most parents can be expected to behave constructively. Of course some parents can be hostile and resentful even when they are expected to be intelligent and thoughtful.

Demonstration lessons are appreciated

Merely telling parents what to do or only giving them written directions will not be as effective as demonstrating the teaching for them. At first, parents may balk at role playing what the teacher is demonstrating, fearing criticism. Later, many parents request that the teacher watch them and critique their teaching efforts. Teachers can nurture this willingness to accept constructive suggestions as the result of someone observing their teaching. It is an important prelude to effective home teaching. It helps to emphasize that children learn a great deal from parents. Children learn without differentiating whether the teaching is appropriate and constructive or inappropriate and destructive. Parents must ultimately accept this responsibility. Failure to understand that they *are* teaching their children every moment interferes with understanding the importance of teaching in the best possible way. Of course some parents have excellent teaching and parenting skills. Teachers should recognize and acknowledge these.

Concentrate on the future

It is crucial for teachers to focus on the future and to avoid inferring that parents have caused their child's problems. Although it is often obvious that the parent's failure to understand basic parenting skills has contributed to the child's problems, it is disastrous to tell them this. They will suspect it. Some parents will experience deep guilt as this awareness dawns. They will need to be reassured that their newly learned skills can be effective in changing behavior and increasing development. They will require frequent sincere approval responses from the professionals who are helping them. Professionals need to avoid anything that reinforces feelings of inadequacy. By avoiding the danger of making parents feel defensive, professionals can minimize parents' tendencies toward denial.

Handicapped and nonhandicapped children are more alike than different

Handicapped and nonhandicapped children are more alike than different. Teachers can help parents to understand that all children exhibit frustrations, misbehave, and refuse to cooperate at times. Parents of a child with a mild handicap often interpret every childish antic as a symptom of some serious problem. Minor infractions of parental rules are seen as major catastrophies. All children, however, behave unpredictably. Most of them learn to manipulate their parents well before they are 2 years old. This comes as a genuine surprise to most parents. Even in the presence of overwhelming evidence, it is difficult for many adults to believe that such little ones are astute observers and efficient managers of parents.

Normally developing children experience many traumas, fears, and aggravations as they learn and grow. Alert parents and teachers seek to allow reasonable challenges. They try to prevent overwhelming demands on young children whenever possible. One "exceptional" parent sums up the need to accept the challenges presented by a developing child:

> A handicapped child takes just the same knowledge and love that a normal child takes, but you have to learn to accept that child for what he is. And if he can't walk, then he can't walk (Hodel, 1981).

METHODS OF PARENT INVOLVEMENT

Just as handicapped children and nonhandicapped children are more alike than different, so are parents of handicapped children and parents of nonhandicapped more alike than different. They have needs, frustrations, hopes, fears, and dreams similar to those of any other parent, although they also have feelings that may be special to exceptional parents. Even so, teachers cannot expect to use the same method of working with all parents just as they cannot expect to use the same method of working with all children. Increasingly attempts are being made to match family needs to available services (Grimm, 1974; Karnes and Zehrbach, 1979).

The boxed material on p. 270 offers a brief description of the most used methods of parent involvement. All of these ways of working with parents may be used at some time in every program. Regularly planned interactions are essential. Teachers must remember, however, that all parents cannot be expected to participate in all available parent involvement activities. Teachers should of course encourage but not demand parents to participate.

One must balance individual needs and capabilities and the goals of parent involvement. Some parents will have a greater need and capacity for cognitive information delivered through lectures, panel discussions, and films.

METHODS OF PARENT INVOLVEMENT

1. Home based teaching, including regular teacher visits, structured lesson planning, observing parent teaching, and evaluating progress and child management guidance.
2. Parent observation in regular and special education classrooms.
3. Passports—notebooks carried between home and school. Both the parents and the teacher make regular notations (see Fig. 9-3).
4. Parent participation as volunteers and aides in the classrooms.
5. Individual parent-teacher conferences and conferences that include extended families.
6. Small group parent meetings planned to encourage parents to work through problems together with a trained group leader or teacher.
7. Larger parent group meetings designed to include media presentation such as films and video tapes. Lectures by specialists may be helpful to some groups of parents. For example, parents of physically handicapped children may request discussions and lectures by physical and occupational therapists.
8. Parenting classes, including commercially available programs and locally developed parent training models.
9. Parents helping parents one-to-one. Often a parent who has experienced and successfully dealt with specific problems can help a "new" parent to cope. The teacher's task is simply to put them in touch with one another.
10. Publication of parent newsletters, assistance on field trips, participation on advisory boards, and using toy lending libraries.

Other parents may most desire and need one-to-one conversations with the teacher when privacy is assured and they can feel comfortably accepted. Still other parents will thrive on being shown how to teach their child.

The remainder of this chapter focuses on the primary considerations to be thought through carefully in making each type of involvement effective. Unique needs are also discussed along with helpful hints for the teachers who must work with these unique needs.

Home based instructional programs

Home based instructional programs offer many advantages. Little children and parents are most natural at home. At home they do not have to develop the feeling of comfortable belonging; they do not have to be transported either by the parents or a school bus. Teachers can take the home life into consideration when planning for the child.

Generally a teacher or trained paraprofessional makes regularly scheduled visits (weekly or monthly) to offer educational services and sometimes social and health services. Parents are encouraged and taught how to teach their own children using household objects or materials following lesson plans prepared and brought by the teachers. Research is demonstrating that the most lasting effects occur when the primary responsibility for teaching is shifted to the parents and when these parents feel responsible for their child's education (Weikart, 1980).

At first, some parents may feel uncomfortable having a special teacher in their homes. Tact, courtesy, and kindness can overcome this initial discomfort very quickly. The teacher or trained paraprofessional becomes a happily anticipated visitor. Interesting games to play, toys to share, and ideas that work usually endear the home teacher to both parents and children.

Model programs. Among the more well-known home based model programs is the Portage Project that serves handicapped children from birth to 6 years of age in rural Wisconsin (Shearer and Shearer, 1972). Home teachers spend about 1½ hours a week in each home providing the parents with teaching cues. Curriculum cards assist the parents in working a minimum of 15 minutes each day with their child. By gradually assuming responsibility for instructional planning and implementation, each parent becomes functionally independent.

Whereas the Portage Project relies on home based instruction as the only formalized instruction for the developmentally delayed children, other models provide home based instruction for children who also attend preschool classrooms. One of the more well-developed programs is the Florida Parent Education Follow Through Program initiated by Gordon and Guinagh (1974). In this model, a trained paraprofessional, often a parent, visits homes and is also an aide in the classroom. Following the directions of the teacher, these visitors are able to facilitate cooperation between classroom and the homes they visit.

One of the successful programs that views parents and educators as resources for each other is the High/Scope program in Ypsilanti, Michigan. This and similar programs have yielded information conducive to longitudinal study. Although data are still being analyzed, reports indicate that a combination of preschool classroom experience and home teaching is yielding positive effects on the development of children through the years (Weikart, 1975).

Because the public schools are beginning to accept the critical role of parent involvement in the success of early education, more and more teachers are being asked to reserve 1 day a week or 1 day a month for home visitations. The success of these visitations is highly dependent on the teacher's training and preparation. This section offers practical suggestions for effective home teaching and discusses important considerations when making home visits. Because only the most critical points are covered, readers are urged to consult the references for more in-depth consideration of home based programs and resources available. Practical suggestions for the home teacher follow:

1. *Be informal, but not too casual.* You are functioning as a professional.
2. *Be prepared.* Have materials, lesson plans, and backup ideas ready. Try to avoid filling out forms to interact more freely. If writing is necessary, explain what you are doing and why.
3. *Be flexible.* If what was planned is inappropriate for any reason, change on the spot. Also encourage parents to vary the lessons to meet their needs, as well as the child's needs.
4. *Carry lesson materials in a picnic basket.* Briefcases look too much like a doctor's medical bag. Be sure to include an appealing game to play and a surprise that the child may keep. Do not plan too much for the parents to do. They have other responsibilities.
5. *Be ready to admire pet frogs, favorite toys, and other family treasures.* Take the time to know what the children and their parents are proud of and what they value most. Compliment the home in some way.
6. *Encourage parents to show or demonstrate what they have accomplished.* Show that their effforts are worthwhile. Express approval and admiration. Avoid direct criticism. Rather, suggest changes by saying something such as "Some of the time you will want to try ___," or "At school we notice that children seem to progress faster when ___."

7. *Do not smoke in the home unless invited to do so.* This can be very irritating to some people.

8. *Avoid confrontations.* Even if the parent insists that what has been suggested won't work or is not something they can or will do, the teacher must not argue or insist that the parent should conform.

9. *Begin and end your visit on time.*

10. *Schedule and discuss the next visit.* Remind the parents that you will review and discuss during the next visit the home teaching activity you have just given them. Be certain the parents can complete the lesson plan. Schedule the next visit and write the date and time on the lesson plan form left with the parents. Assure them that they can reach you by telephone if they should have questions or comments.

11. *Maintain confidentiality.* At all times remember you are a professional. Whatever you observe in the parents' home and any judgments you make are not to be discussed in the teacher's lounge. Families have a right to their privacy and their choice of living style. The effectiveness of visits may depend on your ability to be mature, objective, and professional.

Important considerations when making home visits

1. From the beginning, avoid talking about the children and their special needs when they can possibly overhear. Even completely nonverbal children understand much more than is supposed. Even if they do not understand the words, they will understand the facial expressions, gestures, and body language of the adults. During each home visit, some opportunity for such discussion is useful. If parents are told this in advance, most can arrange for a neighbor or friend to take the child for a time. If this is impractical, an aide should go with the home teacher at least some of the time. The aide can take the child outside or to another part of the home during the time the child is being discussed by parents and teacher.

Remember that these children see you as their "special friend." They need some special attention as they want to feel as valued by the teacher as their parents. Siblings may have the same feelings.

2. Plan to demonstrate at least two or three teaching activities. Even though written suggestions are provided (Fig. 9-2), showing is more effective than merely telling or describing. Only expect the parent to choose one activity a week. Activities accumulate, and by choosing among them parents' interests and time demands can be considered.

Sometimes an older child can be helpful. Teach brothers and sisters the games. Often they can participate with the teaching parent and the child for whom the lesson was planned. Including other children serves two purposes: they are usually excellent teachers, and, by including them, one can avoid jealousy and feelings of being left out.

3. Call attention to particular teaching strategies. It will come as a surprise to many parents that children learn little by failing. It is crucial to teach parents to develop lessons at which their children can succeed. At first, home teachers must be very explicit about the need to avoid lessons that result in failure for the children. Teaching parents how to prompt their children and then to gradually reduce and to fade the prompting is important. This strategy is basic to successful home teaching. Give the parents specific guidelines such as those noted in the boxed material on p. 274.

4. First lessons should be carefully planned so that the parents achieve immediate success. Parents of handicapped children experience a great amount of frustration. They often feel as if they are somehow to blame for their children's problems. They try to teach, but without trained

guidance they may experience little but failure. As a result it is necessary that the first lessons parents are asked to teach be failure proof. It is not helpful for them to watch the teacher teach their child, and then discover later that some mysterious element is lacking when they try to duplicate the lesson.

The home teacher will want to assess the parents' interests, daily routines, skill levels, and abilities to understand, as well as the child's ability level. Parents must be helped to understand how a child's disability affects his or her learning. Discussion and using the curriculum checklist are practical ways of looking at what and how to teach. The helping teacher is setting the stage, providing the prompts, and being the cheering audience as parents succeed in teaching their own child.

5. Be kind. Simple kindness and thoughtfulness will go a long way to make home teaching a success. Some parents will be embarrassed about their homes or will be afraid of criticism. It is important to be blind to the things that are not relevant to teaching the children and to notice things parents are proud of, especially things that they have done for their children.

6. Refer to the child's Individual Education Program (IEP) regularly. Help parents to see how the home teaching lessons relate to the goals and objectives on the Individual Education Program.

7. Help parents to develop behavior management skills. Many parents are embarrassed about their child's misbehavior and attribute it to the handicap. Usually the basis of the problem is not the handicap itself, but rather not knowing how to communicate effectively with the child. If misbehavior is reported at the supermarket, plan some lessons there. The teacher's demonstration of effective controls can be immensely helpful to parents who are frightened and worried.

HOME TEACHING GUIDELINES FOR PARENTS

1. *Be ready to praise.* Praise your child's efforts and successes. Use hugs, pats, smiles, and positive words readily.
2. *Correct with care.* When your child makes mistakes, do not tell him or her that he or she is wrong. Instead, gently show or tell him or her the preferred response. For example, if your child hands you a spoon instead of the requested fork, say, "You've handed me a spoon. Now hand me the fork," instead of "That's not a fork. I asked for the fork."
3. *Find a teachable time and place.* Do not remove a child from an activity in which he or she is involved. Keep the lesson short, from 5 to 15 minutes. Be certain your child is wide awake, not hungry or "keyed up." Prepare a place to work where the child is comfortable and not distracted by sound or sight.
4. *Do not use force.* Do not force your child to continue a lesson. Attention spans vary with the child and with the lesson. Treat your child with the same consideration you would give your friends. If your child senses that you are tense, angry, or critical, he or she will learn to dislike the activities.
5. *Be flexible.* Vary the lesson and methods to fit the child's needs. If one approach does not work, try another. Some learn more quickly while being active; others prefer being more passive. Use as many senses as possible, especially if one or more of the senses is impaired.
6. *Speak clearly.* Use a normal voice when talking to your child. "Baby talk" does not provide a model of the speech or behavior you wish your child to learn.
7. *Be prepared.* Assemble materials and prepare the working space in advance. Do not waste the child's attention span on meaningless activities. Consider taking the phone off the hook during the short lesson period.
8. *Be enthusiastic.* Do not under any circumstances let your child feel that you are working with him or her because "you have to." If you do not feel like working with your child, he or she will feel your tension. Reschedule your lesson. By selecting a rather consistent time each day, you will find it easier to manage your time. If you find you are not enjoying your teaching time, talk this over with your child's teacher. An adjustment in the lessons or the approach may bring greater enjoyment.

Directions for managing the behavior of young children should be explicit. The teacher can give reasons for what is suggested in a manner and in a language that parents understand. Vignette 9-1 shows how this is achieved. Role playing with the parent taking the part of the child will help parents master the needed management skills. Most important, the teacher must explain that behavior is learned. Changing habits and behavior patterns may not be easy and improvement may not be made overnight. Parents may be helped by talking about their problems with other parents who have successfully learned improved child management skills.

8. Never forget that parents know their children better than the teacher does in some ways. Most parents are accurate observers of what their children do and do not do. But their interpretations of the observed behavior is often inappropriate. For example, a child who screams and has a tantrum when denied something that he or she wants may be described by the parents as "bad" or "just like Uncle Will." Usually children who behave in this way have been rewarded by receiving the things they want when they cry. This cause and effect relationship is little understood by many parents. The teacher cannot explain it in a 5-minute lecture!

Chapter 8 enumerated some of the ways

VIGNETTE 9-1: DIRECTIONS TO A PARENT FOR MANAGING A SCREAMER

SCENE: It is time for Ms. McLynn's second home visit. Danny's mother has asked her to help with Danny's screaming. When things don't go exactly the way he wants, he just screams. The neighbors are complaining. Several of them call their children in when Danny comes out.

Mrs. Dickson: "Hello, Ms. McLynn. I'm so glad you could come again so soon."

Ms. McLynn: "Well, I try to go to all of my parents in turn. But if one asks me, I can always return more quickly. Now, let's think about Danny's screaming together. You remember, last week I emphasized that especially with these young children we must work as a team. Unless we are consistent in the way we discipline him at home and at school, he will be even more confused."

Mrs. D.: "Oh yes, I do understand that. That's why I asked you to come back. The morning I visited the classroom he didn't scream once. Here he screams several times every hour!"

Ms. McL.: "The first few days he screamed at school, too. My aides and I have a routine when this happens. Many children try to control us by screaming. One of us picks the child up with no comment, and carries him or her to a small room that has only one chair. Then, the adult puts the child down, shuts the door, and picks up a book, and sits down. No matter how loud the noise is, the adult just reads. As soon as the noise stops, the adult says matter of factly, 'If you are ready, we can go back to the room.' Because of Danny's hearing problem, it helps to gesture toward the room, too. Nothing more is said. Sometimes children begin to scream again, so it's back to reading the book. As soon as the child is quiet, the statement is made again."

Mrs. D.: "How long does it take?"

Ms. McL.: "Some children need to return to the room two or three times in the first week. Rarely more often."

Mrs. D.: "Do you explain to them why?"

Ms. McL.: "Only very briefly. Usually something like 'We can't play if you scream in our room, so we go to our special place until you feel better.'"

Mrs. D.: "That's all?"

Ms. McL.: "That's all. Talking won't do it. Our consistent responses will. Whoever takes the child to the little room remains very quiet, never appears upset, and does not scold."

Mrs. D.: "And how do I do that?"

Ms. McL.: "The first time, do it on faith. After you see it work a few times, you will fully expect it to be effective. Danny will sense this. Remember, you are not punishing him. You are simply communicating that when he screams, he has to go to a certain place alone or with you until he is quiet."

Mrs. D.: "Then, I should stay with him, too?"

Ms. McL.: "Whatever you think is best. Some parents pick the children up and isolate them in a special place, often their own room. If you feel that is safe, it serves the same purpose. But never put him into a dark or dangerous place. Remember, you want to communicate just two things: (1) When you scream, you will never get what you want. (2) When you scream, it bothers us, so you must be away from your friends until you are quiet."

Mrs. D.: "But how will he understand if he can't understand the words?"

Ms. McL.: "He screams because in the past it got him what he wanted. Now, he just has to learn that won't work anymore."

Mrs. D.: "Ok—Please, can I call you if it doesn't work?"

Ms. McL.: "Of course. I'll check back in 3 days."

Dec. 10, Mrs. J. (Susan's mother):

Susan wouldn't eat her breakfast this morning. She didn't seem sick, just not hungry. Could you give her an early snack, please?

Dec. 10, Ms. S. (Susan's teacher at day care):

Susan *was* hungry when she got here. Two glasses of juice and a piece of toast disappeared right away. And then she asked to go "potty." We are making progress. No accidents today! Hooray.

Dec. 11, Mrs. J.:

Ms. R., Susan's home teacher, came yesterday afternoon. She suggested that we continue to work on teaching Susan the names of her clothes. I'm going to put her clothes on the bed, and then tell her to bring me each thing, one at a time. Could you help with this at school, please?

Dec. 11, Ms. S.:

We surely can. Susan brought me her boots and her tote bag when I asked her today. Progress is good.

FIG. 9-3. A passport page used by the daycare teacher, parents, and the home teacher. This page was chosen from notes written during the fourth month of school attendance. Susan is 3 years old and has been described as "developmentally delayed." She uses two-word "sentences" that are partially intelligible. She has frequent "accidents," wetting and soiling herself at home and at school.

teachers can help parents in this essential task. The goal is to assist parents in reinterpreting the behaviors they have called "bad" as something the children have learned and not something "in" them. By the teacher's example and explanations parents can learn to think about their children more constructively. As they do this, the negative behaviors are likely to be replaced with obedience and the charm of childhood.

9. Playfulness and the expression of happiness and joy are essential if children are to achieve their potential. Let the parents observe activities during which the teacher is expressing happiness and joy. Be willing to play with children, enjoying the games they like. This is very effective teaching. Avoid being too serious.

10. Introduce parents to other parents who have similar interests and needs. Even if all of the direct teaching is done in a home teaching arrangement, plan occasional meetings for parents who have similar needs and interests.

11. Communication with all caregivers is essential. In some cases the special teacher may plan and teach lessons to the child in the home as a supplement to the child's attendance at a *regular* preschool or day-care center. When this is the case, a system of reporting what is done can be very useful. Common goals and objectives will be useful. Useful methods of communication include the following:

   a. Phone calls to the child's regular classroom teacher, usually brief, to report on what was accomplished and to suggest carry-over activities.

   b. Written goals and objectives, with copies given to parents and to the preschool or day-care teachers.

   c. A passport notebook with comments and observations made by all concerned (Runge, Walker, and Shea, 1975). This passport notebook may travel with the child and be used by all who are responsible for care and teaching. An example of a page from such a passport notebook is illustrated in Fig. 9-3.

Parents in the classroom

Involving parents in daily classroom activities can be useful in a variety of ways. The teacher is able to model preferred techniques of teaching specific skills and effective approaches to behavior management. Many parents will then be able to translate some of what they have learned about teaching and guiding into more useful interactions in the home environment. Parents with specific skills or talents such as in music or art can be made to feel good about the contributions they can make to the classroom while the teacher is simultaneously guiding their approach to working with children. Parents who accompany classrooms on field trips to such familiar places as the grocery store can observe and ideally generalize ways of using everyday activities to teach their child. Finally, many parents will feel that their child is more like other children than different from them. As they observe progress over time, they will feel encouraged and more hopeful. The first few times parents come to the school will be difficult for them and for their children. Just as the children may cry and touch things that are off limits, so may the parents be upset. Some parents will feel compelled to direct and correct their own children constantly. They may be deeply distressed by every small infraction of the rules. Tears and tantrums are the outward signs of the distress of the children. Nervousness and apologizing for the child's "badness" may be the parents' reaction. With careful planning, the teacher can prevent or at least minimize most of these problems.

First step: parents meet other parents. Before parents begin to observe or participate in the classroom, they can benefit by meeting with "veteran" parents. Parents from previous years, whether or not their children are currently enrolled, can be called on to help. If these experienced parents assist with planning and presenting the program, it will be much more believable and useful to the new parents. The opportunity to talk with other parents who can

---

SAMPLE CLASSROOM PARTICIPATION GUIDELINES

Dear parents,

   As you know, it is very important for you to come to school regularly to help us in the classroom, and to learn more about working with your children at home. But some of you have told me that you felt a little uncomfortable—that you really were not sure what to do sometimes. So I asked one of our "experienced mothers," Laura Brown, to jot down some rules that will help you to feel more sure of what is the "right way." Laura and I talked about these "rules" and she helped me to understand how you feel. Both Laura and I hope you will suggest other things that will make your time at school more useful and enjoyable. These suggestions are just a beginning. Here they are.

Classroom rules for mothers (fathers, grandparents, and aunts, too)

   1. *Don't panic.* The children are allowed to do *some* things at school that they cannot do at home, or that they do not normally do at home. (Using a scissors, putting things into the refrigerator, or helping another child.)
   2. *Don't get "up tight."* If your child "shows off" because you are there, that is perfectly normal, and nobody will blame you. Let Ms. Cane or Ms. McLynn handle your child. They know how tense both of you are at first. They know it is normal.
   3. *Don't talk in front of the children (either at home or school).* Even if you do not think they will understand, never talk about them when they can overhear.
   4. *Take time. Try what the teacher suggests.* It might seem the teacher's way makes matters worse and sometimes it will, at first. But time (lots of it) will make a difference. Ms. McLynn says that with our children we are not just working for this minute. We want them to learn how to use self-control and good judgment. And this takes experience with "logical consequences" of things they do.
   5. *Learn the class rules.* Find our what is a "no-no" and what's all right. For example, Hot Wheels— no riding inside, but the balance toys are okay. Moving the kitchen stuff around is okay, just like we change the room arrangement at home sometimes. Yelling is a "no-no." (That is an "outside voice.") Putting stuff away after you use it is also a rule. But some of them have not learned that yet.

Courtesy Laura Bridgeman.

---

honestly report that they have enjoyed participating in classroom activities is the best preparation for beginners.

   Teachers should plan the program with parents, not for them. Parents themselves can plan the agenda. They must thoughtfully choose items to be discussed and points to be emphasized. Both the nature of the community and the characteristics of the children will influence what needs to be done.

   A letter from the parents who are planning the meeting to the new parents inviting them to come is more effective than a letter from the teacher. This is especially true if the letter from the teacher is duplicated on a faded ditto! One parent group sent handwritten notes to each new parent 1 week in advance. A follow-up phone call, including an offer to pick up the new parents, resulted in nearly 100% attendance.

   Although traditionally mothers have come to school, fathers can be especially helpful. Having one father call another father helps to make it

6. *Ask.* If you are not sure what to do, ask. If you do not know why the teacher does things her way, ask. And do not be afraid to say how you feel. She will listen. Sometimes, she misses something that happens, and it helps if you clue her in. (Remember, do not let the children overhear.) If you have a problem with your child, ask to talk about it with the teacher. She will find a way to talk to you so your child will not overhear. It is also important to tell the teacher if you do not agree with what is happening. Find out why it is happening. The reason will probably make it feel better.

7. *Talk.* Talk to the teacher and the children in the regular way. Ms. McLynn wants you to have "conversations" with the children except during "circle time." These conversations help the children learn. Those words on the bulletin board behind her desk are the cues for words they are working on. Try to use them often while you are talking to the children. Don't try to make them say things "the right way." Conversations should be fun. They help to teach language. Speech lessons are at a separate time, unless Ms. McLynn says otherwise, because trying to make a child correct a speech sound can make things worse. The child may just stop talking to you.

8. *Play with your child and other children at playtime.* You will learn, just as they will. Remember someone else will be playing with your child. It averages out.

9. *Don't feel silly or useless.* It is really important to be there. Cutting stuff, helping clean-up, or just listening are all important. Lots of things are important for the children to learn before kindergarten.

10. *Have an open mind when the teacher or Ms. Cane corrects your child.* They really do care about the children growing up to be solid citizens.

Most important of all: Every time you come you are showing your child that you care about him or her. And you are helping by learning how to be consistent. When both you and the teachers do things the same way most of the time, it makes it easier for the children. Of course, school cannot do it all in just 2½ hours.

P.S. from Ms. McLynn and Ms. Cane: Please do come regularly. There is so much to teach your little ones. We do need your help.

seem less strange. Other family members should be included whenever practical.

Evening meetings are useful to include fathers. Fathers who do shift work or who work at night, however, can be encouraged to come to school during the day. Properly welcomed, fathers have even been known to take a vacation day to come to school.

The orientation meeting. For the orientation meeting the chairperson should be a parent. If at all possible the program presenters should also be parents. Refreshments made by the children are best. Cookies are fun to make and decorate, and concentrated punch is easy to stir. A special touch is added by having the children snip the edges of construction paper or scribble pictures to make placemats.

During the first meeting program presenters can emphasize the importance of parent participation in the classroom. This includes observation visits, conferences, meetings, and regular volunteer work in the classroom. Parents who are genuine believers in the value of their classroom participation communicate this effectively. A sign-up sheet for classroom involvement should be placed in a conspicuous place. By spacing, limit to two the number of parents who visit at the same time. First visits should be short—30 minutes to 1 hour is sufficient. It will surprise most parents that coming to school as often as once a week is desirable. This may not be possible for some, but all parents should be encouraged to come at least once a month.

Teachers may present specific classroom participation guidelines. An example of a letter used for this purpose is found in the boxed material on pp. 278-279. Some parent groups prefer to have a round table discussion, talking about each item of the guidelines. One parent group planned a series of skits to emphasize special points. Of course, parents who are uncomfortable in role playing should not be expected to take part. Many enjoy the chance to act the part of naughty children and equally naughty parents. Then, a repetition of the incident with more appropriate behaviors can be useful. Other groups prefer films or videotapes.

Relaxing and getting acquainted. After the planned meeting, a social time provides the opportunity for the teacher to introduce parents to each other. Name tags, including the name of the child who attends the school, are helpful. Although teachers will want to greet each parent individually, they will also want to encourage parents to talk to each other. Teachers will need to be wise in sharing their time equally among parents. This is not the time for in-depth parent conferences. An announcement to this effect just before the social time begins may prevent problem discussions.

Following up. The day after the meeting a letter from the teacher thanking the parents who participated and pointing out how much was accomplished is necessary. If these are handwritten and mailed, instead of sent with

the children, the effect is much greater. In addition to the notes, a summary of what happened should go home with each child. This summary should be sent to each family whether or not they attended the meeting. The guidelines distributed at the meeting can also be sent home at this time. If at all possible parents who attended the meeting should contact those who did not come. Knowing they were missed is important to many parents.

Parents as observers. All parents will feel unsure at first, even if they hide their feelings well. They will wonder what their children will do, and will expect the worst. Often their children will oblige. Teachers must strive to make parents feel comfortable and welcome. Give their children specific things to do to keep them from seeking attention in undesirable ways. It may be necessary to make it clear that a visit to the classroom is not a time for socializing with the teacher or other parents.

Providing a special place to sit. Teachers need to provide a special place for parents to sit and observe. The actual placement of the chair will depend on what the teacher wishes the parents to observe. If the teacher wishes the parent to observe a child's interaction with a group of children, then the chair must be placed far enough away for the parent to observe comfortably. If the teacher wishes the parent to observe the child as he or she manipulates small objects, then the chair will need to be quite near the child. Some parents will wish to take notes. A clip board and paper should be provided along with a copy of the daily schedule.

Interacting with their own child. Encourage parents to greet their own child, and allow their own child to show them around. These social skills must be taught to many children. Initial awkwardness can yield quickly to confidence and security if the teacher sets the stage and does a bit of managing. Give cues such as "Show Dad where we keep our big blocks. I'll bet he can build a tall tower," or "Show Mother where we keep the easel and the markers. I wonder if she knows how well you can draw." Naturalness, friendliness, and a comfortable feeling for all should be the goal.

If the parents indicate they would enjoy it, encourage them to play a game with their own child and one or two others. A demonstration by the teacher starts the game, but then the teacher should be busy with others to allow the parent the opportunity to develop his or her own style. The intent is to set the stage for parents and children to have a good time, feel at ease, and to remember the visit later with happy memories.

Keeping the visit short. The visit should be short. The time schedule should be understood by everyone before the visit begins. Encourage parents to vary the time of day they visit to create a more complete understanding of their child's educational strengths and weaknesses and conditions of most favorable response.

Providing observation guidelines. Help parents to become astute observers by telling them what to look for. A short list of focus points might be helpful. For example, Ms. McLynn may wish Danny's mother to observe his reaction to sound in the classroom. She could prepare the following short list:

1. What does Danny do when someone calls his name?
2. Does Danny act differently when I stand directly in front of him and speak to him than when he cannot see my face?
3. Does Danny respond to noises made behind him or anywhere out of sight?

Such a list of focus points makes it easier to discuss the observations with everyone focusing on the child's behavior rather than on more subjective aspects of the child such as personality. Mr. Curtis might prepare the following list to help Vicky's parent understand his or her concerns:

1. What is the first thing Vicky did? What is the second?
2. Approximately how long did Vicky stay with each activity?
3. Which activity held Vicky's attention the longest?

A sample of a parent observation form that helps to focus the parent's attention is presented in the box on p. 282.

Demonstrating effective teaching. A productive way of helping a parent to understand how a child learns best is to provide opportunities for the parent to observe a teacher working with the child. Something must be planned to keep the other children busy and happy while the teacher works with one child or a small group. The parent should be given a copy of the lesson plan including the objectives and the procedure to be followed. A place for parent comments is helpful. A useful format is presented on p. 283.

Conducting mini-conferences. Parents should not expect a parent conference per se when they observe or participate. Occasional mini-conferences (5 to 10 minutes long,) however, following an observation are helpful if they can be arranged. This should not take place where the children can overhear. The teacher will want to call attention to the positive aspects of the visit, and make light of any problems. Noting a child's progress is always a good idea. The observation guidelines provide a mutual point of discussion. Parents should be encouraged to ask questions and make comments. They will feel like partners only if their opinions are obviously valued.

If a mini-conference is not possible, the visit may be followed up by a telephone conversation. Parents can also be encouraged to leave written comments or questions in a designated place if there is no time for discussion.

Parents as participants. In some classrooms, parents are encouraged or expected to participate as teacher aides. Chapter 10 is designed to assist teachers make effective use of parents who

---

PARENT OBSERVATION REPORT

Date: _____

Who was involved in this experience? _____

What happened first?

Then what did the child do?

What did you do, or what did another adult caregiver do?

What were the results?

Do you think you or the other adult caregiver might have done something better? Why or why not?

---

regularly volunteer their time and energy over an extended time, and should be reviewed if parents are expected to be aides.

Some parents, however, may be able to work with children in the classroom only occasionally. The purpose of this participation is to help the parent learn to work and play more productively with their child outside of the classroom. The interest checklist found in Chapter 10 is useful in planning to involve parents in classroom activities. Teaching activities to be done by parents must be carefully planned. Directions should be written in brief, clear terms free of

jargon. Care must be taken to use vocabulary easily understood and read by the parent. Although written guidelines are important, the teaching activity should be demonstrated by the teacher first. The lesson must be designed to ensure success.

Tell and show parents how to correct the children if they seem to "fail." Remind them that a continuing goal is to be sure the children recognize that failure in a task is only a clue to try another way. Tell the parents that one of the major purposes in each lesson is to teach children how to use their mistakes to help them learn.

SAMPLE LESSON OBSERVATION FORM

Purpose: The children are learning about two kinds of counting. The first is rote counting. We call it rote counting when we say the numbers in the right order, but do not count things. The second kind of counting helps them to begin to understand that numbers mean amounts such as one is one thing and two is two things.

Objective: The children will learn to count from 1 to 10 saying each number in the correct order.

Procedure: We will begin by saying the numbers in the right order. "Let's count from 1 to 10." Then little by little, the teacher will "hold back" allowing the children to supply the missing numbers. If needed, the missing numbers will be said.

NOTE: The children will receive lots of praise for their efforts. They will never be told that they are wrong. They will just be encouraged to try again. There will be lots of smiles and all will be having fun. Please join in whenever you feel like it.

Your comments (Please tell us what you think and wonder about. We will talk after the lesson for a few minutes. Please try this lesson at home and let us know how it goes.): _____

_____
_____
_____

It is often helpful to ask parents to play a game or teach a lesson that has been done before by the teacher with the children. Children love repetition. If they have experienced the activity before, it will be easier for the parent to conduct the lesson. The activity should be one that is useful for the parent's own child. Suggestions such as the following can be put in a parent handout and can be posted or distributed when parents choose to participate.

Suggestions for parent participants
1. Plan for success for both the parents and the childrn.
2. Choose an activity that can be easily demonstrated. Provide a brief written description of the objective and procedures of the activity.
3. Keep the group small (two or three children).
4. Explain the purpose of the lesson or game. Be specific.
5. Emphasize that learning should be fun even if it is also hard work.
6. Do not emphasize "winning." Little children just like to play. Winning and losing are artificial concepts and interfere with learning.
7. Select a game or activity parents can use at home. Most commercial games or lessons can be duplicated with things found in most homes. Whenever possible, choose an activity that will benefit the child and interest his or her parent.
8. Specifically explain how to manage children's errors and misbehaviors. Demonstrate and talk about various techniques. A mistake or "failure" is merely a clue to try another way.

Parent-teacher conferences

Individual parent-teacher conferences can and should be one of the most effective methods of parent involvement. Inherent in this approach is flexibility. Either the parent or the teacher can request the conference. It can be held at school or at home at any convenient time as long as parents feel the comfort of privacy and confidentiality. The content varies with the needs of the parents, the child, and the teacher. The teacher can individualize the specific suggestions made and the level of the language used. With conferences, parents who cannot read or understand written comments do not miss important information about their child's progress.

Stephens (1979) discusses four sets of behaviors needed by teachers to conduct effective parent-teacher conferences: (1) skills in rapport building; (2) obtaining information from parents; (3) providing parents with helpful information; and (4) summarizing, identifying new objectives, and making recommendations. Developing these skills takes preparation, practice, time, and patience. By being aware of the need to develop competence in these four important behaviors, beginning teachers can focus on developing habits conducive to successful conferencing.

Preparing for the conference. Teachers plan the objectives for the conference with situational needs in mind. For some the objectives will be general, such as merely becoming acquainted and helping to assure the parents that their child is well cared for and progressing. Another conference may be requested by the parent or the teacher because of a specific concern. For example, Mr. Curtis may need to know if Vicky is as inattentive and active at home as she is in the classroom. If he understands her parents' attitudes and reactions, he may be able to work with her family in developing consistency between school and home. Mr. Curtis realizes, however, that his objectives will have to be flexible enough to accommodate the parents' needs as well.

The teacher should be prepared to provide parents with adequate information. Consider the information gathered through the various observation techniques discussed in Chapter 3. Samples of the child's work, anecdotal records, tape recordings, logs, and assessment data should be readily available on request. Special care must be taken to discuss this information in layman's terms.

When conferences are initiated by teachers, personal invitations should be extended by telephone or through letters. A mimeographed note is not very personal. Whenever possible, parents should be given a choice of date and time. A quiet, uninterrupted setting must be prepared with comfortable adult-sized chairs. The teacher should not be seated behind a desk because this only puts a distance between the teacher and a parent who may already be tense. Offering a beverage can make the parent feel more relaxed. Babysitting may need to be arranged because the presence of children distracts the conversation and destroys the confidentiality necessary. Girl Scouts and teacher's aides can help out by taking the child and siblings to the playground or to another room.

Beginning the conference. Often the initial few minutes of a conference are the most uncomfortable and are perhaps the most critical in building the necessary rapport. Initial impressions can create defensiveness that gets in the way of objective thinking and the creation of a productive relationship. Greetings, a handshake, and thanking the parent for coming help the parent to see that the teacher appreciates his or her effort to come. To help the parent feel at ease, it is helpful to begin with nonemotional topics, although these must be brief because the parent is usually anxious to get to the purpose of the meeting.

A time limit to the conference should be made clear so that the parent will not feel rejected when it is necessary to close the conversation. A statement such as the following can establish the time limit of a conference and clarify the teacher's purpose in requesting the meeting: "I am so happy, Ms. Jones, that you are able to share the next 15 minutes with me today. I have so much to tell you about Jamie's progress, and I want to hear how you feel about it."

If the parent has initiated the conference, the teacher might say: "I am so glad, Ms. Dickson, that you felt free to request this conference. I will be free until 4 o'clock and am eager to know where you would like to begin." If the parent hesitates, the teacher should try not to become tense. If the silence or apparent reluctance of the parent to speak seems to go on too long, the teacher should then make a facilitating comment such as "It is sometimes hard to express what we are thinking or feeling." All the while the teacher should try to show by body language that he or she cares, is ready to listen, and is not pushy.

Conducting the conference. Once the purpose of the conference is clarified, the teacher should try to encourage the parent to talk if he or she has said very little. The teacher can make a facilitating comment such as "I thought you might share some of your observations and concerns about Mary so that we might plan a way to work together to help her progress." The teacher should then listen very carefully to whatever the parent says. Parents usually express their primary concerns at this time. The teacher is also given a glimpse of the sophistication level of the parent. The teacher can then gear his or her language to the level of the parents.

Listening carefully. Listening carefully is absolutely critical in the development of productive parent-teacher relationships. Attentive listening not only encourages parents to express themselves, but it demonstrates the teacher's acceptance and concern. Valand (1975) discusses the following four attending skills as basic to effective listening: (1) minimal encouragers to talk, (2) reflection, (3) paraphrasing and summarization, and (4) clarification.

Minimal encouragers to talk are expressions and nonverbal cues that let the speaker know you want to hear more of what he or she has to

say. Gordon (1970) refers to these as door-openers. Typical of these are such comments as "uh-huh," "yes," "that's interesting," and "hmmm." These can be very useful in getting parents to continue talking, but they should not become overused or used stereotypically. The teacher should be certain not to interrupt the parent with these or other comments. Leaning somewhat forward is usually a sign that the teacher is listening and trying to focus on what is being said.

Reflection involves comments that let the parent know the teacher has heard and understood what the parent is saying. It helps to focus the parent's comments by recognizing a specific comment. It is a cue to parents to elaborate on that specific idea, concept, or question. If the reflection also includes the feeling the teacher perceives, then the teacher will be demonstrating the active listening encouraged by Gordon (1970). Consider the following example of a partial reflection and a reflection involving feeling necessary to active listening (Valand, 1975):

Parent: "I had thought that when he began speech therapy, his talking would improve."
Teacher: "Would improve?"
　　　　　or
　　　"You're feeling pretty discouraged."

Lichter (1976) spells out the advantages of active listening for the teacher working with a parent of a handicapped child. In his work with the parents of moderately retarded children, he has found "active listening" to be "a profound way to communicate a willingness to hear, to understand, and to have empathy with someone who is isolated and struggling to be heard" (p. 68). Considering the emotional needs of parents of handicapped children, it is well worth a teacher's time to invest the energy necessary to become a good active listener.

Paraphrasing and summarizing occur when the teacher attempts to repeat to the parent what he or she has said in revised form. This demonstrates that the teacher has heard what the speaker said and gives him or her the chance to clarify any misunderstanding the teacher may have. Finally, clarification completes the process of active listening. It is necessary to clarify what the parent is saying whenever the teacher has any doubts. If it cannot be done through active listening, then it can be done directly by asking, "Are you saying . . .?" or "Do you mean . . .?" Vignette 9-2, which depicts a home conference, illustrates the skills involved in reflection, paraphrasing, summarization, and clarification.

Questioning. Morgan (1977, p. 4) suggests using questions for only two purposes: (1) to obtain specifically needed information or clarification, and (2) to direct the parent's conversation when it runs astray. Questions such as "Can you tell me exactly what Susie did that bothered you so much?" help to focus the conversation and provide additional information. Such an open-ended question, which cannot be answered with a "yes" or "no," encourages a reluctant parent. On the other hand, a closed question, which can be answered with a "yes" or "no," helps to narrow the focus of a disorganized parent. As teachers need to avoid interrogation, they should practice becoming skilled in using productive questions.

Recognizing parents' concerns. The teacher needs to recognize parents' concerns. This chapter has been emphasizing the importance of a warm, caring attitude that conveys understanding. Of course this attitude and the skills to convey it are absolutely essential for an effective parent-teacher conference. Teachers must expect parents to be reluctant at first. They must be given time to learn that the teacher cares. Reflective listening is one way to let parents know that the teacher has heard and understood their concerns. Another is by being prepared and honest. If parents ask a question and the teacher does not know the answer he or she should kindly say so. The teacher should not try to be something he or she is not. The teacher is not a

medical doctor or a psychotherapist. The teacher must not try to pretend otherwise by giving misleading information. The teacher can and should be prepared to make appropriate referrals. A file or notebook listing names and telephone numbers of local agencies can be helpful. The teacher should be careful not to be biased in referrals or to endorse anyone in particular. It is a good idea to obtain a list from the local special education regional office, school psychologist, social worker, nurse, or principal.

Describing childrens' progress. Be organized and positive in describing children's progress. Give specific examples of a child's skills or behavior whenever possible. Encourage parents to discuss individual points of progress and to ask questions. Do not overwhelm them with information or use jargon. Do not be evasive or a fortune teller. The teacher can only discuss what the child will be doing in the classroom, what the child has accomplished, and what might be expected in the immediate next step. The teacher cannot predict how the child will be functioning next year or the year after.

Closing the conference. The teacher has the primary responsibility of ending the conference in conformity with the time limit. Such comments as, "Given the few minutes we have left, could you explain . . .?," or "It is about time to call it a day; do you have any additional questions?" are gentle reminders that the conference must come to an end. Arranging for future contacts, "Let's see, our next regularly scheduled meeting is . . .," and thanking parents for their time certainly helps to bring a conversation to a close. By standing or by closing the child's folder, parents can readily see that time is up. Finally, switching back to social conversation, the teacher can lead the way to the door.

After the conference. Teachers need to allow enough time between conferences to record what has occurred during the conference. This record retains vital information, documents the

VIGNETTE 9-2: A HOME CONFERENCE BETWEEN
PARENT AND TEACHER

SCENE: Matt is a 4 year old who has been described by his mother as "never still" and by his father as "all boy." In the last week the mother reports that several of her favorite plants have crashed to the floor as Matt walked by. "He never does anything mean or on purpose," she said. He bumps into things and is surprised when adults complain or he breaks things.

It is time for Ms. McLynn's first home visit. Matt's mother, Ms. G., greets her at the door.

Ms. G.: "Hello. Matt has been so excited about your coming, and when he heard you knock, he hid under the bed!"

Ms. McL.: "Good to be here, Ms. G. At school Matt is so helpful. I can always count on Matt to see what needs doing, and to do it. He seems to sense the other children's needs, as well as mine."

Ms. G.: "But he is so rough. And always breaking something. My neighbors say he is hyperactive."

Ms. McL.: "What does that mean to them?"

Ms. G.: "Oh, you know, never still. He just can't seem to be quiet for a minute."

Ms. McL.: "But he has been very quiet since I've been here."

Ms. G.: "He's still hiding under the bed. Oh, he can be quiet when *he* wants to be."

Ms. McL.: "So you feel he really does have control of how active he is?"

Ms. G.: "Yes, I guess so. But just tell him to sit still and he bounces all over the place."

Ms. McL.: "You feel he is too active."

Ms. G.: "Yes. And he won't listen when I tell him to sit still. That burns me up."

Ms. McL.: "His constant moving annoys you."

Ms. G.: "You bet it does. What can I do to make him behave? I've tried spanking but he forgets right away."

Ms. McL.: "From watching at school and with what you told me, I'd like to suggest that we both try something. Let's catch him being quiet and gentle."

Ms. G.: "When? How?"

Ms. McL.: "At school I'll keep a special paper on my desk. Everytime he is quiet or gentle I'll say someting like, 'Matt, I like the way you help Missy with her coat. You were so gentle,' or 'Matt, you are doing a good job with that puzzle. You are so quiet that I can hear the birds singing outside.' Than, I'll make a quick note—for example,

9:03—Quiet and gentle. Helped Missy with coat.

9:10—Worked puzzle. Quiet 3 minutes."

Ms. G.: "Well, it can't hurt."

Ms. McL.: "I'll call you in 2 days to see how it's working."

And 2 days later when Ms. McLynn called she was not surprised that Ms. G. could report more quiet and gentle times than noisy ones. So could Ms. McLynn.

visit, and helps create continuity between meetings. Although occasional notes may be taken during the conference, extensive notetaking is unwise because it interferes with listening and often makes parents uncomfortable. Parents should be apprised of any notes that are taken and the purpose they will serve. Only information that can directly be used to improve the instruction of the child is worth recording.

Involving parents in group meetings

In many communities, parent involvement is synonymous with group meetings. If parents are invited to attend scheduled group meetings, then the school has fulfilled its commitment to parent involvement. Little attention is given to whether or not the planned meetings meet the needs of those invited to participate. Such meetings are usually designed to provide educational information to relatively large groups of people. Professionals are invited to speak, films are shown, books are displayed, and refresh-ments are served. The level of vocabulary used may or may not be understood by the audience. Eager parents may be able to resolve their confusion only by taking advantage of the question and answer period. As a result, parents who manage to attend one meeting may not return for the next.

In a study attempting to identify factors that cause parents to avoid involvement, Stile, Cole, and Garner (1979) report such factors as (1) meetings held at inconvenient times or in inconvenient locations, (2) parent participation in planning not encouraged, (3) programs not aimed at "social" needs of parents in addition to skill deficits of children, (4) parents not allowed to organize or run their own programs, and (5) parents threatened by professionals or by situations.

To maximize the value of group meetings, teachers will need to keep in mind these factors. They should realize that group meetings will meet the needs of some, but not all, parents.

Group meetings are often welcomed by parents who wish to meet and talk with other parents who have children with similar handicaps. Other parents attend primarily to seek the knowledge of the experts in the field. Some rather shy parents may enjoy not being the focus of attention whereas other shy parents may be too inhibited to come in the first place. Whereas those parents who linger on are obviously enjoying the experience, some parents may feel awkward socializing or feel pressure to hurry home. Because of the great diversity of individual needs, meetings should be a balance between educational concerns and social involvement. Teachers cannot expect all parents to be equally involved in all activities. They must observe carefully and try to plan activities that will meet the needs of all of the parents at least some of the time.

Rationale for parent education groups. If parents of children with similar problems are brought together, a supportive climate can be developed for families to learn about and share feelings concerning their handicapped children. Parent education groups also enhance the opportunity to provide parents with knowledge in specific skill areas such as home based teaching and child management. Alternative approaches to childrearing can be presented. Parents can more readily become acquainted with local community resources. Finally, teachers have an opportunity to get to know parents in a setting that can be more relaxed than the parents' home or the child's classroom. Fig. 9-4 provides a sample of topics typical of programs designed for parents of young children.

Guidelines for developing successful group meetings

Parents to parents. A review of the literature indicates that parents are increasingly requesting a true partnership in all aspects of the education of their child and themselves (Clements and Alexander, 1975). Parents who feel they have a voice in selecting topics, speakers, times,

dates, and hours of meetings are usually more actively involved. This is why the suggestion was made earlier to involve parents in developing the orientation meeting. Parents who help plan have a tendency to recruit other parents to attend to realize the fruits of their labors. Note that Fig. 9-4 not only presents possible program topics, but it also illustrates one way to assess the interests of parents.

Frequency of meetings. Because large group meetings should be only a part of the total parent involvement program, they should not be called too frequently. Parents cannot handle more than one such meeting a month. If small group meetings involving parents with very similar needs have been developed to offer social and emotional support, more frequent meetings may be desirable. If these meetings are being organized by the parents with the teacher acting as a consultant, the parents will probably create the needed flexibility for these more informal meetings.

Notification of meetings. Large group meetings must be advertised at least 1 month in advance. Multiple media should be used. Written flyers or notes sent home with the children, telephone calls through a calling chain, newspaper articles, and cable television and local radio announcements will be necessary for maximum participation. Follow-up notices approximately 1 week before the meetings will be helpful. Of course, small group meetings with the responsibility for planning rotated among the interested participants will not take such elaborate notification. Usually one telephone call to each participant is sufficient.

Content of meetings. The content of meetings is where the active participation of an advisory group of parents is critical. Parents know what they need and should be encouraged to express their needs. Besides a written needs assessment as illustrated in Fig. 9-4, teachers can be alert to needs expressed during home visitations, parent-teacher conferences, or informal conversa-

Dear Parents:

Listed below are a number of topics that can become the focus of one or more parent meetings. Because we would like to arrange meetings that will be helpful to you, we would appreciate your cooperation in filling out this questionnaire. Please indicate by checking the appropriate spaces below which meetings would interest you enough for you to take the time to join us. Your comments and opinions are really needed. Please complete this form today and return it with your child by Friday.

Sincerely,

Your Parent Planning Committee

		Yes	*No*	*Maybe*
1.	How do children grow and develop			
	a. Learning to talk	[ ]	[ ]	[ ]
	b. Learning to think	[ ]	[ ]	[ ]
	c. Getting along with others	[ ]	[ ]	[ ]
2.	Understanding my child's special needs			
	a. A pediatrician's views	[ ]	[ ]	[ ]
	b. A physical therapist helps	[ ]	[ ]	[ ]
	c. Other:_____	[ ]	[ ]	[ ]
3.	The importance of play			
	a. Helping your child learn to play	[ ]	[ ]	[ ]
	b. Choosing appropriate toys	[ ]	[ ]	[ ]

FIG. 9-4. Sample parent program topics (interest checklist).

			Yes	No	Maybe
4.	Living with your child				
	a.	Eating hassles	[ ]	[ ]	[ ]
	b.	Bedtime nuisances	[ ]	[ ]	[ ]
	c.	Toileting troubles	[ ]	[ ]	[ ]
	d.	The baby-sitter search	[ ]	[ ]	[ ]
	e.	Brothers and sisters	[ ]	[ ]	[ ]
	f.	Other:_____	[ ]	[ ]	[ ]
5.	Nutrition		[ ]	[ ]	[ ]
6.	Safety-first aid		[ ]	[ ]	[ ]
7.	Community resources		[ ]	[ ]	[ ]
8.	Helping my child behave		[ ]	[ ]	[ ]
9.	Parent effectiveness training		[ ]	[ ]	[ ]

10. What we need the most is:

   _____

   _____

11. The best day(s) for meetings are:

   _____ ___AM ___PM   _____ ___AM ___PM

FIG. 9-4, cont'd. Sample parent program topics (interest checklist).

Parents:

Please give us your honest opinion of tonight's meeting by providing a smile or a frown on the clown. Additional comments will be most helpful to us. Your assistance in completing this form and putting it into the box at the door is appreciated.

The Program Committee

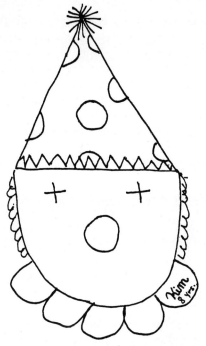

Comments: (Feel free to use the back of the paper, too.)

FIG. 9-5. Sample parent meeting evaluating form.

tion. Speakers need to be dynamic and able to speak on a comprehensible and assimilable level. The best recommendations usually come from the parents. Whenever possible teachers should hear a speaker before requesting his or her assistance with a parent group. Films or videotapes should also be previewed ahead of time.

Child involvement. Teachers should remember that involving children's work or the children themselves lures the parents into attending. Parents will come to see their child in a presentation, their child's work displayed, or their child on a film or a videotape. One Early Childhood Center that had difficulty getting parents to form an advisory group planned an easter egg hunt for the children. While the children were hunting eggs with the supervision of teachers, the director offered the parents refreshments and conducted a brief but successful orientation and organizational meeting.

Variety. Teachers should be aware of the need for variety. Every meeting should not focus on a very serious topic that calls for the complete attention of the parents. Humor and fun are a necessary part of the learning of many parents who must face serious problems every day. Each meeting should involve some socializing and some meetings should be purely social. Some groups of parents will plan and enjoy an occasional potluck dinner involving just the parents or even whole families. Workdays can be a very productive means of fostering informal communication. Some parents will feel much more comfortable in informal clothes painting classroom furniture or making educational toys. Still other parents would gladly organize and conduct a garage sale with proceeds to benefit their children.

Babysitters and carpools. Teachers should recognize the need for babysitters and carpools. Research has already indicated that parents of handicapped children suffer from a lack of relief from physical demands and time constraints. It is thus irresponsible to expect such parents to use their limited babysitting resources to attend a parent meeting (Dunlap, 1979). The planning committee must arrange babysitting through local service clubs, high school students, or other volunteers. Carpools or other transportation arrangements may also increase the attendance at meetings. Such practical matters can be all important to parents who may already have more than they need in the way of problems.

Evaluation. Evaluation is of crucial importance. The atmosphere during group meetings of any size must reflect friendliness, caring, and relaxation. If teachers are tense, then parents will find themselves responding to this tension. Teachers must be alert to activities that lessen tension, that bring smiles to faces, that generate questions, that prompt people to lean toward action, and that are talked about positively during the socializing period. Attendance itself is only one form of evaluation. Evaluation can be informal anecdotal records or logs focusing on the items just mentioned or it can be formal written reactions by the parents. Formal evaluations should be kept to a minimum. Fig. 9-5 illustrates a combination of a formal evaluative procedure using an informal technique that is nonthreatening to both parents and teachers.

SPECIFIC APPROACHES TO PARENT EDUCATION AND TRAINING

Parents seek and need information, guidance, and support that involves practical, specific, day-to-day suggestions on how to promote optimal adjustment for their child. All of the techniques discussed thus far including direct teaching of appropriate behavior, modeling in the classroom and at home, instructional group meetings, and individual parent-teacher conferences are vehicles for delivering practical day-to-day suggestions. The following section discusses yet another approach: more systematic parent education programs. Some revolve around a basic theoretical approach whereas others combine approaches into a packaged program. Lillie (1974) suggests that parent programs fall into one of three basic models: behavioral, psychological insight, or experiential. Only a few of the most used approaches are discussed. References at the end of the chapter will provide more in-depth understanding for interested readers.

Behavioral model

The behavioral model is usually concerned with helping parents to teach or to change specific behaviors. Parents are carefully taught to observe their children's behavior, to measure it, to select target behaviors for change, to administer appropriate reinforcement for desired behavior, to ignore certain inappropriate behaviors, and to model preferred behavior. Trainers are consultants to the parents who themselves employ the behavior change techniques. This approach seems to work best for relatively stable parents who can maintain the high level of consistency necessary for success.

The behavioral approach can be very effective for those who master the techniques and are able regularly to reward positive behavior and ignore the behavior they wish to extinguish. Once parents are successful with this approach they can apply the techniques to a variety of behaviors. This approach can create even greater problems, however, for those who are unable to be consistent in their application of praise or who lack it. Intermittent or inconsistent ignoring of undesirable behavior is actually worse than not ignoring it at all.

Teachers who wish to assist parents in understanding the principles of behavior management may wish to refer to such works as *Parents are Teachers: A Child Management Program* (Becker, 1971); *Effective Parents, Responsible Children: A Guide to Confident Parenting* (Elmers and Artchson, 1977); *Parents, Children, Discipline: A Positive Approach* (Madsen and Madsen, 1972); *Living with Children: New Methods for Parents and Teachers* (Patterson and Gullion, 1968); and *Behavior Modification* (Walker and Shea, 1980). Chapter 8 also discusses behavior management techniques.

Psychological insight model

Whereas the behavioral model is not concerned with why children do what they do, the psychological insight model emphasizes the need to understand the dynamics that occur between parent and child. This approach became widely known through Ginott's works *Between Parent and Child* (1965) and *Between Parent and Teenager* (1971). Students may wish to begin with his *Teacher and Child* (1972) as a means of becoming familiar with some very useful insights into adult-child interaction.

Probably the most popular approach classified by Clements and Alexander (1975) as belonging to the psychological insight model is that of Gordon's *Parent Effectiveness Training* (1970). This is labeled as the "no-lose" approach to childrearing that is thought to be an answer to those parents who do not wish to be either permissive or authoritarian. As discussed in the section on parent-teacher conferences, active listening as taught by Gordon can be extremely helpful when working with parents of handicapped children. Lichter (1976) carefully illustrates how teachers can become effective active listeners. Gordon also advocates understanding who actually "owns" the problem and working out mutually agreed on solutions.

Dreikurs and others present another popular approach to understanding children's behavior and managing it. The concept of allowing children to experience the consequences of their own action is seen by Dreikurs and Grey (1968) as a powerful motivator of proper behavior. Dreikurs and Gordon alike usually give children more credit for being able to be active agents in helping to solve their own behavior problems

A MOTHER TALKS ABOUT THE IMPORTANT THINGS

Be patient. Children need time to learn. Don't rush them. Especially if they make a mess. Don't fuss. Let them know you spill things, too. Encourage them to clean it up, and then let them know what a good job they did—even if it isn't. When you let them know you think they did well, they will try even harder the next time.

If your children try to make a bed, and it really isn't very neat, don't criticize them by telling them so, or by doing it over for them. That is, don't do it over unless you want them to feel that "I'm not good enough." Your main purpose is to make them feel good about themselves. When they feel special, their skills will grow very quickly. Being proud of themselves comes from having you let them know you are proud of them. Saying it is important, but not finding fault is even more important.

And when you have company, please don't ignore the children. Include them for at least some of the time. How else can they learn to be good hosts and hostesses? Of course, don't let them be center stage. Don't allow them to interrupt. But be sure you don't brush them aside, either, Plan ways to include them, and let them learn how to talk to people. Thoughtfulness and being helpful can't be learned unless they have an opportunity to practice.

Trust is important, too. A child wants to trust his or her parents. If you tell them you are going to do something like go to the park, be sure that you do go—even if it's raining. Seeing it in the rain can be a special kind of treat. But if you just don't go, children learn not to trust you. Most of all, be the kind of person you want them to be.

With thanks to Angie's mother, Mrs. Joanna Campbell.

than is the case with those who espouse control primarily through behavior modification. Parents of young handicapped children may indeed need help in avoiding overprotection and the tendency to underestimate their children's abilities to change their own behavior and to solve their own problems.

Experiential model

The experiential model focuses on providing parents with definite opportunities to observe and model appropriate ways to work with their child. Often training sessions are designed to help parents learn to teach specific skills. This is the primary method of the home based programs that demonstrate lessons in the home or the programs that demonstrate lessons in the classroom. Active teaching and academic instruction in the classroom are encouraged (Karnes and Zehrbach, 1979).

Systematic training for effective parenting (STEP)

Systematic Training for Effective Parenting (Dinkmeyer and McKay, 1976) is an example of a packaged parent education program that is receiving considerable use. It comes in a carrying case and features brightly colored, well-illustrated brochures, posters, a leader's manual, and a parent's handbook. This all-inclusive program is designed to help parents promote democratic living through nine group sessions.

Teachers and parent training

Teachers are expected to develop parent involvement programs that facilitate parent participation regarding program objectives, educational goals and objectives, and the implementation of strategies for helping children to develop. Teachers are also the primary source of comfort and education to many parents who strive to cope with the problems generated by raising any young child, let alone a handicapped child. Teachers are limited, however, by time and resources. They cannot and should not be expected to implement parent counseling or to be on call night and day. They can, however, be expected to know about the resources available to parents and to make every possible effort to create opportunities for parents to become involved in their child's education.

This chapter has given a sampling of the variety of procedures, methods, and materials open to teachers for review as they design a multifaceted parent involvement program. The last sections of this chapter provide insights into ways of working with parents who need special consideration.

WORKING WITH PARENTS WITH SPECIAL NEEDS

Some parents may seek guidance on how to handle a particular problem. When this happens, teachers should encourage them to describe exactly what they are concerned about. Often what they need most is help in defining the problem. Once precisely identified, many mountains dissolve into manageable molehills.

It can be helpful to give parents specific things to do and to avoid doing, if they feel upset and ineffective. It is even more supportive, however, to lead them to discover workable solutions by using leading questions. The following questions are useful for this purpose.

1. Did you feel what you did was helpful?
2. What else would you like to try now?
3. Sometimes at school we find it helps if we . . . . Do you find it helpful?
4. Do you think that might be useful at home?
5. How could you "catch your child being good?"
6. When you . . . have you noticed any changes?
7. What have you done that helped the most?

There are no pat answers. Each family is unique. Sometimes parents need to be reminded that rarely only one right way exists to meet a particular challenge. Often parents need to be told that what they did was the best that could be done under the circumstances. Then they can be led to think about alternative solutions. All the while teachers must be prepared to offer referral sources to parents who need help requiring expertise beyond their capabilities.

Helping parents who are reluctant to come to school

Some parents may resist coming to school for any number of reasons. Perhaps they were so discouraged or threatened by their own school experiences that coming to a school is very distasteful. Or they may state very emphatically that it is the teacher's job, not theirs, to teach their child. Others, equally vehement, may assert that nobody is going to tell them how to raise their children. Still others may be threatened and fear embarrassment by the possibility of their child revealing family secrets.

Parents' reactions may depend on where they are in the denial-acceptance continuum outlined earlier in this chapter. Parents who are having difficulty facing their child's limitations may seek to avoid yet another validation of their child's problems by yet another professional. Some parents simply cannot take extra pressure and may develop what Meadow and Meadow (1971) refer to as "parental paralysis" when demands are perceived to be impossible.

Preventing negative interactions. Teachers will want to try to prevent negative interactions. The way in which teachers respond to reluctant parents may determine whether or not they continue to be reluctant. Because of the implementation of Public Law 94-142, most staffing conferences are attended by one or both parents. The way professionals conduct themselves during these conferences can set the stage for the parents' reactions to future contacts with school personnel. Teachers can make special efforts to help keep the conferences in perspective. As Seligman (1979) points out, such meetings must be handled with sensitivity and good judgment. Otherwise, hearing about the child's limitations from each of the professionals may be more than a parent can tolerate. Whenever possible, delicate issues should be handled on a one-to-one basis with someone with whom the parent has developed a rapport. Staffing conferences, like parent-teacher conferences, must provide a balance between positive and negative factors about the child's development.

By developing an attitude of positive regard and helpful skills such as "active listening," teachers can help parents who are intimidated by differential education or social standing. Striking a balance between warmly inviting parents to become involved as respected partners in their child's education and avoiding too much pressure is essential. Some parents will respond to invitations made by other parents. If this technique is tried, teachers must avoid saying to the helping parent "Ms. Smith just won't come to school," or "Ms. Jones just won't do what I tell her." Instead they should say "Ms. Smith hasn't been to our classroom yet. Do you think you could call her and maybe stop by to see her? Perhaps if you explain what we do here and why it is important she will feel more comfortable about coming."

In some cases, fathers may be reluctant to come to school. Another father might be helpful in explaining how much fathers can help to make the preschool experience a great success. Teachers should gently urge mothers to invite fathers. If considerable resistance is expressed, the subject of a formal visit should be dropped. Teachers must respect that role expectations in some families preclude fathers from coming to school. Fathers who will not come to school, however, may like to contribute to their child's education by making something for the class-room. Some fathers will not resist attending an informal function such as a family barbecue.

Finally, teachers must avoid expecting too much of a parent involvement program. They can rejoice in the slow changes in attitudes and behavior that do occur. Being in too much of a hurry can sometimes cause teachers to overlook the quality of what is happening slowly.

Working with parents who abuse or neglect children

The laws on child abuse and child neglect are explicit. If teachers (and others responsible for working with children) notice any signs of abuse or neglect, they must report their suspicions to community or county authorities. Ideally the procedure for dealing with abusive parents should be worked out before it is ever necessary to report abuse. Principals, directors, nurses, and social workers should meet with teachers to plan what to do when they suspect abuse.

Guidelines for teachers of abused children. The following guidelines can be a starting point for a discussion or for developing a policy for working with abusive parents:

1. Be alert for signs of sadness or anger, as well as bruises, burns, and cuts. Listen to what the children say. Be especially alert for changes in behavior that cannot be explained by impending illness or a "happening" at school. Begin *at once* to record specific details of your observations. Be certain to make a written note of the date, time, and manner of observation. These may be necessary if a report must be made to authorities. Keep these confidential and under lock and key.

2. Cigarette burns are usually round. Small round burns should always be investigated.

3. Bruises on legs and buttocks can be the result of falls. The frequency and the severity of the bruises are useful criteria. Even

clumsy children stay unbruised most of the time. If the child is nearly always bruised, be suspicious.

4. Black eyes do result from bumping into things. So do bumps on heads. Again, the severity and the relative frequency of the bruises dictate the degree of teacher concern.

5. Little children usually "tell all," but even 3 year olds can be frightened into lying about how they were hurt. It is not unusual for parents to tell little ones that if they say that mommy or daddy hurt them a big bad person will come and take them away. When this happens, the children's explanations are usually and obviously "dictated." If the story changes, be suspicious.

6. After a report to the proper authorities has been made, the teacher should seek help and guidance from the principal or the director of the school. Next steps with the parents should not be decided by the teacher alone. Home visits should be discontinued at least for some time. This is a needed safety precaution for both the teacher and the parents.

7. On subsequent visits, after conferences with persons who are competent to advise the teacher on what to do and how to do it, teachers should not go alone to the home. An aide should accompany the teacher and should be alert to what is said. Confidential notes made by the teacher after the meeting should not become part of the child's file but should be kept in the teacher's personal possession. These can be destroyed when the need for them is ended.

8. Regardless of the nature or severity of the case, if the child continues to attend school, it is the teacher's responsibility to continue to try to encourage the parents to participate in parent meetings and in volunteering at school. The teacher should

have the help of persons trained and skilled in helping these parents. If the school does not offer this service, the teacher should insist on receiving it from some public or private source. Skill in teaching does not infer that the teacher must be all things to all people. Trying to be so can result in disaster.

Maintaining a perspective. Teachers need to maintain a perspective on the situation. It may be particularly difficult to forgive and forget the abuse or neglect of a young child. Teachers will find it helpful to learn about causes and effects of mental and physical abuse. Professionals from community agencies are often willing to present workshops for teachers. If this cannot be arranged easily, reading about the subject can be useful. Halperin (1979) helps to put the problem into perspective:

Maltreating parents are adults with problems rather than inhuman monsters who delight in hurting their children. They are people who have problems that affect their ability to be good parents rather than hopeless mental and social misfits (p. 65).

Of particular interest to teachers will be the continuing research into the child's contribution to his or her own abuse. Parke and Collmer (1975) discuss a number of ways a child plays a role in the abuse process. For example, there may be genetically determined characteristics or learned behaviors that elicit abuse. Abused children may become repulsive in appearance or difficult to manage. These characteristics may in turn provoke even more of the very abuse that caused their origin.

Adults who maltreat children may have been conditioned to abuse or neglect while growing up. They may be imitating the parenting behavior they once experienced. Often they have failed to internalize the values of the general society in regard to children and childrearing; sometimes the very structure of the family unit precipitates maltreatment. The frustration of daily living frequently combines with other factors to lead parents to abuse or neglect their youngsters.

Head Start policy. Teachers are well advised to heed the policy of Head Start governing the prevention, identification, treatment, and reporting of child abuse and neglect. The policy emphasizes that "Head Start programs will not undertake, on their own, to treat cases of child abuse and neglect. Head Start programs will, on the other hand, cooperate fully with child protective service agencies . . . and make every effort to retain in their programs children allegedly abused or neglected" (Halperin, 1979, p. 191).

Without the help of trained teachers who understand and know how to deal with the special problems of young handicapped children, many parents of these youngsters are stressed and tempted beyond their ability to cope. This is why teachers of these children and their parents must establish a workable partnership early. It is useful for teachers to ask themselves how well they would be able to cope if the situation were reversed and they were the parents instead of the teachers.

Working with parents who are handicapped themselves

In addition to the challenges encountered in working with all parents, many teachers of young children will discover that they are working with parents who are themselves handicapped. It is common to discover parents who can neither read nor write adequately. Often these parents dropped out of school. Typically, they are out of work, frequently in trouble of one kind or another, and usually at odds with other family members most of the time. Some have a great deal of skill at manipulating those who attempt to help them. They know precisely when to appear docile and cooperative and when to be angry and aggressive.

The nature of the handicap or developmental disability of these parents will vary widely. Although overt behaviors may appear to be similar, causes can be very different. It is unwise and dangerous to generalize. Each parent is an individual with unique needs. In some way each one can be helped.

A good place to begin is to avoid difficult and abstract terminology. Information may need to be communicated more than once. Directions given to these parents must be explained and demonstrated. Only one behavior can be modified at a time and only one lesson can be taught at a time. Repetition is usually required. Tact, patience, and continuous praise are essential. Sometimes the best a teacher can do for some mentally handicapped parents or emotionally disturbed parents is to find other professionals trained to help these parents directly.

The very young parent. Many parents are very young themselves. Usually these parents are young girls who have chosen to keep the baby fathered by boys who have since disappeared. The place to begin working with these young girls may be in the classroom, allowing them to play with their children. Merely being there and feeling accepted can work wonders. As they see an adult treat their young child with love and respect, the possibility of behaving that way themselves may seem nearer.

Developmentally disabled parents. All of the suggestions made for working out a partnership with parents are also useful in working with developmentally disabled parents. The following guidelines have also been useful to teachers working with developmentally disabled parents:

1. *Establish priorities.* To help developmentally disabled parents develop effective parenting skills, teachers must choose priorities carefully. The first priority may be to help parents to discontinue yelling and spanking their children for every minor offense. One parent was observed shrieking her child's name and "no" at 1 minute intervals during a 20 minute home visit. Another mother complained that

her child was always "bad." When asked to explain what he was doing that was "bad," she said that he just never stopped running in the house. For this mother, the suggestion that she take him outside to play every day was a brand new idea. Within a short time the indoor running stopped.

2. *Coordinate help.* As soon as possible, discover which other agencies and persons are extending help to these parents. If there are several, get them together if possible to plan for effective communication and concerted action. (After a mother complained everybody was telling her to do something different, the teacher discovered that 15 different persons working for seven agencies were in fact trying to tell her what she should do. The resulting contradictions would have baffled any parent.)

3. *Make frequent, brief contacts.* Telephone calls are better than notes, and 10 minutes with the parent in the home can pay quick dividends.

4. *Avoid lengthy explanations.* Be brief. Be explicit. Show these parents what to do and how to do it. They are usually willing to try, if they understand what is wanted.

5. *Praise and tangible rewards are necessary.* "Parent of the week" and "Child of the day" awards are meaningful.

6. *Sincerity is essential.* There is always something positive to call attention to in any situation. Do not forget to tell parents about every sign of progress you see in their children.

7. *Be aware of frustration.* Many of these parents live with constant frustration. Try to ease some of this, if possible. Merely coming to school at a certain date and time is a major accomplishment if they cannot read. A call to remind them, a marked calendar, or a special tag sent home is useful.

8. *Require little or no reading.* Send only one request or direction in notes, if they can read. A list of things to do will probably be ignored.

9. *Involve developmentally delayed parents.* Whenever possible, include developmentally delayed parents in clasroom observations, volunteer activities, parent conferences, and meetings. Answer their questions in short sentences and with simple language. Supervise their activities closely. It is helpful to remember that they are with their child far more than the teacher. If their teaching skills and behavior management can be improved, great rewards for the children can be achieved.

Working with parents who do not speak English

Teachers are increasingly expected to work with children and parents who do not speak English. Ideally a translator or interpeter should be available to help, but this is rarely possible. Older siblings, however, can be very good translators. Young children who have acquired a different native language may be placed in early childhood special education classes to accelerate their learning of English. All of these people who must learn to speak a second language need understanding and thoughtful help. Trying to understand a new language is difficult at best. If a handicapping condition is also present the problems are greatly complicated.

The suggestions made for working with all parents are equally relevant for parents who do not understand English. Communication, however, may need to be much more "show" than "tell." The example of the teacher's management of children's behavior is quickly grasped by these parents. If their mores and styles of living and working with their children are very different, they will communicate it by ignoring suggestions graciously. It is often useful to encourage these parents to come to school more often than other parents. The very things their children are learning to understand and say also help them to learn the new language more quickly. The time the teacher spends helping these parents is quickly reflected in improved help by them in their homes.

Working with parents who have limited resources

Perhaps the most useful suggestion for working with parents who appear to have financially limited resources is to avoid underestimating what they can do. One mother who appeared to have very little to work with in her home demonstrated remarkable skill in turning household items into teaching toys. This mother only needed ideas. Another family had been accustomed to making do with very little. Vocabulary and language skills were limited. But the father loved to make things out of wood. When the teacher provided wood and nails, he made a very useful workbench for the classroom, and came weekly to show the children how to work with simple tools.

Some of these parents have hidden organizational skills. Given the opportunity, they accept responsibility and the need to change some of their ways of working with their children. Of course there are parents who will not come to school, who will not cooperate, and who resist all efforts to help their children. But there are fewer of these parents than most of us believe.

SUMMARY

Properly trained teachers will recognize and actively work toward involving parents in a partnership of responsibility for their child's development. One of the first links in bridging a link between school and home is for the teacher to recognize the emotional needs of families with handicapped children. Parents often react to the realization that their child has a handicapping condition in stages similar to the emotional adjustment encountered with the loss of a loved one. The alert and informed teacher can help parents work through each stage from initial feelings of shock, disbelief and denial through anger and resentment, bargaining to make it go away, depression and discouragement, and on to acceptance.

Children and members of the extended family can be included in the process of emotional and educational adjustments. Siblings are an especially valuable ally, as children typically accept a handicapped child without jealousy or anxiety. Especially in early sessions with family members, it is important to avoid jargon and technical concepts. Test results should be explained in terms of common behaviors. Developmental checklists help parents to relate their child's behaviors to "normal" development and to envision what and how well their child will be doing when specific objectives are mastered.

A variety of methods of parent involvement were surveyed, such as home based instruction, observations, passports, and meetings. As a source of adaptable ideas, some of the model home based instruction programs were described, such as the Portage Project and High/Scope. For effectiveness in home visits and instruction, teachers learn to use two-way communication, taking time to listen and to observe, as well as to inform and to demonstrate.

Guidelines were provided for working with parents within the classroom under a variety of purposes. With teacher planning, it is possible to create a developmental approach for bringing parents into contact with other parents of handicapped children (the more seasoned veterans), orienting them to observation and eventually participation within the classroom. Parent education groups and parent-teacher conferences can be viewed as requiring special teacher skills rather than simply as an opportunity to chat.

To complement the normal techniques of bonding parent involvement, the chapter concluded with two areas of special consideration. One was the use of alternative theoretical approaches for working with parents. Included were considerations and orientations underlying special models such as the behavioral model, the psychological insight model, and the experiential model. Each has its unique points of emphasis together with a philosophical rationale. Finally, teachers were reminded that some parents of children with handicaps may have special needs themselves. These range from parents who are reluctant to come to school, to parents who are handicapped themselves, to parents who do not speak English, or to parents who abuse or neglect their children. Throughout the chapter, sufficient details have been provided to encourage teachers to pick and choose the type and extent of involvement most appropriate for their parents, their children, and themselves.

DISCUSSION TOPICS AND ACTIVITIES

1. Do additional reading and research into the emotional needs and feelings of parents of handicapped children. Discuss these feelings with class members. If possible, try to empathize with these feelings.
2. Make a list of the public and private institutions in your area whose purpose is to assist exceptional parents cope with their problems. Organize the list as a referral file including contact person, telephone number, and cost and type of services.
3. Assume the role of a handicapped child's parent and do a local telephone survey. Describe your child's condition and ask for information as to where and how to obtain help. Record this information in a file and share it with classmates. Try to get some idea of how parents might feel when in this situation.
4. Review and discuss why parents may feel fearful about their meetings with school personnel. What can teachers do to help relieve these feelings?
5. Prepare and role play an orientation meeting. Try to be as convincing as possible when giving the reasons why you would like to get your children's parents involved.
6. Develop a questionnaire that you can use to determine the interests and needs of parents for parent involvement. Try it out on a few parents. Compare it to that of classmates and revise when necessary.
7. Collect magazine, newspaper, and journal articles about working with parents. Make a file of useful ideas.
8. Role play a home visit with classmates. Share constructive criticism.
9. Consider and discuss the possibility of a values collision between a home visitor and a family. How can such a collision be avoided? Have you ever been involved in such a situation?
10. As a class, discuss the issues of confidentiality, privileged communication, and conversation in the teacher's lounge in relation to parent involvement.
11. Gather and discuss newsletters from local early child-

hood centers. Develop one that may be appropriate for a class you will teach.
12. Develop a happy-gram to be sent home to parents.
13. Write to one or more of the national resource agencies listed in Appendix G for information to begin a parent resource file.

ANNOTATED REFERENCES
Emotional needs of families with handicapped children

Buscaglia, L. *The disabled and their parents: A counseling challenge.* Thorofare, N.J.: Charles B. Slack, Inc., 1975. Everyone who works with handicapped children and their parents should seriously read this book. In a very direct writing style the author makes a demand for competent, reality-based, and sensible guidance. He offers practical, down-to-earth suggestions for improved counseling. Most of all, the author considers handicaps to be made, not born.

Kübler-Ross, E. *On death and dying.* New York: Macmillan, Inc., 1969.
With warm sensitivity, the author depicts the delicate subject of the terminally ill and the struggle to accept death. This remarkable book not only helps the reader to face more professionally and personally the inevitable end of life, but it also lends insight into the stages through which some parents of handicapped children may pass.

Roos, P. Psychological counseling with parents of retarded children. In L. Baruth, and M. Burggraf (Eds.), *Readings in counseling parents of exceptional children.* Guilford, Conn.: Special Learning Corp., 1979, 103-107.
The author clearly describes typical parental reactions to their child's retardation. The author outlines a number of specific suggestions for working with these parents and emphasizes the importance of attentive listening. Consideration is given to using formal test results when working with the parents.

Seligman, M. *Strategies for helping parents of exceptional children.* New York: The Free Press, 1979.
The major purpose of this excellent book is to help teachers become more knowledgeable about the exceptional parents they confer with, and to augment their heightened awareness through the improvement of their own communication abilities. One well-written chapter is devoted to understanding the dynamics of families with an exceptional child. The author offers specific strategies for working with parents, including a section on problem parents and on critical incidents for role playing and discussion.

Methods of parent involvement

Clements, J.E., and Alexander, R.N. Parent training: Bringing it all back home. *Focus on Exceptional Children,* 1975, 7, 1-12.

This concise, informative article places the evolution of parent involvement into perspective. The authors review contemporary trends in parent involvement and various parent training techniques. The authors also illustrate and discuss a model for a school based delivery system of services for parents of exceptional children.

Kroth, R.L. *Communicating with parents of exceptional children: Improving parent-teacher relationships.* Denver: Love Publishing Co., 1975.

This is a book of techniques designed to help teachers understand the child and his or her family, to provide parents with information, and to help parents solve problems. It is aimed at teachers who wish to go beyond individual parent-teacher conferences and report cards. The author emphasizes using appropriate reinforcers as a tool in changing children's behavior, and provides case studies to assist teachers in skill development.

Kroth, R.L., and Simpson, R.L. *Parent conferences as a teaching strategy.* Denver: Love Publishing Co., 1977.

The focus of this book is on adult-teacher interviews or parent-teacher conferences: Specific topics covered include: clarifying values of the interviewer and interviewee, dynamics of the interview process, preparing for the interview and understanding educational data. The authors present a suggested interview format, a recording procedure, and role playing exercises. Actual case histories are used to clarify various points.

Lillie, D.L., and Trohanis, P.L. (Eds.), *Teaching parents to teach.* New York: Walker and Company, 1976.

Theory and practical applications are provided in a series of articles that give a good rationale for parent involvement. These articles are intended to help those who run early childhood programs for handicapped children to develop, organize, and implement parent involvement programs. An extensive annotated bibliography is included.

Michaelis. C.T. *Home and school partnerships in exceptional education.* Rockville, M.D.: Aspen Systems Corporation, 1980.

Writing from the viewpoint of a professional and a parent of a handicapped child, the author is able to present the major communication blocks of home-school interrelationships that must be overcome. Throughout the book, practical recommendations are made to help parents and teachers work together on behalf of handicapped children. Of particular interest is a chapter that translates technical language into common terms.

Morrison, G.S. *Parent involvement in the home, school, and community.* Columbus: Charles E. Merrill Publishing Co., 1978.

This extremely readable text is designed to provide a combination of theory and practical methods for students at all levels. The topic of parent involvement is thoroughly covered. Separate chapters are devoted to parent involvement through home visitations, parent involvement in early childhood programs, and parent involvement with handicapped children.

Nedler, S.E., and McAfee, O.D. *Working with parents: Guidelines for early childhood and elementary teachers.* Belmont, Calif.: Wadsworth Publishing Co., 1979.

This text begins with a historical overview of the parent involvement movement in the United States. Techniques for identifying needs, selecting goals and objectives, developing activities, motivating parents, and evaluating programs follow. The authors give concrete examples of five basic approaches to parent involvement: home-based, school- or center-based, home-school partnerships, parent education, and parents as policy makers.

Rutherford, R.B., and Edgar, E. *Teachers and parents: A guide to interaction and cooperation.* Boston: Allyn and Bacon, Inc., 1979.

This book describes systematic procedures that lead toward solution of student problems through cooperative efforts with parents. The development of trust is thought to be the basic ingredient for cooperation. The authors give attention to applied behavior analysis, interpersonal communication skills, assertiveness, and values clarification.

Simmons-Martin, A. *Chats with Johnny's parents.* Washington, D.C.: The Alexander Graham Bell Association for the Deaf, 1975.

This small book offers examples of parent-teacher conversations concerning a hearing impaired child. It is useful to teachers of all handicapped children.

REFERENCES

Becker, W.C. *Parents are teachers: A child management program.* Champaign, Ill.: Research Press, 1971.

Boyd, D. *The three stages.* New York: National Association for Retarded Childen, 1950.

Buscaglia, L. *The disabled and their parents: A counseling challenge.* Thorofare, N.J.: Charles B. Slack, Inc., 1975.

Chinn, P., Drew, C., and Logan, D. *Mental retardation.* St. Louis: The C.V. Mosby Co., 1979.

Clements, J.E., and Alexander, R.N. Parent training: Bringing it all back home. *Focus on Exceptional Children*, 1975, *7*, 1-12.

Davis, H. Personal communication, 1962.

Dinkmeyer, D., and McKay, G.D. Systematic training for effective parenting. *Leader's Manual.* Circle Pines, Minn.: American Guidance Service, 1976.

Dreikurs, R., and Grey, L. *Logical consequences: A new approach to discipline.* New York: Hawthorn Books, Inc., 1968.

Dunlap, W.R. How do parents of handicapped children view their needs? *Journal of the Division of Early Childhood*, 1979, *1*, 1-10.

Elmers, R., and Artchson, R. *Effective parents, responsible children: A guide to confident parenting.* New York: Mc-Graw-Hill, 1977.

Farber, B. Family organization and crisis: Maintenance of integration in families with a severely retarded child. *Monograph of Society for Research in Child Development,* 1960, *25.*

Frankenburg, W.K., Dodds, J.B., and Fandal, A. *The Denver Developmental Screening Test.* Denver: The University of Colorado Medical Center, 1970.

Ginott, H.G. *Between parent and child.* New York: The Macmillan Publishing Co., 1965.

Ginott, H.G. *Between parent and teenager.* New York: Avon Books, 1971.

Ginott, H.G. *Teacher and child.* New York: The Macmillan Publishing Co., 1972.

Gordon, I.J., and Guinagh, B. *A home learning center approach to early stimulation.* Final report on Project No. Ro1 MH 16037-04. Gainsville, Fl.: University of Florida, Institute for Development of Human Resources, 1974.

Gordon, T. *Parent effectiveness training.* New York: Peter H. Wyden, 1970.

Grimm, J. (Ed.) *Training parents to teach—four models.* (1st Chance for Children), Chapel Hill, N.C.: Technical Assistance Development Systems, 1974, *3.*

Grossman, F.K. Brothers and sisters of retarded children. *Psychology Today,* 1972, 5, 82-84, 102-104.

Halperin, M. *Helping maltreated children: School and community involvement.* St. Louis: The C.V. Mosby Co., 1979.

Hodel, M.B. Parents learn to share with son. *The Intelligencer,* Edwardsville, Ill.: 16 January 1981, 2.

Karnes, M.B., and Zehrbach, R.R. Matching families and services. In R. Piazza, and R. Rothman (eds.), *Pre-school Education for the Handicapped.* Guilford, Conn.: Special Learning Corporation, 1979, 143-146.

Kirk, W. A parent's perspective. *Illinois Regional Resource Center Newsletter,* 1979, *2,* 5-6.

Klein, S.D. Brother to sister: Sister to brother. *The Exceptional Parent,* 1972, *2,* 10-15.

Kübler-Ross, E. *On death and dying.* New York: The Macmillan Publishing Co., 1969.

Lepler, M. Having a handicapped child. *The American Journal of Maternal Child Nursing,* 1978, 32-34.

Lichter, R. Communicating with parents: It begins with listening. *Teaching Exceptional Children,* 1976, *8,* 66-71.

Lillie, D.L. Dimensions in parent programs: An overview. In J. Grimm (Ed.), *Training parents to teach—four models.* (1st Chance for Children), Chapel Hill, N.C.: Technical Assistance Development Systems, 1974, *3.*

Madsen, C.K., and Madsen, C.H. *Parents, children, discipline: A positive approach.* Boston: Allyn and Bacon, 1972.

Meadow, K.P., and Meadow, L. Changing role perceptions for parents of handicapped children. *Exceptional Children,* 1971, *38,* 21-27.

Meier, J. The long range results of early identification and intervention and some salient ethical/social/political considerations. In D. Nasim (Ed.), *Communicator,* Division of Early Childhood, Council for Exceptional Children, 1978, *4,* 28-39.

Michaelis, C.T. *Home and school partnerships in exceptional education.* Rockville, Md.: Aspen Systems Corporation, 1980.

Morgan, W. Skills in working with parents (1240). Champaign, Ill.: University of Illinois, Institute for Research on Exceptional Children, 1977.

Parke, R.D., and Collmer, C.W. Child abuse: An interdisciplinary analysis. In E.M. Hetherington (Ed.), *Review of child development research.* Chicago: University of Chicago Press, 1975, 509-590.

Patterson, G.R., and Gullion, M.E. *Living with children: New methods for parents and teachers.* Champaign, Ill.: Research Press, 1968.

Roos, P. Parents and families of the mentally retarded. In J.M. Kauffman and J.S. Payne (Eds.), *Mental retardation: Introduction and personal perspectives.* Columbus: Charles E. Merrill, 1975.

Roos, P. Psychological counseling with parents of retarded children. In L. Baruth and M. Burggraf (Eds.), *Readings in counseling parents of exceptional children.* Guilford, Conn.: Special Learning Corp., 1979, 103-107.

Runge, A., Walker, J., and Shea, T.M. A passport to positive parent-teacher communication. *Teaching Exceptional Children,* 1975, 7, 91-92.

Searl, S.J. Stages of parent reaction. *The Exceptional Parent,* 1978, *8,* 27-29.

Seligman, M. *Strategies for helping parents of exceptional children.* New York: The Free Press, 1979.

Shearer, M.S., and Shearer, D.E. The Portage Project: A model for early childhood education. *Exceptional Children,* 1972, *39,* 210, 217.

Stephens, T.M. Parent/teacher conferences. *The Directive Teacher,* 1979, *2,* 2.

Stigen, G. *Heartaches and handicaps: An irreverent survival manual for parents.* Palo Alto, Calif.: Science and Behavior Books, Inc., 1976.

Stile, S.W., Cole, J.T., and Garner, A.W. Maximizing parental involvement in programs for exceptional children. *Journal of the Division of Early Childhood Education,* 1979, *1,* 68-92.

Susser, P. Parents are partners. *The Exceptional Parent,* 1974, 41-47.

Tanner, D.C. Loss and grief: Implications for the speech-language pathologist and audiologist. *American Journal of the American Speech and Hearing Association,* 1980, *22,* 916-928.

Valand, M.C. Conducting parent-teacher conferences. (Mimeographed paper). Chapel Hill, N.C.: The University of North Carolina, Chapel Hill training-Outreach Program, 1975.

Walker, J.E., and Shea, T.M. *Behavior modification.* St. Louis: The C.V. Mosby Co., 1980.

Weikart, D.P. Parental involvement through home teaching. *High/Scope Educational Research Foundation Report.* Ypsilanti, Mich.: High/Scope Educational Research Foundation, 1975, 74-75.

Weikart, D.P. (Ed.) *Keys to early childhood education.* Washington D.C.: Capitol Publications, 1980, *1.*

10

Effective use of paraprofessionals in the classroom

It would be difficult to find a teacher of young handicapped children who is not grateful for and even dependent on the help of paraprofessionals and volunteers in the classroom. Teachers who hesitate to sing the praises of those who assist them either have not learned how to incorporate effectively their assistance into the classroom routine or have a unique situation. Teachers must do more than be grateful for the assistance they receive; they must also realize that they have an important responsibility for guiding and developing paraprofessionals. Resourceful work is required to launch a successful volunteer program but teachers typically do not know where to begin. This chapter provides guidelines for effectively developing and using paraprofessionals and volunteers in the classroom.

Paraprofessionals are those who choose to work with youngsters in preschools and day-care centers for little pay, and volunteers choose to do this work for no pay. By definition both do not have the training and expertise necessary to perform as professional teachers. (At times, however, newly certified teachers may accept these jobs because of a lack of certified openings in their area.) Most of these people delight in the charm of children, are patient with their fumbles, and understand their special needs. If the basic qualities of respect and caring are not present from the beginning, however, paraprofessionals and volunteers will not find the work pleasant or rewarding. These underlying qualities cannot be taught. Adults who do not have them should choose other work.

The motivation to serve in and of itself is not enough. Paraprofessionals and volunteers need to be willing to learn new skills. They must accept a willingness to change attitudes and philosophies about how to manage child behavior. Simply responding to special problems according to one's parental experience or values about "good" and "bad" behaviors may run contrary to the professional aims of the institution and the teacher. For example, paraprofessionals and volunteers frequently have strong ideas about discipline and sex issues that may need tempering to be consistent with the goals and philosophy of the teacher. Their basic caring for children is a point of departure. But typically more than good intentions are necessary.

The teacher has the responsibility to explain special needs, to provide specific guidelines, and to demonstrate desired techniques of behavior management. In effect the teacher, when working with paraprofessionals and volunteers, is a leader and a manager. For this adult-to-adult role relationship to work effectively, mutual respect among the participants is needed. Each will bring specific skills, interests, and talents to the tasks to be performed. Each will have a unique role to play in making childrens' experiences happy and educationally appropriate. But it remains the teacher's responsibility to guide, develop, and use the interests, talents, and motivation of any and all paraprofessionals and volunteers who seek to contribute.

WHO ARE THE PARAPROFESSIONALS?

Paraprofessionals, those who lack the full training and certification necessary to teach young children with special needs, provide three levels of assistance (Greer, 1978). The specific category "paraprofessional" refers to persons who are employed by a school for salaries much lower than those received by credentialed teachers. This specifically includes teacher assistants and teacher aides. A *teacher assistant* has limited decision-making authority but is responsible for directly assuming whatever instructional and support tasks are granted by the supervising teacher. Teacher assistants often are involved in directly instructing children as part of their training before becoming professionals.

Teacher aides have less authority and responsibility than teacher assistants. Typically aides are not directly involved in nonsupervised instruction because they may have no teacher training. They commonly handle more routine tasks and nominal instructional activities such as supervising play, feeding, toileting, and preparing materials.

Volunteers provide a broad range of assistance for which they receive no salaries. Nationally over six million nonpaid volunteers are working in schools (Boyer, 1978). As established by the National School Volunteers Program, the following four principal objectives are reached by the tasks performed by volunteers (Carter and Dapper, 1974):

1. Relieving professional staff members of nonteaching duties
2. Providing needed services to individual children that supplement the work of the classroom teacher
3. Enriching the experiences of children beyond what would normally be available (such as sharing special talents)
4. Building improved understanding of school problems in the community and stimulating citizen support for educational improvement

Throughout this chapter the term *paraprofessional* will generally refer to any of the three levels of assistance by those of nonteacher rank. However, where the handling of paraprofessionals and volunteers differs, the distinctions will be clearly stated. For example, schools typically do not have to recruit *paid* teacher aides and teacher assistants. Volunteer recruitment may be a critical element, however, in having sufficient adult resources to carry out needed instructional and support activities within budget limitations. The performance effectiveness of volunteers is not normally evaluated formally. Volunteers are usually thanked and praised for their help. With paraprofessionals who may aspire to become teachers, however, specifying tasks and formalizing the

evaluation of their performance are fundamental parts of the learning-development process.

THE DETERMINANTS OF PARAPROFESSIONAL PERFORMANCE

Recruiting, developing, and effectively using paraprofessionals places the teacher of young children in a role for which he or she may be ill-prepared. Undoubtedly the prevailing emphasis in the education of teachers is toward theories of learning, instructional methods, curricula, and behavior management of children. When paraprofessionals are used in any capacity to supplement and extend pupil-teacher contact, however, the teacher is thrust into the role of leader and manager of adults. In this leadership role the responsibilities of the teacher differ only in degree from many of the functions required of a manger in a business, a hospital, or a government agency.

How does the teacher become a leader and manager of adults in the classroom? To answer this question, it is necessary to focus first on the paraprofessional as a resource. The value of this resource is the potential of the paraprofessional to extend the capacity and effectiveness of the teacher. To achieve this potential the teacher should be able to answer the following question: What affects the behavior of the paraprofessional in the classroom (or behind the scenes) and subsequently his or her performance effectiveness?

We will explore this question by starting with a simple model of human behavior developed by the late psychologist Lewin (1951). He noted that in the most basic way, $B = f(P, E)$. Replacing symbols with words, this reads: "Behavior is a function of the Person and Environment." This suggests that human behavior is a field of dynamic forces. Some of these forces arise within the person, whereas others arise from the environmental situation at any time.

If we are interested in the paraprofessional's behavior, we then must ask: What are the essential qualities of forces in assistants, aides, and volunteers that in part determine how they behave in their supportive role in the classroom? We must also address the qualities of the environmental forces, especially those controllable by the teacher: What are the qualities of the teacher as leader, policy maker, and manager that will also influence the behavior and performance of paraprofessionals?

Forces within the person

To answer the questions about the qualities of paraprofessionals and of the environment, we should consider first an elaboration of specific forces within the paraprofessional, the person about whose performance we are now concerned. Cummings and Schwab (1974) emphasize that the two major forces within an individual most relevant in affecting job performance are abilities and motivation.

Abilities. A person's abilities are reasonably deterministic and stable at any given time. Abilities include special skills, knowledge, and the sum experiences that relate to the particular task or situation people encounter. Ability also includes a capacity for perceiving unexpected situational needs and responding with problem-solving behaviors in a manner that copes with rather than ignores or accentuates the problem. How does the teacher aide respond to the child who has fallen off the climbing apparatus and is crying uncontrollably? Ability may make the difference in response behavior.

Motivation. Motivation, by contrast, is a dynamic quality that potentially can change day by day, even moment by moment. Many factors can alter or create instability in a person's motivational state, such as personal needs, attitudes, family problems, health, interests, and other people. In the school setting, however, the teacher should be concerned about the two qualities that give outward meaning to motivation—the direction and the strength of effort. As stated by Cook (1980):

Motivation itself is intangible, little more than a concept that we use to explain a force within people. More precisely, it is a ubiquitous term used to make inferences about the direction and strength of human behavior. In work organizations (including schools), motivation is said to be reflected in what a person does and the manner in which it is done. (p. 62)

The strength or level of effort exerted by a person is most simply thought of as how hard a person tries. A high level of effort typically is described by adjectives such as "enthusiastic, persevering, committed, conscientious, and hard working" (Cook and Cook, 1981). The direction of effort involves making choices about where to channel (or direct) one's behavior. In tasks that allow some personal discretion about what to do and when to do it, personal motivation often underlies the selection of tasks actually performed. One teacher aide or volunteer may devote considerable time to playing games with the children. Another may prepare and assemble materials for instructional use. Another may volunteer to collect fees and keep records. Yet another may enjoy gathering children around the piano to sing songs. Different people, each with a unique set of interests and ways of promoting their own feelings of personal satisfaction, are motivated to engage in different activities.

Forces within the environment

We have generally explained the concept *environment* as conditions outside the person or as factors that are not part of personal abilities or motivation. In a teaching situation involving using paraprofessionals, however, it is helpful to differentiate *environment* into three factors or qualities. One set of factors (forces) can be thought of as including such elements as the children (their ages, handicaps, personalities, and skills), the physical facilities of the school, the resources available (both materials and funds for special events such as field trips and

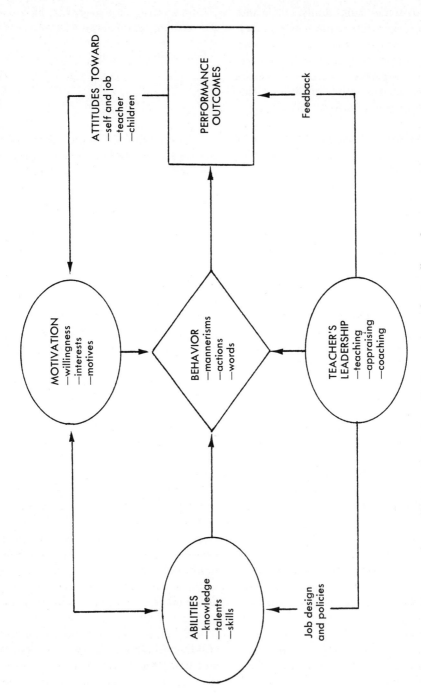

FIG. 10-1. Key factors affecting a paraprofessional's performance.

cooking experiences), and the weather. These are forces in the school. Another set of factors are forces in the paraprofessional's life away from the school, such as family income, personal relationships, and quality of physical and emotional life. These personal environmental forces may also influence work behavior in the school. The third factor is the teacher.

Conditions in the paraprofessional's life away from school are largely beyond the control of the teacher. The teacher can, however, partially control the school conditions. If the school is relatively large, well established, and must meet the needs of children with diverse backgrounds, however, the teacher may find these conditions are also largely uncontrollable. This leaves the teacher's behavior as the major controllable factor that can be used to guide and influence the paraprofessional's behavior.

Fig. 10-1 integrates these key determinants of paraprofessional performance into an interacting network. To achieve the performance desired of paraprofessionals, teachers play critical roles in working with them. These roles include selective recruiting, determining special abilities, helping to develop the potential of others, stimulating effort by clarifying task expectations, providing some variety of challenges, and offering constructive and reinforcing feedback. When considered from this perspective, the teacher truly has a major leadership responsibility (Shank and McElroy, 1970).

PREPARING TO WORK WITH PARAPROFESSIONALS

The remainder of this chapter explores the avenues for successfully working with paraprofessionals through the planning, organization, and leadership skills of the supervising teacher. Before the teacher aide or volunteer can begin to offer a major contribution to the classroom, several essential steps should be taken by the teacher. These include the following:

1. Developing clear and appropriate job descriptions

2. Recruiting selectively to find people with needed job qualities
3. Becoming involved in a thorough orientation program and clearly defining the teacher's responsibilities to teacher aides and volunteers
4. Attempting continually to discover and match classroom responsibilities with the special skills, talents, and interests of paraprofessionals, and to provide evaluative feedback (Karnes and Lee, 1978)

Designing and defining jobs

Designing and defining jobs is the starting point for effectively using paraprofessionals. There are two primary reasons why job design is the appropriate point of departure. First, careful consideration of job design elements provides the criteria for recruiting and selecting paraprofessionals, especially paid teacher aides. Second, everyone works more effectively if they know what they are supposed to do and how and when they are supposed to do the job. Job design thus frames the expectations that are so important to job functioning and role relationships. Because this responsibility falls on teachers, it clarifies in their minds the purposes, tasks, and conditions in which paraprofessionals are to be part of the classroom team. Similarly, a clearly defined set of tasks, responsibilities, and relationships establishes for paraprofessionals the framework within which they are expected to work.

Job design refers to specifying the content and relationships of any job, be it the job of teacher aide, volunteer, teacher, principal, or director. Properly conceived, job design considers both the job holder as a person and the performance contributions expected on behalf of the organization (or classroom). A simple way of thinking about job design characteristics is to borrow concepts from a classical study of group dynamics in which Homans (1950) conceived of any work group (such as teacher, paraprofessionals, or pupils) as a social system. Homans identified three features common to any small work group: activities, interactions, and sentiments. With slight modification, the following are the basics for defining essential job design elements in schools:

1. Activities or tasks. Defines the content of what a job holder is to do. What is the scope or breadth of tasks? To what degree are they to be standardized and routinized instead of creative? How often are they to be performed? What results are expected? How are they to be recognized (by both the paraprofessional and the teacher)?

2. Interactions or role relationships. Defines with whom the job holder is expected to interact, how often (or under what conditions) this is to happen, and the quality of that relationship. What relationship is the paraprofessional to have with the children? With other adults—staff members and parents? What are the paraprofessional's responsibilities and limits of authority relative to the teacher? How much autonomy or freedom (self-initiative) is given the paraprofessional for certain types of tasks? To what extent is teamwork instead of individual action expected?

3. Sentiments or values and attitudes. Defines the conditions under which work is to be performed and the sources of satisfaction available to the job holder. By calling attention to sentiments, the teacher is forced to anticipate and build on essential elements that affect the quality of the paraprofessional's involvement in the classroom such as: What personal rewards are meaningful to the paraprofessional? How is the paraprofessional expected to view sensitive issues such as discipline methods and toilet habits? What values and attitudes held by the paraprofessional will contribute best to the school's objectives and be compatible with those of the teacher?

Developing job task descriptions. It is useful if job specifics relating to job design elements can be expressed in writing. This job description typically conveys more than a trite list of "responsible for" statements. As previously suggested, a written job description provides both the criteria for screening candidates (in the case of teacher aides) and a picture of the job for the candidate. For a starting point in creating a useful statement of job task design, the teacher should think about the ways in which a teacher aide or a volunteer can be useful. One of the easiest ways to develop such a list of task possibilities is to jot down ideas as they occur during the school day. Some of the ways paraprofessionals could be useful might include the following:

1. Preparing the room, including bulletin boards, materials needed for special projects, and daily supplies
2. Greeting the children and assisting with all routines
3. Supervising activities in the classroom and on the playground
4. Nurturing appropriate behavior, including dealing with misbehaviors acceptably and effectively
5. Teaching specific lessons planned and directed by the teacher
6. Preparing, cataloging, and filing educational games and lesson materials
7. Setting up projectors and other media equipment
8. Showing films, slides, and special materials
9. Contacting parents to set up conferences
10. Helping with end of the day routines, including clean up

Once the teacher has identified desirable tasks, he or she should record them to clarify the following: who is to conduct the activity, how often it is to be performed, the manner in which it is to be performed (if standardization or consistency is desired), and how all concerned can recognize successful performance.

Visualizing role relationships. After the teacher has defined activity areas, he or she should think carefully about the role visualized for the paraprofessional. Will the paraprofessional be a creative, warm contributor to the children's learning, or merely the person behind the scenes who prepares materials? Will he or she be encouraged to suggest activities, or be relegated to doing only what the teacher has planned?

The answers to such role relationship questions reflect the philosophy and style of the teacher. Fig. 10-2 depicts the extreme views of interaction that teachers have of themselves in relation to support personnel. A teacher who wants to be the boss and run a tight classroom ought to be aware of this philosophy. Such a situation will definitely restrict the range of

freedom and autonomy given to paraprofessionals (Litman, 1971).

It is helpful if the teacher thinks carefully about his or her role relationship philosophy before completing job descriptions and procedures for paraprofessionals. Whether or not it is recognized and clearly defined, the basic feeling (or sentiment) for what is appropriate and right will determine what the teacher will do in working with support people.

If the teacher discovers that the role assigned to and accepted by the teacher aide reflects a subtle feeling that the teacher aide cannot actually teach carefully planned and supervised lessons, the teacher should experiment. He or

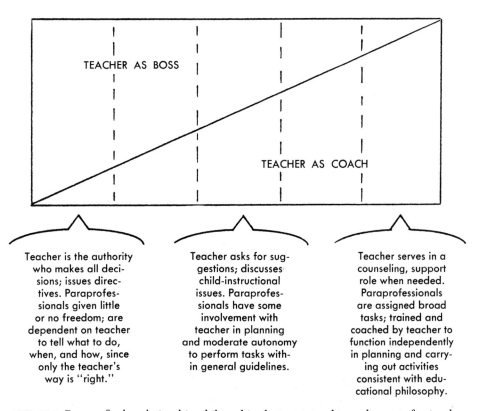

| Teacher is the authority who makes all decisions; issues directives. Paraprofessionals given little or no freedom; are dependent on teacher to tell what to do, when, and how, since only the teacher's way is "right." | Teacher asks for suggestions; discusses child-instructional issues. Paraprofessionals have some involvement with teacher in planning and moderate autonomy to perform tasks within general guidelines. | Teacher serves in a counseling, support role when needed. Paraprofessionals are assigned broad tasks; trained and coached by teacher to function independently in planning and carrying out activities consistent with educational philosophy. |

FIG. 10-2. Range of role relationship philosophies between teacher and paraprofessionals.

she can provide explicit directions, demonstrate what is to be done, and then discuss ways to improve the lesson the next time. This may convince the teacher that given helpful supervision the teacher aide can be an effective assistant teacher. Of course it is always the teacher's responsibility to determine what the lesson should include and what the objectives must be. Techniques of behavior management cannot be left to chance or allowed to be inconsistent. These must be the teacher's responsibility. But with planning, guidance, and supervision, teacher aides can provide excellent teaching. Research (Karnes, 1973) findings indicate that if paraprofessionals are closely supervised, the progress of the children they teach will be comparable to that achieved by an all professional staff.

CHILD INTERACTION GUIDELINES FOR PARAPROFESSIONALS

1. *Create a pleasant atmosphere.* Tense children cannot become effectively involved. Help them feel comfortable by being warm and enthusiastic. If you relax and enjoy yourself, the children will feel this and follow your example.
2. *Your voice is your assistant.* A soft, confident voice elicits a child's attention more quickly than a high or loud one. First gaining eye contact with a child and then speaking directly and softly to him or her will be more effective than shouting across the room.
3. *Be positive.* Instead of saying "Don't spill your milk," it is better to say "Hold your glass with two hands." "Good builders put their tools away carefully" is a better statement than "Don't throw your tools."
4. *Labels are for jelly jars, not for children.* Labels and phrases such as "naughty boy" or "bad girl" make children feel ashamed and unworthy. Children with these feelings cannot learn.
5. *Keep competition out of the classroom.* Nothing is to be gained from fostering competition among young children. Discourage children when they say "I can draw better than Susie" by saying "Each can draw in his or her own special way."
6. *Choices are for choosing.* When it is time to clean up, do not ask the children if they want to clean up. Instead say "It is time to clean up now." If you do not intend to accept no for an answer, do not give them a choice. Give them a choice only when you really want them to choose.
7. *Sharing is not simple.* Preschool-aged children are just learning to share. If they are playing with something, in their minds the toy belongs to them at that moment. Children should be encouraged to ask if they can have a turn and to tell others when they are through playing with something.
8. *Keep your eyes on the children.* Children must be within the visual range of supervising adults at all times. They need and deserve alert supervision, which is not possible when the responsible adult is engaged in adult conversation. If too many children are entering any one play area, then some must be redirected to other areas.
9. *Do not dominate children's activities.* Children should be allowed to use their active imaginations as they experiment with ideas and materials. Unless you are teaching a specific lesson, stay in the background with supportive but not suppressive comments.
10. *Prevention is perfect.* Be alert so you can redirect behavior that can become a problem. Remember that children should not be allowed to hurt themselves or others.

Translating sentiments (values and attitudes) into policy guidelines. Few dedicated teachers would work without some form of lesson plan or curriculum guide. Similarly, the teacher plans in advance the essential performance tasks expected of paraprofessionals and clarifies intended relationships. This enables planned rather than reactive use of these potentially valuable people. For optimum effectiveness, however, the teacher should also plan for and codify the affective behavior expected of paraprofessionals. This means in part explaining (in writing when possible) the ways in which teacher aides and volunteers are to behave to be consistent with the philosophy and educational aims of the teacher and the school.

The most useful way of expressing such sentiments are to provide guidelines for behavior. The boxed material on p. 314 illustrates several specific guidelines that were developed by one preschool director to emphasize the desired behaviors for volunteers to use when interacting with the children. A handout of these (and other) guidelines was given to each volunteer and explained as part of the orientation process. They subsequently served as criteria the teachers could use to discuss successes and problems with the volunteers. By periodically calling attention to specific guidelines, the teachers were able to guide most volunteers to adopt behaviors fairly consistent with the expected patterns.

As suggested by the guidelines in the box, properly codified policies of role behavior state the way or tone of doing the job and *what* is to be done. They can also indicate *when* a particular behavior is considered appropriate. The volunteer who is supervising outdoor play in the vicinity of the sandbox is thus not caught in the dilemma of wondering "What do I do now?" when he or she sees Tony throwing sand.

Because they serve as a frame of reference for feedback, policy guidelines not only help in redirecting a paraprofessional's behavior (when necessary), but they also stimulate job satisfaction. The paraprofessional knows when he or she has done a good job or has handled a difficult situation successfully and consistently with the school's standards. Guidelines also permit teachers to reinforce appropriate behavior. To the extent they allow the paraprofessional to make discretionary choices, the guidelines can help him or her feel more "professional" about being involved in the learning process.

RECRUITING PARAPROFESSIONAL SERVICES

When recruiting paraprofessional services, the teacher should keep in mind the necessary qualities of a successful paraprofessional. Agencies who use volunteers regularly are finding that an increasing number of them are generally mature and highly trained. It is common to find a certified teacher employed as a classroom aide. Most volunteers today are middle-aged, although retirees increasingly are being recognized as valuable assets to the classroom. They are usually devoted to their work and enjoy sharing their vast knowledge and skills gained from years of experience. Volunteer expenses are even tax deductible for some senior citizens. At the other end of the age-experience spectrum are students from elementary school through college who continue to offer their enthusiasm and desire to learn while working with young children (Karnes and Lee, 1978).

Coordinating recruitment efforts

The first step in recruiting and organizing paraprofessional services might be to select a volunteer coordinator. Often a mother will eagerly take such a responsibility. It is helpful to have a coordinator who has previously been an enthusiastic volunteer. The enthusiasm will be most useful in the coordinator's recruiting efforts. The coordinator will also need to have organizational skills and a positive way of working with others (Carter and Dapper, 1974).

SOME SERVICES COMMONLY PROVIDED BY VOLUNTEER WORKERS

Services requiring minimal skills or training:
1. Assisting in decorating rooms
2. Distributing supplies and snacks
3. Helping with clothing and toileting
4. Preparing materials for instructional units
5. Supervising outdoor play
6. Arranging and helping with field trips

Services requiring some skills or training:
1. Typing newsletters, forms, and parent notices
2. Collecting and accounting for pupil fees
3. Instructing in special arts or crafts units
4. Organizing and supervising a classroom library
5. Assisting in health and competency screening programs
6. Interpreting for non-English-speaking parents
7. Making costumes, capes, or other sewn items
8. Leading or accompanying music units

This person, if not the teacher, works with the teacher in making a list of classroom jobs to be done and in determining the time of day service is needed. The coordinator is then in a position to search for individuals who can fill the needs outlined in the job task description. The boxed material shown above lists classroom jobs typically found in preschool or early childhood classrooms.

Recruitment techniques

The volunteer coordinator might begin by telephoning parents of children in the class, members of the Parent-Teacher Organization, and college instructors in the area. Inviting inter-ested individuals to a coffee hour when class-room needs are presented and sign-up contracts are available may speed up the recruitment process. Holding the meeting in the classroom will make job explanations simple and will help generate necessary enthusiasm. If the teacher is not the coordinator, he or she is spared the uncomfortable feelings of asking for help (Brock, 1976).

Personal appearances at gatherings of interested service clubs, senior citizen groups, the Parent-Teacher Organization, new members in the community, college and high school classrooms, and youth organizations can be an effective recruitment technique. The volunteer coordinator should be able to explain clearly what is needed and to answer questions. A coordinator who has been volunteering for some time is often more able to answer questions and to generate enthusiasm. It also helps to have on hand brochures or flyers with illustrated samples of job responsibilities, places and times of volunteering, and the name and telephone number of the contact person. The same flyers can be distributed in the local library, medical offices, and churches. At all times, volunteer coordinators should be prepared to sign up individuals who indicate interest. Fig. 10-3 offers a sample of one type of recruitment contract.

One effective means of reaching a number of individuals who might be interested in volunteering is to include an eye-catching recruitment letter in the report cards of elementary school children and possibly in report cards of older children. The letter should contain a checklist of skills, interests, and talents that can be returned when completed to the teacher by the child. The same letter and checklist can be sent to college students, high school students, and community clubs. In some communities a newspaper advertisement is useful. Fig. 10-4 is an example of a letter and checklist that has been used effectively.

VOLUNTEER CONTRACT

WHEREAS I believe in the value of nurturing and educating young children, and care about their well-being, and

WHEREAS I seek to contribute my personal talents and energies on behalf of helping the teachers and children of the Early Childhood Center, in exchange for the joys of sharing a child's happiness,

THEREFORE, I willingly enter into this agreement to volunteer my personal services to the Early Childhood Center on the following days _____ _____ and times _____,

commencing on the _____ day of _____198___, and continuing until the_____day of _____, 198_____.

THIS AGREEMENT entered into at _____ in the state of _____ between

_____   _____
Volunteer   Date

Who resides at:

_____   _____
                                            Phone
_____

and

_____   _____
Volunteer Coordinator   Date

FIG. 10-3. A volunteer recruitment contract.

Dear Friends:

This letter is sent to you because I believe that you join me in realizing
that children are a most important resource. As a teacher of young children
(ages 3 to 5), I feel a special responsibility to recognize and provide for
individual needs. The more I learn about child growth and development, the
more convinced I become of the need to individualize instruction as much as
possible as soon as possible.

Many of the young children in your child's classroom do need individualized
attention. You have many and varied experiences that you could use to help
our children here at school. We need volunteer teacher aides to help the
children directly and/or to assist the teacher in providing more individual
attention.

A list of possible volunteer responsibilities is attached. Please check
those duties that you would be interested in doing or add any that have not
been included. We invite you to a brief meeting on   or
          to explain the volunteer program in detail. Please
check the date that is most convenient for you and return the checklist to
school by your child.

                              Yours truly,

Name _____   Address _____   Phone _____

I would like to:

[ ] Assist in the classroom   [ ] Other:
[ ] Help on the playground
[ ] Work with an individual child
[ ] Work with small groups of children
[ ] Help with clerical chores
[ ] Prepare instructional materials
[ ] Share my special talent:
[ ] Assist with field trips
[ ] Substitute for regular volunteer
[ ] Babysit for another volunteer

I prefer to help: [ ] At school   [ ] At home

Day(s) I can help: [ ] M.   [ ] Tu.   [ ] W.   [ ] Th.   [ ] F.

Hours I can help: _____ _____ _____ _____ _____

Volunteer meeting I prefer to attend:

[ ]_____   [ ]_____
        (Day and time)   (Day and time)

FIG. 10-4. Volunteer solicitation letter and checklist.

LEARNING THROUGH ORIENTATION IS MUTUAL

Any new teacher aide or volunteer must be socialized into the norms and practices of the teacher and the school. Similarly, the expectations and talents of paraprofessionals can never be comprehensively defined during the recruiting or screening stages. These emerge out of discussion and behavior once in the classroom. What inevitably happens in the early days of the working relationship is the creation of a psychological contract (Schein, 1965). In framing the psychological contract the paraprofessional typically considers the following: "What am I going to get out of my work in this classroom? How can I make use of my talents and interests so that I am doing something worthwhile and will be reasonably satisfied? How can my involvement support the attainment of my personal goals and needs, including learning or growth aspirations?"

The classroom teacher's considerations are more along the following lines: "How can I effectively use this person to complement my own skills, talents, and interests? How can I get him or her to accept my philosophies, policies, and goals? What can I do to motivate and develop in this person the abilities and commitments that will help me and the school realize our educational goals?" The terms and conditions of the contract must be favorable to both.

The socialization process of building an effective working relationship is genuinely a mutual responsibility. Both people have to learn about each other. In the process of communicating (verbally, in writing, and through behaviors), they begin to expand their clarification of mutual role relationships. At its very essence a role is a set of expectations about what is appropriately to be done and what is to be avoided. For paraprofessionals, the role can either be reasonably well defined and stimulating or ambiguous, conflicting, and stifling with noxious jobs and oppressive supervision (see Gattmann

and Henricks, 1973, for a review of changes in roles).

Communication of expectations

Both the teacher and the paraprofessional must communicate their expectations. It is an unusual paraprofessional who does not approach the first day of his or her assignment with some feelings of apprehension. In the classroom life of the teacher aide or volunteer, the relationship with the teacher can make the experience rich and fulfilling or miserable and tedious. To help launch the relationship, a planned orientation meeting reaps greater rewards than the cost of the time invested.

If only one teacher and one teacher aide are involved, the orientation may take place in a pleasant corner of the classroom, or it can take place at a restaurant during a planned lunch hour. In any event, the number of people involved will influence where the meeting takes place and how it is conducted. But the number of people involved should not influence what is discussed.

For a general plan, it is a good idea for the teacher to begin with an overview explanation of his or her philosophy and that of the school. The teacher can then lead into a description of the purposes of the school and the plans to be followed in achieving those purposes. Finally, the teacher must describe procedures and role expectations. Here films, slides, or videotapes can be useful. Later the teacher should provide time for discussion and answering questions.

Stressing the importance of communicating common goals, Boomer (1980) discusses specific key items to be considered in the orientation of paraprofessionals. These include design of classroom space, operation of instructional and office equipment, emergency procedures, and the schedule of activities including the paraprofessionals' hourly responsibilities. One could add to this list the importance of professional conduct. The paraprofessionals who are expected to

WORKING AS A PARAPROFESSIONAL IN AN EARLY CHILDHOOD SPECIAL EDUCATION CLASSROOM

At least one of the paraprofessionals in this classroom would be paid and expected to conform to professional standards. Most paraprofessionals would be extensions of the teacher helping to provide additional individualized instruction. Many would be invited to participate in conferences, would learn to chart children's progress, and would be expected to model unique techniques of instruction. Some may be assigned to handle extra care needs of more severely handicapped children.

behave as professionals will usually do so. This includes being prompt, appropriately dressed, and respectful of all aspects of confidentiality regarding children's characteristics and behaviors.

Discovery and use of special skills and talents

To make the orientation truly an opportunity for two-way communication, the resourceful teacher should encourage new paraprofessionals to reveal their special interests, skills, and talents. Asking about previous work experience is important. Parenting skills and homemaking skills, however, are equally important in preschools and day-care centers. Very few skills cannot be adapted to useful and interesting class-

Name _____

     Mom   *Dad*   WOULD YOU LIKE TO:

1. [ ] [ ] Read a story to some of the children?

2. [ ] [ ] Teach a song or some other musical activity?

3. [ ] [ ] Help children create something in art?

4. [ ] [ ] Bring the family pet to visit school?

5. [ ] [ ] Help set up or supervise a field trip?

6. [ ] [ ] Make a book of a child's story?

7. [ ] [ ] Work puzzles or play games?

8. [ ] [ ] Share your hobby with the class? Hobby

9. [ ] [ ] Show children how to use simple carpenter tools?

10. [ ] [ ] Bring a guitar (or other instrument) and demonstrate?

11. [ ] [ ] Help cut out and paste pictures?

12. [ ] [ ] Teach the children something about your occupation?

13. [ ] [ ] Conduct a simple science experiment?

14. [ ] [ ] Wear a costume from another country and tell about it?

15. [ ] [ ] Bring necessary materials and plant some seeds?

16. [ ] [ ] Demonstrate rug weaving, leather tooling, or other crafts?

17. [ ] [ ] Make jam or churn butter?

18. [ ] [ ] Fix a bulletin board?

19. [ ] [ ] Sew dress up and/or doll clothing?

20. [ ] [ ] Construct special toys-equipment?

And if none of these appeal to you, what would you like to do?

FIG. 10-5. Samples from a parent volunteer checklist.

room activities. Everything from sports to nee-
dlework fits in somewhere. Hobbies can be the
source of exciting lessons. Baking and gardening,
as well as sewing and cleaning, can be the basis
for preschool science and math lessons.

One effective method of discovering the special skills and talents of paraprofessionals is to
develop a simple questionnaire that can be filled
out by potential helpers. Many teachers ask
parents to complete the questionnaire to encourage parent involvement. Others use the
questionnaire with hired teacher aides and with
volunteers. The questionnaire in Fig. 10-5 was
designed to incorporate the needs of an early
childhood center while allowing the respondents
some latitude of choice.

Once the special interests, skills, and talents
of the paraprofessional are known, the teacher
may plan to adapt lesson themes to them. A
teacher aide in one class loved to garden. An
outdoor garden provided lessons in many concepts. Children learned about *straight, front,*
and *back* rows. They learned about plants that
grew *taller* and things that were *shorter.* They
discovered the *shortest* stem and the *longest*
vine. That garden was the basis of science lessons and nutrition themes, as well as a source
of beauty and joy.

Another teacher aide was particularly interested in puppets. She made sock puppets for
each child and taught them basic skills. Puppet
shows enlivened nutrition lessons and language
lessons. Puppets sang the alphabet song and
learned to say "please" and "thank you." Puppets helped with everything and the teacher
aide felt proud of her accomplishment.

When the teacher gives special thought and
care to matching classroom responsibilities with
the paraprofessional's skills and talents, everyone benefits. Ideally a teacher aide will be ready
for anything, and many of them are. But even
when paraprofessionals are willing to do "anything and everything," relationships and performances are better when interests are allowed
to blossom.

WORKING AS A PARAPROFESSIONAL IN A BEHAVIORISTICALLY ORIENTED PROGRAM

In a highly structured behavioristic program,
paraprofessionals might be expected to become
proficient in dispensing both concrete and verbal reinforcement. Some would be expected to
participate in intensive preservice training designed to teach specific instructional strategies
that are to be followed in detail. These would
include behavioral management techniques
and how to use academically oriented procedures.

Most teacher aides are expected to take care
of many routine matters. Taking attendance,
counting milk money or lunch money, and supervising the bathroom are often taken for
granted. Getting lesson materials ready and
cleaning up are duties for many teacher aides.
But they can do much more, given encouragement and opportunity. A teacher aide who plays
the piano may also find pleasure in choosing
songs and musical stories. One who sews will
enjoy introducing simple sewing activities. Outdoor games may be the sports-minded paraprofessional's special delight. If the teacher tells the
paraprofessional that his or her talents and interests are respected and used, the teacher can
generate creative and resourceful suggestions.

DEFINING THE TEACHER'S RESPONSIBILITIES TO TEACHER AIDES OR VOLUNTEERS

This section focuses on defining the teacher's
responsibilities to teacher aides or volunteers.
We have implied, if not stressed, so far the use
of thoughtful and kindly attitudes by the teacher
toward the teacher aide or volunteer. A few of
the commonly accepted responsibilities for
leadership and guidance are summarized in the

SOME RESPONSIBILITIES OF TEACHERS TO PARAPROFESSIONALS

1. To exert active leadership and guidance to build a team of coordinated helpers.
2. To create an atmosphere in which paraprofessionals feel accepted and motivated to perform effectively.
3. To provide ample structure and direction so paraprofessionals know what is expected of them.
4. To hold an orientation session with new paraprofessionals to discuss program goals, procedures, policies, and what to expect of children with special needs.
5. To plan work in advance of the workday, and to build variety into the tasks paraprofessionals are assigned to perform.
6. To provide adequate information so that paraprofessionals can carry out their tasks, and to provide feedback so they know that you know how they are performing.
7. To have on hand the resources paraprofessionals will need to carry out assigned tasks; to show them where to find materials, how to set up an activity, and how to operate any special equipment. To make known any restrictions or special needs necessary to accommodate particular children.
8. To assign tasks within the range of competency of a paraprofessional while providing increased responsibility and autonomy as performance indicates increased competence.
9. To provide opportunities for regularly scheduled meetings between the teacher and the paraprofessional. Such meetings will allow for adequate planning and avoid waiting for a crisis to force communication. Impromptu meetings should not become substitutes for regularly scheduled meetings.

---

boxed material shown above. This genuine caring must not, however, interfere with the teacher's awareness of his or her role as the person on whom ultimate responsibility rests. What is done in and out of the classroom and the way in which it is done are undeniably the teacher's responsibilities. Termination and replacement may be the best solution for the teacher aide who does not share an understanding of this fact. A tug of war for the affections of the children or their parents is destructive and dysfunctional. Differing philosophies of what is "best" for children leads to subtle and disruptive experiences.

Just as the teacher avoids embarrassing or criticizing the teacher aide or volunteer in front of parents and other adults, so must the paraprofessional avoid undermining the teacher. The teacher's responsibility is to make this very clear from the beginning. The teacher must be alert to recognize any overt or covert attempts to interfere with behavior management or teaching methods. Such interference should be dealt with immediately. If free and open discussion of the importance of consistent attitudes and management of children is established in the beginning, future problems will be minimized.

We have aimed most of the suggestions thus far at preparing for the entry of volunteers and teacher aides into the classroom. These activities are essentially of a managerial planning nature: defining essential tasks, developing policy guidelines for paraprofessional conduct, recruiting volunteers, orienting teacher aides and volunteers into the philosophy and ways of the school, while also learning of special talents and interests. What follows is heavily focused on actions the teacher can take to motivate and stretch the abilities of teacher aides and volunteers. These suggestions place the classroom teacher of young handicapped children in a leadership role, guiding, coaching, encouraging, and rewarding the efforts and developing skills of resourceful support personnel. As a starting point, it is useful to think of the teacher as a role model for paraprofessionals (Litman, 1971).

Being an appropriate role model

Teachers must be appropriate role models. A teacher who says one thing and behaves in a different way is inexcusable. What teachers *do* speaks louder than what they *say*. Advising someone to avoid spanking, yelling and fault finding will not achieve the desired results unless the teacher is consistent in avoiding these negative behaviors when interacting with children. What the teacher does will influence the teacher aide's behavior. If a quiet manner is recommended by the teacher, then a quiet voice must be used by the teacher—at least most of the time.

Often it is useful for the teacher to tell the paraprofessional what will be demonstrated, and to pinpoint what is to be observed. The teacher should explain what will be done and why it will be done. Sometimes a particular procedure should be written and available for reference. This is important for new lessons or activities.

After the teacher completes a specific demonstration, the teacher aide will want to practice. Usually (at least at first) the teacher should not observe this practice session. But it is helpful for the teacher to suggest that an observation will be made when the teacher aide feels ready. Allow the aide to take the initiative by extending an invitation such as "Tomorrow when you feel ready for me to watch you, let me know."

Part of a teacher's responsibilities as a role model are to build up, not undermine, the desire and productive energies of paraprofessionals. Just as the teacher's responsibilities

---

> ### WORKING AS A PARAPROFESSIONAL IN A PIAGETIAN CLASSROOM
>
> Paraprofessionals in a Piagetian classroom would most likely function as part of a team. They would participate in small groups and with individual children. A continuous inservice training program would help them understand Piagetian theory and its translation into lesson planning. Team members would be expected to become astute observers and promoters of children's natural curiosity.

---

toward children are to help them to become more fully functioning independently rather than dependently, the same applies to paraprofessionals. But development of the independent skills and motivation of paraprofessionals does not occur through abandonment. A disorganized teacher whose actions reveal he or she has given little thought to how paraprofessionals are to serve confuses and discourages those who seek to help. Perhaps the best way of looking at effective ways in which a teacher can help to develop and encourage a teacher aide or a volunteer is through the eyes of those who work in paraprofessional roles. The boxed material on p. 325 presents just such a perspective in a sensitive but strongly worded message from a practicing teacher aide to teachers generally.

Making sufficient planning time available

The teacher aide who provided the message for the boxed material on p. 325 wrote about the implications of the teacher's planning (or failure to plan) on the motivation of aides. Another facet of paraprofessional motivation and effectiveness comes from the teacher and the teacher aide (or the volunteer) spending some time together to plan. Many federally funded programs in the 1960's and 1970's allowed for

ADVICE FROM A PRESCHOOL AIDE TO TEACHERS

NOTE: The comments that follow were written by an experienced teacher aide. She has worked with a number of different teachers, and has very strong feelings about teacher actions that made her work effective and rewarding, and those that interfered with her own effectiveness.

Treating your aides as if they have no common sense will get you little help. Most aides are more intelligent than they are given credit for. Don't give them only menial chores, but also things that are more gratifying. Give them air to breathe and expand themselves and they will be more help to you as the teacher than you can imagine. One time I worked for a teacher just 1 day a week. Often when I came she said, "Oh! Are you here today? I didn't know you came this week." Really made me feel welcome and useful. Sometimes she just said, "I don't have anything for you to do today. Go see if any of the other teachers have something for you to do." So, planning ahead is important. Teachers complain of "having too much to do": and then they don't make good use of the aide's time because they didn't plan.

Treat your aide as an intelligent person. Aides can do much more than run dittos and wash dirty faces. If you tell them what to do and why and then show them how, they can be really good teachers. Don't expect them to plan the lessons, but with a little help, they can teach little children very effectively. Answer all questions as soon as possible, and answer them as you would any other adult. Don't "talk down" to them. Your college degree doesn't give you the right to belittle their ability to understand. Tell why you do something, and if they don't understand the first time, tell them again in another way. Show them how to do something the right way yourself. Don't just tell them and leave.

Compliment your aide sometimes, but not too much. Too much flattery is insulting. But a genuine "I like the way you showed Susie how to button her coat" helps to make it all worthwhile.

Let your aides learn from their mistakes. Don't "catch them" every time. Just look the other way for a while. Give them a chance to change by themselves. But if they are really doing something wrong, or they are stuck in some way, suggest, "Sometimes it helps to do it this way." And then show them or tell them again.

Never embarrass them in front of the children or parents, or anybody for that matter. If you must correct them, wait until you can do it when you are alone. Smart teachers know how to make suggestions look and sound like compliments. "You really are teaching Tommy how to wash his hands. Do you think he is ready to learn to use the brush?" is a lot better than "Don't you remember, I told you that you should teach the children to brush their fingernails when they wash their hands."

Listen to your aides' comments. Let them have the satisfaction of suggesting things to you sometimes. An occasional "Oh, I'm so glad you suggested that" is better than a hundred insincere things. Ask your aides' opinions sometimes, and then listen.

Do remember, you are the teacher. You are responsible. You are in charge. Aides need to know "their teacher" knows what to do. They need to respect all that education you've had. Give them a chance.

by Robbie Crane
Alton, Illinois

VIGNETTE 10-1: DIALOGUE OF A TEACHER-PARAPROFESSIONAL PLANNING SESSION

THE SCENE: It is after school. The children have gone home. Ms. McLynn and her teacher aide, Ms. Robbie, are talking about a lesson Ms. Robbie just completed.

Ms. Robbie: We were doing the lesson from the kit that you had in the lesson plan. The directions said that we should sit in a circle. Then, each child was supposed to roll the ball to a child of his or her choice and say "I'm rolling the ball to ____" and name the child. But Danny and Terry couldn't do it at all.

Ms. McLynn: Did the others understand?

Ms. Robbie: Most of them did. Some just said, "to Susie," but Danny just threw the ball and Terry wouldn't even do that.

Ms. McLynn: What do you think would have made the lesson better?

Ms. Robbie: I'm not sure what the point of that lesson is. It didn't give a reason for doing it, so I wasn't sure what to emphasize.

Ms. McLynn: Just enjoying an activity is important. Did they seem to like it?

Ms. Robbie: Terry and Danny just seemed confused by the whole thing. When I tried to make them say the whole sentence Danny just got mad and wouldn't do anything. Terry started to cry.

Ms. McLynn: That really wasn't much fun for you either. And lessons are usually enjoyed by all when you teach the children. For now, let's just expect that Danny and Terry are learning by being there and watching the others and hearing them. Probably both of them will learn more than we think in that way. Tomorrow, try the lesson again with that in mind. When it is Danny's turn, ask him "To whom will you roll the ball?" Do this just before you give him the ball. Gesture with a questioning look and a shrug of your shoulders. Talk to him, too, of course. Expect him to point to a child, and say something. Then you say, "to Jimmy" as a model for him, or name whomever he points to. Again, just before you give him the ball, look expectant, and model "to Jimmy" for him again if necessary. Accept any attempt to say anything, now. Later, you can require a better approximation of the speech. Do the same thing for Terry.

Ms. Robbie: What if another child rolls the ball to one of them? Should I take it away from them, and make them listen to me first?

Ms. McLynn: No, but if you have one on each side of you, you could put your hand on the ball while you talk to them. Keep it just as spontaneous and natural as you can. But do contrive it so that they have to say some part of it. As soon as they can do that much, you can make what they say longer—perhaps "rolling to Susie." Part of what they must develop is auditory memory span. Right now, a few sounds are all they can remember. As you play in this way, that skill will grow rapidly.

Ms. Robbie: Okay. I'll try it that way tomorrow.

whole days for teachers and teacher aides to plan together each week. Money was available for regular evaluation and planning sessions. Few programs today include this necessity. Conversely, time for planning often seems a luxury.

As with everything else, teachers must do what they can. Day-to-day planning usually fits into very small time segments. The time after school, lunch periods, and so-called "breaks" become the scarce moments for planning. These daily time constrictions make it necessary that the teacher do overall planning before the school year begins. Necessary planning before the school year starts includes designing record-keeping systems, choosing basic lesson plans, organizing the classroom, scheduling activities, preparing materials, and assigning responsibilities. The paraprofessional must learn how to use the instructional equipment and what to do in case of various emergencies. The paraprofessional's responsibilities within the daily schedule should be written out. Before and after school rarely provide enough time for such comprehensive planning no matter how dedicated the teacher and the teacher aide may be.

Over time, however, teacher aides and even volunteers should be encouraged to plan some of the specific lessons. The teacher identifies the goals and objectives, but the "equivalent practice" (Chapter 4) can be suggested by paraprofessionals. For example, one teacher aide raised tropical fish. With her help, the children planned an aquarium. They learned colors as they chose the stones for the bottom. They discovered water temperature as they planned for the fish. Feeding the fish developed measuring skills and a sense of responsibility.

During the months that the aquarium served as an excellent teaching tool, the teacher and the teacher aide discussed many different ways in which it could be used. More than half of the excellent teaching ideas that evolved originated with the teacher aide. The teacher continued to pinpoint specific objectives that could be achieved, but it was uniquely successful because of the teacher aide's knowledge and enthusiasm to take charge of this project.

Planning sessions need not be overly drawn out. At times they focus on preparing for the next day events for only one or two children. An example of an effective brief planning session is revealed in Vignette 10-1. This scene also shows how a teacher can provide effective feedback in a helpful but nonthreatening manner.

Providing constructive feedback

Just as routine planning time boosts effectiveness, so also does regular and constructive feedback from teacher to paraprofessional. The teacher must build in feedback about how the teacher aide or volunteer is doing. Informal feedback should not be the occasion for a great deal of discussion. It should be specific, clearly stated, and timely. The teacher should identify strengths, behaviors, and attitudes to be changed or developed. The more straightforward the evaluation, the more effective it will be.

Avoid focusing on personalities. Focus on the task behaviors and the procedures that are changeable. For example, telling the teacher aide that he or she is disorganized is not helpful. Explaining why the crayons and scissors should be placed within the reach of each child instead of at the end of the table, however, will help him or her to understand precisely how to become more organized and efficient. The teacher should discuss why specific things are important. If necessary he or she should reteach and demonstrate again. It is especially important for the teacher to evaluate and provide suggestions to the teacher aide with no other adults or children present (or within hearing distance). The teacher's intent is to support and develop the teacher aide's skills, not to undermine needed authority.

It is important not to exaggerate the negative effects of whatever the teacher aide is doing wrong. Rather state what is wanted, why it is desirable, and how it is to be achieved.

The teacher should not forget to reward effort and abilities as part of success. Things easy for the teacher may be difficult for an inexperienced teacher aide. The teacher should not expect everything to be learned at once! Time is needed for practice. Recognition by way of "thank yous" for regular role appropriate behaviors are as important as special rewards for exceptional success. But such spontaneous or informal feedback opportunities do not eliminate the need for periodic formal evaluation of paraprofessional behaviors, especially for teacher aides.

EVALUATING PARAPROFESSIONAL SERVICES

Evaluating paraprofessional services is a critical step in developing improved and successful programs for young children. Informal daily feedback helps create an atmosphere in which the paraprofessional feels secure, worthy, appreciated, and professional. But more formal periodic evaluations are helpful for persons whose service is expected to be ongoing. Formal evaluations not only help personnel development, but also can strengthen program development.

Typically the first evaluation is not too long after initial employment (1 month) to focus on and correct misunderstandings and confused expectations. Such a clarification serves the interests of both parties because an effective evaluation acknowledges that the teacher as well as the paraprofessional can learn from the experience. The time between subsequent evaluations is lengthened to 3 or 4 months. For an experienced teacher aide, once a year may be adequate.

Using self-evaluations

One formal technique is to allow paraprofessionals the opportunity to evaluate their own

contributions and feelings. If the paraprofessional feels comfortable in sharing this self-evaluation with the supervising teacher, chances for growth and development can be enhanced. Perceptions of self-performance are tested against the teacher's observations and expectations. The teacher has the opportunity to provide constructive feedback, to offer encouragement, and to coach. The self-evaluation process may be open ended, or it may be guided by a checklist such as the one illustrated in Fig. 10-6.

As noted in the directions in Figure 10-6, using recent critical incidents is typically a practical technique for clarifying role behaviors and learning. By contrasting a successful event with a not so successful one, a problem-solving approach can emphasize conditions necessary for future success rather than belabor criticism of a past problem. When a teacher aide or volunteer has not been doing something felt necessary (such as failing to listen to children), the teacher can probe the consequences of such behavior. The teacher should be prepared to provide an example of when such a failure or neglect led to

Check the appropriate box for each question as it applies to you. Note
briefly two examples (contrasting if possible) of recent experiences for
each question.

HOW OFTEN DO I . . .	Usually	Some-times	Seldom
1. Follow directions of the classroom teacher?	[ ]	[ ]	[ ]
2. Observe closely techniques used by the teacher and put them into practice when working with children and groups?	[ ]	[ ]	[ ]
3. Offer my services to the teacher when there is an apparent need for help?	[ ]	[ ]	[ ]
4. Plan for assigned tasks with children rather than wing it on a hit-or-miss basis?	[ ]	[ ]	[ ]
5. Observe closely to realize individual children's likes, dislikes, interests, and limitations?	[ ]	[ ]	[ ]
6. Allow children time to think and act on their own before giving directive help?	[ ]	[ ]	[ ]
7. Find opportunities for giving children choices in daily activities?	[ ]	[ ]	[ ]
8. Really listen to what children have to say?	[ ]	[ ]	[ ]
9. Acknowledge children's successes and appropriate behaviors and minimize failures or inappropriate behaviors?	[ ]	[ ]	[ ]
10. Accept suggestions and criticisms without becoming emotionally upset?	[ ]	[ ]	[ ]

FIG. 10-6. Self-evaluation worksheet for paraprofessionals.

an inappropriate consequence. Then both the teacher and the teacher aide should work toward a plan of action for reducing the frequency of the behavior. Behavior management techniques are applicable to more than just children (Sherman and Bushell, 1975).

Teacher-initiated evaluations of aides

Teacher-initiated evaluations of aides are necessary because most people see their own behaviors in a more positive light than do others. The self-evaluation conference potentially thus must deal with distortions in perceptions between the teacher aide and the teacher. As long as the primary reason for evaluation is personal and team improvement, however, the conflict dangers of differing perceptions are reduced. An evaluation initiated by the teacher overcomes the potential clash between views, especially when the teacher uses a form or checklist. Teacher-initiated evaluation, however, can generate anxiety and defensiveness on the part of the person being evaluated. Success in either case hinges on the manner in which the teacher handles the conference.

It is better for the teacher to focus on specific behaviors or behavioral episodes than to discuss generalities such as "dependability" or "interpersonal relations." To do this effectively, the teacher needs to take the time to describe specific behaviors used by the teacher aide that are helping and hindering performance effectiveness. An easy technique for organizing a face-to-face evaluation conference is for the teacher to list a select few behavioral descriptions under the following three focal areas (adapted from Harrison, 1978):

1. If you would increase or do more often the following things, they would help our performance:

2. If you would decrease or stop doing these things, our performance would be better off:

3. To help maintain good performance, keep doing these things much the same as you have been doing:

The teacher and the teacher aide then discuss each of the behaviors to be increased, decreased, or maintained. Specific incidents are used to interpret and demonstrate why the change (or maintenance) would be helpful. The lists for each category should not be too long. The objective is to identify a few important behaviors that conceivably could be changed with concentrated effort. The teacher encourages commitment to some plan of action for changing, but improvement may mean the teacher has to change also if he or she is part of the cause of the problem.

The key to a meaningful evaluation is not what is written but the discussion of the recorded comments between the teacher and the teacher aide. The conference is the basis for developing objectives or intended targets of change (and behavior maintanance) in the future. In a "management by objectives" fashion, any objectives and action plans agreed on by the teacher and the teacher aide can be briefly written, dated, and signed by both (Ora, 1973). Each subsequent review considers progress toward attaining the previously formulated objectives. Collectively these periodic evaluations are the basis for the year-end evaluation required of teacher aides in most school districts. As a psychological benefit, however, the periodic conferences reduce the chances that the teacher will take the teacher aide for granted and encourages professional-like involvement.

A TECHNIQUE FOR AN AIDE'S EVALUATION OF TEACHER

To (Teacher):_____

From (Aide):_____

Date:_____

1. You could help my performance and our team effort if you would increase or do more often the following things:

2. I could do a better job of helping you if you would decrease or stop doing these things:

3. To help maintain good performance, keep doing these things much the same as you have been doing:

FIG. 10-7. A technique for an aide's evaluation of the teacher.

Evaluation of the teacher by the aide

Teachers who are dedicated to developing an effective use of paraprofessional services in the classroom find it valuable to evaluate themselves as responsible models of instructional excellence and supervisors of paraprofessionals. If the teacher and the paraprofessionals have developed a relationship of trust and professionalism, the teacher can gain much from the paraprofessionals' evaluative feedback. Teachers need to know when their directions are not clear, when they are expecting too much, and when they have been unappreciative or unresponsive. Most teachers do not wish to be negative or ineffective. They are human, however, and do err from time to time. Everyone will benefit if a two-way communication of constructive feedback and positive reinforcement is in effect.

Since the objective of an aide's evaluation of the teacher is to improve their role relationship and team performance, the process needs to be kept simple. Teacher aides need to be given an opportunity to capture their thoughts on paper, however, before any face-to-face meeting. This provides the teacher aide the security of having reflected on and organized thoughts about the quality of their role relationship. A time should be scheduled and the teacher aide should be requested to bring in some written comments or feedback. A most effective way of promoting such preparation is to use a simple three-part variation of the technique mentioned in the previous section. Such an evaluation form is presented in Fig. 10-7.

A special advantage comes from the teacher and the teacher aide both using a variation of the same three "increase, decrease, or continue" role behavior issues. The simplicity of this single-page sheet enables both the teacher and the teacher aide to think in parallel terms—what each of them can do to help the other so they both benefit. The concept of increasing, decreasing, or maintaining certain behaviors is easily understood. Not using scales, scores, or rating points reduces the defensiveness or anxiety of either party. The conference focuses on the three levels, inviting objectives and strategies for dealing with the specific identified behaviors. With mutual evaluations everyone can learn and grow.

RECOGNIZING AND REWARDING TIME AND SERVICE

The importance of daily recognition and praise for time and service cannot be overstressed. Teachers must be careful, however, to be sincere and specific in the comments they make. Each time a teacher aide or a volunteer is told specifically what was helpful, he or she is able to clarify future behavior expectations. Consider the difference between the following two statements: (1) "Ms. Jones, I really appreciated your willingness to help today." (2) "Ms. Jones, I really appreciated your quick response and willingness to help the children clean up the spilled paint. If it had been left on the floor 1 minute longer, two or three children would have walked through it and we would really have had a mess." Whereas the first comment was obviously positive it did not tell the teacher aide exactly what was particularly appreciated. The second comment was not only positive but it conveyed to the teacher aide the importance of quick, preventative action. It also helped the teacher aide to know that the teacher is actually observing and really does feel responsible.

Besides daily recognition, paraprofessionals need and deserve some form of more public, tangible recognition and reward. This is especially true of nonpaid volunteers. Many schools choose to publicly honor volunteers at school assemblies, at Parent-Teacher organization meetings, and at specially planned dinners or coffees. A certificate of recognition is often awarded (Fig. 10-8). It is not necessary for the teacher to purchase commercially made certificates. The certificates can be typed, made by

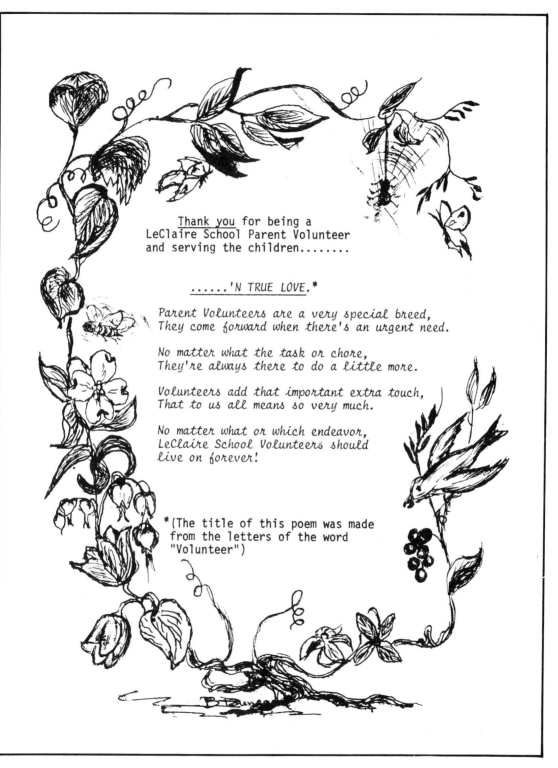

Thank you for being a
LeClaire School Parent Volunteer
and serving the children........

......'N TRUE LOVE.*

Parent Volunteers are a very special breed,
They come forward when there's an urgent need.

No matter what the task or chore,
They're always there to do a little more.

Volunteers add that important extra touch,
That to us all means so very much.

No matter what or which endeavor,
LeClaire School Volunteers should
live on forever!

*(The title of this poem was made
from the letters of the word
"Volunteer")

FIG. 10-8. Example of a parent volunteer "certificate." (Poem by Bettie Duncan, LeClaire School, Edwardsville, Ill.)

teachers, art teachers, or the children themselves.

Names of volunteers and the nature of their service can be listed in the local newspaper or school newsletter. Personal letters from the teacher, principal, or school superintendent are always welcome. One early childhood center hosts a special potluck dinner for the staff members and the volunteers once or twice a year. These are festive occasions that everyone anticipates with pleasure. One elementary school features a "Volunteer of the Week" bulletin board to recognize the contribution of a particular volunteer. Of course permission of the volunteer is obtained first. Another school provides tickets to special performances at the local theater in an effort to say "thank you." The possibilities for volunteer recognition are limited only by imagination and resources.

SUMMARY

Teacher aides and volunteers are potentially valuable resources for extending the teacher's care and development of young children. The extent to which these potentials are realized depends primarily on how the teacher prepares for and develops a working relationship with paraprofessionals. Figure 10-1 presented schematically a way of thinking about the critical components and relationships that affect the outcomes of using paraprofessionals. The Figure focuses attention on the reality that the quality of paraprofessional service depends on *both* the teacher as manager and leader and the teacher aide or volunteer. But the responsibility always totally rests with the teacher, not with the paraprofessional.

To initiate a planned program of using paraprofessionals, it is necessary to design the jobs that assistants and volunteers can do. But job design should not be aimed merely at enabling the teacher to eliminate routine tasks or unpleasant tasks. The teacher should remember that effectiveness also involves the motivation of the person. Since paraprofessionals work more because of a desire to help young children rather than for tangible rewards, the jobs they are expected to do should allow for the growth of their abilities. Feelings of competency and learning reinforce paraprofessionals' motivational desires to work thoughtfully with children and to perform other tasks.

The jobs performed by paraprofessionals typically require interrelationships with either the children or the adult members of the educational team. The teacher should plan the nature of these role relationships so that all participants are behaving appropriately to a common philosophy and a common set of expectations. Guidelines for the ways volunteers and teacher aides are to interact with children should even be formalized in writing.

The following are several advantages to having such job descriptions and policy guidelines in writing and available as handouts: (1) they help in recruiting and selecting paraprofessionals by giving a focused idea of the nature of the work and the working environment; (2) the orientation is focused on those attributes that are important to the teacher and the school; (3) expectations are clarified and made public to minimize future misunderstandings; and (4) they can be a basis for feedback and evaluation about how appropriately the teacher aide or the volunteer is acting in relation to the needs and standards of the teacher.

As a leader, the teacher is a role model for paraprofessionals, especially in helping them to understand how to work with the children. The degree and quality of preparation for using the time and talents of paraprofessionals sets the stage for appropriate behaviors. If the teacher fails to plan how to use a teacher aide's or volunteer's time, paraprofessionals can assume that planning is not a quality necessary for preschools; that their job is basically babysitting; and that if learning should happen to occur, well, then that is also all right.

If the teacher has planned and organized the tasks of paraprofessionals and clarified the ways of working within the classroom, then feedback and evaluation can be a natural part of the experience. Rather than functioning as a punishment or as a "here is what you have been doing wrong" response, frequent feedback and periodic evaluations should be a time for personal development and for strengthening team relationships. Performance evaluation does not have to be a one-way street or something the teacher inflicts on the teacher aide or the volunteer. Quite the contrary, effective teachers will invite teacher aides to evaluate the teacher. After all, the common goal is to discover ways of improving what happens in the classroom and on the playground. If this means the teacher makes some changes in the ways of working with paraprofessionals (for example, being less critical or giving more autonomy), both the teacher and the paraprofessional are probably better off for the change. Similarly teacher aides and volunteers need to be recognized for what they contribute. This extends to formal recognition at year's end and at well-spaced times throughout the year. Teacher recognition of paraprofessionals is a way of saying "Thanks for making my job easier and more successful."

DISCUSSION TOPICS AND ACTIVITIES

1. Role play an interview with a prospective classroom aide. Be alert to questions that help you get to know something about the individual's talents, skills, interests, motives, and biases. Think ahead and be prepared to be explicit about what you will want the teacher aide to do or not to do. Observers may give constructive feedback to the participants by sharing their reactions and what they learned from watching the interaction.
2. Gather or prepare useful techniques for evaluating the success of a paraprofessional program. Refer to Figure 10-7 for suggestions. Check to see that your evaluation elements match the jobs you have designed.
3. Prepare a recruitment letter and an accompanying interest inventory. Discuss with classmates how these can be used effectively. Try your ideas out on public school personnel who are familiar with or merely interested in paraprofessional services.
4. Prepare an agenda for a volunteer orientation meeting. Take turns role playing various stages of the meeting. Discuss how you would make individuals feel welcome, the "musts" you will cover, and the techniques for developing commitments on the part of the participants. Be alert to a tendency to be too technical in your language.

ANNOTATED REFERENCES

Alden, J.W. (Ed.) *Volunteers in education: Future public policy.* Alexandria, Va.: National School Volunteer Program, Inc., 1979.

This book offers considerable practical advice on topics such as volunteer activities, potential participants, program benefits, and cost-effectiveness data. A useful section on the steps needed to plan and establish a successful volunteer program is included. Model programs are examined. Of great value is the annotated bibliography that contains additional examples of model programs.

Brock, H.C. *Parent volunteer programs in early childhood education: A practical approach.* Syracuse, N.Y. Gaylord Bros., Inc., 1976.

This brief book grew out of the author's practical experience in a successful parent involvement program over a 2-year period. A model program is presented including a discussion of legal and financial considerations, selecting goals and objectives, recruitment and training, and evaluation. Numerous samples of field-tested forms are included.

Carter, B., and Dapper, G. *Organizing school volunteer programs.* New York: Citation Press, 1974.

Dapper and Carter provide a useful resource for teachers, administrators, or coordinators who become involved in the organizational aspects of a volunteer program. They present a broad overview offering a variety of approaches to the details of an effective program.

Clough, D.B., and Clough, B.M. *Utilizing teacher aides in the classroom.* Springfield, Ill.: Charles C Thomas Pub., 1978.

The purpose of this book is to assist classroom teachers in the development of managerial and human relations skills necessary in working with noncertified personnel. This is an excellent resource for anyone wishing to gain more in-depth understanding of the major concerns we have discussed in this chapter. These authors effectively use their experiences as a teacher and a principal.

Gattmann, E., and Henricks, W. *The other teacher: Aides to learning.* Belmont, Calif.: Wadsworth Pub. Co., 1973.

The authors offer practical techniques that are directly applicable to the classroom. This book presents an overview of child development, a look at the atypical child, and approaches to teaching basic skills. Each chapter contains an annotated bibliography useful to the teacher aide who wishes to understand the philosophy and the mechanics of teaching. It also contains a helpful glossary.

Lombardo, V.S. *Paraprofessionals in special education.* Springfield, Ill.: Charles C Thomas Pub., 1980.

Lombardo brings the reader up-to-date on the history and present status of paraprofessionals within special education. Chapters are training modules to assist individuals who must train paraprofessionals. The book is basically a guide that would enable a group to receive training through using several learning stations. Upon completion, trainers would be expected to understand the various characteristics of the diagnostic-prescriptive process and the learning characteristics of the primary handicapping conditions. Although the book is intended for those who will work with children older than preschoolers, it can also be useful to trainers of paraprofessionals of younger children.

Rockwell, R.E., and Comer, J.M. *School volunteer program: A manual for coordinators.* Athens, Ohio: Midwest Teacher Corps Network, Ohio University, 1978.

This manual was written in response to requests for specific guidelines to use when setting up and implementing a school volunteer program. The authors discuss and illustrate specific examples of information a school must have before a program is considered, the mechanics necessary to prepare for a volunteer program, initial procedures, and techniques for acknowledging time and effort.

Shank, P.C., and McElroy, W. *The paraprofessionals or teacher aides.* Midland, Mich.: Pendell Pub. Co., 1970.

The authors describe three purposes for this handbook: (1) to provide a guide for selecting, preparing, and assigning teacher aides; (2) to present practical information for teacher aides; and (3) to describe methods of organizing and teaching proven lessons. The authors outline a thorough program of preparation including the critical elements of playground supervision, first aid, and using audio-visual equipment.

Todd, V.E., and Hunter, G.H. *The aide in early childhood education.* New York: Macmillan, Inc., 1973.

The authors of this handbook view anyone working anywhere with a young child as a teacher aide who is an essential part of the young child's early environment. This book was written as a handbook for parents and other teacher aides who guide the learning of young children. It is assumed that teacher aides learn by observing the reactions of young children, need to know various learning activities in common use, and are familiar with the basics of child development. In a sense this book is a basic curriculum guide presenting not only specific lesson ideas but what to say and do in assisting the child to learn. This is a valuable resource for teacher aides who are expected

to be an integral part of lesson planning and implementation.

REFERENCES

Alden, J.W. (Ed.) *Volunteers in education: Future public policy.* Alexandria, Va.: National School Volunteer Program Inc., 1979.

Boomer, L.W. Meeting common goals through effective teacher-paraprofessional communication. *Teaching Exceptional Children*, 1981, *13*, 51-53.

Boyer, W. The U.S. Commissioner of Education's keynote speech to the opening session of National School Volunteers' Conference. Arlington, Va., 1978.

Brock, H.C. *Parent volunteer programs in early childhood education: A practical approach.* Syracuse, N.Y.: Gaylord Bros., 1976.

Carter, B., and Dapper, G. *Organizing school volunteer programs.* New York: Citation Press, 1974.

Chow, S.H.L., and Elmore, P. *Early childhood information unit: Resource manual and program descriptions.* San Francisco: Far West Laboratory for Educational Research and Development, 1973.

Cook, C.W., and Cook, R.E. Strategies for strengthening achievement-success striving. Submitted for publication review.

Cook, C.W. Motivation theories: Toward an integrating model. *Academy of Management Proceedings*, Southwest Division, 1979, 31-35.

Cook, C.W. Guidelines for managing motivation. *Business Horizons*, 1980, *23*, 61-69.

Cummings, L.L., and Schwab, D.P. *Performance in organizations.* Glenvies, Ill.: Scott, Foresman and Co., 1974.

Gattmann, E. and Henricks, W. *The other teacher: Aides to learning.* Belmont, Calif.: Wadsworth, 1973.

Greer, J.V. Utilizing paraprofessionals and volunteers in special education. *Focus on Exceptional Children*, 1978, *10*, 1-15.

Harrison, R. When power conflicts trigger team spirit. In W.L. French, C.H. Bell, Jr., and R.A. Zawacki (Eds.), *Organization development.* Dallas: Business Publications, Inc., 1978.

Homans, G.C. *The human group.* New York: Harcourt, Brace, & Co., Inc., 1950.

Karnes, M.B. Implications of research with disadvantaged children for early intervention with the handicapped. In J.B. Jordan and R.F. Dailey (Eds.), *Not all little wagons are red.* Reston, Va.: The Council for Exceptional Children, 1973.

Karnes, M.B., and Lee, R.C. *Early childhood.* Reston, Va.: The Council for Exceptional Children, 1978.

Lewin, K. *Field theory in social science; selected theoretical papers.* New York: Harper, 1951.

Litman, F. Supervision and the involvement of paraprofessionals in early childhood education. In R.H. Anderson and H.G. Shane (Eds.), *As the twig is bent: Readings in early childhood education.* Boston: Houghton Mifflin, 1971, 368-377.

Ora, J.P. Involvement and training of parent- and citizen-workers in early education for the handicapped. In J.B. Jordan and R.F. Dailey (Eds.), *Not all little wagons are red.* Reston, Va.: The Council for Exceptional Children, 1973.

Rockwell, R.E., and Comer, J.M. *School volunteer program: A manual for coordinators.* Athens, Ohio: Midwest Teacher Corps Network, Ohio University, 1978.

Schein, E.H. *Organizational psychology.* Englewood Cliffs, N.J.: Prentice-Hall, Inc., 1965.

Shank, P.C., and McElroy, W. *The paraprofessionals or teacher aides: Selection, preparation and assignment.* Midland, Mich.: Pendell Publishing, 1970.

Sherman, J.A., and Bushell, D., Jr. Behavior modification as an educational technique. In F.D. Horowitz (Ed.), *Review of child development research* (Vol. 4). Chicago: University of Chicago Press, 1975, 409-462.

APPENDIX

*Developmental guidelines**

The major developmental achievements of children 3, 4, and 5 years of age

Age (years)	Physical	Gross motor	Fine motor	Sensory	Language
3	Heart rate approximately 95 beats/ minute Respiratory rate approximately 24 breaths/minute Blood pressure: systolic 100 mg Hg, diastolic 67 mm Hg (plus or minus 25 mm Hg) Usual weight gain of 1.8 to 2.7 kg (4 to 6 pounds) Usual gain in height of 5 to 6.25 cm (2 to 2.5 inches) May have achieved nighttime control of bowel and bladder	Rides tricycle Jumps off bottom step Stands on one foot for a few seconds Goes up stairs using alternate feet, may still come down using both feet on the step Broad jumps May try to dance, but balance may not be adequate	Builds tower of nine to ten cubes Builds bridge with three cubes Adeptly places small pellets in narrow-necked bottle In drawing, copies a circle, imitates a cross, names what he has drawn, cannot draw stick-man but may make circle with facial features	Able to copy geometric figures Can place geometric forms into respective opening if form board is reversed Reading readiness may be present	Has vocabulary of about 900 words Uses primarily "telegraphic" speech Uses complete sentences of three to four words Talks incessantly regardless of whether anyone is paying attention Repeats sentence of six syllables Constantly asks questions

From L. Whaley and D.L. Wong. *Nursing care of infants and children.* St. Louis: The C.V. Mosby Co., 1979.

*With gratitude to Lucille Whaley and Donna Wong; from L. Whaley and D.L. Wong, *Nursing care of infants and children.* St. Louis, The C.V. Mosby Co., 1979.

Socialization	Cognition	Family relationships
Dresses self almost completely if helped with back buttons and told which shoe is right or left	Is in preconceptual phase	Attempts to please parents and conform to their expectations
Buttons and unbuttons accessible buttons	Is egocentric in thought and behavior	Is less jealous of younger sibling; may be opportune time for birth of additional sibling
Pulls on shoes	Has beginning understanding of time; uses many time-oriented expressions, talks about past and future as much as about present, pretends to tell time	Is aware of family relationships and sex role functions
Has increased attention span		Boys tend to identify more with father or other male figure
Feeds self completely	Has improved concept of space as demonstrated in understanding of prepositions and ability to follow directional command	Has increased ability to separate easily and comfortably from parents for short periods
Pours from a bottle or pitcher		
Can prepare simple meals, such as cold cereal and milk	Has beginning ability to view concepts from another perspective	
Can help to set table, dry dishes without breaking any		
Likes to "help" entertain by passing around food		
May have fears, especially of dark and going to bed		
Knows own sex and appropriate sex of others		
In play, parallel and associative phase; begins to learn simple games and meaning of rules, but follows them according to self-interpretation; speaks to doll, animal, truck, and so on; begins to work out social interaction through play; able to share toys, although expresses idea of "mine" frequently		

Continued.

The major developmental achievements of children 3, 4, and 5 years of age—cont'd

Age (years)	Physical	Gross motor	Fine motor	Sensory	Language
4	Pulse, respiration, and blood pressure decrease very slightly Height and weight gain remain constant Length at birth is doubled	Skips and hops on one foot Catches ball reliably Throws ball overhand Walks down stairs using alternate footing	Imitates a gate with cubes Uses scissors successfully to cut out picture following outline Can lace shoes, but may not be able to tie bow In drawing, copies a square, traces a cross and diamond, adds three parts to stick figure	Maximum potential for development of amblyopia	Has vocabulary of 1500 words or more Uses sentences of four to five words Questioning is at peak Tells exaggerated stories Knows simple songs May be mildly profane if he associates with older children Obeys four prepositional phrases, such as "under," "on top of," beside," "in back of" or "in front of" Names one or more colors Comprehends analogies, such as, "If ice is cold, fire is ___" Repeats four digits Uses words liberally but frequently does not comprehend meaning
5	Pulse, respiration, and blood pressure decrease slightly Growth rate is similar to that of previous year Eruption of permanent dentition	Skips and hops on alternate feet Throws and catches ball well Jumps rope Skates with good balance Walks backward with heel to toe	Ties shoelaces Uses scissors, simple tools, or pencil very well In drawing, copies a diamond and triangle: adds seven to nine parts to stickman; prints a	Minimum potential for development of amblyopia Visual acuity approaches 20/20 (may not	Has vocabulary of about 2100 words Uses sentences of six to eight words, with all parts of speech Names coins (nickel, dime, and so on)

Socialization	Cognition	Family relationships
Very independent Tends to be selfish and impatient Aggressive physically as well as verbally Takes pride in accomplishments Has mood swings Boasts and tattles Shows off dramatically, enjoys entertaining others Tells family tales to others with no restraint Still has many fears In play, is cooperative and associative; imaginary playmates common; uses dramatic, imaginative, and imitative devices; works through unresolved conflicts, such as jealousy toward sibling, anger toward parent, or unconquered fear in himself; sexual exploration and curiosity demonstrated through play, such as being "doctor" or "nurse"	Is in phase of intuitive thought Causality still related to proximity of events Understands time better, especially in terms of sequence of daily events Unable to conserve matter Judges everything according to one dimension, such as height, width, or first Immediate perceptual clues dominate judgment Can choose longer of two lines or heavier of two objects Is beginning to develop less egocentrism and more social awareness May count correctly but has poor mathematic concept of numbers Still believes that thoughts cause events Obeys because parents have set limits, not because of understanding of reason behind right or wrong	Rebels if parents expect too much from him, such as impeccable table manners Takes aggression and frustration out on parents or siblings Do's and don'ts become important May have rivalry with older or younger siblings, may resent older's privileges and younger's invasion of privacy and possessions May run away from home Identifies strongly with parent of opposite sex Is able to run errands outside the home
Less rebellious and quarrelsome than at age 4 years More settled and eager to get down to business Not as open and accessible in thoughts and behavior as in earlier years Independent but trustworthy, not foolhardy	Begins to question what parents think by comparing them to age-mates and other adults May notice prejudice and bias in outside world Is more able to view other's perspective, but tolerates differences rather than understands them	Gets along well with parents Doesn't run away from home May seek out mother more often than at age 4 years for reassurance and security, especially when entering school Is upset not to find parent, for example, when he comes home from school

Continued.

The major developmental achievements of children 3, 4, and 5 years of age—cont'd

Age (years)	Physical	Gross motor	Fine motor	Sensory	Language
5—cont'd	may begin, especially if deciduous tooth eruption was early (before age 6 months First permanent teeth to erupt are four molars, which come in behind the last temporary teeth (often mistaken for temporary molars) Handedness is established (about 90% are right-handed)	Jumps from height of 12 inches, lands on toes Balances on alternate feet with eyes closed	few letters, numbers, or words, such as his first name	be completely achieved until 8 years of age)	Names four or more colors Describes drawing or pictures with much comment and enumeration Asks meaning of words Asks inquisitive questions Can repeat sentence of ten syllables or more Knows names of days of week, months, and other time-associated words Defines words using action as well as description Knows composition of articles, such as, "A shoe is made of ____" Can follow three demands in succession

Socialization	Cognition	Family relationships
Has fewer fears, relies on outer authority to control the world	Tends to be matter-of-fact about differences in others	Tolerates siblings, but finds 3-year-old children a special nuisance
Eager to do things right and to please, tries to "live by the rules"	May begin to show understanding of conservation of numbers through counting objects regardless of arrangement	Begins to question parent's thinking and principles
Acts "manly" or "womanly"	Uses time-oriented words with increased understanding	Strongly identifies with parent of same sex, especially boys with their fathers
Takes increased responsibility for his actions	Very curious about factual information regarding his world	Enjoys doing activities, such as sports, cooking, shopping, and so on, with parent of same sex
Has fairly consistent and polished manners		
Cares for himself totally, occasionally needing supervision in dress or hygiene		
May complain over minor injuries but tries to be brave for major pain		
In play, cooperative; likes rules and tries to follow them but may cheat to avoid losing; begins to notice group conformity and sense of belonging; very industrious, tries to accomplish a goal and feels pride and satisfaction, as well as unhappiness and discontent; may demand to watch television more now that he understands programs better; not ready for concentrated close work or small print because of slight far-sightedness and still unrefined eye-hand coordination; imitative play mimics the portrayed adult like a mirror image; wants to use real objects during play, such as actual ingredients to make cookies rather than sand or mud		

APPENDIX

B

*Find your child's speech and hearing age**

INSTRUCTIONS: Read each question through your child's age group and check yes or no. Add the total and see below.

All yes = *Good!* Your child is developing hearing, speech, and language normally.

1-3 no = *Caution!* Your child may have delayed hearing, speech, and language development.

More than 3 no = *Action!* Take your child for professional help.

Check one		Hearing and understanding	Child's age	Talking	Check one	
Yes	No				Yes	No
☐	☐	Does your child hear and understand most speech in the home?	**5 years**	Does your child say all sounds correctly except perhaps *s* and *th*?	☐	☐
☐	☐	Does your child hear and answer when first called?		Does your child use the same sentence structure as the family?	☐	☐
☐	☐	Does your child hear quiet speech?		Does your child's voice sound clear, like other children's?	☐	☐
☐	☐	Does everyone who knows your child think he/she hears well (teacher, babysitter, grandparent, etc.)?				
☐	☐	Does your child understand conversation easily?	**2½-4 years**	Does your child say most sounds, except perhaps *r*, *s*, *th*, and *l*?	☐	☐
☐	☐	Does your child hear you when you call from another room?		Does your child sometimes repeat words in a sentence?	☐	☐
☐	☐	Does your child hear television or radio at the same loudness level as other members of the family?				
☐	☐	Does your child understand differences in meaning ("go—stop;" "the car pushed the truck—the truck pushed the car")?		Does your child use 200-300 words?	☐	☐
				Does your child use 2-3 word sentences?	☐	☐
				Does your child ask lots of "why" and "what" questions?	☐	☐
☐	☐	Can your child point to pictures in a book upon hearing them named?		Has your child's jargon and repeating disappeared?	☐	☐

*Adapted from public information materials of the American Speech-Language-Hearing Association; used with permission.

Check one		Hearing and understanding	Child's age	Talking	Check one	
Yes	**No**				**Yes**	**No**
☐	☐	Does your child notice sounds (dog barking, telephone ringing, television sound, knocking at door and so on)?		Does your child like to name things?	☐	☐
☐	☐	Can your child follow two requests ("get the ball and put it on the table")?	**1½-2 years**	Does your child have 10-15 words (by age 2)?	☐	☐
				Does your child sometimes repeat requests?	☐	☐
				Does your child ask 1-2 word questions ("where kitty? go bye-bye? more?")?	☐	☐
				Does your child put 2 words together ("more cookie")?	☐	☐
☐	☐	Has your child begun to respond to requests ("come here"; "do you want more")?	**9 months-1 year**	Does your child say words (8-10 words at age 1½; 2-3 words at age 1). (Words may not be clear).	☐	☐
☐	☐	Does your child turn or look up when you call?		Does your child enjoy imitating sounds?	☐	☐
☐	☐	Does your child search or look around when hearing new sounds?		Does your child use jargon (babbling that sounds like real speech)?	☐	☐
☐	☐	Does your child listen to people talking?		Does your child use voice to get attention?	☐	☐
☐	☐	Does your child respond to "no" and her/his name?	**6 months**	Does your child's babbling sound like the parent's speech, only not clear?		
☐	☐	Does your child notice and look around for the source of new sounds?		Does your child make lots of different sounds?	☐	☐
☐	☐	Does your child turn her/his head toward the side where the sound is coming from?				
☐	☐	Does your child try to turn toward the speaker?	**3 months**	Does your child babble?	☐	☐
☐	☐	Does your child smile when spoken to?		Does your child cry differently for different needs?	☐	☐
☐	☐	Does your child stop playing and appear to listen to sounds or speech?		Does your child repeat the same sounds a lot?	☐	☐
☐	☐	Does your child seem to recognize mother's voice?				
☐	☐	Does your child listen to speech?	**Birth**	Does your child coo or gurgle?	☐	☐
☐	☐	Does your child startle or cry at noises?				
☐	☐	Does your child awaken at loud sounds?				
	TOTAL			TOTAL		

Definitions of handicapped children*

(a) As used in this part, the term "handicapped children" means those children evaluated in accordance with 121a.530-121a.534 as being mentally retarded, hard of hearing, deaf, speech impaired, other health impaired, deaf-blind, multihandicapped, or as having specific learning disabilities, who because of those impairments need special education and related services.

(b) The terms used in this definition are defined as follows:

(1) "Deaf" means a hearing impairment which is so severe that the child is impaired in processing linguistic information through hearing, with or without amplification, which adversely affects educational performance.

(2) "Deaf-blind" means concomitant hearing and visual impairments, the combination of which causes such severe communication and other developmental and educational problems that they cannot be accommodated in special education programs solely for deaf or blind children.

(3) "Hard of Hearing" means a hearing impairment, whether permanent or fluctuating, which adversely affects a child's educational performance but which is not included under the definition of "deaf" in this section.

(4) "Mentally retarded" means significantly subaverage general intellectual functioning

existing concurrently with deficits in adaptive behavior and manifested during the developmental period, which adversely affects a child's educational performance.

(5) "Multihandicapped" means concomitant impairment (such as mentally retarded—blind, mentally retarded—orthopedically impaired, etc.), the combination of which causes such severe educational problems that they cannot be accommodated in special education programs solely for one of the impairments. The term does not include deaf-blind children.

(6) "Orthopedically impaired" means a severe orthopedic impairment which adversely affects a child's educational performance. The term includes impairments caused by congenital anomaly (e.g., clubfoot, absence of some member etc.), impairments caused by disease (e.g. poliomyelitis, bone tuberculosis, etc.) and impairments from other causes (e.g., cerebral palsy, amputations, and fractures or burns which cause contractures).

(7) "Other health impaired" means limited strength, vitality or alertness, due to chronic or acute health problems such as a heart condition, tuberculosis, rheumatic fever, nephritis, asthma, sickle cell anemia, hemophilia, epilepsy, lead poisoning, leukemia, or diabetes, which adversely affects a child's educational performance.

(8) "Seriously emotionally disturbed" is defined as follows:

*Federal Register, Vol. 2, No. 163-Tuesday, August 23, 1977 (121a.5).

(i) The term means a condition exhibiting one or more of the following characteristics over a long period of time and to a marked degree, which adversely affects educational performance:

(A) An inability to learn which cannot be explained by intellectual, sensory, or health factors;

(B) An inability to build or maintain satisfactory interpersonal relationships with peers and teachers;

(C) Inappropriate types of behavior or feelings under normal circumstances;

(D) A general pervasive mood of unhappiness or depression; or

(E) A tendency to develop physical symptoms or fears associated with personal or school problems.

(ii) The term includes children who are schizophrenic or autistic. The term does not include children who are socially maladjusted, unless it is determined that they are seriously emotionally disturbed.

(9) "Specific learning disability" means a disorder in one or more of the basic psychological processes involved in understanding or in using language, spoken or written, which may manifest itself in an imperfect ability to listen, think, speak, read, write, spell, or to do mathematical calculations. The term includes such conditions as perceptual handicaps, brain injury, minimal brain dysfunction, dyslexia, and developmental aphasia. The term does not include children who have learning problems which are primarily the result of visual, hearing, or motor handicaps, of mental retardation or emotional disturbances or of environmental, cultural, or economic disadvantage.

(10) "Speech impaired" means a communication disorder such as stuttering, impaired articulation, a language impairment, or a voice impairment, which adversely affects a child's performance.

(11) "Visually handicapped" means a visual impairment which, even with correction, adversely affects a child's educational performance. The term includes both partially seeing and blind children.

Assessment techniques for use with young children: a sampling

AUTHORS' NOTE: We chose the techniques annotated in this section primarily because they could be used by practicing teachers. We gave preference to criterion-referenced techniques because we believe these are most conducive to program planning. We made no attempt to include tests that take specialized training to administer or to interpret properly.

Because our presentation of these techniques is not an endorsement of their effectiveness, potential users are urged to study their characteristics in detail. To determine which techniques are most appropriate to the purpose and population being tested, potential users should examine test manuals and the *Eighth Mental Measurements Yearbook* (Buros, 1978). One should take careful note of the test's validity, reliability, characteristics of the normative sample, performance demands, and utility of the techniques.

Auditory Discrimination Test

AUTHOR: J.M. Wepman

PUBLISHER: Western Psychological Services, 12031 Wilshire Boulevard, Los Angeles, California 90025

AGES: 5 years to 8 years

REQUIRED RESPONSES: Verbal and nonverbal

ADMINISTRATION: Individually by teacher or others trained in diagnostic testing in approximately 15 minutes

SCORING: Easy

DESCRIPTION: This screening test assesses the child's ability to recognize the differences among phonemes used in standard English; the child is used to indicate whether words of a pair are the same or different.

SCORES: Error score

OTHER CONSIDERATIONS: One should use this screening test with caution because young children often have difficulty with the concepts of "same" and "different." The normative population is inadequately described. Examination of the pattern of errors can be helpful to program planning.

Basic Concept Inventory

AUTHOR: S. Engelmann

PUBLISHER: Follett Publishing Company, 1010 West Washington Blvd., Chicago, Illinois 60607

AGES: 3 years to 10 years

REQUIRED RESPONSES: Verbal and nonverbal (considerable verbalization is required)

ADMINISTRATION: Individually by teacher in 15 to 25 minutes

SCORING: Easy

DESCRIPTION: This is a criterion-referenced checklist that assesses necessary basic concepts, pattern awareness, sentence repetition, and comprehension.

OTHER CONSIDERATIONS: It includes racially integrated pictures and suggestions for remediation.

Bayley Scales of Infant Development

AUTHOR: N. Bayley

PUBLISHER: Psychological Corporation, 304 East 45th Street, New York, New York 10017

AGES: 2 months to 2½ years

REQUIRED RESPONSES: Primarily nonverbal

ADMINISTRATION: Individually by trained examiner in approximately 1 hour with the mother present

SCORING: Moderately difficult

DESCRIPTION: This scale consists of three subparts: mental scale, motor scale, and infant behavior record. It is made up of 163 items including sensory-perceptual activities, manipulation and play with objects, learning and problem-solving, the beginning of verbal communication, and motor control.

SCORES: Mental Development Index and Psychomotor Development Index

OTHER CONSIDERATIONS: This is a norm-referenced observation scale with age placements set at the age at which 50% of the normative population passed each item. High internal consistency. Adequate correlation with the Stanford-Binet Intelligence Scale.

Boehm Test of Basic Concepts

AUTHOR: A. E. Boehm

PUBLISHER: The Psychological Corporation, 304 East 45th Street, New York, New York 10017

AGES: 4 years to 8 years

REQUIRED RESPONSES: Nonverbal

ADMINISTRATION: Individually or in small groups by teacher or diagnostician in approximately 30 minutes

SCORING: Easy

DESCRIPTION: This test is intended to measure mastery of basic concepts of time, quantity (numbers), and space (direction, location, orientation, and dimension).

SCORES: Percent correct by grade and socioeconomic level

OTHER CONSIDERATIONS: Children can point to choices rather than marking with a pencil. Directions can be given in Spanish. It is not suitable for a visually impaired child. Teachers will find it useful to develop a class profile of concepts to be mastered. It can be used with the resource guide also developed by Boehm (Appendix E).

Brigance Diagnostic Inventory Early Development

AUTHOR: A. H. Brigance

PUBLISHER: Curriculum Associates, Inc., 5 Esquire Road, North Villerica, Massachusetts 01862

AGES: Up to 7 years

REQUIRED RESPONSES: Nonverbal and verbal

ADMINISTRATION: Individually by teacher or trained paraprofessional either in its entirety or by individual skills, as needed

SCORING: Easy

DESCRIPTION: This criterion-referenced inventory allows the teacher to determine developmental levels in the areas of psychomotor, self-help, communication, general knowledge, and comprehension and academic skills.

SCORES: Developmental ages

OTHER CONSIDERATIONS: It includes developmental record books providing systematic, graphic performance records. Results are readily translated into sequential, individualized lessons.

Carolina Developmental Profile

AUTHORS: D. L. Lillie and G. L. Harbin

PUBLISHER: Kaplan Corporation, 600 Jonestown Road, Winston-Salem, North Carolina 27103

AGES: 2 years to 5 years

REQUIRED RESPONSES.: Verbal and nonverbal

ADMINISTRATION.: Individually by teacher at several different times

SCORING: Easy

DESCRIPTION: This is a criterion-referenced checklist that includes gross motor, fine motor, visual perception, receptive, and expressive language. It is designed to provide a profile of what a child can and cannot do.

SCORES: Developmental ages

OTHER CONSIDERATIONS: It can be used in conjunction with the Developmental Task Instruction System also developed by Lillie.

Cognitive Skills Assessment Battery

AUTHORS: A.E. Boehm and B.R. Slater

PUBLISHER: Teachers College Press, 81 Adams Drive, Totowa, New Jersey 07512

AGES: 3 years to 6 years

REQUIRED RESPONSES: Verbal and nonverbal

ADMINISTRATION: Individually by trained aide or teacher in 20 to 25 minutes

SCORING: Easy

DESCRIPTION: This is a criterion-referenced battery intended to provide a profile of skill competencies from which to develop curriculum. Areas covered include orientation of the child to the environment, identification of body parts, visual-motor coordination, auditory memory, story and picture comprehension, knowledge of shape, number, color letters, and vocabulary.

OTHER CONSIDERATIONS: One can obtain a classroom profile that enables the teacher to match classroom goals to classroom methods and materials.

Comprehensive Identification Process (CIP)

AUTHOR: R.R. Zehrback

PUBLISHER: Scholastic Testing Service, Inc., 480 Meyer Road, Bensenville, Illinois 60106

AGES: 2 years to 5½ years

REQUIRED RESPONSES: Verbal and nonverbal

ADMINISTRATION: Individually by teacher or trained paraprofessional in 30 to 45 minutes. Specialists are recommended for the vision, hearing, and speech and language subtests.

SCORING: Easy to moderately difficult

DESCRIPTION: This screening test samples cognitive-verbal, fine motor, gross motor, speech, language, social-affective, hearing, and visual development.

SCORES: The following three-part system is used to rate the items: pass, evaluate, and refer or rescreen.

OTHER CONSIDERATIONS: Children are screened individually at different stations. Parents' opinion are considered.

Cooperative Preschool Inventory

AUTHOR: B. Caldwell

PUBLISHER: Addison-Wesley Testing Service, South Street, Reading, Massachusetts 01867

AGES: 3 years to 6½ years

REQUIRED RESPONSES: Verbal and nonverbal (heavy verbal emphasis)

ADMINISTRATION: Individually by teacher in 15 minutes

SCORING: Easy

DESCRIPTION: This test was developed to assess readiness in a variety of basic skills important to school success. The 64 items cover four areas: personal-social relationships, associative vocabulary, concepts-numerical, and concepts-sensory.

SCORES: Age percentile norms for the total score

OTHER CONSIDERATIONS: Directions are verbal and can be given in English or Spanish. Subtests are not individually normed, but teachers can refer to them in informally assessing strengths and weaknesses.

Denver Developmental Screening Test

AUTHORS: W.K. Frankenburg, J.B. Dodds, and A. Fandal

PUBLISHER: Ladoca Project and Publishing Foundation, East 51st Avenue and Lincoln Street, Denver, Colorado 80216

AGES: 1 month to 6 years

REQUIRED RESPONSES: Verbal and nonverbal

ADMINISTRATION: Individually by teacher or trained paraprofessional in 15 to 20 minutes

SCORING: Easy

DESCRIPTION: This screening test includes items in personal-social, fine motor-adaptive, language, and gross motor development.

SCORES: Items are scored as passed, failed, refused, or no opportunity. Developmental levels are obtained.

OTHER CONSIDERATIONS: The forms and manual have been translated into Spanish.

Developmental Activities Screening Inventory (DASI)

AUTHORS: R.F. DuBose and M.B. Langley

PUBLISHER: Teaching Resources Corporation, 50 Pond Park Road, Hingham, Massachusetts 02043

AGES: 6 months to 5 years

REQUIRED RESPONSES: Nonverbal

ADMINISTRATION: Individually by teacher in one or two settings. Instructions may be given either visually or verbally.

SCORING: Easy

DESCRIPTION: The 55 test items assess fine-motor control, cause-effect relationships, associations, number concepts, size discriminations, and sequencing.

SCORES: Developmental level and quotient

OTHER CONSIDERATIONS: Tasks can be adapted for use with the visually impaired. Simple remedial programs are suggested in the test manual. Has been used successfully with multihandicapped children.

Developmental Indicators for the Assessment of Learning (DIAL)

AUTHORS: C. Mardell and D. Goldenberg

PUBLISHER: Childcraft Education Corporation, 20 Kilmer Road, Edison, New Jersey 08817

AGES: 2½ years to 5½ years

REQUIRED RESPONSES: Verbal and nonverbal

ADMINISTRATION: Individually by teacher or trained paraprofessional in 25 to 30 minutes

SCORING: Easy

DESCRIPTION: Areas within this prekindergarten screening test include gross motor, fine motor, concepts communication, and social and emotional development.

SCORES: Scaled scores and functional level

OTHER CONSIDERATIONS: Strengths and weaknesses can be recorded on a profile sheet. It is necessary to be cautious when scoring the articulation items.

Developmental Profile

AUTHORS: G. D. Alpern and T. J. Boll

PUBLISHER: Psychological Development Publications, 7150 Lakeside Drive, Indianapolis, Indiana 46278

AGES: 6 months to 12 years

REQUIRED RESPONSES: Rater responses

ADMINISTRATION: Individually rated from direct observation or interview of parents in 30 to 40 minutes

SCORING: Easy

DESCRIPTION: This test is designed to screen quickly for competencies in physical, self-help, social, academic, and communication development.

SCORES: Age norms

OTHER CONSIDERATIONS: Allows for administration, scoring, and interpretation by people without specific training in psychological testing.

Developmental Test of Motor Integration

AUTHORS: K. Beery and N. Buktenica

PUBLISHER: Follett Publishing Company, 1010 West Washington Blvd., Chicago, Illinois 60607

AGES: 2 years to 15 years

REQUIRED RESPONSES: Nonverbal (copying)

ADMINISTRATION: Individually or in small groups in approximately 10 minutes by a teacher, diagnostician, or trained paraprofessional

SCORING: Relatively easy

DESCRIPTION: This test consists of a series of geometric shapes to be copied by the child.

SCORES: Age Equivalent Scores

OTHER CONSIDERATIONS: Whereas the scoring is relatively easy, trained observers are needed to interpret the results. The child must be able to understand and follow oral or pantomimed directions.

Gesell Developmental Schedules

AUTHORS: H. Knobloch and B. Pasamanick (Eds.)

PUBLISHER: Harper and Row, 10 E. 53rd Street, New York, New York 10022

AGES: 4 weeks to 5 years

REQUIRED RESPONSES: Verbal and nonverbal

ADMINISTRATION: Individually by trained diagnosticians in 30 minutes

SCORING: Moderately difficult

DESCRIPTION: Administers a broad array of items including copying figures, naming body parts, following commands, matching forms, naming animals, and writing name, address, and numbers.

SCORES: Developmental age and developmental quotient

OTHER CONSIDERATIONS: Reliability appears to depend on the clinical training and experience of examiners.

Goldman-Fristoe-Woodcock Auditory Skills Test Battery

AUTHORS: R. Goldman, M. Fristoe, and R. Woodcock

PUBLISHER: American Guidance Service, Publishers' Building, Circle Pines, Minnesota 55014

AGES: 3 years to adults

REQUIRED RESPONSES: Verbal

ADMINISTRATION: Individually by teacher with some training in language disorders in approximately 60 minutes or 10 to 15 minutes per test

SCORING: Moderately difficult

DESCRIPTION: This test is designed to assess discrimination of speech sounds under quiet and noisy conditions. Subtests include auditory selective attention, auditory discrimination, auditory memory, and sound-symbol test.

SCORES: Percentile ranks, age equivalents, standard scores, and stanines

OTHER CONSIDERATIONS: Each subtest has a separate profile of performance.

Language and Language Disorders of the Preacademic Child

AUTHOR: T.E. Bangs

PUBLISHER: Western Psychological Services, 12031 Wilshire Boulevard, Los Angeles, California 90025

AGES: 1 month to 6 years

REQUIRED RESPONSES: Verbal

ADMINISTRATION: Individually by trained examiner in 60 to 90 minutes

SCORING: Moderately difficult

DESCRIPTION: This norm-referenced battery is intended to provide a diagnosis, help identify the etiological factors, to present essential information for treatment, and to document gains determined by reassessment. Areas include comprehension, expression, short-term visual and auditory memory, and perceptual-motor performance.

SCORES: Mental age

OTHER CONSIDERATIONS: Also supplies a specific questionnaire for requesting historical information.

Learning Accomplishment Profile

AUTHOR: A. Sanford

PUBLISHER: Kaplan School Supply, 600 Jonestown Road, Winston-Salem, North Carolina 27103

AGES: Up to 6 years

REQUIRED RESPONSES: Nonverbal and verbal

ADMINISTRATION: Individually by teacher or trained paraprofessional

SCORING: Easy

DESCRIPTION: This is a developmental checklist designed to assist in the development of individualized instructional plans. Areas assessed include language, cognition, self-help, gross motor, and fine motor skills.

SCORES: Rate of development equal to developmental age divided by chronological age

OTHER CONSIDERATIONS: As this is a checklist, data on reliability and validity were not reported.

McCarthy Scales of Children's Abilities

AUTHOR: D. McCarthy

PUBLISHER: The Psychological Corporation, 304 East 45th Street, New York, New York 10017

AGES: 2 years to 8 years

REQUIRED RESPONSES: Verbal and nonverbal

ADMINISTRATION: Individually administered by a trained examiner in approximately 1 hour

SCORING: Moderately difficult

DESCRIPTION: This norm-referenced test contains six scales: verbal, quantitative, perceptual-performance, general cognitive, memory, and motor development. Determines strengths, weaknesses, and a general level of cognitive functioning.

SCORES: Scaled scores yielding a General Cognitive Index (GCI)

OTHER CONSIDERATIONS: The term IQ is carefully avoided. Contents are said to be useful with children of both sexes from various ethnic, regional, and socioeconomic groups.

Motor Free Visual Perception Test

AUTHORS: R.P. Colarusso and D.D. Hammill

PUBLISHER: Academic Therapy Publications, 1539 Fourth Street, San Rafael, California 94901

AGES: 5 years to 8 years

REQUIRED RESPONSES: Nonverbal (pointing)

ADMINISTRATION: Individually by teacher or trained paraprofessional in 10 minutes

SCORING: Easy

DESCRIPTION: This test consists of 36 items in the following areas: spatial relationships, visual discrimination, figure-ground, visual closure, and visual memory.

SCORES: Perceptual ages and perceptual quotient

OTHER CONSIDERATIONS: To perform on this test, the child must understand the concepts of "same" and "different." It is useful to assess visual and perceptual abilities without involving significant motor responses.

Move-Grow-Learn (movement skills survey)

AUTHORS: R.E. Orpet and L.L. Heustis

PUBLISHER: Follett Publishing Company, 1010 West Washington Blvd., Chicago, Illinois 60607

AGES: 3 years to 9 years

REQUIRED RESPONSES: Nonverbal

ADMINISTRATION: Individually by teacher through observing the child during classroom, playground, and gymnasium activities.

SCORING: Children are rated on a scale from 1 to 5.

DESCRIPTION: This criterion-referenced rating scale focuses on coordination and rhythm, agility, flexibility, strength, speed, balance, and body awareness.

SCORES: Ratings from minus 1 (severely impaired) to 5 (excellent)

OTHER CONSIDERATIONS: This survey is designed to be used with the Frostig-Maslow Move-Grow-Learn program (Appendix E).

Peabody Individual Achievement Test

AUTHORS: L.M. Dunn and F.C. Markwardt, Jr.

PUBLISHER: American Guidance Service, Publishers' Building, Circle Pines, Minnesota 55014

AGES: 5 years to adult

REQUIRED RESPONSES: Verbal and nonverbal

ADMINISTRATION: Individually by teacher or trained paraprofessional in approximately 30 to 40 minutes

SCORING: Easy

DESCRIPTION: This screening test is designed to assess a child's level of achievement in reading recognition, reading comprehension, mathematics, spelling, and general information.

SCORES: Age and grade equivalents, percentile ranks, and standard scores

OTHER CONSIDERATIONS: Comprehensive examination of the manual is necessary. When the test items are appropriate to kindergarten or first grade curriculum, it may be useful in determining the most appropriate placement for a child.

Peabody Picture Vocabulary Test (PPVT-R)

AUTHORS: L.M. Dunn and L.M. Dunn

PUBLISHER: American Guidance Service, Publishers' Building, Circle Pines, Minnesota 55014

AGES: 2 years to adult

REQUIRED RESPONSES: Nonverbal

ADMINISTRATION: Individually by teachers in 10 to 20 minutes.

SCORING: Easy

DESCRIPTION: This test requires the child to hear a cue word and to point to the one picture out of four that corresponds best to the perceived word. It is a test of hearing vocabulary and receptive language.

SCORES: Percentile ranks, age equivalents, and stanines

OTHER CONSIDERATIONS: A child must have adequate hearing, sight, some degree of motor coordination, and understanding of standard English to respond appropriately. Caution is urged in using this test to measure more than receptive language.

The Portage Guide to Early Education

AUTHORS: Portage Preschool Project

PUBLISHER: CESA 12, Box 564, Portage, Wisconsin 53901

AGES: Up to 6 years

REQUIRED RESPONSES: Nonverbal and verbal

ADMINISTRATION: Individually by teacher or trained paraprofessional in approximately 30 minutes

SCORING: Easy

DESCRIPTION: This criterion-referenced checklist assesses behaviors in five developmental areas: cognitive, self-help, motor, language, and socialization.

SCORES: Developmental levels in years

OTHER CONSIDERATIONS: This checklist combines items from a number of developmental scales and originated as part of the Portage Project, a home based early intervention program. Each skill is referenced to a card that describes how to teach the skill assessed (Appendix E).

Psychoeducational Evaluation of the Preschool Child

AUTHORS: E. Jedrysek, Z. Klapper, L. Pope, and J. Wortis

PUBLISHER: Grune and Stratton, 757 Third Avenue, New York, New York 10017

AGES: 3 years to 6 years

REQUIRED RESPONSES: Verbal and nonverbal

ADMINISTRATION: Individually by teacher in one setting or a number of settings

SCORING: Easy

DESCRIPTION: The five skill areas that include physical functioning and sensory status, perceptual functioning, competence in short term retention, language skills, and cognitive functioning are arranged in developmental sequence. Emphasis is placed on how a child functions.

SCORES: Age and grade norms

OTHER CONSIDERATIONS: This instrument is intended to supplement more formal test results. The purpose of this technique is to provide information to be used in formulating teaching goals. Probes are allowed to encourage modification of test items to obtain the most data possible.

Santa Clara Inventory of Developmental Tasks

AUTHORS: Santa Clara Unified School District

PUBLISHER: Richard L. Zweig, Inc., 20800 Beach Boulevard, Huntington Beach, California 92648

AGES: Preschool to 7 years

REQUIRED RESPONSES: Verbal and nonverbal

ADMINISTRATION: Individually by teacher through observing classroom activities or during a specified time, as needed

SCORING: Easy

DESCRIPTION: Sixty tasks screen development in the following eight areas: motor coordination, visual motor performance, visual perception, visual memory, auditory perception, auditory memory, language development, and conceptual development. A developmental profile is constructed for each child.

SCORES: Each item is scored with a 0 (almost never), 1 (some of the time), or 2 (most of the time).

OTHER CONSIDERATIONS: A resource guide for reteaching of each of the 60 tasks is included. It can also be used with the Santa Clara Plus (Appendix E).

Uzgiris-Hunt Ordinal Scales of Psychological Development

AUTHORS: I. Uzgiris and J.M. Hunt

PUBLISHER: University of Illinois Press, Urbana, Illinois 61801

AGES: 2 weeks to 2 years

REQUIRED RESPONSES: Verbal and nonverbal

ADMINISTRATION: Individually by trained examiner in several sessions

DESCRIPTION: These criterion-referenced scales cover tasks equivalent to Piaget's sensorimotor stage. They relate to the following six areas: visual pursuit and performance, eliciting desired environmental events, vocal and gestural imitation, operational causality, object relations in space, and schemes for relating to objects.

OTHER CONSIDERATIONS: Assistance in interpretation may be obtained from C.J. Dunst. *A clinical and educational manual for use with the Uzgiris and Hunt Scales of infant psychological development.* Baltimore, Md.: University Park Press, 1980.

Vineland Social Maturity Scale

AUTHOR: E.A. Doll

PUBLISHER: American Guidance Service, Publishers' Building, Circle Pines, Minnesota 55014

AGES: 1 month to adult

REQUIRED RESPONSES: Rater responses

ADMINISTRATION: Individually rated through interview with caregivers in 20 to 30 minutes

SCORING: Moderately difficult

DESCRIPTION: Factual information assessing an individual's level of maturity in self-help, self-direction, occupation, communication, locomotion, and socialization are sought by individuals trained in interviewing techniques.

SCORES: Chronological age norms

OTHER CONSIDERATIONS: This scale has been widely used to determine adaptation of mentally retarded individuals. The instrument is in need of revision and updating.

APPENDIX

Instructional programs
for use with young children: a sampling

AUTHORS' NOTE: Many of the prepared curricula and teaching kits available to teachers of young children are useful when planning for and teaching children with special needs. Most of the kits and programs contain a wealth of ideas and related materials. Concepts are developed through games, songs, and activities that young children enjoy. They often give specific instructions for adapting materials to meet special needs.

The materials listed below represent a selection from those most widely used in early childhood education programs. New curricula and related materials appear regularly in this expanding market. Their inclusion here is not an endorsement of their value for use in any specific program. Before purchasing any of these materials, teachers should do a careful analysis of their potential effectiveness.

One must give particular attention to the material's instructional objectives. Are they clearly defined and are they consistent with the classroom objectives? Will the unique needs of involved children be considered? Are objectives carefully sequenced or can they be sequenced to become part of a total developmentally based curriculum? Are the materials conducive to the physical demands of young children and are they cost effective? Is special training necessary to use the materials? Only through careful study

can critical questions such as these be answered. We encourage such study before materials are either purchased or used.

Publisher: *American Guidance Service, Publishers' Building, Circle Pines, Minnesota 55014*

My Friends and Me

AUTHOR: D.E. Davis

DESCRIPTION: This program is designed to help children identify problems, seek solutions, and learn how to get along with others. Songs, picture stories, activity board adventures, and two fuzzy dolls, Candoo and Willdoo, help children learn about themselves and others. Includes related at-home activities.

Peabody Early Experiences Kit (PEEK)

AUTHORS: L.M. Dunn, L.T. Chun, D.C. Crowell, L.M. Dunn, L.G. Alevy, and E.R. Yackel

DESCRIPTION: The PEEK kit contains 250 spirally sequenced lessons that focus on cognitive, social, and oral language development. Puppets, a picture deck, photographs, story cards, songs, posters, and a magnetic fishing pole are among the items included in these imaginative lessons.

Peabody Language Development Kit: Level P

AUTHORS: L.M. Dunn, J.O. Smith, and K. Horton

DESCRIPTION: This kit provides advanced 3 year olds, 4 year olds, and 5 year olds with practice in "labeling language," syntactical and grammatical structure, and logical thinking. The revised edition contains 360 lessons that involve picture cards, puppets, sound books, posters, manikins, magnetic shapes, and plastic fruits and vegetables. Uses a variety of modes of stimulation. Teachers find the pictures to be very appealing and useful in lessons that do not depend on the kit.

Small Wonder

AUTHOR: M.B. Karnes

DESCRIPTION: Small Wonder is a two-part program that fosters emotional, physical, and intellectual growth of infants and toddlers. Activities that include games, exercises, songs, picture stories, and puppet plays emphasize language development. Included is a diary that allows a baby's reaction to each activity to be recorded as a keepsake.

Publisher: *American Science and Engineering, Inc., 20 Overland Street, Boston, Massachusetts 02215*

Early Childhood Curriculum: A Piaget Program

AUTHOR: C. Lavatelli

DESCRIPTION: The purpose of this program is to provide experiences in classification, number, measurement, space, and serialization that are necessary for movement into the Piagetian stage of concrete operations. Gamelike activities initially under teacher direction stimulate work with concrete materials to solve problems and develop associate language. Teacher's guides and kits of materials may be obtained separately for each area.

Publisher: *Bowmar/Noble Publishers, Inc., 4563 Colorado Boulevard, Los Angeles, California 90039*

Early Childhood Series

AUTHORS: N. Curry, R. Jaynes, M. Crume, E. Radlauer, and R. Radlauer

DESCRIPTION: This multimedia program is designed to stimulate the development of self-concept, awareness of the physical environment, and promotion of social interaction. Each of these themes is explored through book-and-record sets, sound filmstrips, and study prints. These components can be purchased separately.

Project Me

AUTHORS: F. Schaefer and I. Chambers

DESCRIPTION: Project Me has been expanded to include at least 11 different sets containing filmstrips, cassettes, and teacher's manuals. Critical concepts of early learning such as body image, visual perception, size discrimination, form perception, directionality, cause and effect, empathy, tolerance, and general recognition of emotions are the targets of instruction. Pictures are projected on to the "Learning Wall," a floor-based screen, creating a total environment into which the child can project himself or herself and react accordingly.

Publisher: *Council for Exceptional Children, 1920 Association Drive, Reston, Virginia 22091*

Learning Language at Home

AUTHOR: M.B. Karnes

DESCRIPTION: This program includes 200 lesson cards with 1,000 activities divided into the following four skill areas: Learning to Do, which builds motor skills through manual expression; Learning to Listen, which builds auditory skills; Learning to Look, which builds visual skills; and Learning to Tell, which builds verbal expression. Each activity is intended to involve parents in the varied learning experiences.

Learning Mathematical Concepts at Home

AUTHOR: M.B. Karnes

DESCRIPTION: Activity cards containing an objective, needed materials, and procedures are divided into seven lesson areas: geometric shapes, sets and one-to-one matching, numbers and counting, numerals, addition and subtraction, patterns and progressions, and measurement. Lessons are sequenced and progress forms are included.

Publisher: *Developmental Learning Materials, P.O. Box 4000, One DLM Park, Allen, Texas 75002*

Body and Self-Awareness Big Box

DESCRIPTION: The Big Box contains 186 activity cards designed to help young children develop an awareness of their own bodies and of their relationship to the space and objects around them. Includes materials to assist in developing positive self-concepts and to express feelings.

Language Big Box

DESCRIPTION: This Big Box contains 24 Developmental Learning Materials products along with 170 activity cards to encourage the most effective use of these products in language development and early childhood education. Included are the familiar association pictures, category and classification cards, same and different cards, and sequential picture cards.

Visual Perception Big Box

DESCRIPTION: Included in the visual perception Big Box are 140 activity cards that focus on color, shape, size, closure, discrimination, eye-hand coordination, and visual-language concepts. Basic Developmental Learning Materials items included are: parquetry, sequencing beads and patterns, sequential picture cards, visual memory cards, and visual discrimination flip books.

Got To Be Me!

AUTHOR: M. Harmin

DESCRIPTION: This unique program is designed to encourage children to become more aware of themselves by discovering their likes and dislikes, strengths and weaknesses, and hopes and fears. Self-expression is stimulated by a series of colorfully illustrated cards containing thought-provoking pictures and unfinished sentences on each side. These 48 pictures are also found in consumable workbooks for older children. A teacher's guide presents additional activities. This program is available in Spanish.

Publisher: *Follett Publishing Company, 1010 West Washington Boulevard, Chicago, Illinois 60607*

The Frostig Program, revised

AUTHOR: M. Frostig

DESCRIPTION: The Frostig program is intended for use with children with known or suspected visual perception problems. Included are 375 spirit masters

and a teacher's guide to activities in the following areas: visual-motor coordination, figure-ground perception, perceptual constancy, position in space, and spatial relationships.

Move-Grow-Learn, revised

AUTHORS: M. Frostig and P. Maslow

DESCRIPTION: 170 exercise cards give directions for a total movement program that improves sensory-motor skills, self-awareness, coordination, agility, strength, flexibility, and balance. A section is devoted to creative movement that stimulates imagination and self-expression. A teacher's guide explains the theoretical basis of this preschool and primary school program.

Publisher: *Melton Peninsula, Inc., 1949 Stemmons Freeway, Suite 690, Dallas, Texas 75207*

The Perceptual Motor Play Program

AUTHORS: H. Goldstein and M. Alter

DESCRIPTION: This program is divided into two phases, exploratory play and social play. Phase one contains activities that include sensory orientation, fine motor exploration, and gross motor exploration. The activity bank in phase two contains 96 task cards with a task analysis of the skills taught. Also includes record sheets, a teacher's manual, and a "How to create materials book."

Publisher: *Milton Bradley Company, 443 Shaker Road, East Long Meadow, Massachusetts 01028*

Game Oriented Activities for Learning (GOAL)

AUTHOR: M. Karnes

DESCRIPTION: The 337 lesson plan cards are divided into the following 11 processing skill areas: auditory and visual reception, auditory and visual association, verbal and manual expression, auditory and visual memory, and grammatic, auditory, and visual closure. Picture cards, situation pictures, templates, posters, animal puzzles, patterns and plans, spin and find games, and "scenes around us" combine into game-like activities to be used with small groups of children.

GOAL: Mathematical Concepts

AUTHOR: M. Karnes

DESCRIPTION: 148 lessons are divided into 8 content areas: geometric shapes, sets and one-to-one matching, whole numbers and rational counting, numerals, addition and subtraction, measurement, metric measurement, and patterns and progressions. Materials include number-numeral tiles, wooden dice, path to math game board, flannel board aids, add-on cubes, place value charts, lotto, shapes templates, and number lines that can be used with small groups of children.

Publisher: *Science Research Associates, Inc., 259 East Erie Street, Chicago, Illinois 60611*

DISTAR Language I

AUTHORS: S. Engelmann, J. Osborn, and T. Engelmann

DESCRIPTION: This program is designed to teach basic language concepts to children in small groups. It is a highly structured instructional system. Teacher presentation books are to be followed precisely. Children are reinforced for staying on a task and for participating together in a series of teacher-directed lessons. Emphasizes concepts necessary for success in school.

Inquisitive Games: Discovering How to Learn; Exploring Number and Space

AUTHOR: H. Sprigle

DESCRIPTION: Discovering How to Learn is designed to help children develop proficiency in classifying, analyzing, generalizing, and problem solving. Strategies including small group activities and games for up to four players emphasize the how and why rather than the what. Focus is on gathering, organizing, and processing information.

Exploring Number and Space is a set of math oriented games and activities to help in the development of preoperational skills as described by Piaget. Small group involvement in sequenced activities encourages comprehending relationships necessary to understanding basic mathematical concepts.

Publisher: *Teaching Resources Corporation, 50 Pond Park Road, Hingham, Massachusetts 02043*

Dubnoff School Program 1

AUTHORS: B. Dubnoff, I. Chambers, and F. Schaefer

DESCRIPTION: This program consists of three levels of small sequential steps that form a complete pre-writing program beginning with single strokes and ending with the transition from manuscript writing to cursive writing. Each level, which includes an instructor's guide, student workbooks with acetates, crayons, and Good Work Awards, can be ordered separately. These perceptual-motor exercises may be used with a whole class or with small groups.

Erie Program

AUTHORS: D.A. Hatton, F.J. Pizzat, and J.M. Pelkowski

DESCRIPTION: Four sets of games emphasizing six basic geometric shapes are included in the Erie Program. These visual-perceptual games use game boards, bingo, templates, worksheets, tracing, and domino activities.

Fairbanks-Robinson Program

AUTHORS: J.S. Fairbanks and J. Robinson

DESCRIPTION: Level 1 of this program is designed to develop the following skills at the preschool level to the early kindergarten level: line reproduction; shape and size perception; coloring; cutting; spatial relationships; figure-ground discrimination; sequencing; and parts-to-whole relationships. Activities include tracing, copying, coloring, cutting, mazes, dot-to-dot designs, and puzzles.

Learning Staircase

AUTHORS: L. Coughran and M. Goff

DESCRIPTION: This program is designed to identify specific deficiencies and to prescribe individualized training tasks within 20 content areas. Each area contains 9 to 82 separate lessons with the task's object, method, materials, and performance criteria. Includes an assessment inventory system, parental report form, and grid pad for record keeping. Also includes, in addition to the usual early childhood content areas, "same and different," "toilet training," and "time."

Publisher: *The MacMillan Company, Front and Brown Street, Riverside, New Jersey 08075*

Early Childhood Discovery Materials

AUTHOR: Bank Street College of Education

DESCRIPTION: The purpose of these materials is to foster the development of language, conceptual, perceptual, and motor skills in young children. Materials are boxed according to such themes as the farm, the park, and the supermarket. Also available are Associated Materials that are used to extend and reinforce specific skills. A teacher's guide presents specific teaching suggestions.

Publisher: *The Psychological Corporation, 304 East 45th Street, New York, New York 10017*

Boehm Resource Guide for Basic Concept Teaching

AUTHOR: A.E. Boehm

DESCRIPTION: This kit is designed to assist in teaching such basic concepts as time, space, and quantity. It contains 65 concept cards that provide pictures illustrating concept relationships; 91 duplicating masters of worksheets; 35 game cards for use in puzzles, matching, and classifying tasks; and a picture book for developing the concept "pair." The Boehm test of basic concepts can be used to determine which lessons will be most appropriate for specific children (Appendix D).

Publisher: *VORT Corporation, P.O. Box 11552, Palo Alto, California 94306*

Hawaii Early Learning Profile (HELP)

DESCRIPTION: HELP consists of two components. Included are charts that cover 6 developmental areas and 650 sequenced skills. These facilitate recording and provide a visual picture of developmental skills for ages up to 3 years. The Activity Guide provides specific learning activities, definitions, and criteria for each of the sequenced skills. Each can be purchased separately.

Publisher: *Richard L. Zweig Associates, Inc., 20800 Beach Boulevard, Huntington Beach, California 92648*

Santa Clara Plus

AUTHOR: J.M. Casey

DESCRIPTION: This kit contains 242 "readiness recipes" with 664 activities for large group, small group, and individual use. Skill areas include motor coordination, visual motor performance, visual perception, visual memory, auditory perception, auditory memory, language development, conceptual development, and social and emotional development. They are arranged in the order of skills measured by the Santa Clara Inventory of Developmental Tasks (Appendix D). Tasks were chosen from Raymond Allen, Inc. "Your green pages." *Early Years Magazine* 1971-1976.

F

Individual materials for use with young children: a sampling

AUTHORS' NOTE: The following chart lists a sampling of individual instructional materials that are useful in early childhood classrooms. The methods of using these materials are dependent on the philosophy and goals of each program and on the individual characteristics of children who are enrolled. The skills listed represent target behaviors within many programs although they may not merit universal agreement. We have made no attempt to provide an exhaustive list of either skills or materials; we simply list resource ideas. They are provided to stimulate imagination and further analysis of available materials.

	Sensory motor development									Perceptual efficiency					
	Balance	Body awareness	Coordination	Controlled movement	Fine-motor dexterity	Laterality	Sensory awareness	Self-help skills	Visual-motor integration	Attention and concentration	Directionality	Visual discrimination	Visual memory	Visualization	Spatial relationships
Abacus					X	X			X				X		X
Association picture cards															
Attribute blocks									X			X	X		X
Balls			X	X					X						
Beads			X	X	X				X			X	X		X
Bean bags		X	X	X		X			X	X	X				X
Blocks			X	X	X				X		X		X		X
Books		X			X	X	X			X		X	X	X	
Bowling set			X	X					X	X	X				X
Cars and trucks			X		X				X		X				X
Chalkboard			X	X	X	X			X	X	X		X	X	X
Clay (Playdough)		X	X	X	X		X	X	X						X
Climbing equipment	X	X	X	X			X	X	X		X				X
Color cubes			X	X	X	X			X		X	X	X	X	X
Crayons			X	X	X	X			X		X				
Dolls		X				X	X	X	X					X	

Communication						Cognition and reading readiness								Social and emotional development					
Auditory discrimination	Auditory memory	Comprehension	Nonverbal expression	Verbal facility	Vocabulary	Academic readiness	Association	Classification	Creativity	Part to whole relationships	Problem solving	Serialization	Quantitative skills	Cooperation	Imitation	Self-control	Self-expression	Self-esteem	Understanding feelings
													X						
		X			X		X	X		X									
		X			X	X	X	X			X		X						
	X					X		X			X	X	X	X	X	X			
														X			X		
		X						X	X		X		X	X	X		X	X	
		X			X	X	X	X					X	X					X
														X	X	X			
		X	X				X	X				X	X	X	X	X	X		
		X				X		X					X	X	X		X		
		X	X					X	X	X				X	X	X	X		X
		X												X	X	X	X		
	X					X		X				X	X	X					
		X	X			X			X				X		X	X	X	X	X
		X	X											X	X		X	X	X

Continued.

	Sensory motor development									Perceptual efficiency					
	Balance	Body awareness	Coordination	Controlled movement	Fine-motor dexterity	Laterality	Sensory awareness	Self-help skills	Visual-motor integration	Attention and concentration	Directionality	Visual discrimination	Visual memory	Visualization	Spatial relationships
Dominoes			X	X	X	X			X		X				X
Dressing frames		X	X	X	X	X		X	X	X	X				X
Dress-up clothes		X	X		X	X	X	X	X					X	
Easel and paints			X	X	X	X	X		X			X		X	X
Etch-a-sketch			X	X	X	X			X	X	X			X	X
Farm animals											X				
Flannel and felt board					X	X			X	X	X	X	X	X	X
Form board					X				X		X		X		X
Geo boards			X	X	X	X			X		X		X		X
Housekeeping equipment		X			X		X	X	X					X	
Hula Hoops	X	X	X	X		X	X		X		X				X
Knob boards					X				X				X		
Lacing boards			X	X	X	X		X	X		X			X	X
Legos			X	X	X				X					X	X
Lotto						X			X	X		X	X		
Magic markers			X	X	X	X			X		X			X	X
Magnetic board				X	X	X			X		X		X	X	X
Match-ups					X				X	X		X		X	
Mirrors		X				X	X	X			X	X	X		X
Musical instruments		X	X	X			X		X	X					
Nesting toys			X	X	X				X			X		X	
Parquetry			X	X	X				X			X	X	X	X
Peg boards			X	X	X	X			X		X		X	X	X
Photographs		X						X					X	X	
Pictures		X									X	X	X	X	
Play store						X		X	X			X	X		
Punching clown				X					X		X				X
Puppets															
Puzzles		X							X	X		X	X	X	X
Records		X		X			X			X					
Sand box				X	X		X	X	X						
Science equipment					X		X		X	X		X	X	X	X
Scissors			X	X	X	X		X	X	X					
Sequence cards					X	X			X			X	X	X	
Shape sorting toys			X	X	X				X			X			X
Sound boxes							X								
Tactile surfaces							X					X	X		
Telephones		X					X	X		X					
Tunnel	X	X		X		X	X		X		X				X
Unifix cubes			X		X	X			X			X	X		X
Water play toys		X			X		X	X	X						
Wheeled toys	X	X	X						X						
Work bench		X	X	X	X	X		X	X	X				X	X
Zoo animals									X					X	

	Communication						Cognition and reading readiness								Social and emotional development					
	Auditory discrimination	Auditory memory	Comprehension	Nonverbal expression	Verbal facility	Vocabulary	Academic readiness	Association	Classification	Creativity	Part to whole relationships	Problem solving	Serialization	Quantitative skills	Cooperation	Imitation	Self-control	Self-expression	Self-esteem	Understanding feelings
							X				X		X	X	X					
																			X	X
			X				X	X							X	X		X	X	X
			X				X	X							X		X	X	X	
			X						X	X					X		X			
			X		X		X	X	X				X					X		
			X		X	X	X	X	X	X	X		X	X				X		
								X	X			X	X	X						
						X						X		X						
			X	X			X	X	X	X			X	X	X	X	X	X	X	
															X				X	
													X	X						
										X					X			X		
										X										
	X	X	X			X	X	X	X				X	X	X					
				X				X	X	X	X				X	X	X	X	X	
				X				X	X	X	X			X	X	X			X	
						X	X	X	X		X	X								
								X		X	X	X				X		X	X	X
	X	X	X	X	X		X	X		X			X		X	X	X	X		
							X			X	X	X	X							
								X		X	X	X			X	X				
													X	X	X	X			X	X
		X		X	X		X		X		X			X		X	X	X	X	X
					X	X		X	X		X			X		X	X	X	X	X
				X				X			X				X	X	X	X	X	X
	X	X	X			X		X					X	X						
	X	X	X		X			X											X	
	X	X	X		X	X	X	X	X		X	X	X	X						
			X			X	X	X	X			X	X	X	X					
					X			X	X					X	X					
					X			X	X					X						
	X	X				X		X	X					X						
	X	X	X		X	X				X					X	X		X		X
															X		X			
						X	X	X						X						
				X	X					X					X	X	X	X		
			X							X					X	X	X	X	X	
		X	X	X				X	X	X					X	X	X	X	X	

National advocacy groups

American Alliance for Health, Physical Education
and Recreation
Room 422
1201 16th Street
Washington, D.C. 20036

Closer Look
Box 1492
Washington, D.C. 20013

Council for Exceptional Children
Information Center
1920 Association Drive
Reston, Virginia 22091

National Center for Law and the Handicapped
1235 North Eddy Street
South Bend, Indiana 46617

Emotional disturbance

American Academy of Child Psychiatry
1800 R Street N.W., Suite 904
Washington, D.C. 20009

American Association of Psychiatric Services for
Children
1701 18th Street, N.W.
Washington, D.C. 20009

American Psychological Association/Division of
Child and Youth Services
1200 17th Street, N.W.
Washington, D.C. 20005

Mental Health Association, National Headquarters
1800 North Kent Street
Arlington, Virginia 22209

National Society for Autistic Children
621 Central Avenue
Albany, New York 12006

Hearing, speech, and language impairments

American Speech and Hearing Association
10801 Rockville Pike
Rockville, Maryland 20852

Alexander Graham Bell Association for the Deaf, Inc.
3417 Volta Place, N.W.
Washington, D.C. 20007

Gallaudet College for the Deaf
The Office of Public Relations
Kendall Green
Washington, D.C. 20002

International Association of Parents of the Deaf
814 Thayer Avenue
Silver Spring, Maryland 20910

International Parents' Organization
Alexander Graham Bell Association for the Deaf, Inc.
3417 Volta Place, N.W.
Washington, D.C. 20007

National Association for Hearing and Speech Action
814 Thayer Avenue
Silver Spring, Maryland 20910

National Association of the Deaf
814 Thayer Avenue
Silver Spring, Maryland 20910

Learning disabilities

Association for Children with Learning Disabilities
4156 Library Road
Pittsburgh, Pennsylvania 15234

Orton Society
8415 Bellona Lane
Towson, Maryland 21204

Mental retardation

American Association for the Education of the Severely/Profoundly Handicapped
1600 W. Armory Way
Seattle, Washington 98119

American Association on Mental Deficiency
5101 Wisconsin Avenue, N.W.
Washington, D.C. 20014

National Association for Retarded Citizens
2709 Avenue E. East
P.O. Box 6109
Arlington, Texas 76011

President's Committee on Mental Retardation
Department of Health and Human Services
Washington, D.C. 20201

Physical and health impairments

American Alliance for Health, Physical Education and Recreation
1201 16th Street
Washington, D.C. 20036

American Diabetes Association
600 Fifth Avenue
New York, New York 10020

American Heart Association
7320 Greenville Avenue
Dallas, Texas 75231

Cystic Fibrosis Foundation
3379 Peachtree Road, N.E.
Atlanta, Georgia 30326

Epilepsy Foundation of America
1828 L Street, N.W.
Washington, D.C. 20036

National Easter Seal Society for Crippled Children and Adults
2023 W. Ogden Avenue
Chicago, Illinois 60612

National Epilepsy League
6 North Michigan Avenue
Chicago, Illinois 60602

National Kidney Foundation
116 East 27th Street
New York, New York 10010

Muscular Dystrophy Association of America
810 Seventh Avenue
New York, New York 10019

The Arthritis Foundation
1212 Avenue of the Americas
New York, New York, 10036

The National Association of the Physically Handicapped
6473 Grandville Avenue
Detroit, Michigan 48228

The National Foundation/March of Dimes
1275 Mamaroneck Avenue
New York, New York 10018

The National Hemophilia Foundation
25 West 39th Street
New York, New York 10018

Visual impairments

American Foundation for the Blind
15 West 16th Street
New York, New York 10011

American Optometric Association
7000 Chippewa Street
St. Louis, Missouri 63119

Association for the Education of the Visually
   Handicapped
919 Walnut Street
Philadelphia, Pennsylvania 19107

Delta Gamma Foundation of the Delta Gamma
   Fraternity
3250 Riverside Drive
P.O. Box 5897
Columbus, Ohio 43221

Library of Congress
Division for the Blind and Physically Handicapped
Reference Department
Washington, D.C. 20542

Lions International
209 North Michigan Avenue
Chicago, Illinois 60601

National Accreditation Council for Agencies Serving
   the Blind and Visually Handicapped
79 Madison Avenue
New York, New York 10016

National Association for the Visually Handicapped
305 East 24th Street
New York, New York 10010

Periodicals relevant to the education of young children

Child Care Quarterly
Behavioral Publications
72 Fifth Avenue
New York, N.Y. 10011

Child Development
Society for Research in Child Development
5801 Ellis Avenue
Chicago, Ill. 60637

Child Education
Evans Brothers Limited
Montague House
Russell Square
London, WCIB 5BX
England

Childhood Education
Association for Childhood Education International
3615 Wisconsin Avenue, N.W.
Washington, D.C. 20016

Children Today
Children's Bureau
Office of Child Development
Office of Human Development
U.S. Department of Education
Washington, D.C. 20013

Children in Contemporary Society
Pittsburgh Association for the Education of Young
   Children
P.O. Box 11173
Pittsburgh, Pa. 15237

Child Welfare
Child Welfare League of America, Inc.
67 Irving Place
New York, N.Y. 10010

Cycles
TADS (Technical Assistance Development System)
625 W. Cameron Avenue
Chapel Hill, N.C. 27514
(Administered by the Bureau of Education for the
   Handicapped)

Day Care and Early Education
Behavioral Publications
72 Fifth Avenue
New York, N.Y. 10011

Early Child Development and Care
Gordon and Breach Science Publishers, Inc.
One Park Avenue
New York, N.Y. 10016

Early Years
Allen Raymond, Inc.
P.O. Box 1223
Darien, Conn. 06820

Educating Children, Early and Middle Years
American Association of Elementary-Kindergarten-
   Nursery Educators
1201 16th Street, N.W.
Washington, D.C. 20036

ERIC-ECE Newsletter
ERIC Clearinghouse on Early Childhood Education
805 W. Pennsylvania
Urbana, Ill. 61801

Exceptional Children
Council for Exceptional Children
920 Association Drive
Reston, Va. 22091
(An additional journal is available for members who belong to the subgroup "Division for Early Childhood.")

The Exceptional Parent
Psy-Ed Corporation
262 Beacon Street
Boston, Mass. 02116

Parent Cooperative Preschools International
Journal Editorial and Publication Office
9111 Alton Parkway
Silver Spring, Maryland 20910

P.E.N. Preschool Education Newsletter
Multi Media Education, Inc.
11 West 42nd Street
New York, N.Y. 10036

Report of Pre-school Education
Capitol Publications, Inc.
2430 Pennsylvania Avenue, N.W.
Washington, D.C. 20037

The Volta Review
The Alexander Graham Bell Association for the Deaf, Inc.
3417 Volta Place, N.W.
Washington, D.C. 20007

Young Children
National Association for the Education of Young Children
1834 Connecticut Avenue, N.W.
Washington, D.C. 20009

Glossary

acuity—Degree to which one is able to hear sounds and see visual images.

adapt—To change or modify while retaining the basic model.

advocate—One who acts on behalf of another.

affective—Pertaining to emotion, feeling, or attitude.

anecdotal record—A factual account of a child's behavior.

articulation—The manner in which speech sounds are produced.

assessment—Either a test or an observation that determines a child's strengths or weaknesses in a particular area of development.

association—The process of relating one concept to another.

atypical—Not typical. Different from the norm or average.

audiologist—A trained professional who measures hearing acuity, diagnoses hearing impairments, and assists in planning for remediation, including hearing aids and educational adaptations.

auditory discrimination—The ability to distinguish one sound from another.

auditory memory—The ability to retain and recall what has been heard.

behavior modification—Systematic, consistent efforts to change an individual's behavior. Carefully planned consequences for specific behaviors are designed to help a learner develop new and more appropriate responses to situations and experiences.

behavioral objective (also referred to as performance objectives)—Identifies exactly what the teacher will do, provide, or restrict; describes the learner's observable behavior; and defines how well the learner must perform.

body awareness (image)—Awareness of one's own body and its position in time and space.

categorical placement—Placement of children according to classification of their suspected disabilities. Classrooms that are categorical usually group children according to disability labels; for example, classes for children who are learning disabled or emotionally disturbed.

child-find—The process of finding and identifying children with handicapping conditions.

chronological age (CA)—A child's actual age in years and months.

classification—Distinguishing characteristics of things; then sorting, matching, or otherwise grouping them.

cognition—Analytical, logical acts of mental behavior that result in the act of knowing.

concepts—Mental images or ideas.

confidentiality—Records and other information about children must not be shown to anyone other than those who have been approved to have the information. Parental consent in writing must be obtained before information can be released to other individuals or facilities.

congenital—Presumed to be present at birth.

correlation—The relationship between factors.

Council for Exceptional Children (CEC)—A national professional organization for anyone working for and with gifted and handicapped children.

criterion—A norm or standard for a behavior or item.

criterion-referenced tests—Tests or observations that compare a child's performance on a particular task to a standard established for that specific task. Such tests identify what a child can and cannot do.

369

cross-categorical programs—A program designed to serve children who have differing handicapping conditions.

curriculum—All of the specific features of a master teaching plan that have been chosen by a particular teacher for his or her classroom. Curricula may vary widely from school to school, but each curriculum reflects the skills, tasks, and behaviors that a school has decided are important for children to acquire.

custodial care—Usually refers to the constant supervision and care of bodily needs provided in institutional settings.

decibel—Unit used to measure hearing intensity or loudness.

decoding—The act of deciphering or obtaining meaning from what is seen or heard.

developmental curriculum checklist—A checklist of behavior often prepared by choosing items from standardized tests or scales. Duplicate items are deleted and those remaining are arranged in a developmental sequence. The checklist is then used as a guide in designing curriculum and in providing a record of individual children's progress through the curriculum.

developmentally disabled (delayed)—Persons who have an identifiable delay in mental or physical development compared with established norms are referred to in this way, rather than as "impaired" or "retarded."

diagnosis—A diagnosis is an effort to find the cause of a problem by observing the child and considering the results of tests.

directionality—The ability to know right from left, up from down, forward from backward, and other directional orientation.

discrimination—The ability to differentiate among similar stimuli.

divergent thinking—Thinking that is unusual, different, and searching.

eclecticism—Method of practice of selecting what seems best from various systems or programs.

echolalia—A habit of repeating (without meaning), or "echoing," what is said by others.

encoding—The act of expressing oneself in words or gestures.

emerging skills—As children learn, they may use a new skill some, but not all of the time. A skill observed at least some of the time is said to be emerging.

en route behaviors—Tasks to be mastered or behaviors to be demonstrated as the child moves from one level of functioning (entry behavior) to a designated goal or objective (terminal behavior).

entry behavior—The level of functioning or behavior already acquired before beginning a series of tasks.

environment—Everything the child encounters. The rooms, furniture, toys, the opportunity to experience new and different places, and the behaviors of those around the child constitute the environment.

equivalent practice—To prevent boredom in repetition, the teacher provides equivalent practice by offering a variety of materials and activities that are designed to develop the same skill. The task must also be at the same level of difficulty and provide the same kind of practice to be equivalent.

etiology—The study of the causes of diseases or disabilities.

evaluation—The process of making value judgments based on behavioral information about the effectiveness of a program in meeting the needs of children enrolled.

expansion—Adults expand a child's utterance by stating the child's idea in a longer phrase or sentence.

expressive language—What is said or written to communicate an idea or a question.

feedback—The receipt of knowledge of results (the effect) of one's own behavior.

figure-ground discrimination—The ability to attend to one aspect of a visual or auditory field while relegating other aspects of the environment to the background.

fine motor skills—Activities with the fingers and hands.

First Chance Programs—Preschool programs for the handicapped funded by the Bureau of Education for the Handicapped.

Free Appropriate Public Education (FAPE)—Designed by Public Law 94-142 to mean special education and related services provided at public expense. Such services are to be described in the individualized education program, are to be appropriate to the child's individual needs, and are to meet requirements of the state agency.

genetic—Having to do with the principles of heredity.

goals—The general statement on the individualized education program that states what teaching is expected to accomplish; for example, "To improve Johnny's fine motor skills."

grammar—The linguistic rules of language.

gross motor skills—Activities using large muscles such as running, climbing, throwing, and jumping.

high risk signals—Those signs that when observed in very young children have been known to be predictive of more than normal likelihood of future handicaps or developmental delays.

hyperactivity—Exceedingly active behavior not typical of most children.

hypertonicity—Condition in which muscles are stretched and constantly excited.

hypoactivity—Opposite of hyperactivity; lethargy.

hypotonicity—Condition in which muscles are limp and do not exhibit resistance to stretching.

identification—The process of finding and screening individuals to determine if they might benefit from specialized services.

Individualized Education Program (IEP)—A written plan that states a child's present level of functioning; specific areas that need special services; annual goals; short-term objectives; services to be provided and the method of evaluation to be implemented. An Individualized Education Program is required for every child receiving services while Public Law 94-142 is in effect.

individualize—Matching a teaching task to the capacity of the particular individual being taught.

innate—Inherent within an individual.

inner language—The language in which thinking occurs. The process of internalizing and organizing experiences that can be expressed by symbols.

instructional objectives—These define specific accomplishments to be achieved. See "Behavioral objectives."

integration—Education of handicapped children with nonhandicapped classmates to the maximum extent appropriate.

interindividual differences—Differences between individuals.

intraindividual differences—Differences in performance within one child on different factors or on the same factor at different times.

labeling—Giving a categorical term (label) to a handicapping condition and to those who exhibit such a condition; for example, "emotionally disturbed" or "mentally retarded."

laterality—Awareness of sidedness; left and right of the body.

least restrictive environment—This is a concept inherent in Public Law 94-142 that requires handicapped children to be educated with nonhandicapped peers in regular educational settings to the maximum extent appropriate.

litigation—The act or process of contesting by law through lawsuits.

locomotor—Pertaining to movement from one location to another.

mainstreaming—The practice of placing children with special needs in regular classrooms whenever appropriate.

mental age—Level of mental functioning. A child with a mental age (MA) of 4-0 is thought to be mentally functioning like a 4 year old.

modality—The pathways through which an individual receives information and thereby learns. Some individuals are thought to learn more quickly through one modality than another; that is, some process auditory information more efficiently than visual information and would thus be classified as auditory learners.

modeling—Providing a demonstration of an expected behavior.

multidisciplinary team (interdisciplinary team)—Professionals with a variety of different skills and training constitute a multidisciplinary team.

multisensory learning—A technique to facilitate learning that employs a combination of sense modalities at the same time.

neurological examination—An examination of sensory or motor responses to determine whether there are impairments of the nervous system.

noncategorical—Grouping children together without labeling or categorizing according to suspected handicaps.

nonlocomotor—Lack of movement from one place to another.

nonverbal ability—Having skill to perform a task that does not involve using words.

norms—A sample of a large number of people's behavior against which a particular behavior can be compared.

norm-referenced tests—These are tests that report a particular child's performance in relation to other children of the same chronological age. Such tests are highly standardized and usually do not include individuals with handicapping conditions in the normative sample against which behavior is being compared.

observable behavior—Behavior that can be seen, heard, or felt.

ocular pursuit—Following an object with the eye.

olfactory—Pertaining to the sense of smell.

ophthalmologist—A physician trained in the diagnosis and treatment of diseases of the eyes.

optometrist—A vision specialist trained to measure refraction and prescribe glasses but not licensed to treat eye diseases.

otologist—A physician trained to treat problems of the ear.

parallel talk—Parents of young children often talk about what their children are doing as it is happening. Their "talk" occurs parallel to what the child is doing. This practice appears to help young children learn language.

paraplegia—Paralysis of both legs.

paraprofessional—A trained assistant to a professional teacher, often referred to as a teacher aide.

pediatrician—A physician whose specialty is working with and treating infants and young children.

percentile rank—The percentage of persons in a normal distribution who score below a particular point.

perception—The process of interpreting what is received by the five senses.

perceptual-motor—The interaction of various channels of perception with motor activity; for example, the act of kicking is a perceptual-motor interaction between sight and gross motor responses.

performance objectives—See "Behavioral objectives."

perseveration—Continuous repetition of the same action characterized by the inability to shift readily from one activity to another.

pincer grasp—Coordination of index finger and thumb.

prognosis—A forecast of the probable course of a disease or illness.

prompting—Using cues and partial cues to build desired behavior. Verbal prompting often involves saying a single sound or word to help a child remember what to say or do. Physical prompting that involves physical assistance or touch can be helpful to initiate a motor or self-help skill. Prompts should be reduced gradually (faded) until they can be eliminated.

prosthesis—Artificial device used to replace a missing body part.

psycholinguistics—The field of study that combines psychology and linguistics to create an understanding of the total language process.

Public Law 94-142—The Education for All Handicapped Children Act (Federal Register, August 23, 1977, Vol. 42, No. 163). See Chapters 2 and 3 for a discussion of this act.

rapport—A harmonious relationship. When working with a child, establishing rapport involves developing a climate or atmosphere in which the child feels comfortable enough to perform as well as possible.

receptive language—The ability to understand the intent and meaning of someone's effort to communicate.

reinforcer—An event or consequence (reward) that increases the likelihood of a behavior being repeated. May be concrete or social.

reliability—Extent to which a test measures a given performance consistently. The degree to which it is dependable, stable, and relatively free from errors of measurement.

residual hearing—Auditory acuity of an individual after an impairment without amplification.

retarded—Traditionally this term was used to describe any individual who was slow to learn or difficult to teach. The term is not precise and is less often used today. Laws specify that one must correlate test scores, adaptive behavior, and other factors before this term can be used appropriately.

reversal—A transposition of letters.

reverse chaining—Begin teaching with the last step of a task and working backwards. Is particularly useful with self-help skills.

rigidity—A type of cerebral palsy characterized by widespread continuous muscle tension. Muscles of the body become very stiff.

rotation—The turning around of letters in a word, such as mistaking d for b.

screening—The process of sorting out from a total group children who may have problems. It is often a part of a total program called Child-Find, or Child-Check. The intent is to test all children with specially designed screening instruments to determine those who need further diagnostic testing and to determine if a problem really does exist.

self-fulfilling prophecy—The tendency for individuals to behave in accordance with views they perceive others to have of them.

sensory motor—The combination of input of sense organs and output of motor activity.

seriation—Ordering according to relative differences.

shaping—A technique of behavior modification in which behaviors that are successive approximations of the target behavior are reinforced until target behavior is acquired.

sorting—Discrimination and separation according to differences.

spasticity—Muscular incoordination resulting from sudden, involuntary contractions of the muscles; a type of cerebral palsy.

spatial relationships—The ability to perceive the position of two or more objects in relation to oneself and in relation to each other.

standardization—The procedure of having standard directions and scoring so that normative data about others who have taken the test can be used.

standardized tests—Tests that are administered in a specifically described standard way, scored in a particular way, and then compared with the performance of a standard group.

stanine—A single digit derived score based on the normal curve. It ranges in value from 1 to 9 with a mean of 5.

stimuli—Information that can be received by the senses.

stuttering—A speech impairment evidenced by hesitations, repetitions, or spasms of breathing.

successive approximation—The process of gradually increasing expectations for a child to display behaviors that are more like the desired target be-

havior; used in shaping behaviors not previously a part of the child's behavior pattern.

tactile—The sense of touch.

target behavior—The terminal objective or final desired behavior that is the goal of shaping when using behavioral (performance) objectives. This same term, when used in relation to behavior modification, refers to the negative behavior to be changed.

task analysis—Breaking down a difficult task into small steps that lead to doing the difficult task. En route behaviors are behavioral objectives that state the individual subskills leading toward the terminal objective or the difficult task.

terminal objective—The behavioral objective that a particular teacher has chosen as the highest level of skill he or she intends to strive toward to help a child or children achieve.

total communication—A philosophy involved in teaching the hearing impaired that includes using aural, manual, and oral methods to ensure effective communication.

trauma—The condition, physical or mental, that results from shock or a violently produced wound or injury.

tremor—Involuntary vibration in large muscles.

utterance—Something that is said or produced orally. It is not necessary that an utterance be spoken correctly to be counted in the child's mean length of utterance (MLU).

validity—The extent to which an instrument measures what it is supposed to measure or what the test giver needs it to measure.

verbal expression—The ability to express one's ideas verbally.

visual association—The process of relating concepts that have been presented visually.

visualization—Imagery; the ability to retrieve a mental image or to produce a mental image.

Author index

Subject index